Franklin Allen   Stewart C. Myers   Richard A. Brealey

W elcome to the *Concise Edition* of *Principles of Corporate Finance.* We are proud of the success of our more comprehensive *Principles of Corporate Finance* text, now in its 9th edition, and we have done our best to make this book even better.

This book may be your first view of the world of modern finance. If so, you will read first for new ideas, for an understanding of how finance theory translates to practice, and occasionally, we hope, for entertainment. But eventually you will be in a position to make financial decisions, not just study them. At that point you can turn to this book as a reference and guide.

Many purchasers of *Principles of Corporate Finance, Concise,* are not new students of finance, but practicing financial managers. Regardless of the reader's experience and responsibilities in finance, we are confident that this book will be a positive-NPV investment.

SOME USEFUL WEB SITES

At the beginning of each part in the book we list a sample of relevant Web sites. Here are some sites that you should find generally useful.

Good sources for financial news:
www.cfonews.com
www.dowjones.com
www.economist.com *The Economist*
www.ft.com *The Financial Times*
online.wsj.com *The Wall Street Journal*—partly restricted to subscribers
www.brint.com Cross-references to press comment on business and financial issues

Web addresses for some other journals that are read by financial managers:
www.businessweek.com
www.cfo.com
www.corporatefinancemag.com
www.euromoney.com Free access on registration
www.forbes.com
money.cnn.com/magazines/fortune *Fortune*
www.institutionalinvestor.com Free access on registration
money.cnn.com
www.risk.net

Some useful sites with market commentary and data on individual firms and stocks:
www.bloomberg.com
www.corporateinformation.com A good international site on company information
finance.yahoo.com An outstanding source of stock price and company information
www.hoovers.com
www.wisi.com Another good international site
www.reportgallery.com Easy access to annual reports

Links to other finance sites:
www.afponline.org
www.ceoexpress.com
www.cob.ohio-state.edu/fin/journal/jofsites.htm Good site maintained by Ohio State College of Business
www.courses.dsu.edu/finance
www.financewise.com
www.finpipe.com

With the purchase of a New Book*

You Can Access the Real Financial Data that the Experts Use!

*Access is available to purchasers of new books only. If you purchased a used book, the site ID may have expired.

This card entitles the purchaser of a new textbook to a semester of access to the Educational Version of Standard & Poor's Market Insight®, a rich online resource featuring hundreds of the most often researched companies in the Market Insight database.

For 1,000 companies, this website provides you:

- Access to six years' worth of fundamental financial data from the renowned Standard & Poor's COMPUSTAT® database
- 12 Excel Analytics Reports, including balance sheets, income statements, ratio reports and cash flow statements; adjusted prices reports, and profitability; forecasted values and monthly valuation data reports
- Access to Financial Highlights Reports including key ratios
- S & P Stock Reports that offer fundamental, quantitative and technical analysis
- EDGAR reports updated throughout the day
- Industry Surveys, written by S & P's Equity analysts
- News feeds (updated hourly) for companies and industries.

STANDARD &POOR'S

Mc Graw Hill **McGraw-Hill Irwin**

Exclusive partnership!

See other side for your unique site ID access code.

Welcome to the Educational Version of Market Insight!

www.mhhe.com/edumarketinsight

Check out your textbook's website for details on how this special offer enhances the value of your purchase!

1. To get started, use your web browser to go to **www.mhhe.com/edumarketinsight**

2. Enter your site ID exactly as it appears below.

3. You may be prompted to enter the site ID for future use—please keep this card.

Your site ID is:

ak147933

STANDARD &POOR'S

ISBN 978-0-07-336758-3
MHID 0-07-336758-3

McGraw-Hill Irwin

*If you purchased a used book, this site ID may have expired.

PRINCIPLES *of* CORPORATE FINANCE

Concise Edition

The McGraw-Hill/Irwin Series in Finance, Insurance and Real Estate

Stephen A. Ross, Franco Modigliani Professor of Finance and Economics, Sloan School of Management, Massachusetts Institute of Technology, Consulting Editor

PRINCIPLES *of* CORPORATE FINANCE

Concise Edition

FIRST EDITION

RICHARD A. BREALEY

Professor of Finance
London Business School

STEWART C. MYERS

Robert C. Merton (1970) Professor of Finance
Sloan School of Management
Massachusetts Institute of Technology

FRANKLIN ALLEN

Nippon Life Professor of Finance
The Wharton School
University of Pennsylvania

Boston   Burr Ridge, IL   Dubuque, IA   New York   San Francisco   St. Louis
Bangkok   Bogotá   Caracas   Kuala Lumpur   Lisbon   London   Madrid   Mexico City
Milan   Montreal   New Delhi   Santiago   Seoul   Singapore   Sydney   Taipei   Toronto

McGraw-Hill
Irwin

PRINCIPLES OF CORPORATE FINANCE, CONCISE EDITION

Published by McGraw-Hill/Irwin, a business unit of The McGraw-Hill Companies, Inc., 1221 Avenue of the Americas, New York, NY, 10020. Copyright © 2009 by The McGraw-Hill Companies, Inc. All rights reserved. No part of this publication may be reproduced or distributed in any form or by any means, or stored in a database or retrieval system, without the prior written consent of The McGraw-Hill Companies, Inc., including, but not limited to, in any network or other electronic storage or transmission, or broadcast for distance learning.

Some ancillaries, including electronic and print components, may not be available to customers outside the United States.

This book is printed on acid-free paper.

1 2 3 4 5 6 7 8 9 0 WCK / WCK 0 9 8

ISBN   978-0-07-340511-7
MHID   0-07-340511-6

Executive editor: *Michele Janicek*
Developmental editor II: *Christina Kouvelis*
Marketing manager: *Ashley Smith*
Media producer: *Greg Bates*
Managing editor: *Lori Koetters*
Lead production supervisor: *Michael R. McCormick*
Senior designer: *Cara David*
Media project manager: *Sri Potluri*
Cover design: *Eric Kass*
Interior design: *Jenny El-Shamy*
Typeface: *10/12 Palatino*
Compositor: *Aptara, Inc.*
Printer: *Quebecor World Versailles Inc.*

Library of Congress Cataloging-in-Publication Data

Brealey, Richard A.
    Principles of corporate finance / Richard A. Brealey, Stewart C. Myers, Franklin Allen.—Concise ed., 1st ed.
        p. cm.—(The McGrawHill/Irwin series in finance, insurance, and real estate)
    Includes index.
    ISBN-13: 978-0-07-340511-7 (alk. paper)
    ISBN-10: 0-07-340511-6 (alk. paper)
    1. Corporations—Finance. I. Myers, Stewart C. II. Allen, Franklin. III. Title.
    HG4026.B6673 2009
    658.15—dc22

                                                                    2007046484

www.mhhe.com

To Our Parents

ABOUT THE AUTHORS

RICHARD A. BREALEY

Professor of Finance at the London Business School. He is the former president of the European Finance Association and a former director of the American Finance Association. He is a fellow of the British Academy and has served as a special adviser to the Governor of the Bank of England and director of a number of financial institutions. Other books written by Professor Brealey include *Introduction to Risk and Return from Common Stocks.*

STEWART C. MYERS

Robert C. Merton (1970) Professor of Finance at MIT's Sloan School of Management. He is past president of the American Finance Association and a research associate of the National Bureau of Economic Research. His research has focused on financing decisions, valuation methods, the cost of capital, and financial aspects of government regulation of business. Dr. Myers is a director of The Brattle Group, Inc., and is active as a financial consultant.

FRANKLIN ALLEN

Nippon Life Professor of Finance at the Wharton School of the University of Pennsylvania. He is past president of the American Finance Association, Western Finance Association, and Society for Financial Studies. His research has focused on financial innovation, asset price bubbles, comparing financial systems, and financial crises. He is a scientific adviser at the Sveriges Riksbank (Sweden's central bank).

PREFACE

The financial manager faces some key decisions: What capital investments should the firm make? Should it pay for these investments by plowing back profits, by issuing common stock, or by borrowing? And what plans can the firm make to ensure that it stays financially strong and healthy? This book presents the basis for answering these questions.

This book is a distillation of the ninth edition of our more comprehensive text, *Principles of Corporate Finance*. Some users of *Principles* have suggested that its coverage is more extensive than they need, and with these comments in mind, we have designed this concise version. We believe that *Concise* provides the essential knowledge base for a financial manager. The first 11 chapters are essentially the same as those in *Principles*. They cover the time value of money, the valuation of bonds and stocks, and practical capital budgeting decisions. The remaining chapters discuss market efficiency, payout policy, capital structure, option valuation, and long- and short-term financial planning. Readers who are familiar with *Principles* will notice a small number of changes in these chapters. The option chapters include a simple example showing how to value an option to expand, but they omit the other book's Appendix on the effect of dilution on option values. In the chapter on short-term financial planning we have

added a description of the money-market instruments that firms use to park surplus cash.

Of course, the decision as to what to include and what to omit was not always easy. We would like to have covered topics such as new issues, mergers, private equity, credit risk, and so on. But the book is meant to be *concise*. We have therefore reviewed the contents of a large number of one-semester finance courses, and been resolute in restricting our coverage to the most commonly taught topics.

We realize that some instructors will prefer a different sequence of topics. We have therefore ensured that the text is modular, so that parts can be introduced in an alternative order. For example, there should be no difficulty in reading the material on financial statement analysis and short-term financial decisions before the chapters on valuation and capital investment.

Throughout the book we have described both the theory and practice of corporate finance. We hardly need to explain why financial managers need to master the practical aspects of their job, but we should spell out why down-to-earth managers need to bother with theory.

Managers learn from experience how to cope with routine problems. But the best managers are also able to respond to change. To do so you need more than time-honored rules of thumb; you must understand *why* companies and financial markets behave the way they do. In other words, you need a *theory* of finance.

Does that sound intimidating? It shouldn't. Good theory helps you to grasp what is going on in the world around you. It helps you to ask the right questions when times change and new problems need to be analyzed. It also tells you which things you do *not* need to worry about. Throughout this book we show how managers use financial theory to solve practical problems.

Of course, the theory presented in this book is not perfect and complete—no theory is. There are some famous controversies where financial economists cannot agree. We have not glossed over these disagreements. We set out the arguments for each side and tell you where we stand.

Much of this book is concerned with understanding what financial managers do and why. But we also say what financial managers *should* do to increase company value. Where theory suggests that financial managers are making mistakes, we say so, while admitting that there may be hidden reasons for their actions. In brief, we have tried to be fair but to pull no punches.

MAKING LEARNING EASIER

Each chapter of the book includes an introductory preview, a summary, and an annotated list of suggestions for further reading. There is a quick and easy quiz, practice questions on both numerical and conceptual topics, and a few challenge questions. Many questions use financial data on actual companies, which the reader can download from Standard & Poor's educational version of Market Insight. Answers to the quiz questions may be found at the end of the book, along with a glossary and tables for calculating present values and pricing options. We have also provided for each chapter concept review questions and have keyed these to the page in the book where the topic is discussed. Sample questions are

shown at the end of each chapter. The full set of Concept Review Questions is available on the book's Web site, **www.mhhe.com/bma1e.**

The book also contains seven end-of-chapter mini-cases. These include specific questions to guide the case analysis. Answers to the mini-cases are available to instructors on the book's Web site.

A number of the tables in the text are shown as Excel spreadsheets. In these cases an equivalent "live" spreadsheet is contained on the book's Web site. Readers can use these live spreadsheets to understand better the calculations behind the table and to see the effect of changing the underlying data. A number of end-of-chapter questions ask the student to use the spreadsheets to check that they understand the effect of changing inputs.

The 20 chapters in this book are divided into 7 parts. Each part includes a short introduction that explains the sequence of topics. Parts 1 to 3 of the book cover valuation and capital investment decisions, and Parts 4 to 6 discuss long-term financing. Part 7 focuses on financial planning and short-term financial decisions.

SUPPLEMENTS

In this edition, we have gone to great lengths to ensure that our supplements are equal in quality and authority to the text itself.

For the Instructor

Instructor's CD-ROM
ISBN 9780073279404
MHID 0073279404

This comprehensive CD contains all the following instructor supplements. We have compiled them in electronic format for easier access and convenience. Print copies are available through your McGraw-Hill representative.

- **Instructor's Manual**   The Instructor's Manual was completed by C. R. Krishnaswamy of Western Michigan University. It contains an overview of each chapter, teaching tips, learning objectives, challenge areas, key terms, and an annotated outline that provides references to the PowerPoint slides.

- **Test Bank** The Test Bank, also developed by C. R. Krishnaswamy, contains multiple-choice and short answer/discussion questions. The level of difficulty is varied and is indicated by using a label of easy, medium, or difficult.

- **Computerized Test Bank** McGraw-Hill's EZ Test is a flexible and easy-to-use electronic testing program. The program allows instructors to create tests from book-specific items. It accommodates a wide range of question types and instructors may add their own questions. Multiple versions of the test can be created and any test can be exported for use with course management systems such as WebCT, BlackBoard, or PageOut. EZ Test Online is a new service and gives you a place to easily administer your EZ Test–created exams and quizzes online. The program is available for Windows and Macintosh environments.

- **PowerPoint Presentation System** Matt Will of the University of Indianapolis prepared the PowerPoint Presentation, which contains exhibits, outlines, key points, and summaries in a visually stimulating collection of slides. You can edit, print, or rearrange the slides to fit the needs of your course.

For the Student

Online Learning Center
www.mhhe.com/bma1e

Find a wealth of information online! This site contains information about the book and the authors as well as teaching and learning materials for the instructor and the student, including:

- **Excel Templates** There are templates for selected exhibits ("live" Excel), as well as various end-of-chapter problems, that have been set as Excel spreadsheets—all denoted by an icon. They correlate with specific concepts in the text and allow students to work through financial problems and gain experience using spreadsheets. End-of-chapter templates were prepared by Peter R. Crabb of Northwest Nazarene University.

- **Interactive FinSims** This valuable asset consists of multiple simulations of key financial topics. Ideal for students to use in order to reinforce their knowledge and gain additional practice to strengthen their skills.

- **Online Quizzes** These multiple-choice questions are provided as an additional testing and reinforcement tool for students. Each quiz is organized by chapter to test the specific concepts presented in that particular chapter. Immediate scoring of the quiz will occur upon submission and the correct answers will be provided.

- **Standard & Poor's Educational Version of Market Insight** McGraw-Hill is proud to partner with Standard & Poor's by offering instructors and students access to the educational version of Market Insight. A passcode card is bound into new books, which gives you access to six years of financial data for over 1,000 companies. Relevant chapters contain end-of-chapter problems that use these data to help you gain a better understanding of practical business situations.

ACKNOWLEDGMENTS
We have a long list of people to thank for their helpful criticism of earlier editions of *Principles* and for assistance in preparing this *Concise* edition. They include Aleijda de Cazenove Balsan, Kedran Garrison, Robert Pindyck, and Gretchen Slemmons at MIT; Stefania Uccheddu at London Business School; Lynda Borucki, Michael Barhum, Marjorie Fischer, Larry Kolbe, Michael Vilbert, Bente Villadsen, and Fiona Wang at The Brattle Group, Inc.; Alex Triantis

at the University of Maryland; Julie Wulf and Jinghua Yan at the University of Pennsylvania; Adam Kolasinski at the University of Washington; and Simon Gervais at Duke University.

We want to express our appreciation to those instructors whose insightful comments and suggestions were invaluable to us during the revision process:

Neyaz Ahmed *University of Maryland*

Noyan Arsen *Koc University*

Jan Bartholdy *ASB, Denmark*

Penny Belk *Loughborough University*

Omar Benkato *Ball State University*

Eric Benrud *University of Baltimore*

Peter Berman *University of New Haven*

Michael Roberts *University of Pennsylvania*

Alon Brav *Duke University*

Jean Canil *University of Adelaide*

John Cooney *Texas Tech University*

Charles Cuny *Washington University, St. Louis*

Adri DeRidder *Gotland University*

William Dimovski *Deakin University, Melbourne*

David Ding *Nanyang Technological University*

Robert Duvic *University of Texas at Austin*

Robert Everett *Johns Hopkins University*

Christopher Geczy *University of Pennsylvania*

Stuart Gillan *University of Delaware*

Felix Goltz *Edhec Business School*

Ning Gong *Melbourne Business School*

Gary Gray *Pennsylvania State University*

C. J. Green *Loughborough University*

Mark Griffiths *Thunderbird, American School of International Management*

Re-Jin Guo *University of Illinois, Chicago*

Winfried Hallerbach *Erasmus University, Rotterdam*

Milton Harris *University of Chicago*

Glenn Henderson *University of Cincinnati*

Donna Hitscherich *Columbia University*

Ronald Hoffmeister *Arizona State University*

Ravi Jagannathan *Northwestern University*

Jarl Kallberg *NYU, Stern School of Business*

Ron Kaniel *Duke University*

Steve Kaplan *University of Chicago*

Arif Khurshed *Manchester Business School*

Ken Kim *University of Wisconsin, Milwaukee*

C. R. Krishnaswamy *Western Michigan University*

George Kutner *Marquette University*

David Lins *University of Illinois, Urbana*

David Lovatt *University of East Anglia*

Debbie Lucas *Northwestern University*

Brian Lucey *Trinity College, Dublin*

Suren Mansinghka *University of California, Irvine*

George McCabe *University of Nebraska*

Joe Messina *San Francisco State University*

Dag Michalsen *BI, Oslo*

Franklin Michello *Middle Tennessee State University*

Peter Moles *University of Edinburgh*

Claus Parum *Copenhagen Business School*

Dilip Patro *Rutgers University*

John Percival *University of Pennsylvania*

Latha Ramchand *University of Houston*

Narendar V. Rao *Northeastern University*

Raghavendra Rau *Purdue University*

Charu Reheja *Vanderbilt University*

Tom Rietz *University of Iowa*

Robert Ritchey *Texas Tech University*

Michael Roberts *University of Pennsylvania*

Mo Rodriguez *Texas Christian University*

John Rozycki *Drake University*

Marc Schauten *Eramus University*

Brad Scott *Webster University*

Jay Shanken *Emory University*

Chander Shekhar *University of Melbourne*

Nejat Seyhun *University of Michigan*

Richard Simonds *Michigan State University*

Bernell Stone *Brigham Young University*

Shrinivasan Sundaram *Ball State University*

Avanidhar Subrahmanyam *University of California, Los Angeles*

Tim Sullivan *Bentley College*

Stephen Todd *Loyola University, Chicago*

Walter Torous *University of California, Los Angeles*

Ilias Tsiakas *University of Warwick*

David Vang *St. Thomas University*

Steve Venti *Dartmouth College*

John Wald *Rutgers University*

Kelly Welch *University of Kansas*

Jill Wetmore *Saginaw Valley State University*

Patrick Wilkie *University of Virginia*

Matt Will *University of Indianapolis*

Art Wilson *George Washington University*

Shee Wong *University of Minnesota, Duluth*

Minhua Yang *University of Central Florida*

This list is surely incomplete. We know how much we owe to our colleagues at the London Business School, MIT's Sloan School of Management, and the University of Pennsylvania's Wharton School. In many cases, the ideas that appear in this book are as much their ideas as ours.

We would also like to thank all those at McGraw-Hill/Irwin who worked on the book, including Michele Janicek, Executive Editor; Christina Kouvelis, Developmental Editor II; Lori Koetters, Managing Editor; Ashley Smith, Marketing Manager; Jennifer Jelinski, Marketing Specialist; Cara David, Designer; Michael McCormick, Senior Production Supervisor; Kerry Bowler, Media Project Manager; and Greg Bates, Media Producer.

Finally, we record the continuing thanks due to our wives, Diana, Maureen, and Sally, who were unaware when they married us that they were also marrying the *Principles of Corporate Finance*.

Richard A. Brealey
Stewart C. Myers
Franklin Allen

GUIDED TOUR

Pedagogical Features

PART INTRODUCTIONS

Introductions to each part explain the links between different concepts. They include real-world examples that provide motivation for the chapters that follow. A listing of pertinent Web sites is provided at **www.mhhe.com/bma1e.**

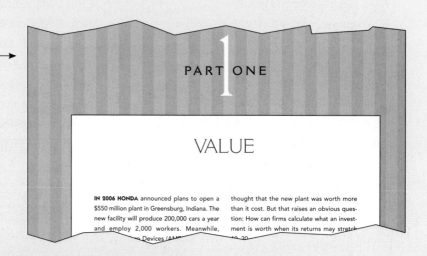

PART ONE
1

VALUE

IN 2006 HONDA announced plans to open a $550 million plant in Greensburg, Indiana. The new facility will produce 200,000 cars a year and employ 2,000 workers. Meanwhile, ... Devices (AM...

thought that the new plant was worth more than it cost. But that raises an obvious question: How can firms calculate what an investment is worth when its returns may stretch ...

FINANCE IN THE NEWS BOXES

Relevant news articles from financial publications appear in various chapters throughout the text. Aimed at bringing real life into the classroom, these boxes provide insight into the business world today.

FINANCE IN THE NEWS

WARREN BUFFETT ON GROWTH AND PROFITABILITY

I thought it would be instructive to go back and look at a couple of industries that transformed this country much earlier in this century: automobiles and aviation. Take automobiles first: I have here one page, out of 70 in total, of car and truck manufacturers that have operated in this country. At one time, there was a Berkshire car and an Omaha car. Naturally I noticed those. But there was also a telephone book of others.

All told, there appear to have been at least 2,000 car makes, in an industry that had an incredible impact on people's lives. If you had foreseen in the earl... ...ndustry would ...

the airplane—another industry whose plainly brilliant future would have caused investors to salivate. So I went back to check out aircraft manufacturers and found that in the 1919–39 period, there were about 300 companies, only a handful still breathing today. Among the planes made then—we must have been the Silicon Valley of that age—were both the Nebraska and the Omaha, two aircraft that even the most loyal Nebraskan no longer relies upon.

Move on to failures of airlines. Here's a list of 129 airlines that in the past 20 years filed for bankruptcy. Continental was smart enough to make that li... ...As of 199...

EXCEL INTEGRATION

Selected exhibits are set as Excel spreadsheets and new end-of-chapter Excel questions are included. The templates are available on the book Web site at **www.mhhe.com/bma1e** and are denoted by an icon.

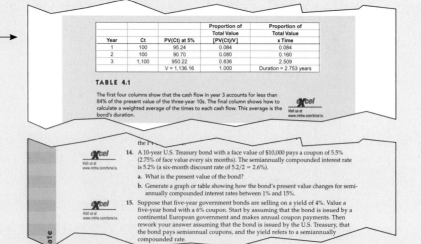

Year	Ct	PV(Ct) at 5%	Proportion of Total Value [PV(Ct)/V]	Proportion of Total Value x Time
1	100	95.24	0.084	0.084
2	100	90.70	0.080	0.160
3	1,100	950.22	0.836	2.509
		V = 1,136.16	1.000	Duration = 2.753 years

TABLE 4.1

The first four columns show that the cash flow in year 3 accounts for less than 84% of the present value of the three-year 10s. The final column shows how to calculate a weighted average of the times to each cash flow. This average is the bond's duration.

excel
Visit us at
www.mhhe.com/bma1e.

14. A 10-year U.S. Treasury bond with a face value of $10,000 pays a coupon of 5.5% (2.75% of face value every six months). The semiannually compounded interest rate is 5.2% (a six-month discount rate of 5.2/2 = 2.6%).

  a. What is the present value of the bond?

  b. Generate a graph or table showing how the bond's present value changes for semiannually compounded interest rates between 1% and 15%.

15. Suppose that five-year government bonds are selling on a yield of 4%. Value a five-year bond with a 6% coupon. Start by assuming that the bond is issued by a continental European government and makes annual coupon payments. Then rework your answer assuming that the bond is issued by the U.S. Treasury, that the bond pays semiannual coupons, and the yield refers to a semiannually compounded rate.

End-of-Chapter Features

WEB PROJECTS

Featured among selected chapters are Web Projects that give students the opportunity to explore financial Web sites on their own to gain familiarity and apply chapter concepts.

WEB PROJECTS

There are dozens of Web sites that provide calculators to help with personal financial decisions. Two good examples are **www.quicken.com** and **www.smartmoney.com**. (*Note:* for both calculators the annual rate is quoted as 12 times the monthly rate.)

1. Suppose that you have $5,000 in the bank and plan to save $500 a month. If you earn a return of 12% a year (1% a month), how much will you have accumulated by the time that you retire in 30 years? Now log in to the Quicken site and find a nice savings calculator. Use this to check your answer.

2. Suppose that you take out a 30-year mortgage loan of $200,000 at an interest rate of 10%. What is your total monthly payment? How much of the first month's payment goes to reduce the size of the loan? How much of the payment after two years goes to reduce the amount of the loan? You can check your answers by logging in to the personal finance page of **www.smartmoney.com** and using the mortgage calculator.

CONCEPT REVIEW QUESTIONS

These questions review the concepts illustrated within each chapter and serve as useful review. The first three questions are featured in the text and additional questions are provided on the book Web site at **www.mhhe.com/bma1e,** as denoted by the instructional banner.

CONCEPT REVIEW QUESTIONS

Visit us at www.mhhe.com

1. Write down the formula for the present value of an investment that produces cash flows of C_1, C_2 and C_3. (page 37)
2. What is the formula for the two-year discount factor, DF_2? (page 37)
3. Can the two-period discount rate (r_2) ever be smaller than the one-period rate (r_1)? (page 38)

For a complete listing of your chapter Concept Review Questions, please visit us at www.mhhe.com/bma1e.

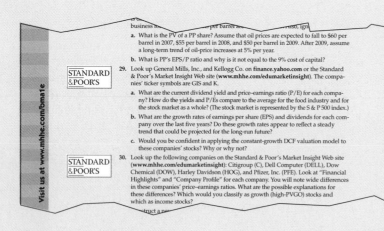

business ... per barrel ar... ...riso, ign...

a. What is the PV of a PP share? Assume that oil prices are expected to fall to $60 per barrel in 2007, $55 per barrel in 2008, and $50 per barrel in 2009. After 2009, assume a long-term trend of oil-price increases at 5% per year.

b. What is PP's EPS/P ratio and why is it not equal to the 9% cost of capital?

STANDARD &POOR'S

29. Look up General Mills, Inc., and Kellogg Co. on **finance.yahoo.com** or the Standard & Poor's Market Insight Web site (**www.mhhe.com/edumarketinsight**). The companies' ticker symbols are GIS and K.

a. What are the current dividend yield and price-earnings ratio (P/E) for each company? How do the yields and P/Es compare to the average for the food industry and for the stock market as a whole? (The stock market is represented by the S & P 500 index.)

b. What are the growth rates of earnings per share (EPS) and dividends for each company over the last five years? Do these growth rates appear to reflect a steady trend that could be projected for the long-run future?

c. Would you be confident in applying the constant-growth DCF valuation model to these companies' stocks? Why or why not?

STANDARD &POOR'S

30. Look up the following companies on the Standard & Poor's Market Insight Web site (**www.mhhe.com/edumarketinsight**): Citigroup (C), Dell Computer (DELL), Dow Chemical (DOW), Harley Davidson (HOG), and Pfizer, Inc. (PFE). Look at "Financial Highlights" and "Company Profile" for each company. You will note wide differences in these companies' price-earnings ratios. What are the possible explanations for these differences? Which would you classify as growth (high-PVGO) stocks and which as income stocks?

...struct a ne...

STANDARD & POOR'S INTEGRATION

Selected chapters include problems that directly incorporate the Educational Version of Market Insight, a service based on S&P's renowned Compustat database. These problems provide you with an easy method of including current, real-world data into your course. An access code is provided FREE with the purchase of a new book.

MINI-CASES

To enhance the concepts discussed within a chapter, updated mini-cases are included in selected chapters so students can apply their knowledge to real-world scenarios.

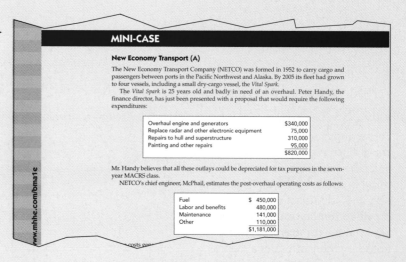

MINI-CASE

New Economy Transport (A)

The New Economy Transport Company (NETCO) was formed in 1952 to carry cargo and passengers between ports in the Pacific Northwest and Alaska. By 2005 its fleet had grown to four vessels, including a small dry-cargo vessel, the *Vital Spark.*

The *Vital Spark* is 25 years old and badly in need of an overhaul. Peter Handy, the finance director, has just been presented with a proposal that would require the following expenditures:

Overhaul engine and generators	$340,000
Replace radar and other electronic equipment	75,000
Repairs to hull and superstructure	310,000
Painting and other repairs	95,000
	$820,000

Mr. Handy believes that all these outlays could be depreciated for tax purposes in the seven-year MACRS class.

NETCO's chief engineer, McPhail, estimates the post-overhaul operating costs as follows:

Fuel	$ 450,000
Labor and benefits	480,000
Maintenance	141,000
Other	110,000
	$1,181,000

...costs gen...

GLOBAL INDEX

Because many concepts in financial management are relevant around the world, this edition provides updated and enhanced international coverage. The Global Index makes this information easy to access.

BRIEF CONTENTS

CONTENTS

CONTENTS

CONTENTS

CONTENTS

PART ONE

1

VALUE

IN 2006 HONDA announced plans to open a $550 million plant in Greensburg, Indiana. The new facility will produce 200,000 cars a year and employ 2,000 workers. Meanwhile, Advanced Micro Devices (AMD) declared its intention to build a multibillion-dollar chip plant in upstate New York.

What was special about these developments? Nothing, except perhaps their size! We cite them because they are typical of the investments in new products and equipment that are being made each day in the United States and the rest of the world.

Presumably, Honda and AMD decided to undertake the investments because they thought that the new plant was worth more than it cost. But that raises an obvious question: How can firms calculate what an investment is worth when its returns may stretch 10, 20, or more years into the future?

This is the topic of Part 1. To set the scene, Chapter 1 shows how businesses are organized and describes the role that the financial manager plays in evaluating investments and finding the money to pay for them. Chapter 2 starts to build a theory of value. By the end of Chapter 7, you should be able to tackle a standard investment decision, such as those faced by Honda and AMD.

Web sites related to this Part appear at www.mhhe.com/bma1e.

CHAPTER ONE

FINANCE AND THE FINANCIAL MANAGER

THIS BOOK IS about financial decisions made by corporations. We should start by saying what these decisions are and why they are important.

Corporations face two broad financial questions: What investments should the firm make? and How should it pay for those investments? The first question involves spending money; the second involves raising it.

The secret of success in financial management is to increase value. That is a simple statement, but not very helpful. It is like advising an investor in the stock market to "Buy low, sell high." The problem is how to do it.

There may be a few activities in which one can read a textbook and then do it, but financial management is not one of them. That is why finance is worth studying. Who wants to work in a field where there is no room for judgment, experience, creativity, and a pinch of luck? Although this book cannot supply any of these items, it does present the concepts and information on which good financial decisions are based, and it shows you how to use the tools of the trade of finance.

We start in this chapter by explaining what a corporation is and introducing you to the responsibilities of its financial managers. We will distinguish *real assets* from *financial assets* and *capital investment decisions* from *financing decisions*. We stress the importance of financial markets, both national and international, to the financial manager.

Finance is about money and markets, but it is also about people. The success of a corporation depends on how well it harnesses everyone to work to a common end. The financial manager must appreciate the conflicting objectives often encountered in financial management. Resolving conflicts is particularly difficult when people have different information. This is an important theme that runs through to the last chapter of this book. In this chapter we will start with some definitions and examples.

1.1   WHAT IS A CORPORATION?

Not all businesses are corporations. Small ventures can be owned and managed by a single individual. These are called *sole proprietorships*. In other cases several people may join to own and manage a *partnership*.[1] However, this book is about *corporate* finance. So we need to explain what a **corporation** is.

In the United States almost all large and medium-sized businesses are organized as corporations. For example, Boeing, Bank of America, Microsoft, and General Electric are corporations. So are businesses such as British Petroleum, Unilever, Nestlé, and Volkswagen in Europe, and Sony in Japan. In each case the firm is owned by stockholders who hold shares in the business.

When a corporation is first established, its shares may all be held by a small group of investors, perhaps the company's managers and a few backers. In this case the shares are not publicly traded and the company is *closely held*. Eventually, when the firm grows and new shares are issued to raise additional capital, its shares will be widely traded. Such corporations are known as *public companies*. Most well-known corporations in the United States are public companies. In many other countries, it's common for large companies to remain in private hands.

By organizing as a corporation, a business can attract a wide variety of investors. Some may hold only a single share worth a few dollars, cast only a single vote, and receive a tiny proportion of profits and dividends. Shareholders may also include giant pension funds and insurance companies whose investment may run to millions of shares and hundreds of millions of dollars, and who are entitled to a correspondingly large number of votes and proportion of profits and dividends.

Although the stockholders own the corporation, they do not manage it. Instead, they vote to elect a *board of directors*. Some of these directors may be drawn from top management, but others are non-executive directors, who are not employed by the firm. The board of directors represents the shareholders. It appoints top management and is supposed to ensure that managers act in the shareholders' best interests.

This *separation of ownership and management* gives corporations permanence.[2] Even if managers quit or are dismissed and replaced, the corporation can survive, and today's stockholders can sell all their shares to new investors without disrupting the operations of the business.

Unlike partnerships and sole proprietorships, corporations have **limited liability**, which means that stockholders cannot be held personally responsible for the firm's debts. When Enron and WorldCom went belly-up in 2001 and 2002—two of the largest bankruptcies ever—no one demanded that their stockholders put up more money to cover the companies' debts. Stockholders can lose their entire investment, but no more.

Although a corporation is owned by its stockholders, it is legally distinct from them. It is based on *articles of incorporation* that set out the purpose of the business, how many shares can be issued, the number of directors to be appointed, and so

---

[1] Many professional businesses, such as accounting and legal firms, are partnerships. Most large investment banks started as partnerships, but eventually these companies and their financing needs grew too large for them to continue in this form. Goldman Sachs, the last of the leading investment-bank partnerships, issued shares and became a public corporation in 1998.

[2] Corporations can be immortal but the law requires partnerships to have a definite end. A partnership agreement must specify an ending date or a procedure for wrapping up the partnership's affairs. A sole proprietorship also will have an end because the proprietor is mortal.

on. These articles must conform to the laws of the state in which the business is incorporated.[3] For many legal purposes, the corporation is considered as a resident of its state. As a legal "person," it can borrow or lend money, and it can sue or be sued. It pays its own taxes (but it cannot vote!).

Because the corporation is distinct from its shareholders, it can do things that partnerships and sole proprietorships cannot. For example, it can raise money by selling new shares to investors and it can buy those shares back. One corporation can make a takeover bid for another and then merge the two businesses.

There are also some *disadvantages* to organizing as a corporation. Managing a corporation's legal machinery and communicating with shareholders can be time-consuming and costly. Furthermore, in the United States there is an important tax drawback. Because the corporation is a separate legal entity, it is taxed separately. So corporations pay tax on their profits, and, in addition, shareholders pay tax on any dividends that they receive from the company. The United States is unusual in this respect. To avoid taxing the same income twice, most other countries give shareholders at least some credit for the tax that the company has already paid.[4]

1.2   THE ROLE OF THE FINANCIAL MANAGER

To carry on business, corporations need an almost endless variety of **real assets.** Many of these assets are tangible, such as machinery, factories, and offices; others are intangible, such as technical expertise, trademarks, and patents. All of them need to be paid for. To obtain the necessary money, the corporation sells claims on its real assets and on the cash those assets will generate. These claims are called **financial assets** or **securities.** For example, if the company borrows money from the bank, the bank gets a written promise that the money will be repaid with interest. Thus the bank trades cash for a financial asset. Financial assets include not only bank loans but also shares of stock, bonds, and a dizzying variety of specialized securities.

The financial manager stands between the firm's operations and the **financial (or capital) markets,** where investors hold the financial assets issued by the firm.[5] The financial manager's role is illustrated in Figure 1.1, which traces the flow of cash from investors to the firm and back to investors again. The flow starts when the firm sells securities to raise cash (arrow 1 in the figure). The cash is used to purchase real assets used in the firm's operations (arrow 2). Later, if the firm does well, the real assets generate cash inflows that more than repay the initial investment (arrow 3). Finally, the cash is either reinvested (arrow 4*a*) or returned to the investors who bought the securities (arrow 4*b*). Of course, the choice between arrows 4*a* and 4*b* is not completely free. For example, if a bank lends money at stage 1, the bank has to be repaid the money plus interest at stage 4*b*.

---

[3] In the United States Delaware has a well-developed and supportive system of corporate law. Even though they may do little business in that state, a high proportion of U. S. corporations are incorporated in Delaware.

[4] We describe some other countries' corporate tax systems in Chapter 13.

[5] You will hear financial managers use the terms *financial markets* and *capital markets* almost synonymously. But *capital markets* are, strictly speaking, the source of long-term financing only. Short-term financing comes from the *money market*. "Short-term" means less than one year. We use the term *financial markets* to refer to all sources of financing.

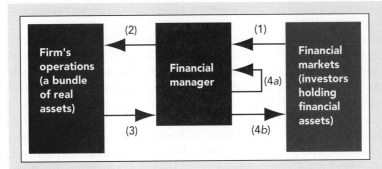

FIGURE 1.1

Flow of cash between financial markets and the firm's operations. Key: (1) Cash raised by selling financial assets to investors; (2) cash invested in the firm's operations and used to purchase real assets; (3) cash generated by the firm's operations; (4a) cash reinvested; (4b) cash returned to investors.

Our diagram takes us back to the financial manager's two basic questions. First, what real assets should the firm invest in? Second, how should the cash for the investment be raised? The answer to the first question is the firm's **investment,** or **capital budgeting, decision.** The answer to the second is the firm's **financing decision.**

Investment and financing decisions are typically *separated*, that is, analyzed independently. When an investment opportunity or "project" is identified, the financial manager first asks whether the project is worth more than the capital required to undertake it. If the answer is yes, he or she then considers how the project should be financed.

But the separation of investment and financing decisions does *not* mean that the financial manager can forget about investors and financial markets when analyzing capital investment projects. As we will see in the next chapter, the fundamental financial objective of the firm is to maximize the value of the cash invested in the firm by its stockholders. Look again at Figure 1.1. Stockholders are happy to contribute cash at arrow 1 only if the decisions made at arrow 2 generate at least adequate returns at arrow 3. "Adequate" means returns at least equal to the returns that stockholders could earn by investing in financial markets. If your firm's projects consistently generate *less* than adequate returns, your shareholders will want their money back.

Financial managers of large corporations need to be men and women of the world. They must decide not only *which* assets their firm should invest in but also *where* those assets should be located. Take Nestlé, for example. It is a Swiss company, but only a small proportion of its production takes place in Switzerland. Its 484 factories are located in 87 countries. Nestlé's managers must therefore know how to evaluate investments in countries with different currencies, interest rates, inflation rates, and tax systems.

The financial markets in which the firm raises money are likewise international. The stockholders of large corporations are scattered around the globe. Shares are traded around the clock in New York, London, Tokyo, and other financial centers. Bonds and bank loans move easily across national borders. Consequently, a corporation that needs to raise cash doesn't have to borrow from its hometown bank. Day-to-day cash management also becomes a complex task for firms that produce or sell in different countries. For example, think of the problems that Nestlé's financial managers face in keeping track of the cash receipts and payments in 87 countries.

We admit that Nestlé is unusual, but few financial managers can close their eyes to international financial issues. So throughout the book we will pay attention to differences in financial systems and examine the problems of investing and raising money internationally.

The financial manager does not work in a vacuum. A wide range of financial institutions has grown up to supply the firm with capital and to offer a variety of other financial services. For example, the firm may go to a bank to raise short-term debt or to an insurance company for a longer-term loan. It may raise cash by selling additional shares to mutual funds, pension funds, and other investors. It may engage an investment bank to advise on a new issue of shares or to assist in merger negotiations. And so on. The firm's financial manager needs a good understanding of how requests will be viewed by these financial institutions. Likewise, to understand the firm's needs and how best to satisfy them, the managers of the financial institutions must themselves have a good grasp of the principles of corporate finance.

In Figure 1.1, financial markets are simply a source of financing for corporations. Speaking more broadly, we can view financial markets as a mechanism for transporting savings from every nook and cranny in the economy to productive investments throughout the economy. But financial markets serve several other important functions.

Financial markets provide liquidity for investors, that is, the ability to trade securities, if necessary on short notice, and the flexibility to align their investment portfolios with their personal goals and preferences. There is no necessary link between the risks and durations of the firm's investments and the risks and durations of shareholder's portfolios. As we will see in Chapter 2, the firm doesn't have to worry about the investment horizons and risk tolerances of its shareholders. The firm can pursue the simple goal of maximizing value.

Financial markets also allow investors to reduce risk by diversification and to adjust their exposure to the market risks that can't be diversified away. The firm doesn't need to diversify, however, because investors can do so on their own. But firms can use financial markets to *manage* risk, for example by hedging particular risks that would otherwise interfere with the firm's operations. We discuss risk and risk management extensively in this book, especially in Chapters 8 through 10.

Financial managers also look to financial markets as a source of information about interest rates, raw material prices, and market values of firms and securities. For example, the financial manager can look to his or her own stock price as a month-to-month report card on the firm's financial performance.

1.3 WHO IS THE FINANCIAL MANAGER?

In this book we will use the term *financial manager* to refer to anyone responsible for a significant investment or financing decision. But only in the smallest firms is a single person responsible for all the decisions discussed in this book. In most cases, responsibility is dispersed. Top management is of course continuously involved in financial decisions. But the engineer who designs a new production facility is also involved: The design determines the kind of real assets the firm will hold. The marketing manager who commits to a major advertising campaign is also making an important investment decision. The campaign is an investment in an intangible asset that is expected to pay off in future sales and earnings.

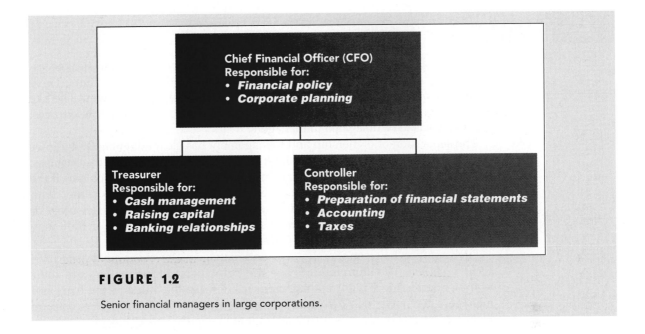

FIGURE 1.2

Senior financial managers in large corporations.

Nevertheless there are some managers who specialize in finance. Their roles are summarized in Figure 1.2. The **treasurer** is responsible for looking after the firm's cash, raising new capital, and maintaining relationships with banks, stockholders, and other investors who hold the firm's securities.

For small firms, the treasurer is likely to be the only financial executive. Larger corporations also have a **controller,** who prepares the financial statements, manages the firm's internal accounting, and looks after its tax obligations. You can see that the treasurer and controller have different functions: The treasurer's main responsibility is to obtain and manage the firm's capital, whereas the controller ensures that the money is used efficiently.

Still larger firms usually appoint a **chief financial officer (CFO)** to oversee both the treasurer's and the controller's work. The CFO is deeply involved in financial policy and corporate planning. Often he or she will have general managerial responsibilities beyond strictly financial issues and may also be a member of the board of directors.

The CFO is usually responsible for organizing and supervising the capital budgeting process. However, major capital investment projects are so closely tied to plans for product development, production, and marketing that managers from these areas are inevitably drawn into planning and analyzing the projects. If the firm has staff members specializing in corporate planning, they too are naturally involved in capital budgeting.

Because of the importance of many financial issues, ultimate decisions often rest by law or by custom with the board of directors. For example, only the board has the legal power to declare a dividend or to sanction a public issue of securities. Boards usually delegate decisions for small or medium-sized investment outlays, but the authority to approve large investments is almost never delegated.

1.4 SEPARATION OF OWNERSHIP AND MANAGEMENT

In large businesses separation of ownership and management is a practical necessity. Major corporations may have hundreds of thousands of shareholders. There is no way for all of them to be actively involved in management: It would be like running New York City through a series of town meetings for all its citizens. Authority has to be delegated to managers.

The separation of ownership and management has clear advantages. It allows share ownership to change without interfering with the operation of the business. It allows the firm to hire professional managers. But it also brings problems if the managers' and owners' objectives differ. You can see the danger: Rather than attending to the wishes of shareholders, managers may seek a more leisurely or luxurious working lifestyle; they may shun unpopular decisions, or they may attempt to build an empire with their shareholders' money.

Such conflicts between shareholders' and managers' objectives create *principal–agent problems*. The shareholders are the principals; the managers are their agents. Shareholders want management to increase the value of the firm, but managers may have their own axes to grind or nests to feather. **Agency costs** are incurred when (1) managers do not attempt to maximize firm value and (2) shareholders incur costs to monitor the managers and influence their actions. Of course, there are no costs when the shareholders are also the managers. That is one of the advantages of a sole proprietorship. Owner–managers have no conflicts of interest.

Conflicts between shareholders and managers are not the only principal–agent problems that the financial manager is likely to encounter. For example, just as shareholders need to encourage managers to work for the shareholders' interests, so senior management needs to think about how to motivate everyone else in the company. In this case senior management are the principals and junior management and other employees are their agents.

Agency costs can also arise in financing. In normal times, the banks and bondholders who lend the company money are united with the shareholders in wanting the company to prosper, but when the firm gets into trouble, this unity of purpose can break down. At such times decisive action may be necessary to rescue the firm, but lenders are concerned to get their money back and are reluctant to see the firm making risky changes that could imperil the safety of their loans. Squabbles may even break out between different lenders as they see the company heading for possible bankruptcy and jostle for a better place in the queue of creditors.

Think of the company's overall value as a pie that is divided among a number of claimants. These include the management and the shareholders, as well as the company's workforce and the banks and investors who have bought the company's debt. The government is a claimant too, since it gets to tax corporate profits.

All these claimants are bound together in a complex web of contracts and understandings. For example, when banks lend money to the firm, they insist on a formal contract stating the rate of interest and repayment dates, perhaps placing restrictions on dividends or additional borrowing. But you can't devise written rules to cover every possible future event. So written contracts are incomplete and need to be supplemented by understandings and by arrangements that help to align the interests of the various parties.

Principal–agent problems would be easier to resolve if everyone had the same information. That is rarely the case in finance. Managers, shareholders, and lenders may all have different information about the value of a real or financial asset, and it may be many years before all the information is revealed. Financial managers need to recognize these *information asymmetries* and find ways to reassure investors that there are no nasty surprises on the way.

Here is one example. Suppose you are the financial manager of a company that has been newly formed to develop and bring to market a drug to cure toetitis. At a meeting with potential investors you present the results of clinical trials, show upbeat reports by an independent market research company, and forecast profits amply sufficient to justify further investment. But the potential investors are still worried that you may know more than they do. What can you do to convince them that you are telling the truth? Just saying "Trust me" won't do the trick. Perhaps you need to *signal* your integrity by putting your money where your mouth is. For example, investors are likely to have more confidence in your plans if they see that you and the other managers have large personal stakes in the new enterprise. Therefore your decision to invest your own money can provide information to investors about the true prospects of the firm. In later chapters we will look more carefully at how corporations tackle the problems created by differences in objectives and information.

Human beings are only human, and even hard-headed financial managers may be subject to congenital biases such as overconfidence or overoptimism. When forecasting, they may place excessive weight on recent experience; they may be tempted to throw good money after bad to rescue a losing project; and so on. Consequently, in this book we will sometimes turn to behavioral psychology for help in explaining seemingly irrational actions of managers and investors.

1.5   TOPICS COVERED IN THIS BOOK

We have mentioned how financial managers face two broad decisions—which real assets the firm should invest in and how to raise the cash to pay for them. Thus, the investment decision typically precedes the financial decision. That is how we have organized this book. Parts 1 to 3 are almost entirely devoted to different aspects of the investment decision. The first topic is how to value real and financial assets, the second is the link between risk and value, and the third is the management of the capital investment process.

Parts 4 to 6 are concerned with financing decisions. We start with a crucial question. Can the financial manager assume that the market will fairly value the firm's securities? There is a lot of evidence that securities are fairly priced, but we will also encounter some puzzling anomalies. Part 5 focuses on two fundamental financing decisions: How much should the firm pay out to its shareholders and how much should it borrow? In Part 6 we move on to look at options and how they are valued. Options may be tacked on to an issue of corporate securities and they often lurk in the *real* assets that the company owns.

Part 7 covers financial planning and short-term financial management. We address a variety of practical topics, including short- and longer-term forecasting, channels for short-term borrowing or investment, and possible homes for any surplus cash.

SUMMARY

In Chapter 2 we will begin with the most basic concepts of asset valuation. However, we should first sum up the principal points made in this introductory chapter.

Large businesses are usually organized as corporations. Corporations have three important features. First, they are legally distinct from their owners and pay their own taxes. Second, corporations provide limited liability, which means that the stockholders who own the corporation cannot be held responsible for the firm's debts. Third, the owners of a corporation are not usually the managers.

The overall task of the financial manager can be broken down into (1) the investment, or capital budgeting, decision and (2) the financing decision. In other words, the firm has to decide (1) what real assets to buy and (2) how to raise the necessary cash.

In small companies there is often only one financial executive, the treasurer. However, most companies have both a treasurer and a controller. The treasurer's job is to obtain and manage the company's financing, while the controller's job is to confirm that the money is used correctly. In large firms there is also a chief financial officer or CFO.

Shareholders want managers to increase the value of the company's stock, but managers may have different objectives. This potential conflict of interest is termed a principal–agent problem. Any loss of value that results from such conflicts is termed an agency cost. Of course there may be other conflicts of interest. For example, the interests of the shareholders may sometimes conflict with those of the firm's banks and bondholders. These and other agency problems become more complicated when agents have more or better information than the principals.

The financial manager plays on an international stage and must understand how international financial markets operate and how to evaluate overseas investments. We discuss international corporate finance at many different points in the chapters that follow.

FURTHER READING

Financial managers read *The Wall Street Journal (WSJ), The Financial Times (FT),* or both daily. You should too. *The Financial Times* is published in Britain, but there are North American and Asian editions as well. There are also European and Asian editions of *The Wall Street Journal. The New York Times* and a few other big-city newspapers have good business and financial sections, but they are no substitute for the *WSJ* or *FT.* The business and financial sections of most United States dailies are, except for local news, nearly worthless for the financial manager.

The Economist, BusinessWeek, Forbes, and *Fortune* contain useful financial sections, and there are several magazines that specialize in finance. These include *Euromoney, Corporate Finance, Journal of Applied Corporate Finance, Risk,* and *CFO Magazine.* This list does not include research journals such as the *Journal of Finance, Journal of Financial Economics, Review of Financial Studies,* and *Financial Management.* In the following chapters we give specific references to pertinent research and to books and articles focused on practical applications.

1. What is meant by limited liability? Do corporations have limited liability? What about sole proprietorships? (page 3)

2. There is an important tax drawback in the United States to organizing as a corporation. What is it? (page 4)

3. Firms invest in real assets and finance them by selling financial assets. Give some examples of each. (page 4)

For a complete listing of your chapter Concept Review Questions, please visit us at www.mhhe.com/bma1e.

QUIZ

1. Read the following passage: "Companies usually buy (*a*) assets. These include both tangible assets such as (*b*) and intangible assets such as (*c*). In order to pay for these assets, they sell (*d*) assets such as (*e*). The decision about which assets to buy is usually termed the (*f*) or (*g*) decision. The decision about how to raise the money is usually termed the (*h*) decision." Now fit each of the following terms into the most appropriate space: *financing, real, bonds, investment, executive airplanes, financial, capital budgeting, brand names.*

2. Vocabulary test. Explain the differences between:
   a. Real and financial assets.
   b. Capital budgeting and financing decisions.
   c. Closely held and public corporations.
   d. Limited and unlimited liability.
   e. Corporation and partnership.

3. Which of the following are real assets, and which are financial?
   a. A share of stock.
   b. A personal IOU.
   c. A trademark.
   d. A factory.
   e. Undeveloped land.
   f. The balance in the firm's checking account.
   g. An experienced and hardworking sales force.
   h. A corporate bond.

4. What are the main *disadvantages* of the corporate form of organization?

5. Which of the following statements more accurately describe the treasurer than the controller?
   a. Likely to be the only financial executive in small firms.
   b. Monitors capital expenditures to make sure that they are not misappropriated.
   c. Responsible for investing the firm's spare cash.
   d. Responsible for arranging any issue of common stock.
   e. Responsible for the company's tax affairs.

Visit us at www.mhhe.com/bma1e

6. Which of the following statements always apply to corporations?
    a. Unlimited liability.
    b. Limited life.
    c. Ownership can be transferred without affecting operations.
    d. Managers can be fired with no effect on ownership.
    e. Shares must be widely traded.
7. In most large corporations, ownership and management are separated. What are the main implications of this separation?

CHAPTER TWO

PRESENT VALUES, THE OBJECTIVES OF THE FIRM, AND CORPORATE GOVERNANCE

COMPANIES INVEST IN a variety of real assets. These include tangible assets such as plant and machinery and intangible assets such as patents and training for employees. The object of the investment, or capital budgeting, decision is to find real assets that are worth more than they cost. In this chapter we will take the first, most basic steps toward understanding how assets are valued.

There are a few cases in which it is not that difficult to estimate asset values. In real estate, for example, you can hire a professional appraiser to do it for you. Suppose you own a warehouse. The odds are that your appraiser's estimate of its value will be within a few percent of what the building would actually sell for.[1] After all, there is continuous activity in the real estate market, and the appraiser's stock-in-trade is knowledge of the prices at which similar properties have recently changed hands. Thus the problem of valuing real estate is simplified by the existence of an active market in which all kinds of properties are bought and sold. For many purposes no formal theory of value is needed. We can take the market's word for it.

But we need to go deeper than that. First, it is important to know how asset values are reached in an active market. Even if you can take the appraiser's word for it, it is important to understand *why* that warehouse is worth, say, $2 million and not a higher or lower figure. Second, the market for most corporate assets is pretty thin. Look in the classified advertisements in *The Wall Street Journal:* It is not often that you see a blast furnace for sale.

Companies are always searching for assets that are worth more to them than to others. That warehouse is worth more to you if you can manage it better than others can. But in that case, looking at the price of similar buildings will not tell you what the warehouse is worth under your management. You need to know how asset values are determined. In other words, you need a theory of value.

This chapter starts to develop that theory. We lead off with a simple numerical example: Should you invest in a new office building in the hope of selling it at a profit next year? You should do so if net present value is positive, that is, if the new building's value today exceeds the investment that

(continued)

is required. A positive net present value implies that the rate of return on your investment is higher than the opportunity cost of capital.

This chapter's first task is to define and explain net present value, rate of return, and opportunity cost of capital. The second task is to explain *why* financial managers need to search for investments with positive net present values. Here we will come to the fundamental objective of corporate finance: maximizing the current value of the firm's shares. We will explain why all shareholders should support this objective and why it makes more sense

than other corporate goals, such as "maximizing profits."

Finally, we turn to the *managers'* objectives and discuss some of the mechanisms that help to align the managers' and stockholders' interests. We ask whether attempts to increase shareholder value need be at the expense of workers, customers, or the community at large.

In this chapter we will stick to the simplest numerical examples to make basic ideas clear. Readers with a taste for complication will find plenty to satisfy them in later chapters.

---

[1] Needless to say, there are some properties that appraisers find nearly impossible to value—for example, nobody knows the potential selling price of the Taj Mahal, the Parthenon, or Windsor Castle.

2.1   INTRODUCTION TO PRESENT VALUE

If you find an investment opportunity, how do you decide whether it is worthwhile? Suppose you come across a vacant lot that you can buy for $50,000. Your real estate adviser thinks there will be a shortage of office space a year from now and that an office building will fetch $420,000. For simplicity, we will assume that this $420,000 is a sure thing. The total cost of buying the land and constructing the building would be $370,000. Thus you would be investing $370,000 now to generate $420,000 a year hence. You should go ahead if the **present value (PV)** of the $420,000 payoff is greater than the investment of $370,000. Therefore, you need to ask, What is the value today of $420,000 to be received one year from now, and is that present value greater than $370,000?

Calculating Future Value and Present Value

The first basic principle of finance is that *a dollar today is worth more than a dollar tomorrow*, because the dollar today can be invested to start earning interest immediately. Financial managers refer to this as the *time value of money*. Suppose that the rate of interest on U.S. government securities is 5% per year. If you invest $400,000 at 5% interest, you will have $400,000 × 1.05 = $420,000 a year from now. The **future value** of $400,000 today is 1.05 × $400,000 = $420,000 a year from now.

In our example, we know the *future* value (the office building that will be worth $420,000), but we need to find the *present* value of that future payoff. Think again of the time value of money. Since $1 in hand today is worth more than $1 next year, $1 next year must be worth *less* than $1 today. Therefore $420,000 next year must be worth less than $420,000 today—but how much less? The answer is $400,000, because investors can put up $400,000 today, earn 5% interest, and get $420,000 next year.

The arithmetic of present value is simple. Just run our future value calculation in reverse. If the interest rate is 5%, then the present value of $420,000 one year from now is $420,000/1.05 = $400,000. To find the present value, we divide the future cash flow by 1.05, or multiply it by 1/1.05. This multiplier (1/1.05 in our example) is called the **discount factor.** In general, if C_1 denotes the expected payoff at date 1 (one year hence), then

$$\text{Present value } (PV) = \text{discount factor} \times C_1$$

This discount factor is the value today of $1 received in the future. It is expressed as the reciprocal of 1 plus a rate of return:

$$\text{Discount factor} = \frac{1}{1 + r}$$

The rate of return r is the reward that investors demand for accepting delayed payment.

To calculate present value, we discount expected payoffs by the rate of return offered by equivalent investment alternatives in the capital market. This rate of return is the **discount rate, hurdle rate,** or **opportunity cost of capital.** It is called the opportunity cost because it is the return foregone by investing in the project rather than investing in securities. In our example the opportunity cost was 5%. Present value was obtained by dividing $420,000 by 1.05:

$$PV = \text{discount factor} \times C_1 = \frac{1}{1 + r} \times C_1 = \frac{420{,}000}{1.05} = \$400{,}000$$

Let us assume that as soon as you have bought the land and begun construction, you decide to sell your project. How much could you sell it for? That is an easy question. Since the property will be worth $420,000 in a year, investors would be willing to pay $400,000 for it today. That is what it would cost them to get a $420,000 payoff from investing in government securities. Of course, you could always sell your property for less, but why sell for less than the market will bear? The $400,000 present value is the only feasible price that satisfies both buyer and seller. Therefore, the present value of the property is also its market price.

Net Present Value

The office building is worth $400,000, but this does not mean you are $400,000 better off. You committed $370,000 and therefore the **net present value (NPV)** is $30,000. Net present value is found by subtracting the required investment:

$$NPV = PV - \text{required investment} = 400{,}000 - 370{,}000 = \$30{,}000$$

In other words, your office development is worth more than it costs—it makes a *net* contribution to value and increases your wealth. The formula for calculating NPV can be written as

$$NPV = C_0 + \frac{C_1}{1 + r}$$

remembering that C_0, the cash flow at time 0 (that is, today), will usually be a negative number. In other words, C_0 is an investment and therefore a cash outflow. In our example, $C_0 = -\$370{,}000$.

Risk and Present Value

We made one unrealistic assumption in our discussion of the office development: Your real estate adviser cannot be certain about the future value of an office building. The $420,000 represents the best forecast, but it is not a sure thing.

If the future value of the building is risky, our calculation of NPV is wrong. Investors could achieve $420,000 with certainty by buying $400,000 worth of U.S. government securities, so they would not buy your building for that amount. You would have to cut your asking price to attract investors' interest.

Here we can invoke a second basic financial principle: *A safe dollar is worth more than a risky one*. Most investors avoid risk when they can do so without sacrificing return. However, the concepts of present value and the opportunity cost of capital still make sense for risky investments. It is still proper to discount the payoff by the rate of return offered by an equivalent investment. But we have to think of *expected* payoffs and the *expected* rates of return on other investments.[2]

Not all investments are equally risky. The office development is more risky than a government security but less risky than a start-up biotech venture. Suppose you believe the project is as risky as investment in the stock market and that stocks are forecasted to return 12%. Then 12% becomes the opportunity cost of capital. That is what you are giving up by not investing in equally risky securities. Now recompute NPV:

$$PV = \frac{420,000}{1.12} = \$375,000$$
$$NPV = PV - 370,000 = \$5,000$$

The office building still makes a net contribution to value, but the increase in your wealth is smaller than in our first calculation, which assumed that the future value of the office building was risk-free.

The value of the office building depends, therefore, on the timing of the cash flows and their uncertainty. The $420,000 payoff would be worth exactly that if it could be realized instantaneously. If the office building is as risk-free as government securities, the one-year delay *reduces value* by $20,000 to $400,000. If the building is as risky as investment in the stock market, then uncertainty further reduces value by $25,000 to $375,000.

If other investors agree with your forecast of a $420,000 payoff and your assessment of its risk, then your property ought to be worth $375,000 once construction is underway. If you tried to sell it for more, there would be no takers, because the property would then offer an expected rate of return lower than the 12% available in the stock market. Thus the office building's present value is also its market value.

Unfortunately, adjusting asset values for both time and uncertainty is often more complicated than our example suggests. Therefore, we will take the two effects separately. For the most part, we will dodge the problem of risk in Chapters 2 through 7, either by treating all cash flows as if they were known with certainty or by talking about expected cash flows and expected rates of return without worrying how risk is defined or measured. Then in Chapter 8 we will turn to the problem of understanding how financial markets cope with risk.

Present Values and Rates of Return

We have decided that construction of the office building is a smart thing to do, since it is worth more than it costs—it has a positive net present value and creates

---

[2] We define "expected" more carefully in Chapter 10. For now think of expected payoff as a realistic forecast, neither optimistic nor pessimistic. Forecasts of expected payoffs are correct on average.

wealth for you. To calculate how much it is worth, we worked out how much you would need to invest directly in securities to achieve the same payoff. The project's present value is equal to its future income discounted at the rate of return offered by these securities.

We can state our decision rule in another way: Our real estate venture is worth undertaking because its rate of return exceeds the cost of capital. The rate of return on the investment in the office building is simply the profit as a proportion of the initial outlay:

$$\text{Return} = \frac{\text{profit}}{\text{investment}} = \frac{420,000 - 370,000}{370,000} = .135, \text{ or } 13.5\%$$

The cost of capital is once again the return foregone by *not* investing in securities. If the office building is as risky as investing in the stock market, the return foregone is 12%. Since the 13.5% return on the office building exceeds the 12% opportunity cost, you should go ahead with the project.

Here, then, we have two equivalent decision rules for capital investment:[3]

- *Net present value rule.* Accept investments that have positive net present values.
- *Rate of return rule.* Accept investments that offer rates of return in excess of their opportunity costs of capital.[4]

The Opportunity Cost of Capital

The opportunity cost of capital is such an important concept that we will give one more example. You are offered the following opportunity: Invest $100,000 today and, depending on the state of the economy at the end of the year, you will receive one of these equally probable payoffs:

Slump	Normal	Boom
$80,000	$110,000	$140,000

Since the three scenarios all have probability 1/3, the expected payoff is

$$C_1 = \left(\frac{1}{3}\right)(80,000 + 110,000 + 140,000) = \$110,000$$

This represents an expected return of 10% on the investment of $100,000. But what's the right discount rate?

You search for a common stock with the same risk as the investment. Stock X turns out to be a perfect match. X's price next year, given a normal economy, is forecasted at $110. The stock price will be lower in a slump and higher in a boom, but to the same degrees as your investment ($80 in a slump and $140 in a boom). You conclude that the risks of stock X and your investment are identical.

---

[3] You might check for yourself that these are equivalent rules. In other words, if the return of $50,000/$370,000 is greater than *r*, then the net present value −$370,000 + [$420,000/(1 + *r*)] *must* be greater than 0.

[4] The two rules can conflict when there are cash flows at more than two dates. We address this problem in Chapter 6.

Stock X's current price is $95.65. It offers an expected rate of return of 15%:

$$\text{Expected return} = \frac{\text{expected profit}}{\text{investment}} = \frac{110 - 95.65}{95.65} = .15, \text{ or } 15\%$$

This is the expected return that you are giving up by investing in the project rather than the stock market. In other words, it is the project's opportunity cost of capital.

To value the project, discount the expected cash flow by the opportunity cost of capital:

$$PV = \frac{110,000}{1.15} = \$95,650$$

This is the amount it would cost investors in the stock market to buy an expected cash flow of $110,000. (They could do this by buying 1,000 shares of stock X.) It is therefore also the sum that investors would be prepared to pay for your project.

To calculate net present value, deduct the initial investment:

$$NPV = 95,650 - 100,000 = -\$4,350$$

The project is worth $4,350 less than it costs. It is *not* worth undertaking. Instead of creating wealth, it would destroy wealth and make you worse off, compared with investing in the stock market.

Notice that you come to the same conclusion if you compare the expected project return with the cost of capital:

$$\text{Expected return on project} = \frac{\text{expected profit}}{\text{investment}} = \frac{110,000 - 100,000}{100,000} = .10, \text{ or } 10\%$$

The 10% expected return on the project is less than the 15% return investors could expect to earn by investing in stock X, so the project is not worthwhile.

Of course in real life it's impossible to restrict the future states of the economy to just "slump," "normal," and "boom." We have also simplified by assuming a perfect match between the payoffs of 1,000 shares of stock X and the payoffs to the investment project. The main point of the example does carry through to real life, however. Remember this: The opportunity cost of capital for an investment project is the expected rate of return demanded by investors in common stocks or other securities subject to the same risks as the project. When you discount the project's expected cash flow at its opportunity cost of capital, the resulting present value is the amount investors would be willing to pay for the project. Any time you find and launch a positive-NPV project (a project with present value exceeding its outlay) you have created wealth.

A Source of Confusion

Here is a possible source of confusion. Suppose a banker approaches. "Your company is a fine and safe business with few debts," she says. "My bank will lend you the $100,000 that you need for the project at 8%." Does that mean that the cost of capital for the project is 8% ? If so, the project would be worth doing. At an 8% cost of capital, PV would be 110,000/1.08 = $101,852 and NPV = 101,852 − 100,000 = +$1,852.

But that can't be right. First, the interest rate on the loan has nothing to do with the risk of the project: It reflects the good health of your existing business. Second, whether you take the loan or not, you still face the choice between the project, which offers an expected return of 10%, or the equally risky stock which gives an expected return of 15%. A financial manager who borrows at 8% and invests at 10% is not smart, but stupid, if the company or its shareholders can borrow at 8% and buy an equally risky investment offering 15%. That is why the 15% expected return on the stock is the opportunity cost of capital for the project.

2.2   FOUNDATIONS OF THE NET PRESENT VALUE RULE

The net present value rule seems sensible enough. It worked for you when you decided to buy that vacant lot and constructed an office building on it. But will the rule work for everybody? Consider another investor who is short on cash and risk-averse. Would she really be willing to part with $370,000 immediately in exchange for a forecasted payoff of $420,000 next year? Or suppose that you're the CFO of a large corporation with many stockholders, who differ widely in age, wealth, and tolerance for risk. How could all those stockholders agree on the value added by a new investment?

Your First Day on the Job   You have just been hired by the stockholder relations department at ExxonMobil. The annual stockholders' meeting is scheduled for your first day of work, and you are asked to attend. The meeting itself seems routine, but you note how carefully the CEO explains ExxonMobil's plans for capital investment. The extra explanation makes sense, you realize, because the planned capital investments exceed $15 billion annually.

After the formal meeting you mingle at the shareholders' coffee hour. You can't help overhearing a rather heated exchange between an elderly woman, evidently retired, and an earnest young man:

Retired woman: The company's spending a fortune on developing new
    fields. Why have they bought a 30% stake in that Sakhalin project in
    Russia? It's going to cost more than $12 billion to develop, and it won't
    pay off for decades. Let someone else look for oil in Russia. I would prefer
    a bigger dividend. The dollar's down and I have to pay for my annual
    trip to Tuscany.

Earnest young man: Would you like to see some pictures of my new daughter
    Michelle? Of course you would—don't worry, I've only got a dozen. I bought
    the ExxonMobil shares for her. She needs diapers, not dividends. Our
    company should invest for the long run. That oil from Russia will pay for
    her college education.

You are tempted to intervene, but hesitate. What should you say? They are only two of many thousands of ExxonMobil shareholders, and even they can't agree. Could the development of new fields be good news for little Michelle and bad news for the retired globetrotter? What about other stockholders? Some may combine long-run objectives with high risk-aversion. Could a risk-averse, long-term investor agree with Michelle's dad on the wisdom of ExxonMobil's investment in an offshore field in eastern Russia?

The answer to these questions is yes: all of ExxonMobil's stockholders should be able to agree on its investment plans, provided that the investments all have positive NPVs and that all stockholders have equal access to capital markets. We now demonstrate that theorem.

FIGURE 2.1

Effects of investing $370,000 in the office-building project. Consumption opportunities are enlarged by the project's $30,000 positive NPV. With the project, you can pick a time pattern of consumption along the outer maroon line, which starts at the project's present value of $400,000. No matter what *your* preferred consumption plan, you are better off with the project.

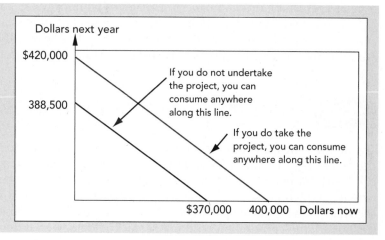

How Capital Markets Reconcile Preferences for Current vs. Future Consumption

You can look forward to a stream of income from your future employment. Unless you have some way of storing or anticipating the income, you will be compelled to consume it as it arrives. If the bulk of your income comes late in life, the result could be hunger now and gluttony later. The capital market solves this problem by allowing you to trade between dollars today and dollars in the future and vice versa. You can therefore consume moderately both now and in the future no matter when your income comes.

Suppose you have a nest egg of exactly $370,000 in cash. You could spend all of it today. You could invest it all at 5% interest and consume 1.05 × $370,000 = $388,500 a year from now. Or you could split the difference, consuming $185,000 now and putting the remaining $185,000 to work at 5%, so you can consume 1.05 × $185,000 = $194,250 next year. Or you could arrange many other blends of present and future consumption. The entire range of possibilities is shown by the blue line in Figure 2.1. The slope of this line is determined by the 5% interest rate.

Now suppose you also have the opportunity to invest your nest egg of $370,000 in the office-building development described earlier. This will produce a surefire $420,000 next year. But that does not mean you can't consume anything today. You can borrow against your future income. With an interest rate of 5%, you can borrow and spend up to $420,000/1.05 = $400,000. By varying the amount you borrow you can obtain any mixture of consumption this year and next. These possible mixtures are shown by the maroon line in Figure 2.1. No matter what your preferences are, you are clearly better off investing in the office building. Investing in the building adds value. It increases your wealth. It moves you up from the blue to the maroon line in Figure 2.1. That is why the NPV rule makes sense. Whenever you accept a positive-NPV investment project, you have extra wealth that can be spent now or in the future.[5]

---

[5] The exact balance between present and future consumption that each individual will choose depends on personal preferences. Readers who are familiar with economic theory will recognize that the choice can be represented by adding indifference curves for each individual to Figure 2.1. The preferred combination of present and future consumption is the point of tangency between the interest rate line and the individual's indifference curve. In other words, each individual will borrow or lend until 1 plus the interest rate equals the marginal rate of time preference (i.e., the slope of the indifference curve). A more formal graphical analysis of investment and the choice between present and future consumption is on the Brealey-Myers-Allen Web site at **www.mhhe.com/bma1e**.

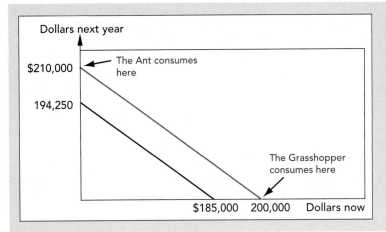

FIGURE 2.2

In this case both the Ant and the Grasshopper have a half-share in the building project. Both are $15,000 richer by undertaking the project. The grasshopper chooses to spend this money now, while the ant prefers to postpone doing so until next year.

We can now see how the existence of a well-functioning capital market allows investors with different time patterns of desired consumption to agree on whether investment projects should be undertaken. Suppose that there are two investors with entirely difference preferences. Think of A as an ant, who wishes to save for the future, and of G as a grasshopper, who would prefer to spend all his wealth on some ephemeral frolic, taking no heed of tomorrow. Each has been offered the opportunity to invest $185,000 in a 50% share in the office building.

You can see from Figure 2.2 that A would clearly be happy to invest in the building. If she invests in the building, she will have .5 × $420,000 = $210,000 to spend at the end of the year. If she invested her $185,000 in the capital market, she would have only 1.05 × $185,000 = $194,250 to spend.[6]

But what about G, who wants money now, not in one year's time? He too is happy to invest, because he can borrow against the future payoff of the investment project. As you can see from Figure 2.2, investing gives him $15,000 more to spend today (210,000/1.05 = $200,000).

The key condition that allows A and G to agree on building the new office is that both have access to a well-functioning, competitive capital market, in which they can borrow and lend at the same rate. Whenever firms discount cash flows at capital market rates, they are implicitly assuming that their shareholders have equal access to competitive capital markets.

It is easy to see how our net present value rule would be damaged if we did not have such a well-functioning capital market. For example, suppose that G could not easily borrow against future income. In that case he might well prefer to spend his cash today rather than invest it in an office building. If A and G were shareholders in the same enterprise, there would be no simple way to reconcile their different objectives.

No one believes unreservedly that capital markets function perfectly. Later in this book we will discuss several cases in which differences in taxation, transaction costs, and other imperfections must be taken into account in financial decision

---

[6] If A did not have $185,000 to invest, it would pay for her to borrow it. At the end of the year she could repay the loan out of the proceeds from her share in the office building. That would leave her with an additional 210,000 − 194,250 = $15,750 to spend. Similarly, it would pay for G to borrow at 5% to invest in a building offering a return of 13.5%.

making. However, we will also discuss research that indicates that, in general, capital markets function fairly well. That is one good reason for relying on net present value as a corporate objective. Another good reason is that net present value makes common sense; we will see that it gives obviously silly answers less frequently than its major competitors. But for now, having glimpsed the problems of imperfect markets, we shall, like an economist in a shipwreck, simply *assume* our life jacket and swim safely to shore.

A Fundamental Result

Our justification of the net present value rule was restricted to two periods and to certain cash flows. However, the rule also makes sense for uncertain cash flows that extend far into the future. The argument goes like this:

1. A financial manager should act in the interests of the firm's owners, its stockholders. Each stockholder wants three things:
   a. To be as rich as possible, that is, to maximize current wealth.
   b. To transform that wealth into whatever time pattern of consumption he or she desires.
   c. To choose the risk characteristics of that consumption plan.
2. But stockholders do not need the financial manager's help to achieve the best time pattern of consumption. They can do that on their own, providing they have free access to competitive capital markets. They can also choose the risk characteristics of their consumption plan by investing in more- or less-risky securities.
3. How can the financial manager help the firm's stockholders? There is only one way: by increasing the market value of each stockholder's stake in the firm. The way to do that is to seize all investment opportunities that have a positive net present value.

In large corporations ownership is spread across thousands of people. As a practical matter they need to delegate control to managers. That's not a problem, though. If there are well-functioning capital markets, the shareholders will all agree that the managers should maximize shareholder wealth by choosing only positive-NPV projects. The shareholders do not have to interfere in day-to-day decisions. All they need to do is to ensure that the firm hires competent managers who have the correct incentives to choose positive-NPV projects. These managers don't need to know the preferences of each shareholder. They just need to follow one simple instruction: Maximize NPV.

In some countries capital markets do not function so well, and shareholders with different time preferences and risk tolerances may disagree about what firms should invest in. This could reduce the demand for shares of widely owned corporations. Such countries generally have more family-owned and state-owned firms and a greater concentration of control and wealth. For example, in Indonesia, the Philippines, and Thailand the largest 10 families control half of corporate assets.[7]

---

[7] See S. Claessens, S. Djankov, and L.H.P. Lang, "The Separation of Ownership and Control in East Asian Corporations," *Journal of Financial Economics* 58 (2000), pp. 81–112, and R. La Porta, F. Lopez-de-Silanes, and A. Shleifer, "Corporate Ownership Around the World," *Journal of Finance* 59 (April 1999), pp. 30–45.

Other Corporate Goals

Sometimes you hear managers speak as if the corporation has other financial goals. For example, they may say that their job is to maximize profits. That sounds reasonable. After all, don't shareholders prefer to own a profitable company rather than an unprofitable one? But taken literally, profit maximization doesn't make sense as a corporate objective. Here are three reasons:

1. Maximizing profits? Which year's profits? Shareholders might not want a manager to increase next year's profits at the expense of profits in later years.

2. A company may be able to increase future profits by cutting its dividend and investing the cash. That is not in the shareholders' interest if the company earns only a low return on the investment.

3. Different accountants may calculate profits in different ways. So you may find that a decision that improves profits in one accountant's eyes will reduce them in another's.

In contrast to maximizing profits, the net present value rule recognizes the time value of money and the difference between project rates of return and opportunity costs of capital. It also focuses on cash flow, and thus is immune to disagreements about accounting profits.

2.3   CORPORATE GOALS AND CORPORATE GOVERNANCE

We have explained that managers can best serve the interests of shareholders by investing in projects with positive net present values. But this takes us back to the principal–agent problem highlighted in Chapter 1. How can the shareholders (the principals) ensure that management (their agents) don't simply look after their own interests? Shareholders can't spend their lives watching managers to check that they are pursuing the shareholders' interests. However, good systems of *corporate governance* can help to ensure that the shareholders' pockets are close to the managers' hearts.

A company's board of directors is elected by the shareholders and is supposed to represent them. Boards of directors are sometimes portrayed as passive stooges who always champion the incumbent management. But when company performance starts to slide and managers do not offer a credible recovery plan, boards do act. In recent years the chief executives of Airbus, Aon, Deutsche Telecom, Dow Jones, Home Depot, Pfizer, Sun Microsystems, and Volkswagen were all forced to step aside when their companies' profitability deteriorated and the need for new strategies became clear.

If shareholders believe that the corporation is underperforming and that the board of directors is not holding managers to task, they can nominate their own candidates for directors and try to get them elected. For example, in 2006 the shareholders of the H. J. Heinz food company voted in two new directors, including Nelson Peltz, who had led a proxy fight seeking to replace incumbent directors. (Such contests are called *proxy fights* because the dissident shareholders try to collect voting proxies from other shareholders.) In 2005, investor Carl Icahn bought a large holding of Blockbuster shares and managed to win seats for himself and two associates on the Blockbuster board. In both cases the new directors were pushing the companies to cut costs and compete more vigorously.

These examples are exceptions to the general rule, however. Proxy fights are expensive and hard to win, and therefore rare. Usually disgruntled stockholders simply take the "Wall Street Walk"—that is, they sell their shares and move on to other investments.

Yet the Wall Street Walk can send a powerful message.

If enough shareholders bail out, the stock price tumbles. This damages top management's reputation and compensation. Part of the top managers' paychecks comes from bonuses tied to the company's earnings or from stock options, which pay off if the stock price rises but are worthless if the price falls below a stated threshold. This motivates managers to increase earnings and the stock price.[8]

If managers and directors do not maximize value, there is always the threat of a takeover. The further a company's stock price falls, due to lax management or wrong-headed policies, the easier it is for another company or group of investors to buy up a majority of the shares. The old management team is then likely to find itself out on the street and its place taken by a fresh team prepared to make the changes needed to realize the company's value.

These arrangements ensure that few managers at the top of major U.S. corporations are lazy or inattentive to stockholders' interests. On the contrary—the pressure to perform can be intense.

Should Managers Look After the Interests of Their Shareholders?

We have described managers as the agents of shareholders. But perhaps this begs the question, Is it desirable for managers to act in the selfish interests of their shareholders? Does a focus on enriching the shareholders mean that managers must act as greedy mercenaries riding roughshod over the weak and helpless?

Most of this book is devoted to financial policies that increase a firm's value. None of these policies requires gallops over the weak and helpless. In most instances, there is little conflict between doing well (maximizing value) and doing good. Profitable firms are those with satisfied customers and loyal employees; firms with dissatisfied customers and a disgruntled workforce will probably end up with declining profits and a low stock price.

Of course, when we say that the objective of the firm is to maximize shareholder wealth, we do not mean that anything goes. The law deters managers from making blatantly dishonest decisions, but most managers are not simply concerned with observing the letter of the law or with keeping to written contracts. In business and finance, as in other day-to-day affairs, there are unwritten, implicit rules of behavior. To work efficiently together, we need to trust each other. Thus huge financial deals are regularly completed on a handshake, and each side knows that the other will not renege later if things turn sour.[9]

---

[8] Some critics say that the incentives created by stock options are excessively powerful, because they tempt managers to try to pump up stock prices so that the options can be cashed in for short-run profits. Managers have also been tempted to tweak the terms and timing of option grants to make the options more valuable. The *scandale du jour* in 2006 was backdating, that is, using hindsight to grant options retroactively to days when the stock price was temporarily low. (The low stock prices meant low option exercise prices, which made the options more valuable. We discuss stock options and backdating in Chapter 17.)

[9] In U.S. law, a contract can be valid even if it is not written down. Of course documentation is prudent, but contracts are enforced if it can be shown that the parties reached a clear understanding and agreement. For example, in 1984, the top management of Getty Oil gave a verbal agreement to merge with Pennzoil. Then Texaco arrived with a higher bid and won the prize. Pennzoil sued—and won—arguing that Texaco had broken up a valid contract.

In many financial transactions, one party has more information than the other. It can be difficult to be sure of the quality of the asset or service that you are buying. This opens up plenty of opportunities for financial sharp practice and outright fraud. The response of honest firms is to distinguish themselves by building long-term relationships with their customers and establishing a name for fair dealing and financial integrity. Major banks and securities firms know that their most valuable asset is their reputation. When something happens to undermine that reputation, the costs can be enormous. Here are two examples.

The Market-Timing Scandal   In the latter half of 2003, the mutual fund industry confronted a market-timing scandal. Market timing exploits the fact that stock markets in different parts of the world close at different times. If there is a strong upward surge in the U.S. stock market, then it is likely that stock prices will rise when markets open in Asia and Europe the next day. Traders who can buy international funds at prices set *before* the surge in U.S. stock prices can often make substantial profits. Similar profits tempt traders who see a sharp fall in the U.S. market and can sell international funds at stale prices. U.S. fund-management companies were not supposed to allow such trading, but some did. When the scandal came to light these companies suffered huge withdrawals, which severely damaged prospects for future revenues and profits. For example, after it was disclosed that managers at Putnam Investments had allowed market-timing trades, the company's funds suffered outflows of $30 billion in two months. Putnam was also fined $100 million and obliged to pay $10 million in compensation.

Citi's Missteps   Citigroup is well known for its worldwide banking operations and competitive internal culture. But that culture spawned trouble. In 2004, Citi's private banking business in Japan was shut down by regulators after charges of money laundering and the sale of excessively risky investments to its Japanese clients. In 2005, its traders in London were accused of manipulating European bond markets with a so-called Dr. Evil trading program. (Citi's CEO, Charles Prince, later called the trades "knuckleheaded.") Citi was also accused of helping the late Chilean dictator Augusto Pinochet hide and manage his personal fortune.

These lapses had hardly any impact on Citigroup's overall revenues and profits. But in March 2005, U.S. banking regulators directed Citigroup not to undertake any large acquisitions until it implemented tighter internal controls and cleared up various regulatory problems. This was a bitter pill to swallow, because Citigroup had planned to grow by acquisitions, particularly overseas.

Citi was the world's largest bank measured by market capitalization, that is, by the aggregate value of all its outstanding common stock. In late 2006 its rival, Bank of America, moved into first place.

Should Firms Be Managed for Shareholders or All Stakeholders?

It is often suggested that firms should be managed on behalf of all stakeholders, not just stockholders. Other stakeholders include employees, customers, suppliers, and the communities where the firm's plants and offices are located.

Different countries take very different views on what the corporation's aims should be. In the United States, the United Kingdom, and other "Anglo-Saxon" economies, the idea of maximizing shareholder value is widely accepted as the

FIGURE 2.3

(*a*) Whose company is it? The views of 378 managers from five countries.
(*b*) Which is more important—job security for employees or shareholder dividends? The views of 399 managers from five countries.

Source: M. Yoshimori, "Whose Company Is It? The Concept of the Corporation in Japan and the West," *Long Range Planning*, Vol. 28 (August 1995), pp. 33–44. Copyright © 1995 with permission from Elsevier Science.

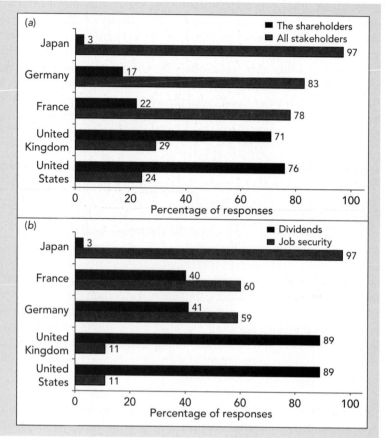

chief financial goal of the firm. In other countries, workers' interests are put forward much more strongly. In Germany, for example, workers in large companies have the right to elect up to half the directors to the companies' supervisory boards. As a result they have a significant role in the governance of the firm and less attention is paid to the shareholders.[10] In Japan managers usually view the interests of shareholders to be on a par with or even subordinate to the interests of employees and customers. For example, Toyota's business philosophy is "to realize stable, long-term growth by working hard to strike a balance between the requirements of people and society, the global environment and the world economy . . . to grow with all of our stakeholders, including our customers, shareholders, employees, and business partners."[11]

Figure 2.3 summarizes the results of interviews with executives from large companies in five countries. Japanese, German, and French executives

---

[10] The following quote from the German banker Carl Fürstenberg (1850–1933) offers an extreme version of how shareholders were once regarded by German managers: "Shareholders are stupid and impertinent—stupid because they give their money to somebody else without any effective control over what the person is doing with it and impertinent because they ask for a dividend as a reward for their stupidity." Quoted by M. Hellwig, "On the Economics and Politics of Corporate Finance and Corporate Control," X. Vives, ed., *Corporate Governance* (Cambridge, UK: Cambridge University Press, 2000), p. 109.

[11] Toyota *Annual Report*, 2003, p. 10.

think that their firms should be run for all stakeholders, while U.S. and U.K. executives say that shareholders come first. When asked about the trade-off between job security and dividends, almost all Japanese executives and the majority of German and French executives believe that job security should come first. By contrast, most U.S. and U.K. executives believe dividends should come first.

As capital markets have become more global, there has been greater pressure for companies in all countries to adopt wealth creation for shareholders as a primary goal. A number of German companies, including DaimlerChrysler and Deutsche Bank, have announced their primary goal as wealth creation for shareholders. In Japan there has been less movement in this direction. For example, the chairman of Toyota has suggested that it would be irresponsible to pursue shareholders' interests. On the other hand, the aggregate market value of Toyota's shares is significantly greater than the market values of GM's and Ford's. So perhaps there is not too much conflict between these goals in practice.

Enron, WorldCom, and SOX

The stock market boom of the late 1990s was followed by a painful crash in the early 2000s. With hindsight we see many stocks, especially telecoms and dot.coms, that traded in the boom at prices far above fundamental values. Why were these prices so high? To some extent it was just a mistake: investors' optimism simply overshot reality. Prices may also have been irrationally high because of "irrational exuberance" and "infectious greed."[12] But in a few cases, including Enron and WorldCom, investors were systematically misled by managers who pumped up their companies' prospects and profits and covered up losses.

Take Enron, for example. At its peak in 2000, the aggregate value of Enron shares was about $60 billion. But by the end of 2001, Enron was bankrupt and its shares worthless. Thus Enron stockholders lost $60 billion. The loss to the overall U.S. economy was *less* than $60 billion, however, because much of that value wasn't there in the first place. Enron made a series of lousy investments and hid massive losses by using misleading accounting and financing schemes. Enron's top management, including its CFO, CEO, and chairman, were later convicted of fraud or conspiracy and sentenced to several years in prison. A similar story unfolded at WorldCom, which cooked its books to sustain an image of profitability and growth. WorldCom's former CEO, Bernie Ebbers, is also in jail.

Enron and WorldCom convinced many investors and most politicians that the U.S. system of corporate governance needed immediate reform. The resulting reforms included the Sarbanes-Oxley Act of 2002 ("SOX"). Among many other provisions, SOX expanded the responsibilities of independent (non-management) directors and required CEOs and CFOs to personally certify the accuracy of their companies' financial statements. Section 404 of SOX requires a detailed annual examination of the company's internal accounting and controls, in an attempt to root out any deficiencies that might lead to misstated financial reports.

---

[12] The quotes are by Alan Greenspan, former chairman of the U.S. Federal Reserve Board.

INTERNATIONAL COMPETITION IN THE BUSINESS OF FINANCE

The British regard London as *the* leading center of international finance. The finance industry, broadly defined, accounts for almost 10% of U.K. Gross Domestic Product (GDP). It's no surprise that the U.K. government wants to keep London competitive and expand London's market share in international finance.

On the other side of the Atlantic, Americans are inclined to argue that New York is in the lead. But the financial services industry is also an important slice of the U.S. economy (about 8% of GDP), and American executives and policymakers worry about international competitiveness.

In November 2006, the Committee on Capital Markets Regulation, an independent panel of financial executives, lawyers, accountants, and economists, released an *Interim Report*, which suggested that "[T]he United States is losing its leading competitive position compared to stock markets and financial centers abroad." The report noted the declining U.S. share of international initial public offerings (IPOs), which fell from 50% of IPO capital raised in 2000 to 5% in 2005. ("International IPO" means a company whose first public share issue is made in a financial market outside its home country. For example, an Italian company might decide to "go public" in London or New York.) The committee also noted the rising use of private financing in the U.S., versus financing by sale of shares or debt in public markets.

The committee recommended more attention to the costs as well as the benefits of regulation and more reliance "on principles-based rules and guidance, rather than the current regime of detailed prescriptive rules." It recommended changes in how SOX is implemented, especially to make Section 404 less rigid and costly.

Many financial managers welcomed these recommendations, but reactions in some other quarters were caustic. Eliot Spitzer, the new governor of New York, promised to "personally appear on Capitol Hill . . . with tens of thousands of investors to defend against these wayward and wrong-headed proposals." Richard Breeden, a former chairman of the Securities and Exchange Commission, called the recommendations "warmed-over, impractical ideas . . . very elegant whining."

On the other hand, London does seem to be gaining business from international companies that are not comfortable about listing their shares and raising capital in the U.S. The U.K. Treasury touts London's "gold-standard regulatory system that is significantly less burdensome. . . . The flexible principles-based regulation of the U.K. imposes fewer costs on firms compared with a rigid-rules-based approach." In crude translation: "Want to make an IPO? Don't like SOX? Come to London."

Sources: See "Interim Report of the Committee on Capital Markets Regulation," November 30, 2006, at **www.capmktsreg.org** and "Financial Services in London: Global Opportunities and Challenges," HM Treasury, March 2006, at **www.hm-treasury.gov.uk.** The comments by Spitzer and Breeden are from the Financial Executives International Web site, **www.fei.org.**

As we write this in 2006, we hear more and more complaints that the post-Enron reforms went too far. The costs of SOX and the burdens of meeting detailed, inflexible regulations are pushing some corporations to return to private (versus public) ownership. The nearby Finance in the News box also notes concerns about the international competitiveness of U.S. financial markets.

These complaints are part of an evolving debate, which we will not settle in the second chapter of this book. But we can pause and ask whether tighter regulation necessarily improves the economic performance of public companies.

Financial markets are supposed to make capital available to companies that can invest at superior returns. Ideally capital should flow so that every positive-NPV project in the entire economy can be financed.

Capital flows through public markets only if investors are protected. Therefore corporate governance must protect shareholders' investments. That means protection against wasteful corporate spending, against excessive managerial pay or perquisites, and against theft and self-dealing (and also against expropriation or punitive regulation or taxation by governments). This line of thinking suggests that more protection of investors would be better and that complete protection would be best.

Complete protection of investors is not feasible, however, because managers must be given the freedom to manage. Dispersed shareholders in a public corporation cannot know what managers are doing or why they are doing it. Investors cannot see the problems and opportunities that the manager sees. The investors cannot watch and second-guess the managers' every move. The most that investors can do is monitor the firm's overall performance and allocate control to intermediaries, particularly the board of directors. The board is closer to the action, of course, but the directors are part-time and cannot manage the company either.

Therefore managers must be given discretion to act on their own analyses and beliefs. Having discretion, they will inevitably consider their own self-interest. Self-interest is not a bad thing: it's an essential motivator, providing that the managers' and investors' incentives are more or less congruent. But incentives will never be perfectly aligned, and heavy-handed attempts to force perfect alignment just won't work. The only way to get perfect alignment is to combine the stockholder and the manager in the same person, as in a sole proprietorship. That's impossible in a public corporation.

Complete protection of investors would not be desirable even if it were feasible. Think of a public corporation as a kind of partnership between insiders—employees and managers—and outside investors. Insiders put up their human capital; investors put up financial capital. If you give the financial capital too much power, the human capital won't show up.

Good protection of investors is essential in a modern economy, but at some point attempts to provide even more protection encounter diminishing returns. More protection increases costs (the costs of SOX Section 404, for example). It also constrains managers' ability to run the business, and may discourage the development of human capital in the firm.

These are difficult trade-offs, and there is no single way to balance the benefits of tighter corporate governance against the costs. For example, as Figure 2.3 suggests, systems of governance vary around the globe. Each of these systems has its proponents and its critics.

SUMMARY

This chapter focuses on the financial objectives of the corporation. We saw that firms can best help their shareholders by accepting all projects with positive net present values and rejecting projects with negative net present values. The net present value of a project measures the wealth created by the project.

To find net present value we first calculate present value. Just discount future cash flow by an appropriate rate r, usually called the discount rate, hurdle rate, or *opportunity cost of capital:*

$$\text{Present value (PV)} = \frac{C_1}{1 + r}$$

Net present value is present value plus any immediate cash flow:

$$\text{Net present value (NPV)} = C_0 + \frac{C_1}{1 + r}$$

Remember that C_0 is negative if the immediate cash flow is an investment, that is, if it is a cash outflow.

The discount rate is determined by rates of return prevailing in capital markets. If the future cash flow is absolutely safe, then the discount rate is the interest rate on safe securities such as U.S. government debt. If the future cash flow is uncertain, then the expected cash flow should be discounted at the expected rate of return offered by equivalent-risk securities. We will talk more about risk and the cost of capital in Chapters 8 to 10.

Cash flows are discounted for two simple reasons: (1) because a dollar today is worth more than a dollar tomorrow, and (2) because a safe dollar is worth more than a risky one. Formulas for PV and NPV are numerical expressions of these ideas. The capital market is the market where safe and risky future cash flows are traded. That is why we look to rates of return prevailing in the capital markets to determine how much to discount for time and risk. By calculating the present value of an asset, we are estimating how much people will pay for it if they have the alternative of investing in the capital markets.

The net present value rule allows efficient separation of ownership and management. A manager who invests only in assets with positive net present values serves the best interests of each one of the firm's shareholders, regardless of differences in their wealth, risk aversion, or preferences for short- or long-term returns. The capital market makes this separation possible. Each shareholder can use the capital market to construct a personal investment plan tailored to his or her own requirements.

There are several institutional arrangements that help to ensure that managers pay close attention to the value of the firm:

- Managers are spurred on by incentive schemes, such as stock options, which pay off big if shareholders gain but are valueless if they do not.
- Managers' actions are subject to the scrutiny of the board of directors.
- Shirkers are likely to find that they are ousted by more energetic managers. This competition may arise within the firm, but poorly performing companies are also more likely to be taken over. The takeover typically brings in a fresh management team.

Managers should play fair by employees, suppliers, and customers, partly because they know it is for the common good, but partly because they know that their firm's most valuable asset is its reputation. Of course ethical issues do arise in financial management, and whenever unscrupulous managers abuse their positions, they harm the economy and society as a whole, because we all trust each other a little less.

In countries such as France, Germany, and Japan, managers give more weight to the interests of all stakeholders, rather than just to shareholders. However, globalization of capital markets has put increasing pressure on companies to pursue shareholders' interests.

The financial manager is asked to pursue financial goals. The firm may trade off financial goals against the goals of other stakeholders, but it cannot make trade-offs rationally unless it knows what the financial goals are. In this book we take maximization of shareholder value as the chief *financial* goal for the firm.

The pioneering works on the net present value rule are:

I. Fisher, *The Theory of Interest* (New York: Augustus M. Kelley, 1965). Reprinted from the 1930 edition.

J. Hirshleifer, "On the Theory of Optimal Investment Decision," *Journal of Political Economy* 66 (August 1958), pp. 329–352.

If you would like to dig deeper into recent controversies about management incentives and corporate governance, we suggest:

J. Brickley, C. W. Smith, Jr., and J. Zimmerman, "Ethics, Incentives and Organizational Design," *Journal of Applied Corporate Finance* 7 (Summer 1994), pp. 8–19.

B. Holmstrom and S. N. Kaplan, "The State of U.S. Corporate Governance: What's Right and What's Wrong?" *Journal of Applied Corporate Finance* 15 (Spring 2003), pp. 8–20.

Journal of Applied Corporate Finance 17 (Fall 2005), a special issue on executive pay and corporate governance.

D. H. Chew, Jr., and S. L. Gillan, *Corporate Governance at the Crossroads: A Book of Readings* (New York: McGraw-Hill, 2005).

FURTHER READING

CONCEPT REVIEW QUESTIONS

1. What is the difference between a discount rate and a discount factor? (page 15)

2. How can risk be incorporated into PVs and NPVs? (page 16)

3. Write down the formulas for an investment's NPV and rate of return. Prove that NPV is positive *only* if the rate of return exceeds the opportunity cost of capital. (page 17)

For a complete listing of your chapter Concept Review Questions, please visit us at www.mhhe.com/bma1e.

QUIZ

1. C_0 is the initial cash flow on an investment, C_1 is the cash flow at the end of one year, and r is the discount rate.

   a. Is C_0 usually positive or negative?

   b. What is the formula for the present value of the investment?

   c. What is the formula for the net present value?

   d. The discount rate equals the *opportunity cost of capital*. Why?

   e. If the investment is risk-free, what is the appropriate measure of r?

2. If the present value of $150 paid at the end of one year is $130, what is the one-year discount factor? What is the discount rate?

3. Calculate the one-year discount factor DF_1 for discount rates of (a) 10%, (b) 20%, and (c) 30%.

4. A merchant pays $100,000 for a load of grain and is certain that it can be resold at the end of one year for $132,000.

   a. What is the return on this investment?

   b. If this return is *lower* than the rate of interest, does the investment have a positive or a negative NPV?

   c. If the rate of interest is 10%, what is the PV of the investment?

   d. What is the NPV?

5. Define the opportunity cost of capital. How in principle would you find the opportunity cost of capital for a risk-free asset? For a risky asset?

6. Look back to the numerical example graphed in Figure 2.2. Suppose the interest rate is 20%. What would the ant (A) and grasshopper (G) do if they both start with $185,000? Would they invest in the office building? Would they borrow or lend? How much and when would each consume?

7. We can imagine the financial manager doing several things on behalf of the firm's stockholders. For example, the manager might:

   a. Make shareholders as wealthy as possible by investing in real assets with positive NPVs.

   b. Modify the firm's investment plan to help shareholders achieve a particular time pattern of consumption.

   c. Choose high- or low-risk assets to match shareholders' risk preferences.

   d. Help balance shareholders' checkbooks.

   But in well-functioning capital markets, shareholders will vote for *only one* of these goals. Which one? Why?

8. Why would one expect managers to act in shareholders' interests? Give some reasons.

PRACTICE QUESTIONS

9. What is the net present value of a *firm's* investment in a U.S. Treasury security yielding 5% and maturing in one year? (*Hint:* What is the opportunity cost of capital? Ignore taxes.)

10. A parcel of land costs $500,000. For an additional $800,000 you can build a motel on the property. The land and motel should be worth $1,500,000 next year. Suppose that common stocks with the same risk as this investment offer a 10% expected return. Would you construct the motel? Why or why not?

11. Calculate the NPV and rate of return for each of the following investments. The opportunity cost of capital is 20% for all four investments.

Investment	Initial Cash Flow, C_0	Cash Flow in Year 1, C_1
1	−10,000	+18,000
2	−5,000	+9,000
3	−5,000	+5,700
4	−2,000	+4,000

   a. Which investment is most valuable?

   b. Suppose each investment would require use of the same parcel of land. Therefore you can take only one. Which one? (*Hint:* What is the firm's objective: to earn a high rate of return or to increase firm value?)

12. In Section 2.1, we analyzed the possible construction of an office building on a plot of land appraised at $50,000. We concluded that this investment had a positive NPV of $5,000 at a discount rate of 12%.

   Suppose E. Coli Associates, a firm of genetic engineers, offers to purchase the land for $58,000, $20,000 paid immediately and $38,000 after one year. U.S. government securities maturing in one year yield 5%.

   a. Assume E. Coli is sure to pay the second $38,000 installment. Should you take its offer or start on the office building? Explain.

   b. Suppose you are *not* sure E. Coli will pay. You observe that other investors demand a 10% return on their loans to E. Coli. Assume that the other investors have correctly assessed the risks that E. Coli will not be able to pay. Should you accept E. Coli's offer?

13. Norman Gerrymander has just received a $1 million bequest. How should he invest it? There are four immediate alternatives.

   a. Investment in one-year U.S. government securities yielding 5%.

   b. A loan to Norman's nephew Gerald, who has for years aspired to open a big Cajun restaurant in Duluth. Gerald had arranged a one-year bank loan for $900,000 at 10%, but asks for a $1 million loan from Norman at 9%.

   c. Investment in the stock market. The expected rate of return is 12%.

   d. Investment in local real estate, which Norman judges is about as risky as the stock market. The opportunity at hand would cost $1 million and is forecasted to be worth $1.1 million after one year.

   Which of these investments have positive NPVs? Which would you advise Norman to take?

14. Show that your answers to Practice Question 13 are consistent with the rate of return rule for investment decisions.

15. Take another look at investment opportunity (d) in Practice Question 13. Suppose a bank offers Norman a $600,000 personal loan at 8%. (Norman is a long-time customer of the bank and has an excellent credit history.) Suppose Norman borrows the money, invests $1 million in real estate opportunity (d) and puts the rest of his money in opportunity (c), the stock market. Is this a smart move? Explain.

16. Ms. Espinoza is retired and depends on her investments for her income. Mr. Liu is a young executive who wants to save for the future. Both are stockholders in Scaled Composites, LLC, which is building SpaceShipOne to take commercial passengers into space. This investment's payoff is many years away. Assume it has a positive NPV for Mr. Liu. Explain why its investment also makes sense for Ms. Espinoza.

17. Answer this question by drawing graphs like Figure 2.1. Casper Milktoast has $200,000 available to support consumption in periods 0 (now) and 1 (next year). He wants to consume *exactly* the same amount in each period. The interest rate is 8%. There is no risk.

   a. How much should he invest, and how much can he consume in each period?

   b. Suppose Casper is given an opportunity to invest up to $200,000 at 10% risk-free. The interest rate stays at 8%. What should he do, and how much can he consume in each period?

   c. What is the NPV of the opportunity in (b)?

18. If a financial institution is caught up in a financial scandal, would you expect its value to fall by more or less than the amount of any fines and settlement payments? Explain.

19. For an outlay of $8 million you can purchase a tanker load of bucolic acid delivered in Rotterdam one year hence. Unfortunately the net cash flow from selling the tanker load will be very sensitive to the growth rate of the world economy:

Slump	Normal	Boom
$8 million	$12 million	$16 million

   a. What is the expected cash flow? Assume the three outcomes for the economy are equally likely.

   b. What is the expected rate of return on the investment in the project?

   c. One share of stock Z is selling for $10. The stock has the following payoffs after one year:

Slump	Normal	Boom
$8	$12	$16

Calculate the expected rate of return offered by stock Z. Explain why this is the opportunity cost of capital for your bucolic acid project.

d. Calculate the project's NPV. Is the project a good investment? Explain why.

CHALLENGE QUESTION

20. In real life the future health of the economy cannot be reduced to three equally probable states like slump, normal, and boom. But we'll keep that simplification for one more example.

Your company has identified two more projects, B and C. Each will require a $5 million outlay immediately. The possible payoffs at year 1, are in millions:

	Slump	Normal	Boom
B	$4	$6	$8
C	5	5.5	6

You have identified the possible payoffs to investors in three stocks, X, Y, and Z:

	Current Price per Share	Payoff at Year 1		
		Slump	Normal	Boom
X	$95.65	$80	$110	$140
Y	40	40	44	48
Z	10	8	12	16

a. What are the expected cash inflows of projects B and C?

b. What are the expected rates of return offered by stocks, X, Y, and Z?

c. What are the opportunity costs of capital for projects B and C? (*Hint:* Calculate the percentage differences, slump versus normal and boom versus normal, for stocks X, Y, and Z. Match up to the percentage differences in B's and C's payoffs.)

d. What are the NPVs of projects B and C?

e. Suppose B and C are launched and $5 million are invested in each. How much will they add to the total market value of your company's shares?

CHAPTER THREE

3

HOW TO CALCULATE PRESENT VALUES

IN CHAPTER 2 we learned how to work out the value of an asset that produces cash exactly one year from now. But we did not explain how to value assets that produce cash two years from now or in several future years. That is the first task for this chapter. We will then have a look at some shortcut methods for calculating present values and at some specialized present value formulas. In particular we will show how to value an investment that makes a steady stream of payments forever (a *perpetuity*) and one that produces a steady stream for a limited period (an *annuity*). We will also look at investments that produce growing streams of payments. You will see how each of these procedures can be used to solve a variety of personal financial decisions. In subsequent chapters we will show how the same techniques are also used by major corporations to value multimillion-dollar investment projects and security issues.

The term *interest rate* sounds straightforward enough, but we will see that it can be defined in various ways. We will explain the distinction between *compound interest* and *simple interest* and we will show the effect of different compounding intervals.

By then you will deserve some payoff for the mental investment you have made in learning how to calculate present values. Therefore we will try out these new tools on bonds and stocks in the next two chapters. After that we will tackle the firm's capital investment decisions at a practical level of detail.

For simplicity, every problem in this chapter is set out in dollars, but the concepts and calculations are identical in euros, yen, or any other currency.

3.1 VALUING LONG-LIVED ASSETS

Do you remember how to calculate the present value (PV) of an asset that produces a cash flow (C_1) one year from now?

$$PV = DF_1 \times C_1 = \frac{C_1}{1 + r_1}$$

The discount factor for the year-1 cash flow is DF_1, and r_1 is the opportunity cost of investing your money for one year. Suppose you will receive a certain cash inflow of $100 next year ($C_1 = 100$) and the rate of interest on one-year U.S. Treasury notes is 7% ($r_1 = .07$). Then present value equals

$$PV = \frac{C_1}{1 + r_1} = \frac{100}{1.07} = \$93.46$$

The present value of a cash flow two years hence can be written in a similar way as

$$PV = DF_2 \times C_2 = \frac{C_2}{(1 + r_2)^2}$$

C_2 is the year-2 cash flow, DF_2 is the discount factor for the year-2 cash flow, and r_2 is the annual rate of interest on money invested for two years. Suppose you get a cash flow of $200 in year 2 ($C_2 = 200$). The rate of interest on two-year Treasury notes is 7.7% per year ($r_2 = .077$); this means that a dollar invested in two-year notes will grow to $1.077^2 = \$1.16$ by the end of two years. The present value of your year-2 cash flow equals

$$PV = \frac{C_2}{(1 + r_2)^2} = \frac{200}{(1.077)^2} = \$172.42$$

Valuing Cash Flows in Several Periods

One of the nice things about present values is that they are all expressed in current dollars—so you can add them up. In other words, the present value of cash flow A + B is equal to the present value of cash flow A plus the present value of cash flow B. For example, suppose you are now offered an investment that produces a cash flow of $100 in year 1 and a further cash flow of $200 in year 2. The one-year interest rate is 7% and the two-year rate is 7.7%. Figure 3.1 shows that the value today of the first year's flow is $C_1/(1 + r_1) = 100/1.07 = \$93.46$ and that the value

FIGURE 3.1

Present value of an investment providing cash flows of $100 in year 1 and $200 in year 2.

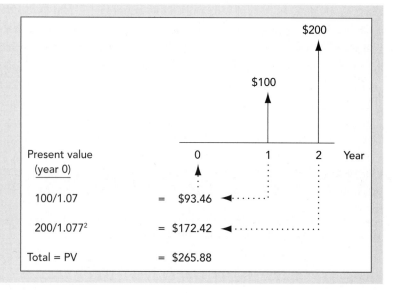

Present value (year 0)		
100/1.07	=	$93.46
200/1.077²	=	$172.42
Total = PV	=	$265.88

of the second year's flow is $C_2/(1 + r_2)^2 = 200/1.077^2 = \$172.42$. Our rule for adding present values tells us that the *total* present value of the investment is

$$PV = \frac{C_1}{1 + r_1} + \frac{C_2}{(1 + r_2)^2} = \frac{100}{1.07} + \frac{200}{1.077^2} = \$265.88$$

We can continue to apply the additivity rule to find the present value of an extended stream of cash flows:

$$PV = \frac{C_1}{1 + r_1} + \frac{C_2}{(1 + r_2)^2} + \frac{C_3}{(1 + r_3)^3} + \cdots$$

This is called the **discounted cash flow** (or **DCF**) formula. A shorthand way to write it is

$$PV = \sum \frac{C_t}{(1 + r_t)^t}$$

where Σ refers to the sum of the series. To find the *net* present value (NPV) we add the (usually negative) initial cash flow, just as in Chapter 2:

$$NPV = C_0 + PV = C_0 + \sum \frac{C_t}{(1 + r_t)^t}$$

Why the Discount Factor Declines as Futurity Increases— And a Digression on Money Machines

If a dollar tomorrow is worth less than a dollar today, one might suspect that a dollar the day after tomorrow should be worth even less. In other words, the discount factor DF_2 should be less than the discount factor DF_1. But is this *necessarily* so, when there is a different interest rate r_t for each period?

Suppose r_1 is 20% and r_2 is 7%. Then

$$DF_1 = \frac{1}{1.20} = .83$$

$$DF_2 = \frac{1}{(1.07)^2} = .87$$

Apparently the dollar received the day after tomorrow is *not* necessarily worth less than the dollar received tomorrow.

But there is something wrong with this example. Anyone who could borrow and lend at these interest rates could become a millionaire overnight. Let us see how such a "money machine" would work. Suppose the first person to spot the opportunity is Hermione Kraft. Ms. Kraft first lends $1,000 for one year at 20%. That is an attractive enough return, but she notices that there is a way to earn an *immediate* surefire profit on her investment. She reasons as follows. Next year she will have $1,200 that can be reinvested for a further year. Although she does not know what interest rates will be at that time, she does know that she can always put the money in a checking account and be certain of having $1,200 at the end of year 2. Her next step, therefore, is to go to her bank and borrow the present value of this $1,200. At 7% interest this present value is

$$PV = \frac{1200}{(1.07)^2} = \$1,048$$

So Ms. Kraft borrows $1,048, invests $1,000, and walks away with a profit of $48. If that does not sound like very much, notice that by borrowing more and investing more she can make much larger profits. For example, if she borrows $21,778,584 and invests $20,778,584, she would become a millionaire.

Of course this story is completely fanciful. Such an opportunity would not last long in well-functioning capital markets. Any bank that allowed you to lend for one year at 20% and borrow for two years at 7% would soon be wiped out by a rush of small investors hoping to become millionaires and a rush of millionaires hoping to become billionaires. There are, however, two lessons to our story. The first is that a dollar tomorrow *cannot* be worth less than a dollar the day after tomorrow. In other words, the value of a dollar received at the end of one year (DF_1) cannot be less than the value of a dollar received at the end of two years (DF_2). There must be some extra gain from lending for two periods rather than one: $(1 + r_2)^2$ cannot be less than $1 + r_1$.[1]

Our second lesson is a more general one and can be summed up by the precept "There is no such thing as a surefire money machine." The technical term for money machine is *arbitrage*. In well-functioning markets, where the costs of buying and selling are low, arbitrage opportunities are eliminated almost instantaneously by investors who try to take advantage of them.[2] Economists have the same idea in mind when they refer to *the law of one price*. By this they mean that two identical assets must sell for the same price, otherwise investors could make arbitrage profits by buying the cheap asset and selling the dear one.

Later in the book we will invoke the *absence* of arbitrage opportunities to prove several useful properties about security prices. That is, we will make statements like "The prices of securities X and Y must be in the following relationship—otherwise there would be potential arbitrage profits and capital markets would not be in equilibrium."

Ruling out arbitrage profits does not require that interest rates be the same for each future period. This relationship between the interest rate and the maturity of the cash flow is called the **term structure of interest rates.** We are going to look at term structure in Chapter 4, but for now we will finesse the issue by assuming that the term structure is "flat"—in other words, the interest rate is the same regardless of the date of the cash flow. This means that we can replace the series of interest rates r_1, $r_2, \ldots, r_t$, etc., with a single rate r and that we can write the present value formula as

$$PV = \frac{C_1}{1 + r} + \frac{C_2}{(1 + r)^2} + \cdots$$

Calculating PVs and NPVs

You have some bad news about your office building venture (the one described at the start of Chapter 2). The contractor says that construction will take two years instead of one and requests payment on the following schedule:

---

[1] The extra return for lending two years rather than one is often referred to as a *forward rate of return*. Our rule implies that the forward rate cannot be negative.

[2] Sometimes you will hear financial people talk about "risk arbitrage." Risk arbitrage generally involves the purchase of one security and the simultaneous sale of a second, similar security in the belief that their prices are out of line. Unlike the returns from pure arbitrage, the returns from risk arbitrage are not locked in. The term "risk arbitrage" is in a way an oxymoron, rather like the terms "graduate student" or "elementary calculus."

1. A $120,000 down payment now. (*Note:* The land, worth $50,000, must also be committed now.)
2. A $100,000 progress payment after one year.
3. A final payment of $100,000 when the building is ready for occupancy at the end of the second year.

Your real estate adviser maintains that despite the delay the building will be worth $420,000 when completed.

All this yields a new set of cash-flow forecasts:

Period	$t = 0$	$t = 1$	$t = 2$
Land	−50,000		
Construction	−120,000	−100,000	−100,000
Payoff			+420,000
Total	$C_0 = -170{,}000$	$C_1 = -100{,}000$	$C_2 = +320{,}000$

If the interest rate is 5%, then NPV is

$$\text{NPV} = C_0 + \frac{C_1}{1 + r} + \frac{C_2}{(1 + r)^2}$$

$$= -170{,}000 - \frac{100{,}000}{1.05} + \frac{320{,}000}{(1.05)^2}$$

Fortunately the news about your office venture is not all bad. The contractor is willing to accept a delayed payment, which means that the present value of the contractor's fee is less than before. This partly offsets the delay in the payoff. As Figure 3.2 shows, the net present value is $25,011—not a substantial decrease from

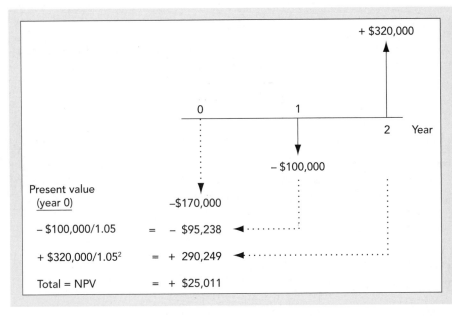

FIGURE 3.2

Calculations showing the net present value of the office building project.

the $30,000 calculated in Chapter 2. Since the net present value is positive, you should still go ahead.[3]

The calculations in Figure 3.2 required just a few keystrokes on a calculator. Real problems can be much more complicated, however, so financial managers usually turn to financial calculators especially programmed for present value calculations or to spreadsheet programs on personal computers. The Web site for this book contains two Web appendices that should get you started in using financial calculators and Excel spreadsheets to solve problems like those in this chapter. In case you should find yourself without a calculator or computer, we have included tables at the end of the book that can be used to solve a variety of present value problems.

3.2   LOOKING FOR SHORTCUTS— PERPETUITIES AND ANNUITIES

How to Value Perpetuities

Sometimes there are shortcuts that make it easy to calculate present values. Let us look at some examples.

On occasion, the British and the French have been known to disagree and sometimes even to fight wars. At the end of some of these wars the British consolidated the debt they had issued during the war. The securities issued in such cases were called consols. Consols are **perpetuities**. These are bonds that the government is under no obligation to repay but that offer a fixed income for each year to perpetuity. The British government is still paying interest on consols issued all those years ago. The annual rate of return on a perpetuity is equal to the promised annual payment divided by the present value:[4]

$$\text{Return} = \frac{\text{cash flow}}{\text{present value}}$$

$$r = \frac{C}{\text{PV}}$$

We can obviously twist this around and find the present value of a perpetuity given the discount rate r and the cash payment C:

$$\text{PV} = \frac{C}{r}$$

---

[3] We assume the cash flows are safe. If they are risky forecasts, the opportunity cost of capital could be higher, say 12%. NPV at 12% is negative.

[4] You can check this by writing down the present value formula

$$\text{PV} = \frac{C}{1+r} + \frac{C}{(1+r)^2} + \frac{C}{(1+r)^3} + \cdots$$

Now let $C/(1+r) = a$ and $1/(1+r) = x$. Then we have (1) PV $= a(1 + x + x^2 + \cdots)$.
Multiplying both sides by x, we have (2) PV$x = a(x + x^2 + \cdots)$.
Subtracting (2) from (1) gives us PV$(1 - x) = a$. Therefore, substituting for a and x,

$$\text{PV}\left(1 - \frac{1}{1+r}\right) = \frac{C}{1+r}$$

Multiplying both sides by $(1 + r)$ and rearranging gives

$$\text{PV} = \frac{C}{r}$$

The year is 2030. You have been fabulously successful and are now a billionaire many times over. It was fortunate indeed that you took that finance course all those years ago. You have decided to follow in the footsteps of two of your heroes, Bill Gates and Warren Buffet. Malaria is still a scourge and you want to help eradicate it and other infectious diseases by endowing a foundation to fund research to combat these diseases. You aim to provide $1 billion a year starting next year. So, if the interest rate is 10%, you are going to have to write a check for

$$\text{Present value of perpetuity} = \frac{C}{r} = \frac{\$1 \text{ billion}}{.1} = \$10 \text{ billion}$$

Two warnings about the perpetuity formula. First, at a quick glance you can easily confuse the formula with the present value of a single payment. A payment of $1 at the end of one year has a present value of $1/(1 + r)$. The perpetuity has a value of $1/r$. These are quite different.

Second, the perpetuity formula tells us the value of a regular stream of payments starting one period from now. Thus your $10 billion endowment would provide the foundation with its first payment in one year's time. If you also want to provide an up-front sum, you will need to lay out an extra $1 billion.

How to Value Annuities

An **annuity** is an asset that pays a fixed sum each year for a specified number of years. The equal-payment house mortgage or installment credit agreement are common examples of annuities.

Figure 3.3 illustrates a simple trick for valuing annuities. The first row represents a perpetuity that produces a cash flow of $1 in each year beginning in year 1. It has a present value of

$$PV = \frac{1}{r}$$

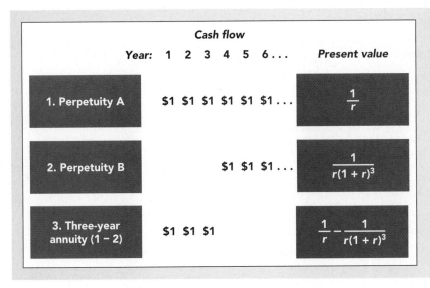

FIGURE 3.3

An annuity that makes payments in each of years 1 through 3 is equal to the difference between two perpetuities.

The second row represents a second perpetuity that produces a cash flow of $1 in each year beginning in year 4. It will have a present value of $1/r$ in year 3 and it therefore has a present value today of

$$PV = \frac{1}{r(1 + r)^3}$$

Both perpetuities provide a cash flow from year 4 onward. The only difference between the two perpetuities is that the first one also provides a cash flow in each of years 1 through 3. In other words, the difference between the two perpetuities is an annuity of $1 for three years. The present value of this annuity is, therefore, the difference between the values of the two perpetuities.[5]

$$PV = \frac{1}{r} - \frac{1}{r(1 + r)^3}$$

The general formula for the value of an annuity that pays $1 a year for each of t years starting in year 1 is

$$\text{Present value of annuity} = \frac{1}{r} - \frac{1}{r(1 + r)^t}$$

This expression is generally known as the t-year annuity factor.[6] Remembering formulas is about as difficult as remembering other people's birthdays. But as long as you bear in mind that an annuity is equivalent to the difference between an immediate and a delayed perpetuity, you shouldn't have any difficulty.

PV Annuities: An Example

Costing an Installment Plan   Most installment plans call for level streams of payments. Suppose that Tiburon Autos offers an "easy payment" scheme on a new Toyota of $5,000 a year, paid at the end of each of the next five years, with no cash down. What is the car really costing you?

First let us do the calculations the slow way, to show that, if the interest rate is 7%, the present value of these payments is $20,501. The time line in Figure 3.4 shows the value of each cash flow and the total present value. The annuity formula, however, is generally quicker:

$$PV = 5{,}000\left[\frac{1}{.07} - \frac{1}{.07(1.07)^5}\right] = 5{,}000 \times 4.100 = \$20{,}501$$

---

[5] Again we can work this out from first principles. We need to calculate the sum of the finite geometric series (1) $PV = a(1 + x + x^2 + \cdots + x^{t-1})$.
where $a = C/(1 + r)$ and $x = 1/(1 + r)$.
Multiplying both sides by x, we have (2) $PVx = a(x + x^2 + \cdots + x^t)$.
Subtracting (2) from (1) gives us $PV(1 - x) = a(1 - x^t)$.
Therefore, substituting for a and x,

$$PV\left(1 - \frac{1}{1+r}\right) = C\left[\frac{1}{1+r} - \frac{1}{(1+r)^{t+1}}\right]$$

Multiplying both sides by $(1 + r)$ and rearranging gives

$$PV = C\left[\frac{1}{r} - \frac{1}{r(1+r)^t}\right]$$

[6] Some people find the following equivalent formula more intuitive:

$$\text{Present value of annuity} = \frac{1}{r}\left[1 - \frac{1}{(1+r)^t}\right]$$

perpetuity formula | $1 starting next year | minus $1 starting at $t + 1$

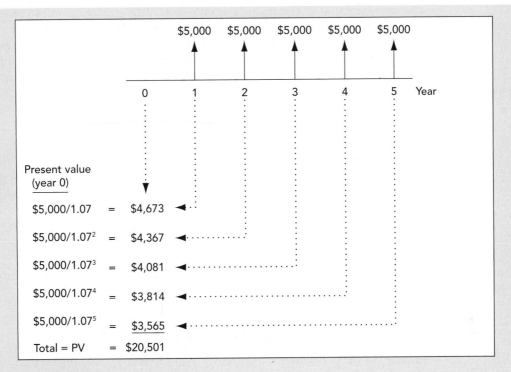

FIGURE 3.4

Calculations showing the year-by-year present value of the installment payments.

Appendix A, Table 3, at the end of the book is a table of annuity factors. You can look there to find the factor of 4.100, if you don't have a calculator or computer handy.

PV Annuities: Another Example

Winning Big at the Lottery   When 13 lucky machinists from Ohio pooled their money to buy Powerball lottery tickets, they won a record $295.7 million. (A fourteenth member of the group pulled out at the last minute to put in his own numbers.) We suspect that the winners received unsolicited congratulations, good wishes, and requests for money from dozens of more or less worthy charities. In response, they could fairly point out that the prize wasn't really worth $295.7 million. That sum was to be repaid in 25 annual installments of $11.828 million each. Assuming that the first payment occurred at the end of one year, what was the present value of the prize? The interest rate at the time was 5.9%.

These payments constitute a 25-year annuity. To value this annuity we simply multiply $11.828 million by the 25-year annuity factor:

$$PV = 11.828 \times 25\text{-year annuity factor}$$
$$= 11.828 \times \left[\frac{1}{r} - \frac{1}{r(1 + r)^{25}} \right]$$

At an interest rate of 5.9%, the annuity factor is

$$\left[\frac{1}{.059} - \frac{1}{.059(1.059)^{25}} \right] = 12.9057$$

The present value of the cash payments is $11.828 × 12.9057 = $152.6 million, much below the well-trumpeted prize, but still not a bad day's haul.

Lottery operators generally make arrangements for winners with big spending plans to take an equivalent lump sum. In our example the winners could either take the $295.7 million spread over 25 years or receive $152.6 million up front. Both arrangements had the same present value.

PV Annuities Due

When we used the annuity formula to value the Powerball lottery prize, we presupposed that the first payment was made at the end of one year. In fact, the first of the 25 yearly payments was made immediately. How does this change the value of the prize?

If we discount each cash flow by one less year, the present value is increased by the multiple $(1 + r)$. In the case of the lottery prize the value becomes 152.6 × $(1 + r)$ = 152.6 × 1.059 = $161.6 million.

A level stream of payments starting immediately is called an **annuity due.** An annuity due is worth $(1 + r)$ times the value of an ordinary annuity.

Calculating Annual Payments: An Example

Finding Mortgage Payments   Annuity problems can be confusing on first acquaintance, but you will find that with practice they are generally straightforward. Here is an example, where you need to use the annuity formula to find the amount of the payment given the present value.

Suppose that you take out a $250,000 house mortgage from your local savings bank. The bank requires you to repay the mortgage in equal annual installments over the next 30 years. It must therefore set the annual payments so that they have a present value of $250,000. Thus

$$PV = \text{mortgage payment} \times \text{30-year annuity factor} = \$250,000$$
$$\text{Mortgage payment} = \$250,000/\text{30-year annuity factor}$$

Suppose that the interest rate is 12% a year. Then

$$\text{30-year annuity factor} = \left[\frac{1}{.12} - \frac{1}{.12(1.12)^{30}}\right] = 8.055$$

and

$$\text{Mortgage payment} = 250,000/8.055 = \$31,037$$

The mortgage loan is an example of an *amortizing loan.* "Amortizing" means that part of the regular payment is used to pay interest on the loan and part is used to reduce the amount of the loan.

Table 3.1 illustrates another amortizing loan. This time it is a four-year loan of $1,000 with an interest rate of 10% and annual payments. The annual payment needed to repay the loan is $315.47. In other words, $1,000 divided by the four-year annuity factor is $315.47. At the end of the first year, the interest charge is 10% of $1,000, or $100. So $100 of the first payment is absorbed by interest, and the remaining $215.47 is used to reduce (or "amortize") the loan balance to $784.53.

Year	Beginning-of-Year Balance	Year-end Interest on Balance	Total Year-end Payment	Amortization of Loan	End-of-Year Balance
1	$1,000.00	$100.00	$315.47	$215.47	$784.53
2	784.53	78.45	315.47	237.02	547.51
3	547.51	54.75	315.47	260.72	286.79
4	286.79	28.68	315.47	286.79	0

TABLE 3.1

An example of an amortizing loan. If you borrow $1,000 at an interest rate of 10%, you would need to make an annual payment of $315.47 over 4 years to repay that loan with interest.

Next year, the outstanding balance is lower, so the interest charge is only $78.45. Therefore $315.47 − 78.45 = $237.02 can be applied to amortization. Because the loan is progressively paid off, the fraction of each payment devoted to interest steadily falls over time, while the fraction used to reduce the loan increases. By the end of year 4 the amortization is just enough to reduce the balance of the loan to zero.

Future Value of an Annuity: An Example

Sometimes you need to calculate the *future* value of a level stream of payments. Perhaps your ambition is to buy a sailboat; something like a 40-foot Beneteau would fit the bill very well. But that means some serious saving. You estimate that, once you start work, you could save $20,000 a year out of your income and earn a return of 8% on these savings. How much will you have available to spend after five years?

We are looking here at a level stream of cash flows—an annuity. We have seen that there is a shortcut formula to calculate the *present* value of an annuity. So there ought to be a similar formula for calculating the *future value* of a level stream of cash flows.

Think first how much your savings are worth today. You will set aside $20,000 in each of the next five years. The present value of this five-year annuity is therefore equal to

$$PV = \$20,000 \times \text{5-year annuity factor}$$

$$= \$20,000 \times \left[\frac{1}{.08} - \frac{1}{.08(1.08)^5} \right] = \$79,854$$

Now think how much you would have after five years if you invested $79,854 today. Simple! Just multiply by $(1.08)^5$:

$$\text{Value at end of year 5} = \$79,854 \times 1.08^5 = \$117,332$$

You should be able to buy yourself a nice boat for $117,000.

We calculated the future value of an annuity by first calculating its present value and then multiplying by $(1 + r)^t$. The general formula for the future value of a level stream of cash flows of $1 a year for t years is, therefore,

$$\text{Future value of annuity} = \left[\frac{1}{r} - \frac{1}{r(1 + r)^t} \right] \times (1 + r)^t = \frac{(1 + r)^t - 1}{r}$$

3.3   MORE SHORTCUTS—GROWING PERPETUITIES AND ANNUITIES

Growing Perpetuities

You now know how to value level streams of cash flows, but you often need to value a stream of cash flows that grows at a constant rate. For example, think back to your plans to donate $10 billion to fight malaria and other infectious diseases. Unfortunately, you made no allowance for the growth in salaries and other costs, which will probably average about 4% a year starting in year 1. Therefore, instead of providing $1 billion a year in perpetuity, you must provide $1 billion in year 1, 1.04 × $1 billion in year 2, and so on. If we call the growth rate in costs g, we can write down the present value of this stream of cash flows as follows:

$$PV = \frac{C_1}{1 + r} + \frac{C_2}{(1 + r)^2} + \frac{C_3}{(1 + r)^3} + \cdots$$

$$= \frac{C_1}{1 + r} + \frac{C_1(1 + g)}{(1 + r)^2} + \frac{C_1(1 + g)^2}{(1 + r)^3} + \cdots$$

Fortunately, there is a simple formula for the sum of this geometric series.[7] If we assume that r is greater than g, our clumsy-looking calculation simplifies to

$$\text{Present value of growing perpetuity} = \frac{C_1}{r - g}$$

Therefore, if you want to provide a perpetual stream of income that keeps pace with the growth rate in costs, the amount that you must set aside today is

$$PV = \frac{C_1}{r - g} = \frac{\$1 \text{ billion}}{.10 - .04} = \$16.667 \text{ billion}$$

Growing Annuities

You are contemplating membership in the St. Swithin's and Ancient Golf Club. The annual membership dues for the coming year are $5,000, but you can make an up-front payment of $12,750, which will provide you with membership for the next three years. Which is the better deal? The answer depends on how rapidly membership fees are likely to increase over the three-year period. For example, suppose that fees are payable at the end of each year and are expected to increase by 6% per annum. The discount rate is 10%.

The problem is to calculate the value of a three-year stream of cash flows that grows at the rate of $g = .06$ each year. Of course, you could calculate each year's

---

[7] We need to calculate the sum of an infinite geometric series $PV = a(1 + x + x^2 + \cdots)$ where $a = C_1/(1 + r)$ and $x = (1 + g)/(1 + r)$. In footnote 4 we showed that the sum of such a series is $a/(1 - x)$. Substituting for a and x in this formula,

$$PV = \frac{C_1}{r - g}$$

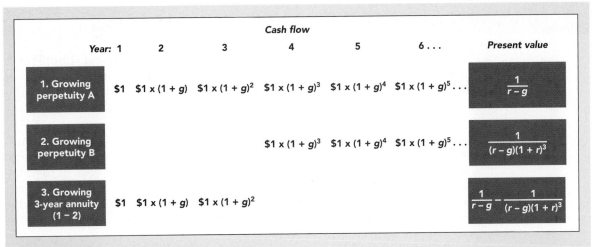

FIGURE 3.5

A three-year stream of cash flows that grows at the rate g is equal to the difference between two growing perpetuities.

cash flow and discount it at 10%. The alternative is to employ the same trick that we used to find the formula for an ordinary annuity. This is illustrated in Figure 3.5. The first row shows the value of a perpetuity that produces a cash flow of $1 in year 1, $1 \times (1 + g)$ in year 2, and so on. It has a present value of

$$PV = \frac{\$1}{(r - g)}$$

The second row shows a similar growing perpetuity that produces its first cash flow of $1 \times (1 + g)^3$ in year 4. It *will* have a present value of $1 \times (1 + g)^3/(r - g)$ in year 3 and therefore has a value today of

$$PV = \frac{\$1}{(r - g)} \times \frac{(1 + g)^3}{(1 + r)^3}$$

The third row in the figure shows that the difference between the two sets of cash flows consists of a three-year stream of a cash flows beginning with $1 in year 1 and growing each year at the rate of g. Its value is equal to the difference between our two growing perpetuities:

$$PV = \frac{\$1}{(r - g)} - \frac{\$1}{(r - g)} \times \frac{(1 + g)^3}{(1 + r)^3}$$

In our golf club example, the present value of the three annual membership dues would be

$$PV = [1/(.10 - .06) - (1.06)^3/(.10 - .06)(1.10)^3] \times \$5,000$$

$$= 2.629 \times \$5,000 = \$13,146$$

If you can find the cash, you would be better off paying now for a three-year membership.

3.4   COMPOUND INTEREST AND PRESENT VALUES

There is an important distinction between **compound interest** and **simple interest.** When money is invested at compound interest, each interest payment is reinvested to earn more interest in subsequent periods. In contrast, the opportunity to earn interest on interest is not provided by an investment that pays only simple interest.

Table 3.2 compares the growth of $100 invested at compound versus simple interest. Notice that in the simple interest case, *the interest is paid only on the initial investment of $100.* Your wealth therefore increases by just $10 a year. In the compound interest case, you earn 10% on your initial investment in the first year, which gives you a balance at the end of the year of $100 \times 1.10 = \$110$. Then in the second year you earn 10% on this $110, which gives you a balance at the end of the second year of $100 \times 1.10^2 = \$121$.

Table 3.2 shows that the difference between simple and compound interest is nil for a one-period investment, trivial for a two-period investment, but overwhelming for an investment of 10 years or more. A sum of $100 invested during the American Revolution and earning compound interest of 10% a year would now be worth over $330 billion. If only your ancestors could have put away a few cents.

The two top lines in Figure 3.6 compare the results of investing $100 at 10% simple interest and at 10% compound interest. It looks as if the rate of growth is constant under simple interest and accelerates under compound interest. However, this is an optical illusion. We know that under compound interest our wealth grows at a *constant* rate of 10%. Figure 3.7 is in fact a more useful presentation. Here the numbers are plotted on a semilogarithmic scale and the constant compound growth rates show up as straight lines.

In the United States you have to be careful to understand the way in which rates are quoted for consumers. The truth-in-lending laws require that when quoting an annual interest rate, companies should use an **annual percentage rate** or **APR.**

	Simple Interest			Compound Interest			
Year	Starting Balance	+ Interest	= Ending Balance	Starting Balance	+	Ending Interest	= Balance
1	$100	+ 10	= $110	$100	+	10	= $110
2	110	+ 10	= 120	110	+	11	= 121
3	120	+ 10	= 130	121	+	12.1	= 133.1
4	130	+ 10	= 140	133.1	+	13.3	= 146.4
10	190	+ 10	= 200	236	+	24	= 259
100	1,090	+ 10	= 1,100	1,252,783	+	125,278	= 1,378,061
200	2,090	+ 10	= 2,100	17,264,116,042	+	1,726,411,604	= 18,990,527,646
230	2,390	+ 10	= 2,400	301,248,505,631	+	30,124,850,563	= 331,373,356,194

TABLE 3.2

Value of $100 invested at 10% simple and compound interest.

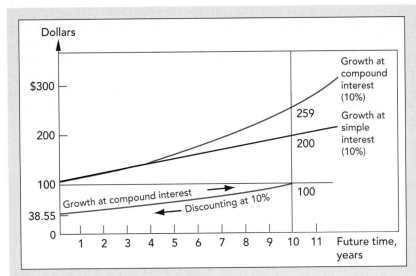

FIGURE 3.6

Compound interest versus simple interest. The top two ascending lines show the growth of $100 invested at simple and compound interest. The longer the funds are invested, the greater the advantage with compound interest. The bottom line shows that $38.55 must be invested now to obtain $100 after 10 periods. Conversely, the present value of $100 to be received after 10 years is $38.55.

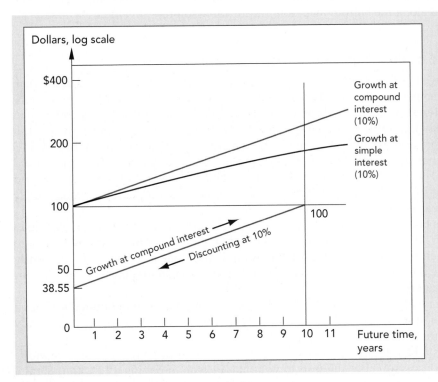

FIGURE 3.7

The same story as Figure 3.6, except that the vertical scale is logarithmic. A constant compound rate of growth means a straight ascending line. This graph makes clear that the growth rate of funds invested at simple interest actually *declines* as time passes.

For example, if interest of 1% per month is charged on your credit card loan, the company will quote an APR of 12%. But you know that this quoted APR really means that you are paying 1% every month, and that this will cumulate over the year to an effective interest rate of $1.01^{12} - 1 = .1268$, or 12.68%.[8]

$$EAR = \left[1 + \frac{APR}{m}\right]^m - 1$$

_____

[8] APRs are calculated differently in other countries. For example, in the European Union APRs must be expressed as annually compounded rates and are therefore higher.

The financial issues faced by corporations almost always involve compound interest rather than simple interest, and therefore financial people generally assume that you are talking about compound interest unless you specify otherwise. Discounting is a process of compound interest. Some people find it intuitively helpful to replace the question, What is the present value of $100 to be received 10 years from now, if the opportunity cost of capital is 10%? with the question, How much would I have to invest now in order to receive $100 after 10 years, given an interest rate of 10%? The answer to the first question is

$$PV = \frac{100}{(1.10)^{10}} = \$38.55$$

And the answer to the second question is

$$\text{Investment} \times (1.10)^{10} = \$100$$

$$\text{Investment} = \frac{100}{(1.10)^{10}} = \$38.55$$

The bottom lines in Figures 3.6 and 3.7 show the growth path of an initial investment of $38.55 to its terminal value of $100. One can think of discounting as traveling *back* along the bottom line, from future value to present value.

A Note on Compounding Intervals

So far we have implicitly assumed that each cash flow occurs at the end of the year. This is sometimes the case. For example, in France and Germany most corporations pay interest on their bonds annually. However, in the United States and Britain most pay interest semiannually. In these countries, the investor can earn an additional six months' interest on the first payment, so that an investment of $100 in a bond that paid interest of 10% per annum compounded semiannually would amount to $105 after the first six months, and by the end of the year it would amount to $1.05^2 \times 100 = \$110.25$. In other words, 10% compounded semiannually is equivalent to 10.25% compounded annually.

Let's take another example. Suppose a U.S. bank offers you an automobile loan with an APR of 6%. If you are required to pay interest monthly, you will need to pay each month one-twelfth of the annual rate, that is, $6/12 = .5\%$ a month. Because the monthly return is compounded, the true annual interest rate on your loan is not 6%, but $1.005^{12} - 1 = .0617$, or 6.17%.

In general, an investment of $1 at a rate of r per annum compounded m times a year amounts by the end of the year to $[1 + (r/m)]^m$, and the equivalent annually compounded rate of interest is $[1 + (r/m)]^m - 1$.

Let's return to our earlier example of a 30-year mortgage. Suppose the mortgage salesperson now suggests to you that, instead of paying a 12% annual rate, it would be more convenient and cheaper for you to have a 1% monthly rate. It would be more convenient because you are paid monthly, and the mortgage payments could be deducted directly from your bank account each month. Since there will be $30 \times 12 = 360$ payments, the salesperson calculates the amount of each payment by dividing the value of the loan by the 360-month annuity factor:

$$\text{360-month annuity factor} = \left[\frac{1}{.01} - \frac{1}{.01(1.01)^{360}}\right] = 97.218$$

Therefore,

$$\text{Monthly mortgage payment} = \text{value of loan}/360\text{-month annuity factor}$$
$$= 250{,}000/97.218 = \$\,2{,}572$$

The salesperson, therefore, points out that your yearly payments would be reduced from \$31,037 to just $12 \times 2{,}572 = \$30{,}864$.

By now you should be able to see through this kind of ploy. The salesperson's argument ignores the time value of money! It is true that the total amount of the payments is less with the monthly scheme, but the payments start earlier. The annual rate that is equivalent to 1% a month is not 12% but $1.01^{12} - 1 = 12.68\%$, as we saw in our credit card example.

Continuous Compounding

In the case of our automobile loan example interest was compounded $m = 12$ times a year and the interest rate was 6%. The annually compounded rate was therefore $[1 + (r/m)]^m - 1 = [1 + .06/12]^{12} - 1 = .0617$, or 6.17%. Instead of compounding interest monthly, the rate could be compounded weekly ($m = 52$) or daily ($m = 365$). In fact there is no limit to how frequent payments could be or how short the compounding interval. One can imagine a situation where the payments are spread evenly and continuously throughout the year, and the interest rate is continuously compounded.[9] In this case m is infinite.

It turns out that there are many occasions in finance when continuous compounding is useful. As we will see shortly, one application is in capital budgeting. Another important application is in option pricing models, such as the Black–Scholes model that we will introduce in Chapter 18. These are continuous time models. So you will find that most computer programs for calculating option values will ask for the continuously compounded interest rate.

It may seem that a lot of calculations would be needed to find a continuously compounded interest rate. However, think back to your high school algebra. You may recall that as m approaches infinity $[1 + (r/m)]^m$ approaches $(2.718)^r$. The figure 2.718—or e, as it is called—is the base for natural logarithms. Therefore, \$1 invested at a continuously compounded rate of r will grow to $e^r = (2.718)^r$ by the end of the first year. By the end of t years it will grow to $e^{rt} = (2.718)^{rt}$.

Example 1 Suppose you invest \$1 at a continuously compounded rate of 11% ($r = .11$) for one year ($t = 1$). The end-year value is $e^{.11}$, or \$1.116. In other words, investing at 11% a year *continuously* compounded is exactly the same as investing at 11.6% a year *annually* compounded.

Example 2 Suppose you invest \$1 at a continuously compounded rate of 11% ($r = .11$) for two years ($t = 2$). The final value of the investment is $e^{rt} = e^{.22}$, or \$1.246.

---

[9] When we talk about *continuous* payments, we are pretending that money can be dispensed in a continuous stream like water out of a faucet. One can never quite do this. For example, instead of paying out \$1 billion every year to combat malaria, you could pay out about \$1 million every $8\frac{3}{4}$ hours or \$10,000 every $5\frac{1}{4}$ minutes or \$10 every $3\frac{1}{6}$ seconds but you could not pay it out *continuously*. Financial managers *pretend* that payments are continuous rather than hourly, daily, or weekly because (1) it simplifies the calculations, and (2) it gives a very close approximation to the NPV of frequent payments.

Sometimes it may be more reasonable to assume that the cash flows from a project are spread evenly over the year rather than occurring at the year's end. It is easy to adapt our previous formulas to handle this. For example, suppose that we wish to compute the present value of a perpetuity of C dollars a year. We already know that if the payment is made at the end of the year, we divide the payment by the *annually* compounded rate of r:

$$PV = \frac{C}{r}$$

If the same total payment is made in an even stream throughout the year, we use the same formula but substitute the *continuously* compounded rate.

Example 3   Suppose the annually compounded rate is 18.5%. The present value of a $100 perpetuity, with each cash flow received at the end of the year, is 100/.185 = $540.54. If the cash flow is received continuously, we must divide $100 by 17%, because 17% continuously compounded is equivalent to 18.5% annually compounded ($e^{.17} = 1.185$). The present value of the continuous cash flow stream is 100/.17 = $588.24. Investors are prepared to pay more for the continuous cash payments because the cash starts to flow in immediately.

For any other continuous payments, we can always use our formula for valuing annuities. For instance, suppose that you have thought again about your donation and have decided to fund a vaccination program in emerging countries, which will cost $1 billion a year, starting immediately, and spread evenly over 20 years. Previously, we used the annually compounded rate of 10%; now we must use the continuously compounded rate of $r = 9.53\%$ ($e^{.0953} = 1.10$). To cover such an expenditure, then, you need to set aside the following sum:[10]

$$PV = C\left(\frac{1}{r} - \frac{1}{r} \times \frac{1}{e^{rt}}\right)$$

$$= \$1 \text{ billion} \left(\frac{1}{.0953} - \frac{1}{.0953} \times \frac{1}{6.727}\right) = \$1 \text{ billion} \times 8.932 = \$8.932 \text{ billion}$$

If you look back at our earlier discussion of annuities, you will notice that the present value of $1 billion paid at the *end* of each of the 20 years was $8.514 billion. Therefore, it costs you $418 million—or 5%—more to provide a continuous payment stream.

Often in finance we need only a ballpark estimate of present value. An error of 5% in a present value calculation may be perfectly acceptable. In such cases it doesn't usually matter whether we assume that cash flows occur at the end of the year or in a continuous stream. At other times precision matters, and we do need to worry about the exact frequency of the cash flows.

---

[10] Remember that an annuity is simply the difference between a perpetuity received today and a perpetuity received in year t. A continuous stream of C dollars a year in perpetuity is worth C/r, where r is the continuously compounded rate. Our annuity, then, is worth

$$PV = \frac{C}{r} - \text{present value of } \frac{C}{r} \text{ received in year } t$$

Since r is the continuously compounded rate, C/r received in year t is worth $(C/r) \times (1/e^{rt})$ today. Our annuity formula is therefore

$$PV = \frac{C}{r} - \frac{C}{r} \times \frac{1}{e^{rt}}$$

sometimes written as

$$\frac{C}{r}(1 - e^{-rt})$$

The difficult thing in any present value exercise is to set up the problem correctly. Once you have done that, you must be able to do the calculations, but they are not difficult. Now that you have worked through this chapter, all you should need is a little practice.

SUMMARY

The basic present value formula for an asset that pays off in several periods is the following obvious extension of our one-period formula:

$$PV = \frac{C_1}{1 + r_1} + \frac{C_2}{(1 + r_2)^2} + \cdots$$

You can always work out any present value using this formula, but when the discount rate is the same for each maturity, there may be some shortcuts that can reduce the tedium. Take a look at Table 3.3, which summarizes some of these shortcuts. Notice that the first cash flow of an annuity due occurs immediately. All of the other formulas assume that the first cash flow occurs at the end of one year.

Our next step was to show that discounting is a process of compound interest. Present value is the amount that we would have to invest now at compound interest r in order to produce the cash flows C_1, C_2, etc. When someone offers to lend us a dollar at an annual rate of r, we should always check how frequently the interest is to be compounded. If the compounding interval is annual, we will have to repay $(1 + r)^t$ dollars; on the other hand, if the compounding period is continuous, we will have to repay 2.718^{rt} (or, as it is usually expressed, e^{rt}) dollars. In capital budgeting we often assume that the cash flows occur at the end of each year, and therefore we discount them at an annually compounded rate of interest. Sometimes, however, it may be better to assume that they are spread evenly over the year; in this case we must make use of continuous compounding.

We introduced in this chapter two very important ideas that we will come across several times again. The first is that you can add present values: If your

	Cash flow, $						Present value
Year:	**0**	**1**	**2 . . .**	**. . . t − 1**	**t**	**t + 1 . . .**	
Perpetuity		1	1 . . .	1	1	1 . . .	$\dfrac{1}{r}$
t-period annuity		1	1 . . .	1	1		$\dfrac{1}{r} - \dfrac{1}{r(1 + r)^t}$
t-period annuity due	1	1	1 . . .	1			$(1 + r)\left(\dfrac{1}{r} - \dfrac{1}{r(1 + r)^t}\right)$
Growing perpetuity		1	$1 \times (1 + g)$	$1 \times (1 + g)^{t-2}$	$1 \times (1 + g)^{t-1}$	$1 \times (1 + g)^t \cdots$	$\dfrac{1}{r - g}$
t-period growing annuity		1	$1 \times (1 + g)$	$1 \times (1 + g)^{t-2}$	$1 \times (1 + g)^{t-1}$		$\dfrac{1}{r - g} - \dfrac{1}{r - g} \times \dfrac{(1 + g)^t}{(1 + r)^t}$

TABLE 3.3

Some useful shortcut formulas.

formula for the present value of A + B is not the same as your formula for the present value of A plus the present value of B, you have made a mistake. The second idea is that arbitrage opportunities or money machines are rare and soon vanish. If you think you have found one, go back and check your calculations.

WEB PROJECTS

There are dozens of Web sites that provide calculators to help with personal financial decisions. Two good examples are **www.quicken.com** and **www.smartmoney.com**. (*Note:* for both calculators the annual rate is quoted as 12 times the monthly rate.)

1. Suppose that you have $5,000 in the bank and plan to save $500 a month. If you earn a return of 12% a year (1% a month), how much will you have accumulated by the time that you retire in 30 years? Now log in to the Quicken site and find a nice savings calculator. Use this to check your answer.

2. Suppose that you take out a 30-year mortgage loan of $200,000 at an interest rate of 10%. What is your total monthly payment? How much of the first month's payment goes to reduce the size of the loan? How much of the payment after two years goes to reduce the amount of the loan? You can check your answers by logging in to the personal finance page of **www.smartmoney.com** and using the mortgage calculator.

CONCEPT REVIEW QUESTIONS

1. Write down the formula for the present value of an investment that produces cash flows of C_1, C_2 and C_3. (page 37)

2. What is the formula for the two-year discount factor, DF_2? (page 37)

3. Can the two-period discount rate (r_2) ever be smaller than the one-period rate (r_1)? (page 38)

For a complete listing of your chapter Concept Review Questions, please visit us at www.mhhe.com/bma1e.

QUIZ

1. At an interest rate of 12%, the six-year discount factor is .507. How many dollars is $.507 worth in six years if invested at 12%?

2. If the PV of $139 is $125, what is the discount factor?

3. If the cost of capital is 9%, what is the PV of $374 paid in year 9?

4. A project produces a cash flow of $432 in year 1, $137 in year 2, and $797 in year 3. If the cost of capital is 15%, what is the project's PV?

5. If you invest $100 at an interest rate of 15%, how much will you have at the end of eight years?

6. An investment costs $1,548 and pays $138 in perpetuity. If the interest rate is 9%, what is the NPV?

7. A common stock will pay a cash dividend of $4 next year. After that, the dividends are expected to increase indefinitely at 4% per year. If the discount rate is 14%, what is the PV of the stream of dividend payments?

8. The interest rate is 10%.

   a. What is the PV of an asset that pays $1 a year in perpetuity?

   b. The value of an asset that appreciates at 10% per annum approximately doubles in seven years. What is the approximate PV of an asset that pays $1 a year in perpetuity beginning in year 8?

   c. What is the approximate PV of an asset that pays $1 a year for each of the next seven years?

   d. A piece of land produces an income that grows by 5% per annum. If the first year's income is $10,000, what is the value of the land?

9. a. The cost of a new automobile is $10,000. If the interest rate is 5%, how much would you have to set aside now to provide this sum in five years?

   b. You have to pay $12,000 a year in school fees at the end of each of the next six years. If the interest rate is 8%, how much do you need to set aside today to cover these bills?

   c. You have invested $60,476 at 8%. After paying the above school fees, how much would remain at the end of the six years?

10. The continuously compounded interest rate is 12%.

    a. You invest $1,000 at this rate. What is the investment worth after five years?

    b. What is the PV of $5 million to be received in eight years?

    c. What is the PV of a continuous stream of cash flows, amounting to $2,000 per year, starting immediately and continuing for 15 years?

11. You are quoted an interest rate of 6% on an investment of $10 million. What is the value of your investment after four years if interest is compounded:

    a. Annually? b. Monthly? or c. Continuously?

PRACTICE QUESTIONS

12. What is the PV of $100 received in:

    a. Year 10 (at a discount rate of 1%).

    b. Year 10 (at a discount rate of 13%).

    c. Year 15 (at a discount rate of 25%).

    d. Each of years 1 through 3 (at a discount rate of 12%).

13. a. If the one-year discount factor is .905, what is the one-year interest rate?

    b. If the two-year interest rate is 10.5%, what is the two-year discount factor?

    c. Given these one- and two-year discount factors, calculate the two-year annuity factor.

    d. If the PV of $10 a year for three years is $24.65, what is the three-year annuity factor?

    e. From your answers to (c) and (d), calculate the three-year discount factor.

14. A factory costs $800,000. You reckon that it will produce an inflow after operating costs of $170,000 a year for 10 years. If the opportunity cost of capital is 14%, what is the net present value of the factory? What will the factory be worth at the end of five years?

15. A machine costs $380,000 and is expected to produce the following cash flows:

Year	1	2	3	4	5	6	7	8	9	10
Cash flow ($000s)	50	57	75	80	85	92	92	80	68	50

Visit us at
www.mhhe.com/bma1e.

If the cost of capital is 12%, what is the machine's NPV?

16. Mike Polanski is 30 years of age and his salary next year will be $40,000. Mike forecasts that his salary will increase at a steady rate of 5% per annum until his retirement at age 60.

    a. If the discount rate is 8%, what is the PV of these future salary payments?

    b. If Mike saves 5% of his salary each year and invests these savings at an interest rate of 8%, how much will he have saved by age 60?

    c. If Mike plans to spend these savings in even amounts over the subsequent 20 years, how much can he spend each year?

17. A factory costs $400,000. It will produce an inflow after operating costs of $100,000 in year 1, $200,000 in year 2, and $300,000 in year 3. The opportunity cost of capital is 12%. Calculate the NPV.

Visit us at
www.mhhe.com/bma1e.

18. Halcyon Lines is considering the purchase of a new bulk carrier for $8 million. The forecasted revenues are $5 million a year and operating costs are $4 million. A major refit costing $2 million will be required after both the fifth and tenth years. After 15 years, the ship is expected to be sold for scrap at $1.5 million. If the discount rate is 8%, what is the ship's NPV?

19. As winner of a breakfast cereal competition, you can choose one of the following prizes:

    a. $100,000 now.

    b. $180,000 at the end of five years.

    c. $11,400 a year forever.

    d. $19,000 for each of 10 years.

    e. $6,500 next year and increasing thereafter by 5% a year forever.

If the interest rate is 12%, which is the most valuable prize?

20. Siegfried Basset is 65 years of age and has a life expectancy of 12 more years. He wishes to invest $20,000 in an annuity that will make a level payment at the end of each year until his death. If the interest rate is 8%, what income can Mr. Basset expect to receive each year?

21. David and Helen Zhang are saving to buy a boat at the end of five years. If the boat costs $20,000 and they can earn 10% a year on their savings, how much do they need to put aside at the end of years 1 through 5?

22. Kangaroo Autos is offering free credit on a new $10,000 car. You pay $1,000 down and then $300 a month for the next 30 months. Turtle Motors next door does not offer free credit but will give you $1,000 off the list price. If the rate of interest is 10% a year, (about .83% a month) which company is offering the better deal?

23. Recalculate the NPV of the office building venture in Section 3.1 at interest rates of 5, 10, and 15%. Plot the points on a graph with NPV on the vertical axis and the discount rates on the horizontal axis. At what discount rate (approximately) would the project have zero NPV? Check your answer.

24. If the interest rate is 7%, what is the value of the following three investments?

    a. An investment that offers you $100 a year in perpetuity with the payment at the *end* of each year.

    b. A similar investment with the payment at the *beginning* of each year.

    c. A similar investment with the payment spread evenly over each year.

25. Refer back to Section 3.2. If the rate of interest is 8% rather than 10%, how much would you need to set aside to provide each of the following?

    a. $1 billion at the end of each year in perpetuity.

    b. A perpetuity that pays $1 billion at the end of the first year and that grows at 4% a year.

    c. $1 billion at the end of each year for 20 years.

    d. $1 billion a year spread evenly over 20 years.

26. How much will you have at the end of 20 years if you invest $100 today at 15% *annually* compounded? How much will you have if you invest at 15% *continuously* compounded?

27. You have just read an advertisement stating, "Pay us $100 a year for 10 years and we will pay you $100 a year thereafter in perpetuity." If this is a fair deal, what is the rate of interest?

28. Which would you prefer?

    a. An investment paying interest of 12% compounded annually.

    b. An investment paying interest of 11.7% compounded semiannually.

    c. An investment paying 11.5% compounded continuously.

    Work out the value of each of these investments after 1, 5, and 20 years.

29. In 1880 five aboriginal trackers were each promised the equivalent of 100 Australian dollars for helping to capture the notorious outlaw Ned Kelley. In 1993 the grand-daughters of two of the trackers claimed that this reward had not been paid. The prime minister of Victoria stated that, if this was true, the government would be happy to pay the $100. However, the granddaughters also claimed that they were entitled to compound interest. How much was each entitled to if the interest rate was 5%? What if it was 10%?

30. A leasing contract calls for an immediate payment of $100,000 and nine subsequent $100,000 semiannual payments at six-month intervals. What is the PV of these payments if the *annual* discount rate is 8%?

31. Several years ago *The Wall Street Journal* reported that the winner of the Massachusetts State Lottery prize had the misfortune to be both bankrupt and in prison for fraud. The prize was $9,420,713, to be paid in 19 equal annual installments. (There were 20 installments, but the winner had already received the first payment.) The bankruptcy court judge ruled that the prize should be sold off to the highest bidder and the proceeds used to pay off the creditors.

Visit us at
www.mhhe.com/bma1e.

    a. If the interest rate was 8%, how much would you have been prepared to bid for the prize?

    b. Enhance Reinsurance Company was reported to have offered $4.2 million. Use Excel to find the return that the company was looking for.

32. A mortgage requires you to pay $70,000 at the end of each of the next eight years. The interest rate is 8%.

    a. What is the present value of these payments?

    b. Calculate for each year the loan balance that remains outstanding, the interest payment on the loan, and the reduction in the loan balance.

33. You estimate that by the time you retire in 35 years, you will have accumulated savings of $2 million. If the interest rate is 8% and you live 15 years after retirement, what annual level of expenditure will those savings support?

    Unfortunately, inflation will eat into the value of your retirement income. Assume a 4% inflation rate and work out a spending program for your retirement that will allow you to increase your expenditure in line with inflation.

34. The *annually* compounded discount rate is 5.5%. You are asked to calculate the present value of a 12-year annuity with payments of $50,000 per year. Calculate PV for each of the following cases.

    a. The annuity payments arrive at one-year intervals. The first payment arrives one year from now.

    b. The first payment arrives in six months. Following payments arrive at one-year intervals (i.e., at 18 months, 30 months, etc.).

Visit us at www.mhhe.com/bma1e

35. Dear Financial Adviser,

My spouse and I are each 62 and hope to retire in three years. After retirement we will receive $7,500 per month after taxes from our employers' pension plans and $1,500 per month after taxes from Social Security. Unfortunately our monthly living expenses are $15,000. Our social obligations preclude further economies.

We have $1,000,000 invested in a high-grade, tax-free municipal-bond mutual fund. The return on the fund is 3.5% per year. We plan to make annual withdrawals from the mutual fund to cover the difference between our pension and Social Security income and our living expenses. How many years before we run out of money?

Sincerely,

Luxury Challenged

Marblehead, MA

You can assume that the withdrawals (one per year) will sit in a checking account (no interest). The couple will use the account to cover the monthly shortfalls.

CHALLENGE QUESTIONS

36. Here are two useful rules of thumb. The "Rule of 72" says that with discrete compounding the time it takes for an investment to double in value is roughly 72/interest rate (in percent). The "Rule of 69" says that with continuous compounding the time that it takes to double is exactly 69.3/interest rate (in percent).

  a. If the annually compounded interest rate is 12%, use the Rule of 72 to calculate roughly how long it takes before your money doubles. Now work it out exactly.

  b. Can you prove the Rule of 69?

Visit us at
www.mhhe.com/bma1e.

37. Use Excel to construct your own set of annuity tables.

38. You own an oil pipeline which will generate a $2 million cash return over the coming year. The pipeline's operating costs are negligible, and it is expected to last for a very long time. Unfortunately, the volume of oil shipped is declining, and cash flows are expected to decline by 4% per year. The discount rate is 10%.

  a. What is the PV of the pipeline's cash flows if its cash flows are assumed to last forever?

  b. What is the PV of the cash flows if the pipeline is scrapped after 20 years?

CHAPTER FOUR

VALUING BONDS

INVESTMENT IN NEW plant and equipment requires money—often a lot of money. Sometimes firms can retain and accumulate earnings to cover the cost of investment, but often they need to raise extra cash from investors. If they choose not to sell additional shares of common stock, the cash has to come from borrowing. If cash is needed for only for a short while, they may borrow from a bank. If they need cash for long-term investments, they generally issue bonds, which are simply long-term loans.

Companies are not the only bond issuers. Municipalities also raise money by selling bonds. So do national governments. There is always some risk that a company or municipality will not be able to come up with the cash to repay its bonds, but investors in government issues can be confident that the promised payments will be made in full and on time.[1]

This chapter focuses on how government bonds are valued and on the interest rates that governments pay when they borrow. The markets for these bonds are huge. The aggregate principal amount of outstanding U.S. Treasury securities in mid-2006 was about $8.4 trillion.[2] The corresponding amounts for Germany and the U.K. were about €1.1 trillion and £.4 trillion, respectively. The markets are also sophisticated. Bond traders make massive trades motivated by tiny price discrepancies.

The interest rates on governments bonds are benchmarks for all interest rates. Companies can't borrow at the same low interest rates as governments, but when government rates go up or down, corporate rates follow more or less proportionally. Therefore financial managers had better understand how the government rates are determined and what happens when they change.

Government bonds pay a schedule of cash flows representing interest and repayment of principal. There is no uncertainty about either the amounts or timing. So valuation of government bonds should be simple, just a matter of discounting at the risk-free interest rate, right? Wrong: There's not one risk-free interest rate, but dozens, depending on maturity, and you will find that bond traders may refer to "spot interest rates" or "yields to maturity," which are not the same thing.

(*continued*)

---

[1] This is true only if the government bond is issued in the country's own currency. When governments borrow in another country's currency, investors cannot be absolutely sure of repayment.

[2] This includes $3.6 trillion held by government bodies.

This book is not for bond traders, but if you are to be involved in managing the company's debt, you will have to get beyond the mechanics of discounting. Professional financial managers understand the bond pages in the financial press and know what bond dealers mean when they quote spot rates or yields to maturity. They realize why short-term rates are usually lower (but sometimes higher) than long-term rates and why the longest-term bond prices are most sensitive to fluctuations in interest rates. They can distinguish real (inflation-adjusted) interest rates and nominal (money) rates and anticipate how future inflation can affect interest rates. We cover all these topics in this chapter.

4.1   USING THE PRESENT VALUE FORMULA TO VALUE BONDS

If you own a bond, you are entitled to a fixed set of cash payoffs: Each year until the bond matures, you collect an interest payment; then at maturity, you also get back the face value of the bond, which is called the **principal.** Therefore, when the bond matures, you receive both the principal and interest.

A Short Trip to Germany to Value a Government Bond

We will start our discussion of bond values with a visit to Germany, where the government issues long-term bonds known as "bunds" (short for *Bundesanleihen*). These bonds pay interest and principal in euros (€s). For example, suppose that in July 2006 you decided to buy €100 face value of the 5% bund maturing in July 2012. Each year until 2012 you are entitled to an interest payment of .05 × 100 = €5. This amount is the bond's **coupon.**[3] When the bond matures in 2012 the government pays you the final €5 interest, plus the €100 face value. Your first coupon payment is in one year's time in July 2007. So the cash flows from owning the bonds are as follows:

Cash Flows (€)					
2007	**2008**	**2009**	**2010**	**2011**	**2012**
€5	€5	€5	€5	€5	€105

What is the present value of these payoffs? To determine that, you need to look at the return offered by similar securities. In July 2006 other medium-term German government bonds offered a return of about 3.8%. That is what you were giving up when you bought the 5% bonds. Therefore to value the 5% bonds, you must discount the cash flows at 3.8%:

$$PV = \frac{5}{1.038} + \frac{5}{1.038^2} + \frac{5}{1.038^3} + \frac{5}{1.038^4} + \frac{5}{1.038^5} + \frac{105}{1.038^6} = €106.33$$

---

[3] Bonds used to come with coupons attached, which had to be clipped off and presented to the issuer to obtain the interest payments. This is still the case with *bearer bonds,* where the only evidence of indebtedness is the bond itself. In many parts of the world bearer bonds are still issued and are popular with investors who would rather remain anonymous. The alternative is to issue *registered bonds,* in which case the identity of the bond's owner is recorded and the coupon payments are sent automatically. Bunds are registered bonds.

Bond prices are usually expressed as a percentage of face value. Thus we can say that your 5% bund is worth 106.33%.

You may have noticed a shortcut way to value this bond. Your purchase is like a package of two investments. The first investment pays off the six annual coupon payments of €5 each and the second pays off the €100 face value at maturity. Therefore, you can use the annuity formula to value the coupon payments and add on the present value of the final payment:

$$PV(bond) = PV(coupon\ payments) + PV(final\ payment)$$
$$= (coupon \times 6\text{-year annuity factor}) + (final\ payment \times discount\ factor)$$
$$= 5\left[\frac{1}{.038} - \frac{1}{.038(1.038)^6}\right] + \frac{100}{(1.038)^6} = 26.38 + 79.95 = €106.33$$

Any bond can be valued as a package of an annuity (the coupon payments) and a single repayment (the repayment of the face value).

Rather than asking the value of the bond, we could have phrased our question the other way around: If the price of the bond is 106.33%, what return do investors expect? In that case, you need to find the value of y that solves the following equation:

$$106.33 = \frac{5}{1+y} + \frac{5}{(1+y)^2} + \frac{5}{(1+y)^3} + \frac{5}{(1+y)^4} + \frac{5}{(1+y)^5} + \frac{105}{(1+y)^6}$$

The rate y is called the bond's **yield to maturity.** The yield to maturity on our bond is 3.8%. If you buy the bond at 106.33% and hold it to maturity, you will earn a return of 3.8% over the six years. That figure reflects both the regular interest payment that you receive and the fact that you are paying more for the bond today (€106.33) than you will receive back at maturity (€100).

The only *general* procedure for calculating the yield to maturity is trial and error. You guess at an interest rate and calculate the present value of the bond's payments. If the present value is greater than the actual price, your discount rate must have been too low, and you need to try a higher rate. The more practical solution is to use a spreadsheet program or a specially programmed calculator to calculate the yield.

Back to the United States: Semiannual Coupons and Bond Prices

Just like the German government, the U.S. Treasury periodically raises money by auctioning new issues of bonds. Some of these issues do not mature for 30 years; others, known as *notes*, mature in 10 years or less. The government also issues short-term loans that mature in less than a year. These are known as Treasury bills.

We will look at an example of a U.S. government note. In 2004 the Treasury issued 4.0% notes maturing in 2009. Treasury bonds have a face value of $1,000 so, if you own the 4s of 2009, the Treasury gives you back $1,000 when the bond matures. You can also look forward to a regular interest payment, but, in contrast to our German bond, interest on Treasury bonds is paid *semiannually*.[4] Thus, the 4s of 2009 provide a coupon payment of 4.0/2 = 2.0% of face value every six months.

Once issued, Treasury bonds are widely traded through a network of dealers and the prices at which you can buy or sell the bonds are shown each day in the

[4] The frequency of interest payments varies from country to country. For example, most euro bonds pay interest annually, while bonds in the U.K., Canada, and Japan, generally pay interest semiannually.

FIGURE 4.1

Treasury bond quotes from *The Wall Street Journal*, June 2006.

Source: *The Wall Street Journal*, June 2006 © Dow Jones, Inc.

Treasury Bonds, Notes and Bills

Explanatory Notes

Representative Over-the-Counter quotation based on transactions of $1 million or more. Treasury bond, note and bill quotes are as of mid-afternoon. Colons in bid-and-asked quotes represent 32nds; 101:01 means 101 1/32. Net changes in 32nds. n-Treasury note. i-Inflation-Indexed issue. Treasury bill quotes in hundredths, quoted on terms of a rate of discount. Days to maturity calculated from settlement date. All yields are to maturity and based on the asked quote. Latest 13-week and 26-week bills are boldfaced. For bonds callable prior to maturity, yields are computed to the earliest call date for issues quoted above par and to the maturity date for issues below par. *When issued.
Source: eSpeed/Cantor Fitzgerald

U.S. Treasury strips as of 3 p.m. Eastern time, also based on transactions of $1 million or more. Colons in bid and asked quotes represent 32nds; 99:01 means 99 1/32. Net changes in 32nds. Yields calculated on the asked quotation. ci-stripped coupon interest. bp-Treasury bond, stripped principal. np-Treasury note, stripped principal. For bonds callable prior to maturity, yields are computed to the earliest call date for issues quoted above par and to the maturity date for issues below par.
Source: Bear, Stearns & Co. via Street Software Technology Inc.

Government Bonds & Notes

RATE	MATURITY MO/YR	BID	ASKED	CHG	ASK YLD
2.750	Jun 06n	99:28	99:29	...	4.36
7.000	Jul 06n	100:04	100:05	...	4.91
2.750	Jul 06n	99:22	99:23	...	4.72
2.375	Aug 06n	99:17	99:18	...	4.78
2.375	Aug 06n	99:13	99:14	...	4.92
2.500	Sep 06n	99:07	99:08	...	5.03
6.500	Oct 06n	100:14	100:15	...	5.04
2.500	Oct 06n	99:00	99:01	...	5.04
2.625	Nov 06n	98:30	98:31	...	5.12
3.500	Nov 06n	99:10	99:11	...	5.08
2.875	Nov 06n	98:30	98:31	-1	5.11
3.000	Dec 06n	98:26	98:27	...	5.17
3.375	Jan 07i	100:18	100:19	-1	2.32
3.125	Jan 07n	98:23	98:24	...	5.15
2.250	Feb 07n	98:02	98:03	...	5.13
6.250	Feb 07n	100:21	100:22	-1	5.16
3.375	Feb 07n	98:24	98:25	...	5.13
3.750	Mar 07n	98:29	98:30	...	5.12
3.625	Apr 07n	98:22	98:23	...	5.13
6.625	May 07n	101:10	101:11	...	5.11
4.375	May 07n	99:09	99:10	-1	5.13
3.125	May 07n	98:06	98:07	...	5.11
3.500	May 07n	98:15	98:16	...	5.11
3.625	Jun 07n	98:15	98:16	-1	5.10
3.875	Jul 07n	98:21	98:22	...	5.08
2.750	Aug 07n	97:11	97:12	...	5.08
3.250	Aug 07n	97:29	97:30	...	5.06
6.125	Aug 07n	101:05	101:06	...	5.06
4.000	Aug 07n	98:23	98:24	...	5.07
4.000	Sep 07n	98:20	98:21	-1	5.07
4.250	Oct 07n	98:29	98:30	-1	5.04
3.000	Nov 07n	97:06	97:07	...	5.05
4.250	Nov 07n	98:27	98:28	-1	5.04
4.375	Dec 07n	99:00	99:01	...	5.03
3.625	Jan 08i	102:05	102:06	-1	2.21
4.375	Jan 08n	98:30	98:31	-1	5.03
3.000	Feb 08n	96:24	96:25	-1	5.02
5.500	Feb 08n	100:26	100:27	...	4.96
3.375	Feb 08n	97:11	97:12	-1	5.02
4.625	Feb 08n	99:10	99:11	-1	5.02
4.625	Mar 08n	99:09	99:10	-1	5.02
4.875	Apr 08n	99:23	99:24	-1	5.01
2.625	May 08n	95:21	95:22	...	5.01
3.750	May 08n	97:22	97:23	-1	5.00
5.625	May 08n	101:03	101:04	-1	4.99
4.875	**May 08n**	**99:22**	**99:23**	**-1**	**5.02**
3.250	Aug 08n	96:14	96:15	-1	4.97
4.125	Aug 08n	98:10	98:11	-1	4.93
3.125	Sep 08n	96:02	96:03	-1	4.97
3.125	Oct 08n	95:30	95:31	-1	4.96
3.375	Nov 08n	96:11	96:12	-1	4.97
4.750	Nov 08n	99:14	99:15	-1	4.98
4.375	Nov 08n	98:19	98:20	-1	4.98
3.375	Dec 08n	96:08	96:09	-1	4.96
3.250	Jan 09n	95:27	95:28	-1	4.96
3.875	Jan 09i	104:03	104:04	-2	2.22
4.500	Feb 09n	98:25	98:26	-1	4.98
3.000	Feb 09n	95:03	95:04	-1	4.97
2.625	Mar 09n	94:01	94:02	-1	4.96
3.125	Apr 09n	95:05	95:06	-1	4.96
3.875	May 09n	97:01	97:02	-1	4.96
5.500	May 09n	101:16	101:17	-1	4.92
4.875	May 09n	99:22	99:23	-1	4.97
4.000	Jun 09n	97:10	97:11	-1	4.96

financial press. Figure 4.1 is an excerpt from the bond quotation page of *The Wall Street Journal*. Look at the entry for our 4.0% Treasury bond maturing in June 2009. The **asked price** of 97:11 is the price you need to pay to buy the bond from a dealer. This price is quoted in 32nds rather than decimals. Thus a price of 97:11 means that each bond costs 97 and 11/32, or 97.34375% of face value. The face value of the bond is $1,000, so each bond costs $973.4375.[5]

The **bid price** is the price investors receive if they sell the bond to a dealer. The dealer earns her living by charging a *spread* between the bid and the asked price. Notice that the spread for the 4% bonds is only 1/32, or about .03%, of the bond's value.

The next column in Figure 4.1 shows the change in price since the previous day. The price of the 4.0% bonds has fallen by 1/32. Finally, the column "Ask Yld" shows the **ask yield to maturity.** Because interest is semiannual, yields on U.S. bonds are

[5] The quoted bond price is known as the *flat* (or *clean*) price. The price that the bond buyer actually pays (sometimes called the *full* or *dirty price*) is equal to the flat price *plus* the interest that the seller has already earned on the bond since the last interest payment. The precise method for calculating this *accrued interest* varies from one type of bond to another. You need to use the flat price to calculate the yield.

usually quoted as semiannually compounded yields. Thus, if you buy the 4.0% bond at the asked price and hold it to maturity, you will earn a semiannually compounded return of 4.96%. This is equivalent to a yield over six months of 4.96/2 = 2.48%.

We can now repeat the present value calculations that we did for the German government bond. We just need to recognize that bonds in the United States have a face value of $1,000, that their coupons are paid semiannually, and that the quoted yield is a semiannually compounded rate.

Here are the cash flows from the 4s of 2009:

Cash Flows ($)					
Dec 2006	Jun 2007	Dec 2007	Jun 2008	Dec 2008	June 2009
$20	$20	$20	$20	$20	$1,020

If investors demand a semiannual return of 2.48% for investing in three-year bonds, then the present value of these cash flows is

$$PV = \frac{20}{1.0248} + \frac{20}{1.0248^2} + \frac{20}{1.0248^3} + \frac{20}{1.0248^4} + \frac{20}{1.0248^5} + \frac{1020}{1.0248^6} = \$973.54$$

Each bond is worth $973.54, or 97.35% of face value (the slight difference from the figure in *The Wall Street Journal* is simply due to rounding error).

4.2   HOW BOND PRICES VARY WITH INTEREST RATES

As interest rates change, so do bond prices. For example, suppose that investors demanded a yield of 3% on three-year Treasury bonds. What would be the price of the 4s of 2009? Just repeat the last calculation with a six-month yield of 1.5%:

$$PV = \frac{20}{1.015} + \frac{20}{1.015^2} + \frac{20}{1.015^3} + \frac{20}{1.015^4} + \frac{20}{1.015^5} + \frac{1020}{1.015^6} = \$1,028.49$$

or 102.85% of face value. The lower interest rate results in a higher bond price.

The solid line in Figure 4.2 shows the value of our 4% bond for different interest rates. You can see that as yields fall, bond prices rise. When the yield is equal to the bond's coupon (4%), the bond sells for exactly its face value. When the yield is higher than 4%, the bond sells at a discount to face value. When the yield is lower, the bond sells at a premium.

Bond investors cross their fingers that market interest rates will fall, so that the price of their securities will rise. If they are *unlucky* and the interest rates jump up, the value of their investment declines. Any such change in interest rates is likely to have only a modest effect on the value of near-term cash flows, but it will have a much greater effect on the value of distant cash flows. Thus the price of long-term bonds is affected more by changing interest rates than is the price of short-term bonds.

Duration and Bond Volatility

But what do we mean by the phrases "long-term" and "short-term" bonds? A coupon bond that matures in year 30 makes payments in *each* of years 1 through 30. Therefore, it is somewhat misleading to describe the bond as a 30-year bond; the average time to each cash flow is less than 30 years.

FIGURE 4.2

The value of the three-year 4% bond falls as interest rates rise.

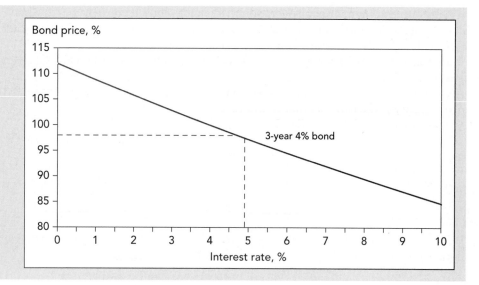

Year	Ct	PV(Ct) at 5%	Proportion of Total Value [PV(Ct)/V]	Proportion of Total Value x Time
1	100	95.24	0.084	0.084
2	100	90.70	0.080	0.160
3	1,100	950.22	0.836	2.509
		V = 1,136.16	1.000	Duration = 2.753 years

TABLE 4.1

The first four columns show that the cash flow in year 3 accounts for less than 84% of the present value of the three-year 10s. The final column shows how to calculate a weighted average of the times to each cash flow. This average is the bond's duration.

Visit us at
www.mhhe.com/bma1e.

Consider a simple three-year bond that pays interest of 10% once a year. The first three columns of Table 4.1 calculate the present value (V) of this bond assuming a yield to maturity of 5%. The total value of the bond is $1,136.16.

The fourth column shows the contribution of each payment to the bond's value. Notice that the cash flow in year 3 accounts for less than 84% of the value. The remaining 16% comes from the earlier cash flows.

Bond analysts often use the term **duration** to describe the average time to each payment. If we call the total value of the bond V, then duration is calculated as follows:[6]

$$\text{Duration} = \frac{[1 \times \text{PV}(C_1)]}{V} + \frac{[2 \times \text{PV}(C_2)]}{V} + \frac{[3 \times \text{PV}(C_3)]}{V} + \cdots$$

---

[6] This measure is also known as *Macaulay duration* after its inventor.

The final column of Table 4.1 shows that for our three-year 10% bond,

$$\text{Duration} = (1 \times .084) + (2 \times .080) + (3 \times .836) = 2.753 \text{ years}$$

The bond's maturity is three years but the weighted average time to each cash flow is only 2.753 years.

Suppose we take another three-year bond. This time the coupon payment is 4%. The maturity is the same as that of the 10% bond, but the first two years' coupon payments account for a smaller fraction of the value. In this sense the bond is a longer bond. The duration of the three-year 4% bonds is 2.884 years.

Consider now what happens to the price of the 10% and 4% bonds as interest rates change:

	3-year 10% bond		3-year 4% bond	
	New Price	Change	New Price	Change
Yield falls .5%	1151.19	+1.32%	986.26	+1.39%
Yield rises .5%	1121.41	−1.30	959.53	−1.36
Difference		2.62		2.75

A 1 percentage-point variation in yield causes the price of the 10s to change by 2.62%. We can say that the 10s have a **volatility** of 2.62%, while the 4s have a volatility of 2.75%.

Notice that the 4% bonds have the greater volatility and that they also have the longer duration. In fact, a bond's volatility is directly related to its duration: [7]

$$\text{Volatility (\%)} = \frac{\text{duration}}{1 + \text{yield}}$$

In the case of the 10s,

$$\text{Volatility (\%)} = \frac{2.753}{1.05} = 2.62$$

Figure 4.3 shows how changing interest rates affect the prices of a 3-year 4% bond and a 30-year 4% bond. Each bond's volatility is simply the slope of the line relating the bond price to the interest rate. The 30-year bond has a much longer duration than the 3-year bond and is correspondingly more volatile. This shows up in the steeper curve in Figure 4.3. Notice also that the bond's volatility changes as the interest rate changes. Volatility is higher at lower interest rates (the curve is steeper), and it is lower at higher rates (the curve is flatter).[8]

A Cautionary Note

Bond volatility measures the effect on bond prices of a shift in interest rates. For example, we calculated that the three-year 10s had a volatility of 2.62. This means

---

[7] For this reason volatility is also called *modified duration*.

[8] Bond investors refer to this feature as the bond's *convexity*.

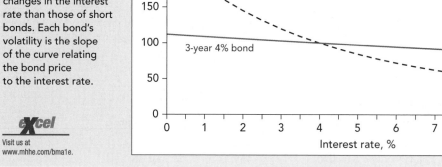

FIGURE 4.3

Plots of the prices of 3-year and 30-year 4% bonds. Notice that prices of the long bonds are more sensitive to changes in the interest rate than those of short bonds. Each bond's volatility is the slope of the curve relating the bond price to the interest rate.

e**X**cel

Visit us at
www.mhhe.com/bma1e.

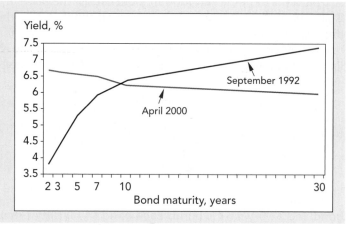

FIGURE 4.4

Short- and long-term interest rates do not always move in parallel. Between September 1992 and April 2000 U.S. short-term rates rose sharply while long-term rates declined.

that a 1 percentage-point change in interest rates leads to a 2.62% change in the bond price:

$$\text{Change in bond price} = 2.62 \times \text{change in interest rates}$$

Once you understand how your firm will be affected by interest rate changes, you can consider whether it is worth protecting against these risks.

If the yields on all bonds moved in precise lockstep, then the volatility measure would capture *exactly* the effect of interest rate changes on bond prices. However, Figure 4.4 illustrates that short- and long-term interest rates do *not* always move in perfect unison. Between 1992 and 2000 short-term interest rates nearly doubled while long-term rates declined. As a result, the term structure, which initially sloped steeply upward, shifted to a downward slope. Because short- and long-term yields do not move in parallel, a single measure of volatility cannot be the whole story, and managers may need to worry not just about the risks of an overall change in interest rates but also about shifts in the shape of the term structure.

4.3 THE TERM STRUCTURE OF INTEREST RATES

We now need to look more carefully at the relationship between short- and long-term rates of interest. Consider a simple loan that pays \$1 at time 1. The present value of this loan is

$$PV = \frac{1}{1 + r_1}$$

Thus we discount the cash flow at r_1, today's rate for a one-period loan. This rate is often called today's one-period **spot rate.**

   If we have a loan that pays \$1 at both time 1 and time 2, present value is

$$PV = \frac{1}{1 + r_1} + \frac{1}{(1 + r_2)^2}$$

This is identical to the calculations that we performed at the start of Chapter 3 where we valued a series of risk-free cash flows. The first period's cash flow is discounted at today's one-period spot rate and the second period's flow is discounted at today's two-period spot rate. The series of spot rates r_1, r_2, etc., is one way of expressing the **term structure** of interest rates.

The Yield to Maturity and the Term Structure

Rather than discounting each of the payments at a different rate of interest, we could instead find a single rate that would produce the same present value. That is what we did in Section 4.1 when we calculated the yield to maturity on the German and U.S. government bonds. In the case of our simple two-year loan, we could write the present value in terms of the yield to maturity as

$$PV = \frac{1}{1 + y} + \frac{1}{(1 + y)^2}$$

Financial managers who want a quick, summary measure of interest rates look in the financial press at the yield to maturity on government bonds. Or they may refer to the **yield curve,** which summarizes how bond yields vary with the bond's maturity. Thus managers may make broad generalizations such as "If we take out a five-year loan, we will have to pay an interest rate (i.e., yield) of 5%."

   Throughout this book, we too will use the yield to maturity to summarize the return required by bond investors. But you also need to understand the measure's limitations when the spot rates r_1, r_2, etc., are not equal. The yield to maturity resembles an average of these different spot rates and, like any average, it may hide some useful information. If you wish to understand why different bonds sell at different prices, you may need to dig deeper and look at the separate interest rates for one-year cash flows, two-year cash flows, and so on. In other words, you may need to look at the *spot* rates of interest.

Example   Here is an example where comparing the yields of two bonds is potentially misleading. It is 2009. You are contemplating an investment in U.S. Treasuries and come across the following quotations for two bonds:

Bond	Price as % of Face Value	Yield to Maturity
5s of 2014	85.211	8.78%
10s of 2014	105.429	8.62

Does the higher yield on the 5s of 2014 mean that they are a better buy? The only way to know for sure is to use the spot rates of interest to calculate the bonds' present values. This is done in Table 4.2, assuming for simplicity annual coupon payments.

The important assumption in Table 4.2 is that long-term interest rates are higher than short-term interest rates. We have assumed that the one-year interest rate is $r_1 = .05$, the two year rate is $r_2 = .06$, and so on. When each year's cash flow is discounted at the rate appropriate for that year, we see that each bond's present value is equal to the quoted price. Thus each bond is fairly priced.

If both bonds are fairly priced, why do the 5s have a higher yield? Because for each dollar that you invest in the 5s, you receive relatively little cash inflow in the first four years and a relatively high cash inflow in the final year. Therefore, although the two bonds have identical maturity dates, the 5s provide a greater proportion of their cash flows in 2014. In this sense the 5s are a longer-term investment than the 10s. Their higher yield to maturity just reflects the fact that long-term interest rates are higher than short-term rates.

Notice the reason that the yield to maturity in this example is misleading. When the yield is calculated, the *same* rate is used to discount *all* payments on the bond. But in our example bondholders demand *different* rates of return (r_1, r_2, etc.) for cash flows that occur at different dates. Since the cash flows on the two bonds are also not identical, the bonds have different yields to maturity, and the yield to maturity on the 5s of 2014 offers only a rough guide to the appropriate yield on the 10s of 2014.

		Present Value Calculations			
		5s of 2014		10s of 2014	
Year	Spot Interest Rate	Cash Flow	PV	Cash Flow	PV
2010	$r_1 = .05$	$ 50	$ 47.62	$ 100	$ 95.24
2011	$r_2 = .06$	50	44.50	100	89.00
2012	$r_3 = .07$	50	40.81	100	81.63
2013	$r_4 = .08$	50	36.75	100	73.50
2014	$r_5 = .09$	1050	682.43	1100	714.92
		Totals	$852.11		$1,054.29

TABLE 4.2

Calculating present values of two bonds when long-term interest rates are higher than short-term rates.

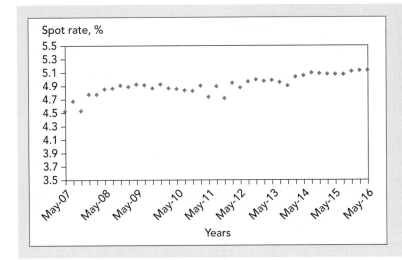

FIGURE 4.5

Spot rates on U.S. Treasury strips, June 2006.

Measuring the Term Structure

You can think of the spot rate, r_t, as the rate of interest on a bond that makes a single payment at time t. Such bonds do exist. They are known as **stripped bonds,** or **strips.** On request the Treasury will split a normal coupon bond into a package of mini-bonds, each of which makes just one cash payment. Thus, our 5% bonds of 2014 could be exchanged for five coupon strips each paying $50 and a principal strip paying $1,000.

The prices of strips are shown each day in the financial press. For example, in June 2006 a 10-year strip cost $609.06, and it will make a single payment of $1,000 in the summer of 2016. Hence the 10-year spot rate was $(1000/609.06)^{1/10} - 1 = .0508$, or 5.08%.[9]

In Figure 4.5 we have used the prices of strips with different maturities to plot the term structure of spot rates from 1 to 10 years. You can see that investors required a somewhat higher interest rate for lending for 10 years rather than 1.

4.4   EXPLAINING THE TERM STRUCTURE

The term structure that we showed in Figure 4.5 was upward-sloping. In other words, long-term rates of interest were higher than short-term rates. This is the more common pattern, but sometimes it is the other way around, with short rates higher than long rates. Why do we get these shifts in term structure?

Let us look at a simple example. Suppose that the one-year spot rate (r_1) is 5% and the two-year spot rate is higher at $r_2 = 6\%$. If you invest in a one-year Treasury strip, you would earn the one-year spot rate, so that by the end of the year each dollar that you invested would have grown to $\$(1 + r_1) = \$1.05$. If instead you were prepared to invest for two years, you would earn the two-year spot rate of r_2, and by the end of the two years each dollar would have grown to $\$(1 + r_2)^2 = \$1.06^2 = \$1.1236$. By

---

[9] This is an annually compounded rate. The yields quoted by U.S. bond dealers are semiannually compounded rates.

FIGURE 4.6

An investor can invest either in a two-year loan (*a*) or in two successive one-year loans (*b*). The expectations theory says that in equilibrium the expected payoffs from these two strategies must be equal. In other words, the forward rate, f_2, must equal the expected spot rate, $_1r_2$.

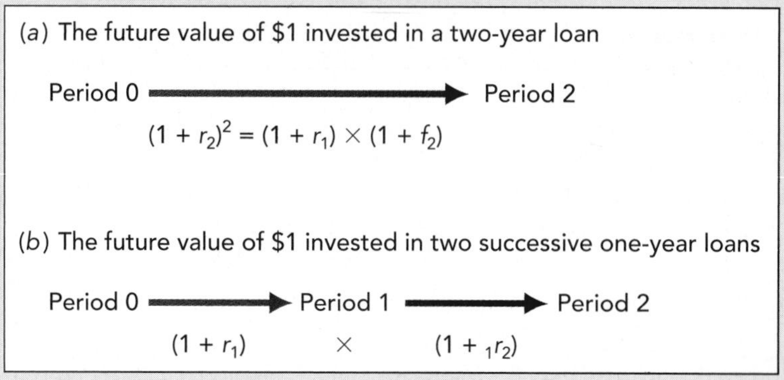

(*a*) The future value of $1 invested in a two-year loan

Period 0 ⟶ Period 2

$$(1 + r_2)^2 = (1 + r_1) \times (1 + f_2)$$

(*b*) The future value of $1 invested in two successive one-year loans

Period 0 ⟶ Period 1 ⟶ Period 2

$$(1 + r_1) \qquad \times \qquad (1 + {}_1r_2)$$

keeping your money invested for that second year, your savings grow from $1.05 to $1.1236, an increase of 7.01%. This extra 7.01% that you earn by keeping your money invested for two years rather than one is termed the **forward interest rate** or f_2.

Notice how we calculated the forward rate. When you invest for one year, each dollar grows to $$(1 + r_1)$. When you invest for two years, each dollar grows to $$(1 + r_2)^2$. Therefore, the extra return that you earn for that second year is $f_2 = (1 + r_2)^2/(1 + r_1) - 1$. In our example,

$$f_2 = (1 + r_2)^2/(1 + r_1) - 1 = (1 + .06)^2/(1 + .05) - 1 = .0701, \text{ or } 7.01\%$$

If you twist this equation around, you can obtain an expression for the two-year spot rate, r_2, in terms of the one-year spot rate, r_1, and the forward rate, f_2:

$$(1 + r_2)^2 = (1 + r_1)(1 + f_2)$$

In other words, you can think of the two-year investment as earning the one-year spot rate for the first year and the extra return, or forward rate, for the second year.

The Expectations Theory

Would you be happy to earn an extra 7% for investing for two years rather than one? The answer depends on how you expect interest rates to change over the coming year. Suppose, for example, that you were confident that interest rates would rise sharply, so that at the end of the year the one-year rate would be 8%. In that case, rather than investing in a two-year bond and earning an extra 7% for the second year, you would do better to invest in a one-year bond and, when that matured, to reinvest the cash for a further year at 8%. If other investors shared your view, no one would be prepared to hold the two-year bond and its price would fall. It would stop falling only when the extra return from holding the two-year bond equalled the expected future one-year rate. Let us call this expected rate $_1r_2$—that is, the spot rate at year 1 on a loan maturing at the end of year 2.[10] Figure 4.6 shows that at that point investors would earn the same expected return from investing in a two-year loan as from investing in two successive one-year loans.

---

[10] Be careful to distinguish $_1r_2$ from r_2, the spot interest rate on a bond held from time 0 to time 2. The quantity $_1r_2$ is a one-year spot rate established at time 1.

This is known as the **expectations theory** of the term structure. It states that in equilibrium the forward interest rate f_2 must equal the expected one-year spot rate $_1r_2$. The expectations theory implies that the *only* reason for an upward-sloping term structure is that investors expect short-term interest rates to rise; the *only* reason for a declining term structure is that investors expect short-term rates to fall.[11] The expectations theory also implies that investing in a succession of short-term bonds gives exactly the same expected return as investing in long-term bonds.

If short-term interest rates are significantly lower than long-term rates, it is tempting to borrow short-term rather than long-term. The expectations theory implies that such naïve strategies won't work. If short-term rates are lower than long-term rates, then investors must be expecting interest rates to rise. When the term structure is upward-sloping, you are likely to make money by borrowing short only if investors are *overestimating* future increases in interest rates.

Even on a casual glance the expectations theory does not seem to be the complete explanation of term structure. For example, if we look back over the period 1900–2006, we find that the return on long-term U.S. Treasury bonds was on average about 1.2 percentage points higher than the return on short-term Treasury bills.[12] Perhaps short-term interest rates stayed lower than investors expected, but it seems more likely that investors wanted some extra return for holding long bonds and that on average they got it. If so, the expectations theory is wrong.

These days the expectations theory has few strict adherents, but most economists believe that expectations about future interest rates have an important effect on term structure. For example, you often hear market commentators remark that the forward interest rate over the next few months is higher than the current spot rate and conclude that the market is expecting the Fed to raise interest rates.

There is quite a bit of evidence for this type of reasoning. Suppose that every month from 1950 to 2005 you used the three-month forward rate of interest to predict the change in the corresponding spot rate over these three months. You would have found on average that the steeper the term structure, the more the spot rate rose. It looks as if the expectations theory has some truth to it even if it is not the whole truth.

Introducing Risk

What does the expectations theory leave out? The most obvious answer is "risk." If you are confident about the future level of interest rates, you will simply choose the strategy that offers the highest return. But, if you are not sure of your forecasts, you may well opt for a less risky strategy even if it means giving up some return.

Remember that the prices of long-duration bonds are more volatile than those of short-term bonds. A sharp increase in interest rates can easily knock 30% or 40% off the price of long-term bonds. For some investors this extra volatility may not be a concern. For example, pension funds and life insurance companies with long-term liabilities may prefer to lock in future returns by investing in long-term bonds. However, the volatility of long-term bonds *does* create extra risk for investors who do not have such long-term obligations. These investors will be prepared to hold long bonds only if they offer the compensation of a higher return. In this case

---

[11] This follows from our example. If the one-year spot rate, r_1, exceeds the two-year spot rate, r_2, then r_1 also exceeds the forward rate, f_2. If the forward rate equals the expected spot rate, $_1r_2$, then r_1 must also exceed $_1r_2$.

[12] Treasury bills are short-term government debts with a maximum maturity of six months.

the forward rate must be *higher* than the expected spot rate and the term structure will be upward-sloping more often than not. Of course, if future spot rates are expected to fall, the term structure could be downward-sloping and still reward investors for lending long. But the additional reward for risk offered by long bonds would result in a less dramatic downward slope.

Inflation and Term Structure

There is one other thing that you need to think about when comparing the risk of different bonds. Although the cash flows on every U.S. Treasury bond are certain, you can't be sure what that money will buy. That depends on the rate of inflation.

Suppose you are saving for your retirement. Which of the following strategies is the more risky? Invest in a succession of one-year Treasury bonds or invest in a 20-year bond?

If you buy the 20-year bond, you know what money you will have at the end of the period but you will be making a long-term bet on inflation. Inflation may seem benign now but who knows what it will be like in 10 or 20 years? This uncertainty about inflation may make it more risky for you to fix today the rates at which you will lend in the distant future.

You can reduce this uncertainty by investing in successive short-term bonds. You do not know the interest rate at which you will be able to reinvest your money at the end of each year, but at least you know that it will incorporate the latest information about inflation in the coming year. So, if inflation takes off, it is likely that you will be able to reinvest your money at a higher interest rate.

Here then we have another reason that long-term bonds may offer a risk premium. If inflation creates an additional source of risk for long-term lenders, borrowers must offer some extra incentive if they want investors to lend long. That is why we often see a steeply upward-sloping term structure when inflation is particularly uncertain.

4.5   REAL AND NOMINAL RATES OF INTEREST

It is now time to review more carefully the relation between inflation and interest rates. Suppose you invest $1,000 in a one-year bond that makes a single payment of $1,100 at the end of the year. Your cash flow is certain, but the government makes no promises about what that money will buy. If the prices of goods and services increase by more than 10%, you will have lost ground in terms of the goods that you can buy.

Several indexes are used to track the general level of prices. The best known is the Consumer Price Index, or CPI, which measures the number of dollars that it takes to pay for a typical family's purchases. The change in the CPI from one year to the next measures the rate of inflation. Figure 4.7 shows the rate of inflation in the United States since 1900. Inflation touched a peak at the end of World War I, when it reached 21%. This figure, however, pales into insignificance compared with inflation in Germany in 1923, which was more than 20,000,000,000% a year (or about 5% per day). Of course prices do not always rise. For example, in recent years Japan and Hong Kong have both faced a problem of deflation. The United States experienced severe deflation in the Great Depression when prices fell by 24% in three years.

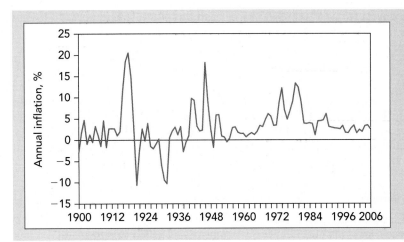

FIGURE 4.7

Annual rates of inflation in the United States from 1900–2006.

Source: E. Dimson, P. R. Marsh, and M. Staunton, *Triumph of the Optimists: 101 Years of Investment Returns* (Princeton, NJ: Princeton University Press, 2002), with updates provided by the authors. Reprinted by permission of Princeton University Press.

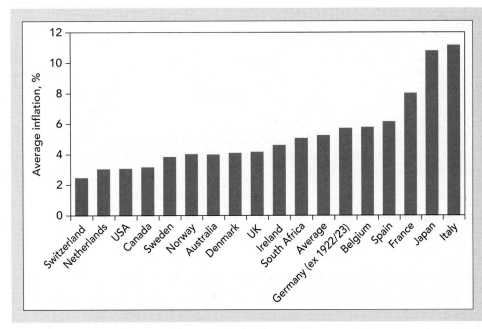

FIGURE 4.8

Average rates of inflation in 17 countries from 1900–2006.

Source: E. Dimson, P. R. Marsh, and M. Staunton, *Triumph of the Optimists: 101 Years of Investment Returns* (Princeton, NJ: Princeton University Press, 2002), with updates provided by the authors. Reprinted by permission of Princeton University Press.

The average inflation rate in the United States between 1900 and 2006 was 3.1%. As you can see from Figure 4.8, among major economies the U.S. has been almost top of the class in holding inflation in check. Those countries that have been torn by war have generally experienced much higher inflation. For example, in Italy and Japan inflation since 1900 has averaged about 11% a year.

Economists sometimes talk about current, or nominal, dollars versus constant, or real, dollars. For example, the *nominal* cash flow from your one-year bond is $1,100. But suppose prices of goods rise over the year by 6%; then each dollar will buy you 6% fewer goods next year than it does today. So at the end of the year $1,100 will buy the same quantity of goods as 1,100/1.06 = $1,037.74 today. The nominal payoff on the bond is $1,100, but the *real* payoff is only $1,037.74.

The general formula for converting nominal cash flows at a future period t to real cash flows is

$$\text{Real cash flow}_t = \frac{\text{nominal cash flow}_t}{(1 + \text{inflation rate})^t}$$

For example, if you were to invest that $1,000 in a 20-year bond with a 10% coupon, then your final year's payment would still be $1,100, but with an inflation rate of 6% a year, the real value of that payoff would be $1,100/1.06^{20} = \$342.99$.

When a bond dealer says that your bond yields 10%, she is quoting a nominal interest rate. That rate tells you how rapidly your money will grow:

Invest Current Dollars		Receive Period-1 Dollars	Result
1,000	→	1,100	10% *nominal* rate of return

However, with an inflation rate of 6%, you are only 3.774% better off at the end of the year than at the start:

Invest Current Dollars		Expected Real Value of Period-1 Dollars	Result
1,000	→	1,037.74	3.774% expected *real* rate of return

Thus, we could say, "The bank account offers a 10% nominal rate of return," or "It offers a 3.774% expected real rate of return." The formula for calculating the real rate of return is

$$1 + r_{\text{real}} = (1 + r_{\text{nominal}})/(1 + \text{inflation rate})$$

In our example,[13]

$$1.03774 = 1.10/1.06$$

Indexed Bonds and the Real Rate of Interest

Most bonds are like our U.S. Treasury bonds; they promise you a fixed *nominal* rate of interest. The *real* interest rate that you receive is uncertain and depends on inflation. If the inflation rate turns out to be higher than you expected, the real return on your bonds will be lower than forecasted.

You *can* nail down a real return; you do so by buying an indexed bond whose payments are linked to inflation. Indexed bonds have been around in many other countries for decades, but they were almost unknown in the United States until 1997 when the U.S. Treasury began to issue inflation-indexed bonds known as TIPS (Treasury Inflation-Protected Securities).[14]

---

[13] A common rule of thumb states that $r_{\text{real}} = r_{\text{nominal}} - $ inflation rate. In our example this gives $r_{\text{real}} = .10 - .06 = .04$, or 4%. This is not a bad approximation to the true real interest rate of 3.774%. But there are countries where inflation is large (sometimes 100% or more). In such cases it pays to use the full formula.

[14] Indexed bonds were not completely unknown in the United States before 1997. For example, in 1780 American Revolutionary soldiers were compensated with indexed bonds that paid the value of "five bushels of corn, 68 pounds and four-seventh parts of a pound of beef, ten pounds of sheep's wool, and sixteen pounds of sole leather."

The real cash flows on TIPS are fixed, but the nominal cash flows (interest and principal) increase as the Consumer Price Index increases. For example, suppose that the U.S. Treasury issues 3% 20-year TIPS at a price of 100. If during the first year the Consumer Price Index rises by (say) 10%, then the coupon payment on the bond would increase by 10% to $(1.1 \times 3) = 3.3\%$. And the final payment of principal would also increase in the same proportion to $(1.1 \times 100) = 110\%$. Thus, an investor who buys the bond at the issue price and holds it to maturity can be assured of a real yield of 3%.

As we write this in the summer of 2006, long-term TIPS offer a yield of about 2.3%. This yield is a *real* yield: It measures the extra goods your investment will allow you to buy. The 2.3% yield on TIPS is about 2.8% less than the nominal yield on nominal Treasury bonds. If the annual inflation rate proves to be higher than 2.8%, you will earn a higher return by holding long-term TIPS; if the inflation rate is less than 2.8%, you will be better off with nominal bonds.

The real yield that investors demand depends on people's willingness to save (the supply of capital)[15] and the opportunities for productive investment by governments and businesses (the demand for capital). For example, suppose that investment opportunities generally improve. Firms have more good projects, so they are willing to invest more than previously at the current interest rate. Therefore, the rate has to rise to induce individuals to save the additional amount that firms want to invest.[16] Conversely, if investment opportunities deteriorate, there will be a fall in the real interest rate.

This implies that the required real rate of interest depends on real phenomena. A high aggregate willingness to save may be associated with high aggregate wealth (because wealthy people usually save more), an uneven distribution of wealth (an even distribution would mean fewer rich people who do most of the saving), and a high proportion of middle-aged people (the young don't need to save and the old don't want to—"You can't take it with you"). Correspondingly a high propensity to invest may be associated with a high level of industrial activity or major technological advances.

Real interest rates do change but they do so gradually. We can see this by looking at the U.K. where the government has issued indexed bonds since 1982. The (maroon) line in Figure 4.9 shows that the (real) yield on these bonds has fluctuated within a relatively narrow range, while the yield on nominal government bonds (the blue line) has declined dramatically.

Inflation and Nominal Interest Rates

How does the inflation outlook affect the nominal rate of interest? Here is how the economist Irving Fisher answered the question. Suppose that consumers are equally happy with 100 apples today or 105 apples in a year's time. In this case the real or "apple" interest rate is 5%. If the price of apples is constant at (say) $1 each, then we will be equally happy to receive $100 today or $105 at the end of the year. That extra $5 will allow us to buy 5% more apples at the end of the year than we could buy today.

---

[15] Some of this saving may be done indirectly. For example, if you hold 100 shares of IBM stock, and IBM plows back $1.00 a share, IBM is saving $100 on your behalf. The government may also oblige you to save by raising taxes to invest in roads, hospitals, and so on.

[16] We assume that investors save more as interest rates rise. It doesn't have to be that way; here is an extreme example of how a higher interest rate could mean less saving. Suppose that 20 years hence you will need $50,000 at current prices for your children's college expenses. How much will you have to set aside today to cover this obligation? The answer is the present value of a real expenditure of $50,000 after 20 years, or $50,000/(1 + \text{real interest rate})^{20}$. The higher the real interest rate, the lower the present value and the less you have to set aside.

FIGURE 4.9

The maroon line shows the real yield on long-term indexed bonds issued by the U.K. government. The blue line shows the yield on long-term nominal bonds. Notice that the real yield has been much more stable than the nominal yield.

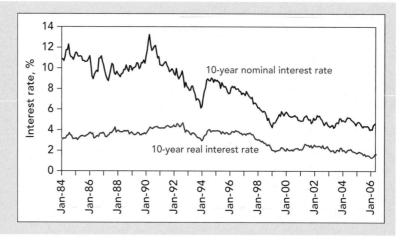

But suppose now that the apple price is expected to increase by 10% to $1.10 each. In that case we would *not* be happy to give up $100 today for the promise of $105 next year. To buy 105 apples in a year's time, we will need to receive 1.10 × $105 = $115.50. In other words, the nominal rate of interest must increase by the expected rate of inflation to 15.50%.

This is Fisher's theory: A change in the expected inflation rate will cause the same proportionate change in the *nominal* interest rate; it has no effect on the required real interest rate. The formula relating the nominal interest rate and expected inflation is

$$1 + r_{nominal} = (1 + r_{real})(1 + i)$$

where r_{real} is the real interest rate that consumers require and i is the expected inflation rate. In our example, the prospect of inflation causes $1 + r_{nominal}$ to rise to 1.05 × 1.10 = 1.155.

Nominal interest rates cannot be negative; if they were, everyone would prefer to hold cash, which pays zero interest. But what about *real* rates? For example, is it possible for the money rate of interest to be 5% and the expected rate of inflation to be 10%, thus giving a negative real interest rate? If this happens, you may be able to make money in the following way: You borrow $100 at an interest rate of 5% and use the money to buy apples. You store the apples and sell them at the end of the year for $110, which leaves you enough to pay off your loan plus $5 for yourself.

Since easy ways to make money are rare, we can conclude that if it doesn't cost anything to store goods, the money rate of interest can't be less than the expected rise in prices. But many goods are even more expensive to store than apples, and others can't be stored at all (you can't store haircuts, for example). For these goods the money interest rate can be less than the expected price rise.

How Well Does Fisher's Theory Explain Interest Rates?

Not all economists would agree with Fisher that the real rate of interest is unaffected by the inflation rate. For example, if changes in prices are associated with

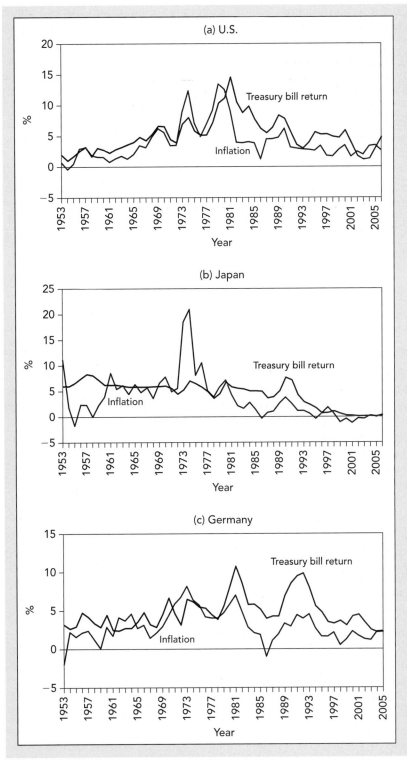

FIGURE 4.10

The return on Treasury bills and the rate of inflation in the U.S., Japan, and Germany, 1953–2006.

Source: E. Dimson, P. R. Marsh, and M. Staunton, *Triumph of the Optimists: 101 Years of Investment Returns* (Princeton, NJ.: Princeton University Press, 2002), with updates provided by the authors. Reprinted by permission of Princeton University Press.

changes in the level of industrial activity, then in inflationary conditions I might want more or less than 105 apples in a year's time to compensate me for the loss of 100 today.

We wish we could show you the past behavior of interest rates and *expected* inflation. Instead we have done the next best thing and plotted in Figure 4.10 the return on Treasury bills (short-term government debt) against *actual* inflation for the U.S., Japan, and Germany. Notice that since 1953 the return on Treasury bills has generally been a little above the rate of inflation. Investors in each country earned an average real return of between 1% and 2% during this period.

Look now at the relationship between the rate of inflation and the Treasury bill rate. Figure 4.10 shows that investors have for the most part demanded a higher rate of interest when inflation has been high.[17] So it looks as if Fisher's theory provides at least a useful rule of thumb for financial managers. If the expected inflation rate changes, it is a good bet that there will be a corresponding change in the interest rate.

---

[17] The principal exception occurred in Japan in 1973–74, when rapid monetary growth was followed by the oil crisis.

SUMMARY

Bonds are simply long-term loans. If you own a bond, you are entitled to a regular interest (or *coupon*) payment and at maturity you get back the bond's face value (or *principal*). In the United States bond interest is generally paid every six months but in other countries the interest may be paid annually.

The value of any bond is equal to the cash payments discounted at the spot rates of interest. For example, the value of a 10-year bond with a 5% coupon paid annually equals

$$\text{PV (\% of face value)} = \frac{5}{1 + r_1} + \frac{5}{(1 + r_2)^2} + \cdots + \frac{105}{(1 + r_{10})^{10}}$$

Bond dealers commonly use the yield to maturity on a bond to summarize its prospective return. To calculate the yield to maturity on the 10-year 5s, you need to solve for y in the following equation:

$$\text{Bond price} = \frac{5}{1 + y} + \frac{5}{(1 + y)^2} + \cdots + \frac{105}{(1 + y)^{10}}$$

The yield to maturity, y, is like an average of the spot interest rates, r_1, r_2, etc. Like most averages it can be a useful summary measure, but it can also hide a lot of useful information. If you want to dig deeper, we suggest that you refer to yields on stripped bonds as measures of the spot rates of interest.

A bond's maturity tells you when you receive your final payment, but it is also useful to know the *average* time to each payment. This is called the bond's *duration*. Duration is important because there is a direct relationship between the duration of a bond and its volatility. A change in interest rates has a greater effect on the price of a bond with a longer duration.

The one-period spot rate, r_1, may be very different from the two-period spot rate, r_2. In other words, investors may want a different annual rate of return for lending for one year rather than for two years. Why is this? The *expectations theory* says that bonds are priced so that an investor who holds a succession of short bonds can expect the same return as another investor who holds a long bond. The expectations theory predicts that r_2 will exceed r_1 only if next period's one-year interest rate is expected to rise.

The expectations theory cannot be a complete explanation of term structure if investors are worried about risk. Long bonds may be a safe haven for investors with long-term fixed liabilities. But other investors may not like the extra volatility of long-term bonds or may be concerned that a sudden burst of inflation may largely wipe out the real value of these bonds. Such investors will be prepared to hold long-term bonds only if they offer the compensation of a higher rate of interest.

Bonds promise a fixed money payment but the *real* interest rate that they provide depends on inflation. The real interest rate that investors require is determined by the demand for capital and the supply of savings. The demand for capital comes from governments and firms that want to invest in new projects. The supply of savings comes from individuals who are willing to consume tomorrow rather than today. The equilibrium interest rate is the rate that produces a balance between the demand and supply.

The best-known theory about the effect of inflation on interest rates was suggested by Irving Fisher. He argued that the nominal, or money, rate of interest is equal to the required real rate plus the expected (and unrelated) rate of inflation. If the expected inflation rate increases by 1%, so too will the money rate of interest. During the past 50 years Fisher's simple theory has not done a bad job of explaining changes in short-term interest rates in the United States, Japan, and Germany.

When you buy a U.S. Treasury bond, you can be confident that you will get your money back. When you lend to a company, you face the risk that it will go belly-up and will not be able to repay its bonds. We sidestepped the issue of default risk in this chapter, but bear in mind that companies need to compensate investors for this risk with a higher rate of interest.

FURTHER READING

A general text on debt markets is:

S. Sundaresan, *Fixed Income Markets and Their Derivatives*, 2nd ed. (Cincinnati, OH: South-Western Publishing, 2001).

Schaefer's paper is a good review of duration and how it is used to hedge fixed liabilities:

S. M. Schaefer, "Immunisation and Duration: A Review of Theory, Performance and Application," in J. M. Stern and D. H. Chew, Jr., *The Revolution in Corporate Finance* (Oxford: Basil Blackwell, 1986).

WEB PROJECT

Log on to **www.smartmoney.com** and find *The Living Yield Curve*, which provides a moving picture of the term structure. How does today's yield curve compare with the average? Do short-term interest rates move more or less than long-term rates? Why do you think this is the case?

CONCEPT REVIEW QUESTIONS

1. Fill in the blanks: The market value of a bond is the present value of its _____ and _____ payments. (page 60)
2. What is meant by a bond's yield to maturity and how is it calculated? (page 61)
3. If interest rates rise, do bond prices rise or fall? (page 63)

For a complete listing of your chapter Concept Review Questions, please visit us at www.mhhe.com/bma1e

QUIZ

1. A 10-year bond is issued with a face value of $1,000, paying interest of $60 a year. If market yields increase shortly after the T-bond is issued, what happens to the bond's
   a. Coupon rate?
   b. Price?
   c. Yield to maturity?

2. A bond with a coupon rate of 8% is selling at a price of 97%. Is the bond's yield to maturity more or less than 8%?

3. In August 2006 Treasury 12.5s of 2014 offered a semiannually compounded yield of 8.669%. Recognizing that coupons are paid semiannually, calculate the bond's price.

4. Here are the prices of three bonds with 10-year maturities:

Bond Coupon (%)	Price (%)
2	81.62
4	98.39
8	133.42

   If coupons are paid annually, which bond offered the highest yield to maturity? Which had the lowest? Which bonds had the longest and shortest durations?

5. a. What is the formula for the value of a two-year, 5% bond in terms of spot rates?
   b. What is the formula for its value in terms of yield to maturity?
   c. If the two-year spot rate is higher than the one-year rate, is the yield to maturity greater or less than the two-year spot rate?
   d. In each of the following sentences choose the correct term from within the parentheses:
   - "The (yield-to-maturity/spot-rate) formula discounts all cash flows from one bond at the same rate even though they occur at different points in time."
   - "The (yield-to-maturity/spot-rate) formula discounts all cash flows received at the same point in time at the same rate even though the cash flows may come from different bonds."

6. Construct some simple examples to illustrate your answers to the following:
   a. If interest rates rise, do bond prices rise or fall?
   b. If the bond yield is greater than the coupon, is the price of the bond greater or less than 100?
   c. If the price of a bond exceeds 100, is the yield greater or less than the coupon?
   d. Do high-coupon bonds sell at higher or lower prices than low-coupon bonds?
   e. If interest rates change, does the price of high-coupon bonds change proportionately more than that of low-coupon bonds?

7. The following table shows the prices of a sample of U.S. Treasury strips in August 2006. Each strip makes a single payment of $1,000 at maturity.

   a. Calculate the annually compounded, spot interest rate for each year.

   b. Is the term structure upward- or downward-sloping or flat?

   c. Would you expect the yield on a coupon bond maturing in August 2010 to be higher or lower than the yield on the 2010 strip?

   d. Calculate the annually compounded, one-year forward rate of interest for August 2008. Now do the same for August 2009.

Maturity	Price (%)
August 2007	95.53
August 2008	91.07
August 2009	86.2
August 2010	81.08

8. a. An 8%, five-year bond yields 6%. If the yield remains unchanged, what will be its price one year hence? Assume annual coupon payments.

   b. What is the total return to an investor who held the bond over this year?

   c. What can you deduce about the relationship between the bond return over a particular period and the yields to maturity at the start and end of that period?

9. True or false? Explain.

   a. Longer-maturity bonds necessarily have longer durations.

   b. The longer a bond's duration, the lower its volatility.

   c. Other things equal, the lower the bond coupon, the higher its volatility.

   d. If interest rates rise, bond durations rise also.

10. Calculate the durations and volatilities of securities A, B, and C. Their cash flows are shown below. The interest rate is 8%.

Visit us at
www.mhhe.com/bma1e.

	Period 1	Period 2	Period 3
A	40	40	40
B	20	20	120
C	10	10	110

11. a. Suppose that the one-year spot rate of interest at time 0 is 1% and the two-year spot rate is 3%. What is the forward rate of interest for year 2?

   b. What does the expectations theory of term structure say about the relationship between the forward rate and the one-year spot rate at time 1?

   c. Over a very long period of time, the term structure in the United States has been on average upward-sloping. Is this evidence for or against the expectations theory?

   d. If longer-term bonds are more risky than short-term bonds, what can you deduce about the relationship between the forward rate and the one-year spot rate at time 1?

   e. If you have to meet long-term liabilities (college tuition for your children, for example), is it safer to invest in long- or short-term bonds? Assume inflation is predictable.

   f. If inflation is very uncertain and you have to meet long-term real liabilities, is it safer to invest in long- or short-term bonds?

PRACTICE QUESTIONS

12. A 10-year German government bond (bund) has a face value of €100 and an annual coupon rate of 5%. Assume that the interest rate (in euros) is equal to 6% per year. What is the bond's PV?

13. Look again at Practice Problem 12. Suppose that the German bund paid interest semi-annually like a U.S. bond. (The bond would pay .025 × 100 = €2.5 every six months.) What is the PV in this case?

Visit us at
www.mhhe.com/bma1e.

14. A 10-year U.S. Treasury bond with a face value of $10,000 pays a coupon of 5.5% (2.75% of face value every six months). The semiannually compounded interest rate is 5.2% (a six-month discount rate of 5.2/2 = 2.6%).

   a. What is the present value of the bond?

   b. Generate a graph or table showing how the bond's present value changes for semi-annually compounded interest rates between 1% and 15%.

Visit us at
www.mhhe.com/bma1e.

15. Suppose that five-year government bonds are selling on a yield of 4%. Value a five-year bond with a 6% coupon. Start by assuming that the bond is issued by a continental European government and makes annual coupon payments. Then rework your answer assuming that the bond is issued by the U.S. Treasury, that the bond pays semiannual coupons, and the yield refers to a semiannually compounded rate.

Visit us at
www.mhhe.com/bma1e.

16. Refer again to Practice Problem 15. How would the bond value in each case change if interest rates fall to 3%?

Visit us at
www.mhhe.com/bma1e.

17. A six-year government bond makes annual coupon payments of 5% and offers a yield of 3% annually compounded. Suppose that one year later the bond still yields 3%. What return has the bondholder earned over the 12-month period? Now suppose that the bond yields 2% at the end of the year. What return would the bondholder earn in this case?

Visit us at
www.mhhe.com/bma1e.

18. A 6% six-year bond yields 12% and a 10% six-year bond yields 8%. Calculate the six-year spot rate. Assume annual coupon payments. (*Hint:* What would be your cash flows if you bought 1.2 10% bonds?)

19. Is the yield on high-coupon bonds more likely to be higher than that on low-coupon bonds when the term structure is upward-sloping or when it is downward-sloping? Explain.

20. The one-year spot rate is $r_1 = 6\%$, and the forward rate for a one-year loan maturing in year 2 is $f_2 = 6.4\%$. Similarly, $f_3 = 7.1\%$, $f_4 = 7.3\%$, and $f_5 = 8.2\%$. What are the spot rates r_2, r_3, r_4, and r_5? If the expectations hypothesis holds, what can you say about expected future interest rates?

21. Suppose your company will receive $100 million at $t = 4$ but must make a $107 million payment at $t = 5$. Assume the spot and forward rates from Practice Problem 20. Show how the company can lock in the interest rate at which it will invest at $t = 4$. Will the $100 million, invested at this locked-in rate, be sufficient to cover the $107 million liability?

Visit us at
www.mhhe.com/bma1e.

22. Use the rates from Practice Problem 20 one more time. Consider the following bonds, each with a five-year maturity. Calculate the yield to maturity for each. Which is the better investment (or are they equally attractive)? Each has $1,000 face value and pays coupons annually.

Coupon (%)	Price (%)
5	92.07
7	100.31
12	120.92

23. You have estimated spot rates as follows:

Year	Spot Rate
1	$r_1 = 5.00\%$
2	$r_2 = 5.40\%$
3	$r_3 = 5.70\%$
4	$r_4 = 5.90\%$
5	$r_5 = 6.00\%$

    a. What are the discount factors for each date (that is, the present value of $1 paid in year t)?

    b. What are the forward rates for each period?

    c. Calculate the PV of the following bonds assuming annual coupons:

       i. 5%, two-year bond.

       ii. 5%, five-year bond.

       iii. 10%, five-year bond.

    d. Explain intuitively why the yield to maturity on the 10% bond is less than that on the 5% bond.

    e. What should be the yield to maturity on a five-year zero-coupon bond?

    f. Show that the correct yield to maturity on a five-year annuity is 5.75%.

    g. Explain intuitively why the yield on the five-year bonds described in part (c) must lie between the yield on a five-year zero-coupon bond and a five-year annuity.

24. Look at the spot interest rates shown in Practice Problem 23. Suppose that someone told you that the six-year spot interest rate was 4.80%. Why would you not believe him? How could you make money if he was right? What is the minimum sensible value for the six-year spot rate?

25. Look again at the spot interest rates shown in Practice Problem 23. What can you deduce about the one-year spot interest rate in four years if

    a. The expectations theory of term structure is right?

    b. Investing in long-term bonds carries additional risks?

26. Look up prices of 10 U.S. Treasury bonds with different coupons and different maturities. Calculate how their prices would change if their yields to maturity increased by 1 percentage point. Are long- or short-term bonds most affected by the change in yields? Are high- or low-coupon bonds most affected?

27. In Section 4.2 we stated that the duration of the three-year 4% bond was 2.884 years. Construct a table like Table 4.1 to show that this is so.

28. Find the "live" spreadsheet for Table 4.1 on this book's Web site, **www.mhhe.com/bma1e.** Show how duration and volatility change if (a) the bond's coupon is 8% of face value and (b) the bond's yield is 6%. Explain your finding.

29. The formula for the duration of a perpetual bond that makes an equal payment each year in perpetuity is (1 + yield)/yield. If bonds yield 5%, which has the longer duration—a perpetual bond or a 15-year zero-coupon bond? What if the yield is 10%?

30. You have just been fired as CEO. As consolation the board of directors gives you a five-year consulting contract at $150,000 per year. What is the duration of this contract if your personal borrowing rate is 9%? Use duration to calculate the change in the contract's present value for a .5% increase in your borrowing rate.

CHALLENGE
QUESTIONS

Visit us at
www.mhhe.com/bma1e.

Visit us at
www.mhhe.com/bma1e.

31. Write a spreadsheet program to construct a series of bond tables that show the present value of a bond given the coupon rate, maturity, and yield to maturity. Assume that coupon payments are semiannual and yields are compounded semiannually.

32. Find the arbitrage opportunity (opportunities?). Assume for simplicity that coupons are paid annually. In each case the face value of the bond is $1,000.

Bond	Maturity (years)	Coupon ($)	Price ($)
A	3	zero	751.30
B	4	50	842.30
C	4	120	1,065.28
D	4	100	980.57
E	3	140	1,120.12
F	3	70	1,001.62
G	2	zero	834.00

33. The duration of a bond that makes an equal payment each year in perpetuity is $(1 + \text{yield})/\text{yield}$. Prove it.

34. What is the duration of a common stock whose dividends are expected to grow at a constant rate in perpetuity?

Visit us at
www.mhhe.com/bma1e.

35. a. What spot and forward rates are embedded in the following Treasury bonds? The price of one-year (zero-coupon) Treasury bills is 93.46%. Assume for simplicity that bonds make only annual payments. (*Hint:* Can you devise a mixture of long and short positions in these bonds that gives a cash payoff only in year 2? In year 3?)

Coupon (%)	Maturity (years)	Price (%)
4	2	94.92
8	3	103.64

b. A three-year bond with a 4% coupon is selling at 95.00%. Is there a profit opportunity here? If so, how would you take advantage of it?

CHAPTER FIVE

THE VALUE OF COMMON STOCKS

WE SHOULD WARN you that being a financial expert has its occupational hazards. One is being cornered at cocktail parties by people who are eager to explain their system for making creamy profits by investing in common stocks. Fortunately, these bores go into temporary hibernation whenever the market goes down.

We may exaggerate the perils of the trade. The point is that there is no easy way to ensure superior investment performance. Later in the book we will show that in well-functioning capital markets changes in security prices are fundamentally unpredictable. Therefore, in this chapter, when we propose to use the concept of present value to price common stocks, we are not promising you a key to investment success; we simply believe that the idea can help you to understand why some investments are priced higher than others.

Why should you care? If you want to know the value of a firm's stock, why can't you look up the stock price in the newspaper? Unfortunately, that is not always possible. For example, you may be the founder of a successful business. You currently own all the shares but are thinking of going public by selling off shares to other investors. You and your

advisers need to estimate the price at which those shares can be sold.

There is also another, deeper reason why managers need to understand how shares are valued. If a firm acts in its shareholders' interest, it should accept those investments that increase the value of their stake in the firm. But in order to do this, it is necessary to understand what determines the shares' value.

We begin with a look at how stocks are traded. Then we explain the basic principles of share valuation and the use of discounted-cash-flow (DCF) models to estimate expected rates of return.

These principles lead us to the fundamental difference between growth and income stocks. A growth stock doesn't just grow; it is also expected to earn rates of return higher than the cost of capital on its future investments. It's the *combination* of growth and superior returns that generates high price–earnings ratios for growth stocks. We show examples of price–earnings and earning–price ratios for growth and income stocks. Finally we show how DCF models can be extended to value entire businesses rather than individual shares.

(continued)

Still another warning: Everybody knows that common stocks are risky and that some are more risky than others. Therefore, investors will not commit funds to stocks unless the expected rates of return are commensurate with the risks. But we say next to nothing in this chapter about the linkages between risk and expected return. A more careful treatment of risk starts in Chapter 8.

5.1 HOW COMMON STOCKS ARE TRADED

General Electric (GE) has about 10.3 billion shares outstanding and at last count these shares were owned by about 5 million shareholders. They included large pension funds and insurance companies that each own several million shares, as well as individuals who own a handful of shares. If you owned one GE share, you would own .00000001% of the company and have a claim on the same tiny fraction of GE's profits. Of course, the more shares you own, the larger your "share" of the company.

If GE wishes to raise additional capital, it may do so either by borrowing or by selling new shares to investors. Sales of new shares to raise new capital are said to occur in the *primary market*. But most trades in GE shares take place in existing shares, which investors buy from each other. These trades do not raise new capital for the firm. This market for secondhand shares is known as the *secondary market*. The principal secondary marketplace for GE shares is the New York Stock Exchange (NYSE). This is the largest stock exchange in the world and trades, on an average day, nearly 2 billion shares in some 2,800 companies.

GE and other large U.S. companies are also traded on foreign exchanges. GE is traded in London and on the Euronext exchange in Paris, for example. At the same time many foreign companies trade in the U.S. Toyota and Fiat trade on the NYSE, as do Air France KLM, Brasil Telecom, Canadian Pacific Railway, Nokia, Taiwan Semiconductor, Royal Dutch Shell, and more than 400 others.

Suppose that you are the head trader for a pension fund that wishes to buy 100,000 GE shares. You contact your broker, who then relays the order to the floor of the NYSE. Trading in each stock is the responsibility of a *specialist*, who keeps a record of orders to buy and sell. When your order arrives, the specialist checks this record to see if an investor is prepared to sell at your price. Alternatively, the specialist may be able to get you a better deal from one of the brokers who is gathered around or may sell you some of his or her own stock. If no one is prepared to sell at your price, the specialist makes a note of your order and executes it as soon as possible.

The NYSE is not the only stock market in the United States. For example, many stocks are traded *over the counter* by a network of dealers, who display the prices at which they are prepared to trade on a system of computer terminals known as Nasdaq (National Association of Securities Dealers Automated Quotations System). If you like the price that you see on the Nasdaq screen, you simply strike a bargain with the dealer.

The NYSE and Nasdaq illustrate the two principal types of exchange. The NYSE is an **auction market** in which the specialist acts as an auctioneer, who matches up would-be buyers and sellers. Most major exchanges around the world, such as the Tokyo Stock Exchange, the London Stock Exchange, and the Frankfurt Exchange, are organized as auction markets, but the auctioneer in these cases is a computer rather than a specialist.[1] That means there is no stock exchange floor to show on the evening news and no one needs to ring a bell to start trading. Nasdaq is an example of a **dealer market,** in which all trades take place between the investor and one of a group of dealers. Dealer markets are relatively rare for trading equities, but dealers are active in trading many other financial instruments. For example, most bonds are traded in dealer markets.

The prices at which stocks trade are summarized in the daily press. Here, for example, is how *The Wall Street Journal* recorded a day's trading in GE in November 2006:

| 52-week | | | | | | | |
Hi	Lo	Stock (DIV)	Yld %	PE	Vol 100s	Close	Net Chg
36.48	32.06	Gen Elec 1.00	2.8	21	267992	35.27	0.50

You can see that on this day investors traded a total of $267{,}992 \times 100 = 26{,}799{,}200$ shares of GE stock. By the close of the day the stock traded at $35.27 a share, up $0.50 from the day before. Since there were 10.3 billion shares of GE outstanding, investors were placing a total value on the stock of $363 billion.

Buying stocks is a risky occupation. GE's stock price was not that volatile in 2005 and 2006—the price range was only $32.06 to $36.48. But the stock price had peaked at about $60 in 2001. An unfortunate investor who had bought in at $60 would have lost 41% of his or her investment. Of course, you don't come across such people at cocktail parties; they either keep quiet or aren't invited.

The Wall Street Journal also provides three other facts about GE's stock. GE pays an annual dividend of $1.00 a share, the dividend yield on the stock is 2.8%, and the ratio of the stock price to earnings (P/E ratio) is 21. We will explain shortly why investors pay attention to these figures.

Most of the trading on the NYSE and other major exchanges is in ordinary common stocks, but other securities are traded also, including preferred shares, which offer a fixed dividend, and warrants, which offer the investor an option to buy common stock. In addition investors can choose from hundreds of *exchange-traded funds* (ETFs), which are portfolios of stocks that can be bought or sold in a single trade. These include SPDRs (Standard & Poor's Depository Receipts or "spiders"), which are portfolios tracking several Standard & Poor's stock-market indexes, including the benchmark S&P 500. You can buy DIAMONDS, which track the Dow Jones Industrial Average; QUBES or QQQQs, which track the Nasdaq 100 index, as well as ETFs that track specific industries or commodities. You can also buy shares in closed-end mutual funds[2] that invest in portfolios of securities. These include country funds, for example the Mexico and Chile funds, that invest in portfolios of stocks in specific countries.

---

[1] Trades are still made face to face on the floor of the NYSE, but computerized trading is expanding rapidly. In 2006 the NYSE merged with Archepelago, an electronic trading system, and transformed itself into a public corporation. The NYSE Group is expanding internationally by merging with Euronext, an electronic trading system in Europe.

[2] *Closed-end* mutual funds issue shares that are traded on stock exchanges. *Open-end* funds are not traded on exchanges. Investors in open-end funds transact directly with the fund. The fund issues new shares to investors and redeems shares from investors who want to withdraw money from the fund.

5.2   HOW COMMON STOCKS ARE VALUED

Think back to the last chapter, where we described how to value future cash flows. The discounted-cash-flow (DCF) formula for the present value of a stock is just the same as it is for the present value of any other asset. We just discount the cash flows by the return that can be earned in the capital market on securities of comparable risk. Shareholders receive cash from the company in the form of a stream of dividends. So

$$PV(\text{stock}) = PV(\text{expected future dividends})$$

At first sight this statement may seem surprising. When investors buy stocks, they usually expect to receive a dividend, but they also hope to make a capital gain. Why does our formula for present value say nothing about capital gains? As we now explain, there is no inconsistency.

Today's Price

The cash payoff to owners of common stocks comes in two forms: (1) cash dividends and (2) capital gains or losses. Suppose that the current price of a share is P_0, that the expected price at the end of a year is P_1, and that the expected dividend per share is DIV_1. The rate of return that investors expect from this share over the next year is defined as the expected dividend per share DIV_1 plus the expected price appreciation per share $P_1 - P_0$, all divided by the price at the start of the year P_0:

$$\text{Expected return} = r = \frac{DIV_1 + P_1 - P_0}{P_0}$$

Suppose Fledgling Electronics stock is selling for $100 a share ($P_0 = 100$). Investors expect a $5 cash dividend over the next year ($DIV_1 = 5$). They also expect the stock to sell for $110 a year hence ($P_1 = 110$). Then the expected return to the stockholders is 15%:

$$r = \frac{5 + 110 - 100}{100} = .15, \text{ or } 15\%$$

On the other hand, if you are given investors' forecasts of dividend and price and the expected return offered by other equally risky stocks, you can predict today's price:

$$\text{Price} = P_0 = \frac{DIV_1 + P_1}{1 + r}$$

For Fledgling Electronics $DIV_1 = 5$ and $P_1 = 110$. If r, the expected return for Fledgling is 15%, then today's price should be $100:

$$P_0 = \frac{5 + 110}{1.15} = \$100$$

What exactly is the discount rate, r, in this calculation? It's called the **market capitalization rate** or **cost of equity capital**, which are just alternative names for the opportunity cost of capital, defined as the expected return on other securities with the same risks as Fledgling shares.

Many stocks will be safer than Fledgling, and many riskier. But among the thousands of traded stocks there will be a group with essentially the same risks. Call this group Fledgling's *risk class*. Then all stocks in the risk class have to be priced to offer the same expected rate of return.

Let's suppose that the other securities in Fledgling's risk class all offer the same 15% expected return. Then $100 per share has to be the right price for Fledgling stock. In fact it is the only possible price. What if Fledgling's price were above $P_0 = \$100$? In this case investors would shift their capital to the other securities and in the process would force down the price of Fledgling stock. If P_0 were less than $100, the process would reverse. Investors would rush to buy, forcing the price up to $100.

We conclude that at each point in time *all securities in an equivalent risk class are priced to offer the same expected return.* This is a condition for equilibrium in well-functioning capital markets. It is also common sense.

But What Determines Next Year's Price?

We have managed to explain today's stock price P_0 in terms of the dividend DIV_1 and the expected price next year P_1. Future stock prices are not easy things to forecast directly. But think about what determines next year's price. If our price formula holds now, it ought to hold then as well:

$$P_1 = \frac{DIV_2 + P_2}{1 + r}$$

That is, a year from now investors will be looking out at dividends in year 2 and price at the end of year 2. Thus we can forecast P_1 by forecasting DIV_2 and P_2, and we can express P_0 in terms of DIV_1, DIV_2, and P_2:

$$P_0 = \frac{1}{1 + r}(DIV_1 + P_1) = \frac{1}{1 + r}\left(DIV_1 + \frac{DIV_2 + P_2}{1 + r}\right) = \frac{DIV_1}{1 + r} + \frac{DIV_2 + P_2}{(1 + r)^2}$$

Take Fledgling Electronics. A plausible explanation why investors expect its stock price to rise by the end of the first year is that they expect higher dividends and still more capital gains in the second. For example, suppose that they are looking today for dividends of $5.50 in year 2 and a subsequent price of $121. That implies a price at the end of year 1 of

$$P_1 = \frac{5.50 + 121}{1.15} = \$110$$

Today's price can then be computed either from our original formula

$$P_0 = \frac{DIV_1 + P_1}{1 + r} = \frac{5.00 + 110}{1.15} = \$100$$

or from our expanded formula

$$P_0 = \frac{DIV_1}{1 + r} + \frac{DIV_2 + P_2}{(1 + r)^2} = \frac{5.00}{1.15} + \frac{5.50 + 121}{(1.15)^2} = \$100$$

We have succeeded in relating today's price to the forecasted dividends for two years (DIV_1 and DIV_2) plus the forecasted price at the end of the *second* year (P_2). You will not be surprised to learn that we could go on to replace P_2 by

$(DIV_3 + P_3)/(1 + r)$ and relate today's price to the forecasted dividends for three years (DIV_1, DIV_2, and DIV_3) plus the forecasted price at the end of the *third* year (P_3). In fact we can look as far out into the future as we like, removing Ps as we go. Let us call this final period H. This gives us a general stock price formula:

$$P_0 = \frac{DIV_1}{1 + r} + \frac{DIV_2}{(1 + r)^2} + \cdots + \frac{DIV_H + P_H}{(1 + r)^H}$$

$$= \sum_{t=1}^{H} \frac{DIV_t}{(1 + r)^t} + \frac{P_H}{(1 + r)^H}$$

The expression $\sum_{t=1}^{H}$ indicates the sum of the discounted dividends from year 1 to year H.

Table 5.1 continues the Fledgling Electronics example for various time horizons, assuming that the dividends are expected to increase at a steady 10% compound rate. The expected price P_t increases at the same rate each year. Each line in the table represents an application of our general formula for a different value of H. Figure 5.1 is a graph of the table. Each column shows the present value of the dividends up to the time horizon and the present value of the price at the horizon. As the horizon recedes, the dividend stream accounts for an increasing proportion of present value, but the *total* present value of dividends plus terminal price always equals $100.

How far out could we look? In principle the horizon period H could be infinitely distant. Common stocks do not expire of old age. Barring such corporate hazards as bankruptcy or acquisition, they are immortal. (For example, one of the

| Horizon Period (H) | Expected Future Values | | Present Values | | |
	Dividend (DIV_t)	Price (P_t)	Cumulative Dividends	Future Price	Total
0	—	100	—	—	100
1	5.00	110	4.35	95.65	100
2	5.50	121	8.51	91.49	100
3	6.05	133.10	12.48	87.52	100
4	6.66	146.41	16.29	83.71	100
10	11.79	259.37	35.89	64.11	100
20	30.58	672.75	58.89	41.11	100
50	533.59	11,739.09	89.17	10.83	100
100	62,639.15	1,378,061.23	98.83	1.17	100

TABLE 5.1

Applying the stock valuation formula to Fledgling Electronics.

Assumptions:
1. Dividends increase at 10% per year, compounded.
2. Capitalization rate is 15%.

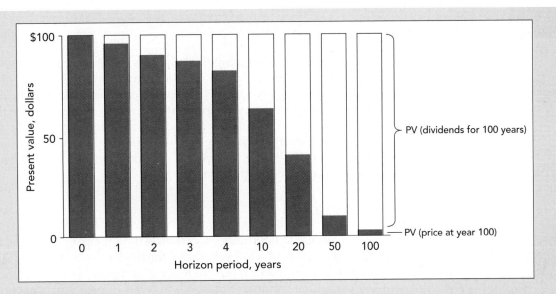

FIGURE 5.1

As your horizon recedes, the present value of the future price (shaded area) declines but the present value of the stream of dividends (unshaded area) increases. The total present value (future price and dividends) remains the same.

earliest corporations, the Hudson's Bay Company, was incorporated in 1670 and is still going strong as a major Canadian retailer.) As H approaches infinity, the present value of the terminal price ought to approach zero, as it does in the final column of Figure 5.1. We can, therefore, forget about the terminal price entirely and express today's price as the present value of a perpetual stream of cash dividends. This is usually written as

$$P_0 = \sum_{t=1}^{\infty} \frac{\text{DIV}_t}{(1 + r)^t}$$

where ∞ indicates infinity.

This discounted-cash-flow (DCF) formula for the present value of a stock is just the same as it is for the present value of any other asset. We just discount the cash flows—in this case the dividend stream—by the return that can be earned in the capital market on securities of equivalent risk. Some find the DCF formula implausible because it seems to ignore capital gains. But we know that the formula was *derived* from the assumption that price in any period is determined by expected dividends *and* capital gains over the next period.

Notice that it is *not* correct to say that the value of a share is equal to the sum of the discounted stream of earnings per share. Earnings are generally larger than dividends because part of those earnings is reinvested in new plant, equipment, and working capital. Discounting earnings would recognize the rewards of that investment (a higher *future* dividend) but not the sacrifice (a lower dividend *today*). The correct formulation states that share value is equal to the discounted stream of dividends per share.

Share Value = discounted stream of dividends per share

5.3   ESTIMATING THE COST OF EQUITY CAPITAL

In Chapter 3 we encountered some simplified versions of the basic present value formula. Let us see whether they offer any insights into stock values. Suppose, for example, that we forecast a constant growth rate for a company's dividends. This does not preclude year-to-year deviations from the trend: It means only that *expected* dividends grow at a constant rate. Such an investment would be just another example of the growing perpetuity that we valued in Chapter 3. To find its present value we must divide the first year's cash payment by the difference between the discount rate and the growth rate:

$$P_0 = \frac{DIV_1}{r - g} \quad \checkmark$$

Remember that we can use this formula only when g, the anticipated growth rate, is less than r, the discount rate. As g approaches r, the stock price becomes infinite. Obviously r must be greater than g if growth really is perpetual.

Our growing perpetuity formula explains P_0 in terms of next year's expected dividend DIV_1, the projected growth trend g, and the expected rate of return on other securities of comparable risk r. Alternatively, the formula can be turned around to obtain an estimate of r from DIV_1, P_0, and g:

$$r = \frac{DIV_1}{P_0} + g$$

The expected return equals the **dividend yield** (DIV_1/P_0) plus the expected rate of growth in dividends (g).

These two formulas are much easier to work with than the general statement that "price equals the present value of expected future dividends."[3] Here is a practical example.

Using the DCF Model to Set Gas and Electricity Prices

The prices charged by local electric and gas utilities are regulated by state commissions. The regulators try to keep consumer prices down but are supposed to allow the utilities to earn a fair rate of return. But what is fair? It is usually interpreted as r, the market capitalization rate for the firm's common stock. That is, the fair rate of return on equity for a public utility ought to be the cost of equity, that is, the rate offered by securities that have the same risk as the utility's common stock.[4]

Small variations in estimates of this return can have large effects on the prices charged to the customers and on the firm's profits. So both utilities and regulators work hard to estimate the cost of equity accurately. They've noticed that utilities

---

[3] These formulas were first developed in 1938 by Williams and were rediscovered by Gordon and Shapiro. See J. B. Williams, *The Theory of Investment Value* (Cambridge, MA: Harvard University Press, 1938); and M. J. Gordon and E. Shapiro, "Capital Equipment Analysis: The Required Rate of Profit," *Management Science* 3 (October 1956), pp. 102–110.

[4] This is the accepted interpretation of the U.S. Supreme Court's directive in 1944 that "the returns to the equity owner [of a regulated business] should be commensurate with returns on investments in other enterprises having corresponding risks." *Federal Power Commission v. Hope Natural Gas Company*, 302 U.S. 591 at 603.

are mature, stable companies that ought to offer tailor-made cases for application of the constant-growth DCF formula.[5]

Suppose you wished to estimate the cost of equity for Northwest Natural Gas, a local natural gas distribution company. Its stock was selling for $41.67 per share at the start of 2007. Dividend payments for the next year were expected to be $1.49 a share. Thus it was a simple matter to calculate the first half of the DCF formula:

$$\text{Dividend yield} = \frac{DIV_1}{P_0} = \frac{1.49}{41.67} = .036, \text{ or } 3.6\%$$

The hard part is estimating g, the expected rate of dividend growth. One option is to consult the views of security analysts who study the prospects for each company. Analysts are rarely prepared to stick their necks out by forecasting dividends to kingdom come, but they often forecast growth rates over the next five years, and these estimates may provide an indication of the expected long-run growth path. In the case of Northwest, analysts in 2007 were forecasting an annual growth of 5.1%.[6] This, together with the dividend yield, gave an estimate of the cost of equity capital:

$$r = \frac{DIV_1}{P_0} + g = .036 + .051 = .087, \text{ or } 8.7\%$$

An alternative approach to estimating long-run growth starts with the **payout ratio,** the ratio of dividends to earnings per share (EPS). For Northwest, this was forecasted at 62%. In other words, each year the company was plowing back into the business about 38% of earnings per share:

$$\text{Plowback ratio} = 1 - \text{payout ratio} = 1 - \frac{DIV}{EPS} = 1 - .62 = .38$$

Also, Northwest's ratio of earnings per share to book equity per share was about 10%. This is its **return on equity,** or **ROE:**

$$\text{Return on equity} = ROE = \frac{EPS}{\text{book equity per share}} = .10$$

If Northwest earns 10% of book equity and reinvests 38% of income, then book equity will increase by $.38 \times .10 = .038$, or 3.8%. Earnings and dividends per share will also increase by 3.8%:

$$\text{Dividend growth rate} = g = \text{plowback ratio} \times ROE = .38 \times .10 = .038$$

That gives a second estimate of the market capitalization rate:

$$r = \frac{DIV_1}{P_0} + g = .036 + .038 = .074, \text{ or } 7.4\%$$

---

[5] There are many exceptions to this statement. For example, Pacific Gas & Electric (PG&E), which serves northern California, used to be a mature, stable company until the California energy crisis of 2000 sent wholesale electric prices sky-high. PG&E was not allowed to pass these price increases on to retail customers. The company lost more than $3.5 billion in 2000 and was forced to declare bankruptcy in 2001. PG&E emerged from bankruptcy in 2004, but we may have to wait a while before it is again a suitable subject for the constant-growth DCF formula.

[6] In this calculation we're assuming that earnings and dividends are forecasted to grow forever at the same rate g. We'll show how to relax this assumption later in this chapter. The growth rate was based on the average earnings growth forecasted by Value Line and IBES. IBES compiles and averages forecasts made by security analysts. Value Line publishes its own analysts' forecasts.

Although these estimates of Northwest's cost of equity seem reasonable, there are obvious dangers in analyzing any single firm's stock with the constant-growth DCF formula. First, the underlying assumption of regular future growth is at best an approximation. Second, even if it is an acceptable approximation, errors inevitably creep into the estimate of g.

Remember, Northwest's cost of equity is not its personal property. In well-functioning capital markets investors capitalize the dividends of all securities in Northwest's risk class at exactly the same rate. But any estimate of r for a single common stock is "noisy" and subject to error. Good practice does not put too much weight on single-company cost-of-equity estimates. It collects samples of similar companies, estimates r for each, and takes an average. The average gives a more reliable benchmark for decision making.

The next-to-last column of Table 5.2 gives DCF cost-of-equity estimates for Northwest and eight other gas distribution companies. These are all stable, mature companies for which the constant-growth DCF formula *ought* to work. Notice the variation in the cost-of-equity estimates. Some of the variation may reflect differences in the risk, but some is just noise. The average estimate is 9.9%.

Table 5.3 gives another example of DCF cost-of-equity estimates, this time for U.S. railroads in 2005.

Estimates of this kind are only as good as the long-term forecasts on which they are based. For example, several studies have observed that security analysts are subject to behavioral biases and their forecasts tend to be over-optimistic. If so, such DCF estimates of the cost of equity should be regarded as upper estimates of the true figure.

Company	Stock Price	Dividend Annual Rate[a]	Dividend Yield	Long-Term Growth Rate	DCF Cost of Equity	Multistage DCF Cost of Equity[b]
AGL Resources Inc	$39.32	$1.48	3.8%	4.0%	7.7%	8.8%
Atmos Energy Corp	32.34	1.51	4.7	6.5	11.2	9.6
Laclede Group Inc	36.24	1.49	4.1	4.6	8.7	9.1
New Jersey Resources Corp	51.60	1.50	2.9	5.5	8.4	8.1
Northwest Natural Gas Co	41.67	1.49	3.6	5.1	8.7	8.6
Piedmont Natural Gas Co	27.98	1.49	5.3	4.9	10.2	8.7
South Jersey Industries Inc	33.47	1.51	4.5	6.2	10.7	8.1
Southwest Gas Corp	38.24	1.56	4.1	9.8	13.9	8.2
WGL Holdings Inc	33.13	1.48	4.5	4.3	8.8	9.2
				Average:	9.9%	8.6%

TABLE 5.2

Cost-of-equity estimates for local gas distribution companies at the start of 2007. The long-term growth rate is based on security analysts' forecasts. In the multistage DCF model, growth after 2011 is assumed to adjust gradually to the estimated long-term growth rate of Gross Domestic Product (GDP).

[a] Projected dividends, based on current dividend and one year's growth.
[b] Long-term GDP growth forecasted at 3.6%.
Source: The Brattle Group, Inc.

	Average Dividend Yield[a]	Forecasted Growth Rate[b]	Cost of Equity[c]
Burlington Northern Santa Fe	1.47%	12.74%	14.21%
CSX	1.06	15.52	16.58
Norfolk Southern	1.41	14.92	16.34
Union Pacific	1.91	12.67	14.57
Weighted average[d]			15.18

TABLE 5.3

Cost-of-equity estimates for U.S. railroads, 2005. The estimates use the constant-growth DCF model, which in this case probably overestimates the railroads' true cost of equity because the forecasted growth rates cannot be sustained in perpetuity.

[a] Average of monthly dividend yields during 2005.
[b] Based on IBES averages of security analysts' growth forecasts.
[c] Some rows do not add up because of rounding.
[d] Weights based on total market values of the railroads' common stock.
Source: U.S. Surface Transportation Board, "Railroad Cost of Capital—2005," September 15, 2006.

Dangers Lurk in Constant-Growth Formulas

The simple constant-growth DCF formula is an extremely useful rule of thumb, but no more than that. Naive trust in the formula has led many financial analysts to silly conclusions.

We have stressed the difficulty of estimating r by analysis of one stock only. Try to use a large sample of equivalent-risk securities. Even that may not work, but at least it gives the analyst a fighting chance, because the inevitable errors in estimating r for a single security tend to balance out across a broad sample.

In addition, resist the temptation to apply the formula to firms having high current rates of growth. Such growth can rarely be sustained indefinitely, but the constant-growth DCF formula assumes it can. This erroneous assumption leads to an overestimate of r. Table 5.3 is probably an example of such an overestimate. The four largest U.S. railroads were expanding rapidly in 2005 and 2006 as they recovered from a period of low profitability. Security analysts were forecasting continued recovery and earnings growth at 12% to 15% for the next few years. But the rate of growth was bound to slow down when the recovery was completed. Thus analysts and investors were not assuming a single future growth rate, but at least two: a near-term rate of rapid growth, then a transition to a moderate long-term growth rate. There was no basis for assuming 12% to 15% growth in perpetuity.

DCF Valuation with Varying Growth Rates   Consider Growth-Tech, Inc., a firm with $DIV_1 = \$.50$ and $P_0 = \$50$. The firm has plowed back 80% of earnings and has had a return on equity (ROE) of 25%. This means that *in the past*

$$\text{Dividend growth rate} = \text{plowback ratio} \times \text{ROE} = .80 \times .25 = .20$$

The temptation is to assume that the future long-term growth rate g also equals .20. This would imply

$$r = \frac{.50}{50.00} + .20 = .21$$

TABLE 5.4

Forecasted earnings and dividends for Growth-Tech. Note the changes in year 3: ROE and earnings drop, but payout ratio increases, causing a big jump in dividends. However, subsequent growth in earnings and dividends falls to 8% per year. Note that the increase in equity equals the earnings not paid out as dividends.

	Year			
	1	2	3	4
Book equity	10.00	12.00	14.40	15.55
Earnings per share, EPS	2.50	3.00	2.30	2.49
Return on equity, ROE	.25	.25	.16	.16
Payout ratio	.20	.20	.50	.50
Dividends per share, DIV	.50	.60	1.15	1.24
Growth rate of dividends (%)	—	20	92	8

But this is silly. No firm can continue growing at 20% per year forever, except possibly under extreme inflationary conditions. Eventually, profitability will fall and the firm will respond by investing less.

In real life the return on equity will decline gradually over time, but for simplicity let's assume it suddenly drops to 16% at year 3 and the firm responds by plowing back only 50% of earnings. Then g drops to $.50 \times .16 = .08$.

Table 5.4 shows what's going on. Growth-Tech starts year 1 with book equity of $10.00 per share. It earns $2.50, pays out 50 cents as dividends, and plows back $2. Thus it starts year 2 with book equity of $10 + 2 = $12. After another year at the same ROE and payout, it starts year 3 with equity of $14.40. However, ROE drops to .16, and the firm earns only $2.30. Dividends go up to $1.15, because the payout ratio increases, but the firm has only $1.15 to plow back. Therefore subsequent growth in earnings and dividends drops to 8%.

Now we can use our general DCF formula:

$$P_0 = \frac{DIV_1}{1 + r} + \frac{DIV_2}{(1 + r)^2} + \frac{DIV_3 + P_3}{(1 + r)^3}$$

Investors in year 3 will view Growth-Tech as offering 8% per year dividend growth. So we can use the constant-growth formula to calculate P_3:

$$P_3 = \frac{DIV_4}{r - .08}$$

$$P_0 = \frac{DIV_1}{1 + r} + \frac{DIV_2}{(1 + r)^2} + \frac{DIV_3}{(1 + r)^3} + \frac{1}{(1 + r)^3} \frac{DIV_4}{r - .08}$$

$$= \frac{.50}{1 + r} + \frac{.60}{(1 + r)^2} + \frac{1.15}{(1 + r)^3} + \frac{1}{(1 + r)^3} \frac{1.24}{r - .08}$$

We have to use trial and error to find the value of r that makes P_0 equal $50. It turns out that the r implicit in these more realistic forecasts is approximately .099, quite a difference from our "constant-growth" estimate of .21.

Our present value calculations for Growth-Tech used a *two-stage* DCF valuation model. In the first stage (years 1 and 2), Growth-Tech is highly profitable (ROE = 25%), and it plows back 80% of earnings. Book equity, earnings, and dividends increase by 20% per year. In the second stage, starting in year 3, profitability and plowback decline, and earnings settle into long-term growth at 8%. Dividends jump up to $1.15 in year 3, and then also grow at 8%.

	Year			
	1	**2**	**3**	**4**
Book equity at start of year	10.00	10.40	10.82	11.25
Earnings per share, EPS	.40	.73	1.08	1.12
Return on equity, ROE	.04	.07	.10	.10
Dividends per share, DIV	0	.31	.65	.67
Growth rate of dividends (%)	—	—	110	4

TABLE 5.5

Forecasted earnings and dividends for Phoenix.com. The company can initiate and increase dividends as profitability (ROE) recovers. Note that the increase in book equity equals the earnings not paid out as dividends.

Growth rates can vary for many reasons. Sometimes growth is high in the short run not because the firm is unusually profitable, but because it is recovering from an episode of *low* profitability. Table 5.5 displays projected earnings and dividends for Phoenix.com, which is gradually regaining financial health after a near meltdown. The company's equity is growing at a moderate 4%. ROE in year 1 is only 4%, however, so Phoenix has to reinvest all its earnings, leaving no cash for dividends. As profitability increases in years 2 and 3, an increasing dividend can be paid. Finally, starting in year 4, Phoenix settles into steady-state growth, with equity, earnings, and dividends all increasing at 4% per year.

Assume the cost of equity is 10%. Then Phoenix shares should be worth $9.13 per share:

$$P_0 = \underbrace{\frac{0}{1.1} + \frac{.31}{(1.1)^2} + \frac{.65}{(1.1)^3}}_{\text{PV (first-stage dividends)}} + \underbrace{\frac{1}{(1.1)^3}\frac{.67}{(.10-.04)}}_{\text{PV (second-stage dividends)}} = \$9.13$$

You could go on to valuation models with three or more stages. For example, the far-right column of Table 5.2 presents multistage DCF estimates of the cost of equity for our old friend Northwest and eight other local gas distribution companies. In this case the long-term growth rates reported in the table do not continue forever. After 2011, each company's growth rate gradually adjusts to an estimated long-term growth rate for Gross Domestic Product (GDP). From 2017 on, all firms' dividends are forecasted to grow with GDP at 5.3%. The resulting cost-of-equity estimates average out to 8.6%, somewhat lower than the estimates from the simple, perpetual-growth model. The dispersion of the cost-of-equity estimates is reduced, however.

We must leave you with two more warnings about DCF formulas for valuing common stocks or estimating the cost of equity. First, it's almost always worthwhile to lay out a simple spreadsheet, like Table 5.4 or 5.5, to ensure that your dividend projections are consistent with the company's earnings and required investments. Second, be careful about using DCF valuation formulas to test whether the market is correct in its assessment of a stock's value. If your estimate of the value is different from that of the market, it is probably because you have used poor dividend forecasts. Remember what we said at the beginning of this chapter about simple ways of making money on the stock market: There aren't any.

5.4 THE LINK BETWEEN STOCK PRICE AND EARNINGS PER SHARE

Investors separate *growth stocks* from *income stocks.* They buy growth stocks primarily for the expectation of capital gains, and they are interested in the future growth of earnings rather than in next year's dividends. They buy income stocks primarily for the cash dividends. Let us see whether these distinctions make sense.

Imagine first the case of a company that does not grow at all. It does not plow back any earnings and simply produces a constant stream of dividends. Its stock would resemble the perpetual bond described in Chapter 3. Remember that the return on a perpetuity is equal to the yearly cash flow divided by the present value. The expected return on our share would thus be equal to the yearly dividend divided by the share price (i.e., the dividend yield). Since all the earnings are paid out as dividends, the expected return is also equal to the earnings per share divided by the share price (i.e., the earnings–price ratio). For example, if the dividend is $10 a share and the stock price is $100, we have

$$\text{Expected return} = \text{dividend yield} = \text{earnings–price ratio}$$
$$= \frac{DIV_1}{P_0} \qquad = \frac{EPS_1}{P_0}$$
$$= \frac{10.00}{100} \qquad = .10$$

The price equals

$$P_0 = \frac{DIV_1}{r} = \frac{EPS_1}{r} = \frac{10.00}{.10} = 100$$

The expected return for *growing* firms can *also* equal the earnings–price ratio. The key is whether earnings are reinvested to provide a return equal to the market capitalization rate. For example, suppose our monotonous company suddenly hears of an opportunity to invest $10 a share next year. This would mean no dividend at $t = 1$. However, the company expects that in each subsequent year the project would earn $1 per share, so that the dividend could be increased to $11 a share.

Let us assume that this investment opportunity has about the same risk as the existing business. Then we can discount its cash flow at the 10% rate to find its net present value at year 1:

$$\text{Net present value per share at year 1} = -10 + \frac{1}{.10} = 0$$

Thus the investment opportunity will make no contribution to the company's value. Its prospective return is equal to the opportunity cost of capital.

What effect will the decision to undertake the project have on the company's share price? Clearly none. The reduction in value caused by the nil dividend in year 1 is exactly offset by the increase in value caused by the extra dividends in later years. Therefore, once again the market capitalization rate equals the earnings–price ratio:

$$r = \frac{EPS_1}{P_0} = \frac{10}{100} = .10$$

Project Rate of Return	Incremental Cash Flow, C	Project NPV in Year 1[a]	Project's Impact on Share Price in Year 0[b]	Share Price in Year 0, P_0	$\dfrac{EPS_1}{P_0}$	r
.05	$ .50	−$ 5.00	−$ 4.55	$ 95.45	.105	.10
.10	1.00	0	0	100.00	.10	.10
.15	1.50	+ 5.00	+ 4.55	104.55	.096	.10
.20	2.00	+ 10.00	+ 9.09	109.09	.092	.10

TABLE 5.6

Effect on stock price of investing an additional $10 in year 1 at different rates of return. Notice that the earnings–price ratio overestimates r when the project has negative NPV and underestimates it when the project has positive NPV.

[a] Project costs $10.00 ($EPS_1$). NPV $= -10 + C/r$, where $r = .10$.
[b] NPV is calculated at year 1. To find the impact on P_0, discount for one year at $r = .10$.

Table 5.6 repeats our example for different assumptions about the cash flow generated by the new project. Note that the earnings–price ratio, measured in terms of EPS_1, next year's expected earnings, equals the market capitalization rate (r) *only* when the new project's NPV = 0. This is an extremely important point—managers frequently make poor financial decisions because they confuse earnings–price ratios with the market capitalization rate.

In general, we can think of stock price as the capitalized value of average earnings under a no-growth policy, plus **PVGO**, the **net present value of growth opportunities:**

$$P_0 = \frac{EPS_1}{r} + PVGO$$

The earnings–price ratio, therefore, equals

$$\frac{EPS}{P_0} = r\left(1 - \frac{PVGO}{P_0}\right)$$

It will underestimate r if PVGO is positive and overestimate it if PVGO is negative. The latter case is less likely, since firms are rarely forced to take projects with negative net present values.

Calculating the Present Value of Growth Opportunities for Fledgling Electronics

In our last example both dividends and earnings were expected to grow, but this growth made no net contribution to the stock price. The stock was in this sense an "income stock." Be careful not to equate firm performance with the growth in earnings per share. A company that reinvests earnings at below the market capitalization rate r may increase earnings but will certainly reduce the share value.

Now let us turn to that well-known growth stock, Fledgling Electronics. You may remember that Fledgling's market capitalization rate, r, is 15%. The company is expected to pay a dividend of $5 in the first year, and thereafter the dividend is predicted to increase indefinitely by 10% a year. We can, therefore, use the simplified constant-growth formula to work out Fledgling's price:

$$P_0 = \frac{DIV_1}{r - g} = \frac{5}{.15 - .10} = \$100$$

Suppose that Fledgling has earnings per share of $EPS_1 = \$8.33$. Its payout ratio is then

$$\text{Payout ratio} = \frac{DIV_1}{EPS_1} = \frac{5.00}{8.33} = .6$$

In other words, the company is plowing back $1 - .6$, or 40% of earnings. Suppose also that Fledgling's ratio of earnings to book equity is ROE = .25. This explains the growth rate of 10%:

$$\text{Growth rate} = g = \text{plowback ratio} \times \text{ROE} = .4 \times .25 = .10$$

The capitalized value of Fledgling's earnings per share if it had a no-growth policy would be

$$\frac{EPS_1}{r} = \frac{8.33}{.15} = \$55.56$$

But we know that the value of Fledgling stock is $100. The difference of $44.44 must be the amount that investors are paying for growth opportunities. Let's see if we can explain that figure.

Each year Fledgling plows back 40% of its earnings into new assets. In the first year Fledgling invests $3.33 at a permanent 25% return on equity. Thus the cash generated by this investment is $.25 \times 3.33 = \$.83$ per year starting at $t = 2$. The net present value of the investment as of $t = 1$ is

$$NPV_1 = -3.33 + \frac{.83}{.15} = \$2.22$$

Everything is the same in year 2 except that Fledgling will invest $3.67, 10% more than in year 1 (remember $g = .10$). Therefore at $t = 2$ an investment is made with a net present value of

$$NPV_2 = -3.67 + \frac{.83 \times 1.10}{.15} = \$2.44$$

Thus the payoff to the owners of Fledgling Electronics stock can be represented as the sum of (1) a level stream of earnings, which could be paid out as cash dividends if the firm did not grow, and (2) a set of tickets, one for each future year, representing the opportunity to make investments having positive NPVs. We know that the first component of the value of the share is

$$\text{Present value of level stream of earnings} = \frac{EPS_1}{r} = \frac{8.33}{.15} = \$55.56$$

The first ticket is worth $2.22 in $t = 1$, the second is worth $2.22 \times 1.10 = \$2.44$ in $t = 2$, the third is worth $2.44 \times 1.10 = \$2.69$ in $t = 3$. These are the forecasted cash values of the tickets. We know how to value a stream of future cash values that grows at 10% per year: Use the constant-growth DCF formula, replacing the fore-casted dividends with forecasted ticket values:

$$\text{Present value of growth opportunities} = \text{PVGO} = \frac{\text{NPV}_1}{r-g} = \frac{2.22}{.15-.10} = \$44.44$$

Now everything checks:

$$
\begin{aligned}
\text{Share price} &= \text{present value of level stream of earnings} \\
&\quad + \text{present value of growth opportunities} \\
&= \frac{\text{EPS}_1}{r} + \text{PVGO} \\
&= \$55.56 + \$44.44 \\
&= \$100
\end{aligned}
$$

Why is Fledgling Electronics a growth stock? Not because it is expanding at 10% per year. It is a growth stock because the net present value of its future investments accounts for a significant fraction (about 44%) of the stock's price.

Stock prices today reflect investors' expectations of future operating *and invest-ment* performance. Growth stocks sell at high price–earnings ratios because investors are willing to pay now for expected superior returns on investments that have not yet been made.

Examples of Growth Opportunities

Almost everyone regards Microsoft as a growth stock and mature firms like Cummins or Dow Chemical as income stocks. Let's check that out. Table 5.7 shows estimates of PVGO for these and several other stocks at the start of 2007. Take Cummins as an example. We can approximate its PVGO by subtracting the value

Stock	Stock Price, P	EPS[a]	Cost of Equity, r[b]	PVGO = P − EPS/r	PVGO, Percent of Stock Price
Income stocks:					
Cummins, Inc. ($)	118.18	12.03	.157	41.56	35%
Dow Chemical ($)	39.90	4.11	.125	7.02	18
Unilever (£)	14.16	0.896	.091	4.31	30
Scottish Power (£)	7.40	0.462	.097	2.64	36
Growth stocks:					
Microsoft ($)	29.86	1.57	.123	17.10	57
Starbucks ($)	35.42	0.985	.092	24.71	70
e2v Technologies (£)	3.80	0.234	.15	2.24	59
Logica (£)	1.85	0.111	.159	1.15	62

TABLE 5.7

Estimated PVGOs

[a] EPS is defined as the average earnings under a no-growth policy. As an estimate of EPS, we used the average of the current and forecasted earnings per share. *Source:* Yahoo! Finance **(finance.yahoo.com).** Reproduced with permission of Yahoo! Inc. © 2007 by Yahoo! Inc. Yahoo! and the Yahoo! logo are trademarks of Yahoo! Inc.
[b] The market capitalization rate was estimated by using the capital asset pricing model. We describe this model and how to use it in Chapters 9 and 10. For this example, we used a market risk premium of 7% and a risk-free interest rate of 5% (U.S.) and 5.5% (U.K.).

of its existing business from its stock price. The existing business is assumed to generate a level stream of future earnings, which is valued by dividing forecasted EPS of about $12 per share by an estimated cost of equity of 15.7%.[7] The resulting PVGO of $41.60 per share is 35% of the stock price. A similar calculation for Microsoft gives PVGO as 57% of its stock price.

Table 5.7 also includes PVGO estimates for several other companies, including two mature companies and two high-tech growth companies from the U.K. Notice that PVGO accounts for well over half the value of the growth companies' shares. Investors expected these companies to invest heavily, grow rapidly, *and* earn returns well above their costs of capital.

5.5   VALUING A BUSINESS BY DISCOUNTED CASH FLOW

Investors routinely buy and sell shares of common stock. Companies frequently buy and sell entire businesses or major stakes in businesses. For example, in 2006 the Forbes family, owners of the company that publishes *Forbes* magazine, sold a 40% stake to Elevation Partners, an investment partnership that included Bono, the lead singer for the rock band U2. The price was over $200 million. You can be sure that the Forbes family, Bono, and their respective advisers burned a lot of midnight oil to make sure that the deal was fairly priced.

Do the discounted-cash-flow formulas we presented in this chapter work for entire businesses as well as for shares of common stock? Sure: It doesn't matter whether you forecast dividends per share or the total free cash flow of a business. Value today always equals future cash flow discounted at the opportunity cost of capital.

Valuing the Concatenator Business

Rumor has it that Establishment Industries is interested in buying your company's concatenator manufacturing operation. Your company is willing to sell if it can get the full value of this rapidly growing business. The problem is to figure out what its true present value is.

Table 5.8 gives a forecast of **free cash flow** (FCF) for the concatenator business. Free cash flow is the amount of cash that a firm can pay out to investors after paying for all investments necessary for growth. As we will see, free cash flow can be negative for rapidly growing businesses.

Table 5.8 is similar to Table 5.4, which forecasted earnings and dividends per share for Growth-Tech, based on assumptions about Growth-Tech's equity per share, return on equity, and the growth of its business. For the concatenator business, we also have assumptions about assets, profitability—in this case, after-tax operating earnings relative to assets—and growth. Growth starts out at a rapid 20% per year, then falls in two steps to a moderate 6% rate for the long run. The growth rate determines the net additional investment required to expand assets, and the profitability rate determines the earnings thrown off by the business.[8]

---

[7] We are treating EPS as a level stream of nominal earnings, like coupon payments on a perpetual bond. The alternative is to project a level stream of real (inflation-adjusted) earnings, which would be valued at a real discount rate. Use of a lower real discount rate would increase the value of the existing business and reduce PVGO. The growth companies at the bottom of Table 5.7 would still have more PVGO than the mature companies at the top of the table, however.

[8] Table 5.8 shows *net* investment, which is total investment less depreciation. We are assuming that investment for replacement of existing assets is covered by depreciation and that net investment is devoted to growth.

	Year									
	1	**2**	**3**	**4**	**5**	**6**	**7**	**8**	**9**	**10**
Asset value	10.00	12.00	14.40	17.28	20.74	23.43	26.47	28.05	29.73	31.51
Earnings	1.20	1.44	1.73	2.07	2.49	2.81	3.18	3.36	3.57	3.78
Investment	2.00	2.40	2.88	3.46	2.69	3.04	1.59	1.68	1.78	1.89
Free cash flow	−.80	−.96	−1.15	−1.39	−.20	−.23	1.59	1.68	1.79	1.89
Earnings growth from previous period (%)	20	20	20	20	20	13	13	6	6	6

TABLE 5.8

Forecasts of free cash flow, in $ millions, for the Concatenator Manufacturing Division. Rapid expansion in years 1–6 means that free cash flow is negative, because required additional investment outstrips earnings. Free cash flow turns positive when growth slows down after year 6.

Notes:
1. Starting asset value is $10 million. Assets required for the business grow initially at 20% per year, then at 13%, and finally at 6%.
2. Profitability (earnings/asset values) is constant at 12%.
3. Free cash flow equals earnings minus net investment. Net investment equals total capital expenditures less depreciation. Note that earnings are also calculated net of depreciation.

Free cash flow, the next to last line in Table 5.8, is negative in years 1 through 6. The concatenator business is paying a negative dividend to the parent company; it is absorbing more cash than it is throwing off.

Is that a bad sign? Not really: The business is running a cash deficit not because it is unprofitable, but because it is growing so fast. Rapid growth is good news, not bad, so long as the business is earning more than the opportunity cost of capital. Your company, or Establishment Industries, will be happy to invest an extra $800,000 in the concatenator business next year, so long as the business offers a superior rate of return.

Valuation Format

The value of a business is usually computed as the discounted value of free cash flows out to a *valuation horizon(H)*, plus the forecasted value of the business at the horizon, also discounted back to present value. That is,

$$PV = \underbrace{\frac{FCF_1}{1+r} + \frac{FCF_2}{(1+r)^2} + \cdots + \frac{FCF_H}{(1+r)^H}}_{PV(\text{free cash flow})} + \underbrace{\frac{PV_H}{(1+r)^H}}_{PV(\text{horizon value})}$$

Of course, the concatenator business will continue after the horizon, but it's not practical to forecast free cash flow year by year to infinity. PV_H stands in for free cash flow in periods $H+1$, $H+2$, etc.

Valuation horizons are often chosen arbitrarily. Sometimes the boss tells everybody to use 10 years because that's a round number. We will try year 6, because growth of the concatenator business seems to settle down to a long-run trend after year 7.

Estimating Horizon Value

There are several common formulas or rules of thumb for estimating horizon value. First, let us try the constant-growth DCF formula. This requires free cash flow for year 7, which we have from Table 5.8, a long-run growth rate, which appears to be 6%, and a discount rate, which some high-priced consultant has told us is 10%. Therefore,

$$\text{PV (horizon value)} = \frac{1}{(1.1)^6}\left(\frac{1.59}{.10 - .06}\right) = 22.4$$

The present value of the near-term free cash flows is

$$\text{PV(cash flows)} = -\frac{.80}{1.1} - \frac{.96}{(1.1)^2} - \frac{1.15}{(1.1)^3} - \frac{1.39}{(1.1)^4} - \frac{.20}{(1.1)^5} - \frac{.23}{(1.1)^6}$$
$$= -3.6$$

and, therefore, the present value of the business is

$$\text{PV(business)} = \text{PV(free cash flow)} + \text{PV(horizon value)}$$
$$= -3.6 \qquad\qquad + 22.4$$
$$= \$18.8 \text{ million}$$

Now, are we done? Well, the mechanics of this calculation are perfect. But doesn't it make you just a little nervous to find that 119% of the value of the business rests on the horizon value? Moreover, a little checking shows that the horizon value can change dramatically in response to apparently minor changes in assumptions. For example, if the long-run growth rate is 8% rather than 6%, the value of the business increases from $18.8 to $26.3 million.[9]

In other words, it's easy for a discounted-cash-flow business valuation to be mechanically perfect and practically wrong. Smart financial managers try to check their results by calculating horizon value in different ways.

Horizon Value Based on P/E Ratios   Suppose you can observe stock prices for mature manufacturing companies whose scale, risk, and growth prospects today roughly match those projected for the concatenator business in year 6. Suppose further that these companies tend to sell at price–earnings ratios of about 11. Then you could reasonably guess that the price–earnings ratio of a mature concatenator operation will likewise be 11. That implies:

$$\text{PV(horizon value)} = \frac{1}{(1.1)^6}\,(11 \times 3.18) = 19.7$$
$$\text{PV(business)} = -3.6 + 19.7 = \$16.1 \text{ million}$$

Horizon Value Based on Market–Book Ratios   Suppose also that the market–book ratios of the sample of mature manufacturing companies tend to cluster around

---

[9] If long-run growth is 8% rather than 6%, an extra 2% of period-7 assets will have to be plowed back into the concatenator business. This reduces free cash flow by $.53 million to $1.06 million. So,

$$\text{PV(horizon value)} = \frac{1}{(1.1)^6}\left(\frac{1.06}{.10 - .08}\right) = \$29.9$$
$$\text{PV(business)} = -3.6 + 29.9 = \$26.3 \text{ million}$$

1.4. (The market–book ratio is just the ratio of stock price to book value per share.) If the concatenator business market–book ratio is 1.4 in year 6,

$$PV(\text{horizon value}) = \frac{1}{(1.1)^6}(1.4 \times 23.43) = 18.5$$

$$PV(\text{business}) = -3.6 + 18.5 = \$14.9 \text{ million}$$

It's easy to poke holes in these last two calculations. Book value, for example, often is a poor measure of the true value of a company's assets. It can fall far behind actual asset values when there is rapid inflation, and it often entirely misses important intangible assets, such as your patents for concatenator design. Earnings may also be biased by inflation and a long list of arbitrary accounting choices. Finally, you never know when you have found a sample of truly similar companies.

But remember, the purpose of discounted cash flow is to estimate market value—to estimate what investors would pay for a stock or business. When you can *observe* what they actually pay for similar companies, that's valuable evidence. Try to figure out a way to use it. One way to use it is through valuation rules of thumb, based on price–earnings or market–book ratios. A rule of thumb, artfully employed, sometimes beats a complex discounted-cash-flow calculation hands down.

A Further Reality Check

Here is another approach to valuing a business. It is based on what you have learned about price–earnings ratios and the present value of growth opportunities.

Suppose the valuation horizon is set not by looking for the first year of stable growth, but by asking when the industry is likely to settle into competitive equilibrium. You might go to the operating manager most familiar with the concatenator business and ask:

> Sooner or later you and your competitors will be on an equal footing when it comes to major new investments. You may still be earning a superior return on your core business, but you will find that introductions of new products or attempts to expand sales of existing products trigger intense resistance from competitors who are just about as smart and efficient as you are. Give a realistic assessment of when that time will come.

"That time" is the horizon after which PVGO, the net present value of subsequent growth opportunities, is zero. After all, PVGO is positive only when investments can be expected to earn more than the cost of capital. When your competition catches up, that happy prospect disappears.

We know that present value in any period equals the capitalized value of next period's earnings, plus PVGO:

$$PV_t = \frac{\text{earnings}_{t+1}}{r} + PVGO$$

But what if PVGO = 0? At the horizon period H, then,

$$PV_H = \frac{\text{earnings}_{H+1}}{r}$$

In other words, when the competition catches up, the price–earnings ratio equals $1/r$, because PVGO disappears.

Suppose that competition is expected to catch up in and after period 9. Then we can calculate the horizon value at period 8 as the present value of a level stream of earnings starting in period 9 and continuing indefinitely. The resulting value for the concatenator business is:[10]

$$PV(\text{horizon value}) = \frac{1}{(1 + r)^8} \left(\frac{\text{earnings in period 9}}{r} \right)$$

$$= \frac{1}{(1.1)^8} \left(\frac{3.57}{.10} \right)$$

$$= \$16.7 \text{ million}$$

$$PV(\text{business}) = -2.0 + 16.7 = \$14.7 \text{ million}$$

We now have four estimates of what Establishment Industries ought to pay for the concatenator business. The estimates reflect four different methods of estimating horizon value. There is no best method, although in many cases we put most weight on the last method, which sets the horizon date at the point when management expects PVGO to disappear. The last method forces managers to remember that sooner or later competition catches up.

Our calculated values for the concatenator business range from $14.7 to $18.8 million, a difference of about $4 million. The width of the range may be disquieting, but it is not unusual. Discounted-cash-flow formulas only estimate market value, and the estimates change as forecasts and assumptions change. Managers cannot know market value for sure until an actual transaction takes place.

---

[10] Three additional points about this calculation: First, the PV of free cash flow before the horizon improves to −$2.0 million because inflows in years 7 and 8 are now included. Second, if competition really catches up by year 9, then the earnings shown for year 10 in Figure 5.8 are too high, since they include a 12% return on the investment in year 9. Competition would allow only the 10% cost of capital. Third, we assume earnings in year 9 of $3.57, 12% on assets of $29.73. But competition might force down the rate of return on existing assets in addition to returns on new investment. That is, earnings in year 9 could be only $2.97 (10% of $29.73). Practice Problem 31 explores these possibilities.

SUMMARY

In this chapter we have used our newfound knowledge of present values to examine the market price of common stocks. The value of a stock is equal to the stream of cash payments discounted at the rate of return that investors expect to receive on other securities with equivalent risks.

Common stocks do not have a fixed maturity; their cash payments consist of an indefinite stream of dividends. Therefore, the present value of a common stock is

$$PV = \sum_{t=1}^{\infty} \frac{DIV_t}{(1 + r)^t}$$

However, we did not just *assume* that investors purchase common stocks solely for dividends. In fact, we began with the assumption that investors have relatively short horizons and invest for both dividends and capital gains. Our fundamental valuation formula is, therefore,

$$P_0 = \frac{DIV_1 + P_1}{1 + r}$$

This is a condition of market equilibrium. If it did not hold, the share would be overpriced or underpriced, and investors would rush to sell or buy it. The flood of sellers or buyers would force the price to adjust so that the fundamental valuation formula holds.

This formula will hold in each future period as well as the present. That allowed us to express next year's forecasted price in terms of the subsequent stream of dividends DIV_2, DIV_3, . . .

We also made use of the formula for a growing perpetuity presented in Chapter 3. If dividends are expected to grow forever at a constant rate of g, then

$$P_0 = \frac{DIV_1}{r - g}$$

It is often helpful to twist this formula around and use it to estimate the market capitalization rate r, given P_0 and estimates of DIV_1 and g:

$$r = \frac{DIV_1}{P_0} + g$$

Remember, however, that this formula rests on a *very* strict assumption: constant dividend growth in perpetuity. This may be an acceptable assumption for mature, low-risk firms, but for many firms, near-term growth is unsustainably high. In that case, you may wish to use a *two-stage* DCF formula, where near-term dividends are forecasted and valued, and the constant-growth DCF formula is used to forecast the value of the shares at the start of the long run. The near-term dividends and the future share value are then discounted to present value.

The general DCF formula can be transformed into a statement about earnings and growth opportunities:

$$P_0 = \frac{EPS_1}{r} + PVGO$$

The ratio EPS_1/r is the capitalized value of the earnings per share that the firm would generate under a no-growth policy. PVGO is the net present value of the investments that the firm will make in order to grow. A growth stock is one for which PVGO is large relative to the capitalized value of EPS. Most growth stocks are stocks of rapidly expanding firms, but expansion alone does not create a high PVGO. What matters is the profitability of the new investments.

The same formulas that we used to value common shares can also be used to value entire businesses. In that case, we discount not dividends per share but the entire free cash flow generated by the business. Usually a two-stage DCF model is deployed. Free cash flows are forecasted out to a horizon and discounted to present value. Then a horizon value is forecasted, discounted, and added to the value of the free cash flows. The sum is the value of the business.

Valuing a business is simple in principle but not so easy in practice. Forecasting reasonable horizon values is particularly difficult. The usual assumption is moderate long-run growth after the horizon, which allows use of the growing-perpetuity DCF formula at the horizon. Horizon values can also be calculated by assuming "normal" price–earnings or market-to-book ratios at the horizon date.

In earlier chapters you should have acquired—we hope painlessly—a knowledge of the basic principles of valuing assets and a facility with the mechanics of discounting. Now you know something of how common stocks are valued and market capitalization rates estimated. In Chapter 6 we can begin to apply all this knowledge in a more specific analysis of capital budgeting decisions.

FURTHER READING

J. B. Williams's original work remains very readable. See particularly Chapter V of:

J. B. Williams, *The Theory of Investment Value* (Cambridge, MA: Harvard University Press, 1938).

Leibowitz and Kogelman call PVGO the "franchise factor." They analyze it in detail in:

M. L. Leibowitz and S. Kogelman, "Inside the P/E Ratio: The Franchise Factor," *Financial Analysts Journal* 46 (November–December 1990), pp. 17–35.

Myers and Borucki cover the practical problems encountered in estimating DCF costs of equity for regulated companies; Harris and Marston report DCF estimates of rates of return for the stock market as a whole:

S. C. Myers and L. S. Borucki, "Discounted Cash Flow Estimates of the Cost of Equity Capital—A Case Study," *Financial Markets, Institutions and Instruments* 3 (August 1994), pp. 9–45.

R. S. Harris and F. C. Marston: "The Market Risk Premium: Expectational Estimates Using Analysts' Forecasts," *Journal of Applied Finance*, 11 (2001), pp. 6–16.

CONCEPT REVIEW QUESTIONS

1. What is the difference between the primary and secondary markets for a corporation's shares? (page 86)

2. Write down the general DCF formula for the value of a stock. (page 91)

3. The present value of a stock should not depend on how long the investor expects to hold it. Explain why. (page 91)

For a complete listing of your chapter Concept Review Questions, please visit us at www.mhhe.com/bma1e.

QUIZ

1. True or false?

   a. All stocks in an equivalent-risk class are priced to offer the same expected rate of return.

   b. The value of a share equals the PV of future dividends per share.

2. Respond briefly to the following statement:

   "You say stock price equals the present value of future dividends? That's crazy! All the investors I know are looking for capital gains."

3. Company X is expected to pay an end-of-year dividend of $5 a share. After the dividend its stock is expected to sell at $110. If the market capitalization rate is 8%, what is the current stock price?

Visit us at www.mhhe.com/bma1e

4. Company Y does not plow back any earnings and is expected to produce a level dividend stream of $5 a share. If the current stock price is $40, what is the market capitalization rate?

5. Company Z's earnings and dividends per share are expected to grow indefinitely by 5% a year. If next year's dividend is $10 and the market capitalization rate is 8%, what is the current stock price?

6. Company Z-prime is like Z in all respects save one: Its growth will stop after year 4. In year 5 and afterward, it will pay out all earnings as dividends. What is Z-prime's stock price? Assume next year's EPS is $15.

7. If company Z (see Quiz Problem 5) were to distribute all its earnings, it could maintain a level dividend stream of $15 a share. How much is the market actually paying per share for growth opportunities?

8. Consider three investors:

   a. Mr. Single invests for one year.

   b. Ms. Double invests for two years.

   c. Mrs. Triple invests for three years.

   Assume each invests in company Z (see Quiz Problem 5). Show that each expects to earn a rate of return of 8% per year.

9. True or false? Explain.

   a. The value of a share equals the discounted stream of future earnings per share.

   b. The value of a share equals the PV of earnings per share assuming the firm does not grow, plus the NPV of future growth opportunities.

10. Under what conditions does r, a stock's market capitalization rate, equal its earnings–price ratio EPS_1/P_0?

11. What do financial managers mean by "free cash flow"? How is free cash flow calculated? Briefly explain.

12. What is meant by the "horizon value" of a business? How can it be estimated?

13. Suppose the horizon date is set at a time when the firm will run out of positive-NPV investment opportunities. How would you calculate the horizon value? (*Hint:* What is the P/EPS ratio when PVGO = 0?)

---

14. Look in a recent issue of *The Wall Street Journal* at "NYSE-Composite Transactions."

   a. What is the latest price of IBM stock?

   b. What are the annual dividend payment and the dividend yield on IBM stock?

   c. What would the yield be if IBM changed its yearly dividend to $1.50?

   d. What is the P/E on IBM stock?

   e. Use the P/E to calculate IBM's earnings per share.

   f. Is IBM's P/E higher or lower than that of ExxonMobil?

   g. What are the possible reasons for the difference in P/E?

15. Rework Table 5.1 under the assumption that the dividend on Fledgling Electronics is $10 next year and that it is expected to grow by 5% a year. The capitalization rate is 15%.

16. Consider the following three stocks:

   a. Stock A is expected to provide a dividend of $10 a share forever.

   b. Stock B is expected to pay a dividend of $5 next year. Thereafter, dividend growth is expected to be 4% a year forever.

PRACTICE
QUESTIONS

Visit us at
www.mhhe.com/bma1e.

c. Stock C is expected to pay a dividend of $5 next year. Thereafter, dividend growth is expected to be 20% a year for five years (i.e., until year 6) and zero thereafter.

If the market capitalization rate for each stock is 10%, which stock is the most valuable? What if the capitalization rate is 7%?

17. Pharmecology is about to pay a dividend of $1.35 per share. It's a mature company, but future EPS and dividends are expected to grow with inflation, which is forecasted at 2.75% per year.

   a. What is Pharmecology's current stock price? The nominal cost of capital is 9.5%.

   b. Redo part(a) using forecasted real dividends and a real discount rate.

18. Company Q's current return on equity (ROE) is 14%. It pays out one-half of earnings as cash dividends (payout ratio = .5). Current book value per share is $50. Book value per share will grow as Q reinvests earnings.

   Assume that the ROE and payout ratio stay constant for the next four years. After that, competition forces ROE down to 11.5% and the payout ratio increases to 0.8. The cost of capital is 11.5%

   a. What are Q's EPS and dividends next year? How will EPS and dividends grow in years 2, 3, 4, 5 and subsequent years?

   b. What is Q's stock worth per share? How does that value depend on the payout ratio and growth rate after year 4?

19. Mexican Motors stock sells for 200 pesos per share and next year's dividend is 8.5 pesos. Security analysts are forecasting earnings growth of 7.5% per year for the next five years.

   a. Assume that earnings and dividends are expected to grow at 7.5% in perpetuity. What rate of return are investors expecting?

   b. Mexican Motors has generally earned about 12% on book equity (ROE = .12) and paid out 50% of earnings as dividends. Suppose it maintains the same ROE and payout ratio in the long-run future. What is the implication for g? For r? Should you revise your answer to part(a) of this question?

20. In mid-2006, after a year of sharply higher oil prices, major oil companies were selling at unusually low price–earnings (P/E) ratios. In October, for example, *The Wall Street Journal* reported P/Es of 5 for ConocoPhillips and 6 for Marathon Oil. Recall that these reported P/Es equal current price divided by EPS for the prior year.

   a. What are the possible reasons for the low P/Es? (*Hint:* What if investors expected future oil prices to decline?)

   b. Look again in *The Wall Street Journal* or another source of stock-market data. How have P/Es for these companies changed since October 2006? How do you interpret or explain the changes?

21. In August 2006, *The Wall Street Journal* reported a P/E of 63 for Textron, a mature conglomerate that would not normally be regarded as a high-growth company. It turns out that Textron had recently announced a large, one-time loss from discontinued operations. This loss caused a large, one-time reduction in reported earnings. Does this example suggest why extremely high P/EPS ratios can be misleading? Explain briefly.

22. Phoenix Corp. faltered in the recent recession but has recovered since. EPS and dividends have grown rapidly since 2014.

	2014	2015	2016	2017	2018
EPS	$.75	2.00	2.50	2.60	2.65
Dividends	$ 0	1.00	2.00	2.30	2.65
Dividend growth	—	—	100%	15%	15%

The figures for 2017 and 2018 are of course forecasts. Phoenix's stock price today in 2016 is $21.75. Phoenix's recovery will be complete in 2018, and there will be *no further growth* in EPS or dividends.

A security analyst forecasts *next year's* rate of return on Phoenix stock as follows:

$$r = \frac{DIV}{P} + g = \frac{2.30}{21.75} + .15 = .256, \text{ about } 26\%$$

What's wrong with the security analyst's forecast? What is the actual expected rate of return over the next year?

23. Each of the following formulas for determining shareholders' required rate of return can be right or wrong depending on the circumstances:

   a. $r = \dfrac{DIV_1}{P_0} + g$

   b. $r = \dfrac{EPS_1}{P_0}$

   For each formula construct a *simple* numerical example showing that the formula can give wrong answers and explain why the error occurs. Then construct another simple numerical example for which the formula gives the right answer.

24. Alpha Corp's earnings and dividends are growing at 15% per year. Beta Corp's earnings and dividends are growing at 8% per year. The companies' assets, earnings, and dividends per share are now (at date 0) exactly the same. Yet PVGO accounts for a greater fraction of Beta Corp's stock price. How is this possible? (*Hint:* There is more than one possible explanation.)

25. Look again at the financial forecasts for Growth-Tech given in Table 5.4. This time assume you *know* that the opportunity cost of capital is $r = .12$ (discard the .099 figure calculated in the text). Assume you do *not* know Growth-Tech's stock value. Otherwise follow the assumptions given in the text.

   a. Calculate the value of Growth-Tech stock.

   b. What part of that value reflects the discounted value of P_3, the price forecasted for year 3?

   c. What part of P_3 reflects the present value of growth opportunities (PVGO) after year 3?

   d. Suppose that competition will catch up with Growth-Tech by year 4, so that it can earn only its cost of capital on any investments made in year 4 or subsequently. What is Growth-Tech stock worth now under this assumption? (Make additional assumptions if necessary.)

26. Compost Science, Inc. (CSI), is in the business of converting Boston's sewage sludge into fertilizer. The business is not in itself very profitable. However, to induce CSI to remain in business, the Metropolitan District Commission (MDC) has agreed to pay whatever amount is necessary to yield CSI a 10% book return on equity. At the end of the year CSI is expected to pay a $4 dividend. It has been reinvesting 40% of earnings and growing at 4% a year.

   a. Suppose CSI continues on this growth trend. What is the expected long-run rate of return from purchasing the stock at $100? What part of the $100 price is attributable to the present value of growth opportunities?

   b. Now the MDC announces a plan for CSI to treat Cambridge sewage. CSI's plant will, therefore, be expanded gradually over five years. This means that CSI will have to reinvest 80% of its earnings for five years. Starting in year 6, however, it will again be able to pay out 60% of earnings. What will be CSI's stock price once this announcement is made and its consequences for CSI are known?

27. Update the calculations in Table 5.7 for Cummins, Dow Chemical, Microsoft, and Starbucks. For simplicity use the costs of equity in the table. You will need to track down an updated EPS forecast, from MSN Money (**www.moneycentral.MSN.com**) or Yahoo! (**finance.yahoo.com**), for example.

28. Permian Partners (PP) produces from aging oil fields in west Texas. Production is 1.8 million barrels per year in 2006, but production is declining at 7% per year for the foreseeable future. Costs of production, transportation, and administration add up to $25 per barrel. The average oil price was $65 per barrel in 2006.

    PP has 7 million shares outstanding. The cost of capital is 9%. All of PP's net income is distributed as dividends. For simplicity assume that the company will stay in business forever and that costs per barrel are constant at $25. Also, ignore taxes.

    a. What is the PV of a PP share? Assume that oil prices are expected to fall to $60 per barrel in 2007, $55 per barrel in 2008, and $50 per barrel in 2009. After 2009, assume a long-term trend of oil-price increases at 5% per year.

    b. What is PP's EPS/P ratio and why is it not equal to the 9% cost of capital?

STANDARD &POOR'S

29. Look up General Mills, Inc., and Kellogg Co. on **finance.yahoo.com** or the Standard & Poor's Market Insight Web site (**www.mhhe.com/edumarketinsight**). The companies' ticker symbols are GIS and K.

    a. What are the current dividend yield and price–earnings ratio (P/E) for each company? How do the yields and P/Es compare to the average for the food industry and for the stock market as a whole? (The stock market is represented by the S & P 500 index.)

    b. What are the growth rates of earnings per share (EPS) and dividends for each company over the last five years? Do these growth rates appear to reflect a steady trend that could be projected for the long-run future?

    c. Would you be confident in applying the constant-growth DCF valuation model to these companies' stocks? Why or why not?

STANDARD &POOR'S

30. Look up the following companies on the Standard & Poor's Market Insight Web site (**www.mhhe.com/edumarketinsight**): Citigroup (C), Dell Computer (DELL), Dow Chemical (DOW), Harley Davidson (HOG), and Pfizer, Inc. (PFE). Look at "Financial Highlights" and "Company Profile" for each company. You will note wide differences in these companies' price–earnings ratios. What are the possible explanations for these differences? Which would you classify as growth (high-PVGO) stocks and which as income stocks?

31. Construct a new version of Table 5.8, assuming that competition drives down profitability (on existing assets as well as new investment) to 11.5% in year 6, 11% in year 7, 10.5% in year 8 and 8% in year 9 and all later years. What is the value of the concatenator business?

CHALLENGE QUESTIONS

32. The constant-growth DCF formula

$$P_0 = \frac{DIV_1}{r - g}$$

    is sometimes written as

$$P_0 = \frac{ROE(1 - b)BVPS}{r - bROE}$$

    where BVPS is book equity value per share, b is the plowback ratio, and ROE is the ratio of earnings per share to BVPS. Use this equation to show how the price-to-book ratio varies as ROE changes. What is price-to-book when ROE = r?

33. Portfolio managers are frequently paid a proportion of the funds under management. Suppose you manage a $100 million equity portfolio offering a dividend yield (DIV_1/P_0)

of 5%. Dividends and portfolio value are expected to grow at a constant rate. Your annual fee for managing this portfolio is .5% of portfolio value and is calculated at the end of each year. Assuming that you will continue to manage the portfolio from now to eternity, what is the present value of the management contract? How would the contract value change if you invested in stocks with a 4% yield?

34. Suppose the concatenator division, which we valued based on Table 5.8, is spun off as an independent company, Concatco, with 1 million shares of common stock outstanding. What would each share sell for? Before answering, notice the negative free cash flows for years 1 to 6. The PV of these cash flows is −$3.6 million. Assume that this shortfall will have to be financed by additional shares issued in the near future. Also assume for simplicity that the $3.6 million earns interest at 10% and is sufficient to cover the negative free cash flows in Table 5.8. Concatco will pay no dividends in years 1 to 6, but will pay out all free cash flow starting in year 7.

   Now calculate the value of each of the 1 million existing Concatco shares. Briefly explain your answer. (*Hints:* Suppose the existing stockholders, who own 1 million shares, buy newly issued shares to cover the $3.6 million financing requirement. In other words, the $3.6 million comes directly out of existing stockholders' wallets. What's the value per share? Now suppose instead that the $3.6 million comes from new investors, who buy shares at a fair price. Does your answer change?)

MINI-CASE

Reeby Sports

Ten years ago, in 1998, George Reeby founded a small mail-order company selling high-quality sports equipment. Since those early days Reeby Sports has grown steadily and been consistently profitable. The company has issued 2 million shares, all of which are owned by George Reeby and his five children.

For some months George has been wondering whether the time has come to take the company public. This would allow him to cash in on part of his investment and would make it easier for the firm to raise capital should it wish to expand in the future.

But how much are the shares worth? George's first instinct is to look at the firm's balance sheet, which shows that the book value of the equity is $26.34 million, or $13.17 per share. A share price of $13.17 would put the stock on a P/E ratio of 6.6. That is quite a bit lower than the 13.1 P/E ratio of Reeby's larger rival, Molly Sports.

George suspects that book value is not necessarily a good guide to a share's market value. He thinks of his daughter Jenny, who works in an investment bank. She would undoubtedly know what the shares are worth. He decides to phone her after she finishes work that evening at 9 o'clock or before she starts the next day at 6.00 A.M.

Before phoning, George jots down some basic data on the company's profitability. After recovering from its early losses, the company has earned a return that is higher than its estimated 10% cost of capital. George is fairly confident that the company could continue to grow fairly steadily for the next six to eight years. In fact he feels that the company's growth has been somewhat held back in the last few years by the demands from two of the children for the company to make large dividend payments. Perhaps, if the company went public, it could hold back on dividends and plow more money back into the business.

There are some clouds on the horizon. Competition is increasing and only that morning Molly Sports announced plans to form a mail-order division. George is worried that beyond the next six or so years it might become difficult to find worthwhile investment opportunities.

George realizes that Jenny will need to know much more about the prospects for the business before she can put a final figure on the value of Reeby Sports, but he hopes that the information is sufficient for her to give a preliminary indication of the value of the shares.

	1999	2000	2001	2002	2003	2004	2005	2006	2007	2008E
Earnings per share, $	−2.10	−0.70	0.23	0.81	1.10	1.30	1.52	1.64	2.00	2.03
Dividend, $	0.00	0.00	0.00	0.20	0.20	0.30	0.30	0.60	0.60	0.80
Book value per share, $	9.80	7.70	7.00	7.61	8.51	9.51	10.73	11.77	13.17	14.40
ROE, %	−27.10	−7.1	3.0	11.6	14.5	15.3	16.0	15.3	17.0	15.4

QUESTIONS

1. Help Jenny to forecast dividend payments for Reeby Sports and to estimate the value of the stock. You do not need to provide a single figure. For example, you may wish to calculate two figures, one on the assumption that the opportunity for further profitable investment is reduced in year 6 and another on the assumption that it is reduced in year 8.

2. How much of your estimate of the value of Reeby's stock comes from the present value of growth opportunities?

CHAPTER SIX

6

WHY NET PRESENT VALUE LEADS TO BETTER INVESTMENT DECISIONS THAN OTHER CRITERIA

A **COMPANY'S SHAREHOLDERS** prefer to be rich rather than poor. Therefore, they want the firm to invest in every project that is worth more than it costs. The difference between a project's value and its cost is its *net present value (NPV)*. Companies can best help their shareholders by investing in all projects with a positive NPV and rejecting those with a negative NPV.

We start this chapter with a review of the net present value rule. We then turn to some other measures that companies may look at when making investment decisions. The first two of these measures, the project's payback period and its book rate of return, are little better than rules of thumb, easy to calculate and easy to communicate. Although there is a place for rules of thumb in this world, an engineer needs something more accurate when designing a 100-story building, and a financial manager needs more than a rule of thumb when making a substantial capital investment decision.

Instead of calculating a project's NPV, companies often compare the expected rate of return from investing in the project with the return that shareholders could earn on equivalent-risk investments in the capital market. The company accepts those projects that provide a higher return than shareholders could earn for themselves. If used correctly, this rate of return rule should always identify projects that increase firm value. However, we shall see that the rule sets several traps for the unwary.

We conclude the chapter by showing how to cope with situations when the firm has only limited capital. This raises two problems. One is computational. In simple cases we just choose those projects that give the highest NPV per dollar invested, but more elaborate techniques are sometimes needed to sort through the possible alternatives. The other problem is to decide whether capital rationing really exists and whether it invalidates the net present value rule. Guess what? NPV, properly interpreted, wins out in the end.

6.1   A REVIEW OF THE BASICS

Vegetron's chief financial officer (CFO) is wondering how to analyze a proposed $1 million investment in a new venture called project X. He asks what you think.

Your response should be as follows: "First, forecast the cash flows generated by project X over its economic life. Second, determine the appropriate opportunity cost of capital. This should reflect both the time value of money and the risk involved in project X. Third, use this opportunity cost of capital to discount the project's future cash flows. The sum of the discounted cash flows is called present value (PV). Fourth, calculate *net* present value (NPV) by subtracting the $1 million investment from PV. Invest in project X if its NPV is greater than zero."

However, Vegetron's CFO is unmoved by your sagacity. He asks why NPV is so important.

Your reply: "Let us look at what is best for Vegetron stockholders. They want you to make their Vegetron shares as valuable as possible.

"Right now Vegetron's total market value (price per share times the number of shares outstanding) is $10 million. That includes $1 million cash we can invest in project X. The value of Vegetron's other assets and opportunities must therefore be $9 million. We have to decide whether it is better to keep the $1 million cash and reject project X or to spend the cash and accept the project. Let us call the value of the new project PV. Then the choice is as follows:

Asset	Market Value ($ millions)	
	Reject Project X	Accept Project X
Cash	1	0
Other assets	9	9
Project X	0	PV
	10	9 + PV

"Clearly project X is worthwhile if its present value, PV, is greater than $1 million, that is, if net present value is positive."

CFO: "How do I know that the PV of project X will actually show up in Vegetron's market value?"

Your reply: "Suppose we set up a new, independent firm X, whose only asset is project X. What would be the market value of firm X?

"Investors would forecast the dividends firm X would pay and discount those dividends by the expected rate of return of securities having similar risks. We know that stock prices are equal to the present value of forecasted dividends.

"Since project X is the only asset, the dividend payments we would expect firm X to pay are exactly the cash flows we have forecasted for project X. Moreover, the rate investors would use to discount firm X's dividends is exactly the rate we should use to discount project X's cash flows.

"I agree that firm X is entirely hypothetical. But if project X is accepted, investors holding Vegetron stock will really hold a portfolio of project X and the firm's other assets. We know the other assets are worth $9 million considered as a separate venture. Since asset values add up, we can easily figure out the portfolio value once we calculate the value of project X as a separate venture.

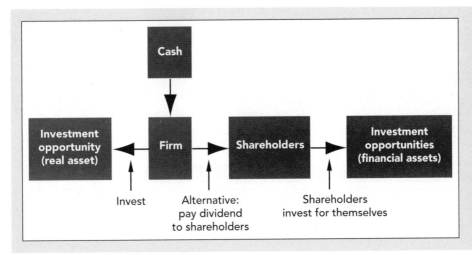

FIGURE 6.1

The firm can either keep and reinvest cash or return it to investors. (Arrows represent possible cash flows or transfers.) If cash is reinvested, the opportunity cost is the expected rate of return that shareholders could have obtained by investing in financial assets.

"By calculating the present value of project X, we are replicating the process by which the common stock of firm X would be valued in capital markets."

CFO: "The one thing I don't understand is where the discount rate comes from."

Your reply: "I agree that the discount rate is difficult to measure precisely. But it is easy to see what we are *trying* to measure. The discount rate is the opportunity cost of investing in the project rather than in the capital market. In other words, instead of accepting a project, the firm can always give the cash to the shareholders and let them invest it in financial assets.

"You can see the trade-off (Figure 6.1). The opportunity cost of taking the project is the return shareholders could have earned had they invested the funds on their own. When we discount the project's cash flows by the expected rate of return on financial assets, we are measuring how much investors would be prepared to pay for your project."

"But which financial assets?" Vegetron's CFO queries. "The fact that investors expect only 12% on IBM stock does not mean that we should purchase Fly-by-Night Electronics if it offers 13%."

Your reply: "The opportunity-cost concept makes sense only if assets of equivalent risk are compared. In general, you should identify financial assets with risks equivalent to the project under consideration, estimate the expected rate of return on these assets, and use this rate as the opportunity cost."

Net Present Value's Competitors

When you advised the CFO to calculate the project's NPV, you were in good company. These days 75% of firms always, or almost always, calculate net present value when deciding on investment projects. However, as you can see from Figure 6.2, NPV is not the only investment criterion that companies use, and firms often look at more than one measure of a project's attractiveness.

About three-quarters of firms calculate the project's internal rate of return (or IRR); that is roughly the same proportion as use NPV. The IRR rule is a close relative of NPV and, when used properly, it will give the same answer. You therefore need to understand the IRR rule and how to take care when using it.

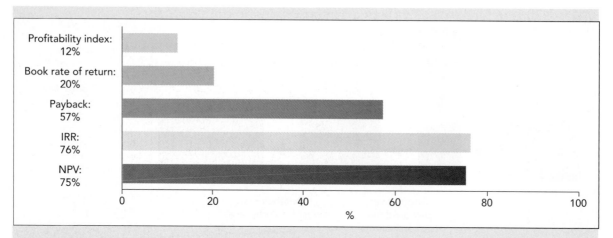

FIGURE 6.2

Survey evidence on the percentage of CFOs who always, or almost always, use a particular technique for evaluating investment projects.

Source: Reprinted from J. R. Graham and C. R. Harvey, "The Theory and Practice of Finance: Evidence from the Field," *Journal of Financial Economics* 61 (2001), pp. 187–243, © 2001 with permission from Elsevier Science.

A large part of this chapter is concerned with explaining the IRR rule, but first we will look at two other measures of a project's attractiveness—the project's payback and its book rate of return. As we will see, both measures have obvious defects. Few companies rely on them to make their investment decisions, but they do use them as supplementary measures that may help to distinguish the marginal project from the no-brainer.

Later in the chapter we will also come across one further investment measure, the profitability index. As you can see from Figure 6.2, it is not often used, but you will find that there are circumstances in which this measure has some special advantages.

Three Points to Remember about NPV

As we look at these alternative criteria, it is worth keeping in mind the following key features of the net present value rule. First, the NPV rule recognizes that *a dollar today is worth more than a dollar tomorrow,* because the dollar today can be invested to start earning interest immediately. Any investment rule that does not recognize the *time value of money* cannot be sensible. Second, net present value depends solely on the *forecasted cash flows* from the project and the *opportunity cost of capital.* Any investment rule that is affected by the manager's tastes, the company's choice of accounting method, the profitability of the company's existing business, or the profitability of other independent projects will lead to inferior decisions. Third, *because present values are all measured in today's dollars, you can add them up.* Therefore, if you have two projects A and B, the net present value of the combined investment is

$$NPV(A + B) = NPV(A) + NPV(B)$$

This adding-up property has important implications. Suppose project B has a negative NPV. If you tack it onto project A, the joint project (A + B) must have a lower NPV than A on its own. Therefore, you are unlikely to be misled into accepting a poor project (B) just because it is packaged with a good one (A). As we shall see, the alternative measures do not have this property. If you are not careful, you may be tricked into deciding that a package of a good and a bad project is better than the good project on its own.

NPV Depends on Cash Flow, Not on Book Returns

Net present value depends only on the project's cash flows and the opportunity cost of capital. But when companies report to shareholders, they do not simply show the cash flows. They also report book—that is, accounting—income and book assets.

Financial managers sometimes use these numbers to calculate a book (or accounting) rate of return on a proposed investment. In other words, they look at the prospective book income as a proportion of the book value of the assets that the firm is proposing to acquire:

$$\text{Book rate of return} = \frac{\text{book income}}{\text{book assets}}$$

Cash flows and book income are often very different. For example, the accountant labels some cash outflows as *capital investments* and others as *operating expenses*. The operating expenses are, of course, deducted immediately from each year's income. The capital expenditures are put on the firm's balance sheet and then depreciated. The annual depreciation charge is deducted from each year's income. Thus the book rate of return depends on which items the accountant chooses to treat as capital investments and how rapidly they are depreciated.[1]

Now the merits of an investment project do not depend on how accountants classify the cash flows[2] and few companies these days make investment decisions just on the basis of the book rate of return. But managers know that the company's shareholders pay considerable attention to book measures of profitability and naturally they think (and worry) about how major projects would affect the company's book return. Those projects that will reduce the company's book return may be scrutinized more carefully by senior management.

You can see the dangers here. The company's book rate of return may not be a good measure of true profitability. It is also an *average* across all of the firm's activities. The average profitability of past investments is not usually the right hurdle for new investments. Think of a firm that has been exceptionally lucky and successful. Say its average book return is 24%, double shareholders' 12% opportunity cost of capital. Should it demand that all *new* investments offer 24% or better? Clearly not: That would mean passing up many positive-NPV opportunities with rates of return between 12 and 24%.

---

[1] This chapter's mini-case contains simple illustrations of how book rates of return are calculated and of the difference between accounting income and project cash flow. Read the case if you wish to refresh your understanding of these topics. Better still, do the case calculations.

[2] Of course, the depreciation method used for tax purposes does have cash consequences that should be taken into account in calculating NPV. We cover depreciation and taxes in the next chapter.

| 6.2 | PAYBACK |

Some companies require that the initial outlay on any project should be recoverable within a specified period. The **payback period** of a project is found by counting the number of years it takes before the cumulative forecasted cash flow equals the initial investment.

Consider the following three projects:

| | Cash Flows ($) | | | | Payback | |
Project	C_0	C_1	C_2	C_3	Period (years)	NPV at 10%
A	−2,000	500	500	5,000	3	+2,624
B	−2,000	500	1,800	0	2	−58
C	−2,000	1,800	500	0	2	+50

Project A involves an initial investment of $2,000 ($C_0 = -2,000$) followed by cash inflows during the next three years. Suppose the opportunity cost of capital is 10%. Then project A has an NPV of +$2,624:

$$NPV(A) = -2,000 + \frac{500}{1.10} + \frac{500}{1.10^2} + \frac{5,000}{1.10^3} = +\$2,624$$

Project B also requires an initial investment of $2,000 but produces a cash inflow of $500 in year 1 and $1,800 in year 2. At a 10% opportunity cost of capital project B has an NPV of −$58:

$$NPV(B) = -2,000 + \frac{500}{1.10} + \frac{1,800}{1.10^2} = -\$58$$

The third project, C, involves the same initial outlay as the other two projects but its first-period cash flow is larger. It has an NPV of +$50.

$$NPV(C) = -2,000 + \frac{1,800}{1.10} + \frac{500}{1.10^2} = +\$50$$

The net present value rule tells us to accept projects A and C but to reject project B.

The Payback Rule

Now look at how rapidly each project pays back its initial investment. With project A you take three years to recover the $2,000 investment; with projects B and C you take only two years. If the firm used the *payback rule* with a cutoff period of two years, it would accept only projects B and C; if it used the payback rule with a cutoff period of three or more years, it would accept all three projects. Therefore, regardless of the choice of cutoff period, the payback rule gives answers different from the net present value rule.

You can see why payback can give misleading answers:

1. *The payback rule ignores all cash flows after the cutoff date.* If the cutoff date is two years, the payback rule rejects project A regardless of the size of the cash inflow in year 3.

2. *The payback rule gives equal weight to all cash flows before the cutoff date.* The payback rule says that projects B and C are equally attractive, but because C's cash inflows occur earlier, C has the higher net present value at any discount rate.

In order to use the payback rule, a firm has to decide on an appropriate cutoff date. If it uses the same cutoff regardless of project life, it will tend to accept many poor short-lived projects and reject many good long-lived ones.

Occasionally companies discount the cash flows before they compute the payback period. The discounted cash flows for our three projects are as follows:

	Discounted Cash Flows ($)				Discounted Payback Period (years)	NPV at 20%
Project	C_0	C_1	C_2	C_3		
A	−2,000	500/1.10 = 455	$500/1.10^2$ = 413	$5,000/1.10^3$ = 3,757	3	+2,624
B	−2,000	500/1.10 = 455	$1,800/1.10^2$ = 1,488		—	−58
C	−2,000	1,800/1.10 = 1,636	$500/1.10^2$ = 413		2	+50

The *discounted payback rule* asks, How many years does the project have to last in order for it to make sense in terms of net present value? You can see that the value of the cash inflows from project B never exceeds the initial outlay and would always be rejected under the discounted payback rule. Thus the discounted payback rule will never accept a negative-NPV project. On the other hand, it still takes no account of cash flows after the cutoff date, so that good long-term projects such as A continue to risk rejection.

The simplicity of payback makes it an easy device for *describing* investment projects. Managers talk casually about quick-payback projects in the same way that investors talk about high-P/E common stocks, but the payback period of a project does not usually govern their decisions. Some managers, particularly in small firms, *do* use payback in judging investment proposals. We don't know why. Maybe these managers don't believe the more distant cash-flow forecasts and in frustration decide to discard entirely all forecasts beyond the payback period.

6.3   INTERNAL (OR DISCOUNTED-CASH-FLOW) RATE OF RETURN

Whereas payback and return on book are ad hoc measures, internal rate of return has a much more respectable ancestry and is recommended in many finance texts. If, therefore, we dwell more on its deficiencies, it is not because they are more numerous but because they are less obvious.

In Chapter 2 we noted that the net present value rule could also be expressed in terms of rate of return, which would lead to the following rule: "Accept investment opportunities offering rates of return in excess of their opportunity costs of capital." That statement, properly interpreted, is absolutely correct. However, interpretation is not always easy for long-lived investment projects.

There is no ambiguity in defining the true rate of return of an investment that generates a single payoff after one period:

$$\text{Rate of return} = \frac{\text{payoff}}{\text{investment}} - 1$$

Alternatively, we could write down the NPV of the investment and find the discount rate that makes NPV = 0.

$$\text{NPV} = C_0 + \frac{C_1}{1 + \text{discount rate}} = 0$$

implies

$$\text{Discount rate} = \frac{C_1}{-C_0} - 1$$

Of course C_1 is the payoff and $-C_0$ is the required investment, and so our two equations say exactly the same thing. *The discount rate that makes NPV = 0 is also the rate of return.*

Unfortunately, there is no wholly satisfactory way of defining the true rate of return of a long-lived asset. The best available concept is the so-called **discounted-cash-flow (DCF) rate of return** or **internal rate of return (IRR)**. The internal rate of return is used frequently in finance. It can be a handy measure, but, as we shall see, it can also be a misleading measure. You should, therefore, know how to calculate it and how to use it properly.

Calculating the IRR

The internal rate of return is defined as the rate of discount that makes NPV = 0. This means that to find the IRR for an investment project lasting T years, we must solve for IRR in the following expression:

$$\text{NPV} = C_0 + \frac{C_1}{1 + \text{IRR}} + \frac{C_2}{(1 + \text{IRR})^2} + \cdots + \frac{C_T}{(1 + \text{IRR})^T} = 0$$

Actual calculation of IRR usually involves trial and error. For example, consider a project that produces the following flows:

Cash Flows ($)		
C_0	C_1	C_2
−4,000	+2,000	+4,000

The internal rate of return is IRR in the equation

$$\text{NPV} = -4,000 + \frac{2,000}{1 + \text{IRR}} + \frac{4,000}{(1 + \text{IRR})^2} = 0$$

Let us arbitrarily try a zero discount rate. In this case NPV is not zero but +$2,000:

$$\text{NPV} = -4,000 + \frac{2,000}{1.0} + \frac{4,000}{(1.0)^2} = +\$2,000$$

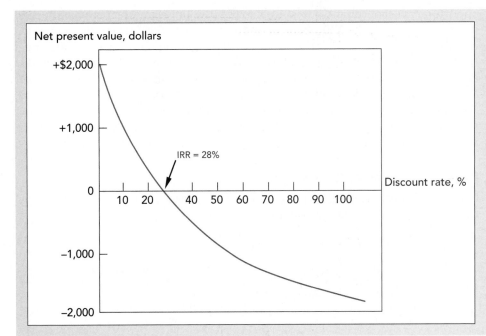

FIGURE 6.3

This project costs $4,000 and then produces cash inflows of $2,000 in year 1 and $4,000 in year 2. Its internal rate of return (IRR) is 28%, the rate of discount at which NPV is zero.

The NPV is positive; therefore, the IRR must be greater than zero. The next step might be to try a discount rate of 50%. In this case net present value is −$889:

$$\text{NPV} = -4{,}000 + \frac{2{,}000}{1.50} + \frac{4{,}000}{(1.50)^2} = -\$889$$

The NPV is negative; therefore, the IRR must be less than 50%. In Figure 6.3 we have plotted the net present values implied by a range of discount rates. From this we can see that a discount rate of 28% gives the desired net present value of zero. Therefore IRR is 28%.

The easiest way to calculate IRR, if you have to do it by hand, is to plot three or four combinations of NPV and discount rate on a graph like Figure 6.3, connect the points with a smooth line, and read off the discount rate at which NPV = 0. It is of course quicker and more accurate to use a computer or a specially programmed calculator, and this is what most financial managers do.

Some people confuse the internal rate of return and the opportunity cost of capital because both appear as discount rates in the NPV formula. The internal rate of return is a *profitability measure* that depends solely on the amount and timing of the project cash flows. The opportunity cost of capital is a *standard of profitability* that we use to calculate how much the project is worth. The opportunity cost of capital is established in capital markets. It is the expected rate of return offered by other assets with the same risk as the project being evaluated.

The IRR Rule

The internal rate of return rule is to accept an investment project if the opportunity cost of capital is less than the internal rate of return. You can see the reasoning behind this idea if you look again at Figure 6.3. If the opportunity cost of capital is less than the 28% IRR, then the project has a *positive* NPV when discounted at the opportunity cost of capital. If it is equal to the IRR, the project has a *zero* NPV. And if it is greater than the IRR, the project has a *negative* NPV. Therefore, when we compare the opportunity cost of capital with the IRR on our project, we are effectively asking whether our project has a positive NPV. This is true not only for our example. The rule will give the same answer as the net present value rule *whenever the NPV of a project is a smoothly declining function of the discount rate.*

Many firms use internal rate of return as a criterion in preference to net present value. We think that this is a pity. Although, properly stated, the two criteria are formally equivalent, the internal rate of return rule contains several pitfalls.

Pitfall 1—Lending or Borrowing?

Not all cash-flow streams have NPVs that decline as the discount rate increases. Consider the following projects A and B:

Project	Cash Flows ($)		IRR	NPV at 10%
	C_0	C_1		
A	−1,000	+1,500	+50%	+364
B	+1,000	−1,500	+50%	−364

Each project has an IRR of 50%. (In other words, $-1{,}000 + 1{,}500/1.50 = 0$ *and* $+1{,}000 - 1{,}500/1.50 = 0$.)

Does this mean that they are equally attractive? Clearly not, for in the case of A, where we are initially paying out $1,000, we are *lending* money at 50%, in the case of B, where we are initially receiving $1,000, we are *borrowing* money at 50%. When we lend money, we want a *high* rate of return; when we borrow money, we want a *low* rate of return.

If you plot a graph like Figure 6.3 for project B, you will find that NPV increases as the discount rate increases. Obviously the internal rate of return rule, as we stated it above, won't work in this case; we have to look for an IRR *less* than the opportunity cost of capital.

Pitfall 2—Multiple Rates of Return

Helmsley Iron is proposing to develop a new strip mine in Western Australia. The mine involves an initial investment of $A600 million and is expected to produce a cash inflow of $A120 million a year for the next nine years. At the end of that time the company will incur $A150 million of cleanup costs. Thus the cash flows from the project are:

Cash Flows (millions of Australian dollars)				
C_0	C_1	...	C_9	C_{10}
−600	120		120	−150

Helmsley calculates the project's IRR and its NPV as follows:

IRR (%)	NPV at 10%
−44.0 *and* 11.6	$A33 million

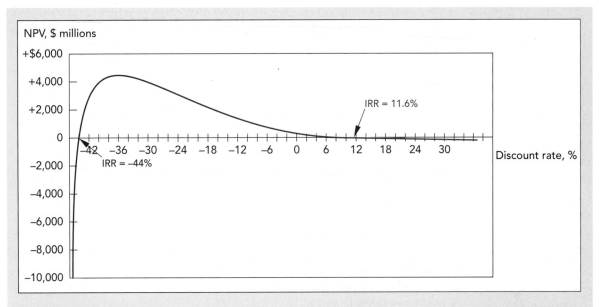

FIGURE 6.4

Helmsley Iron's mine has two internal rates of return. NPV = 0 when the discount rate is −44% *and* when it is +11.6%.

Note that there are *two* discount rates that make NPV = 0. That is, *each* of the following statements holds:

$$NPV = -600 + \frac{120}{.56} + \frac{120}{.56^2} + \cdots + \frac{120}{.56^9} - \frac{150}{.56^{10}} = 0$$

$$NPV = -600 + \frac{120}{1.116} + \frac{120}{1.116^2} + \cdots + \frac{120}{1.116^9} - \frac{150}{1.116^{10}} = 0$$

In other words, the investment has an IRR of both −44.0 *and* 11.6%. Figure 6.4 shows how this comes about. As the discount rate increases, NPV initially rises and then declines. The reason for this is the double change in the sign of the cash-flow stream. There can be as many internal rates of return for a project as there are changes in the sign of the cash flows.[3]

Decommissioning and clean-up costs can sometimes be huge. Phillips Petroleum has estimated that it will need to spend $1 billion to remove its Norwegian offshore oil platforms. It can cost over $300 million to decommission a nuclear power plant. These are obvious instances where cash flows go from positive to negative, but you can probably think of a number of other cases where the company needs to plan for later expenditures. Ships periodically need to go into dry dock for a refit, hotels may receive a major face-lift, machine parts may need replacement, and so on.

Whenever the cash-flow stream is expected to change sign more than once, the company typically sees more than one IRR.

---

[3] By Descartes's "rule of signs" there can be as many different solutions to a polynomial as there are changes of sign.

As if this is not difficult enough, there are also cases in which *no* internal rate of return exists. For example, project C has a positive net present value at all discount rates:

Project	Cash Flows ($)			IRR (%)	NPV at 10%
	C_0	C_1	C_2		
C	+1,000	−3,000	+2,500	None	+339

A number of adaptations of the IRR rule have been devised for such cases. Not only are they inadequate, but they also are unnecessary, for the simple solution is to use net present value.[4]

Pitfall 3—Mutually Exclusive Projects

Firms often have to choose from among several alternative ways of doing the same job or using the same facility. In other words, they need to choose from among **mutually exclusive projects.** Here too the IRR rule can be misleading.
    Consider projects D and E:

Project	Cash Flows ($)		IRR (%)	NPV at 10%
	C_0	C_1		
D	−10,000	+20,000	100	+ 8,182
E	−20,000	+35,000	75	+11,818

Perhaps project D is a manually controlled machine tool and project E is the same tool with the addition of computer control. Both are good investments, but E has the higher NPV and is, therefore, better. However, the IRR rule seems to indicate that if you have to choose, you should go for D since it has the higher IRR. If you follow the IRR rule, you have the satisfaction of earning a 100% rate of return; if you follow the NPV rule, you are $11,818 richer.
    You can salvage the IRR rule in these cases by looking at the internal rate of return on the incremental flows. Here is how to do it: First, consider the smaller project (D in our example). It has an IRR of 100%, which is well in excess of the 10% opportunity cost of capital. You know, therefore, that D is acceptable. You

---

[4] Companies sometimes get around the problem of multiple rates of return by discounting the later cash flows back at the cost of capital until there remains only one change in the sign of the cash flows. A *modified internal rate of return* can then be calculated on this revised series. In our example, the modified IRR is calculated as follows:

1. Calculate the present value of the year 9 and 10 cash flows in year 8:
$$\text{PV in year 9} = +120/1.1 − 150/1.1^2 = −14.9$$

2. Add to the year 8 cash flow the present value of subsequent cash flows:
$$C_8 + \text{PV (subsequent cash flows)} = +120 − 14.9 = 105.1$$

3. Since there is now only one change in the sign of the cash flows, the revised series has a unique rate of return, which is 11.5%:
$$\text{NPV} = −600 + \frac{120}{1.115} + \frac{120}{1.115^2} + \cdots + \frac{120}{1.115^7} + \frac{105.1}{1.115^8} = 0$$

Since the modified IRR of 11.5% is greater than the cost of capital (and the initial cash flow is negative), the project has a positive NPV when valued at the cost of capital.
    Of course, it would be much easier in such cases to abandon the IRR rule and just calculate project NPV.

now ask yourself whether it is worth making the additional $10,000 investment in E. The incremental flows from undertaking E rather than D are as follows:

Project	Cash Flows ($)		IRR (%)	NPV at 10%
	C_0	C_1		
E − D	−10,000	+15,000	50	+3,636

The IRR on the incremental investment is 50%, which is also well in excess of the 10% opportunity cost of capital. So you should prefer project E to project D.[5]

Unless you look at the incremental expenditure, IRR is unreliable in ranking projects of different scale. It is also unreliable in ranking projects that offer different patterns of cash flow over time. For example, suppose the firm can take project F or project G but not both (ignore H for the moment):

Project	Cash Flows ($)						Etc.	IRR (%)	NPV at 10%
	C_0	C_1	C_2	C_3	C_4	C_5			
F	−9,000	+6,000	+5,000	+4,000	0	0	...	33	3,592
G	−9,000	+1,800	+1,800	+1,800	+1,800	+1,800	...	20	9,000
H		−6,000	+1,200	+1,200	+1,200	+1,200	...	20	6,000

Project F has a higher IRR, but project G has the higher NPV. Figure 6.5 shows why the two rules give different answers. The blue line gives the net present value of project F at different rates of discount. Since a discount rate of 33% produces a net present value of zero, this is the internal rate of return for project F. Similarly, the maroon line shows the net present value of project G at different discount rates. The IRR of project G is 20%. (We assume project G's cash flows continue indefinitely.) Note that project G has a higher NPV so long as the opportunity cost of capital is less than 15.6%.

The reason that IRR is misleading is that the total cash inflow of project G is larger but tends to occur later. Therefore, when the discount rate is low, G has the higher NPV; when the discount rate is high, F has the higher NPV. (You can see from Figure 6.5 that the two projects have the *same* NPV when the discount rate is 15.6%.) The internal rates of return on the two projects tell us that at a discount rate of 20% G has a zero NPV (IRR = 20%) and F has a positive NPV. Thus if the opportunity cost of capital were 20%, investors would place a higher value on the shorter-lived project F. But in our example the opportunity cost of capital is not 20% but 10%. Investors are prepared to pay relatively high prices for longer-lived securities, and so they will pay a relatively high price for the longer-lived project. At a 10% cost of capital, an investment in G has an NPV of $9,000 and an investment in F has an NPV of only $3,592.[6]

---

[5] You may, however, find that you have jumped out of the frying pan into the fire. The series of incremental cash flows may involve several changes in sign. In this case there are likely to be multiple IRRs and you will be forced to use the NPV rule after all.

[6] It is often suggested that the choice between the net present value rule and the internal rate of return rule should depend on the probable reinvestment rate. This is wrong. The prospective return on another *independent* investment should *never* be allowed to influence the investment decision.

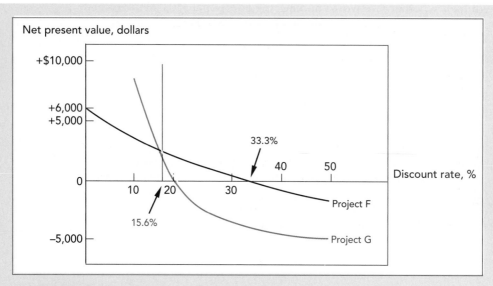

FIGURE 6.5

The IRR of project F exceeds that of project G, but the NPV of project F is higher *only* if the discount rate is greater than 15.6%.

This is a favorite example of ours. We have gotten many businesspeople's reaction to it. When asked to choose between F and G, many choose F. The reason seems to be the rapid payback generated by project F. In other words, they believe that if they take F, they will also be able to take a later project like H (note that H can be financed using the cash flows from F), whereas if they take G, they won't have money enough for H. In other words they implicitly assume that it is a *shortage of capital* that forces the choice between F and G. When this implicit assumption is brought out, they usually admit that G is better if there is no capital shortage.

But the introduction of capital constraints raises two further questions. The first stems from the fact that most of the executives preferring F to G work for firms that would have no difficulty raising more capital. Why would a manager at IBM, say, choose F on the grounds of limited capital? IBM can raise plenty of capital and can take project H regardless of whether F or G is chosen; therefore H should not affect the choice between F and G. The answer seems to be that large firms usually impose capital budgets on divisions and subdivisions as a part of the firm's planning and control system. Since the system is complicated and cumbersome, the budgets are not easily altered, and so they are perceived as real constraints by middle management.

The second question is this. If there is a capital constraint, either real or self-imposed, should IRR be used to rank projects? The answer is no. The problem in this case is to find the package of investment projects that satisfies the capital constraint and has the largest net present value. The IRR rule will not identify this package. As we will show in the next section, the only practical and general way to do so is to use the technique of linear programming.

When we have to choose between projects F and G, it is easiest to compare the net present values. But if your heart is set on the IRR rule, you can use it as long as you look at the internal rate of return on the incremental flows. The procedure is exactly the same as we showed above. First, you check that project F has a satisfactory IRR. Then you look at the return on the additional investment in G.

| Project | Cash Flows ($) | | | | | | | IRR (%) | NPV at 10% |
	C_0	C_1	C_2	C_3	C_4	C_5	Etc.		
G – F	0	−4,200	−3,200	−2,200	+1,800	+1,800	. . .	15.6	+5,408

The IRR on the incremental investment in G is 15.6%. Since this is greater than the opportunity cost of capital, you should undertake G rather than F.

Pitfall 4—What Happens When We Can't Finesse the Term Structure of Interest Rates?

We have simplified our discussion of capital budgeting by assuming that the opportunity cost of capital is the same for all the cash flows, $C_1, C_2, C_3,$ etc. Remember our most general formula for calculating net present value:

$$NPV = C_0 + \frac{C_1}{1 + r_1} + \frac{C_2}{(1 + r_2)^2} + \frac{C_3}{(1 + r_3)^3} + \cdots$$

In other words, we discount C_1 at the opportunity cost of capital for one year, C_2 at the opportunity cost of capital for two years, and so on. The IRR rule tells us to accept a project if the IRR is greater than the opportunity cost of capital. But what do we do when we have several opportunity costs? Do we compare IRR with $r_1, r_2, r_3, \ldots$? Actually we would have to compute a complex weighted average of these rates to obtain a number comparable to IRR.

What does this mean for capital budgeting? It means trouble for the IRR rule whenever the term structure of interest rates becomes important. In a situation where it is important, we have to compare the project IRR with the expected IRR (yield to maturity) offered by a traded security that (1) is equivalent in risk to the project and (2) offers the same time pattern of cash flows as the project. Such a comparison is easier said than done.

Many firms use the IRR, thereby implicitly assuming that there is no difference between short-term and long-term rates of interest. They do this for the same reason that we have so far finessed the term structure: simplicity.[7]

The Verdict on IRR

We have given four examples of things that can go wrong with IRR. We spent much less space on payback or return on book. Does this mean that IRR is worse than the other two measures? Quite the contrary. There is little point in dwelling

---

[7] In Chapter 10 we will look at some other cases in which it would be misleading to use the same discount rate for both short-term and long-term cash flows.

on the deficiencies of payback or return on book. They are clearly ad hoc measures that often lead to silly conclusions. The IRR rule has a much more respectable ancestry. It is less easy to use than NPV, but, used properly, it gives the same answer.

Nowadays few large corporations use the payback period or return on book as their primary measure of project attractiveness. Most use discounted cash flow or "DCF," and for many companies DCF means IRR, not NPV. For "normal" investment projects with an initial cash outflow followed by a series of cash inflows, there is no difficulty in using the internal rate of return to make a simple accept/reject decision. However, we think that financial managers need to worry more about Pitfall 3. Financial managers never see all possible projects. Most projects are proposed by operating managers. A company that instructs nonfinancial managers to look first at project IRRs prompts a search for those projects with the highest IRRs rather than the highest NPVs. It also encourages managers to *modify* projects so that their IRRs are higher. Where do you typically find the highest IRRs? In short-lived projects requiring little up-front investment. Such projects may not add much to the value of the firm.

We don't know why so many companies pay such close attention to the internal rate of return, but we suspect that it may reflect the fact that management does not trust the forecasts it receives. Suppose that two plant managers approach you with proposals for two new investments. Both have a positive NPV of $1,400 at the company's 8% cost of capital, but you nevertheless decide to accept project A and reject B. Are you being irrational?

The cash flows for the two projects and their NPVs are set out in the table below. You can see that, although both proposals have the same NPV, project A involves an investment of $9,000, while B requires an investment of $9 million. Investing $9,000 to make $1,400 is clearly an attractive proposition, and this shows up in A's IRR of nearly 16%. Investing $9 million to make $1,400 might also be worth doing if you could be *sure* of the plant manager's forecasts, but there is almost no room for error in project B. You could spend time and money checking the cash-flow forecasts, but is it really worth the effort? Most managers would look at the IRR and decide that, if the cost of capital is 8%, a project that offers a return of 8.01% is not worth the worrying time.

Alternatively, management may conclude that project A is a clear winner that is worth undertaking right away, but in the case of project B it may make sense to wait and see whether the decision looks more clear-cut in a year's time.[8] Management postpones the decision on projects such as B by setting a hurdle rate for the IRR that is higher than the cost of capital.

Project	Cash Flows ($ thousands)				NPV at 8%	IRR (%)
	C_0	C_1	C_2	C_3		
A	−9.0	2.9	4.0	5.4	1.4	15.58
B	−9,000	2,560	3,540	4,530	1.4	8.01

---

[8] When projects are clear winners (Project A), it generally pays to invest right away and capture the cash flows. However, in the case of marginal projects (project B), the option to wait and see can be valuable. The techniques of option valuation that we describe in Chapter 18 can help managers to decide *when* to invest.

6.4	CHOOSING CAPITAL INVESTMENTS WHEN RESOURCES ARE LIMITED

Our entire discussion of methods of capital budgeting has rested on the proposition that the wealth of a firm's shareholders is highest if the firm accepts *every* project that has a positive net present value. Suppose, however, that there are limitations on the investment program that prevent the company from undertaking all such projects. Economists call this *capital rationing*. When capital is rationed, we need a method of selecting the package of projects that is within the company's resources yet gives the highest possible net present value.

An Easy Problem in Capital Rationing

Let us start with a simple example. The opportunity cost of capital is 10%, and our company has the following opportunities:

	Cash Flows ($ millions)			
Project	C_0	C_1	C_2	NPV at 10%
A	−10	+30	+5	21
B	−5	+5	+20	16
C	−5	+5	+15	12

All three projects are attractive, but suppose that the firm is limited to spending $10 million. In that case, it can invest *either* in project A *or* in projects B and C, but it cannot invest in all three. Although individually B and C have lower net present values than project A, when taken together they have the higher net present value. Here we cannot choose between projects solely on the basis of net present values. When funds are limited, we need to concentrate on getting the biggest bang for our buck. In other words, we must pick the projects that offer the highest net present value per dollar of initial outlay. This ratio is known as the **profitability index:**[9]

$$\text{Profitability index} = \frac{\text{net present value}}{\text{investment}}$$

For our three projects the profitability index is calculated as follows:[10]

Project	Investment ($ millions)	NPV ($ millions)	Profitability Index
A	10	21	2.1
B	5	16	3.2
C	5	12	2.4

---

[9] If a project requires outlays in two or more periods, the denominator should be the present value of the outlays. A few companies do not discount the benefits or costs before calculating the profitability index. The less said about these companies the better.

[10] Sometimes the profitability index is defined as the ratio of the present value to initial outlay, that is, as PV/investment. This measure is also known as the *benefit–cost ratio*. To calculate the benefit–cost ratio, simply add 1.0 to each profitability index. Project rankings are unchanged.

Project B has the highest profitability index and C has the next highest. Therefore, if our budget limit is $10 million, we should accept these two projects.[11]

Unfortunately, there are some limitations to this simple ranking method. One of the most serious is that it breaks down whenever more than one resource is rationed.[12] For example, suppose that the firm can raise only $10 million for investment in *each* of years 0 and 1 and that the menu of possible projects is expanded to include an investment next year in project D:

Project	Cash Flows ($ millions)			NPV at 10%	Profitability Index
	C_0	C_1	C_2		
A	−10	+30	+5	21	2.1
B	−5	+5	+20	16	3.2
C	−5	+5	+15	12	2.4
D	0	−40	+60	13	0.4

One strategy is to accept projects B and C; however, if we do this, we cannot also accept D, which costs more than our budget limit for period 1. An alternative is to accept project A in period 0. Although this has a lower net present value than the combination of B and C, it provides a $30 million positive cash flow in period 1. When this is added to the $10 million budget, we can also afford to undertake D next year. A and D have *lower* profitability indexes than B and C, but they have a *higher* total net present value.

The reason that ranking on the profitability index fails in this example is that resources are constrained in each of two periods. In fact, this ranking method is inadequate whenever there is *any* other constraint on the choice of projects. This means that it cannot cope with cases in which two projects are mutually exclusive or in which one project is dependent on another.

For example, suppose that you have a long menu of possible projects starting this year and next. There is a limit on how much you can invest in each year. Perhaps also you can't undertake both project alpha and beta (they both require the same piece of land), and you can't invest in project gamma unless you invest in delta (gamma is simply an add-on to delta). You need to find the package of projects that satisfies all these constraints and gives the highest NPV.

One way to tackle such a problem is to work through all possible combinations of projects. For each combination you first check whether the projects satisfy the constraints and then calculate the net present value. But it is smarter to recognize that linear programming (LP) techniques are specially designed to search through such possible combinations and that you can hand the problem to a computer that is equipped to solve LPs.[13]

---

[11] If a project has a positive profitability index, it must also have a positive NPV. Therefore, firms sometimes use the profitability index to select projects when capital is *not* limited. However, like the IRR, the profitability index can be misleading when used to choose between mutually exclusive projects. For example, suppose you were forced to choose between (1) investing $100 in a project whose payoffs have a present value of $200 or (2) investing $1 million in a project whose payoffs have a present value of $1.5 million. The first investment has the higher profitability index; the second makes you richer.

[12] It may also break down if it causes some money to be left over. It might be better to spend all the available funds even if this involves accepting a project with a slightly lower NPV.

[13] On our Web site at **www.mhhe.com/bma1e** we show how linear programming can be used to select from the four projects in our earlier example.

Uses of Capital Rationing Models

Linear programming models seem tailor-made for solving capital budgeting problems when resources are limited. Why then are they not universally accepted either in theory or in practice? One reason is that these models can turn out to be very complex. Second, as with any sophisticated long-range planning tool, there is the general problem of getting good data. It is just not worth applying costly, sophisticated methods to poor data. Furthermore, these models are based on the assumption that all future investment opportunities are known. In reality, the discovery of investment ideas is an unfolding process.

Our most serious misgivings center on the basic assumption that capital is limited. When we come to discuss company financing, we shall see that most large corporations do not face capital rationing and can raise large sums of money on fair terms. Why then do many company presidents tell their subordinates that capital is limited? If they are right, the capital market is seriously imperfect. What then are they doing maximizing NPV?[14] We might be tempted to suppose that if capital is not rationed, they do not *need* to use linear programming and, if it is rationed, then surely they *ought* not to use it. But that would be too quick a judgment. Let us look at this problem more deliberately.

Soft Rationing   Many firms' capital constraints are "soft." They reflect no imperfections in capital markets. Instead they are provisional limits adopted by management as an aid to financial control.

Some ambitious divisional managers habitually overstate their investment opportunities. Rather than trying to distinguish which projects really are worthwhile, headquarters may find it simpler to impose an upper limit on divisional expenditures and thereby force the divisions to set their own priorities. In such instances budget limits are a rough but effective way of dealing with biased cash-flow forecasts. In other cases management may believe that very rapid corporate growth could impose intolerable strains on management and the organization. Since it is difficult to quantify such constraints explicitly, the budget limit may be used as a proxy.

Because such budget limits have nothing to do with any inefficiency in the capital market, there is no contradiction in using an LP model in the division to maximize net present value subject to the budget constraint. On the other hand, there is not much point in elaborate selection procedures if the cash-flow forecasts of the division are seriously biased.

Even if capital is not rationed, other resources may be. The availability of management time, skilled labor, or even other capital equipment often constitutes an important constraint on a company's growth.

Hard Rationing   Soft rationing should never cost the firm anything. If capital constraints become tight enough to hurt—in the sense that projects with significant positive NPVs are passed up—then the firm raises more money and loosens the constraint. But what if it *can't* raise more money—what if it faces *hard* rationing?

Hard rationing implies market imperfections, but that does not necessarily mean we have to throw away net present value as a criterion for capital budgeting. It depends on the nature of the imperfection.

Arizona Aquaculture, Inc. (AAI), borrows as much as the banks will lend it, yet it still has good investment opportunities. This is not hard rationing so long as

---

[14] Don't forget that in Chapter 2 we had to assume perfect capital markets to derive the NPV rule.

AAI can issue stock. But perhaps it can't. Perhaps the founder and majority share-holder vetoes the idea from fear of losing control of the firm. Perhaps a stock issue would bring costly red tape or legal complications.[15]

This does not invalidate the NPV rule. AAI's *shareholders* can borrow or lend, sell their shares, or buy more. They have free access to security markets. The type of portfolio they hold is independent of AAI's financing or investment decisions. The only way AAI can help its shareholders is to make them richer. Thus AAI should invest its available cash in the package of projects having the largest aggregate net present value.

A barrier between the firm and capital markets does not undermine net present value so long as the barrier is the *only* market imperfection. The important thing is that the firm's *shareholders* have free access to well-functioning capital markets.

The net present value rule *is* undermined when imperfections restrict share-holders' portfolio choice. Suppose that Nevada Aquaculture, Inc. (NAI), is solely owned by its founder, Alexander Turbot. Mr. Turbot has no cash or credit remaining, but he is convinced that expansion of his operation is a high-NPV investment. He has tried to sell stock but has found that prospective investors, skeptical of prospects for fish farming in the desert, offer him much less than he thinks his firm is worth. For Mr. Turbot capital markets hardly exist. It makes little sense for him to discount prospective cash flows at a market opportunity cost of capital.

----

[15] A majority owner who is "locked in" and has much personal wealth tied up in AAI may be effectively cut off from capital markets. The NPV rule may not make sense to such an owner, though it will to the other shareholders.

SUMMARY

If you are going to persuade your company to use the net present value rule, you must be prepared to explain why other rules may *not* lead to correct decisions. That is why we have examined three alternative investment criteria in this chapter.

Some firms look at the book rate of return on the project. In this case the company decides which cash payments are capital expenditures and picks the appropriate rate to depreciate these expenditures. It then calculates the ratio of book income to the book value of the investment. Few companies nowadays base their investment decision simply on the book rate of return, but shareholders pay attention to book measures of firm profitability and some managers therefore look with a jaundiced eye on projects that would damage the company's book rate of return.

Some companies use the payback method to make investment decisions. In other words, they accept only those projects that recover their initial investment within some specified period. Payback is an ad hoc rule. It ignores the timing of cash flows within the payback period, and it ignores subsequent cash flows entirely. It therefore takes no account of the opportunity cost of capital.

The internal rate of return (IRR) is defined as the rate of discount at which a project would have zero NPV. It is a handy measure and widely used in finance; you should therefore know how to calculate it. The IRR rule states that companies should accept any investment offering an IRR in excess of the opportunity cost of capital. The IRR rule is, like net present value, a technique based on discounted cash flows. It will therefore give the correct answer if properly used. The problem is that it is easily misapplied. There are four things to look out for:

1. *Lending or borrowing?* If a project offers positive cash flows followed by negative flows, NPV can *rise* as the discount rate is increased. You should accept such projects if their IRR is *less* than the opportunity cost of capital.

2. *Multiple rates of return.* If there is more than one change in the sign of the cash flows, the project may have several IRRs or no IRR at all.

3. *Mutually exclusive projects.* The IRR rule may give the wrong ranking of mutually exclusive projects that differ in economic life or in scale of required investment. If you insist on using IRR to rank mutually exclusive projects, you must examine the IRR on each incremental investment.

4. *The cost of capital for near-term cash flows may be different from the cost for distant cash flows.* The IRR rule requires you to compare the project's IRR with the opportunity cost of capital. But sometimes there is an opportunity cost of capital for one-year cash flows, a different cost of capital for two-year cash flows, and so on. In these cases there is no simple yardstick for evaluating the IRR of a project.

If you are going to the expense of collecting cash-flow forecasts, you might as well use them properly. Ad hoc criteria should therefore have no role in the firm's decisions, and discounted cash flow methods should be employed in preference to other techniques. Having said that, we must be careful not to exaggerate the payoff of proper technique. Technique is important, but it is by no means the only determinant of the success of a capital expenditure program. If the forecasts of cash flows are poor, even the most careful application of the net present value rule will fail.

In developing the NPV rule, we assumed that the company can maximize shareholder wealth by accepting every project that is worth more than it costs. But, if capital is strictly limited, then it may not be possible to take every project with a positive NPV. If capital is rationed in only one period, then the firm should follow a simple rule: Calculate each project's profitability index, which is the project's net present value per dollar of investment. Then pick the projects with the highest profitability indexes until you run out of capital. Unfortunately, this procedure fails when capital is rationed in more than one period or when there are other constraints on project choice. The only general solution is linear programming.

Hard capital rationing always reflects a market imperfection—a barrier between the firm and capital markets. If that barrier also implies that the firm's shareholders lack free access to a well-functioning capital market, the very foundations of net present value crumble. Fortunately, hard rationing is rare for corporations in the United States. Many firms do use soft capital rationing, however. That is, they set up self-imposed limits as a means of financial planning and control.

For a survey of capital budgeting procedures, see:
J. Graham and C. Harvey, "How CFOs Make Capital Budgeting and Capital Structure Decisions," *Journal of Applied Corporate Finance* 15 (spring 2002), pp. 8–23.

FURTHER READING

Visit us at www.mhhe.com/bma1e

CONCEPT REVIEW QUESTIONS

1. "Most firms use only one measure of a project's attractiveness." True or false? (page 117)

2. "Payback gives too much weight to cash flows that occur after the cutoff date." True or false? (page 120)

3. How is the discounted payback period calculated? Does discounted payback solve the deficiencies of the payback rule? (page 121)

For a complete listing of your chapter Concept Review Questions, please visit us at www.mhhe.com/bma1e.

QUIZ

1. **a.** What is the payback period on each of the following projects?

Project	Cash Flows ($)				
	C_0	C_1	C_2	C_3	C_4
A	−5,000	+1,000	+1,000	+3,000	0
B	−1,000	0	+1,000	+2,000	+3,000
C	−5,000	+1,000	+1,000	+3,000	+5,000

  b. *Given* that you wish to use the payback rule with a cutoff period of two years, which projects would you accept?

  c. If you use a cutoff period of three years, which projects would you accept?

  d. If the opportunity cost of capital is 10%, which projects have positive NPVs?

  e. "If a firm uses a single cutoff period for all projects, it is likely to accept too many short-lived projects." True or false?

  f. If the firm uses the discounted-payback rule, will it accept any negative-NPV projects? Will it turn down positive-NPV projects? Explain.

2. Write down the equation defining a project's internal rate of return (IRR). In practice how is IRR calculated?

3. **a.** Calculate the net present value of the following project for discount rates of 0, 50, and 100%:

Cash Flows ($)		
C_0	C_1	C_2
−6,750	+4,500	+18,000

  b. What is the IRR of the project?

4. You have the chance to participate in a project that produces the following cash flows:

Cash Flows ($)		
C_0	C_1	C_2
+5,000	+4,000	−11,000

The internal rate of return is 13%. If the opportunity cost of capital is 10%, would you accept the offer?

5. Consider a project with the following cash flows:

C_0	C_1	C_2
−100	+200	−75

    a. How many internal rates of return does this project have?

    b. Which of the following numbers is the project IRR:
       (i) −50%; (ii) −12%; (iii) +5%; (iv) +50%?

    c. The opportunity cost of capital is 20%. Is this an attractive project? Briefly explain.

6. Consider projects Alpha and Beta:

	Cash Flows ($)			
Project	C_0	C_1	C_2	**IRR (%)**
Alpha	−400,000	+241,000	+293,000	21
Beta	−200,000	+131,000	+172,000	31

The opportunity cost of capital is 8%.
    Suppose you can undertake Alpha or Beta, but not both. Use the IRR rule to make the choice. (*Hint:* What's the incremental investment in Alpha?)

7. Suppose you have the following investment opportunities, but only $90,000 available for investment. Which projects should you take?

Project	NPV	Investment
1	5,000	10,000
2	5,000	5,000
3	10,000	90,000
4	15,000	60,000
5	15,000	75,000
6	3,000	15,000

8. Consider the following projects:

PRACTICE QUESTIONS

	Cash Flows ($)					
Project	C_0	C_1	C_2	C_3	C_4	C_5
A	−1,000	+1,000	0	0	0	0
B	−2,000	+1,000	+1,000	+4,000	+1,000	+1,000
C	−3,000	+1,000	+1,000	0	+1,000	+1,000

    a. If the opportunity cost of capital is 10%, which projects have a positive NPV?

    b. Calculate the payback period for each project.

    c. Which project(s) would a firm using the payback rule accept if the cutoff period is three years?

    d. Calculate the discounted payback period for each project.

    e. Which project(s) would a firm using the discounted payback rule accept if the cutoff period was three years?

9. Respond to the following comments:

    a. "I like the IRR rule. I can use it to rank projects without having to specify a discount rate."

    b. "I like the payback rule. As long as the minimum payback period is short, the rule makes sure that the company takes no borderline projects. That reduces risk."

10. Calculate the IRR (or IRRs) for the following project:

C_0	C_1	C_2	C_3
−3,000	+3,500	+4,000	−4,000

For what range of discount rates does the project have positive NPV?

11. Consider the following two mutually exclusive projects:

	Cash Flows ($)			
Project	C_0	C_1	C_2	C_3
A	−100	+60	+60	0
B	−110	0	0	+140

    a. Calculate the NPV of each project for discount rates of 0, 10, and 20%. Plot these on a graph with NPV on the vertical axis and discount rate on the horizontal axis.

    b. What is the approximate IRR for each project?

    c. In what circumstances should the company accept project A?

    d. Calculate the NPV of the incremental investment (B − A) for discount rates of 0, 10, and 20%. Plot these on your graph. Show that the circumstances in which you would accept A are also those in which the IRR on the incremental investment is less than the opportunity cost of capital.

12. Mr. Cyrus Clops, the president of Giant Enterprises, has to make a choice between two possible investments:

	Cash Flows ($ thousands)			
Project	C_0	C_1	C_2	IRR (%)
A	−400	+250	+300	23
B	−200	+140	+179	36

The opportunity cost of capital is 9%. Mr. Clops is tempted to take B, which has the higher IRR.

    a. Explain to Mr. Clops why this is not the correct procedure.

    b. Show him how to adapt the IRR rule to choose the best project.

    c. Show him that this project also has the higher NPV.

13. The Titanic Shipbuilding Company has a noncancelable contract to build a small cargo vessel. Construction involves a cash outlay of $250,000 at the end of each of the next two years. At the end of the third year the company will receive payment of $650,000. The company can speed up construction by working an extra shift. In this case there will be a cash outlay of $550,000 at the end of the first year followed by a cash payment of $650,000 at the end of the second year. Use the IRR rule to show the (approximate) range of opportunity costs of capital at which the company should work the extra shift.

14. Look again at projects D and E in Section 6.3. Assume that the projects are mutually exclusive and that the opportunity cost of capital is 10%.

   a. Calculate the profitability index for each project.

   b. Show how the profitability-index rule can be used to select the superior project.

15. Borghia Pharmaceuticals has $1 million allocated for capital expenditures. Which of the following projects should the company accept to stay within the $1 million budget? How much does the budget limit cost the company in terms of its market value? The opportunity cost of capital for each project is 11%.

Project	Investment ($ thousands)	NPV ($ thousands)	IRR (%)
1	300	66	17.2
2	200	−4	10.7
3	250	43	16.6
4	100	14	12.1
5	100	7	11.8
6	350	63	18.0
7	400	48	13.5

[Handwritten annotations: PI = NPV/Investment; 0.22, −0.02, 0.172, 0.140, 0.070, 0.180, 0.120; 1,3,4,6; WAPI]

CHALLENGE QUESTIONS

16. Some people believe firmly, even passionately, that ranking projects on IRR is OK if each project's cash flows can be reinvested at the project's IRR. They also say that the NPV rule "assumes that cash flows are reinvested at the opportunity cost of capital." Think carefully about these statements. Are they true? Are they helpful?

17. Look again at the project cash flows in Practice Question 10. Calculate the modified IRR as defined in footnote 4 in Section 6.3. Assume the cost of capital is 12%.

   Now try the following variation on the modified IRR concept. Figure out the fraction x such that x times C_1 and C_2 has the same present value as (minus) C_3.

   $$xC_1 + \frac{xC_2}{1.12} = -\frac{C_3}{1.12^2}$$

   Define the modified project IRR as the solution of

   $$C_0 + \frac{(1 - x)C_1}{1 + IRR} + \frac{(1 - x)C_2}{(1 + IRR)^2} = 0$$

   Now you have two modified IRRs. Which is more meaningful? If you can't decide, what do you conclude about the usefulness of modified IRRs?

18. Consider the following capital rationing problem:

Project	C_0	C_1	C_2	NPV
W	−10,000	−10,000	0	+6,700
X	0	−20,000	+5,000	+9,000
Y	−10,000	+5,000	+5,000	+0
Z	−15,000	+5,000	+4,000	−1,500
Financing available	20,000	20,000	20,000	

   Set up this problem as a linear program and solve it.

   You can allow partial investments, that is, $0 \leq x \leq 1$. Calculate and interpret the shadow prices[16] on the capital constraints.

---

[16] A shadow price is the marginal change in the objective for a marginal change in the constraint.

MINI-CASE

Vegetron's CFO Calls Again

(The first episode of this story was presented in Section 6.1.)

Later that afternoon, Vegetron's CFO bursts into your office in a state of anxious confusion. The problem, he explains, is a last-minute proposal for a change in the design of the fermentation tanks that Vegetron will build to extract hydrated zirconium from a stockpile of powdered ore. The CFO has brought a printout (Table 6.1) of the forecasted revenues, costs, income, and book rates of return for the standard, low-temperature design. Vegetron's engineers have just proposed an alternative high-temperature design that will extract most of the hydrated zirconium over a shorter period, five instead of seven years. The forecasts for the high-temperature method are given in Table 6.2.[17]

CFO: Why do these engineers always have a bright idea at the last minute? But you've got to admit the high-temperature process looks good. We'll get a faster payback, and the rate of return beats Vegetron's 9% cost of capital in every year except the first. Let's see, income is $30,000 per year. Average investment is half the $400,000 capital outlay, or $200,000, so the average rate of return is 30,000/200,000, or 15%—a lot better than the 9% hurdle rate. The average rate of return for the low-temperature process is not that good, only 28,000/200,000, or 14%. Of course we might get a higher rate of return for the low-temperature proposal if we depreciated the investment faster—do you think we should try that?

TABLE 6.1

Income statement and book rates of return for high-temperature extraction of hydrated zirconium ($ thousands).

* Straight-line depreciation over five years is 400/5 = 80, or $80,000 per year.
† Capital investment is $400,000 in year 0.

	Year				
	1	2	3	4	5
1. Revenue	180	180	180	180	180
2. Operating costs	70	70	70	70	70
3. Depreciation*	80	80	80	80	80
4. Net income	30	30	30	30	30
5. Start-of-year book value†	400	320	240	160	80
6. Book rate of return (4 ÷ 5)	7.5%	9.4%	12.5%	18.75%	37.5%

TABLE 6.2

Income statement and book rates of return for low-temperature extraction of hydrated zirconium ($ thousands).

* Rounded. Straight-line depreciation over seven years is 400/7 = 57.14, or $57,140 per year.
† Capital investment is $400,000 in year 0.

	Year						
	1	2	3	4	5	6	7
1. Revenue	140	140	140	140	140	140	140
2. Operating costs	55	55	55	55	55	55	55
3. Depreciation*	57	57	57	57	57	57	57
4. Net income	28	28	28	28	28	28	28
5. Start-of-year book value†	400	343	286	229	171	114	57
6. Book rate of return (4 ÷ 5)	7%	8.2%	9.8%	12.2%	16.4%	24.6%	49.1%

---

[17] For simplicity we have ignored taxes. There will be plenty about taxes in Chapter 7.

You: Let's not fixate on book accounting numbers. Book income is not the same as cash flow to Vegetron or its investors. Book rates of return don't measure the true rate of return.

CFO: But people use accounting numbers all the time. We have to publish them in our annual report to investors.

You: Accounting numbers have many valid uses, but they're not a sound basis for capital investment decisions. Accounting changes can have big effects on book income or rate of return, even when cash flows are unchanged.

Here's an example. Suppose the accountant depreciates the capital investment for the low-temperature process over six years rather than seven. Then income for years 1 to 6 goes down, because depreciation is higher. Income for year 7 goes up because the depreciation for that year becomes zero. But there is no effect on year-to-year cash flows, because depreciation is not a cash outlay. It is simply the accountant's device for spreading out the "recovery" of the up-front capital outlay over the life of the project.

CFO: So how do we get cash flows?

You: In these cases it's easy. Depreciation is the only noncash entry in your spreadsheets (Tables 6.1 and 6.2), so we can just leave it out of the calculation. Cash flow equals revenue minus operating costs. For the high-temperature process, annual cash flow is:

$$\text{Cash flow} = \text{revenue} - \text{operating cost} = 180 - 70 = 110, \text{ or } \$110,000$$

CFO: In effect you're adding back depreciation, because depreciation is a noncash accounting expense.

You: Right. You could also do it that way:

$$\text{Cash flow} = \text{net income} + \text{depreciation} = 30 + 80 = 110, \text{ or } \$110,000$$

CFO: Of course. I remember all this now, but book returns seem important when someone shoves them in front of your nose.

You: It's not clear which project is better. The high-temperature process appears to be less efficient. It has higher operating costs and generates less total revenue over the life of the project, but of course it generates more cash flow in years 1 to 5.

CFO: Maybe the processes are equally good from a financial point of view. If so we'll stick with the low-temperature process rather than switching at the last minute.

You: We'll have to lay out the cash flows and calculate NPV for each process.

CFO: OK, do that. I'll be back in a half hour—and I also want to see each project's true, DCF rate of return.

QUESTIONS

1. Are the book rates of return reported in Table 6.1 useful inputs for the capital investment decision?

2. Calculate NPV and IRR for each process. What is your recommendation? Be ready to explain to the CFO.

CHAPTER SEVEN

MAKING INVESTMENT DECISIONS WITH THE NET PRESENT VALUE RULE

IN LATE 2003 Boeing announced its intention to produce and market the 787 Dreamliner. The decision committed Boeing and its partners to a substantial capital investment, involving 3 million square feet of additional facilities. But, barring any technical glitches, it looks as if Boeing will earn a good return on this investment. As we write this in January 2007, Boeing has booked orders for 471 Dreamliners, making it one of the most successful aircraft launches in history.

How does a company, such as Boeing, decide to go ahead with the launch of a new airliner? We know the answer in principle. The company needs to forecast the project's cash flows and discount them at the opportunity cost of capital to arrive at the project's NPV. A project with a positive NPV increases shareholder value.

But those cash flow forecasts do not arrive on a silver platter. First, the company's managers need answers to a number of basic questions. How soon can the company get the plane into production? How many planes are likely to be sold each year and at what price? How much does the firm need to invest in new production facilities, and what is the projected production cost? How long will the model stay in production, and what happens to the plant and equipment at the end of that time?

These predictions need to be checked for completeness and accuracy, and then pulled together to produce a single set of cash-flow forecasts. That requires careful tracking of taxes, changes in working capital, inflation, and the end-of-project salvage values of plant, property, and equipment. The financial manager must also ferret out hidden cash flows and take care to reject accounting entries that look like cash flows but truly are not.

Our first task in this chapter is to look at how to develop a set of project cash flows. We will then work through a realistic and comprehensive example of a capital investment analysis.

We conclude the chapter by looking at how the financial manager should apply the present value rule when choosing between investment in plant and equipment with different economic lives. For example, suppose you must decide between machine Y with a 5-year useful life and Z with a 10-year life.

The present value of Y's lifetime investment and operating costs is naturally less than Z's because Z will last twice as long. Does that necessarily make Y the better choice? Of course not. You will find that, when you are faced with this type of problem, the trick is to transform the present value of the costs into an *equivalent annual cost*, that is, the total cost per year of buying and operating the asset.

7.1   APPLYING THE NET PRESENT VALUE RULE

Boeing's decision to produce the 787 required a heavy up-front investment in new production facilities. But often the largest investments involve the acquisition of intangible assets. Consider, for example, the expenditure by major banks on information technology, or IT (computers, software, and telecommunications). These projects can soak up hundreds of millions of dollars. Yet much of the expenditure goes to intangibles such as system design, programming, testing, and training. Think also of the huge expenditure by pharmaceutical companies on research and development (R&D). Pfizer, one of the largest pharmaceutical companies, spent $7.6 billion on R&D in 2006. The R&D cost of bringing *one* new prescription drug to market has been estimated at $800 million.

Expenditures on intangible assets such as IT and R&D are investments just like expenditures on new plant and equipment. In each case the company is making an up-front expenditure in the expectation that it will generate a stream of future profits. Ideally, firms should apply the same criteria to any capital investment, regardless of whether it involves a tangible or intangible asset.

We have seen that an investment in any asset creates wealth if the discounted value of the future cash flows exceeds the up-front cost. But up to this point we have glossed over the problem of *what* to discount. When you are faced with this problem, you should always stick to three general rules:

1. Only cash flow is relevant.
2. Always estimate cash flows on an incremental basis.
3. Be consistent in your treatment of inflation.

We will discuss each of these rules in turn.

Only Cash Flow Is Relevant

The first and most important point: Net present value depends on future cash flows. Cash flow is the simplest possible concept; it is just the difference between cash received and cash paid out. Many people nevertheless confuse cash flow with accounting income.

Income statements are intended to show how well the company is performing. Therefore, accountants *start* with "dollars in" and "dollars out," but to obtain accounting income they adjust these inputs in two ways. First, they try to show profit as it is *earned* rather than when the company and its customers get around to paying their bills. Second, they sort cash outflows into two categories: current expenses and capital expenses. They deduct current expenses when calculating income but do not deduct capital expenses. There is a good reason for this. If the firm lays out a large amount of money on a big capital project, you do not conclude that the firm is performing poorly, even though a lot of cash is going out the door. Therefore, the accountant does not deduct capital expenditure when calculating the year's income but, instead, depreciates it over several years.

As a result of these adjustments, income includes some cash flows and excludes others, and it is reduced by depreciation charges, which are not cash flows at all. It is not always easy to translate the customary accounting data back into actual dollars—dollars you can buy beer with. If you are in doubt about what is a cash flow, simply count the dollars coming in and take away the dollars going out. Don't assume without checking that you can find cash flow by routine manipulations of accounting data.

Always estimate cash flows on an after-tax basis. Some firms do not deduct tax payments. They try to offset this mistake by discounting the cash flows before taxes at a rate higher than the opportunity cost of capital. Unfortunately, there is no reliable formula for making such adjustments to the discount rate.

You should also make sure that cash flows are recorded only when they occur and not when work is undertaken or a liability is incurred. For example, taxes should be discounted from their actual payment date, not from the time when the tax liability is recorded in the firm's books.

Estimate Cash Flows on an Incremental Basis

The value of a project depends on *all* the additional cash flows that follow from project acceptance. Here are some things to watch for when you are deciding which cash flows should be included:

Do Not Confuse Average with Incremental Payoffs   Most managers naturally hesitate to throw good money after bad. For example, they are reluctant to invest more money in a losing division. But occasionally you will encounter turnaround opportunities in which the *incremental* NPV on investment in a loser is strongly positive.

Conversely, it does not always make sense to throw good money after good. A division with an outstanding past profitability record may have run out of good opportunities. You would not pay a large sum for a 20-year-old horse, sentiment aside, regardless of how many races that horse had won or how many champions it had sired.

Here is another example illustrating the difference between average and incremental returns: Suppose that a railroad bridge is in urgent need of repair. With the bridge the railroad can continue to operate; without the bridge it can't. In this case the payoff from the repair work consists of all the benefits of operating the railroad. The incremental NPV of such an investment may be enormous. Of course, these benefits should be net of all other costs and all subsequent repairs; otherwise the company may be misled into rebuilding an unprofitable railroad piece by piece.

Include All Incidental Effects   It is important to consider a project's effects on the remainder of the firm's business. For example, suppose Sony proposes to launch PlayStation 4, a new version of its video game console. Demand for the new product will almost certainly cut into sales of Sony's existing consoles. This incidental effect needs to be factored into the incremental cash flows. Of course, Sony may reason that it needs to go ahead with the new product because its existing product line is likely to come under increasing threat from competitors. So, even if it decides not to produce the new PlayStation, there is no guarantee that sales of the existing consoles will continue at their present level. Sooner or later they will decline.

Sometimes a new project will *help* the firm's existing business. Suppose that you are the financial manager of an airline that is considering opening a new short-haul route from Peoria, Illinois, to Chicago's O'Hare Airport. When considered in isolation, the new route may have a negative NPV. But once you allow for the additional business that the new route brings to your other traffic out of O'Hare, it may be a very worthwhile investment.

These incidental effects can extend into the far future. When GE, Pratt & Whitney, or Rolls Royce commits to the design and production of a new jet engine, cash inflows are not limited to revenues from engine sales. Once sold, an engine may be in service for 20 years or more, and during that time there is a steady demand for replacement parts. Some engine manufacturers also run profitable service and overhaul facilities. Finally, once an engine is proven in service, there are opportunities to offer modified or improved versions for other uses. All these "downstream" activities generate significant incremental cash inflows.

Do Not Forget Working Capital Requirements   Net working capital (often referred to simply as *working capital*) is the difference between a company's short-term assets and liabilities. The principal short-term assets are accounts receivable (customers' unpaid bills) and inventories of raw materials and finished goods. The principal short-term liabilities are accounts payable (bills that *you* have not paid). Most projects entail an additional investment in working capital. This investment should, therefore, be recognized in your cash-flow forecasts. By the same token, when the project comes to an end, you can usually recover some of the investment. This is treated as a cash inflow. We will supply a numerical example of working-capital investment later in this chapter.

Include Opportunity Costs   The cost of a resource may be relevant to the investment decision even when no cash changes hands. For example, suppose a new manufacturing operation uses land that could otherwise be sold for $100,000. This resource is not free: It has an opportunity cost, which is the cash it could generate for the company if the project were rejected and the resource were sold or put to some other productive use.

This example prompts us to warn you against judging projects on the basis of "before versus after." The proper comparison is "with or without." A manager comparing before versus after might not assign any value to the land because the firm owns it both before and after:

Before	Take Project	After	Cash Flow, Before versus After
Firm owns land	→	Firm still owns land	0

The proper comparison, with or without, is as follows:

With	Take Project	After	Cash Flow, with Project
Firm owns land	→	Firm still owns land	0

Without	Do Not Take Project	After	Cash Flow, without Project
	→	Firm sells land for $100,000	$100,000

Comparing the two possible "afters," we see that the firm gives up $100,000 by undertaking the project. This reasoning still holds if the land will not be sold but is worth $100,000 to the firm in some other use.

Sometimes opportunity costs may be very difficult to estimate; however, where the resource can be freely traded, its opportunity cost is simply equal to the market price. Why? It cannot be otherwise. If the value of a parcel of land to the firm is less than its market price, the firm will sell it. On the other hand, the opportunity cost of using land in a particular project cannot exceed the cost of buying an equivalent parcel to replace it.

Forget Sunk Costs   Sunk costs are like spilled milk: They are past and irreversible outflows. Because sunk costs are bygones, they cannot be affected by the decision to accept or reject the project, and so they should be ignored.

For example, when Lockheed sought a federal guarantee for a bank loan to continue development of the TriStar airplane, the company and its supporters argued it would be foolish to abandon a project on which nearly $1 billion had already been spent. Some of Lockheed's critics countered that it would be equally foolish to continue with a project that offered no prospect of a satisfactory return on that $1 billion. Both groups were guilty of the *sunk-cost fallacy*; the $1 billion was irrecoverable and, therefore, irrelevant.

Beware of Allocated Overhead Costs   We have already mentioned that the accountant's objective is not always the same as the investment analyst's. A case in point is the allocation of overhead costs. Overheads include such items as supervisory salaries, rent, heat, and light. These overheads may not be related to any particular project, but they have to be paid for somehow. Therefore, when the accountant assigns costs to the firm's projects, a charge for overhead is usually made. Now our principle of incremental cash flows says that in investment appraisal we should include only the *extra* expenses that would result from the project. A project may generate extra overhead expenses; then again, it may not. We should be cautious about assuming that the accountant's allocation of overheads represents the true extra expenses that would be incurred.

Treat Inflation Consistently

As we pointed out in Chapter 4, interest rates are usually quoted in *nominal* rather than *real* terms. For example, if you buy an 8% Treasury bond, the government promises to pay you $80 interest each year, but it does not promise what that $80 will buy. Investors take inflation into account when they decide what is an acceptable rate of interest.

If the discount rate is stated in nominal terms, then consistency requires that cash flows should also be estimated in nominal terms, taking account of trends in selling price, labor and materials costs, etc. This calls for more than simply applying a single assumed inflation rate to all components of cash flow. Labor costs per hour of work, for example, normally increase at a faster rate than the consumer price index because of improvements in productivity. Tax savings from depreciation do *not* increase with inflation; they are constant in nominal terms because tax law in the United States allows only the original cost of assets to be depreciated.

Of course, there is nothing wrong with discounting real cash flows at a real discount rate. In fact this is standard procedure in countries with high and volatile inflation. Here is a simple example showing that real and nominal discounting, properly applied, always give the same present value.

Suppose your firm usually forecasts cash flows in nominal terms and discounts at a 15% nominal rate. In this particular case, however, you are given project cash flows in real terms, that is, current dollars:

Real Cash Flows ($ thousands)			
C_0	C_1	C_2	C_3
−100	+35	+50	+30

It would be inconsistent to discount these real cash flows at the 15% nominal rate. You have two alternatives: Either restate the cash flows in nominal terms and discount at 15%, or restate the discount rate in real terms and use it to discount the real cash flows.

Assume that inflation is projected at 10% a year. Then the cash flow for year 1, which is $35,000 in current dollars, will be $35,000 \times 1.10 = \$38,500$ in year-1 dollars. Similarly the cash flow for year 2 will be $50,000 \times (1.10)^2 = \$60,500$ in year-2 dollars, and so on. If we discount these nominal cash flows at the 15% nominal discount rate, we have

$$NPV = -100 + \frac{38.5}{1.15} + \frac{60.5}{(1.15)^2} + \frac{39.9}{(1.15)^3} = 5.5, \text{ or } \$5,500$$

Instead of converting the cash-flow forecasts into nominal terms, we could convert the discount rate into real terms by using the following relationship: $(1 + \text{nominal rate}) = (1 + \text{real rate})(1 + \text{inflation rate})$

$$\text{Real discount rate} = \frac{1 + \text{nominal discount rate}}{1 + \text{inflation rate}} - 1$$

In our example this gives

$$\text{Real discount rate} = \frac{1.15}{1.10} - 1 = .045, \text{ or } 4.5\%$$

If we now discount the real cash flows by the real discount rate, we have an NPV of $5,500, just as before:

$$NPV = -100 + \frac{35}{1.045} + \frac{50}{(1.045)^2} + \frac{30}{(1.045)^3} = 5.5, \text{ or } \$5,500$$

The message of all this is quite simple. Discount nominal cash flows at a nominal discount rate. Discount real cash flows at a real rate. *Never* mix real cash flows with nominal discount rates or nominal flows with real rates.

7.2 EXAMPLE—IM&C'S FERTILIZER PROJECT

As the newly appointed financial manager of International Mulch and Compost Company (IM&C), you are about to analyze a proposal for marketing guano as a garden fertilizer. (IM&C's planned advertising campaign features a rustic gentleman who steps out of a vegetable patch singing, "All my troubles have guano way.")[1]

---

[1] Sorry.

		Period							
		0	**1**	**2**	**3**	**4**	**5**	**6**	**7**
1	Capital investment	10,000							-1,949[a]
2	Accumulated depreciation		1,583	3,167	4,750	6,333	7,917	9,500	0
3	Year-end book value	10,000	8,417	6,833	5,250	3,667	2,083	500	0
4	Working capital		550	1,289	3,261	4,890	3,583	2,002	0
5	Total book value (3 + 4)		8,967	8,122	8,511	8,557	5,666	2,502	0
6	Sales		523	12,887	32,610	48,901	35,834	19,717	
7	Cost of goods sold[b]		837	7,729	19,552	29,345	21,492	11,830	
8	Other costs[c]	4,000	2,200	1,210	1,331	1,464	1,611	1,772	
9	Depreciation		1,583	1,583	1,583	1,583	1,583	1,583	0
10	Pretax profit (6 - 7 - 8 - 9)	-4,000	-4,097	2,365	10,144	16,509	11,148	4,532	1,449[d]
11	Tax at 35%	-1,400	-1,434	828	3,550	5,778	3,902	1,586	507
12	Profit after tax (10 - 11)	-2,600	-2,663	1,537	6,593	10,731	7,246	2,946	942

TABLE 7.1

IM&C's guano project—projections ($ thousands) reflecting inflation and assuming straight-line depreciation.

[a] Salvage value.
[b] We have departed from the usual income-statement format by *not* including depreciation in cost of goods sold. Instead, we break out depreciation separately (see line 9).
[c] Start-up costs in years 0 and 1, and general and administrative costs in years 1 to 6.
[d] The difference between the salvage value and the ending book value of $500 is a taxable profit.

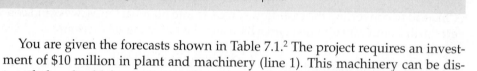

eXcel

Visit us at
www.mhhe.com/bma1e.

You are given the forecasts shown in Table 7.1.[2] The project requires an investment of $10 million in plant and machinery (line 1). This machinery can be dismantled and sold for net proceeds estimated at $1.949 million in year 7 (line 1, column 7). This amount is your forecast of the plant's *salvage value.*

Whoever prepared Table 7.1 depreciated the capital investment over six years to an arbitrary salvage value of $500,000, which is less than your forecast of salvage value. *Straight-line depreciation* was assumed. Under this method annual depreciation equals a constant proportion of the initial investment less salvage value ($9.5 million). If we call the depreciable life T, then the straight-line depreciation in year t is

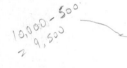

Depreciation in year $t = 1/T \times$ depreciable amount $= 1/6 \times 9.5 = \$1.583$ million

Lines 6 through 12 in Table 7.1 show a simplified income statement for the guano project.[3] This will be our starting point for estimating cash flow. All the entries in the table are nominal amounts. In other words, IM&C's managers have taken into account the likely effect of inflation on prices and costs.

Table 7.2 derives cash-flow forecasts from the investment and income data given in Table 7.1. Cash flow from operations is defined as sales less cost of goods sold, other costs, and taxes. The remaining cash flows include the changes in working capital, the initial capital investment, and the recovery of your estimated salvage value. If, as you expect, the salvage value turns out higher than the depreciated value of the machinery, you will have to pay tax on the difference. So you must also include this figure in your cash-flow forecast.

---

[2] "Live" Excel versions of Tables 7.1, 7.2, 7.4, 7.5, and 7.6 are available on the book's Web site, **www.mhhe.com/bma1e.**

[3] We have departed from the usual income-statement format by separating depreciation from costs of goods sold.

		Period							
		0	1	2	3	4	5	6	7
1	Sales		523	12,887	32,610	48,901	35,834	19,717	
2	Cost of goods sold		837	7,729	19,552	29,345	21,492	11,830	
3	Other costs	4,000	2,200	1,210	1,331	1,464	1,611	1,772	
4	Tax on operations	-1,400	-1,434	828	3,550	5,778	3,902	1,586	
5	Cash flow from operations (1 - 2 - 3 - 4)	-2,600	-1,080	3,120	8,177	12,314	8,829	4,529	
6	Change in working capital		-550	-739	-1,972	-1,629	1,307	1,581	2,002
7	Capital investment and disposal	-10,000							1,442[a]
8	Net cash flow (5 + 6 + 7)	-12,600	-1,630	2,381	6,205	10,685	10,136	6,110	3,444
9	Present value at 20%	-12,600	-1,358	1,654	3,591	5,153	4,074	2,046	961
	Net present value =	+3,520 (sum of 9)							

TABLE 7.2

Visit us at
www.mhhe.com/bma1e.

IM&C's guano project—initial cash-flow analysis assuming straight-line depreciation ($ thousands).

[a] Salvage value of $1,949 less tax of $507 on the difference between salvage value and ending book value.

$$\hookrightarrow (1,949 - 500) \times 0.35$$

IM&C estimates the nominal opportunity cost of capital for projects of this type as 20%. When all cash flows are added up and discounted, the guano project is seen to offer a net present value of about $3.5 million:

$$NPV = -12,600 - \frac{1,630}{1.20} + \frac{2,381}{(1.20)^2} + \frac{6,205}{(1.20)^3} + \frac{10,685}{(1.20)^4} + \frac{10,136}{(1.20)^5}$$
$$+ \frac{6,110}{(1.20)^6} + \frac{3,444}{(1.20)^7} = +3,520, \text{ or } \$3,520,000$$

Separating Investment and Financing Decisions

Our analysis of the guano project takes no notice of how that project is financed. It may be that IM&C will decide to finance partly by debt, but if it does we will not subtract the debt proceeds from the required investment, nor will we recognize interest and principal payments as cash outflows. We analyze the project as if it were all-equity-financed, treating all cash outflows as coming from stockholders and all cash inflows as going to them.

We approach the problem in this way so that we can separate the analysis of the investment decision from the financing decision. But this does not mean that the financing decision can be ignored. We will explain in Chapter 16 how to recognize the effect of financing choices on project values.

Investments in Working Capital

Now here is an important point. You can see from line 6 of Table 7.2 that working capital increases in the early and middle years of the project. What is working capital? you may ask, and why does it increase?

Working capital summarizes the net investment in short-term assets associated with a firm, business, or project. Its most important components are *inventory, accounts receivable,* and *accounts payable.* The guano project's requirements for working capital in year 2 might be as follows:

$$\text{Working capital} = \text{inventory} + \text{accounts receivable} - \text{accounts payable}$$
$$\$1{,}289 \quad = \quad 635 \quad + \quad 1{,}030 \quad - \quad 376$$

Why does working capital increase? There are several possibilities:

1. Sales recorded on the income statement overstate actual cash receipts from guano shipments because sales are increasing and customers are slow to pay their bills. Therefore, accounts receivable increase.
2. It takes several months for processed guano to age properly. Thus, as projected sales increase, larger inventories have to be held in the aging sheds.
3. An offsetting effect occurs if payments for materials and services used in guano production are delayed. In this case accounts payable will increase.

The additional investment in working capital from year 2 to 3 might be

$$\begin{array}{ccccccc} \text{Additional} & & & & \text{increase in} & & \text{increase in} \\ \text{investment in} & = & \text{increase in} & + & \text{accounts} & - & \text{accounts} \\ \text{working capital} & & \text{inventory} & & \text{receivable} & & \text{payable} \\ \$1{,}972 & = & 972 & + & 1{,}500 & - & 500 \end{array}$$

A more detailed cash-flow forecast for year 3 would look like Table 7.3.

Working capital is one of the most common sources of confusion in estimating project cash flows. Here are the most common mistakes:

1. *Forgetting about working capital entirely.* We hope you never fall into that trap.
2. *Forgetting that working capital may change during the life of the project.* Imagine that you sell $100,000 of goods one year and that customers pay six months late. You will therefore have $50,000 of unpaid bills. Now you increase prices by 10%, so revenues increase to $110,000. If customers continue to pay six months late, unpaid bills increase to $55,000, and therefore you need to make an *additional* investment in working capital of $5,000.
3. *Forgetting that working capital is recovered at the end of the project.* When the project comes to an end, inventories are run down, any unpaid bills are

Cash Flows		Data from Forecasted Income Statement		Working-Capital Changes
Cash inflow	=	Sales	−	Increase in accounts receivable
$31,110	=	32,610	−	1,500
Cash outflow	=	Cost of goods sold, other costs, and taxes	+	Increase in inventory net of increase in accounts payable
$24,905	=	(19,552 + 1,331 + 3,550)	+	(972 − 500)
		Net cash flow = cash inflow − cash outflow		
		$6,205 = 31,110 − 24,905		

TABLE 7.3

Details of cash-flow forecast for IM&C's guano project in year 3 ($ thousands).

(you hope) paid off, and you recover your investment in working capital. This generates a cash *inflow*.

There is an alternative to worrying about changes in working capital. You can estimate cash flow directly by counting the dollars coming in from customers and deducting the dollars going out to suppliers. You would also deduct all cash spent on production, including cash spent for goods held in inventory. In other words,

1. If you replace each year's sales with that year's cash payments received from customers, you don't have to worry about accounts receivable.
2. If you replace cost of goods sold with cash payments for labor, materials, and other costs of production, you don't have to keep track of inventory or accounts payable.

However, you would still have to construct a projected income statement to estimate taxes.

We discuss the links between cash flow and working capital in much greater detail in Chapter 20.

A Further Note on Depreciation

Depreciation is a noncash expense; it is important only because it reduces taxable income. It provides an annual *tax shield* equal to the product of depreciation and the marginal tax rate:

$$\text{Tax shield} = \text{depreciation} \times \text{tax rate}$$
$$= 1{,}583 \times .35 = 554, \text{ or } \$554{,}000$$

The present value of the tax shields ($554,000 for six years) is $1,842,000 at a 20% discount rate.

Now if IM&C could just get those tax shields sooner, they would be worth more, right? Fortunately tax law allows corporations to do just that: It allows *accelerated depreciation*.

The current rules for tax depreciation in the United States were set by the Tax Reform Act of 1986, which established a Modified Accelerated Cost Recovery System (MACRS). Table 7.4 summarizes the tax depreciation schedules. Note that there are six schedules, one for each recovery period class. Most industrial equipment falls into the five- and seven-year classes. To keep things simple, we will assume that all the guano project's investment goes into five-year assets. Thus, IM&C can write off 20% of its depreciable investment in year 1, as soon as the assets are placed in service, then 32% of depreciable investment in year 2, and so on. Here are the tax shields for the guano project:

	Year					
	1	**2**	**3**	**4**	**5**	**6**
Tax depreciation (MACRS percentage × depreciable investment)	2,000	3,200	1,920	1,152	1,152	576
Tax shield (tax depreciation × tax rate, $T_c = .35$)	700	1,120	672	403	403	202

Year(s)	3-year	5-year	7-year	10-year	15-year	20-year
			Tax Depreciation Schedules by Recovery-Period Class			
1	33.33	20.00	14.29	10.00	5.00	3.75
2	44.45	32.00	24.49	18.00	9.50	7.22
3	14.81	19.20	17.49	14.40	8.55	6.68
4	7.41	11.52	12.49	11.52	7.70	6.18
5		11.52	8.93	9.22	6.93	5.71
6		5.76	8.92	7.37	6.23	5.28
7			8.93	6.55	5.90	4.89
8			4.45	6.55	5.90	4.52
9				6.56	5.90	4.46
10				6.55	5.90	4.46
11				3.29	5.90	4.46
12					5.90	4.46
13					5.91	4.46
14					5.90	4.46
15					5.91	4.46
16					2.99	4.46
17-20						4.46
21						2.23

Visit us at
www.mhhe.com/bma1e.

TABLE 7.4

Tax depreciation allowed under the modified accelerated cost recovery system
(MACRS) (figures in percent of depreciable investment).

Notes:
1. Tax depreciation is lower in the first and last years because assets are assumed to be in
   service for only six months.
2. Real property is depreciated straight-line over 27.5 years for residential property and
   31.5 years for nonresidential property.

The present value of these tax shields is $2,174,000, about $331,000 higher than
under the straight-line method.

Table 7.5 recalculates the guano project's impact on IM&C's future tax bills, and
Table 7.6 shows revised after-tax cash flows and present value. This time we have
incorporated realistic assumptions about taxes as well as inflation. We of course
arrive at a higher NPV than in Table 7.2, because that table ignored the additional
present value of accelerated depreciation.

There is one possible additional problem lurking in the woodwork behind Table
7.5: In the United States there is an *alternative minimum tax,* which can limit or
defer the tax shields of accelerated depreciation or other *tax preference* items. We
would rather not get into the intricacies of the alternative minimum tax here, but
make a mental note not to sign off on a capital budgeting analysis without checking whether your company is subject to this tax.

A Final Comment on Taxes

All large U.S. corporations keep two separate sets of books, one for stockholders
and one for the Internal Revenue Service. It is common to use straight-line depreciation on the stockholder books and accelerated depreciation on the tax books.
The IRS doesn't object to this, and it makes the firm's reported earnings higher

					Period			
		0	1	2	3	4	5	6	7
1	Sales[a]		523	12,887	32,610	48,901	35,834	19,717	
2	Cost of goods sold[a]		837	7,729	19,552	29,345	21,492	11,830	
3	Other costs[a]	4,000	2,200	1,210	1,331	1,464	1,611	1,772	
4	Tax depreciation		2,000	3,200	1,920	1,152	1,152	576	
5	Pretax profit (1 - 2 - 3 - 4)	-4,000	-4,514	748	9,807	16,940	11,579	5,539	1,949[b]
6	Tax at 35%[c]	-1,400	-1,580	262	3,432	5,929	4,053	1,939	682

TABLE 7.5

eXcel

Visit us at
www.mhhe.com/bma1e.

Tax payments on IM&C's guano project ($ thousands).

[a] From Table 7.1.
[b] Salvage value is zero, for tax purposes, after all tax depreciation has been taken. Thus, IM&C will have to pay tax on the full salvage value of $1,949.
[c] A negative tax payment means a cash *inflow*, assuming IM&C can use the tax loss on its guano project to shield income from other projects.

					Period			
	0	1	2	3	4	5	6	7
Sales[a]		523	12,887	32,610	48,901	35,834	19,717	
Cost of goods sold[a]		837	7,729	19,552	29,345	21,492	11,830	
Other costs[a]	4,000	2,200	1,210	1,331	1,464	1,611	1,772	
Tax[b]	-1,400	-1,580	262	3,432	5,929	4,053	1,939	682
Cash flow from operations (1 - 2 - 3 - 4)	-2,600	-934	3,686	8,295	12,163	8,678	4,176	-682
Change in working capital		-550	-739	-1,972	-1,629	1,307	1,581	2,002
Capital investment and disposal	-10,000							1,949[a]
Net cash flow (5 + 6 + 7)	-12,600	-1,484	2,947	6,323	10,534	9,985	5,757	3,269
Present value at 20%	-12,600	-1,237	2,047	3,659	5,080	4,013	1,928	912
Net present value =	3,802	(sum of 9)						

TABLE 7.6

eXcel

Visit us at
www.mhhe.com/bma1e.

IM&C's guano project—revised cash-flow analysis ($ thousands).

[a] From Table 7.1.
[b] From Table 7.5.

than if accelerated depreciation were used everywhere. There are many other differences between tax books and shareholder books.[4]

The financial analyst must be careful to remember which set of books he or she is looking at. In capital budgeting only the tax books are relevant, but to an outside analyst only the shareholder books are available.

---

[4] This separation of tax accounts from shareholder accounts is not found worldwide. In Japan, for example, taxes reported to shareholders must equal taxes paid to the government; ditto for France and many other European countries.

Project Analysis

Let us review. Several pages ago, you embarked on an analysis of IM&C's guano project. You started with a simplified statement of assets and income for the project that you used to develop a series of cash-flow forecasts. Then you remembered accelerated depreciation and had to recalculate cash flows and NPV.

You were lucky to get away with just two NPV calculations. In real situations, it often takes several tries to purge all inconsistencies and mistakes. Then you may want to analyze some alternatives. For example, should you go for a larger or smaller project? Would it be better to market the fertilizer through wholesalers or directly to the consumer? Should you build 90,000-square-foot aging sheds for the guano in northern South Dakota rather than the planned 100,000-square-foot sheds in southern North Dakota? In each case your choice should be the one offering the highest NPV. Sometimes the alternatives are not immediately obvious. For example, perhaps the plan calls for two costly high-speed packing lines. But, if demand for guano is seasonal, it may pay to install just one high-speed line to cope with the base demand and two slower but cheaper lines simply to cope with the summer rush. You won't know the answer until you have compared NPVs.

You will also need to ask some "what if" questions. How would NPV be affected if inflation rages out of control? What if technical problems delay start-up? What if gardeners prefer chemical fertilizers to your natural product? Managers employ a variety of techniques to develop a better understanding of how such unpleasant surprises could damage NPV. For example, they might undertake a *sensitivity analysis*, in which they look at how far the project could be knocked off course by bad news about one of the variables. Or they might construct different *scenarios* and estimate the effect of each on NPV. Another technique, known as *break-even analysis*, is to explore how far sales could fall short of forecast before the project went into the red.

In Chapter 11 we will practice using each of these "what if" techniques. You will find that project analysis is much more than one or two NPV calculations.[5]

Calculating NPV in Other Countries and Currencies

Our guano project was undertaken in the United States by a U.S. company. But the principles of capital investment are the same worldwide. For example, suppose that you are the financial manager of the German company, K.G.R. Ökologische Naturdüngemittel GmbH (KGR), that is faced with a similar opportunity to make a €10 million investment in Germany. What changes?

1. KGR must also produce a set of cash-flow forecasts, but in this case the project cash flows are stated in euros, the Eurozone currency.
2. In developing these forecasts, the company needs to recognize that prices and costs will be influenced by the German inflation rate.
3. Profits from KGR's project are liable to the German rate of corporate tax.
4. KGR must use the German system of depreciation allowances. In common with many other countries, Germany allows firms to choose between two methods of depreciation—the straight-line system and the declining-balance system. KGR opts for the declining-balance method and writes off 30% of the depreciated value of the equipment each year (the maximum allowed under current German tax rules). Thus, in the first year, KGR writes off .30 × 10 = €3

---

[5] In the meantime you might like to get ahead of the game by viewing the live spreadsheets for the guano project and seeing how NPV would change with a shortfall in sales or an unexpected rise in costs.

million and the written-down value of the equipment falls to $10 - 3 = €7$ million. In year 2, KGR writes off $.30 × 7 = €2.1$ million and the written-down value is further reduced to $7 - 2.1 = €4.9$ million. In year 4 KGR observes that depreciation would be higher if it could switch to straight-line depreciation and write off the balance of €3.43 million over the remaining three years of the equipment's life. Fortunately, German tax law allows it to do this. Therefore, KGR's depreciation allowance each year is calculated as follows:

	Year					
	1	2	3	4	5	6
Written-down value, start of year (€ millions)	10	7	4.9	3.43	2.29	1.14
Depreciation (€ millions)	$.3 × 10$ $= 3$	$.3 × 7$ $= 2.1$	$.3 × 4.9$ $= 1.47$	$3.43/3$ $= 1.14$	$3.43/3$ $= 1.14$	$3.43/3$ $= 1.14$
Written-down value, end of year (€ millions)	$10 - 3$ $= 7$	$7 - 2.1$ $= 4.9$	$4.9 - 1.47$ $= 3.43$	$3.43 - 1.14$ $= 2.29$	$2.29 - 1.14$ $= 1.14$	$1.14 - 1.14$ $= 0$

Notice that KGR's depreciation deduction declines for the first few years and then flattens out. That is also the case with the U.S. MACRS system of depreciation. In fact, MACRS is just another example of the declining-balance method with a later switch to straight-line.

7.3 EQUIVALENT ANNUAL COSTS

When you calculate NPV, you transform future, year-by-year cash flows into a lump-sum value expressed in today's dollars (or euros, or other relevant currency). But sometimes it's helpful to reverse the calculation, transforming an investment today into an equivalent stream of future cash flows. Consider the following example.

Investing to Produce Reformulated Gasoline at California Refineries

In the early 1990s, the California Air Resources Board (CARB) started planning its "Phase 2" requirements for reformulated gasoline (RFG). RFG is gasoline blended to tight specifications designed to reduce pollution from motor vehicles. CARB consulted with refiners, environmentalists, and other interested parties to design these specifications.

As the outline for the Phase 2 requirements emerged, refiners realized that substantial capital investments would be required to upgrade California refineries. What might these investments mean for the retail price of gasoline? A refiner might ask: "Suppose my company invests $400 million to upgrade our refinery to meet Phase 2. How much extra revenue would we need every year to recover that cost?" Let's see if we can help the refiner out.

Assume $400 million of capital investment and a real (inflation-adjusted) cost of capital of 7%. The new equipment lasts for 25 years, and does not change raw-material and operating costs.

How much additional revenue does it take to cover the $400 million investment? The answer is simple: Just find the 25-year annuity with a present value equal to $400 million.

PV of annuity = annuity payment × 25-year annuity factor

At a 7% cost of capital, the 25-year annuity factor is 11.65.

$$\$400 \text{ million} = \text{annuity payment} \times 11.65$$
$$\text{Annuity payment} = \$34.3 \text{ million per year}[6]$$

This annuity is called an **equivalent annual cost.** Equivalent annual cost is the annual cash flow sufficient to recover a capital investment, including the cost of capital for that investment, over the investment's economic life.

Equivalent annual costs are handy—and sometimes essential—tools of finance. Here is a further example.

Choosing Between Long- and Short-Lived Equipment

Suppose the firm is forced to choose between two machines, A and B. The two machines are designed differently but have identical capacity and do exactly the same job. Machine A costs $15,000 and will last three years. It costs $5,000 per year to run. Machine B is an economy model costing only $10,000, but it will last only two years and costs $6,000 per year to run. These are real cash flows: The costs are forecasted in dollars of constant purchasing power.

Because the two machines produce exactly the same product, the only way to choose between them is on the basis of cost. Suppose we compute the present value of cost:

Machine	Costs ($ thousands)				PV at 6% ($ thousands)
	C_0	C_1	C_2	C_3	
A	+15	+5	+5	+5	28.37
B	+10	+6	+6		21.00

Should we take machine B, the one with the lower present value of costs? Not necessarily, because B will have to be replaced a year earlier than A. In other words, the timing of a future investment decision is contingent on today's choice of A or B.

So, a machine with total PV(costs) of $21,000 spread over three years (0, 1, and 2) is not necessarily better than a competing machine with PV(costs) of $28,370 spread over four years (0 through 3). We have to convert total PV(costs) to a cost per year, that is, to an equivalent annual cost. For machine A, the annual cost turns out to be 10.61, or $10,610 per year:

Machine	Costs ($ thousands)				PV at 6% ($ thousands)
	C_0	C_1	C_2	C_3	
Machine A	+15	+5	+5	+5	28.37
Equivalent annual cost		+10.61	+10.61	+10.61	28.37

---

[6] For simplicity we have ignored taxes. Taxes would enter this calculation in two ways. First, the $400 million investment would generate depreciation tax shields. The easiest way to handle these tax shields is to calculate their PV and subtract it from the initial outlay. For example, if the PV of depreciation tax shields is $83 million, equivalent annual cost would be calculated on an after-tax investment base of $400 − 83 = $317 million. Second, our annuity payment is after-tax. To actually achieve after-tax revenues of, say, $34.3 million, the refiner would have to achieve pretax revenue sufficient to pay tax and have $34.3 million left over. If the tax rate is 35%, the required pretax revenue is 34.3/(1 − .35) = $52.8 million. Note how the after-tax figure is "grossed up" by dividing by one minus the tax rate.

We calculated the equivalent annual cost by finding the three-year annuity with the same present value as A's lifetime costs.

$$\text{PV of annuity} = \text{PV of A's costs} = 28.37$$
$$= \text{annuity payment} \times \text{three-year annuity factor}$$

The annuity factor is 2.673 for three years and a 6% real cost of capital, so

$$\text{Annuity payment} = \frac{28.37}{2.673} = 10.61$$

A similar calculation for machine B gives:

	Costs ($ thousands)			
	C_0	C_1	C_2	PV at 6% ($ thousands)
Machine B	+10	+6	+6	21.00
Equivalent annual cost		+11.45	+11.45	21.00

Machine A is better, because its equivalent annual cost is less ($10,610 versus $11,450 for machine B).

You can think of the equivalent annual cost of machine A or B as an annual rental charge. Suppose the financial manager is asked to *rent* machine A to the plant manager actually in charge of production. There will be three equal rental payments starting in year 1. The three payments must recover both the original cost of machine A in year 0 and the cost of running it in years 1 to 3. Therefore the financial manager has to make sure that the rental payments are worth $28,370, the total PV(costs) of machine A. You can see that the financial manager would calculate a fair rental payment equal to machine A's equivalent annual cost.

Our rule for choosing between plant and equipment with different economic lives is, therefore, to select the asset with the lowest fair rental charge, that is, the lowest equivalent annual cost.

Equivalent Annual Cost and Inflation   The equivalent annual costs we just calculated are *real* annuities based on forecasted *real* costs and a 6% *real* discount rate. We could, of course, restate the annuities in nominal terms. Suppose the expected inflation rate is 5%; we multiply the first cash flow of the annuity by 1.05, the second by $(1.05)^2 = 1.105$, and so on.

		C_0	C_1	C_2	C_3
A	Real annuity		10.61	10.61	10.61
	Nominal cash flow		11.14	11.70	12.28
B	Real annuity		11.45	11.45	
	Nominal cash flow		12.02	12.62	

Note that B is still inferior to A. Of course the present values of the nominal and real cash flows are identical. Just remember to discount the real annuity at the real rate and the equivalent nominal cash flows at the consistent nominal rate.[7]

---

[7] The nominal discount rate is

$$r_{nominal} = (1 + r_{real})(1 + \text{inflation rate}) - 1$$
$$= (1.06)(1.05) - 1 = .113, \text{ or } 11.3\%$$

Discounting the nominal annuities at this rate gives the same present values as discounting the real annuities at 6%.

When you use equivalent annual costs simply for comparison of costs per period, as we did for machines A and B, we strongly recommend doing the calculations in real terms.[8] But if you actually rent out the machine to the plant manager, or anyone else, be careful to specify that the rental payments be "indexed" to inflation. If inflation runs on at 5% per year and rental payments do not increase proportionally, then the real value of the rental payments must decline and will not cover the full cost of buying and operating the machine.

Equivalent Annual Cost and Technological Change   So far we have the following simple rule: Two or more streams of cash outflows with different lengths or time patterns can be compared by converting their present values to equivalent annual costs. Just remember to do the calculations in real terms.

Now any rule this simple cannot be completely general. For example, when we evaluated machine A versus machine B, we implicitly assumed that their fair rental charges would *continue* at $10,610 versus $11,450. This will be so only if the *real* costs of buying and operating the machines stay the same.

Suppose that this is not the case. Suppose that thanks to technological improvements new machines each year cost 20% less in real terms to buy and operate. In this case future owners of brand-new, lower-cost machines will be able to cut their rental cost by 20%, and owners of old machines will be forced to match this reduction. Thus, we now need to ask: If the real level of rents declines by 20% a year, how much will it cost to rent each machine?

If the rent for year 1 is $rent_1$, rent for year 2 is $rent_2 = .8 \times rent_1$. $Rent_3$ is $.8 \times rent_2$, or $.64 \times rent_1$. The owner of each machine must set the rents sufficiently high to recover the present value of the costs. In the case of machine A,

$$\text{PV of renting machine A} = \frac{rent_1}{1.06} + \frac{rent_2}{(1.06)^2} + \frac{rent_3}{(1.06)^3} = 28.37$$

$$= \frac{rent_1}{1.06} + \frac{.8(rent_1)}{(1.06)^2} + \frac{.64(rent_1)}{(1.06)^3} = 28.37$$

$$rent_1 = 12.94, \text{ or } \$12,940$$

For machine B,

$$\text{PV of renting machine B} = \frac{rent_1}{1.06} + \frac{.8(rent_1)}{(1.06)^2} = 21.00$$

$$rent_1 = 12.69, \text{ or } \$12,690$$

The merits of the two machines are now reversed. Once we recognize that technology is expected to reduce the real costs of new machines, then it pays to buy the shorter-lived machine B rather than become locked into an aging technology with machine A in year 3.

You can imagine other complications. Perhaps machine C will arrive in year 1 with an even lower equivalent annual cost. You would then need to consider scrapping or selling machine B at year 1 (more on this decision below). The financial manager could not choose between machines A and B in year 0 without taking a detailed look at what each machine could be replaced with.

---

[8] Do *not* calculate equivalent annual costs as level *nominal* annuities. This procedure can give incorrect rankings of true equivalent annual costs at high inflation rates. See Challenge Question 28 at the end of this chapter for an example.

Comparing equivalent annual costs should never be a mechanical exercise; always think about the assumptions that are implicit in the comparison. Finally, remember why equivalent annual costs are necessary in the first place. The reason is that A and B will be replaced at different future dates. The choice between them therefore affects future investment decisions. If subsequent decisions are not affected by the initial choice (for example, because neither machine will be replaced) then we do *not need to take future decisions into account.*[9]

Equivalent Annual Cost and Taxes   We have not mentioned taxes. But you surely realized that machine A and B's lifetime costs should be calculated after-tax, recognizing that operating costs are tax-deductible and that capital investment generates depreciation tax shields.

Deciding When to Replace an Existing Machine

The previous example took the life of each machine as fixed. In practice the point at which equipment is replaced reflects economic considerations rather than total physical collapse. *We* must decide when to replace. The machine will rarely decide for us.

Here is a common problem. You are operating an elderly machine that is expected to produce a net cash *inflow* of $4,000 in the coming year and $4,000 next year. After that it will give up the ghost. You can replace it now with a new machine, which costs $15,000 but is much more efficient and will provide a cash inflow of $8,000 a year for three years. You want to know whether you should replace your equipment now or wait a year.

We can calculate the NPV of the new machine and also its *equivalent annual cash flow,* that is, the three-year annuity that has the same net present value:

	Cash Flows ($ thousands)				
	C_0	C_1	C_2	C_3	NPV at 6% ($ thousands)
New machine	−15	+8	+8	+8	6.38
Equivalent annual cash flow		+2.387	+2.387	+2.387	6.38

In other words, the cash flows of the new machine are equivalent to an annuity of $2,387 per year. So we can equally well ask at what point we would want to replace our old machine with a new one producing $2,387 a year. When the question is put this way, the answer is obvious. As long as your old machine can generate a cash flow of $4,000 a year, who wants to put in its place a new one that generates only $2,387 a year?

It is a simple matter to incorporate salvage values into this calculation. Suppose that the current salvage value is $8,000 and next year's value is $7,000. Let us see where you come out next year if you wait and then sell. On one hand, you gain $7,000, but you lose today's salvage value *plus* a year's return on that money. That is, $8,000 \times 1.06 = \$8,480$. Your net loss is $8,480 - 7,000 = \$1,480$, which only partly offsets the operating gain. You should not replace yet.

---

[9] However, if neither machine will be replaced, then we have to consider the extra revenue generated by machine A in its third year, when it will be operating but B will not.

Remember that the logic of such comparisons requires that the new machine be the best of the available alternatives and that it in turn be replaced at the optimal point.

Cost of Excess Capacity   Any firm with a centralized information system (computer servers, storage, software, and telecommunication links) encounters many proposals for using it. Recently installed systems tend to have excess capacity, and since the immediate marginal costs of using them seem to be negligible, management often encourages new uses. Sooner or later, however, the load on a system increases to the point at which management must either terminate the uses it originally encouraged or invest in another system several years earlier than it had planned. Such problems can be avoided if a proper charge is made for the use of spare capacity.

Suppose we have a new investment project that requires heavy use of an existing information system. The effect of adopting the project is to bring the purchase date of a new, more capable system forward from year 4 to year 3. This new system has a life of five years, and at a discount rate of 6% the present value of the cost of buying and operating it is $500,000.

We begin by converting the $500,000 present value of cost of the new system to an equivalent annual cost of $118,700 for each of five years.[10] Of course, when the new system in turn wears out, we will replace it with another. So we face the prospect of future information-system expenses of $118,700 a year. If we undertake the new project, the series of expenses begins in year 4; if we do not undertake it, the series begins in year 5. The new project, therefore, results in an *additional* cost of $118,700 in year 4. This has a present value of $118,700/(1.06)^4$, or about $94,000. This cost is properly charged against the new project. When we recognize it, the NPV of the project may prove to be negative. If so, we still need to check whether it is worthwhile undertaking the project now and abandoning it later, when the excess capacity of the present system disappears.

---

[10] The present value of $118,700 a year for five years discounted at 6% is $500,000.

SUMMARY

By now present value calculations should be a matter of routine. However, forecasting project cash flows will never be routine. Here is a checklist that will help you to avoid mistakes:

1. Discount cash flows, not profits.
   a. Remember that depreciation is not a cash flow (though it may affect tax payments).
   b. Concentrate on cash flows after taxes. Stay alert for differences between tax depreciation and depreciation used in reports to shareholders.
   c. Exclude debt interest or the cost of repaying a loan from the project cash flows. This enables you to separate the investment from the financing decision.
   d. Remember the investment in working capital. As sales increase, the firm may need to make additional investments in working capital, and as the project comes to an end, it will recover those investments.
   e. Beware of allocated overhead charges for heat, light, and so on. These may not reflect the incremental costs of the project.

2. Estimate the project's *incremental* cash flows—that is, the difference between the cash flows with the project and those without the project.

   a. Include all indirect effects of the project, such as its impact on the sales of the firm's other products.

   b. Forget sunk costs.

   c. Include *opportunity costs,* such as the value of land that you would otherwise sell.

3. Treat inflation consistently.

   a. If cash flows are forecasted in nominal terms, use a nominal discount rate.

   b. Discount real cash flows at a real rate.

These principles of valuing capital investments are the same worldwide, but inputs and assumptions vary by country and currency. For example, cash flows from a project in Germany would be in euros, not dollars, and would be forecasted after German taxes.

   When we assessed the guano project, we transformed the series of future cash flows into a single measure of their present value. Sometimes it is useful to reverse this calculation and to convert the present value into a stream of annual cash flows. For example, when choosing between two machines with unequal lives, you need to ask which one has the lower equivalent annual cost. Think of this equivalent annual cost as the regular rental payment that the financial manager would need to charge for use of the machine. Choose machine A over B, other things equal, if A has the lower equivalent annual cost. Remember, though, to calculate equivalent annual costs in real terms and adjust for technological change if necessary.

Visit us at www.mhhe.com/bma1e

CONCEPT REVIEW QUESTIONS

1. Why should the financial manager *include* opportunity costs but *ignore* sunk costs when evaluating a proposed capital investment? Give an example of each case. (pages 145–146)

2. Suppose a forgetful manager makes the mistake of discounting nominal project cash flows at a real discount rate. Inflation is projected at 4% per year. Does the manager overestimate or underestimate NPV? Assume that the project's NPV is positive with proper discounting. (pages 146–147)

3. What does it mean to "separate investment and financing decisions"? Are interest payments treated as an expense in a standard NPV analysis? (page 149)

For a complete listing of your chapter Concept Review Questions, please visit us at www.mhhe.com/bma1e.

QUIZ

1. Which of the following should be treated as incremental cash flows when deciding whether to invest in a new manufacturing plant? The site is already owned by the company, but existing buildings would need to be demolished.

   a. The market value of the site and existing buildings.

   b. Demolition costs and site clearance.

   c. The cost of a new access road put in last year.

   d. Lost earnings on other products due to executive time spent on the new facility.

   e. A proportion of the cost of leasing the president's jet airplane.

f. Future depreciation of the new plant.

g. The reduction in the corporation's tax bill resulting from tax depreciation of the new plant.

h. The initial investment in inventories of raw materials.

i. Money already spent on engineering design of the new plant.

2. Mr. Art Deco will be paid $100,000 one year hence. This is a nominal flow, which he discounts at an 8% nominal discount rate:

$$PV = \frac{100,000}{1.08} = \$92,593$$

The inflation rate is 4%.

Calculate the PV of Mr. Deco's payment using the equivalent *real* cash flow and *real* discount rate. (*Hint:* You should get exactly the same answer as he did.)

3. True or false?

a. A project's depreciation tax shields depend on the actual future rate of inflation.

b. Project cash flows should take account of interest paid on any borrowing undertaken to finance the project.

c. In the U.S., income reported to the tax authorities must equal income reported to shareholders.

d. Accelerated depreciation reduces near-term project cash flows and therefore reduces project NPV.

4. How does the PV of depreciation tax shields vary across the recovery-period classes shown in Table 7.4? Give a general answer; then check it by calculating the PVs of depreciation tax shields in the five-year and seven-year classes. The tax rate is 35% and the discount rate is 10%.

5. The following table tracks the main components of working capital over the life of a four-year project.

	2007	2008	2009	2010	2011
Accounts receivable	0	150,000	225,000	190,000	0
Inventory	75,000	130,000	130,000	95,000	0
Accounts payable	25,000	50,000	50,000	35,000	0

Calculate net working capital and the cash inflows and outflows due to investment in working capital.

6. When appraising mutually exclusive investments in plant and equipment, financial managers calculate the investments' equivalent annual costs and rank the investments on this basis. Why is this necessary? Why not just compare the investments' NPVs? Explain briefly.

7. Air conditioning for a college dormitory will cost $1.5 million to install and $200,000 per year to operate. The system should last 25 years. The real cost of capital is 5%, and the college pays no taxes. What is the equivalent annual cost?

8. Machines A and B are mutually exclusive and are expected to produce the following real cash flows:

Machine	Cash Flows ($ thousands)			
	C_0	C_1	C_2	C_3
A	−100	+110	+121	
B	−120	+110	+121	+133

The real opportunity cost of capital is 10%.

a. Calculate the NPV of each machine.

b. Calculate the equivalent annual cash flow from each machine.

c. Which machine should you buy?

9. Machine C was purchased five years ago for $200,000 and produces an annual cash flow of $80,000. It has no salvage value but is expected to last another five years. The company can replace machine C with machine B (see Quiz Question 8) *either* now *or* at the end of five years. Which should it do?

PRACTICE QUESTIONS

10. Restate the net cash flows in Table 7.6 in real terms. Discount the restated cash flows at a real discount rate. Assume a 20% *nominal* rate and 10% expected inflation. NPV should be unchanged at +3,802, or $3,802,000.

11. In 1898 Simon North announced plans to construct a funeral home on land he owned and rented out as a storage area for railway carts. (A local newspaper commended Mr. North for not putting the cart before the hearse.) Rental income from the site barely covered real estate taxes, but the site was valued at $45,000. However, Mr. North had refused several offers for the land and planned to continue renting it out if for some reason the funeral home was not built. Therefore he did not include the value of the land as an outlay in his NPV analysis of the funeral home. Was this the correct procedure? Explain.

12. Each of the following statements is true. Explain why they are consistent.

a. When a company introduces a new product, or expands production of an existing product, investment in net working capital is usually an important cash outflow.

b. Forecasting changes in net working capital is not necessary if the timing of *all* cash inflows and outflows is carefully specified.

13. Ms. T. Potts, the treasurer of Ideal China, has a problem. The company has just ordered a new kiln for $400,000. Of this sum, $50,000 is described by the supplier as an installation cost. Ms. Potts does not know whether the Internal Revenue Service (IRS) will permit the company to treat this cost as a tax-deductible current expense or as a capital investment. In the latter case, the company could depreciate the $50,000 using the five-year MACRS tax depreciation schedule. How will the IRS's decision affect the after-tax cost of the kiln? The tax rate is 35% and the opportunity cost of capital is 5%.

Visit us at www.mhhe.com/bma1e.

14. A project requires an initial investment of $100,000 and is expected to produce a cash inflow before tax of $26,000 per year for five years. Company A has substantial accumulated tax losses and is unlikely to pay taxes in the foreseeable future. Company B pays corporate taxes at a rate of 35% and can depreciate the investment for tax purposes using the five-year MACRS tax depreciation schedule. Suppose the opportunity cost of capital is 8%. Ignore inflation.

a. Calculate project NPV for each company.

b. What is the IRR of the after-tax cash flows for each company? What does comparison of the IRRs suggest is the effective corporate tax rate?

Visit us at www.mhhe.com/bma1e.

15. Go to the "live" Excel spreadsheet versions of Tables 7.1, 7.5, and 7.6 at **www.mhhe.com/bma1e.**

a. How does the guano project's NPV change if IM&C is forced to use the seven-year MACRS tax depreciation schedule?

b. New engineering estimates raise the possibility that capital investment will be more than $10 million, perhaps as much as $15 million. On the other hand, you believe that the 20% cost of capital is unrealistically high and that the true cost of capital is about 11%. Is the project still attractive under these alternative assumptions?

Visit us at www.mhhe.com/bma1e.

Visit us at www.mhhe.com/bma1e

c. Continue with the assumed $15 million capital investment and the 11% cost of capital. What if sales, cost of goods sold, and net working capital are each 10% higher in every year? Recalculate NPV. (*Note:* Enter the revised sales, cost, and working-capital forecasts in the spreadsheet for Table 7.1.)

16. A widget manufacturer currently produces 200,000 units a year. It buys widget lids from an outside supplier at a price of $2 a lid. The plant manager believes that it would be cheaper to make these lids rather than buy them. Direct production costs are estimated to be only $1.50 a lid. The necessary machinery would cost $150,000 and would last 10 years. This investment could be written off for tax purposes using the seven-year tax depreciation schedule. The plant manager estimates that the operation would require additional working capital of $30,000 but argues that this sum can be ignored since it is recoverable at the end of the 10 years. If the company pays tax at a rate of 35% and the opportunity cost of capital is 15%, would you support the plant manager's proposal? State clearly any additional assumptions that you need to make.

Visit us at
www.mhhe.com/bma1e.

17. Reliable Electric is considering a proposal to manufacture a new type of industrial electric motor which would replace most of its existing product line. A research breakthrough has given Reliable a two-year lead on its competitors. The project proposal is summarized in Table 7.7.

a. Read the notes to the table carefully. Which entries make sense? Which do not? Why or why not?

	2006	2007	2008	2009–2016
1. Capital expenditure	−10,400			
2. Research and development	−2,000			
3. Working capital	−4,000			
4. Revenue		8,000	16,000	40,000
5. Operating costs		−4,000	−8,000	−20,000
6. Overhead		−800	−1,600	−4,000
7. Depreciation		−1,040	−1,040	−1,040
8. Interest		−2,160	−2,160	−2,160
9. Income	−2,000	0	3,200	12,800
10. Tax	0	0	420	4,480
11. Net cash flow	−16,400	0	2,780	8,320
12. Net present value = +13,932				

TABLE 7.7

Cash flows and present value of Reliable Electric's proposed investment ($ thousands). See Practice Problem 17.

Notes:
1. *Capital expenditure:* $8 million for new machinery and $2.4 million for a warehouse extension. The full cost of the extension has been charged to this project, although only about half of the space is currently needed. Since the new machinery will be housed in an existing factory building, no charge has been made for land and building.
2. *Research and development:* $1.82 million spent in 2005. This figure was corrected for 10% inflation from the time of expenditure to date. Thus 1.82 × 1.1 = $2 million.
3. *Working capital:* Initial investment in inventories.
4. *Revenue:* These figures assume sales of 2,000 motors in 2007, 4,000 in 2008, and 10,000 per year from 2009 through 2016. The initial unit price of $4,000 is forecasted to remain constant in real terms.
5. *Operating costs:* These include all direct and indirect costs. Indirect costs (heat, light, power, fringe benefits, etc.) are assumed to be 200% of direct labor costs. Operating costs per unit are forecasted to remain constant in real terms at $2,000.
6. *Overhead:* Marketing and administrative costs, assumed equal to 10% of revenue.
7. *Depreciation:* Straight-line for 10 years.
8. *Interest:* Charged on capital expenditure and working capital at Reliable's current borrowing rate of 15%.
9. *Income:* Revenue less the sum of research and development, operating costs, overhead, depreciation, and interest.
10. *Tax:* 35% of income. However, income is negative in 2006. This loss is carried forward and deducted from taxable income in 2008.
11. *Net cash flow:* Assumed equal to income less tax.
12. *Net present value:* NPV of net cash flow at a 15% discount rate.

   b. What additional information would you need to construct a version of Table 7.7 that makes sense?

   c. Construct such a table and recalculate NPV. Make additional assumptions as necessary.

18. Marsha Jones has bought a used Mercedes horse transporter for her Connecticut estate. It cost $35,000. The object is to save on horse transporter rentals.

   Marsha had been renting a transporter every other week for $200 per day plus $1.00 per mile. Most of the trips are 80 or 100 miles in total. Marsha usually gives the driver a $40 tip. With the new transporter she will only have to pay for diesel fuel and maintenance, at about $.45 per mile. Insurance costs for Marsha's transporter are $1,200 per year.

   The transporter will probably be worth $15,000 (in real terms) after eight years, when Marsha's horse Nike will be ready to retire.

   Is the transporter a positive-NPV investment? Assume a nominal discount rate of 9% and a 3% forecasted inflation rate. Marsha's transporter is a personal outlay, not a business or financial investment, so taxes can be ignored.

19. United Pigpen is considering a proposal to manufacture high-protein hog feed. The project would make use of an existing warehouse, which is currently rented out to a neighboring firm. The next year's rental charge on the warehouse is $100,000, and thereafter the rent is expected to grow in line with inflation at 4% a year. In addition to using the warehouse, the proposal envisages an investment in plant and equipment of $1.2 million. This could be depreciated for tax purposes straight-line over 10 years. However, Pigpen expects to terminate the project at the end of eight years and to resell the plant and equipment in year 8 for $400,000. Finally, the project requires an initial investment in working capital of $350,000. Thereafter, working capital is forecasted to be 10% of sales in each of years 1 through 7.

   Year 1 sales of hog feed are expected to be $4.2 million, and thereafter sales are forecasted to grow by 5% a year, slightly faster than the inflation rate. Manufacturing costs are expected to be 90% of sales, and profits are subject to tax at 35%. The cost of capital is 12%.

   What is the NPV of Pigpen's project?

Visit us at
www.mhhe.com/bma1e.

20. In the International Mulch and Compost example (Section 7.2), we assumed that losses on the project could be used to offset taxable profits elswhere in the corporation. Suppose that the losses had to be carried forward and offset against future taxable profits from the project. How would the project NPV change? What is the value of the company's ability to use the tax deductions immediately?

21. As a result of improvements in product engineering, United Automation is able to sell one of its two milling machines. Both machines perform the same function but differ in age. The newer machine could be sold today for $50,000. Its operating costs are $20,000 a year, but in five years the machine will require a $20,000 overhaul. Thereafter operating costs will be $30,000 until the machine is finally sold in year 10 for $5,000.

   The older machine could be sold today for $25,000. If it is kept, it will need an immediate $20,000 overhaul. Thereafter operating costs will be $30,000 a year until the machine is finally sold in year 5 for $5,000.

   Both machines are fully depreciated for tax purposes. The company pays tax at 35%. Cash flows have been forecasted in real terms. The real cost of capital is 12%.

   Which machine should United Automation sell? Explain the assumptions underlying your answer.

22. Hayden Inc. has a number of copiers that were bought four years ago for $20,000. Currently maintenance costs $2,000 a year, but the maintenance agreement expires at the end of two years and thereafter the annual maintenance charge will rise to $8,000. The machines have a current resale value of $8,000, but at the end of year 2 their value will have fallen to $3,500. By the end of year 6 the machines will be valueless and would be scrapped.

Visit us at
www.mhhe.com/bma1e.

Hayden is considering replacing the copiers with new machines that would do essentially the same job. These machines cost $25,000, and the company can take out an eight-year maintenance contract for $1,000 a year. The machines will have no value by the end of the eight years and will be scrapped.

Both machines are depreciated by using seven-year MACRS, and the tax rate is 35%. Assume for simplicity that the inflation rate is zero. The real cost of capital is 7%. When should Hayden replace its copiers?

23. Return to the start of Section 7.3, where we calculated the equivalent annual cost of producing reformulated gasoline in California. Capital investment was $400 million. Suppose this amount can be depreciated for tax purposes on the 10-year MACRS schedule from Table 7.4. The marginal tax rate, including California taxes, is 39%, the cost of capital is 7%, and there is no inflation. The refinery improvements have an economic life of 25 years.

    a. Calculate the after-tax equivalent annual cost. (*Hint:* It's easiest to use the PV of depreciation tax shields as an offset to the initial investment.)

    b. How much extra would retail gasoline customers have to pay to cover this equivalent annual cost? (*Note:* Extra income from higher retail prices would be taxed.)

24. The Borstal Company has to choose between two machines that do the same job but have different lives. The two machines have the following costs:

Year	Machine A	Machine B
0	$40,000	$50,000
1	10,000	8,000
2	10,000	8,000
3	10,000 + replace	8,000
4		8,000 + replace

These costs are expressed in real terms.

    a. Suppose you are Borstal's financial manager. If you had to buy one or the other machine and rent it to the production manager for that machine's economic life, what annual rental payment would you have to charge? Assume a 6% real discount rate and ignore taxes.

    b. Which machine should Borstal buy?

    c. Usually the rental payments you derived in part (a) are just hypothetical—a way of calculating and interpreting equivalent annual cost. Suppose you actually do buy one of the machines and rent it to the production manager. How much would you actually have to charge in each future year if there is steady 8% per year inflation? (*Note:* The rental payments calculated in part (a) are real cash flows. You would have to mark up those payments to cover inflation.)

25. Look again at your calculations for Practice Problem 24 above. Suppose that technological change is expected to reduce costs by 10% per year. There will be new machines in year 1 that cost 10% less to buy and operate than A and B. In year 2 there will be a second crop of new machines incorporating a further 10% reduction, and so on. How does this change the equivalent annual costs of machines A and B?

26. The president's executive jet is not fully utilized. You judge that its use by other officers would increase direct operating costs by only $20,000 a year and would save $100,000 a year in airline bills. On the other hand, you believe that with the increased use the company will need to replace the jet at the end of three years rather than four. A new jet costs $1.1 million and (at its current low rate of use) has a life of six years. Assume that the company does not pay taxes. All cash flows are forecasted in real terms. The real opportunity cost of capital is 8%. Should you try to persuade the president to allow other officers to use the plane?

27. One measure of the effective tax rate is the difference between the IRRs of pretax and after-tax cash flows, divided by the pretax IRR. Consider, for example, an investment I generating a perpetual stream of pretax cash flows C. The pretax IRR is C/I, and the after-tax IRR is $C(1 - T_C)/I$, where T_C is the statutory tax rate. The effective rate, call it T_E, is

$$T_E = \frac{C/I - C(1 - T_c)/I}{C/I} = T_c$$

In this case the effective rate equals the statutory rate.

   a. Calculate T_E for the guano project in Section 7.2.

   b. How does the effective rate depend on the tax depreciation schedule? On the inflation rate?

   c. Consider a project where all of the up-front investment is treated as an expense for tax purposes. For example, R&D and marketing outlays are always expensed in the United States. They create no tax depreciation. What is the effective tax rate for such a project?

28. We warned that equivalent annual costs should be calculated in real terms. We did not fully explain why. This problem will show you.

   Look back to the cash flows for machines A and B (in "Choosing between Long- and Short-Lived Equipment"). The present values of purchase and operating costs are 28.37 (over three years for A) and 21.00 (over two years for B). The real discount rate is 6% and the inflation rate is 5%.

   a. Calculate the three- and two-year *level nominal* annuities which have present values of 28.37 and 21.00. Explain why these annuities are *not* realistic estimates of equivalent annual costs. (*Hint:* In real life machinery rentals increase with inflation.)

   b. Suppose the inflation rate increases to 25%. The real interest rate stays at 6%. Recalculate the level nominal annuities. Note that the *ranking* of machines A and B appears to change. Why?

29. In December 2005 Mid-American Energy brought online one of the largest wind farms in the world. It cost an estimated $386 million and the 257 turbines have a total capacity of 360.5 megawatts (mW). Wind speeds fluctuate and most wind farms are expected to operate at an average of only 35% of their rated capacity. In this case, at an electricity price of $55 per megawatt-hour (mWh), the project will produce revenues in the first year of $60.8 million (i.e., .35 × 8,760 hours × 360.5 mW × $55 per mWh). A reasonable estimate of maintenance and other costs is about $18.9 million in the first year of operation. Thereafter, revenues and costs should increase with inflation by around 3% a year.

   Conventional power stations can be depreciated using 20-year MACRS, and their profits are taxed at 35%. Suppose that the project will last 20 years and the cost of capital is 12%. To encourage renewable energy sources, the government offers several tax breaks for wind farms.

   a. How large a tax break (if any) was needed to make Mid-American's investment a positive-NPV venture?

   b. Some wind farm operators assume a capacity factor of 30% rather than 35%. How would this lower capacity factor alter project NPV?

MINI-CASE

New Economy Transport (A)

The New Economy Transport Company (NETCO) was formed in 1952 to carry cargo and passengers between ports in the Pacific Northwest and Alaska. By 2005 its fleet had grown to four vessels, including a small dry-cargo vessel, the *Vital Spark*.

The *Vital Spark* is 25 years old and badly in need of an overhaul. Peter Handy, the finance director, has just been presented with a proposal that would require the following expenditures:

Overhaul engine and generators	$340,000
Replace radar and other electronic equipment	75,000
Repairs to hull and superstructure	310,000
Painting and other repairs	95,000
	$820,000

Mr. Handy believes that all these outlays could be depreciated for tax purposes in the seven-year MACRS class.

NETCO's chief engineer, McPhail, estimates the post-overhaul operating costs as follows:

Fuel	$ 450,000
Labor and benefits	480,000
Maintenance	141,000
Other	110,000
	$1,181,000

These costs generally increase with inflation, which is forecasted at 2.5% a year.

The *Vital Spark* is carried on NETCO's books at a net depreciated value of only $100,000, but could probably be sold "as is," along with an extensive inventory of spare parts, for $200,000. The book value of the spare parts inventory is $40,000. Sale of the *Vital Spark* would generate an immediate tax liability on the difference between sale price and book value.

The chief engineer also suggests installation of a brand-new engine and control system, which would cost an extra $600,000.[11] This additional equipment would not substantially improve the *Vital Spark*'s performance, but would result in the following reduced annual fuel, labor, and maintenance costs:

Fuel	$ 400,000
Labor and benefits	405,000
Maintenance	105,000
Other	110,000
	$1,020,000

Overhaul of the *Vital Spark* would take it out of service for several months. The overhauled vessel would resume commercial service next year. Based on past experience, Mr. Handy believes that it would generate revenues of about $1.4 million next year, increasing with inflation thereafter.

But the *Vital Spark* cannot continue forever. Even if overhauled, its useful life is probably no more than 10 years, 12 years at the most. Its salvage value when finally taken out of service will be trivial.

---

[11] This additional outlay would also qualify for tax depreciation in the seven-year MACRS class.

NETCO is a conservatively financed firm in a mature business. It normally evaluates capital investments using an 11% cost of capital. This is a nominal, not a real, rate. NETCO's tax rate is 35%.

QUESTION

1. Calculate the NPV of the proposed overhaul of the *Vital Spark*, with and without the new engine and control system. To do the calculation, you will have to prepare a spreadsheet table showing all costs after taxes over the vessel's remaining economic life. Take special care with your assumptions about depreciation tax shields and inflation.

New Economy Transport (B)

There is no question that the *Vital Spark* needs an overhaul soon. However, Mr. Handy feels it unwise to proceed without also considering the purchase of a new vessel. Cohn and Doyle, Inc., a Wisconsin shipyard, has approached NETCO with a design incorporating a Kort nozzle, extensively automated navigation and power control systems, and much more comfortable accommodations for the crew. Estimated annual operating costs of the new vessel are:

Fuel	$380,000
Labor and benefits	330,000
Maintenance	70,000
Other	105,000
	$885,000

The crew would require additional training to handle the new vessel's more complex and sophisticated equipment. Training would probably cost $50,000 next year.

The estimated operating costs for the new vessel assume that it would be operated in the same way as the *Vital Spark*. However, the new vessel should be able to handle a larger load on some routes, which could generate additional revenues, net of additional out-of-pocket costs, of as much as $100,000 per year. Moreover, a new vessel would have a useful service life of 20 years or more.

Cohn and Doyle offered the new vessel for a fixed price of $3,000,000, payable half immediately and half on delivery next year.

Mr. Handy stepped out on the foredeck of the *Vital Spark* as she chugged down the Cook Inlet. "A rusty old tub," he muttered, "but she's never let us down. I'll bet we could keep her going until next year while Cohn and Doyle are building her replacement. We could use up the spare parts to keep her going. We might even be able to sell or scrap her for book value when her replacement arrives.

"But how do I compare the NPV of a new ship with the old *Vital Spark*? Sure, I could run a 20-year NPV spreadsheet, but I don't have a clue how the replacement will be used in 2020 or 2025. Maybe I could compare the overall *cost* of overhauling and operating the *Vital Spark* to the cost of buying and operating the proposed replacement."

QUESTIONS

1. Calculate and compare the equivalent annual costs of (a) overhauling and operating the *Vital Spark* for 12 more years, and (b) buying and operating the proposed replacement vessel for 20 years. What should Mr. Handy do if the replacement's annual costs are the same or lower?

2. Suppose the replacement's equivalent annual costs are higher than the *Vital Spark*'s. What additional information should Mr. Handy seek in this case?

Visit us at www.mhhe.com/bma1e

PART TWO

RISK

AMAZON.COM STOCK STARTED trading in May 1997 at a price of $1.73. By December 1999, the stock price had risen to $107. Within little more than a year it had slumped to $8.40. As of February 2007, it was back up to $37. These gyrations in Amazon's stock price were unusually large, but they remind us how risky investment in common stocks can be.

Most investors are not adrenaline junkies; they don't enjoy taking risks. Therefore they require a higher expected return from risky investments. Companies recognize this in their capital budgeting decisions. An investment in a risky new project adds value only if the expected return is higher than investors could expect from an equally risky investment in the capital market.

But that raises two questions. How should risk be measured? And what is the relationship between risk and expected return? We tackle these two questions in Part 2.

Web sites related to this Part appear at www.mhhe.com/bma1e.

8

INTRODUCTION TO RISK, RETURN, AND THE OPPORTUNITY COST OF CAPITAL

WE HAVE MANAGED to go through seven chapters without directly addressing the problem of risk, but now the jig is up. We can no longer be satisfied with vague statements like "The opportunity cost of capital depends on the risk of the project." We need to know how risk is defined, what the links are between risk and the opportunity cost of capital, and how the financial manager can cope with risk in practical situations.

In this chapter we concentrate on the first of these issues and leave the other two to Chapters 9 and 10. We start by summarizing more than 100 years of evidence on rates of return in capital markets. Then we take a first look at investment risks and show how they can be reduced by portfolio diversification. We introduce you to beta, the standard risk measure for individual securities.

The themes of this chapter, then, are portfolio risk, security risk, and diversification. For the most part, we take the view of the individual investor. But at the end of the chapter we turn the problem around and ask whether diversification makes sense as a corporate objective.

8.1 OVER A CENTURY OF CAPITAL MARKET HISTORY IN ONE EASY LESSON

Financial analysts are blessed with an enormous quantity of data. There are comprehensive databases of the prices of U.S. stocks, bonds, options, commodities, as well as huge amounts of data for securities in other countries. We will focus on a

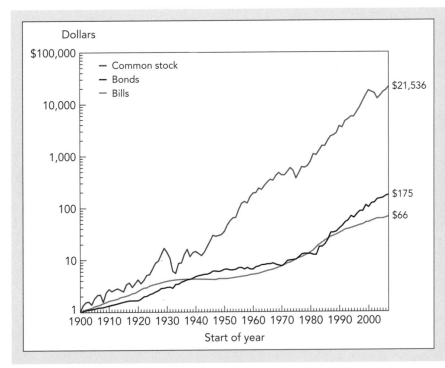

FIGURE 8.1

How an investment of $1 at the start of 1900 would have grown, assuming reinvestment of all dividend and interest payments.

Source: E. Dimson, P. R. Marsh, and M. Staunton, *Triumph of the Optimists: 101 Years of Investment Returns* (Princeton, NJ: Princeton University Press, 2002), © 2002 Reprinted by permission of Princeton University Press; with updates provided by the authors.

study by Dimson, Marsh, and Staunton that measures the historical performance of three portfolios of U.S. securities:[1]

1. A portfolio of Treasury bills, that is, U.S. government debt securities maturing in less than one year.[2]
2. A portfolio of U.S. government bonds.
3. A portfolio of U.S. common stocks.

These investments offer different degrees of risk. Treasury bills are about as safe an investment as you can make. There is no risk of default, and their short maturity means that the prices of Treasury bills are relatively stable. In fact, an investor who wishes to lend money for, say, three months can achieve a perfectly certain payoff by purchasing a Treasury bill maturing in three months. However, the investor cannot lock in a *real* rate of return: There is still some uncertainty about inflation.

By switching to long-term government bonds, the investor acquires an asset whose price fluctuates as interest rates vary. (Bond prices fall when interest rates rise and rise when interest rates fall.) An investor who shifts from bonds to common stocks shares in all the ups and downs of the issuing companies.

Figure 8.1 shows how your money would have grown if you had invested $1 at the start of 1900 and reinvested all dividend or interest income in each of the three portfolios.[3] Figure 8.2 is identical except that it depicts the growth in the *real* value of the portfolio. We will focus here on nominal values.

---

[1] See E. Dimson, P. R. Marsh, and M. Staunton, *Triumph of the Optimists: 101 Years of Investment Returns* (Princeton, NJ: Princeton University Press, 2002).

[2] Treasury bills were not issued before 1919. Before that date the interest rate used is the commercial paper rate.

[3] Portfolio values are plotted on a log scale. If they were not, the ending values for the common stock portfolio would run off the top of the page.

FIGURE 8.2

How an investment of $1 at the start of 1900 would have grown in real terms, assuming reinvestment of all dividend and interest payments. Compare this plot with Figure 8.1, and note how inflation has eroded the purchasing power of returns to investors.

Source: E. Dimson, P. R. Marsh, and M. Staunton, *Triumph of the Optimists: 101 Years of Investment Returns* (Princeton, NJ: Princeton University Press, 2002), © 2002 Reprinted by permission of Princeton University Press; with updates provided by the authors.

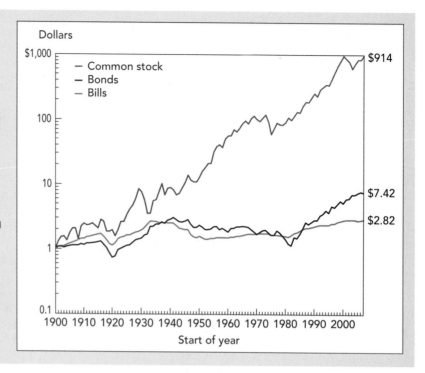

TABLE 8.1

Average rates of return on U.S. Treasury bills, government bonds, and common stocks, 1900–2006 (figures in % per year)

Source: E. Dimson, P. R. Marsh, and M. Staunton, *Triumph of the Optimists: 101 Years of Investment Returns,* (Princeton, NJ: Princeton University Press, 2002), © 2002 Reprinted by permission of Princeton University Press; with updates provided by the authors.

	Average Annual Rate of Return		Average Risk Premium (Extra Return versus Treasury Bills)
	Nominal	**Real**	
Treasury bills	4.0	1.1	0
Government bonds	5.2	2.4	1.2
Common stocks	11.7	8.5	7.6

Investment performance coincides with our intuitive risk ranking. A dollar invested in the safest investment, Treasury bills, would have grown to $66 by the end of 2006, barely enough to keep up with inflation. An investment in long-term Treasury bonds would have produced $175. Common stocks were in a class by themselves. An investor who placed a dollar in the stocks of large U.S. firms would have received $21,536.

We can also calculate the rate of return from these portfolios for each year from 1900 to 2006. This rate of return reflects both cash receipts—dividends or interest—and the capital gains or losses realized during the year. Averages of the 107 annual rates of return for each portfolio are shown in Table 8.1.

Since 1900 Treasury bills have provided the lowest average return—4.0% per year in *nominal* terms and 1.1% in *real* terms. In other words, the average rate of inflation over this period was about 3% per year. Common stocks were again the winners. Stocks of major corporations provided an average nominal return of 11.7%. By taking on the risk of common stocks, investors earned a risk premium of $11.7 - 4.0 = 7.6\%$ over the return on Treasury bills.[4]

You may ask why we look back over such a long period to measure average rates of return. The reason is that annual rates of return for common stocks fluctuate so much that averages taken over short periods are meaningless. Our only hope of gaining insights from historical rates of return is to look at a very long period.[5]

Arithmetic Averages and Compound Annual Returns

Notice that the average returns shown in Table 8.1 are arithmetic averages. In other words, we simply added the 107 annual returns and divided by 107. The arithmetic average is higher than the compound annual return over the period. The 107-year compound annual return for the S&P index was 9.8%.[6]

The proper uses of arithmetic and compound rates of return from past investments are often misunderstood. Therefore, we call a brief time-out for a clarifying example.

Suppose that the price of Big Oil's common stock is $100. There is an equal chance that at the end of the year the stock will be worth $90, $110, or $130. Therefore, the return could be -10%, $+10\%$, or $+30\%$ (we assume that Big Oil does not pay a dividend). The *expected* return is $\frac{1}{3}(-10 + 10 + 30) = +10\%$.

If we run the process in reverse and discount the expected cash flow by the expected rate of return, we obtain the value of Big Oil's stock:

$$PV = \frac{110}{1.10} = \$100$$

The expected return of 10% is therefore the correct rate at which to discount the expected cash flow from Big Oil's stock. It is also the opportunity cost of capital for investments that have the same degree of risk as Big Oil.

Now suppose that we observe the returns on Big Oil stock over a large number of years. If the odds are unchanged, the return will be -10% in a third of the years, $+10\%$ in a further third, and $+30\%$ in the remaining years. The arithmetic average of these yearly returns is

$$\frac{-10 + 10 + 30}{3} = +10\%$$

---

[4] Figures don't add due to rounding.

[5] We cannot be sure that this period is truly representative and that the average is not distorted by a few unusually high or low returns. The reliability of an estimate of the average is usually measured by its *standard error*. For example, the standard error of our estimate of the average risk premium on common stocks is 1.9%. There is a 95% chance that the *true* average is within plus or minus 2 standard errors of the 7.6% estimate. In other words, if you said that the true average was between 3.8 and 11.4%, you would have a 95% chance of being right. *Technical note:* The standard error of the average is equal to the standard deviation divided by the square root of the number of observations. In our case the standard deviation is 19.8%, and therefore the standard error is $19.8/\sqrt{107} = 1.9$.

[6] This was calculated from $(1 + r)^{107} = 21{,}536$, which implies $r = .098$. *Technical note:* For lognormally distributed returns the annual compound return is equal to the arithmetic average return minus half the variance. For example, the annual standard deviation of returns on the U.S. market was about .20, or 20%. Variance was therefore $.20^2$, or .04. The compound annual return is $.04/2 = .02$, or 2 percentage points less than the arithmetic average.

Thus the arithmetic average of the returns correctly measures the opportunity cost of capital for investments of similar risk to Big Oil stock.[7]

The average compound annual return[8] on Big Oil stock would be

$$(.9 \times 1.1 \times 1.3)^{1/3} - 1 = .088, \text{ or } 8.8\%,$$

which is *less* than the opportunity cost of capital. Investors would not be willing to invest in a project that offered an 8.8% expected return if they could get an expected return of 10% in the capital markets. The net present value of such a project would be

$$NPV = -100 + \frac{108.8}{1.1} = -1.1$$

Moral: If the cost of capital is estimated from historical returns or risk premiums, use arithmetic averages, not compound annual rates of return.[9]

Using Historical Evidence to Evaluate Today's Cost of Capital

Suppose there is an investment project that you *know*—don't ask how—has the same risk as Standard and Poor's Composite Index. We will say that it has the same degree of risk as the *market portfolio,* although this is speaking somewhat loosely, because the index does not include all risky securities. What rate should you use to discount this project's forecasted cash flows?

Clearly you should use the currently expected rate of return on the market portfolio; that is the return investors would forgo by investing in the proposed project. Let us call this market return r_m. One way to estimate r_m is to assume that the future will be like the past and that today's investors expect to receive the same "normal" rates of return revealed by the averages shown in Table 8.1. In this case, you would set r_m at 11.7%, the average of past market returns.

Unfortunately, this is *not* the way to do it; r_m is not likely to be stable over time. Remember that it is the sum of the risk-free interest rate r_f and a premium for risk. We know that r_f varies. For example, in 1981 the interest rate on Treasury bills was about 15%. It is difficult to believe that investors in that year were content to hold common stocks offering an expected return of only 11.7%.

If you need to estimate the return that investors expect to receive, a more sensible procedure is to take the interest rate on Treasury bills and add 7.6%, the average *risk premium* shown in Table 8.1. For example, in mid-2006 the interest rate on Treasury bills was about 5%. Adding on the average risk premium, therefore, gives

$$r_m(2006) = r_f(2006) + \text{normal risk premium}$$
$$= .05 + .076 = .126, \text{ or } 12.6\%$$

---

[7] You sometimes hear that the arithmetic average correctly measures the opportunity cost of capital for one-year cash flows, but not for more distant ones. Let us check. Suppose that you expect to receive a cash flow of $121 in year 2. We know that one-year hence investors will value that cash flow by discounting at 10% (the arithmetic average of possible returns). In other words, at the end of the year they will be willing to pay $PV_1 = 121/1.10 = \$110$ for the expected cash flow. But we already know how to value an asset that pays off $110 in year 1—just discount at the 10% opportunity cost of capital. Thus $PV_0 = PV_1/1.10 = 110/1.1 = \$100$. Our example demonstrates that the arithmetic average (10% in our example) provides a correct measure of the opportunity cost of capital regardless of the timing of the cash flow.

[8] The compound annual return is often referred to as the *geometric average* return.

[9] Our discussion above assumed that we *knew* that the returns of -10, $+10$, and $+30\%$ were equally likely. For an analysis of the effect of uncertainty about the expected return see I. A. Cooper, "Arithmetic Versus Geometric Mean Estimators: Setting Discount Rates for Capital Budgeting," *European Financial Management* 2 (July 1996), pp. 157–167.

The crucial assumption here is that there is a normal, stable risk premium on the market portfolio, so that the expected *future* risk premium can be measured by the average past risk premium.

Even with over 100 years of data, we can't estimate the market risk premium exactly; nor can we be sure that investors today are demanding the same reward for risk that they were 50 or 100 years ago. All this leaves plenty of room for argument about what the risk premium *really* is.[10]

Many financial managers and economists believe that long-run historical returns are the best measure available. Others have a gut instinct that investors don't need such a large risk premium to persuade them to hold common stocks.[11] For example, surveys of chief financial officers commonly suggest that they expect a market risk premium that is several percentage points below the historical average.[12]

If you believe that the expected market risk premium is less than the historical average, you probably also believe that history has been unexpectedly kind to investors in the United States and that their good luck is unlikely to be repeated. Here are two reasons that history *may* overstate the risk premium that investors demand today.

Reason 1   Since 1900 the United States has been among the world's most prosperous countries. Other economies have languished or been wracked by war or civil unrest. By focusing on equity returns in the United States, we may obtain a biased view of what investors expected. Perhaps the historical averages miss the possibility that the United States could have turned out to be one of these less-fortunate countries.[13]

Figure 8.3 sheds some light on this issue. It is taken from a comprehensive study by Dimson, Marsh, and Staunton of market returns in 17 countries and shows the average risk premium in each country between 1900 and 2006.[14] There is no evidence here that U.S. investors have been particularly fortunate; the USA was just about average in terms of returns.

In Figure 8.3 Danish stocks come bottom of the league; the average risk premium in Denmark was only 4.9%. The clear winner was Italy with a premium of 11.0%. Some of these differences between countries may reflect differences in risk. For example, Italian stocks have been particularly variable and investors

---

[10] Some of the disagreements simply reflect the fact that the risk premium is sometimes defined in different ways. Some measure the average difference between stock returns and the returns (or yields) on long-term bonds. Others measure the difference between the compound rate of growth on stocks and the interest rate. As we explained above, this is not an appropriate measure of the cost of capital.

[11] There is some theory behind this instinct. The high risk premium earned in the market seems to imply that investors are extremely risk-averse. If that is true, investors ought to cut back their consumption when stock prices fall and wealth decreases. But the evidence suggests that when stock prices fall, investors spend at nearly the same rate. This is difficult to reconcile with high risk aversion and a high market risk premium. See R. Mehra and E. Prescott, "The Equity Premium: A Puzzle," *Journal of Monetary Economics* 15 (1985), pp. 145–161.

[12] It is difficult to interpret the responses to such surveys precisely. The best known is conducted every quarter by Duke University and *CFO* magazine and reported on at **www.cfosurvey.org**. On average since inception CFOs have predicted a 10-year return on U.S. equities of 3.7% in excess of the return on 10-year Treasury bonds. However, respondents appear to have interpreted the question as asking for their forecast of the *compound* annual return. In this case the comparable *expected* (arithmetic average) premium over *bills* is probably 2 or 3 percentage points higher at about 6%. For a description of the survey data, see J. R. Graham and C. Harvey, "The Long-Run Equity Risk Premium," *Finance Research Letters* 2 (2005), pp. 185–194.

[13] This possibility was suggested in P. Jorion and W. N. Goetzmann, "Global Stock Markets in the Twentieth Century," *Journal of Finance* 54 (June 1999), pp. 953–980.

[14] See E. Dimson, P. R. Marsh, and M. Staunton, *Triumph of the Optimists: 101 Years of Investment Returns* (Princeton, NJ: Princeton University Press, 2002).

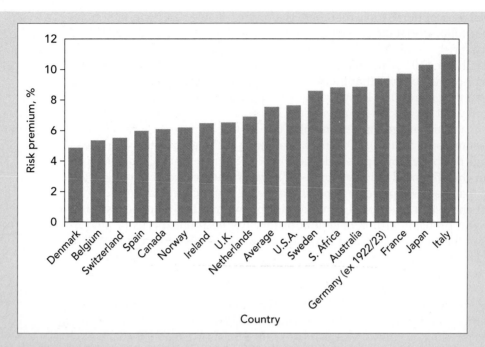

FIGURE 8.3

Average market risk premia (nominal return on stocks minus nominal return on bills), 1900–2006.

Source: E. Dimson, P. R. Marsh, and M. Staunton, *Triumph of the Optimists: 101 Years of Investment Returns* (Princeton, NJ: Princeton University Press, 2002), with updates provided by the authors. © 2002 Reprinted by permission of Princeton University Press.

may have required a higher return to compensate. But remember how difficult it is to make precise estimates of what investors expected. You probably would not be too far out if you concluded that the *expected* risk premium was the same in each country.

Reason 2 Stock prices in the United States have for some years outpaced the growth in company dividends or earnings. For example, between 1950 and 2000 dividend yields in the United States fell from 7.2% to 1.1%. It seems unlikely that investors *expected* such a sharp decline in yields, in which case some part of the actual return during this period was *unexpected*.

Some believe that the low dividend yields at the turn of the century reflected optimism that the new economy would lead to a golden age of prosperity and surging profits, but others attribute the low yields to a reduction in the market risk premium. Perhaps the growth in mutual funds has made it easier for individuals to diversify away part of their risk, or perhaps pension funds and other financial institutions have found that they also could reduce their risk by investing part of their funds overseas. If these investors can eliminate more of their risk than in the past, they may become content with a lower return.

To see how a rise in stock prices can stem from a fall in the risk premium, suppose that a stock is expected to pay a dividend next year of $12 ($DIV_1 = 12$). The stock yields 3% and the dividend is expected to grow indefinitely by 7% a year ($g = .07$). Therefore the total return that investors expect is $r = 3 + 7 = 10\%$. We can find the stock's value by plugging these numbers into the constant-growth formula that we introduced in Chapter 3:

$$PV = DIV_1/(r - g) = 12/(.10 - .07) = \$400$$

Imagine that investors now revise downward their required return to $r = 9\%$. The dividend yield falls to 2% and the value of the stock rises to

$$PV = DIV_1/(r - g) = 12/(.09 - .07) = \$600$$

Thus a fall from 10% to 9% in the required return leads to a 50% rise in the stock price. If we include this price rise in our measures of past returns, we will be doubly wrong in our estimate of the risk premium. First, we will overestimate the return that investors required in the past. Second, we will fail to recognize that the return investors require in the future is lower than they needed in the past.

Dividend Yields and the Risk Premium

If there has been a downward shift in the return that investors have required, then past returns will provide an overestimate of the risk premium. We can't wholly get around this difficulty, but we can get another clue to the risk premium by going back to the constant-growth model that we discussed in Chapter 5. If stock prices are expected to keep pace with the growth in dividends, then the expected market return is equal to the dividend yield plus the expected dividend growth—that is, $r = DIV_1/P_0 + g$. Dividend yields in the United States have averaged 4.4% since 1900, and the annual growth in dividends has averaged about 5.6%. If this dividend growth is representative of what investors *expected*, then the expected market return over this period was $DIV_1/P_0 + g = 4.4 + 5.6 = 10.0\%$, or 6.0% above the risk-free interest rate. This figure is 1.6% lower than the *realized* risk premium reported in Table 8.1.[15]

Dividend yields have averaged 4.4% since 1900, but, as you can see from Figure 8.4, they have fluctuated quite sharply. At the end of 1917, stocks were offering a yield of 9.0%; by 2000 the yield had plunged to just 1.1%. You sometimes hear financial managers suggest that in years such as 2000, when dividend yields were low, capital was relatively cheap. Is there any truth to this? Should companies be adjusting their cost of capital to reflect these fluctuations in yield?

Notice that there are only two possible reasons for the yield changes in Figure 8.4. One is that in some years investors were unusually optimistic or pessimistic about g, the future growth in dividends. The other is that r, the required return, was unusually high or low. Economists who have studied the behavior of dividend yields have concluded that very little of the variation is related to the subsequent rate of dividend growth. If they are right, the level of yields ought to be telling us something about the return that investors require.

This in fact appears to be the case. A reduction in the dividend yield seems to herald a reduction in the risk premium that investors can expect over the following few years. So, when yields are relatively low, companies may be justified in shaving their estimate of required returns over the next year or so. However,

---

[15] See E. F. Fama and K. R. French, "The Equity Premium," *Journal of Finance* 57 (April 2002), pp. 637–659. Fama and French quote even lower estimates of the risk premium, particularly for the second half of the period. The difference partly reflects the fact that they define the risk premium as the difference between market returns and the commercial paper rate. Except for the years 1900–1918, the interest rates used in Table 8.1 are the rates on U.S. Treasury bills.

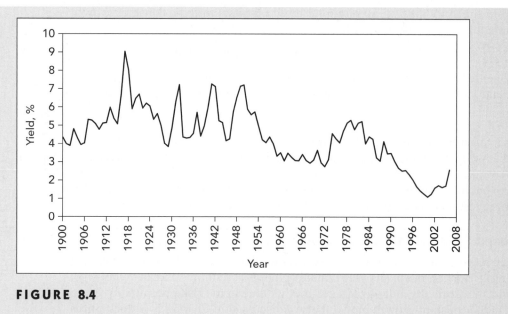

FIGURE 8.4

Dividend yields in the U.S.A. since 1900.

changes in the dividend yield tell companies next to nothing about the expected risk premium over the next 10 or 20 years. It seems that, when estimating the discount rate for longer term investments, a firm can safely ignore year-to-year fluctuations in the dividend yield.

Out of this debate only one firm conclusion emerges: Do not trust anyone who claims to *know* what returns investors expect. History contains some clues, but ultimately we have to judge whether investors on average have received what they expected. Many financial economists rely on the evidence of history and therefore work with a risk premium of about 7.5%. The remainder generally use a somewhat lower figure. Brealey, Myers, and Allen have no official position on the issue, but we believe that a range of 5% to 8% is reasonable for the risk premium in the United States.

8.2   MEASURING PORTFOLIO RISK

You now have a couple of benchmarks. You know the discount rate for safe projects, and you have an estimate of the rate for average-risk projects. But you *don't* know yet how to estimate discount rates for assets that do not fit these simple cases. To do that, you have to learn (1) how to measure risk and (2) the relationship between risks borne and risk premiums demanded.

Figure 8.5 shows the 107 annual rates of return for U.S. common stocks. The fluctuations in year-to-year returns are remarkably wide. The highest annual return was 57.6% in 1933—a partial rebound from the stock market crash of 1929–1932. However, there were losses exceeding 25% in five years, the worst being the −43.9% return in 1931.

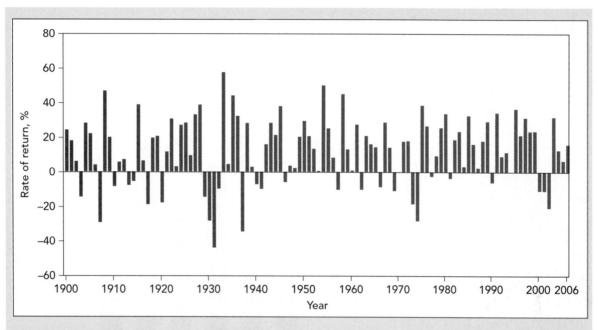

FIGURE 8.5

The stock market has been a profitable but extremely variable investment.

Source: E. Dimson, P. R. Marsh, and M. Staunton, *Triumph of the Optimists: 101 Years of Investment Returns* (Princeton, NJ: Princeton University Press, 2002), with updates provided by the authors. © 2002 Reprinted by permission of Princeton University Press.

Another way of presenting these data is by a histogram or frequency distribution. This is done in Figure 8.6, where the variability of year-to-year returns shows up in the wide "spread" of outcomes.

Variance and Standard Deviation

The standard statistical measures of spread are **variance** and **standard deviation.** The variance of the market return is the expected squared deviation from the expected return. In other words,

$$\text{Variance } (\tilde{r}_m) = \text{the expected value of } (\tilde{r}_m - r_m)^2$$

where $\tilde{r}_m$ is the actual return and r_m is the expected return.[16] The standard deviation is simply the square root of the variance:

$$\text{Standard deviation of } \tilde{r}_m = \sqrt{\text{variance } (\tilde{r}_m)}$$

Standard deviation is often denoted by σ and variance by σ^2.

---

[16] One more technical point: When variance is estimated from a sample of *observed* returns, we add the squared deviations and divide by $N - 1$, where N is the number of observations. We divide by $N - 1$ rather than N to correct for what is called *the loss of a degree of freedom.* The formula is

$$\text{Variance } (\tilde{r}_m) = \frac{1}{N-1} \sum_{t=1}^{N} (\tilde{r}_{mt} - r_m)^2$$

where $\tilde{r}_{mt}$ is the market return in period t and r_m is the mean of the values of $\tilde{r}_{mt}$.

FIGURE 8.6

Histogram of the annual rates of return from the stock market in the United States, 1900–2006, showing the wide spread of returns from invest-ment in common stocks.

Source: E. Dimson, P. R. Marsh, and M. Staunton, *Triumph of the Optimists: 101 Years of Investment Returns,* (Princeton, NJ: Princeton University Press, 2002), with updates provided by the authors. © 2002 Reprinted by permission of Princeton University Press.

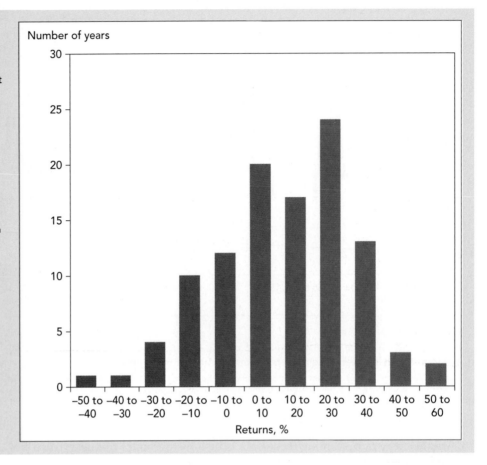

Here is a very simple example showing how variance and standard deviation are calculated. Suppose that you are offered the chance to play the following game. You start by investing $100. Then two coins are flipped. For each head that comes up you get back your starting balance *plus* 20%, and for each tail that comes up you get back your starting balance *less* 10%. Clearly there are four equally likely outcomes:

- Head + head: You gain 40%.
- Head + tail: You gain 10%.
- Tail + head: You gain 10%.
- Tail + tail: You lose 20%.

There is a chance of 1 in 4, or .25, that you will make 40%; a chance of 2 in 4, or .5, that you will make 10%; and a chance of 1 in 4, or .25, that you will lose 20%. The game's expected return is, therefore, a weighted average of the possible outcomes:

$$\text{Expected return} = (.25 \times 40) + (.5 \times 10) + (.25 \times -20) = +10\%$$

Table 8.2 shows that the variance of the percentage returns is 450. Standard devia-tion is the square root of 450, or 21. This figure is in the same units as the rate of return, so we can say that the game's variability is 21%.

(1) Percent Rate of Return ($\tilde{r}$)	(2) Deviation from Expected Return ($\tilde{r} - r$)	(3) Squared Deviation ($\tilde{r} - r$)^2	(4) Probability	(5) Probability $\times$ Squared Deviation
+40	+30	900	.25	225
+10	0	0	.5	0
−20	−30	900	.25	225

Variance = expected value of $(\tilde{r} - r)^2 = 450$

Standard deviation = $\sqrt{\text{variance}} = \sqrt{450} = 21$

TABLE 8.2

The coin-tossing game: Calculating variance and standard deviation.

One way of defining uncertainty is to say that more things can happen than will happen. The risk of an asset can be completely expressed, as we did for the coin-tossing game, by writing all possible outcomes and the probability of each. In practice this is cumbersome and often impossible. Therefore we use variance or standard deviation to summarize the spread of possible outcomes.[17]

These measures are natural indexes of risk.[18] If the outcome of the coin-tossing game had been certain, the standard deviation would have been zero. The actual standard deviation is positive because we *don't* know what will happen.

Or think of a second game, the same as the first except that each head means a 35% gain and each tail means a 25% loss. Again, there are four equally likely outcomes:

- Head + head: You gain 70%.
- Head + tail: You gain 10%.
- Tail + head: You gain 10%.
- Tail + tail: You lose 50%.

For this game the expected return is 10%, the same as that of the first game. But its standard deviation is double that of the first game, 42 versus 21%. By this measure the second game is twice as risky as the first.

Measuring Variability

In principle, you could estimate the variability of any portfolio of stocks or bonds by the procedure just described. You would identify the possible outcomes, assign a probability to each outcome, and grind through the calculations. But where do the probabilities come from? You can't look them up in the newspaper; newspapers seem to go out of their way to avoid definite statements about prospects for securities. We once saw an article headlined "Bond Prices Possibly Set to Move Sharply Either Way." Stockbrokers are much the same. Yours may

---

[17] Which of the two we use is solely a matter of convenience. Since standard deviation is in the same units as the rate of return, it is generally more convenient to use standard deviation. However, when we are talking about the *proportion* of risk that is due to some factor, it is less confusing to work in terms of the variance.

[18] As we explain in Chapter 9, standard deviation and variance are the correct measures of risk if the returns are normally distributed.

respond to your query about possible market outcomes with a statement like this:

> The market currently appears to be undergoing a period of consolidation. For the intermediate term, we would take a constructive view, provided economic recovery continues. The market could be up 20% a year from now, perhaps more if inflation continues low. On the other hand, . . .

The Delphic oracle gave advice, but no probabilities.

Most financial analysts start by observing past variability. Of course, there is no risk in hindsight, but it is reasonable to assume that portfolios with histories of high variability also have the least predictable future performance.

The annual standard deviations and variances observed for our three portfolios over the period 1900–2006 were:[19]

Portfolio	Standard Deviation (σ)	Variance (σ^2)
Treasury bills	2.8	7.8
Government bonds	8.1	66.4
Common stocks	19.8	391.5

As expected, Treasury bills were the least variable security, and common stocks were the most variable. Government bonds hold the middle ground.

You may find it interesting to compare the coin-tossing game and the stock market as alternative investments. The stock market generated an average annual return of 11.7% with a standard deviation of 19.8%. The game offers 10% and 21%, respectively—slightly lower return and about the same variability. Your gambling friends may have come up with a crude representation of the stock market.

Figure 8.7 compares the standard deviation of stock market returns in 17 countries over the same 107-year period. Canada occupies low field with a standard deviation of 16.7%, but most of the other countries cluster together with percentage standard deviations in the low 20s.

Of course, there is no reason to suppose that the market's variability should stay the same over more than a century. For example, Germany, Italy, and Japan now have much more stable economies and markets than they did in the years leading up to and including the Second World War. As you can see from Figure 8.8 variability in the United States is also clearly less now than in the Great Depression of the 1930s.[20]

---

[19] In discussing the riskiness of *bonds,* be careful to specify the time period and whether you are speaking in real or nominal terms. The *nominal* return on a long-term government bond is absolutely certain to an investor who holds on until maturity; in other words, it is risk-free if you forget about inflation. After all, the government can always print money to pay off its debts. However, the real return on Treasury securities is uncertain because no one knows how much each future dollar will buy.

The bond returns were measured annually. The returns reflect year-to-year changes in bond prices as well as interest received. The *one-year* returns on long-term bonds are risky in *both* real and nominal terms.

[20] These estimates are derived from *monthly* rates of return. Annual observations are insufficient for estimating variability decade by decade. The monthly variance is converted to an annual variance by multiplying by 12. That is, the variance of the monthly return is one-twelfth of the annual variance. The longer you hold a security or portfolio, the more risk you have to bear.

This conversion assumes that successive monthly returns are statistically independent. This is, in fact, a good assumption, as we will show in Chapter 12.

Because variance is approximately proportional to the length of time interval over which a security or portfolio return is measured, standard deviation is proportional to the square root of the interval.

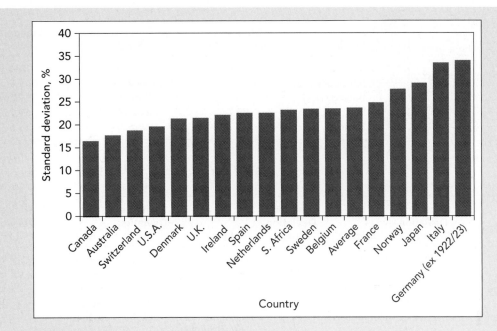

FIGURE 8.7

The risk (standard deviation of annual returns) of markets around the world, 1900–2006.

Source: E. Dimson, P. R. Marsh, and M. Staunton, *Triumph of the Optimists: 101 Years of Global Investment Returns* (Princeton, NJ: Princeton University Press, 2002), with updates provided by the authors. © 2002 Reprinted by permission of Princeton University Press.

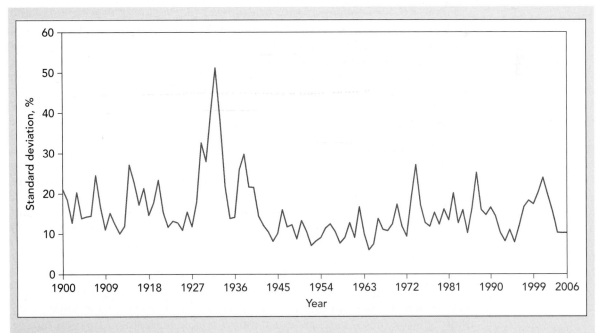

FIGURE 8.8

Annualized standard deviation of the preceding 52 weekly changes in the Dow Jones Industrial Average, 1900–2006.

TABLE 8.3

Standard deviations for selected U.S. common stocks, July 2001– June 2006 (figures in percent per year)

Stock	Standard Deviation (σ)	Stock	Standard Deviation (σ)
Amazon	56.0	Microsoft	24.4
Starbucks	29.9	Wal-Mart	19.8
Boeing	29.8	Pfizer	19.2
IBM	29.7	ExxonMobil	19.2
Disney	27.7	Heinz	16.5

Stock	Standard Deviation (σ)	Market	Standard Deviation (σ)	Stock	Standard Deviation (σ)	Market	Standard Deviation (σ)
Alcan	29.7	Canada	12.3	LVMH	31.0	France	19.4
BP	18.4	U.K.	14.1	Nestlé	13.8	Switzerland	22.8
Deutsche Bank	30.1	Germany	9.8	Nokia	42.1	Finland	27.8
Fiat	35.9	Italy	21.1	Sony	32.5	Japan	17.7
Heineken	17.2	Netherlands	22.8	Telefonica de Argentina	84.4	Argentina	43.9

TABLE 8.4

Standard deviation for selected foreign stocks and market indexes, July 2001–June 2006 (figures in percent per year).

Figure 8.8 does not support the widespread impression of especially volatile stock prices in recent years. However, there were brief episodes of extremely high volatility. On Black Monday, October 19, 1987, the U.S. market fell by 23% *on a single day*. The standard deviation of the market for the week surrounding Black Monday was equivalent to 89% per year. Fortunately, volatility dropped back to normal levels within a few weeks after the crash.

How Diversification Reduces Risk

We can calculate our measures of variability equally well for individual securities and portfolios of securities. Of course, the level of variability over 100 years is less interesting for specific companies than for the market portfolio—it is a rare company that faces the same business risks today as it did a century ago.

Table 8.3 presents estimated standard deviations for 10 well-known common stocks for a recent five-year period.[21] Do these standard deviations look high to you? They should. The market portfolio's standard deviation was about 16% during this period. Of our individual stocks only Heinz came close to this figure. Amazon.com was over three times more variable than the market portfolio.

Take a look also at Table 8.4, which shows the standard deviations of some well-known stocks from different countries and of the markets in which they trade. Some of these stocks are much more variable than others, but you can see

---

[21] These standard deviations are also calculated from monthly data.

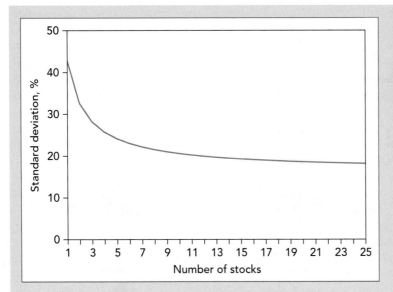

FIGURE 8.9

The risk (standard deviation) of randomly selected portfolios containing different numbers of New York Stock Exchange stocks. Notice that diversification reduces risk rapidly at first, then more slowly.

that once again the individual stocks are for the most part more variable than the market indexes.

This raises an important question: The market portfolio is made up of individual stocks, so why doesn't its variability reflect the average variability of its components? The answer is that *diversification reduces variability*.

Even a little diversification can provide a substantial reduction in variability. Suppose you calculate and compare the standard deviations between 2000 and 2005 of one-stock portfolios, two-stock portfolios, five-stock portfolios, etc. You can see from Figure 8.9 that diversification can cut the variability of returns about in half. Notice also that you can get most of this benefit with relatively few stocks: The improvement is much smaller when the number of securities is increased beyond, say, 20 or 30.[22]

Diversification works because prices of different stocks do not move exactly together. Statisticians make the same point when they say that stock price changes are less than perfectly correlated. Look, for example, at Figure 8.10. The first two panels show histograms of the monthly returns for IBM and Boeing stock over the 60-month period ending June 2006. As we showed in Table 8.3, during this period the standard deviation of their monthly returns was about 30%. Nevertheless, if you had invested all your cash in IBM, there would have been six occasions that you would have lost at least 10% of your investment. If you had put all your money in Boeing stock, you would have lost at least 10% of your investment on five occasions. Now look at the third histogram in Figure 8.10, which shows the distribution of monthly returns on a portfolio that was evenly distributed between IBM and Boeing. On many occasions a decline

---

[22] There is some evidence that in recent years stocks have become individually more risky but have moved less closely together. Consequently, the benefits of diversification have increased. See J. Y. Campbell, M. Lettau, B. G. Malkiel, and Y. Xu, "Have Individual Stocks Become More Volatile? An Empirical Exploration of Idiosyncratic Risk," *Journal of Finance* 56 (February 2001), pp. 1–43.

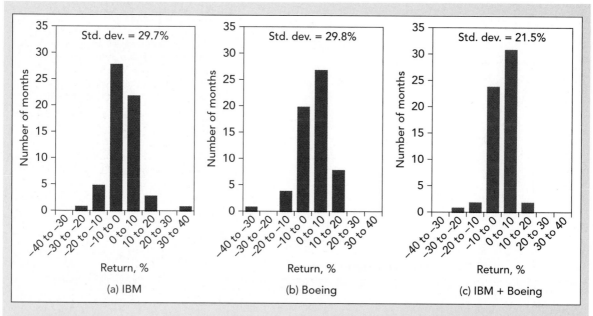

FIGURE 8.10

The spread of returns from a portfolio with equal holdings in IBM and Boeing is less than the spread of returns from the individual stocks. These returns run from July 2001 to June 2006.

in the value of one stock was offset by a rise in the price of the other,[23] so that even this limited diversification would have evened out many of the peaks and the troughs. For example, the odds of losing more than 10% in any month would have roughly halved. This shows up in the lower standard deviation of the two-stock portfolio.

The risk that potentially can be eliminated by diversification is called **unique risk**.[24] Unique risk stems from the fact that many of the perils that surround an individual company are peculiar to that company and perhaps its immediate competitors. But there is also some risk that you can't avoid, regardless of how much you diversify. This risk is generally known as **market risk**.[25] Market risk stems from the fact that there are other economywide perils that threaten all businesses. That is why stocks have a tendency to move together. And that is why investors are exposed to market uncertainties, no matter how many stocks they hold.

In Figure 8.11 we have divided risk into its two parts—unique risk and market risk. If you have only a single stock, unique risk is very important; but once you have a portfolio of 20 or more stocks, diversification has done the bulk of its work. For a reasonably well-diversified portfolio, only market risk matters. Therefore, the predominant source of uncertainty for a diversified investor is that the market will rise or plummet, carrying the investor's portfolio with it.

---

[23] Over this period the correlation between the returns on the two stocks was .05.

[24] Unique risk may be called *unsystematic risk, residual risk, specific risk,* or *diversifiable risk.*

[25] Market risk may be called *systematic risk* or *undiversifiable risk.*

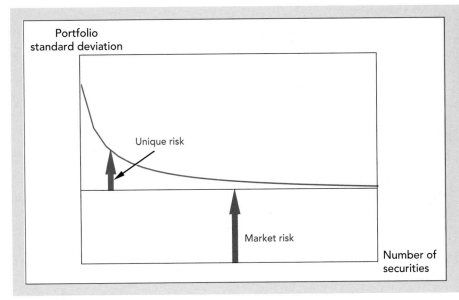

FIGURE 8.11

Diversification eliminates unique risk. But there is some risk that diversification *cannot* eliminate. This is called *market risk*.

8.3   CALCULATING PORTFOLIO RISK

We have given you an intuitive idea of how diversification reduces risk, but to understand fully the effect of diversification, you need to know how the risk of a portfolio depends on the risk of the individual shares.

Suppose that 60% of your portfolio is invested in Wal-Mart and the remainder is invested in IBM. You expect that over the coming year Wal-Mart will give a return of 10% and IBM, 15%. The expected return on your portfolio is simply a weighted average of the expected returns on the individual stocks:[26]

$$\text{Expected portfolio return} = (.60 \times 10) + (.40 \times 15) = 12\% = (x_1 r_1) + (x_2 r_2)$$

[handwritten margin notes: x_1 — portfolio weight of 1st asset; r_1 — expected return of 1st asset]

Calculating the expected portfolio return is easy. The hard part is to work out the risk of your portfolio. In the past the standard deviation of returns was 19.8% for Wal-Mart and 29.7% for IBM. You believe that these figures are a good representation of the spread of possible *future* outcomes. At first you may be inclined to assume that the standard deviation of the portfolio is a weighted average of the standard deviations of the two stocks, that is, $(.60 \times 19.8) + (.40 \times 29.7) = 23.8\%$. That would be correct *only* if the prices of the two stocks moved in perfect lockstep. In any other case, diversification reduces the risk below this figure.

The exact procedure for calculating the risk of a two-stock portfolio is given in Figure 8.12. You need to fill in four boxes. To complete the top-left box, you weight the variance of the returns on stock 1 (σ_1^2) by the *square* of the proportion invested in it (x_1^2). Similarly, to complete the bottom-right box, you weight the

---

[26] Let's check this. Suppose you invest $60 in Wal-Mart and $40 in IBM. The expected dollar return on your Wal-Mart holding is $.10 \times 60 = \$6.00$, and on IBM it is $.15 \times .4 = \$6.00$. The expected dollar return on your portfolio is $6.00 + 6.00 = \$12.00$. The portfolio *rate* of return is $12.00/100 = 0.12$, or 12%.

FIGURE 8.12

The variance of a two-stock portfolio is the sum of these four boxes. x_1, x_2 = proportions invested in stocks 1 and 2; σ_1^2, σ_2^2 = variances of stock returns; σ_{12} = covariance of returns $(\rho_{12}\sigma_1\sigma_2)$; ρ_{12} = correlation between returns on stocks 1 and 2.

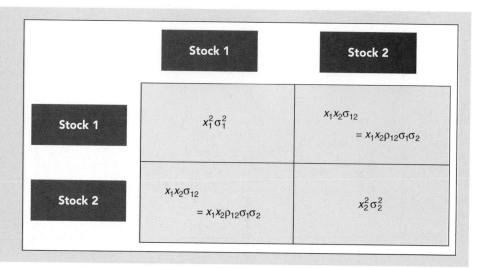

variance of the returns on stock 2 (σ_2^2) by the *square* of the proportion invested in stock 2 (x_2^2).

The entries in these diagonal boxes depend on the variances of stocks 1 and 2; the entries in the other two boxes depend on their **covariance.** As you might guess, the covariance is a measure of the degree to which the two stocks "covary." The covariance can be expressed as the product of the correlation coefficient ρ_{12} and the two standard deviations:[27]

$$\text{Covariance between stocks 1 and 2} = \sigma_{12} = \rho_{12}\sigma_1\sigma_2$$

For the most part stocks tend to move together. In this case the correlation coefficient ρ_{12} is positive, and therefore the covariance σ_{12} is also positive. If the prospects of the stocks were wholly unrelated, both the correlation coefficient and the covariance would be zero; and if the stocks tended to move in opposite directions, the correlation coefficient and the covariance would be negative. Just as you weighted the variances by the square of the proportion invested, so you must weight the covariance by the *product* of the two proportionate holdings x_1 and x_2.

Once you have completed these four boxes, you simply add the entries to obtain the portfolio variance:

$$\text{Portfolio variance} = x_1^2\sigma_1^2 + x_2^2\sigma_2^2 + 2(x_1x_2\rho_{12}\,\sigma_1\sigma_2)$$

The portfolio standard deviation is, of course, the square root of the variance.

Now you can try putting in some figures for Wal-Mart and IBM. We said earlier that if the two stocks were perfectly correlated, the standard deviation of the portfolio would lie 40% of the way between the standard deviations of the two stocks. Let us check this out by filling in the boxes with $\rho_{12} = +1$.

---

[27] Another way to define the covariance is as follows:

$$\text{Covariance between stocks 1 and 2} = \sigma_{12} = \text{expected value of } (\tilde{r}_1 - r_1) \times (\tilde{r}_2 - r_2)$$

Note that any security's covariance with itself is just its variance:

$$\sigma_{11} = \text{expected value of } (\tilde{r}_1 - r_1) \times (\tilde{r}_1 - r_1)$$
$$= \text{expected value of } (\tilde{r}_1 - r_1)^2 = \text{variance of stock 1} = \sigma_1^2$$

	Wal-Mart	**IBM**
Wal-Mart	$x_1^2\sigma_1^2 = (.6)^2 \times (19.8)^2$	$x_1x_2\rho_{12}\sigma_1\sigma_2$ $= (.6) \times (.4) \times 1 \times (19.8) \times (29.7)$
IBM	$x_1x_2\rho_{12}\sigma_1\sigma_2$ $= (.6) \times (.4) \times 1 \times (19.8) \times (29.7)$	$x_2^2\sigma_2^2 = (.4)^2 \times (29.7)^2$

The variance of your portfolio is the sum of these entries:

$$\text{Portfolio variance} = [(.6)^2 \times (19.8)^2] + [(.4)^2 \times (29.7)^2] + 2(.6 \times .4 \times 1 \times 19.8 \times 29.7)$$
$$= 564.5$$

The standard deviation is $\sqrt{564.5} = 23.8\%$, or 40% of the way between 19.8 and 29.7.

Wal-Mart and IBM do not move in perfect lockstep. If past experience is any guide, the correlation between the two stocks is about .35. If we go through the same exercise again with $\rho_{12} = .35$, we find

$$\text{Portfolio variance} = [(.6)^2 \times (19.8)^2] + [(.4)^2 \times (29.7)^2]$$
$$+ 2(.6 \times .4 \times .35 \times 19.8 \times 29.7) = 381.1$$

The standard deviation is $\sqrt{381.1} = 19.5\%$. The risk is now less than 40% of the way between 19.8 and 29.7. In fact, it is a fraction less than the risk of investing in Wal-Mart alone.

The greatest payoff to diversification comes when the two stocks are negatively correlated. Unfortunately, this almost never occurs with real stocks, but just for illustration, let us assume it for Wal-Mart and IBM. And as long as we are being unrealistic, we might as well go whole hog and assume perfect negative correlation ($\rho_{12} = -1$). In this case,

$$\text{Portfolio variance} = [(.6)^2 \times (19.8)^2] + [(.4)^2 \times (29.7)^2]$$
$$+ 2(.6 \times .4 \times (-1) \times 19.8 \times 29.7) = 0$$

When there is perfect negative correlation, there is always a portfolio strategy (represented by a particular set of portfolio weights) that will completely eliminate risk.[28] It's too bad perfect negative correlation doesn't really occur between common stocks.

General Formula for Computing Portfolio Risk

The method for calculating portfolio risk can easily be extended to portfolios of three or more securities. We just have to fill in a larger number of boxes. Each of those down the diagonal—the shaded boxes in Figure 8.13—contains the variance weighted by the square of the proportion invested. Each of the other boxes contains the covariance between that pair of securities, weighted by the product of the proportions invested.[29]

---

[28] Since the standard deviation of IBM is 1.5 times that of Wal-Mart, you need to invest 1.5 times more in Wal-Mart to eliminate risk in this two-stock portfolio.

[29] The formal equivalent to "add up all the boxes" is

$$\text{Portfolio variance} = \sum_{i=1}^{N}\sum_{j=1}^{N} x_ix_j\sigma_{ij}$$

Notice that when $i = j$, σ_{ij} is just the variance of stock i.

FIGURE 8.13

To find the variance of an N-stock portfolio, we must add the entries in a matrix like this. The diagonal cells contain variance terms $(x_i^2 \sigma_i^2)$, and the off-diagonal cells contain covariance terms $(x_i x_j \sigma_{ij})$.

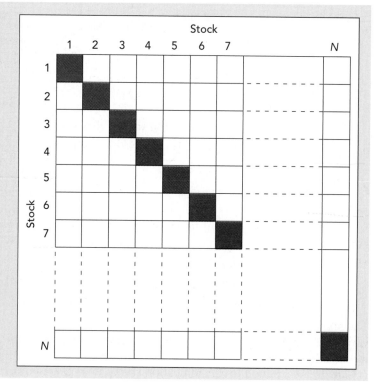

Limits to Diversification

Did you notice in Figure 8.13 how much more important the covariances become as we add more securities to the portfolio? When there are just two securities, there are equal numbers of variance boxes and of covariance boxes. When there are many securities, the number of covariances is much larger than the number of variances. Thus the variability of a well-diversified portfolio reflects mainly the covariances.

Suppose we are dealing with portfolios in which equal investments are made in each of N stocks. The proportion invested in each stock is, therefore, $1/N$. So in each variance box we have $(1/N)^2$ times the variance, and in each covariance box we have $(1/N)^2$ times the covariance. There are N variance boxes and $N^2 - N$ covariance boxes. Therefore,

$$\text{Portfolio variance} = N\left(\frac{1}{N}\right)^2 \times \text{average variance}$$

$$+ (N^2 - N)\left(\frac{1}{N}\right)^2 \times \text{average covariance}$$

$$= \frac{1}{N} \times \text{average variance} + \left(1 - \frac{1}{N}\right) \times \text{average covariance}$$

Notice that as N increases, the portfolio variance steadily approaches the average covariance. If the average covariance were zero, it would be possible to eliminate *all* risk by holding a sufficient number of securities. Unfortunately common stocks move together, not independently. Thus most of the stocks that the investor can actually buy are tied together in a web of positive covariances that set the limit to the benefits of diversification. Now we can understand the precise meaning of the market risk portrayed in Figure 8.11. It is the average covariance that constitutes the bedrock of risk remaining after diversification has done its work.

8.4 HOW INDIVIDUAL SECURITIES AFFECT PORTFOLIO RISK

We presented earlier some data on the variability of 10 individual U.S. securities. Amazon.com had the highest standard deviation and Heinz had the lowest. If you had held Amazon on its own, the spread of possible returns would have been more than three times greater than if you had held Heinz on its own. But that is not a very interesting fact. Wise investors don't put all their eggs into just one basket: They reduce their risk by diversification. They are therefore interested in the effect that each stock will have on the risk of their portfolio.

This brings us to one of the principal themes of this chapter. *The risk of a well-diversified portfolio depends on the market risk of the securities included in the portfolio.* Tattoo that statement on your forehead if you can't remember it any other way. It is one of the most important ideas in this book.

Market Risk Is Measured by Beta

If you want to know the contribution of an individual security to the risk of a well-diversified portfolio, it is no good thinking about how risky that security is if held in isolation—you need to measure its *market risk*, and that boils down to measuring how sensitive it is to market movements. This sensitivity is called **beta (β)**.

Stocks with betas greater than 1.0 tend to amplify the overall movements of the market. Stocks with betas between 0 and 1.0 tend to move in the same direction as the market, but not as far. Of course, the market is the portfolio of all stocks, so the "average" stock has a beta of 1.0. Table 8.5 reports betas for the 10 well-known common stocks we referred to earlier.

Over the five years from mid-2001 to mid-2006, Disney had a beta of 1.26. If the future resembles the past, this means that *on average* when the market rises

Stock	Beta (β)	Stock	Beta (β)
Amazon	2.20	Starbucks	.69
IBM	1.59	ExxonMobil	.65
Disney	1.26	Wal-Mart	.57
Microsoft	1.13	Pfizer	.55
Boeing	1.09	Heinz	.36

TABLE 8.5

Betas for selected U.S. common stocks, July 2001–June 2006.

FIGURE 8.14

The return on Disney stock changes on average by 1.26% for each additional 1% change in the market return. Beta is therefore 1.26.

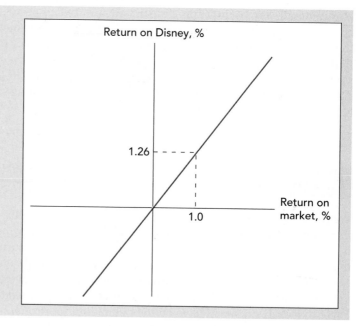

an extra 1%, Disney's stock price will rise by an extra 1.26%. When the market falls an extra 2%, Disney's stock prices will fall an extra 2 × 1.26 = 2.52%. Thus a line fitted to a plot of Disney's returns versus market returns has a slope of 1.26. See Figure 8.14.

Of course Disney's stock returns are not perfectly correlated with market returns. The company is also subject to unique risk, so the actual returns will be scattered about the line in Figure 8.14. Sometimes Disney will head south while the market goes north, and vice versa.

Of the 10 stocks in Table 8.5 Disney has one of the highest betas. Heinz is at the other extreme. A line fitted to a plot of Heinz's returns versus market returns would be less steep: Its slope would be only .36. Notice that many of the stocks that have high standard deviations also have high betas. But that is not always so. For example, Starbucks, which has a relatively high standard deviation, has joined the low-beta stocks in the right-hand column of Table 8.5. It seems that while Starbucks is a risky investment if held on its own, it makes a relatively low contribution to the risk of a diversified portfolio.

Just as we can measure how the returns of a U.S. stock are affected by fluctuations in the U.S. market, so we can measure how stocks in other countries are affected by movements in *their* markets. Table 8.6 shows the betas for the sample of stocks from other countries.

Why Security Betas Determine Portfolio Risk

Let us review the two crucial points about security risk and portfolio risk:

- Market risk accounts for most of the risk of a well-diversified portfolio.
- The beta of an individual security measures its sensitivity to market movements.

TABLE 8.6

Stock	Beta (β)	Stock	Beta (β)
Alcan	1.54	LVMH	1.26
BP	.71	Nestlé	.17
Deutsche Bank	.53	Nokia	1.44
Fiat	1.01	Sony	1.05
Heineken	.31	Telefonica de Argentina	1.05

Betas for foreign stocks, July 2001–June 2006 (beta is measured relative to the stock's home market).

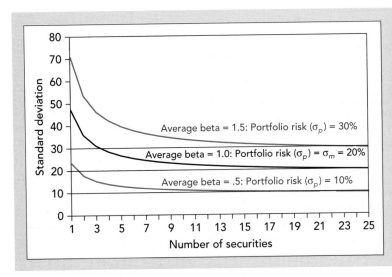

FIGURE 8.15

The blue line shows that a well-diversified portfolio of randomly selected stocks ends up with β = 1 and a standard deviation equal to the market's—in this case 20%. The upper maroon line shows that a well-diversified portfolio with β = 1.5 has a standard deviation of about 30%—1.5 times that of the market. The lower maroon line shows that a well-diversified portfolio with β = .5 has a standard deviation of about 10%—half that of the market.

It is easy to see where we are headed: In a portfolio context, a security's risk is measured by beta. Perhaps we could just jump to that conclusion, but we would rather explain it. Here is an intuitive explanation. We provide a more technical one in footnote 31.

Where's Bedrock?   Look back to Figure 8.11, which shows how the standard deviation of portfolio return depends on the number of securities in the portfolio. With more securities, and therefore better diversification, portfolio risk declines until all unique risk is eliminated and only the bedrock of market risk remains.

Where's bedrock? It depends on the average beta of the securities selected.

Suppose we constructed a portfolio containing a large number of stocks—500, say—drawn randomly from the whole market. What would we get? The market itself, or a portfolio *very* close to it. The portfolio beta would be 1.0, and the correlation with the market would be 1.0. If the standard deviation of the market were 20% (roughly its average for 1900–2006), then the portfolio standard deviation would also be 20%. This is shown by the blue line in Figure 8.15.

But suppose we constructed the portfolio from a large group of stocks with an average beta of 1.5. Again we would end up with a 500-stock portfolio with virtually no unique risk—a portfolio that moves almost in lockstep with the market. However, *this* portfolio's standard deviation would be 30%, 1.5 times that of the market.[30] A well-diversified portfolio with a beta of 1.5 will amplify every market move by 50% and end up with 150% of the market's risk. The upper maroon line in Figure 8.15 shows this case.

Of course, we could repeat the same experiment with stocks with a beta of .5 and end up with a well-diversified portfolio half as risky as the market. You can see this also in Figure 8.15.

The general point is this: The risk of a well-diversified portfolio is proportional to the portfolio beta, which equals the average beta of the securities included in the portfolio. This shows you how portfolio risk is driven by security betas.

Calculating Beta   A statistician would define the beta of stock i as

$$\beta_i = \sigma_{im}/\sigma_m^2$$

where σ_{im} is the *covariance* between the stock returns and the market returns and σ_m^2 is the variance of the returns on the market. It turns out that this ratio of covariance to variance measures a stock's contribution to portfolio risk.[31]

Here is a simple example of how to do the calculations. Columns 2 and 3 in Table 8.7 show the returns over a particular six-month period on the market and the stock of the Anchovy Queen restaurant chain. You can see that, although both investments provided an average return of 2%, Anchovy Queen's stock was particularly sensitive to market movements, rising more when the market rises and falling more when the market falls.

Columns 4 and 5 show the deviations of each month's return from the average. To calculate the market variance, we need to average the squared deviations of the market returns (column 6). And to calculate the covariance between the stock returns and the market, we need to average the product of the two deviations (column 7). Beta is the ratio of the covariance to the market variance, or 76/50.67 = 1.50. A diversified portfolio of stocks with the same beta as Anchovy Queen would be one-and-a-half times as volatile as the market.

---

[30] A 500-stock portfolio with β = 1.5 would still have some unique risk because it would be unduly concentrated in high-beta industries. Its actual standard deviation would be a bit higher than 30%. If that worries you, relax; we will show you in Chapter 9 how you can construct a fully diversified portfolio with a beta of 1.5 by borrowing and investing in the market portfolio.

[31] To understand why, skip back to Figure 8.13. Each row of boxes in Figure 8.13 represents the contribution of that particular security to the portfolio's risk. For example, the contribution of stock 1 is

$$x_1 x_1 \sigma_{11} + x_1 x_2 \sigma_{12} + \cdots = x_1(x_1 \sigma_{11} + x_2 \sigma_{12} + \cdots)$$

where x_i is the proportion invested in stock i, and σ_{ij} is the covariance between stocks i and j (note: σ_{ii} is equal to the variance of stock i). In other words, the contribution of stock 1 to portfolio risk is equal to the relative size of the holding (x_1) times the average covariance between stock 1 and all the stocks in the portfolio. We can write this more concisely by saying that the contribution of stock 1 to portfolio risk is equal to the holding size (x_1) times the covariance between stock 1 and the entire portfolio (σ_{1p}).

To find stock 1's *relative* contribution to risk we simply divide by the portfolio variance to give $x_1(\sigma_{1p}/\sigma_p^2)$. In other words, it is equal to the holding size (x_1) times the beta of stock 1 relative to the portfolio (σ_{1p}/σ_p^2).

We can calculate the beta of a stock relative to *any* portfolio by simply taking its covariance with the portfolio and dividing by the portfolio's variance. If we wish to find a stock's beta *relative to the market portfolio* we just calculate its covariance with the market portfolio and divide by the variance of the market:

$$\text{Beta relative to market portfolio (or, more simply, beta)} = \frac{\text{covariance with the market}}{\text{variance of market}} = \frac{\sigma_{im}}{\sigma_m^2}$$

(1)	(2)	(3)	(4)	(5)	(6)	(7)
						Product of
			Deviation	Deviation	Squared	deviations
			from	from average	deviation	from average
	Market	Anchovy Q	average	Anchovy Q	from average	returns
Month	return	return	market return	return	market return	(cols 4 × 5)
1	−8%	−11%	−10	−13	100	130
2	4	8	2	6	4	12
3	12	19	10	17	100	170
4	−6	−13	−8	−15	64	120
5	2	3	0	1	0	0
6	8	6	6	4	36	24
Average	2	2		Total	304	456
			Variance = σ_m^2 = 304/6 = 50.67			
			Covariance = σ_{im} = 456/6 = 76			
			Beta (β) = σ_{im}/σ_m^2 = 76/50.67 = 1.5			

TABLE 8.7

e**X**cel

Visit us at
www.mhhe.com/bma1e.

Calculating the variance of the market returns and the covariance between the returns on the market and those of Anchovy Queen. Beta is the ratio of the variance to the covariance (i.e., $\beta = \sigma_{im}/\sigma_m^2$)

8.5   DIVERSIFICATION AND VALUE ADDITIVITY

We have seen that diversification reduces risk and, therefore, makes sense for investors. But does it also make sense for the firm? Is a diversified firm more attractive to investors than an undiversified one? If it is, we have an *extremely* disturbing result. If diversification is an appropriate corporate objective, each project has to be analyzed as a potential addition to the firm's portfolio of assets. The value of the diversified package would be greater than the sum of the parts. So present values would no longer add.

Diversification is undoubtedly a good thing, but that does not mean that firms should practice it. If investors were *not* able to hold a large number of securities, then they might want firms to diversify for them. But investors *can* diversify.[32] In many ways they can do so more easily than firms. Individuals can invest in the steel industry this week and pull out next week. A firm cannot do that. To be sure, the individual would have to pay brokerage fees on the purchase and sale of steel company shares, but think of the time and expense for a firm to acquire a steel company or to start up a new steel-making operation.

You can probably see where we are heading. If investors can diversify on their own account, they will not pay any *extra* for firms that diversify. And if they have a sufficiently wide choice of securities, they will not pay any *less* because they are unable to invest separately in each factory. Therefore, in countries like

---

[32] One of the simplest ways for an individual to diversify is to buy shares in a mutual fund that holds a diversified portfolio.

the United States, which have large and competitive capital markets, diversification does not add to a firm's value or subtract from it. The total value is the sum of its parts.

This conclusion is important for corporate finance, because it justifies adding present values. The concept of *value additivity* is so important that we will give a formal definition of it. If the capital market establishes a value PV(A) for asset A and PV(B) for B, the market value of a firm that holds only these two assets is

$$PV(AB) = PV(A) + PV(B)$$

A three-asset firm combining assets A, B, and C would be worth PV(ABC) = PV(A) + PV(B) + PV(C), and so on for any number of assets.

We have relied on intuitive arguments for value additivity. But the concept is a general one that can be proved formally by several different routes. The concept seems to be widely accepted, for thousands of managers add thousands of present values daily, usually without thinking about it.

SUMMARY

Our review of capital market history showed that the returns to investors have varied according to the risks they have borne. At one extreme, very safe securities like U.S. Treasury bills have provided an average return over 107 years of only 4.0% a year. The riskiest securities that we looked at were common stocks. The stock market provided an average return of 11.7%, a premium of 7.6% over the safe rate of interest.

This gives us two benchmarks for the opportunity cost of capital. If we are evaluating a safe project, we discount at the current risk-free rate of interest. If we are evaluating a project of average risk, we discount at the expected return on the average common stock. Historical evidence suggests that this return is 7.6% above the risk-free rate, but many financial managers and economists opt for a lower figure. That still leaves us with a lot of assets that don't fit these simple cases. Before we can deal with them, we need to learn how to measure risk.

Risk is best judged in a portfolio context. Most investors do not put all their eggs into one basket: They diversify. Thus the effective risk of any security cannot be judged by an examination of that security alone. Part of the uncertainty about the security's return is diversified away when the security is grouped with others in a portfolio.

Risk in investment means that future returns are unpredictable. This spread of possible outcomes is usually measured by standard deviation. The standard deviation of the *market portfolio,* generally represented by the Standard and Poor's Composite Index, is around 15% to 20% a year.

Most individual stocks have higher standard deviations than this, but much of their variability represents *unique* risk that can be eliminated by diversification. Diversification cannot eliminate *market* risk. Diversified portfolios are exposed to variation in the general level of the market.

A security's contribution to the risk of a well-diversified portfolio depends on how the security is liable to be affected by a general market decline. This sensitivity to market movements is known as *beta* (β). Beta measures the amount that investors expect the stock price to change for each additional 1% change in the market. The average beta of all stocks is 1.0. A stock with a beta greater than 1 is unusually sensitive to market movements; a stock with a beta below 1 is unusually insensitive to market movements. The standard deviation of a well-diversified portfolio is proportional to its beta. Thus a diversified portfolio invested in stocks with a beta of 2.0 will have twice the risk of a diversified portfolio with a beta of 1.0.

One theme of this chapter is that diversification is a good thing *for the investor.* This does not imply that *firms* should diversify. Corporate diversification is redundant if investors can diversify on their own account. Since diversification does not affect the firm value, present values add even when risk is explicitly considered. Thanks to *value additivity*, the net present value rule for capital budgeting works even under uncertainty. In this chapter we have introduced you to a number of formulas. They are reproduced in the endpapers to the book. You should take a look and check that you understand them.

FURTHER READING

A very valuable record of the performance of United States securities since 1926 is:

Ibbotson Associates, Inc., *Stocks, Bonds, Bills, and Inflation, 2007 Yearbook* (Ibbotson Associates, 2007).

For international evidence on market returns, see:

E. Dimson, P. R. Marsh, and M. Staunton, "The Worldwide Equity Premium: A Smaller Puzzle," in R. Mehra (ed.), *Handbook of Investments: Equity Risk Premium* 1 (North Holland, 2007).

E. Dimson, P. R. Marsh, and M. Staunton, *Triumph of the Optimists: 101 Years of Global Equity Returns* (Princeton University Press, 2002).

For a somewhat technical survey of the literature on the market risk premium, see:

M. J. Brennan, "Corporate Investment Policy," in G. M. Constantinides, M. Harris, and R. M. Stulz (eds.), *Handbook of the Economics of Finance* (Elsevier Science, 2003).

Books on the risk premium include:

B. Cornell, *The Equity Risk Premium: The Long-Run Future of the Stock Market* New York: Wiley, 1999).

R. Ibbotson, W. Goetzmann, and B. Kogut, *The Equity Risk Premium: Research and Practice* (Oxford University Press, 2004).

There have been several studies of the way that standard deviation is reduced by diversification, including:

M. Statman, "How Many Stocks Make a Diversified Portfolio?" *Journal of Financial and Quantitative Analysis* 22 (September 1987), pp. 353–364.

CONCEPT REVIEW QUESTIONS

1. Explain the difference between the arithmetic average and the compound annual return. Which one is higher? (page 175)

2. If stock prices rise faster than dividends, one possible explanation is that the cost of capital has fallen. Explain why. Would an average of past returns over- or underestimate the cost of capital? (page 179)

3. What are the formulas for the variance and standard deviation of returns? (page 181)

For a complete listing of your chapter Concept Review Questions, please visit us at www.mhhe.com/bma1e.

QUIZ

1. A game of chance offers the following odds and payoffs. Each play of the game costs $100, so the net profit per play is the payoff less $100.

Probability	Payoff	Net Profit
.10	$500	$400
.50	100	0
.40	0	−100

What are the expected cash payoff and expected rate of return? Calculate the variance and standard deviation of this rate of return.

2. The following table shows the nominal returns on the U.S. stocks and the rate of inflation.

   a. What was the standard deviation of the market returns?

   b. Calculate the average real return.

Year	Nominal Return (%)	Inflation (%)
2002	−20.9	2.4
2003	+31.6	1.9
2004	+12.5	3.3
2005	+6.4	3.4
2006	+15.8	2.5

3. Stephen Oblonsky, ace mutual fund manager, produced the following percentage rates of return from 2002 to 2006. Rates of return on the market are given for comparison.

	2002	2003	2004	2005	2006
Mr. Oblonsky	−12.1	+28.2	+11.0	+8.9	+15.0
S&P 500	−20.9	+31.6	+12.5	+6.4	+15.8

Calculate the average return and standard deviation of Mr. Oblonsky's mutual fund. Did he do better or worse than the market by these measures?

4. True or false?

   a. Investors prefer diversified companies because they are less risky.

   b. If stocks were perfectly positively correlated, diversification would not reduce risk.

   c. Diversification over a large number of assets completely eliminates risk.

   d. Diversification works only when assets are uncorrelated.

   e. A stock with a high standard deviation may contribute less to portfolio risk than a stock with a lower standard deviation.

   f. The contribution of a stock to the risk of a well-diversified portfolio depends on its market risk.

   g. A well-diversified portfolio with a beta of 2.0 is twice as risky as the market portfolio.

   h. An undiversified portfolio with a beta of 2.0 is less than twice as risky as the market portfolio.

5. In which of the following situations would you get the largest reduction in risk by spreading your investment across two stocks?

   a. The two shares are perfectly correlated.

   b. There is no correlation.

c. There is modest negative correlation.

d. There is perfect negative correlation.

6. To calculate the variance of a three-stock portfolio, you need to add nine boxes:

Use the same symbols that we used in this chapter; for example, x_1 = proportion invested in stock 1 and σ_{12} = covariance between stocks 1 and 2. Now complete the nine boxes.

7. Suppose the standard deviation of the market return is 20%.

a. What is the standard deviation of returns on a well-diversified portfolio with a beta of 1.3?

b. What is the standard deviation of returns on a well-diversified portfolio with a beta of 0?

c. A well-diversified portfolio has a standard deviation of 15%. What is its beta?

d. A poorly diversified portfolio has a standard deviation of 20%. What can you say about its beta?

8. A portfolio contains equal investments in 10 stocks. Five have a beta of 1.2; the remainder have a beta of 1.4. What is the portfolio beta?

a. 1.3.

b. Greater than 1.3 because the portfolio is not completely diversified.

c. Less than 1.3 because diversification reduces beta.

9. What is the beta of each of the stocks shown in Table 8.8?

Stock	Stock Return if Market Return Is:	
	−10%	**+10%**
A	0	+20
B	−20	+20
C	−30	0
D	+15	+15
E	+10	−10

TABLE 8.8

See Quiz Question 9.

10. Here are inflation rates and U.S. stock market and Treasury bill returns between 1929 and 1933:

Year	Inflation	Stock Market Return	T-Bill Return
1929	−2	−14.5	4.8
1930	−6.0	−28.3	2.4
1931	−9.5	−43.9	1.1
1932	−10.3	−9.9	1.0
1933	.5	57.3	.3

PRACTICE QUESTIONS

Visit us at
www.mhhe.com/bma1e.

a. What was the real return on the stock market in each year?

b. What was the average real return?

c. What was the risk premium in each year?

d. What was the average risk premium?

e. What was the standard deviation of the risk premium?

11. You can find monthly adjusted prices for most or all of the companies in Table 8.3 on Standard & Poor's Market Insight Web site (**www.mhhe.com/edumarketinsight**) or on **finance.yahoo.com.** Download the prices for three of these companies to an Excel spreadsheet. Calculate each company's variance and standard deviation of the monthly returns. The Excel functions are VAR and STDEV. Convert the standard deviations from monthly to annual units by multiplying by the square root of 12. How has the stand-alone risk of these stocks changed, compared with the figures reported in Table 8.3?

12. Each of the following statements is dangerous or misleading. Explain why.

a. A long-term United States government bond is always absolutely safe.

b. All investors should prefer stocks to bonds because stocks offer higher long-run rates of return.

c. The best practical forecast of future rates of return on the stock market is a 5- or 10-year average of historical returns.

13. Hippique s.a., which owns a stable of racehorses, has just invested in a mysterious black stallion with great form but disputed bloodlines. Some experts in horseflesh predict the horse will win the coveted Prix de Bidet; others argue that it should be put out to grass. Is this a risky investment for Hippique shareholders? Explain.

14. Lonesome Gulch Mines has a standard deviation of 42% per year and a beta of +.10. Amalgamated Copper has a standard deviation of 31% a year and a beta of +.66. Explain why Lonesome Gulch is the safer investment for a diversified investor.

Visit us at www.mhhe.com/bma1e.

15. Lambeth Walk invests 60% of his funds in stock I and the balance in stock J. The standard deviation of returns on I is 10%, and on J it is 20%. Calculate the variance of portfolio returns, assuming

a. The correlation between the returns is 1.0.

b. The correlation is .5.

c. The correlation is 0.

Visit us at www.mhhe.com/bma1e.

16. a. How many variance terms and how many covariance terms do you need to calculate the risk of a 100-share portfolio?

b. Suppose all stocks had a standard deviation of 30% and a correlation with each other of .4. What is the standard deviation of the returns on a portfolio that has equal holdings in 50 stocks?

c. What is the standard deviation of a fully diversified portfolio of such stocks?

17. Suppose that the standard deviation of returns from a typical share is about .40 (or 40%) a year. The correlation between the returns of each pair of shares is about .3.

a. Calculate the variance and standard deviation of the returns on a portfolio that has equal investments in 2 shares, 3 shares, and so on, up to 10 shares.

b. Use your estimates to draw a graph like Figure 8.11. How large is the underlying market risk that cannot be diversified away?

c. Now repeat the problem, assuming that the correlation between each pair of stocks is zero.

18. Download to a spreadsheet monthly adjusted prices for Coca-Cola, Citigroup, and Pfizer from **finance.yahoo.com** or from Standard & Poor's Market Insight Web site (**www.mhhe.com/edumarketinsight**).

a. Calculate the annual standard deviation of returns for each company, using the most recent three years of monthly returns. Use the Excel function STDEV. Multiply by the square root of 12 to convert to annual units.

b. Use the Excel function CORREL to calculate the correlation coefficient between the monthly returns for each pair of stocks.

c. Calculate the standard deviation of returns for a portfolio with equal investments in each of the three stocks.

19. Table 8.9 shows standard deviations and correlation coefficients for seven stocks from different countries. Calculate the variance of a portfolio with equal investments in each stock.

20. Most of the companies in Table 8.5 are covered either in **finance.yahoo.com** or in the Standard & Poor's Market Insight Web site (**www.mhhe.com/edumarketinsight**). For those that are covered, you can easily calculate beta. Download the "Monthly Adjusted Prices" spreadsheet, and note the columns for returns on the stock and the S&P 500 index. Beta is calculated by the Excel function SLOPE, where the "y" range refers to the company's return (the dependent variable) and the "x" range refers to the market returns (the independent variable). Calculate the betas. How have they changed from the betas reported in Table 8.5?

21. Your eccentric Aunt Claudia has left you $50,000 in Alcan shares plus $50,000 cash. Unfortunately her will requires that the Alcan stock not be sold for one year and the $50,000 cash must be entirely invested in one of the stocks shown in Table 8.9. What is the safest attainable portfolio under these restrictions?

22. There are few, if any, real companies with negative betas. But suppose you found one with $\beta = -.25$.

    a. How would you expect this stock's rate of return to change if the overall market rose by an extra 5%? What if the market fell by an extra 5%?

    b. You have $1 million invested in a well-diversified portfolio of stocks. Now you receive an additional $20,000 bequest. Which of the following actions will yield the safest overall portfolio return?

       i. Invest $20,000 in Treasury bills (which have $\beta = 0$).

       ii. Invest $20,000 in stocks with $\beta = 1$.

       iii. Invest $20,000 in the stock with $\beta = -.25$.

      Explain your answer.

| | Correlation Coefficients | | | | | | | |
	Alcan	BP	Deutsche Bank	Fiat	Heineken	LVMH	Nestlé	Standard Deviation
Alcan	1.00	.34	.53	.30	.20	.53	.08	29.7%
BP		1.00	.44	.26	.20	.27	.29	18.4
Deutsche Bank			1.00	.52	.22	.56	.24	30.1
Fiat				1.00	.17	.42	.26	35.9
Heineken					1.00	.33	.50	17.2
LVMH						1.00	.31	31.0
Nestle							1.00	13.8

TABLE 8.9

Standard deviations of returns and correlation coefficients for a sample of seven stocks.

Note: Correlations and standard deviations are calculated using returns in each country's own currency; in other words, they assume that the investor is protected against exchange risk.

23. You can form a portfolio of two assets, A and B, whose returns have the following characteristics:

Stock	Expected Return	Standard Deviation	Correlation
A	10%	20%	
			.5
B	15	40	

If you demand an expected return of 12%, what are the portfolio weights? What is the portfolio's standard deviation?

STANDARD
&POOR'S

24. Download "Monthly Adjusted Prices" for General Motors (GM) and Harley-Davidson (HOG) from either **finance.yahoo.com** or the Standard & Poor's Market Insight Web site (**www.mhhe.com/edumarketinsight**).

   a. Calculate each company's beta, following the procedure described in Practice Problem 20.

   b. Calculate the annual standard deviation of the market from the monthly returns for the S&P 500. Use the Excel function STDEV, and multiply by the square root of 12 to convert to annual units. Also calculate the annual standard deviations for GM and HOG.

   c. Let's assume that your answers to (a) and (b) are good forecasts. What would be the standard deviation of a well-diversified portfolio of stocks with betas equal to Harley-Davidson's beta? How about a well-diversified portfolio of stocks with GM's beta?

   d. How much of the total risk of GM was unique risk? How much of HOG's?

   e. Now use the monthly prices for General Motors and Harley-Davidson and calculate the covariance and correlation coefficient between the two sets of returns.

CHALLENGE
QUESTIONS

25. Here are some historical data on the risk characteristics of Dell and Home Depot:

	Dell	Home Depot
β (beta)	1.25	1.53
Yearly standard deviation of return (%)	29.32	29.27

Assume the standard deviation of the return on the market was 15%.

   a. The correlation coefficient of Dell's return versus Home Depot's is .59. What is the standard deviation of a portfolio invested half in Dell and half in Home Depot?

   b. What is the standard deviation of a portfolio invested one-third in Dell, one-third in Home Depot, and one-third in risk-free Treasury bills?

   c. What is the standard deviation if the portfolio is split evenly between Dell and Home Depot and is financed at 50% margin, i.e., the investor puts up only 50% of the total amount and borrows the balance from the broker?

   d. What is the *approximate* standard deviation of a portfolio composed of 100 stocks with betas of 1.25 like Dell? How about 100 stocks like Home Depot? (*Hint:* Part (d) should not require anything but the simplest arithmetic to answer.)

26. Suppose that Treasury bills offer a return of about 6% and the expected market risk premium is 8.5%. The standard deviation of Treasury-bill returns is zero and the standard deviation of market returns is 20%. Use the formula for portfolio risk to calculate the standard deviation of portfolios with different proportions in Treasury bills and

the market. (*Note:* The covariance of two rates of return must be zero when the standard deviation of one return is zero.) Graph the expected returns and standard deviations.

27. Select two bank stocks and two oil stocks and then calculate the returns for 60 recent months. (Monthly stock price and index data can be obtained from **finance.yahoo.com.**)

   a. Use the Excel SDEV and CORREL functions to calculate the standard deviation of monthly returns for each of these stocks and the correlation between each pair of stocks.

   b. Use your results to find the standard deviation of a portfolio that is evenly divided between different pairs of stocks. Do you reduce risk more by diversifying across stocks in the same industry or those in different industries?

28. Calculate the beta of each of the stocks in Table 8.9 relative to a portfolio with equal investments in each stock.

Visit us at
www.mhhe.com/bma1e.

CHAPTER NINE

RISK AND RETURN

IN CHAPTER 8 we began to come to grips with the problem of measuring risk. Here is the story so far.

The stock market is risky because there is a spread of possible outcomes. The usual measure of this spread is the standard deviation or variance. The risk of any stock can be broken down into two parts. There is the *unique risk* that is peculiar to that stock, and there is the *market risk* that is associated with marketwide variations. Investors can eliminate unique risk by holding a well-diversified portfolio, but they cannot eliminate market risk. *All* the risk of a fully diversified portfolio is market risk.

A stock's contribution to the risk of a fully diversified portfolio depends on its sensitivity to market changes. This sensitivity is generally known as *beta*. A security with a beta of 1.0 has average market risk—a well-diversified portfolio of such securities has the same standard deviation as the market index. A security with a beta of .5 has below-average market risk—a well-diversified portfolio of these securities tends to move half as far as the market moves and has half the market's standard deviation.

In this chapter we build on this newfound knowledge. We present leading theories linking risk and return in a competitive economy, and we show how these theories can be used to estimate the returns required by investors in different stock market investments. We start with the most widely used theory, the capital asset pricing model, which builds directly on the ideas developed in the last chapter. We will also look at another class of models, known as arbitrage pricing or factor models. Then in Chapter 10 we show how these ideas can help the financial manager cope with risk in practical capital budgeting situations.

<table>
<tr><td>9.1</td><td>HARRY MARKOWITZ AND THE BIRTH OF PORTFOLIO THEORY</td></tr>
</table>

Most of the ideas in Chapter 8 date back to an article written in 1952 by Harry Markowitz.[1] Markowitz drew attention to the common practice of portfolio diversification and showed exactly how an investor can reduce the standard deviation of portfolio returns by choosing stocks that do not move exactly together. But

---

[1] H. M. Markowitz, "Portfolio Selection," *Journal of Finance 7* (March 1952), pp. 77–91.

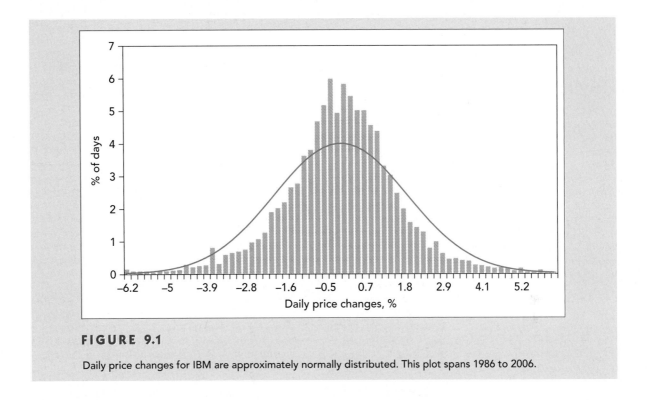

FIGURE 9.1

Daily price changes for IBM are approximately normally distributed. This plot spans 1986 to 2006.

Markowitz did not stop there; he went on to work out the basic principles of port-folio construction. These principles are the foundation for much of what has been written about the relationship between risk and return.

We begin with Figure 9.1, which shows a histogram of the daily returns on IBM stock from 1986 to 2006. On this histogram we have superimposed a bell-shaped nor-mal distribution. The result is typical: When measured over some fairly short interval, the past rates of return on any stock conform fairly closely to a normal distribution.[2]

Normal distributions can be completely defined by two numbers. One is the average or expected return; the other is the variance or standard deviation. Now you can see why in Chapter 8 we discussed the calculation of expected return and standard deviation. They are not just arbitrary measures: If returns are normally distributed, expected return and standard deviation are the *only* two measures that an investor need consider.

Figure 9.2 pictures the distribution of possible returns from three investments. A and B offer an expected return of 10%, but A has the much wider spread of pos-sible outcomes. Its standard deviation is 15%; the standard deviation of B is 7.5%. Most investors dislike uncertainty and would therefore prefer B to A.

Now compare investments B and C. This time both have the *same* standard deviation, but the expected return is 20% from stock C and only 10% from stock B. Most investors like high expected return and would therefore prefer C to B.

---

[2] If you were to measure returns over *long* intervals, the distribution would be skewed. For example, you would encounter returns greater than 100% but none less than −100%. The distribution of returns over periods of, say, one year would be better approximated by a *lognormal* distribution. The lognormal distribution, like the normal, is com-pletely specified by its mean and standard deviation.

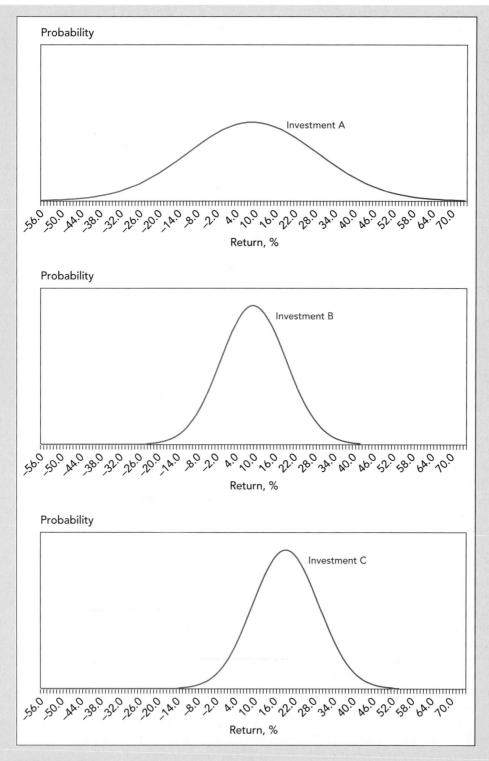

FIGURE 9.2

Investments A and B both have an *expected* return of 10% but because investment A has the greater spread of *possible* returns, it is more risky than B. We can measure this spread by the standard deviation. Investment A has a standard deviation of 15%; B, 7.5%. Most investors would prefer B to A. Investments B and C both have the same standard deviation, but C offers a higher expected return. Most investors would prefer C to B.

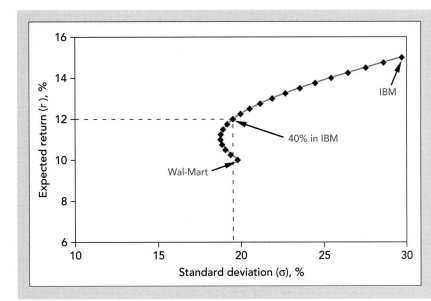

FIGURE 9.3

The curved line illustrates how expected return and standard deviation change as you hold different combinations of two stocks. For example, if you invest 40% of your money in IBM and the remainder in Wal-Mart, your expected return is 12%, which is 40% of the way between the expected returns on the two stocks. The standard deviation is 19.5%, which is less than 40% of the way between the standard deviations of the two stocks. This is because diversification reduces risk.

Combining Stocks into Portfolios

Suppose that you are wondering whether to invest in shares of Wal-Mart or IBM. You decide that Wal-Mart offers an expected return of 10% and IBM offers an expected return of 15%. After looking back at the past variability of the two stocks, you also decide that the standard deviation of returns is 19.8% for Wal-Mart and 29.7% for IBM. IBM offers the higher expected return, but it is more risky.

Now there is no reason to restrict yourself to holding only one stock. For example, in Section 8.3 we analyzed what would happen if you invested 60% of your money in Wal-Mart and 40% in IBM. The expected return on this portfolio is 12%, which is simply a weighted average of the expected returns on the two holdings. What about the risk of such a portfolio? We know that thanks to diversification the portfolio risk is less than the average of the risks of the separate stocks. In fact, on the basis of past experience the standard deviation of this portfolio is 19.5%.[3]

In Figure 9.3 we have plotted the expected return and risk that you could achieve by different combinations of the two stocks. Which of these combinations is best? That depends on your stomach. If you want to stake all on getting rich quickly, you will do best to put all your money in IBM. If you want a more peaceful life, you should invest most of your money in Wal-Mart. To minimize risk you should keep a small investment in IBM.[4]

In practice, you are not limited to investing in only two stocks. For example, suppose that you can choose a portfolio from any of the stocks listed in the first

---

[3] We pointed out in Section 8.3 that the correlation between the returns of Wal-Mart and IBM has been about .35. The variance of a portfolio which is invested 60% in Wal-Mart and 40% in IBM is

$$\text{Variance} = x_1^2\sigma_1^2 + x_2^2\sigma_2^2 + 2x_1x_2\rho_{12}\sigma_1\sigma_2$$
$$= [(.6)^2 \times (19.8)^2] + [(.4)^2 \times (29.7)^2] + 2(.6 \times .4 \times .35 \times 19.8 \times 29.7)$$
$$= 381.1$$

The portfolio standard deviation is $\sqrt{381.1} = 19.5\%$.

[4] The portfolio with the minimum risk has 78.4% in Wal-Mart. We assume in Figure 9.3 that you may not take negative positions in either stock, i.e., we rule out short sales.

Stock	Expected Return	Standard Deviation	Efficient Portfolios—Percentages Allocated to Each Stock			
			A	B	C	D
Amazon.com	23.1%	56.0%	100	52.2	19.2	1.0
IBM	15.0	29.7		33.8	9.4	
Disney	13.4	27.7				
Microsoft	14.2	24.4		13.7	25.8	1.9
Boeing	11.7	29.8				
Starbucks	12.3	29.9				5.9
ExxonMobil	7.9	19.2				16.7
Wal-Mart	10.0	19.8				23.7
Pfizer	8.0	19.2				15.1
Heinz	10.6	16.5		.2	45.6	35.6
Expected portfolio return			23.1	19.1	14.3	9.9
Portfolio standard deviation			56.0	36.1	17.8	10.6

TABLE 9.1

Examples of efficient portfolios chosen from 10 stocks.

Note: Standard deviations and the correlations between stock returns were estimated from monthly stock returns, July 2001–June 2006. Efficient portfolios are calculated assuming that short sales are prohibited.

column of Table 9.1. After analyzing the prospects for each firm, you come up with the return forecasts shown in the second column of the table. You use data for the past five years to estimate the risk of each stock (column 3) and the correlation between the returns on each pair of stocks.[5]

Now turn to Figure 9.4. Each diamond marks the combination of risk and return offered by a different individual security. For example, Amazon.com (marked "A" in the figure) has the highest standard deviation; it also offers the highest expected return. It is represented by the diamond at the upper right of Figure 9.4.

By mixing investment in individual securities, you can obtain an even wider selection of risk and return: in fact, *anywhere* in the shaded area in Figure 9.4. But where in the shaded area is best? Well, what is your goal? Which direction do you want to go? The answer should be obvious: You want to go up (to increase expected return) and to the left (to reduce risk). Go as far as you can, and you will end up with one of the portfolios that lies along the heavy solid line. Markowitz called them **efficient portfolios.** These portfolios are clearly better than any in the interior of the shaded area.

We will not calculate this set of efficient portfolios here, but you may be interested in how to do it. Think back to the capital rationing problem in Section 6.4. There we wanted to deploy a limited amount of capital investment in a mixture of projects to give the highest total NPV. Here we want to deploy an investor's funds to give the highest expected return for a given standard deviation. In principle, both problems

---

[5] There are 45 different correlation coefficients, so we have not listed them in Table 9.1.

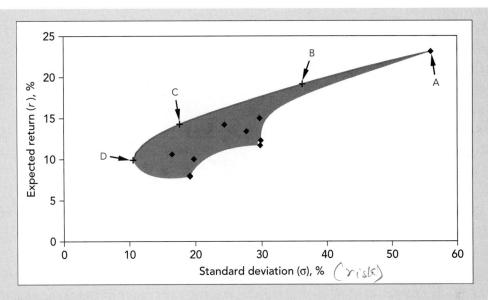

FIGURE 9.4

Each diamond shows the expected return and standard deviation of 1 of the 10 stocks in Table 9.1. The shaded area shows the possible combinations of expected return and standard deviation from investing in a *mixture* of these stocks. If you like high expected returns and dislike high standard deviations, you will prefer portfolios along the heavy line. These are *efficient* portfolios. We have marked the four efficient portfolios described in Table 9.1 (A, B, C, and D).

can be solved by hunting and pecking—but only in principle. To solve the capital rationing problem, we can employ linear programming; to solve the portfolio problem, we would turn to a variant of linear programming known as *quadratic programming*. Given the expected return and standard deviation for each stock, as well as the correlation between each pair of stocks, we could give a computer a standard quadratic program and tell it to calculate the set of efficient portfolios.

Four of these efficient portfolios are marked in Figure 9.4. Their compositions are summarized in Table 9.1. Portfolio A offers the highest expected return; A is invested entirely in one stock, Amazon.com. Portfolio D offers the minimum risk; you can see from Table 9.1 that it has a large holding in Heinz, which has had the lowest standard deviation. Notice that D also has a small holding in Amazon.com, even though this stock is individually very risky. The reason? On past evidence the fortunes of Amazon are only weakly correlated with those of the other stocks in the portfolio and therefore Amazon provides additional diversification.

Table 9.1 also shows the compositions of two other efficient portfolios B and C with intermediate levels of risk and expected return.

We Introduce Borrowing and Lending

Of course, large investment funds can choose from thousands of stocks and thereby achieve a wider choice of risk and return. This choice is represented in Figure 9.5 by the shaded, broken-egg-shaped area. The set of efficient portfolios is again marked by the heavy curved line.

FIGURE 9.5

Lending and borrowing extend the range of investment possibilities. If you invest in portfolio S and lend or borrow at the risk-free interest rate, r_f, you can achieve any point along the straight line from r_f through S. This gives you a higher expected return for any level of risk than if you just invest in common stocks.

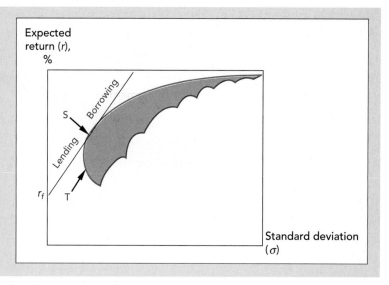

Now we introduce yet another possibility. Suppose that you can also lend or borrow money at some risk-free rate of interest r_f. If you invest some of your money in Treasury bills (i.e., lend money) and place the remainder in common stock portfolio S, you can obtain any combination of expected return and risk along the straight line joining r_f and S in Figure 9.5. Since borrowing is merely negative lending, you can extend the range of possibilities to the right of S by borrowing funds at an interest rate of r_f and investing them as well as your own money in portfolio S.

Let us put some numbers on this. Suppose that portfolio S has an expected return of 15% and a standard deviation of 16%. Treasury bills offer an interest rate (r_f) of 5% and are risk-free (i.e., their standard deviation is zero). If you invest half your money in portfolio S and lend the remainder at 5%, the expected return on your investment is halfway between the expected return on S and the interest rate on Treasury bills:

$$r = (½ \times \text{expected return on S}) + (½ \times \text{interest rate})$$
$$= 10\%$$

And the standard deviation is halfway between the standard deviation of S and the standard deviation of Treasury bills[6]:

$$\sigma = (½ \times \text{standard deviation of S}) + (½ \times \text{standard deviation of bills})$$
$$= 8\%$$

Or suppose that you decide to go for the big time: You borrow at the Treasury bill rate an amount equal to your initial wealth, and you invest everything in

---

[6] If you want to check this, write down the formula for the standard deviation of a two-stock portfolio:

$$\text{Standard deviation} = \sqrt{x_1^2 \sigma_1^2 + x_2^2 \sigma_2^2 + 2x_1 x_2 \rho_{12} \sigma_1 \sigma_2}$$

Now see what happens when security 2 is riskless, i.e., when $\sigma_2 = 0$.

portfolio S. You have twice your own money invested in S, but you have to *pay* interest on the loan. Therefore your expected return is

$$r = (2 \times \text{expected return on S}) - (1 \times \text{interest rate})$$
$$= 25\%$$

And the standard deviation of your investment is

$$\sigma = (2 \times \text{standard deviation of S}) - (1 \times \text{standard deviation of bills})$$
$$= 32\%$$

You can see from Figure 9.5 that when you lend a portion of your money, you end up partway between r_f and S; if you can borrow money at the risk-free rate, you can extend your possibilities beyond S. You can also see that regardless of the level of risk you choose, you can get the highest expected return by a mixture of portfolio S and borrowing or lending. S is the *best* efficient portfolio. There is no reason ever to hold, say, portfolio T.

If you have a graph of efficient portfolios, as in Figure 9.5, finding this best efficient portfolio is easy. Start on the vertical axis at r_f and draw the steepest line you can to the curved heavy line of efficient portfolios. That line will be tangent to the heavy line. The efficient portfolio at the tangency point is better than all the others. Notice that it offers the highest *ratio* of risk premium to standard deviation. This ratio of the risk premium to the standard deviation is called the *Sharpe ratio:*

$$\text{Sharpe ratio} = \frac{\text{Risk premium}}{\text{Standard deviation}} = \frac{r_P - r_f}{\sigma_P}$$

Investors track Sharpe ratios to measure the risk-adjusted performance of investment managers. (Take a look at the mini-case at the end of this chapter.)

We can now separate the investor's job into two stages. First, the best portfolio of common stocks must be selected—S in our example. Second, this portfolio must be blended with borrowing or lending to obtain an exposure to risk that suits the particular investor's taste. Each investor, therefore, should put money into just two benchmark investments—a risky portfolio S and a risk-free loan (borrowing or lending).

What does portfolio S look like? If you have better information than your rivals, you will want the portfolio to include relatively large investments in the stocks you think are undervalued. But in a competitive market you are unlikely to have a monopoly of good ideas. In that case there is no reason to hold a different portfolio of common stocks from anybody else. In other words, you might just as well hold the market portfolio. That is why many professional investors invest in a market-index portfolio and why most others hold well-diversified portfolios.

9.2 THE RELATIONSHIP BETWEEN RISK AND RETURN

In Chapter 8 we looked at the returns on selected investments. The least risky investment was U.S. Treasury bills. Since the return on Treasury bills is fixed, it is unaffected by what happens to the market. In other words, Treasury bills have a beta of 0. We also considered a much riskier investment, the market portfolio of common stocks. This has average market risk: Its beta is 1.0.

FIGURE 9.6

The capital asset pricing model states that the expected risk premium on each investment is proportional to its beta. This means that each investment should lie on the sloping security market line connecting Treasury bills and the market portfolio.

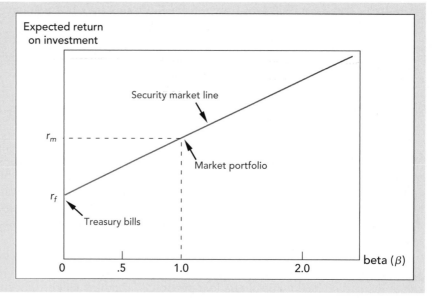

Wise investors don't take risks just for fun. They are playing with real money. Therefore, they require a higher return from the market portfolio than from Treasury bills. The difference between the return on the market and the interest rate is termed the *market risk premium.* Since 1900 the market risk premium ($r_m - r_f$) has averaged 7.6% a year.

In Figure 9.6 we have plotted the risk and expected return from Treasury bills and the market portfolio. You can see that Treasury bills have a beta of 0 and a risk premium of 0.[7] The market portfolio has a beta of 1.0 and a risk premium of $r_m - r_f$. This gives us two benchmarks for the expected risk premium. But what is the expected risk premium when beta is not 0 or 1?

In the mid-1960s three economists—William Sharpe, John Lintner, and Jack Treynor—produced an answer to this question.[8] Their answer is known as the **capital asset pricing model,** or **CAPM.** The model's message is both startling and simple. In a competitive market, the expected risk premium varies in direct proportion to beta. This means that in Figure 9.6 all investments must plot along the sloping line, known as the **security market line.** The expected risk premium on an investment with a beta of .5 is, therefore, *half* the expected risk premium on the market; the expected risk premium on an investment with a beta of 2.0 is *twice* the expected risk premium on the market. We can write this relationship as

Expected risk premium on stock = beta × expected risk premium on market

$$r - r_f = \beta(r_m - r_f)$$

---

[7] Remember that the risk premium is the difference between the investment's expected return and the risk-free rate. For Treasury bills, the difference is zero.

[8] W. F. Sharpe, "Capital Asset Prices: A Theory of Market Equilibrium under Conditions of Risk," *Journal of Finance* 19 (September 1964), pp. 425–442 and J. Lintner, "The Valuation of Risk Assets and the Selection of Risky Investments in Stock Portfolios and Capital Budgets," *Review of Economics and Statistics* 47 (February 1965), pp. 13–37. Treynor's article has not been published.

Stock	Beta (β)	Expected Return $[r_f + \beta(r_m - r_f)]$
Amazon.com	2.20	20.4%
IBM	1.59	16.1
Disney	1.26	13.8
Microsoft	1.13	12.9
Boeing	1.09	12.6
Starbucks	.69	9.8
ExxonMobil	.65	9.6
Wal-Mart	.57	9.0
Pfizer	.55	8.9
Heinz	.36	7.5

TABLE 9.2

These estimates of the returns expected by investors in October 2006 were based on the capital asset pricing model. We assumed 5% for the interest rate r_f and 7% for the expected risk premium $r_m - r_f$.

Some Estimates of Expected Returns

Before we tell you where the formula comes from, let us use it to figure out what returns investors are looking for from particular stocks. To do this, we need three numbers: β, r_f, and $r_m - r_f$. We gave you estimates of the betas of 10 stocks in Table 8.5. In October 2006 the interest rate on Treasury bills was about 5%.

How about the market risk premium? As we pointed out in the last chapter, we can't measure $r_m - r_f$ with precision. From past evidence it appears to be 7.6%, although many economists and financial managers would forecast a lower figure. Let us use 7% in this example.

Table 9.2 puts these numbers together to give an estimate of the expected return on each stock. The stock with the highest beta in our sample is Amazon.com. Our estimate of the expected return from Amazon is 20.4%. The stock with the lowest beta is Heinz. Our estimate of its expected return is 7.5%, 2.5% more than the interest rate on Treasury bills.

You can also use the capital asset pricing model to find the discount rate for a new capital investment. For example, suppose that you are analyzing a proposal by Pfizer to expand its capacity. At what rate should you discount the forecast cash flows? According to Table 9.2, investors are looking for a return of 8.9% from businesses with the risk of Pfizer. So the cost of capital for a further investment in the same business is 8.9%.[9]

In practice, choosing a discount rate is seldom so easy. (After all, you can't expect to be paid a fat salary just for plugging numbers into a formula.) For example, you must learn how to adjust for the extra risk caused by company borrowing. You will also need to consider the difference between short- and long-term interest rates. If short-term rates and long-term rates are very different, a cost of capital based on the short-term rate may be inappropriate for long-term capital investments. But these refinements can wait until later.[10]

---

[9] Remember that instead of investing in plant and machinery, the firm could return the money to the shareholders. The opportunity cost of investing is the return that shareholders could expect to earn by buying financial assets. This expected return depends on the market risk of the assets.

[10] Tax issues arise because a corporation must pay tax on income from an investment in Treasury bills or other interest-paying securities. It turns out that the correct discount rate for risk-free investments is the *after-tax* Treasury bill rate. We come back to this point in Chapter 16.

Various other points on the practical use of betas and the capital asset pricing model are covered in Chapter 10.

Review of the Capital Asset Pricing Model

Let us review the basic principles of portfolio selection:

1. Investors like high expected return and low standard deviation. Common stock portfolios that offer the highest expected return for a given standard deviation are known as *efficient portfolios*.

2. If the investor can lend or borrow at the risk-free rate of interest, one efficient portfolio is better than all the others: the portfolio that offers the highest ratio of risk premium to standard deviation (that is, portfolio S in Figure 9.5). A risk-averse investor will put part of his money in this efficient portfolio and part in the risk-free asset. A risk-tolerant investor may put all her money in this portfolio or she may borrow and put in even more.

3. The composition of this best efficient portfolio depends on the investor's assessments of expected returns, standard deviations, and correlations. But suppose everybody has the same information and the same assessments. If there is no superior information, each investor should hold the same portfolio as everybody else; in other words, everyone should hold the market portfolio.

Now let us go back to the risk of individual stocks:

4. Do not look at the risk of a stock in isolation but at its contribution to portfolio risk. This contribution depends on the stock's sensitivity to changes in the value of the portfolio.

5. A stock's sensitivity to changes in the value of the *market* portfolio is known as *beta*. Beta, therefore, measures the marginal contribution of a stock to the risk of the market portfolio.

Now if everyone holds the market portfolio, and if beta measures each security's contribution to the market portfolio risk, then it is no surprise that the risk premium demanded by investors is proportional to beta. That is what the CAPM says.

What If a Stock Did Not Lie on the Security Market Line?

Imagine that you encounter stock A in Figure 9.7. Would you buy it? We hope not[11]—if you want an investment with a beta of .5, you could get a higher expected return by investing half your money in Treasury bills and half in the market portfolio. If everybody shares your view of the stock's prospects, the price of A will have to fall until the expected return matches what you could get elsewhere.

What about stock B in Figure 9.7? Would you be tempted by its high return? You wouldn't if you were smart. You could get a higher expected return for the same beta by borrowing 50 cents for every dollar of your own money and investing in the market portfolio. Again, if everybody agrees with your assessment, the price of stock B cannot hold. It will have to fall until the expected return on B is equal to the expected return on the combination of borrowing and investment in the market portfolio.

We have made our point. An investor can always obtain an expected risk premium of $\beta(r_m - r_f)$ by holding a mixture of the market portfolio and a risk-free loan. So in well-functioning markets nobody will hold a stock that offers an expected

---

[11] Unless, of course, we were trying to sell it.

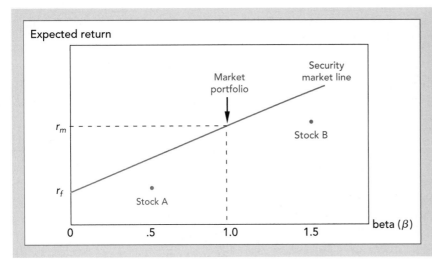

FIGURE 9.7

In equilibrium no stock can lie below the security market line. For example, instead of buying stock A, investors would prefer to lend part of their money and put the balance in the market portfolio. And instead of buying stock B, they would prefer to borrow and invest in the market portfolio.

risk premium of *less* than $\beta(r_m - r_f)$. But what about the other possibility? Are there stocks that offer a higher expected risk premium? In other words, are there any that lie above the security market line in Figure 9.7? If we take all stocks together, we have the market portfolio. Therefore, we know that stocks *on average* lie on the line. Since none lies *below* the line, then there also can't be any that lie *above* the line. Thus each and every stock must lie on the security market line and offer an expected risk premium of

$$r - r_f = \beta(r_m - r_f)$$

9.3   VALIDITY AND ROLE OF THE CAPITAL ASSET PRICING MODEL

Any economic model is a simplified statement of reality. We need to simplify in order to interpret what is going on around us. But we also need to know how much faith we can place in our model.

Let us begin with some matters about which there is broad agreement. First, few people quarrel with the idea that investors require some extra return for taking on risk. That is why common stocks have given on average a higher return than U.S. Treasury bills. Who would want to invest in risky common stocks if they offered only the *same* expected return as bills? We would not, and we suspect you would not either.

Second, investors do appear to be concerned principally with those risks that they cannot eliminate by diversification. If this were not so, we should find that stock prices increase whenever two companies merge to spread their risks. And we should find that investment companies which invest in the shares of other firms are more highly valued than the shares they hold. But we do not observe either phenomenon. Mergers undertaken just to spread risk do not increase stock prices, and investment companies are no more highly valued than the stocks they hold.

The capital asset pricing model captures these ideas in a simple way. That is why financial managers find it a convenient tool for coming to grips with the

FIGURE 9.8

The capital asset pricing model states that the expected risk premium from any investment should lie on the security market line. The dots show the actual average risk premiums from portfolios with different betas. The high-beta portfolios generated higher average returns, just as predicted by the CAPM. But the high-beta portfolios plotted below the market line, and the low-beta portfolios plotted above. A line fitted to the 10 portfolio returns would be "flatter" than the market line.

Source: F. Black, "Beta and Return," *Journal of Portfolio Management* 20 (Fall 1993), pp. 8–18. © 1993 Institutional Investor. Used with permission. We are grateful to Adam Kolasinski for updating the calculations.

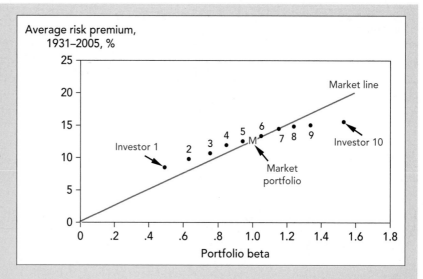

slippery notion of risk and why nearly three-quarters of them use it to estimate the cost of capital.[12] It is also why economists often use the capital asset pricing model to demonstrate important ideas in finance even when there are other ways to prove these ideas. But that does not mean that the capital asset pricing model is ultimate truth. We will see later that it has several unsatisfactory features, and we will look at some alternative theories. Nobody knows whether one of these alternative theories is eventually going to come out on top or whether there are other, better models of risk and return that have not yet seen the light of day.

Tests of the Capital Asset Pricing Model

Imagine that in 1931 ten investors gathered together in a Wall Street bar and agreed to establish investment trust funds for their children. Each investor decided to follow a different strategy. Investor 1 opted to buy the 10% of the New York Stock Exchange stocks with the lowest estimated betas; investor 2 chose the 10% with the next-lowest betas; and so on, up to investor 10, who proposed to buy the stocks with the highest betas. They also planned that at the end of each year they would reestimate the betas of all NYSE stocks and reconstitute their portfolios.[13] And so they parted with much cordiality and good wishes.

In time the 10 investors all passed away, but their children agreed to meet in early 2006 in the same bar to compare the performance of their portfolios. Figure 9.8 shows how they had fared. Investor 1's portfolio turned out to be much less risky than the market; its beta was only .49. However, investor 1 also realized the lowest return, 8.5% above the risk-free rate of interest. At the other extreme, the beta of

---

[12] See J. R. Graham and C. R. Harvey, "The Theory and Practice of Corporate Finance: Evidence from the Field," *Journal of Financial Economics* 61 (2001), pp. 187–243. A number of the managers surveyed reported using more than one method to estimate the cost of capital. Seventy-three percent used the capital asset pricing model, while 39% stated they used the average historical stock return and 34% used the capital asset pricing model with some extra risk factors.

[13] Betas were estimated using returns over the previous 60 months.

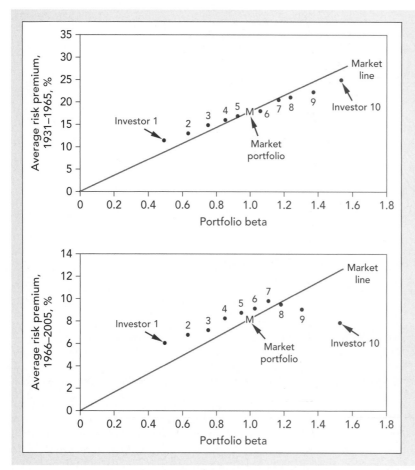

FIGURE 9.9

The relationship between beta and actual average return has been much weaker since the mid-1960s. In particular stocks with the highest betas have provided poor returns.

Source: F. Black, "Beta and Return," *Journal of Portfolio Management* 20 (Fall 1993), pp. 8–18. © 1993 Institutional Investor. Used with permission. We are grateful to Adam Kolasinski for updating the calculations.

investor 10's portfolio was 1.53, about three times that of investor 1's portfolio. But investor 10 was rewarded with the highest return, averaging 15.6% a year above the interest rate. So over this 75-year period returns did indeed increase with beta.

As you can see from Figure 9.8, the market portfolio over the same 75-year period provided an average return of 12.5% above the interest rate[14] and (of course) had a beta of 1.0. The CAPM predicts that the risk premium should increase in proportion to beta, so that the returns of each portfolio should lie on the upward-sloping security market line in Figure 9.8. Since the market provided a risk premium of 12.5%, investor 1's portfolio, with a beta of .49, should have provided a risk premium of about 6% and investor 10's portfolio, with a beta of 1.53, should have given a premium of over 19%. You can see that, while high-beta stocks performed better than low-beta stocks, the difference was not as great as the CAPM predicts.

Although Figure 9.8 provides broad support for the CAPM, critics have pointed out that the slope of the line has been particularly flat in recent years. For example, Figure 9.9 shows how our 10 investors fared between 1966 and 2005. Now it is less

---

[14] In Figure 9.8 the stocks in the "market portfolio" are weighted equally. Since the stocks of small firms have provided higher average returns than those of large firms, the risk premium on an equally weighted index is higher than on a value-weighted index. This is one reason for the difference between the 12.5% market risk premium in Figure 9.8 and the 7.6% premium reported in Table 8.1.

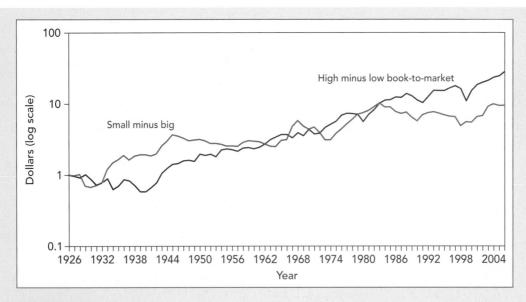

FIGURE 9.10

The maroon line shows the cumulative difference between the returns on small-firm and large-firm stocks. The blue line shows the cumulative difference between the returns on high book-to-market-value stocks (i.e., value stocks) and low book-to-market-value stocks (i.e., growth stocks).

Source: Kenneth French's Web site, **mba.tuck.dartmouth.edu/pages/faculty/ken.french/data_library.html**. Used with permission.

clear who is buying the drinks: Returns are pretty much in line with the CAPM with the important exception of the two highest-risk portfolios. Investor 10, who rode the roller coaster of a high-beta portfolio, earned a return that was below that of the market. Of course, before 1966 the line was correspondingly steeper. This is also shown in Figure 9.9.

What is going on here? It is hard to say. Defenders of the capital asset pricing model emphasize that it is concerned with *expected* returns, whereas we can observe only *actual* returns. Actual stock returns reflect expectations, but they also embody lots of "noise"—the steady flow of surprises that conceal whether on average investors have received the returns they expected. This noise may make it impossible to judge whether the model holds better in one period than another.[15] Perhaps the best that we can do is to focus on the longest period for which there is reasonable data. This would take us back to Figure 9.8, which suggests that expected returns do indeed increase with beta, though less rapidly than the simple version of the CAPM predicts.[16]

The CAPM has also come under fire on a second front: Although return has not risen with beta in recent years, it has been related to other measures. For example, the maroon line in Figure 9.10 shows the cumulative difference between the

---

[15] A second problem with testing the model is that the market portfolio should contain all risky investments, including stocks, bonds, commodities, real estate—even human capital. Most market indexes contain only a sample of common stocks.

[16] We say "simple version" because Fischer Black has shown that if there are borrowing restrictions, there should still exist a positive relationship between expected return and beta, but the security market line would be less steep as a result. See F. Black, "Capital Market Equilibrium with Restricted Borrowing," *Journal of Business* 45 (July 1972), pp. 444–455.

returns on small-firm stocks and large-firm stocks. If you had bought the shares with the smallest market capitalizations and sold those with the largest capitalizations, this is how your wealth would have changed. You can see that small-cap stocks did not always do well, but over the long haul their owners have made substantially higher returns. Since the end of 1926 the average annual difference between the returns on the two groups of stocks has been 3.7%.

Now look at the blue line in Figure 9.10, which shows the cumulative difference between the returns on value stocks and growth stocks. Value stocks here are defined as those with high ratios of book value to market value. Growth stocks are those with low ratios of book to market. Notice that value stocks have provided a higher long-run return than growth stocks.[17] Since 1926 the average annual difference between the returns on value and growth stocks has been 5.2%.

Figure 9.10 does not fit well with the CAPM, which predicts that beta is the *only* reason that expected returns differ. It seems that investors saw risks in "small-cap" stocks and value stocks that were not captured by beta.[18] Take value stocks, for example. Many of these stocks may have sold below book value because the firms were in serious trouble; if the economy slowed unexpectedly, the firms might have collapsed altogether. Therefore, investors, whose jobs could also be on the line in a recession, may have regarded these stocks as particularly risky and demanded compensation in the form of higher expected returns. If that were the case, the simple version of the CAPM cannot be the whole truth.

Again, it is hard to judge how seriously the CAPM is damaged by this finding. The relationship among stock returns and firm size and book-to-market ratio has been well documented. However, if you look long and hard at past returns, you are bound to find some strategy that just by chance would have worked in the past. This practice is known as "data-mining" or "data snooping." Maybe the size and book-to-market effects are simply chance results that stem from data snooping. If so, they should have vanished once they were discovered. There is some evidence that this is the case. If you look again at Figure 9.10, you will see that in the past 20 years small-firm stocks have underperformed just about as often as they have overperformed.

There is no doubt that the evidence on the CAPM is less convincing than scholars once thought. But it will be hard to reject the CAPM beyond all reasonable doubt. Since data and statistics are unlikely to give final answers, the plausibility of the CAPM *theory* will have to be weighed along with the empirical "facts."

Assumptions behind the Capital Asset Pricing Model

The capital asset pricing model rests on several assumptions that we did not fully spell out. For example, we assumed that investment in U.S. Treasury bills is risk-free. It is true that there is little chance of default, but bills do not guarantee a *real*

---

[17] Fama and French calculated the returns on portfolios designed to take advantage of the size effect and the book-to-market effect. See E. F. Fama and K. R. French, "The Cross-Section of Expected Stock Returns," *Journal of Financial Economics* 47 (June 1992), pp. 427–465. When calculating the returns on these portfolios, Fama and French control for differences in firm size when comparing stocks with low and high book-to-market ratios. Similarly, they control for differences in the book-to-market ratio when comparing small- and large-firm stocks. For details of the methodology and updated returns on the size and book-to-market factors see Kenneth French's Web site (**mba.tuck.dartmouth.edu/pages/faculty/ken.french/data_library.html**).

[18] An investor who bought small-company stocks and sold large-company stocks would have incurred some risk. Her portfolio would have had a beta of .20. This is not nearly large enough to explain the difference in returns. There is no simple relationship between the return on the value- and growth-stock portfolios and beta.

return. There is still some uncertainty about inflation. Another assumption was that investors can *borrow* money at the same rate of interest at which they can lend. Generally borrowing rates are higher than lending rates.

It turns out that many of these assumptions are not crucial, and with a little pushing and pulling it is possible to modify the capital asset pricing model to handle them. The really important idea is that investors are content to invest their money in a limited number of benchmark portfolios. (In the basic CAPM these benchmarks are Treasury bills and the market portfolio.)

In these modified CAPMs expected return still depends on market risk, but the definition of market risk depends on the nature of the benchmark portfolios. In practice, none of these alternative capital asset pricing models is as widely used as the standard version.

9.4 SOME ALTERNATIVE THEORIES

The capital asset pricing model pictures investors as solely concerned with the level and uncertainty of their future wealth. But this could be too simplistic. For example, investors may become accustomed to a particular standard of living, so that poverty tomorrow may be particularly difficult to bear if one were wealthy yesterday. Behavioral psychologists have also observed that investors do not focus solely on the *current* value of their holdings, but look back at whether their investments are showing a profit. A gain, however small, may be an additional source of satisfaction. The capital asset pricing model does not allow for the possibility that investors may take account of the price at which they purchased stock and feel elated when their investment is in the black and depressed when it is in the red.[19]

Consumption Betas versus Market Betas

For most people wealth is not an end in itself. What good is wealth if you cannot spend it? People invest now to provide future consumption for themselves or for their families and heirs. The most important risks are those that might force a cutback of future consumption.

Douglas Breeden has developed a model in which a security's risk is measured by its sensitivity to changes in investors' consumption. If he is right, a stock's expected return should move in line with its *consumption beta* rather than its market beta. Figure 9.11 summarizes the chief differences between the standard and consumption CAPMs. In the standard model investors are concerned exclusively with the amount and uncertainty of their future wealth. Each investor's wealth ends up perfectly correlated with the return on the market portfolio; the demand for stocks and other risky assets is thus determined by their market risk. The deeper motive for investing—to provide for consumption—is outside the model.

---

[19] We will discuss aversion to loss again in Chapter 12. The implications for asset pricing are explored in S. Benartzi and R. Thaler, "Myopic Loss Aversion and the Equity Premium Puzzle," *Quarterly Journal of Economics* 110 (1995), pp. 75–92; and in N. Barberis, M. Huang, and T. Santos, "Prospect Theory and Asset Prices," *Quarterly Journal of Economics* 116 (2001), pp. 1–53.

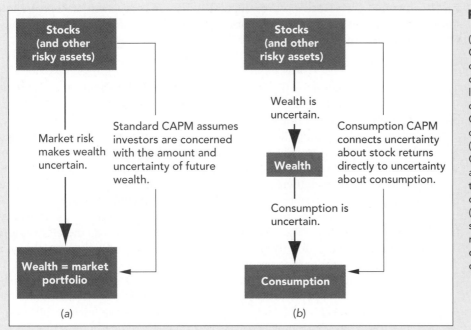

FIGURE 9.11

(a) The standard CAPM concentrates on how stocks contribute to the level and uncertainty of investor's wealth. Consumption is outside the model. (b) The consumption CAPM defines risk as a stock's contribution to uncertainty about consumption. Wealth (the intermediate step between stock returns and consumption) drops out of the model.

In the consumption CAPM, uncertainty about stock returns is connected directly to uncertainty about consumption. Of course, consumption depends on wealth (portfolio value), but wealth does not appear explicitly in the model.

The consumption CAPM has several appealing features. For example, you do not have to identify the market or any other benchmark portfolio. You don't have to worry that Standard and Poor's Composite Index does not track returns on all risky investments.

However, you do have to be able to measure consumption. *Quick:* How much did you consume last month? It is easy to count the hamburgers and movie tickets, but what about the depreciation on your car or washing machine or the daily cost of your homeowner's insurance policy? We suspect that your estimate of total consumption will rest on rough or arbitrary allocations and assumptions. And if it is hard for you to put a dollar value on your total consumption, think of the task facing a government statistician asked to estimate month-by-month consumption for all of us.

In contrast to stock prices, estimated aggregate consumption changes smoothly and gradually over time. Consequently, the volatility of consumption appears too low to explain the past average rates of return on common stocks unless one assumes unreasonably high investor risk aversion. This may reflect our poor measures of consumption or perhaps poor models of how individuals distribute consumption over time. Unless these problems can be solved, it seems unlikely that the consumption CAPM will gain practical use.

Arbitrage Pricing Theory

The capital asset pricing theory begins with an analysis of how investors construct efficient portfolios. Stephen Ross's **arbitrage pricing theory,** or **APT,** comes from a different family entirely. It does not ask which portfolios are efficient. Instead, it starts by *assuming* that each stock's return depends partly on pervasive macroeconomic influences or "factors" and partly on "noise"—events that are unique to that company. Moreover, the return is assumed to obey the following simple relationship:

$$\text{Return} = a + b_1(r_{\text{factor 1}}) + b_2(r_{\text{factor 2}}) + b_3(r_{\text{factor 3}}) + \cdots + \text{noise}$$

The theory does not say what the factors are: There could be an oil price factor, an interest-rate factor, and so on. The return on the market portfolio *might* serve as one factor, but then again it might not.

Some stocks will be more sensitive to a particular factor than other stocks. ExxonMobil would be more sensitive to an oil factor than, say, Coca-Cola. If factor 1 picks up unexpected changes in oil prices, b_1 will be higher for ExxonMobil.

For any individual stock there are two sources of risk. First is the risk that stems from the pervasive macroeconomic factors. This cannot be eliminated by diversification. Second is the risk arising from possible events that are unique to the company. Diversification eliminates unique risk, and diversified investors can therefore ignore it when deciding whether to buy or sell a stock. The expected risk premium on a stock is affected by factor or macroeconomic risk; it is *not* affected by unique risk.

Arbitrage pricing theory states that the expected risk premium on a stock should depend on the expected risk premium associated with each factor and the stock's sensitivity to each of the factors (b_1, b_2, b_3, etc.). Thus the formula is[20]

$$\begin{aligned}\text{Expected risk premium} &= r - r_f \\ &= b_1(r_{\text{factor 1}} - r_f) + b_2(r_{\text{factor 2}} - r_f) + \cdots\end{aligned}$$

Notice that this formula makes two statements:

1. If you plug in a value of zero for each of the b's in the formula, the expected risk premium is zero. A diversified portfolio that is constructed to have zero sensitivity to each macroeconomic factor is essentially risk-free and therefore must be priced to offer the risk-free rate of interest. If the portfolio offered a higher return, investors could make a risk-free (or "arbitrage") profit by borrowing to buy the portfolio. If it offered a lower return, you could make an arbitrage profit by running the strategy in reverse; in other words, you would *sell* the diversified zero-sensitivity portfolio and *invest* the proceeds in U.S. Treasury bills.

2. A diversified portfolio that is constructed to have exposure to, say, factor 1, will offer a risk premium, which will vary in direct proportion to the portfolio's sensitivity to that factor. For example, imagine that you construct two portfolios, A and B, that are affected only by factor 1. If portfolio A is twice as sensitive to factor 1 as portfolio B, portfolio A must offer twice the risk premium. Therefore, if you divided your money equally between U.S. Treasury bills and portfolio A, your combined portfolio would have exactly the same sensitivity to factor 1 as portfolio B and would offer the same risk premium.

   Suppose that the arbitrage pricing formula did *not* hold. For example, suppose that the combination of Treasury bills and portfolio A offered a higher return. In that case investors could make an arbitrage profit by selling portfolio B and investing the proceeds in the mixture of bills and portfolio A.

---

[20] There may be some macroeconomic factors that investors are simply not worried about. For example, some macroeconomists believe that money supply doesn't matter and therefore investors are not worried about inflation. Such factors would not command a risk premium. They would drop out of the APT formula for expected return.

The arbitrage that we have described applies to well-diversified portfolios, where the unique risk has been diversified away. But if the arbitrage pricing relationship holds for all diversified portfolios, it must generally hold for the individual stocks. Each stock must offer an expected return commensurate with its contribution to portfolio risk. In the APT, this contribution depends on the sensitivity of the stock's return to unexpected changes in the macroeconomic factors.

A Comparison of the Capital Asset Pricing Model and Arbitrage Pricing Theory

Like the capital asset pricing model, arbitrage pricing theory stresses that expected return depends on the risk stemming from economywide influences and is not affected by unique risk. You can think of the factors in arbitrage pricing as representing special portfolios of stocks that tend to be subject to a common influence. If the expected risk premium on each of these portfolios is proportional to the portfolio's market beta, then the arbitrage pricing theory and the capital asset pricing model will give the same answer. In any other case they will not.

How do the two theories stack up? Arbitrage pricing has some attractive features. For example, the market portfolio that plays such a central role in the capital asset pricing model does not feature in arbitrage pricing theory.[21] So we do not have to worry about the problem of measuring the market portfolio, and in principle we can test the arbitrage pricing theory even if we have data on only a sample of risky assets.

Unfortunately you win some and lose some. Arbitrage pricing theory does not tell us what the underlying factors are—unlike the capital asset pricing model, which collapses *all* macroeconomic risks into a well-defined *single* factor, the return on the market portfolio.

The Three-Factor Model

Look back at the equation for APT. To estimate expected returns, you first need to follow three steps:

Step 1: Identify a reasonably short list of macroeconomic factors that could affect stock returns;

Step 2: Estimate the expected risk premium on each of these factors ($r_{factor 1} - r_f$, etc.); and

Step 3: Measure the sensitivity of each stock to the factors (b_1, b_2, etc.).

One way to shortcut this process is to take advantage of the research by Fama and French, which showed that stocks of small firms and those with a high book-to-market ratio have provided above-average returns. This could simply be a coincidence. But there is also some evidence that these factors are related to company profitability and therefore may be picking up risk factors that are left out of the simple CAPM.[22]

---

[21] Of course, the market portfolio *may* turn out to be one of the factors, but that is not a necessary implication of arbitrage pricing theory.

[22] E. F. Fama and K. R. French, "Size and Book-to-Market Factors in Earnings and Returns," *Journal of Finance* 50 (1995), pp. 131–155.

If investors do demand an extra return for taking on exposure to these factors, then we have a measure of the expected return that looks very much like arbitrage pricing theory:

$$r - r_f = b_{\text{market}} \left(r_{\text{market factor}}\right) + b_{\text{size}}\left(r_{\text{size factor}}\right) + b_{\text{book-to-market}} \left(r_{\text{book-to-market factor}}\right)$$

This is commonly known as the Fama–French three-factor model. Using it to estimate expected returns is the same as applying the arbitrage pricing theory. Here is an example.[23]

Step 1: Identify the Factors   Fama and French have already identified the three factors that appear to determine expected returns. The returns on each of these factors are

Factor	Measured by
Market factor	Return on market index *minus* risk-free interest rate
Size factor	Return on small-firm stocks *less* return on large-firm stocks
Book-to-market factor	Return on high book-to-market-ratio stocks *less* return on low book-to-market-ratio stocks

Step 2: Estimate the Risk Premium for Each Factor   We will keep to our figure of 7% for the market risk premium. History may provide a guide to the risk premium for the other two factors. As we saw earlier, between 1926 and 2006 the difference between the annual returns on small and large capitalization stocks averaged 3.7% a year, while the difference between the returns on stocks with high and low book-to-market ratios averaged 5.2%.

Step 3: Estimate the Factor Sensitivities   Some stocks are more sensitive than others to fluctuations in the returns on the three factors. You can see this from the first three columns of numbers in Table 9.3, which show some estimates of the factor sensitivities of 10 industry groups for the 60 months ending in June 2006. For example, an increase of 1% in the return on the book-to-market factor *reduces* the return on computer stocks by 1.07% but *increases* the return on utility stocks by .63%. In other words, when value stocks (high book-to-market) outperform growth stocks (low book-to-market), computer stocks tend to perform relatively badly and utility stocks do relatively well.

Once you have estimated the factor sensitivities, it is a simple matter to multiply each of them by the expected factor return and add up the results. For example, the expected risk premium on computer stocks is $r - r_f = (1.67 \times 7) + (.39 \times 3.7) - (1.07 \times 5.2) = 7.6\%$. To calculate the return that investors expected in 2006 we need to add on the risk-free interest rate of about 5%. Thus the three-factor model suggests that expected return on computer stocks in 2006 was $5 + 7.6 = 12.6\%$.

Compare this figure with the expected return estimate using the capital asset pricing model (the final column of Table 9.3). The three-factor model provides a

---

[23] The three-factor model was first used to estimate the cost of capital for different industry groups by Fama and French. See E. F. Fama and K. R. French, "Industry Costs of Equity," *Journal of Financial Economics* 43 (1997), pp. 153–193. Fama and French emphasize the imprecision in using either the CAPM or an APT-style model to estimate the returns that investors expect.

| | Three-Factor Model | | | | CAPM |
| | Factor Sensitivities | | | | |
	b_{market}	b_{size}	$b_{book-to-market}$	Expected Return*	Expected Return**
Autos	1.51	.31	1.08	22.3%	14.9%
Banks	.92	−.17	.13	11.5	11.0
Chemicals	1.04	.01	.26	13.7	12.0
Computers	1.67	.39	−1.07	12.6	18.7
Construction	.41	1.12	1.05	17.5	14.1
Food	.43	−.09	.28	9.1	7.5
Oil and gas	.77	.21	.73	15.0	9.9
Pharmaceuticals	.68	−.62	−.43	5.2	9.1
Telecoms	1.36	−.81	−.05	11.3	13.0
Utilities	.71	.13	.63	13.7	9.5

TABLE 9.3

Estimates of expected equity returns for selected industries using the Fama–French three-factor model and the CAPM.

* The expected return equals the risk-free interest rate plus the factor sensitivities multiplied by the factor risk premia, that is $5 + (b_{market} \times 7) + (b_{size} \times 3.7) + (b_{book-to-market} \times 5.2)$.

** Estimated as $r_f + \beta(r_m - r_f)$, that is $5 + \beta \times 7$. Note that β was estimated from a simple regression and may differ from the values shown for b_{market}.

substantially lower estimate of the expected return for computer stocks. Why? Largely because computer stocks have a low exposure (−1.07) to the book-to-market factor.

SUMMARY

The basic principles of portfolio selection boil down to a commonsense statement that investors try to increase the expected return on their portfolios and to reduce the standard deviation of that return. A portfolio that gives the highest expected return for a given standard deviation, or the lowest standard deviation for a given expected return, is known as an *efficient portfolio*. To work out which portfolios are efficient, an investor must be able to state the expected return and standard deviation of each stock and the degree of correlation between each pair of stocks.

Investors who are restricted to holding common stocks should choose efficient portfolios that suit their attitudes to risk. But investors who can also borrow and lend at the risk-free rate of interest should choose the *best* common stock portfolio *regardless* of their attitudes to risk. Having done that, they can then set the risk of their overall portfolio by deciding what proportion of their money they are willing to invest in stocks. The best efficient portfolio offers the highest ratio of forecasted risk premium to portfolio standard deviation.

For an investor who has only the same opportunities and information as everybody else, the best stock portfolio is the same as the best stock portfolio for other investors. In other words, he or she should invest in a mixture of the market portfolio and a risk-free loan (i.e., borrowing or lending).

A stock's marginal contribution to portfolio risk is measured by its sensitivity to changes in the value of the portfolio. The marginal contribution of a stock to the risk of the *market portfolio* is measured by *beta*. That is the fundamental idea behind the capital asset pricing model (CAPM), which concludes that each security's expected risk premium should increase in proportion to its beta:

$$\text{Expected risk premium} = \text{beta} \times \text{market risk premium}$$
$$r - r_f = \beta(r_m - r_f)$$

The capital asset pricing theory is the best-known model of risk and return. It is plausible and widely used but far from perfect. Actual returns are related to beta over the long run, but the relationship is not as strong as the CAPM predicts, and other factors seem to explain returns better since the mid-1960s. Stocks of small companies, and stocks with high book values relative to market prices, appear to have risks not captured by the CAPM.

The CAPM has also been criticized for its strong simplifying assumptions. A more recent theory called the *consumption* capital asset pricing model suggests that security risk reflects the sensitivity of returns to changes in investors' *consumption*. This theory calls for a consumption beta rather than a beta relative to the market portfolio.

The arbitrage pricing theory offers an alternative theory of risk and return. It states that the expected risk premium on a stock should depend on the stock's exposure to several pervasive macroeconomic factors that affect stock returns:

$$\text{Expected risk premium} = b_1(r_{\text{factor 1}} - r_f) + b_2(r_{\text{factor 2}} - r_f) + \cdots$$

Here b's represent the individual security's sensitivities to the factors, and $r_{\text{factor}} - r_f$ is the risk premium demanded by investors who are exposed to this factor.

Arbitrage pricing theory does not say what these factors are. It asks for economists to hunt for unknown game with their statistical tool kits. Fama and French have suggested three factors:

- The return on the market portfolio less the risk-free rate of interest.
- The difference between the return on small- and large-firm stocks.
- The difference between the return on stocks with high book-to-market ratios and stocks with low book-to-market ratios.

In the Fama–French three-factor model, the expected return on each stock depends on its exposure to these three factors.

Each of these different models of risk and return has its fan club. However, all financial economists agree on two basic ideas: (1) Investors require extra expected return for taking on risk, and (2) they appear to be concerned predominantly with the risk that they cannot eliminate by diversification.

FURTHER READING

The pioneering article on portfolio selection is:
H. M. Markowitz, "Portfolio Selection," *Journal of Finance* 7 (March 1952), pp. 77–91.

There are a number of textbooks on portfolio selection that explain both Markowitz's original theory and some ingenious simplified versions. See, for example:
E. J. Elton, M. J. Gruber, S. J. Brown, and W. N. Goetzmann: *Modern Portfolio Theory and Investment Analysis*, 6th ed. (New York: John Wiley & Sons, 2002).

Of the three pioneering articles on the capital asset pricing model, Jack Treynor's has never been published. The other two articles are:
W. F. Sharpe, "Capital Asset Prices: A Theory of Market Equilibrium under Conditions of Risk," *Journal of Finance* 19 (September 1964), pp. 425–442.

J. Lintner, "The Valuation of Risk Assets and the Selection of Risky Investments in Stock Portfolios and Capital Budgets," *Review of Economics and Statistics* 47 (February 1965), pp. 13–37.

The subsequent literature on the capital asset pricing model is enormous. There are dozens of published tests of the capital asset pricing model. Fisher Black's paper is a very readable example. Discussions of the theory tend to be more uncompromising. Two excellent but advanced examples are Campbell's survey paper and Cochrane's book. The text by Copeland et al. provides somewhat more detail than this chapter on asset pricing models:

T. E. Copeland, J. F. Weston, and K. Shastri, *Financial Theory and Corporate Policy*, 4th ed. (Pearson Addison Wesley, 2005).

F. Black, "Beta and Return," *Journal of Portfolio Management* 20 (Fall 1993), pp. 8–18.

J. Y. Campbell, "Asset Pricing at the Millennium," *Journal of Finance* 55 (August 2000), pp. 1515–1567.

J. H. Cochrane, *Asset Pricing* (Princeton, NJ: Princeton University Press, 2005).

The most accessible implementation of APT is:

E. J. Elton, M. J. Gruber, and J. Mei, "Cost of Capital Using Arbitrage Pricing Theory: A Case Study of Nine New York Utilities," *Financial Markets, Institutions, and Instruments* 3 (August 1994), pp. 46–73.

CONCEPT REVIEW QUESTIONS

1. If stock returns are normally distributed, the distribution can be completely defined by two numbers. What are they? (page 207)

2. What is meant by "the set of efficient portfolios"? (page 210)

3. If an investor can borrow and lend at the same rate of interest, should the choice of a common stock portfolio depend on the investor's willingness to bear risk? Why or why not? (pages 212–213)

For a complete listing of your chapter Concept Review Questions, please visit us at www.mhhe.com/bma1e.

Visit us at www.mhhe.com/bma1e

QUIZ

1. Here are returns and standard deviations for four investments.

	Return	Standard Deviation
Treasury bills	6 %	0%
Stock P	10	14
Stock Q	14.5	28
Stock R	21.0	26

Calculate the standard deviations of the following portfolios.

a. 50% in Treasury bills, 50% in stock P.

b. 50% each in Q and R, assuming the shares have

- perfect positive correlation
- perfect negative correlation
- no correlation

FIGURE 9.12

See Quiz
Question 3.

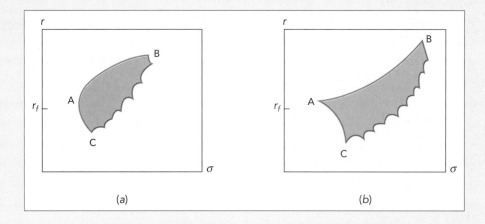

(a)   (b)

    c. Plot a figure like Figure 9.3 for Q and R, assuming a correlation coefficient of .5.

    d. Stock Q has a lower return than R but a higher standard deviation. Does that mean that Q's price is too high or that R's price is too low?

2. For each of the following pairs of investments, state which would always be preferred by a rational investor (assuming that these are the *only* investments available to the investor):

    a. Portfolio A $r = 18\%$ $\sigma = 20\%$
        Portfolio B $r = 14\%$ $\sigma = 20\%$

    b. Portfolio C $r = 15\%$ $\sigma = 18\%$
        Portfolio D $r = 13\%$ $\sigma = 8\%$

    c. Portfolio E $r = 14\%$ $\sigma = 16\%$
        Portfolio F $r = 14\%$ $\sigma = 10\%$

3. Figure 9.12 purports to show the range of attainable combinations of expected return and standard deviation.

    a. Which diagram is incorrectly drawn and why?

    b. Which is the efficient set of portfolios?

    c. If r_f is the rate of interest, mark with an X the optimal stock portfolio.

4. **a.** Plot the following risky portfolios on a graph:

	Portfolio							
	A	**B**	**C**	**D**	**E**	**F**	**G**	**H**
Expected return (r), %	10	12.5	15	16	17	18	18	20
Standard deviation (σ), %	23	21	25	29	29	32	35	45

    b. Five of these portfolios are efficient, and three are not. Which are *in*efficient ones?

    c. Suppose you can also borrow and lend at an interest rate of 12%. Which of the above portfolios has the highest Sharpe ratio?

    d. Suppose you are prepared to tolerate a standard deviation of 25%. What is the maximum expected return that you can achieve if you cannot borrow or lend?

e. What is your optimal strategy if you can borrow or lend at 12% and are prepared to tolerate a standard deviation of 25%? What is the maximum expected return that you can achieve with this risk?

5. Suppose that the Treasury bill rate is 4% and the expected return on the market is 10%. Use the betas in Table 9.2.

   a. Calculate the expected return from Microsoft.

   b. Find the highest expected return that is offered by one of these stocks.

   c. Find the lowest expected return that is offered by one of these stocks.

   d. Would IBM offer a higher or lower expected return if the interest rate were 6% rather than 4%? Assume that the expected market return stays at 10%.

   e. Would ExxonMobil offer a higher or lower expected return if the interest rate were 8%?

6. True or false?

   a. The CAPM implies that if you could find an investment with a negative beta, its expected return would be less than the interest rate.

   b. The expected return on an investment with a beta of 2.0 is twice as high as the expected return on the market.

   c. If a stock lies below the security market line, it is undervalued.

7. Consider a three-factor APT model. The factors and associated risk premiums are

Factor	Risk Premium
Change in GNP	5%
Change in energy prices	−1
Change in long-term interest rates	+2

Calculate expected rates of return on the following stocks. The risk-free interest rate is 7%.

   a. A stock whose return is uncorrelated with all three factors.

   b. A stock with average exposure to each factor (i.e., with $b = 1$ for each).

   c. A pure-play energy stock with high exposure to the energy factor ($b = 2$) but zero exposure to the other two factors.

   d. An aluminum company stock with average sensitivity to changes in interest rates and GNP, but negative exposure of $b = -1.5$ to the energy factor. (The aluminum company is energy-intensive and suffers when energy prices rise.)

8. True or false? Explain or qualify as necessary.

   a. Investors demand higher expected rates of return on stocks with more variable rates of return.

   b. The CAPM predicts that a security with a beta of 0 will offer a zero expected return.

   c. An investor who puts $10,000 in Treasury bills and $20,000 in the market portfolio will have a beta of 2.0.

   d. Investors demand higher expected rates of return from stocks with returns that are highly exposed to macroeconomic risk.

   e. Investors demand higher expected rates of return from stocks with returns that are very sensitive to fluctuations in the stock market.

PRACTICE QUESTIONS

9. Look back at the calculation for Wal-Mart and IBM in Section 9.1. Recalculate the expected portfolio return and standard deviation for different values of x_1 and x_2, assuming the correlation coefficient $\rho_{12} = 0$. Plot the range of possible combinations of expected return and standard deviation as in Figure 9.3. Repeat the problem for $\rho_{12} = +1$ and for $\rho_{12} = -1$.

10. Mark Harrywitz proposes to invest in two shares, X and Y. He expects a return of 12% from X and 8% from Y. The standard deviation of returns is 8% for X and 5% for Y. The correlation coefficient between the returns is .2.

    a. Compute the expected return and standard deviation of the following portfolios:

Portfolio	Percentage in X	Percentage in Y
1	50	50
2	25	75
3	75	25

    b. Sketch the set of portfolios composed of X and Y.

    c. Suppose that Mr. Harrywitz can also borrow or lend at an interest rate of 5%. Show on your sketch how this alters his opportunities. Given that he can borrow or lend, what proportions of the common stock portfolio should be invested in X and Y?

11. Ebenezer Scrooge has invested 60% of his money in share A and the remainder in share B. He assesses their prospects as follows:

	A	B
Expected return (%)	15	20
Standard deviation (%)	20	22
Correlation between returns	.5	

    a. What are the expected return and standard deviation of returns on his portfolio?

    b. How would your answer change if the correlation coefficient was 0 or −.5?

    c. Is Mr. Scrooge's portfolio better or worse than one invested entirely in share A, or is it not possible to say?

12. When we calculated the efficient portfolios in Table 9.1, we assumed that the investor could not hold short positions (that is, have negative holdings). The book Web site (**www.mhhe.com/bma1e**) contains an Excel program for calculating the efficient frontier with short sales. (We are grateful to Simon Gervais for providing us with a copy of this program.)

    a. Look at the efficient portfolios constructed from the 10 stocks in Table 9.1. How does the possibility of short sales improve the choices open to the investor?

    b. Now download "Monthly Adjusted Prices" for 10 different stocks from **finance. yahoo.com** or from the Standard & Poor's Market Insight Web site (**www.mhhe. com/edumarketinsight**) and enter the past returns into the Excel program. (The program will take up to 10 years of returns.) Enter some plausible figures for the expected return on each stock and find the set of efficient portfolios.

13. Download "Monthly Adjusted Prices" for General Motors (GM) and Harley-Davidson (HOG) from **finance.yahoo.com** or from the Standard & Poor's Market Insight Web site (**www.mhhe.com/edumarketinsight**). Use the Excel function SLOPE to calculate beta for each company. (See Chapter 8, Practice Problem 11 for details.)

   a. Suppose the S&P 500 index falls unexpectedly by 5%. By how much would you expect GM or HOG to fall?

   b. Which is the riskier company for the well-diversified investor? How much riskier?

   c. Suppose the Treasury bill rate is 4% and the expected return on the S&P 500 is 11%. Use the CAPM to forecast the expected rate of return on each stock.

14. Download the "Monthly Adjusted Prices" spreadsheets for Boeing and Pfizer from the Standard & Poor's Market Insight Web site (**www.mhhe.com/edumarketinsight**).

   a. Calculate the annual standard deviation for each company, using the most recent three years of monthly returns. Use the Excel function STDEV. Multiply by the square root of 12 to convert to annual units.

   b. Use the Excel function CORREL to calculate the correlation coefficient between the stocks' monthly returns.

   c. Use the CAPM to estimate expected rates of return. Calculate betas, or use the most recent beta reported under "Monthly Valuation Data" on the Market Insight Web site. Use the current Treasury bill rate and a reasonable estimate of the market risk premium.

   d. Construct a graph like Figure 9.3. What combination of Boeing and Pfizer has the lowest portfolio risk? What is the expected return for this minimum-risk portfolio?

15. The Treasury bill rate is 4%, and the expected return on the market portfolio is 12%. Using the capital asset pricing model: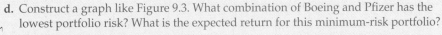

   a. Draw a graph similar to Figure 9.6 showing how the expected return varies with beta.

   b. What is the risk premium on the market?

   c. What is the required return on an investment with a beta of 1.5?

   d. If an investment with a beta of .8 offers an expected return of 9.8%, does it have a positive NPV?

   e. If the market expects a return of 11.2% from stock X, what is its beta?

16. Most of the companies in Table 9.2 are covered in the Standard & Poor's Market Insight Web site (**www.mhhe.com/edumarketinsight**). For those that are covered, use the Excel SLOPE function to recalculate betas from the monthly returns on the "Monthly Adjusted Prices" spreadsheets. Use as many monthly returns as available, up to a maximum of 60 months. Recalculate expected rates of return from the CAPM formula, using a current risk-free rate and a market risk premium of 7%. How have the expected returns changed from the figures reported in Table 9.2?

17. Go to **finance.yahoo.com** or to the Standard & Poor's Market Insight Web site (**www.mhhe.com/edumarketinsight**), and find a low-risk income stock—ExxonMobil or Kellogg might be a good candidate. Estimate the company's beta to confirm that it is well below 1.0. Use monthly rates of return for the most recent three years. For the same period, estimate the annual standard deviation for the stock, the standard deviation for the S&P 500, and the correlation coefficient between returns on the stock and the S&P 500. (The Excel functions are given in Practice Problems above.) Forecast the expected rate of return for the stock, assuming the CAPM holds, with a market return of 12% and a risk-free rate of 5%.

   a. Plot a graph like Figure 9.5 showing the combinations of risk and return from a portfolio invested in your low-risk stock and in the market. Vary the fraction invested in the stock from zero to 100%.

b. Suppose you can borrow or lend at 5%. Would you invest in some combination of your low-risk stock and the market? Or would you simply invest in the market? Explain.

c. Suppose you forecast a return on the stock that is 5 percentage points higher than the CAPM return used in part (a). Redo parts (a) and (b) with this higher forecasted return.

d. Find a high-beta stock and redo parts (a), (b), and (c).

18. Percival Hygiene has $10 million invested in long-term corporate bonds. This bond portfolio's expected annual rate of return is 9%, and the annual standard deviation is 10%.

Amanda Reckonwith, Percival's financial adviser, recommends that Percival consider investing in an index fund that closely tracks the Standard and Poor's 500 index. The index has an expected return of 14%, and its standard deviation is 16%.

a. Suppose Percival puts all his money in a combination of the index fund and Treasury bills. Can he thereby improve his expected rate of return without changing the risk of his portfolio? The Treasury bill yield is 6%.

b. Could Percival do even better by investing equal amounts in the corporate bond portfolio and the index fund? The correlation between the bond portfolio and the index fund is +.1.

19. Some true or false questions about the APT:

a. The APT factors cannot reflect diversifiable risks.

b. The market rate of return cannot be an APT factor.

c. There is no theory that specifically identifies the APT factors.

d. The APT model could be true but not very useful, for example, if the relevant factors change unpredictably.

20. Consider the following simplified APT model:

Factor	Expected Risk Premium
Market	6.4%
Interest rate	−.6
Yield spread	5.1

Calculate the expected return for the following stocks. Assume $r_f = 5\%$.

	Factor Risk Exposures		
	Market	Interest Rate	Yield Spread
Stock	(b_1)	(b_2)	(b_3)
P	1.0	−2.0	−.2
P^2	1.2	0	.3
P^3	.3	.5	1.0

21. Look again at Practice Problem 20. Consider a portfolio with equal investments in stocks P, P^2, and P^3.

a. What are the factor risk exposures for the portfolio?

b. What is the portfolio's expected return?

22. The following table shows the sensitivity of four stocks to the three Fama–French factors in the five years to June 2006. Estimate the expected return on each stock assuming that the interest rate is 5%, the expected risk premium on the market is 7.6%, the expected risk premium on the size factor is 3.7%, and the expected risk premium on the book-to-market factor is 5.2%. (These were the realized premia from 1926–2006.)

| Factor | Factor Sensitivities | | | |
	Coca-Cola	Ford	Pfizer	Microsoft
Market	.36	2.00	.58	.89
Size*	−.23	−.03	−.47	−.07
Book-to-market†	.38	1.10	−.15	−1.17

* Return on small-firm stocks less return on large-firm stocks.
† Return on high book-to-market-ratio stocks less return on low book-to-market-ratio stocks.

23. In footnote 4 we noted that the minimum-risk portfolio contained an investment of 78.4% in Wal-Mart and 21.6 in IBM. Prove it. (*Hint:* You need a little calculus to do so.)

24. Look again at the set of efficient portfolios that we calculated in Section 9.1.

   a. If the interest rate is 10%, which of the four efficient portfolios should you hold?

   b. What is the beta of each holding relative to that portfolio? (*Hint:* If a portfolio is efficient, the expected risk premium on each holding must be proportional to the beta of the stock *relative to that portfolio.*)

   c. How would your answers to (a) and (b) change if the interest rate were 5%?

25. The following question illustrates the APT. Imagine that there are only two pervasive macroeconomic factors. Investments X, Y, and Z have the following sensitivities to these two factors:

Investment	b_1	b_2
X	1.75	.25
Y	−1.00	2.00
Z	2.00	1.00

We assume that the expected risk premium is 4% on factor 1 and 8% on factor 2. Treasury bills obviously offer zero risk premium.

   a. According to the APT, what is the risk premium on each of the three stocks?

   b. Suppose you buy $200 of X and $50 of Y and sell $150 of Z. What is the sensitivity of your portfolio to each of the two factors? What is the expected risk premium?

   c. Suppose you buy $80 of X and $60 of Y and sell $40 of Z. What is the sensitivity of your portfolio to each of the two factors? What is the expected risk premium?

   d. Finally, suppose you buy $160 of X and $20 of Y and sell $80 of Z. What is your portfolio's sensitivity now to each of the two factors? And what is the expected risk premium?

   e. Suggest two possible ways that you could construct a fund that has a sensitivity of .5 to factor 1 only. (*Hint:* One portfolio contains an investment in Treasury bills.) Now compare the risk premiums on each of these two investments.

CHALLENGE QUESTIONS

Visit us at www.mhhe.com/bma1e

f. Suppose that the APT did *not* hold and that X offered a risk premium of 8%, Y offered a premium of 14%, and Z offered a premium of 16%. Devise an investment that has zero sensitivity to each factor and that has a positive risk premium.

MINI-CASE

John and Marsha on Portfolio Selection

The scene: John and Marsha hold hands in a cozy French restaurant in downtown Manhattan, several years before the mini-case in Chapter 10. Marsha is a futures-market trader. John manages a $125 million common-stock portfolio for a large pension fund. They have just ordered tournedos financiere for the main course and flan financiere for dessert. John reads the financial pages of *The Wall Street Journal* by candlelight.

John: Wow! Potato futures hit their daily limit. Let's add an order of gratin Dauphinoise. Did you manage to hedge the forward interest rate on that euro loan?

Marsha: John, please fold up that paper. (*He does so reluctantly.*) John, I love you. Will you marry me?

John: Oh, Marsha, I love you too, but . . . there's something you must know about me—something I've never told anyone.

Marsha (concerned):   John, what is it?

John: I think I'm a closet indexer.

Marsha: What? Why?

John: My portfolio returns always seem to track the S&P 500 market index. Sometimes I do a little better, occasionally a little worse. But the correlation between my returns and the market returns is over 90%.

Marsha: What's wrong with that? Your client wants a diversified portfolio of large-cap stocks. Of course your portfolio will follow the market.

John: Why doesn't my client just buy an index fund? Why are they paying *me?* Am I really adding value by active management? I try, but I guess I'm just an . . . indexer.

Marsha: Oh, John, I know you're adding value. You were a star security analyst.

John: It's not easy to find stocks that are truly over- or undervalued. I have firm opinions about a few, of course.

Marsha: You were explaining why Pioneer Gypsum is a good buy. And you're bullish on Global Mining.

John: Right, Pioneer. (*Pulls handwritten notes from his coat pocket.*) Stock price $87.50. I estimate the expected return as 11% with an annual standard deviation of 32%.

Marsha: Only 11%? You're forecasting a market return of 12.5%.

John: Yes, I'm using a market risk premium of 7.5% and the risk-free interest rate is about 5%. That gives 12.5%. But Pioneer's beta is only .65. I was going to buy 30,000 shares this morning, but I lost my nerve. I've got to stay diversified.

Marsha: Have you tried modern portfolio theory?

John: MPT? Not practical. Looks great in textbooks, where they show efficient frontiers with 5 or 10 stocks. But I choose from hundreds, maybe thousands, of stocks. Where do I get the inputs for 1,000 stocks? That's a million variances and covariances!

Marsha: Actually only about 500,000, dear. The covariances above the diagonal are the same as the covariances below. But you're right, most of the estimates would be out-of-date or just garbage.

John: To say nothing about the expected returns. Garbage in, garbage out.

Marsha: But John, you don't need to solve for 1,000 portfolio weights. You only need a handful. Here's the trick: Take your benchmark, the S&P 500, as security 1. That's what you would end up with as an indexer. Then consider a few securities you really know something about. Pioneer could be security 2, for example. Global, security 3. And so on. Then you could put your wonderful financial mind to work.

John: I get it: Active management means selling off some of the benchmark portfolio and investing the proceeds in specific stocks like Pioneer. But how do I decide whether Pioneer really improves the portfolio? Even if it does, how much should I buy?

Marsha: Just maximize the Sharpe ratio, dear.

John: I've got it! The answer is yes!

Marsha: What's the question?

John: You asked me to marry you. The answer is yes. Where should we go on our honeymoon?

Marsha: How about Australia? I'd love to visit the Melbourne Stock Exchange.

QUESTIONS

1. Table 9.4 reproduces John's notes on Pioneer Gypsum and Global Mining. Calculate the expected return, risk premium, and standard deviation of a portfolio invested partly in the market and partly in Pioneer. (You can calculate the necessary inputs from the betas and standard deviations given in the table.) Does adding Pioneer to the market benchmark improve the Sharpe ratio? How much should John invest in Pioneer and how much in the market?

	Pioneer Gypsum	Global Mining
Expected return	11.0%	12.9%
Standard deviation	32%	20%
Beta	.65	1.22
Stock price	$87.50	$105.00

TABLE 9.4

John's notes on Pioneer Gypsum and Global Mining.

2. Repeat the analysis for Global Mining. What should John do in this case? Assume that Global accounts for .75% of the S&P index.

CHAPTER TEN

CAPITAL BUDGETING AND RISK

LONG BEFORE THE development of modern theories linking risk and return, smart financial managers adjusted for risk in capital budgeting. They knew that risky projects are, other things equal, less valuable than safe ones—that is just common sense. Therefore they demanded higher rates of return from risky projects, or they based their decisions about risky projects on conservative forecasts of project cash flows.

Today most companies start with the *company cost of capital* as a benchmark risk-adjusted discount rate for new investments. The company cost of capital is the opportunity cost of capital for investment in the firm as a whole. It is usually calculated as a weighted average cost of capital, that is, the average rate of return demanded by investors in the company's debt and equity securities. Our first task in this chapter is to explain when the company cost of capital can, and cannot, be used to discount project cash flows. We shall see that it is the right discount rate for projects that have the same risk as the company's existing business. But if a project is riskier than the firm as it stands, the cost of capital *for the project* should be higher. Conversely, the project cost of capital for a safe project is lower.

The hardest part of estimating the company cost of capital is figuring out the expected rate of return to investors in the firm's stock. Many firms turn to

the capital asset pricing model (CAPM) for an answer. The CAPM states that expected return equals the risk-free interest rate r_f plus a risk premium that depends on beta and the market risk premium $r_m - r_f$:

$$\text{Expected return} = r_f + \text{beta} \times (r_m - r_f)$$

We used this formula in the last chapter to estimate expected rates of return on a sample of common stocks, but we provided little guidance on how to estimate beta. Unfortunately, you cannot look up beta in a newspaper or see it clearly by tracking a few day-by-day or month-by-month changes in stock price. But you can usually get an approximate measure by looking at how the stock price has responded on average to historical market fluctuations. Smart financial managers also look at average betas for portfolios of similar companies. Betas estimated for portfolios are more accurate than betas estimated for individual companies.

Sometimes you do not have a beta, or you get beta estimates that are just statistical garbage. In those cases, you can assess the project's operating leverage (its ratio of fixed to variable cost) and you can ask whether the project's future cash flows will be unusually sensitive to the business cycle. Cyclical projects with high operating leverage have high betas. But be careful not to confuse diversifiable risk with market risk. Diversifiable risk does not increase the cost of capital.

Betas vary from project to project. They can also vary over time. Some projects are riskier in youth than in old age, for example, and we may need a higher discount rate for the start-up stage of a project. But in most cases financial managers assume that project risk is the same in every future period and use a single risk-adjusted discount rate for all future cash flows. We will use *certainty equivalents* to illustrate how risk accumulates over time for ordinary projects.

We close the chapter with a brief look at risk and discount rates for international projects.

10.1 COMPANY AND PROJECT COSTS OF CAPITAL

The **company cost of capital** is defined as the expected return on a portfolio of all the company's existing securities. It is the opportunity cost of capital for investment in the firm's assets, and therefore the appropriate discount rate for the firm's average-risk projects.

If the firm has no significant amount of debt outstanding, then the company cost of capital is just the expected rate of return on the firm's stock. Many large, successful companies fit this special case, including Microsoft. In Table 9.2 we estimated that investors require a return of 12.9% from Microsoft common stock. If Microsoft is contemplating an expansion of the firm's existing business, it would make sense to discount the forecasted cash flows at 12.9%.

The company cost of capital is *not* the correct discount rate if the new projects are more or less risky than the firm's existing business. Each project should in principle be evaluated at its *own* opportunity cost of capital. This is a clear implication of the value-additivity principle introduced in Chapter 8. For a firm composed of assets A and B, the firm value is

$$\text{Firm value} = PV(AB) = PV(A) + PV(B)$$
$$= \text{sum of separate asset values}$$

Here PV(A) and PV(B) are valued just as if they were mini-firms in which stockholders could invest directly. Investors would value A by discounting its forecasted cash flows at a rate reflecting the risk of A. They would value B by discounting at a rate reflecting the risk of B. The two discount rates will, in general, be different. If the present value of an asset depended on the identity of the company that bought it, present values would *not* add up, and we know they do add up. (Consider a portfolio of $1 million invested in Pfizer and $1 million invested in Bank of America. Would any reasonable investor say that the portfolio is worth anything more or less than $2 million?)

If the firm considers investing in a third project C, it should also value C as if C were a mini-firm. That is, the firm should discount the cash flows of C at the expected rate of return that investors would demand to make a separate investment in C. *The true cost of capital depends on the use to which that capital is put.*

This means that Microsoft should accept any project that more than compensates for the project's beta. In other words, Microsoft should accept any project lying above the upward-sloping security market line that links expected return to risk in Figure 10.1. If the project is high-risk, Microsoft needs a higher prospective return than if the project is low-risk. Now contrast the company cost of capital rule, which accepts any project *regardless of its risk* as long as it offers a higher

FIGURE 10.1

A comparison between the company cost of capital rule and the required return under the capital asset pricing model. Microsoft's company cost of capital is about 12.9%. This is the correct discount rate only if the project beta is 1.13. In general, the correct discount rate increases as project beta increases. Microsoft should accept projects with rates of return above the security market line relating required return to beta.

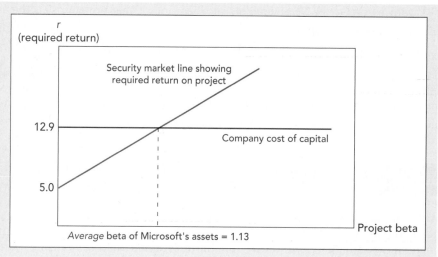

return than the *company's* cost of capital. In terms of Figure 10.1, the rule tells Microsoft to accept any project above the horizontal cost of capital line, that is, any project offering a return of more than 12.9%.

It is clearly silly to suggest that Microsoft should demand the same rate of return from a very safe project as from a very risky one. If Microsoft used the company cost of capital rule, it would reject many good low-risk projects and accept many poor high-risk projects. It is also silly to suggest that just because another company has a low company cost of capital, it is justified in accepting projects that Microsoft would reject.

The notion that each company needs only one discount rate or cost of capital is widespread, but far from universal. Many firms require different returns from different categories of investment. For example, discount rates might be set as follows:

Category	Discount Rate
Speculative ventures	30%
New products	20
Expansion of existing business	15 (company cost of capital)
Cost improvement, known technology	10

Perfect Pitch and the Cost of Capital

The true cost of capital depends on project risk, not on the company undertaking the project. So why is so much time spent estimating the company cost of capital?

There are two reasons. First, many (maybe most) projects can be treated as average risk, that is, no more or less risky than the average of the company's other assets. For these projects the company cost of capital is the right discount rate. Second, the company cost of capital is a useful starting point for setting discount rates for unusually risky or safe projects. It is easier to add to, or subtract from, the company cost of capital than to estimate each project's cost of capital from scratch.

There is a good musical analogy here. Most of us, lacking perfect pitch, need a well-defined reference point, like middle C, before we can sing on key. But anyone who can carry a tune gets *relative* pitches right. Businesspeople have good intuition about *relative* risks, at least in industries they are used to, but not about absolute risk or required rates of return. Therefore, they set a companywide cost of capital as a benchmark. This is not the right hurdle rate for everything the company does, but adjustments can be made for more or less risky ventures.

That said, we have to admit that many large companies use the company cost of capital not just as a benchmark, but also as an all-purpose discount rate for every project proposal. Measuring differences in risk is difficult to do objectively, and financial managers shy away from intracorporate squabbles. ("My projects are safer than yours! I want a lower discount rate!" "No they're not! Your projects are riskier than a naked call option!"[1])

When firms force use of a single company cost of capital, risk adjustment shifts from the discount rate to project cash flows. Top management may demand extra-conservative cash-flow forecasts from extra-risky projects. They may refuse to sign off on an extra-risky project unless NPV, computed at the company cost of capital, is well above zero. Rough and ready risk adjustments are better than none at all.

Debt and the Company Cost of Capital

We defined the company cost of capital as "the expected return on a portfolio of all the company's existing securities." That portfolio usually includes debt as well as equity. Thus the cost of capital is estimated as a blend of the cost of debt (the interest rate) and the cost of equity (the expected rate of return demanded by investors in the firm's common stock).

If you owned a portfolio of all the firm's securities—100% of the debt and 100% of the equity—you would own the firm's assets lock, stock, and barrel. You would not share the cash flows with anyone; every dollar of cash the firm paid out would be paid to you. You can think of the company cost of capital as the expected return on this hypothetical portfolio. To calculate it, you just take a weighted average of the expected returns on the debt and the equity:

$$\text{Company cost of capital} = r_{assets} = r_{portfolio}$$
$$= \frac{\text{debt}}{\text{debt} + \text{equity}} r_{debt} + \frac{\text{equity}}{\text{debt} + \text{equity}} r_{equity}$$

For example, suppose that the firm's market-value balance sheet is:

Asset value	100	Debt value (D)	30
		Equity value (E)	70
Asset value	100	Firm value (V)	100

Note that the values of debt and equity add up to the firm value ($D + E = V$) and that the firm value equals the asset value. These figures are *market* values, not *book* (i.e., accounting) values: The market value of the firm's equity is often very different from its book value.

---

[1] A "naked" call option is an option purchased with no offsetting (hedging) position in the underlying stock or in other options. We will get to options in Chapter 17.

If investors expect a return of 7.5% on the debt and 15% on the equity, then the expected return on the assets must be

$$r_{assets} = \frac{D}{V}r_{debt} + \frac{E}{V}r_{equity}$$

$$= \left(\frac{30}{100} \times 7.5\right) + \left(\frac{70}{100} \times 15\right) = 12.75\%$$

If the firm is contemplating investment in a project that has the same risk as the firm's existing business, the opportunity cost of capital for this project is the same as the firm's cost of capital; in other words, it is 12.75%.

Note that the company cost of capital is not the cost of debt, and not the cost of equity, but an average. Thus the blend is typically called the **weighted-average cost of capital** or "WACC." Estimating WACC can be just a trifle complicated, particularly when taxes are incorporated and changes in debt ratios must be considered. For example, since interest is a tax-deductible expense for corporations, the after-tax cost of debt is $r_D(1 - T_c)$, where T_c is the corporate tax rate. So

$$\text{After-tax WACC} = r_D(1 - T_c)\frac{D}{V} + r_E\frac{E}{V}$$

We defer these complications to Chapters 14 and 16. In this chapter we will concentrate on measuring the cost of equity. But please do not try to estimate and use the weighted-average cost of capital for any practical purpose until you have at least read Chapters 14 and 16.

10.2   MEASURING THE COST OF EQUITY

Suppose that you are considering an across-the-board expansion by your firm. Such an investment would have about the same degree of risk as the existing business. Therefore you should discount projected cash flows at a weighted-average cost of capital. To calculate the weighted-average cost of capital, you need an estimate of the cost of equity.

You decide to use the capital asset pricing model (CAPM). Here you are in good company: as we saw in the last chapter, most large U.S. companies do use the CAPM to estimate the cost of equity.[2] The CAPM says that

$$\text{Expected stock return} = r_f + \beta(r_m - r_f)$$

Now you have to estimate beta. Let us see how that is done in practice.

Estimating Beta

In principle we are interested in the future beta of the company's stock, but lacking a crystal ball, we turn first to historical evidence. For example, look at the scatter diagram at the top left of Figure 10.2. Each dot represents the return on Intel stock and the return on the market in a particular month. The plot starts in July 1996 and runs to June 2001, so there are 60 dots in all.

---

[2] The CAPM is not the last word on risk and return, of course, but the principles and procedures covered in this chapter work just as well with other models such as the Fama–French three-factor model.

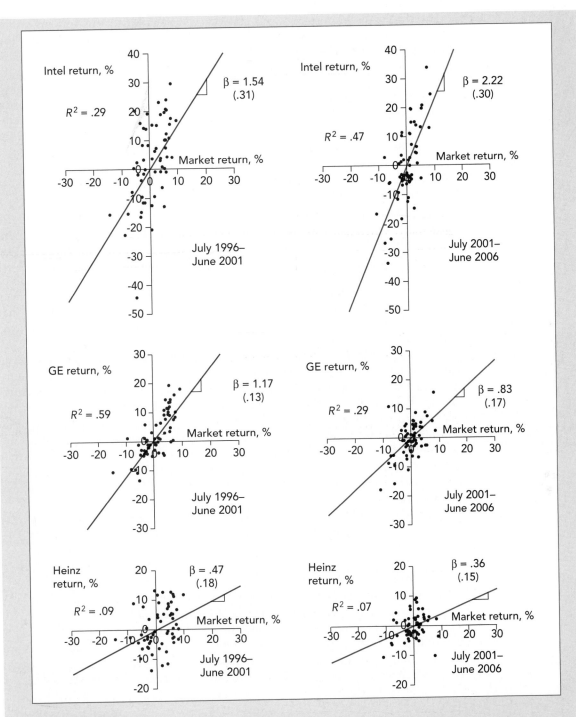

FIGURE 10.2

We have used past returns to estimate the betas of three stocks for the periods July 1996 to June 2001 (left-hand diagrams) and July 2001 to June 2006 (right-hand diagrams). Beta is the slope of the fitted line. Notice that in both periods Intel had the highest beta and Heinz the lowest. Standard errors are in parentheses below the betas. The standard error shows the range of possible error in the beta estimate. We also report the proportion of total risk that is due to market movements (R^2).

The second diagram on the left shows a similar plot for the returns on GE stock, and the third shows a plot for Heinz. In each case we have fitted a line through the points. The slope of this line is an estimate of beta.[3] It tells us how much on average the stock price changed for each additional 1% change in the market index.

The right-hand diagrams show similar plots for the same three stocks during the subsequent period ending in June 2006. Although the slopes varied from the first period to the second, there is little doubt that Heinz's beta is much less than Intel's or that GE's beta falls somewhere between the two. If you had used the past beta of each stock to predict its future beta, you would not have been too far off for GE and Heinz, although you missed on Intel's beta, which increased by about .7 to 2.22 in the later period.

Only a small portion of each stock's total risk comes from movements in the market. The rest is unique risk, which shows up in the scatter of points around the fitted lines in Figure 10.2. R-squared (R^2) measures the proportion of the total variance in the stock's returns that can be explained by market movements. For example, from 2001 to 2006, the R^2 for Intel was .47. In other words, about half of Intel's risk was market risk and half was unique risk. The variance of the returns on Intel stock was 1,901.[4] So we could say that the variance in stock returns that was due to the market was .47 × 1,901 = 893, and the variance of unique returns was .53 × 1,901 = 1,008.

The estimates of beta shown in Figure 10.2 are just that. They are based on the stocks' returns in 60 particular months. The noise in the returns can obscure the true beta. Therefore, statisticians calculate the *standard error* of the estimated beta to show the extent of possible mismeasurement. Then they set up a *confidence interval* of the estimated value plus or minus two standard errors. For example, the standard error of GE's estimated beta in the most recent period is .17. Thus the confidence interval for GE's beta is .83 plus or minus 2 × .17. If you state that the *true* beta for GE is between .49 and 1.17, you have a 95% chance of being right. Notice that we can be more confident of our estimate of Heinz's beta and less confident of Intel's.

Usually you will have more information (and thus more confidence) than this simple calculation suggests. For example, you know that Heinz's estimated beta was well below 1 in the previous period, while Intel's estimated beta was well above 1. Nevertheless, there is always a large margin for error when estimating the beta for individual stocks.

Fortunately, the estimation errors tend to cancel out when you estimate betas of *portfolios*.[5] That is why financial managers often turn to *industry betas*. For example, Table 10.1 shows estimates of beta and the standard errors of these estimates for the common stocks of six large railroad companies. Four of the standard errors are above .2, large enough to preclude a precise estimate of any particular railroad's beta. However, the table also shows the estimated beta for a portfolio of all six

---

[3] Notice that you must regress the *returns* on the stock on the market *returns*. You would get a very similar estimate if you simply used the percentage *changes* in the stock price and the market index. But sometimes analysts make the mistake of regressing the stock price *level* on the *level* of the index and obtain nonsense results.

[4] This is an annual figure; we annualized the monthly variance by multiplying by 12 (see footnote 20 in Chapter 8). The standard deviation was $\sqrt{1,901} = 43.6\%$.

[5] If the observations are independent, the standard error of the estimated mean beta declines in proportion to the square root of the number of stocks in the portfolio.

	β_{equity}	Standard Error
Burlington Northern Santa Fe	0.83	0.19
Canadian Pacific	0.90	0.31
CSX	0.99	0.20
Kansas City Southern	1.02	0.24
Norfolk Southern	0.78	0.26
Union Pacific	0.69	0.18
Industry portfolio	0.87	0.16

TABLE 10.1

Estimates of betas and standard errors for a sample of large railroad companies and for an equally weighted portfolio of these companies, based on monthly returns from October 2001 to September 2006. The precision of the portfolio beta is better than that of the betas of the individual companies (note the lower standard error for the portfolio).

railroad stocks. Notice that the estimated industry beta is somewhat more reliable. This shows up in the lower standard error.

The Expected Return on Union Pacific Corporation's Common Stock

Suppose that in late 2006 you had been asked to estimate the company cost of capital of Union Pacific. Table 10.1 provides two clues about the true beta of Union Pacific's stock: the direct estimate of .69 and the average estimate for the industry of .87. We will use the industry average of .87.[6]

The next issue is what value to use for the risk-free interest rate. The CAPM works period by period and calls for a short-term interest rate. In October 2006 short-term and long-term interest rates were both around 5.0%. The question is, Could a discount rate based on a short-term rate of 5.0% give the right discount rate for cash flows 10 or 20 years in the future?

Well, now that you mention it, probably not. But you cannot use the long-term rate either, because the market risk premium was defined and measured as the average difference between market returns and *short-term* Treasury bill rates. We suggest that you start by estimating the expected return from Treasury bills over the life of the project. In Chapter 4 we observed that investors require a risk premium for holding long-term bonds rather than bills. Table 8.1 showed that over the past century this risk premium has averaged about 1.2%. So to get a rough but reasonable estimate of the expected long-term return from investing in Treasury bills, we need to subtract 1.2% from the current yield rate on long-term bonds. In our example

$$\text{Expected long-term return from bills} = \text{yield on long-term bonds} - 1.2\%$$
$$= 5.0 - 1.2 = 3.8\%$$

This is a plausible estimate of the expected average future return on Treasury bills. We therefore use this rate in our example.

Sometimes the long-term Treasury rate is used without adjustment. If this shortcut is used, then the market risk premium must be restated as the average difference between market returns and *long-term* Treasury returns.

---

[6] Comparing the beta of Union Pacific with those of the other railroads would be misleading if Union Pacific had a materially higher or lower debt ratio. Fortunately, its debt ratio was about average for the sample in Table 10.1.

Returning to our Union Pacific example, suppose you decide to use a market risk premium of 7%. Then the resulting estimate for Union Pacific's cost of equity is about 9.9%:

$$\text{Cost of equity} = \text{expected return} = r_f + \beta(r_m - r_f)$$
$$= 3.8 + .87 \times 7.0 = 9.9\%$$

It is always useful to get a check on such estimates. In this case, we can look back to Table 5.3, which presents cost-of-equity estimates based on the constant-growth DCF formula for Union Pacific and the railroad average. These DCF estimates are considerably higher, at 14.6% for Union Pacific and 15.2% for the industry. Are the DCF estimates too high (as we suspect), or the CAPM estimates too low? You could look to further checks, using DCF models with varying future growth rates[7] or perhaps the three-factor model. We showed in Section 9.4 how the three-factor model can be used to estimate expected returns.

10.3   SETTING DISCOUNT RATES WHEN YOU DON'T HAVE A BETA

Stock or industry betas provide a rough guide to the risk encountered in various lines of business. But an asset beta for the railroad business can take you only so far. Not all investments made in that industry are average-risk. And if you are the first to use railroad-track networks as interplanetary transmission antennas, you will not even have a useful industry beta to start with.

In some cases an asset is publicly traded. If so we can estimate risk from past prices. Suppose your company wants to assess the risk of investing in commercial real estate, for example, in a large office building for company headquarters. Here the company can turn to indexes of real estate prices and returns derived from sales and appraisals of commercial properties.[8]

What should a manager do if the asset has no such convenient price record? What if the proposed investment is not close enough to business as usual to justify using a company cost of capital?

These cases clearly call for judgment. For managers making that kind of judgment, we offer three pieces of advice.

1. *Avoid fudge factors.* Don't give in to the temptation to add fudge factors to the discount rate to offset things that could go wrong with the proposed investment. Adjust cash-flow forecasts first.
2. *Think about the determinants of asset betas.* Often the characteristics of high- and low-beta assets can be observed when the beta itself cannot be.
3. *Don't be fooled by diversifiable risk.*

Let us expand on these points.

---

[7] The average growth rate in Table 5.3 is about 14%, a high rate to project in perpetuity. A multistage DCF model would generate cost-of-equity estimates closer to the CAPM estimate.

[8] See Chapter 23 in D. Geltner, N. G. Miller, J. Clayton, and P. Eichholtz, *Commercial Real Estate Analysis and Investments*, 2nd ed. (South-Western College Publishing, 2006).

Avoid Fudge Factors in Discount Rates

We have defined risk, from the investor's viewpoint, as the standard deviation of portfolio return or the beta of a common stock or other security. But in everyday usage *risk* simply equals "bad outcome." People think of the risks of a project as a list of things that can go wrong. For example,

- A geologist looking for oil worries about the risk of a dry hole.
- A pharmaceutical manufacturer worries about the risk that a new drug that cures baldness may not be approved by the Food and Drug Administration.
- The owner of a resort hotel in a politically unstable part of the world worries about the risk of expropriation.

Managers often add fudge factors to discount rates to offset worries such as these.

This sort of adjustment makes us nervous. First, the bad outcomes we cited appear to reflect unique (i.e., diversifiable) risks that would not affect the expected rate of return demanded by investors. Second, the need for a discount rate adjustment usually arises because managers fail to give bad outcomes their due weight in cash-flow forecasts. The managers then try to offset that mistake by adding a fudge factor to the discount rate.

Example   Project Z will produce just one cash flow, forecasted at $1 million at year 1. It is regarded as average risk, suitable for discounting at a 10% company cost of capital:

$$PV = \frac{C_1}{1 + r} = \frac{1{,}000{,}000}{1.1} = \$909{,}100$$

But now you discover that the company's engineers are behind schedule in developing the technology required for the project. They are confident it will work, but they admit to a small chance that it will not. You still see the *most likely* outcome as $1 million, but you also see some chance that project Z will generate *zero* cash flow next year.

Now the project's prospects are clouded by your new worry about technology. It must be worth less than the $909,100 you calculated before that worry arose. But how much less? There is *some* discount rate (10% plus a fudge factor) that will give the right value, but we do not know what that adjusted discount rate is.

We suggest you reconsider your original $1 million forecast for project Z's cash flow. Project cash flows are supposed to be *unbiased* forecasts that give due weight to all possible outcomes, favorable and unfavorable. Managers making unbiased forecasts are correct on average. Sometimes their forecasts will turn out high, other times low, but their errors will average out over many projects.

If you forecast a cash flow of $1 million for projects like Z, you will overestimate the average cash flow, because every now and then you will hit a zero. Those zeros should be "averaged in" to your forecasts.

For many projects, the most likely cash flow is also the unbiased forecast. If there are three possible outcomes with the probabilities shown below, the unbiased forecast is $1 million. (The unbiased forecast is the sum of the probability-weighted cash flows.)

Possible Cash Flow	Probability	Probability-Weighted Cash Flow	Unbiased Forecast
1.2	.25	.3 ⎫	
1.0	.50	.5 ⎬	1.0, or $1 million
.8	.25	.2 ⎭	

This might describe the initial prospects of project Z. But if technological uncertainty introduces a 10% chance of a zero cash flow, the unbiased forecast could drop to $900,000:

Possible Cash Flow	Probability	Probability-Weighted Cash Flow	Unbiased Forecast
1.2	.225	.27 ⎫	
1.0	.45	.45 ⎪	
.8	.225	.18 ⎬	.90, or $900,000
0	.10	.0 ⎭	

The present value is

$$PV = \frac{.90}{1.1} = .818, \text{ or } \$818,000$$

Now, of course, you can figure out the right fudge factor to add to the discount rate to apply to the original $1 million forecast to get the correct answer. But you have to think through possible cash flows to get that fudge factor; and once you have thought through the cash flows, you don't *need* the fudge factor.

Managers often work out a range of possible outcomes for major projects, sometimes with explicit probabilities attached. We give more elaborate examples and further discussion in Chapter 11. But even when a range of outcomes and probabilities is not explicitly written down, the manager can still consider the good and bad outcomes as well as the most likely one. When the bad outcomes outweigh the good, the cash-flow forecast should be reduced until balance is regained.

Step 1, then, is to do your best to make unbiased forecasts of a project's cash flows. Step 2 is to consider whether *investors* would regard the project as more or less risky than typical for a company or division. Here our advice is to search for characteristics of the asset that are associated with high or low betas. We wish we had a more fundamental scientific understanding of what these characteristics are. We see business risks surfacing in capital markets, but as yet there is no satisfactory theory describing how these risks are generated. Nevertheless, some things are known.

What Determines Asset Betas?

Cyclicality   Many people intuitively associate risk with the variability of book, or accounting, earnings. But much of this variability reflects unique or diversifiable risk. Lone prospectors in search of gold look forward to extremely uncertain future earnings, but whether they strike it rich is not likely to depend on the performance of the market portfolio. Even if they do find gold, they do not bear much market risk. Therefore, an investment in gold prospecting has a high standard deviation but a relatively low beta.

What really counts is the strength of the relationship between the firm's earnings and the aggregate earnings on all real assets. We can measure this either by the *accounting beta* or by the *cash-flow beta*. These are just like a real beta except that changes in book earnings or cash flow are used in place of rates of return on securities. We would predict that firms with high accounting or cash-flow betas should also have high stock betas—and the prediction is correct.

This means that cyclical firms—firms whose revenues and earnings are strongly dependent on the state of the business cycle—tend to be high-beta firms. Thus you should demand a higher rate of return from investments whose performance is strongly tied to the performance of the economy.

Operating Leverage   A production facility with high fixed costs, relative to variable costs, is said to have high *operating leverage*. High operating leverage means high risk. Let us see how this works.

The cash flows generated by any productive asset can be broken down into revenue, fixed costs, and variable costs:

$$\text{Cash flow} = \text{revenue} - \text{fixed cost} - \text{variable cost}$$

Costs are variable if they depend on the rate of output. Examples are raw materials, sales commissions, and some labor and maintenance costs. Fixed costs are cash outflows that occur regardless of whether the asset is active or idle, for example, property taxes or the wages of workers under contract.

We can break down the asset's present value in the same way:

$$\text{PV(asset)} = \text{PV(revenue)} - \text{PV(fixed cost)} - \text{PV(variable cost)}$$

Or equivalently

$$\text{PV(revenue)} = \text{PV(fixed cost)} + \text{PV(variable cost)} + \text{PV(asset)}$$

Those who *receive* the fixed costs are like debtholders in the project; they simply get a fixed payment. Those who receive the net cash flows from the asset are like holders of common stock; they get whatever is left after payment of the fixed costs.

We can now figure out how the asset's beta is related to the betas of the values of revenue and costs. The beta of PV(revenue) is a weighted average of the betas of its component parts:

$$\beta_{\text{revenue}} = \beta_{\text{fixed cost}} \frac{\text{PV(fixed cost)}}{\text{PV(revenue)}}$$
$$+ \beta_{\text{variable cost}} \frac{\text{PV(variable cost)}}{\text{PV(revenue)}} + \beta_{\text{assets}} \frac{\text{PV(asset)}}{\text{PV(revenue)}}$$

The fixed-cost beta should be about zero; whoever receives the fixed costs receives a fixed stream of cash flows.[9] The betas of the revenues and variable costs should be approximately the same, because they respond to the same underlying variable,

---

[9] The cash flows are not absolutely safe, of course. The firm may be able to shut down the plant and avoid the fixed costs entirely. We discuss this abandonment option in Chapter 11.

the rate of output. Therefore, we can substitute $\beta_{\text{variable cost}}$ and solve for the asset beta. Remember that $\beta_{\text{fixed cost}} = 0$.

$$\beta_{\text{assets}} = \beta_{\text{revenue}} \frac{\text{PV(revenue)} - \text{PV(variable cost)}}{\text{PV(asset)}}$$

$$= \beta_{\text{revenue}} \left[1 + \frac{\text{PV(fixed cost)}}{\text{PV(asset)}} \right]$$

Thus, given the cyclicality of revenues (reflected in β_{revenue}), the asset beta is proportional to the ratio of the present value of fixed costs to the present value of the project.

Now you have a rule of thumb for judging the relative risks of alternative designs or technologies for producing the same project. Other things being equal, the alternative with the higher ratio of fixed costs to project value will have the higher project beta. Empirical tests confirm that companies with high operating leverage actually do have high betas.[10]

Other Factors   So far we have focused on risk arising from cash flows. This cash flow risk is not the only risk. A project's value is equal to the expected cash flows discounted at the risk-adjusted discount rate r. If either the risk-free rate or the market risk premium changes, then r will change and so will the project value. A project with very long-term cash flows is more exposed to such shifts in the discount rate than one with short-term cash flows. This project will, therefore, have a high beta even though it may not have high operating leverage and cyclicality.[11]

You cannot hope to estimate the relative risk of assets with any precision, but good managers examine any project from a variety of angles and look for clues as to its riskiness. They know that high market risk is a characteristic of cyclical ventures, of projects with high fixed costs and of projects that are sensitive to market-wide changes in the discount rate. They think about the major uncertainties affecting the economy and consider how projects are affected by these uncertainties.

Finally, do not confuse beta with diversifiable risk. A project may look extra-risky viewed at close range, but if the project's uncertainties are not correlated with the market or other macroeconomic risks, then the project is only average-risk to a diversified investor.

10.4   CERTAINTY EQUIVALENTS—ANOTHER WAY TO ADJUST FOR RISK

In practical capital budgeting, a single discount rate is usually applied to all future cash flows. For example, the financial manager might use the capital asset pricing model to estimate the cost of capital and then use this figure to discount each year's expected cash flow.

---

[10] See B. Lev, "On the Association between Operating Leverage and Risk," "*Journal of Financial and Quantitative Analysis* 9 (September 1974), pp. 627–642; and G. N. Mandelker and S. G. Rhee, "The Impact of the Degrees of Operating and Financial Leverage on Systematic Risk of Common Stock," *Journal of Financial and Quantitative Analysis* 19 (March 1984), pp. 45–57.

[11] See J. Y. Campbell and J. Mei, "Where Do Betas Come From? Asset Price Dynamics and the Sources of Systematic Risk," *Review of Financial Studies* 6 (Fall 1993), pp. 567–592.

Among other things, the use of a constant discount rate assumes that project risk does not change over time, but remains constant year-in and year-out. We know that this cannot be strictly true, for the risks that companies are exposed to are constantly shifting. We are venturing here onto somewhat difficult ground, but there is a way to think about risk that can suggest a route through. It involves converting the expected cash flows to **certainty equivalents.** First we work through an example showing what certainty equivalents are. Then, as a reward for your investment, we will use certainty equivalents to uncover what you are really assuming when you discount a series of future cash flows at a single risk-adjusted discount rate. We also value a project where risk changes over time and ordinary discounting fails.[12]

Valuation by Certainty Equivalents

Think back to the simple real estate investment that we used in Chapter 2 to introduce the concept of present value. You are considering construction of an office building that you plan to sell after one year for $420,000. That cash flow is uncertain with the same risk as the market, so $\beta = 1$. Given $r_f = 5\%$ and $r_m - r_f = 7\%$, you discount at a risk-adjusted discount rate of $5 + 1 \times 7 = 12\%$ rather than the 5% risk-free rate of interest. This gives a present value of $420,000/1.12 = \$375,000$.

Suppose a real estate company now approaches and offers to fix the price at which it will buy the building from you at the end of the year. This guarantee would remove any uncertainty about the payoff on your investment. So you would accept a lower figure than the uncertain payoff of $420,000. But how much less? If the building has a present value of $375,000 and the interest rate is 5%, then

$$PV = \frac{\text{Certain cash flow}}{1.05} = 375,000$$

$$\text{Certain cash flow} = \$393,750$$

In other words, a certain cash flow of $393,750 has exactly the same present value as an expected but uncertain cash flow of $420,000. The cash flow of $393,750 is therefore known as the *certainty-equivalent cash flow.* To compensate for both the delayed payoff and the uncertainty in real estate prices, you need a return of $420,000 - 375,000 = \$45,000$. One part of this difference compensates for the time value of money. The other part ($420,000 - 393,750 = \$26,250$) is a markdown or "haircut" to compensate for the risk attached to the forecasted cash flow of $420,000.

Our example illustrates two ways to value a risky cash flow C_1:

Method 1: Discount the risky cash flow at a *risk-adjusted discount rate r that is greater than r_f.*[13] The risk-adjusted discount rate adjusts for both time and risk. This is illustrated by the clockwise route in Figure 10.3.

Method 2: Find the certainty-equivalent cash flow and discount at the risk-free interest rate r_f. When you use this method, you need to ask, What is the smallest *certain* payoff for which I would exchange the risky cash flow C_1? This

---

[12] Your investment will be rewarded further when we cover options in Chapters 17 and 18. Option pricing formulas discount certainty equivalents.

[13] The discount rate r can be less than r_f for assets with negative betas. But actual betas are almost always positive.

FIGURE 10.3

Two ways to calculate present value. "Haircut for risk" is financial slang referring to the reduction of the cash flow from its forecasted value to its certainty equivalent.

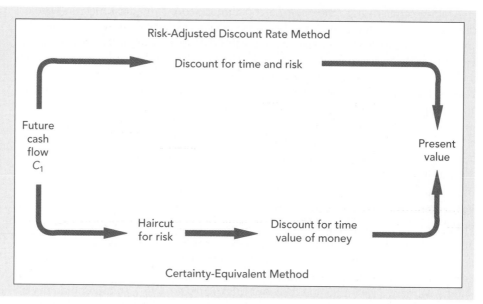

is called the *certainty equivalent* of C_1, denoted by CEQ_1.[14] Since CEQ_1 is the value equivalent of a safe cash flow, it is discounted at the risk-free rate. The certainty-equivalent method makes *separate* adjustments for risk and time. This is illustrated by the counterclockwise route in Figure 10.3.

We now have two identical expressions for PV:

$$PV = \frac{C_1}{1 + r} = \frac{CEQ_1}{1 + r_f}$$

For cash flows two, three, or t years away,

$$PV = \frac{C_t}{(1 + r)^t} = \frac{CEQ_t}{(1 + r_f)^t}$$

When to Use a Single Risk-Adjusted Discount Rate for Long-Lived Assets

We are now in a position to examine what is implied when a constant risk-adjusted discount rate, r, is used to calculate a present value.

Consider two simple projects. Project A is expected to produce a cash flow of $100 million for each of three years. The risk-free interest rate is 6%, the market risk premium is 8%, and project A's beta is .75. You therefore calculate A's opportunity cost of capital as follows:

$$r = r_f + \beta(r_m - r_f)$$
$$= 6 + .75(8) = 12\%$$

---

[14] CEQ_1 can be calculated directly from the capital asset pricing model. The certainty-equivalent form of the CAPM states that the certainty-equivalent value of the cash flow, C_1, is $C_1 - \lambda$ cov $(\tilde{C}_1, \tilde{r}_m)$. Cov$(\tilde{C}_1, \tilde{r}_m)$ is the covariance between the uncertain cash flow, $\tilde{C}_1$, and the return on the market, $\tilde{r}_m$. Lambda, λ, is a measure of the market price of risk. It is defined as $(r_m - r_f)/\sigma_m^2$. For example, if $r_m - r_f = .08$ and the standard deviation of market returns is $\sigma_m = .20$, then lambda $= .08/.20^2 = 2$. We show on our Web site (**www.mhhe.com/bma1e**) how the CAPM formula can be twisted around into this certainty-equivalent form.

Discounting at 12% gives the following present value for each cash flow:

Project A		
Year	Cash Flow	PV at 12%
1	100	89.3
2	100	79.7
3	100	71.2
	Total PV	240.2

Now compare these figures with the cash flows of project B. Notice that B's cash flows are lower than A's; but B's flows are safe, and therefore they are discounted at the risk-free interest rate. The *present value* of each year's cash flow is identical for the two projects.

Project B		
Year	Cash Flow	PV at 6%
1	94.6	89.3
2	89.6	79.7
3	84.8	71.2
	Total PV	240.2

In year 1 project A has a risky cash flow of 100. This has the same PV as the safe cash flow of 94.6 from project B. Therefore 94.6 is the certainty equivalent of 100. Since the two cash flows have the same PV, investors must be willing to give up $100 - 94.6 = 5.4$ in expected year-1 income in order to get rid of the uncertainty.

In year 2 project A has a risky cash flow of 100, and B has a safe cash flow of 89.6. Again both flows have the same PV. Thus, to eliminate the uncertainty in year 2, investors are prepared to give up $100 - 89.6 = 10.4$ of future income. To eliminate uncertainty in year 3, they are willing to give up $100 - 84.8 = 15.2$ of future income.

To value project A, you discounted each cash flow at the same risk-adjusted discount rate of 12%. Now you can see what is implied when you did that. By using a constant rate, you effectively made a larger deduction for risk from the later cash flows:

Year	Forecasted Cash Flow for Project A	Certainty-Equivalent Cash Flow	Deduction for Risk
1	100	94.6	5.4
2	100	89.6	10.4
3	100	84.8	15.2

The second cash flow is riskier than the first because it is exposed to two years of market risk. The third cash flow is riskier still because it is exposed to three years of market risk. This increased risk is reflected in the certainty equivalents that decline by a constant proportion each period.

Therefore, use of a constant risk-adjusted discount rate for a stream of cash flows assumes that risk accumulates at a constant rate as you look farther out into the future.

A Common Mistake

You sometimes hear people say that because distant cash flows are riskier, they should be discounted at a higher rate than earlier cash flows. That is quite wrong: We have just seen that using the same risk-adjusted discount rate for each year's cash flow implies a larger deduction for risk from the later cash flows. The reason is that the discount rate compensates for the risk borne *per period.* The more distant the cash flows, the greater the number of periods and the larger the *total* risk adjustment.

When You Cannot Use a Single Risk-Adjusted Discount Rate for Long-Lived Assets

Sometimes you will encounter problems where the use of a single risk-adjusted discount rate will get you into trouble. For example, later in the book we will look at how options are valued. Because an option's risk is continually changing, the certainty-equivalent method needs to be used.

Here is a disguised, simplified, and somewhat exaggerated version of an actual project proposal that one of the authors was asked to analyze. The scientists at Vegetron have come up with an electric mop, and the firm is ready to go ahead with pilot production and test marketing. The preliminary phase will take one year and cost $125,000. Management feels that there is only a 50% chance that pilot production and market tests will be successful. If they are, then Vegetron will build a $1 million plant that would generate an expected annual cash flow in perpetuity of $250,000 a year after taxes. If they are not successful, the project will have to be dropped.

The expected cash flows (in thousands of dollars) are

$$C_0 = -125$$
$$C_1 = 50\% \text{ chance of } -1{,}000 \text{ and } 50\% \text{ chance of } 0$$
$$= .5(-1{,}000) + .5(0) = -500$$
$$C_t \text{ for } t = 2, 3, \ldots = 50\% \text{ chance of } 250 \text{ and } 50\% \text{ chance of } 0$$
$$= .5(250) + .5(0) = 125$$

Management has little experience with consumer products and considers this a project of extremely high risk.[15] Therefore management discounts the cash flows at 25%, rather than at Vegetron's normal 10% standard:

$$\text{NPV} = -125 - \frac{500}{1.25} + \sum_{t=2}^{\infty} \frac{125}{(1.25)^t} = -125; \text{ or } -\$125{,}000$$

This seems to show that the project is not worthwhile.

---

[15] We will assume that they mean high *market risk* and that the difference between 25% and 10% is *not* a fudge factor introduced to offset optimistic cash-flow forecasts.

Management's analysis is open to criticism if the first year's experiment resolves a high proportion of the risk. If the test phase is a failure, then there is no risk at all—the project is *certain* to be worthless. If it is a success, there could well be only normal risk from then on. That means there is a 50% chance that in one year Vegetron will have the opportunity to invest in a project of *normal* risk, for which the *normal* discount rate of 10% would be appropriate. Thus the firm has a 50% chance to invest $1 million in a project with a net present value of $1.5 million:

$$\text{Success} \rightarrow \text{NPV} = -1,000 + \frac{250}{.10} = +1,500 \text{ (50\% chance)}$$

Pilot production
and market tests

$$\text{Failure} \rightarrow \text{NPV} = 0 \text{ (50\% chance)}$$

Thus we could view the project as offering an expected payoff of .5(1,500)+.5(0) = 750, or $750,000, at $t = 1$ on a $125,000 investment at $t = 0$. Of course, the certainty equivalent of the payoff is less than $750,000, but the difference would have to be very large to justify rejecting the project. For example, if the certainty equivalent is half the forecasted cash flow and the risk-free rate is 7%, the project is worth $225,500:

$$\text{NPV} = C_0 + \frac{\text{CEQ}_1}{1 + r}$$

$$= -125 + \frac{.5(750)}{1.07} = 225.5, \text{ or } \$225,500$$

This is not bad for a $125,000 investment—and quite a change from the negative-NPV that management got by discounting all future cash flows at 25%.

10.5   DISCOUNT RATES FOR INTERNATIONAL PROJECTS

We have shown how the CAPM can help to estimate the cost of capital for domestic investments by U.S. companies. But can we extend the procedure to allow for investments in different countries? The answer is yes in principle, but naturally there are complications.

Foreign Investments Are Not Always Riskier

Pop quiz: Which is riskier for an investor in the United States—the Standard and Poor's Composite Index or the stock market in Egypt? If you answer Egypt, you are right, but *only* if risk is defined as *total* volatility (standard deviation). But does investment in Egypt have a high *beta*? How much does it add to the risk of a diversified portfolio held in the United States?

Table 10.2 shows estimated betas for the Egyptian market and for markets in eight other countries. The standard deviations of returns in these markets were significantly more than the U.S. market, but only Brazil and Turkey had a beta greater than 1. The reason is low correlation. For example, the standard deviation of the Chinese market was 1.96 times that of the Standard and Poor's index, but the correlation coefficient was only .02. The beta was 1.96 × .02 = .04.

TABLE 10.2

Betas of nine country indexes versus the U.S. market, calculated from monthly returns, February 2002–January 2007. Despite high volatility, many of the betas are less than 1. The reason is the relatively low correlation with the U.S. market.

[a] Ratio of standard deviations of country index to Standard & Poor's Composite Index.
[b] Beta is the ratio of covariance to variance. Covariance can be written as $\sigma_{IM} = \rho_{IM}\,\sigma_I\,\sigma_M$; $\beta = \rho_{IM}\,\sigma_I\,\sigma_M/\sigma_M^2 = \rho\,(\sigma_I/\sigma_M)$, where I indicates the country index and M indicates the U.S. market.

	Ratio of Standard Deviations[a]	Correlation Coefficient	Beta[b]
Argentina	2.36	.32	.75
Brazil	2.10	.64	1.34
China	1.96	.02	.04
Egypt	1.49	.09	.14
India	1.80	.39	.70
Indonesia	1.71	.34	.58
Mexico	1.36	.68	.93
Sri Lanka	2.07	−.06	−.13
Turkey	2.96	.53	1.57

Table 10.2 does not prove that investment abroad is always safer than at home. But it should remind you always to distinguish between diversifiable and market risk. The opportunity cost of capital should depend on market risk.

Foreign Investment in the United States

Suppose that Lafarge, the giant French producer of building materials, is considering a new plant in Bordeaux. The financial manager forecasts euro cash flows from the project and discounts these cash flows at the euro cost of capital. She computes that cost of capital in the same way as her counterpart in a U.S. building materials company. She estimates Lafarge's beta and the beta of a portfolio of French building material companies. However, she calculates these betas relative to the *French* market index. Suppose that both measures point to a beta of .94 and that the expected return on the French market is 7% above the euro interest rate. Then Lafarge needs to discount the euro cash flows from the new plant at .94 × 7 = 6.6% above the euro interest rate.

That is straightforward. But now suppose that Lafarge considers expanding into the United States. Once again the financial manager measures beta relative to the French market index. But the fortunes of a U.S. plant will be less closely tied to the fluctuations in the French market. So the beta of a U.S. plant relative to the French index will be less than .94. But how much less? One useful guide is the beta of U.S. building material stocks *relative to the French market*. This beta has been about .54.[16] If this estimate is right, then Lafarge should discount the euro cash flows from its U.S. project at .54 × 7 = 3.8% above the euro interest rate.

Why does Lafarge's manager measure the beta of its investments relative to the French index, whereas her U.S. counterpart measures the beta relative to the U.S. index? The answer lies in Section 8.4, where we explained that risk cannot be considered in isolation; it depends on the other securities in the investor's portfolio.

---

[16] This is the beta of a portfolio of U.S. building material companies relative to the French market, calculated from five years of monthly data from January 2002 to December 2006.

Beta measures risk *relative to the investor's portfolio*. If U.S. investors already hold the U.S. market, an additional dollar invested at home is just more of the same. But, if French investors hold the French market, an investment in the United States can reduce their risk. That explains why investment in a new plant in the United States is likely to have lower risk for Lafarge's shareholders than it would for Martin Marietta's shareholders. It also explains why Lafarge shareholders are willing to accept a lower return from such an investment than the shareholders of Martin Marietta.[17]

When a company measures risk relative to its domestic market, its managers are implicitly assuming that shareholders simply hold domestic stocks. That is not a bad approximation, particularly in the case of the United States.[18] Although U.S. investors can reduce their risk by holding an internationally diversified portfolio of shares, they generally invest only a small proportion of their money overseas. Why they are so shy is a puzzle.[19] It looks as if they are worried about the costs of investing overseas, but we do not understand what these costs include. Maybe it is more difficult to figure out which foreign shares to buy. Or perhaps investors are worried that a foreign government will expropriate their shares, restrict dividend payments, or catch them by a change in the tax law.

However, the world is getting smaller, and investors everywhere are increasing their holdings of foreign securities. Large American financial institutions have substantially increased their overseas investments, and literally dozens of funds have been set up for individuals who want to invest abroad. For example, you can now buy funds that specialize in investment in emerging capital markets such as Vietnam, Peru, or Hungary. As investors increase their holdings of overseas stocks, it becomes less appropriate to measure risk relative to the domestic market and more important to measure the risk of any investment relative to the portfolios that they actually hold.

Who knows? Perhaps in a few years investors will hold internationally diversified portfolios, and later editions of this book will recommend that firms calculate betas relative to the world market. If investors throughout the world held the world portfolio, then French and U.S. companies would both demand the same return from an investment in the United States, in France, or in Egypt.

Do Some Countries Have a Lower Cost of Capital?

Some countries enjoy much lower rates of interest than others. For example, as we write this the long-term interest rate in Japan is about 1.7%, in the United States it is 4.8%. People often conclude from this that Japanese companies enjoy a lower cost of capital.

This view is one part confusion and one part probable truth. The confusion arises because the interest rate in Japan is measured in yen and the rate in the United States is measured in dollars. You would not say that a 10-inch-high rabbit was taller than a 9-foot elephant. You would be comparing their height in different

---

[17] When an investor holds an efficient portfolio, the expected reward for risk on each stock in the portfolio is proportional to its beta *relative to the portfolio*. So, if the French market index is an efficient portfolio for French investors, then these investors will want Lafarge to invest in a new plant if the expected reward is proportional to its beta relative to the French market index.

[18] But it can sometimes be a bad approximation elsewhere. For small countries with open financial borders—Luxembourg, for example—a beta calculated relative to the local market has little value. Few investors in Luxembourg hold only local stocks.

[19] For an explanation of the cost of capital for international investments when there are costs to international diversification, see I. A. Cooper and E. Kaplanis, "Home Bias in Equity Portfolios and the Cost of Capital for Multinational Firms," *Journal of Applied Corporate Finance* 8 (Fall 1995), pp. 95–102.

units. In the same way it makes no sense to compare an interest rate in yen with a rate in dollars. The units are different.

But suppose that in each case you measure the interest rate in *real* terms. Then you are comparing like with like, and it does make sense to ask whether the costs of overseas investment can cause the *real* cost of capital to be lower in Japan. In 2007 financial institutions borrowed an estimated $200 billion in Japan and reinvested it at higher rates elsewhere.[20] These trades are known as *carry trades*. This huge volume of carry trades suggested that investors believed that the real cost of capital was indeed lower in Japan than in some other countries.

---

[20] See "Yen Low Sparks Carry Trade Alert," *Financial Times*, January 30, 2007.

SUMMARY

In Chapter 9 we set out some basic principles for valuing risky assets. In this chapter we have shown you how to apply these principles to practical situations.

The problem is easiest when you believe that the project has the same market risk as the company's existing assets. In this case, the required return equals the required return on a portfolio of all the company's existing securities. This is called the *company cost of capital*.

The company cost of capital is the cost of capital for investment in the firm as a whole. It is usually calculated as a weighted-average cost of capital, that is, the average rate of return demanded by investors in the company's debt and equity securities. But in this chapter we focused mostly on the firm's cost of equity. We defined risk as beta, and we used the capital asset pricing model to estimate expected returns.

The most common way to estimate the beta of a stock is to figure out how the stock price has responded to market changes in the past. Of course, this will give you only an estimate of the stock's true beta. You may get a more reliable figure if you calculate an industry beta for a group of similar companies.

The company cost of capital is the correct discount rate for projects that have the same risk as the company's existing business. Many firms, however, use the company cost of capital to discount the forecasted cash flows on all new projects. This is a dangerous procedure. In principle, each project should be evaluated at its own opportunity cost of capital; the true cost of capital depends on the use to which the capital is put. If we wish to estimate the cost of capital for a particular project, it is *project risk* that counts. Of course the company cost of capital is fine as a discount rate for average-risk projects. It is also a useful starting point for estimating discount rates for safer or riskier projects.

Then we turned to the problem of assessing project risk. We provided several clues for managers seeking project betas. First, avoid adding fudge factors to discount rates to offset worries about bad project outcomes. Adjust cash-flow forecasts to give due weight to bad outcomes as well as good; *then* ask whether the chance of bad outcomes adds to the project's market risk. Second, you can often identify the characteristics of a high- or low-beta project even when the project beta cannot be calculated directly. For example, you can try to figure out how much the cash flows are affected by the overall performance of the economy: Cyclical investments are generally high-beta investments. You can also look at the project's operating leverage: Fixed production charges work like fixed debt charges; that is, they increase beta.Third, don't be fooled by diversifiable project risk. Don't increase the discount rate to off-set risks that can be diversified away in stockholders' portfolios.

There is one more fence to jump. Most projects produce cash flows for several years. Firms generally use the same risk-adjusted rate to discount each of these cash flows. When they do this, they are implicitly assuming that cumulative risk increases at a constant rate as you look further into the future. That assumption is usually reasonable. It is precisely true when the project's future beta will be constant, that is, when risk *per period* is constant.

But exceptions sometimes prove the rule. Be on the alert for projects where risk clearly does not increase steadily. In these cases, you should break the project into segments within which the same discount rate can be reasonably used. Or you should use the certainty-equivalent version of the DCF model, which allows separate risk adjustments to each period's cash flow.

These basic principles apply internationally, but of course there are complications. The risk of a stock or real asset may depend on who's investing. For example, a Swiss investor would calculate a lower beta for Merck than an investor in the United States. Conversely, the U.S. investor would calculate a lower beta for a Swiss pharmaceutical company than a Swiss investor. Both investors see lower risk abroad because of the less-than-perfect correlation between the two countries' markets.

If all investors held the world market portfolio, none of this would matter. But there is a strong home-country bias. Perhaps some investors stay at home because they regard foreign investment as risky. We suspect they confuse total risk with market risk. For example, we showed examples of countries with extremely volatile stock markets. Most of these markets were nevertheless low-beta investments for an investor holding the U.S. market. Again, the reason was low correlation between markets.

FURTHER READING

There is a good review article by Rubinstein on the application of the capital asset pricing model to capital investment decisions:

M. E. Rubinstein, "A Mean-Variance Synthesis of Corporate Financial Theory," *Journal of Finance* 28 (March 1973), pp. 167–182.

Fama's article digs deeper into the implicit assumptions underlying ordinary DCF calculations. Cornell reconsiders the relative risks of near-term vs. distant cash flows.

E. F. Fama, "Discounting Under Uncertainty," *Journal of Business* 69 (October 1996), pp. 415–428.

B. Cornell, "Risk, Duration and Capital Budgeting: New Evidence on Some Old Questions," *Journal of Business* 72 (April 1999), pp. 183–200.

CONCEPT REVIEW QUESTIONS

1. Write out the formula for the company cost of capital, ignoring taxes. For what projects is this the correct discount rate? (page 241)

2. What are the advantages of an industry cost of capital rather than a cost of capital estimated for a single firm? (page 244)

3. Explain carefully how you would estimate beta for a publicly traded stock. (pages 242–244)

For a complete listing of your chapter Concept Review Questions, please visit us at www.mhhe.com/bma1e.

Visit us at www.mhhe.com/bma1e

QUIZ

1. Suppose a firm uses its company cost of capital to evaluate all projects. Will it underestimate or overestimate the value of high-risk projects?

2. Look back to the top-right panel of Figure 10.2. What proportion of Intel's return was explained by market movements? What proportion was unique or diversifiable risk? How does the unique risk show up in the plot? What is the range of possible error in the beta estimate?

3. A company is financed 40% by risk-free debt. The interest rate is 10%, the expected market return is 18%, and the stock's beta is .5. What is the company cost of capital?

4. Gonzalez Farms is breeding a new, genetically engineered potato that should produce low-calorie French fries. Unfortunately the breeding program is not complete, and the new potato will have to be approved by the U.S. Food and Drug Administration. The overall probability of success in breeding and testing is only about 50%. The investment required is $15 million.

   Gonzalez Farms's ordinary cost of capital is 12%. How should the company forecast and discount future cash flows from the low-calorie potato? Should it use a discount rate greater than 12%? How about 24%, to account for the 50% chance of failure? Explain briefly.

5. True or false?

   a. Distant cash flows are riskier than near-term cash flows. Therefore long-term projects require higher risk-adjusted discount rates.

   b. Financial managers should always use the same risk-adjusted discount rate for short- and long-lived projects.

6. Which of these companies is likely to have the higher cost of capital?

   a. A's sales force is paid a fixed annual rate; B's is paid on a commission basis.

   b. C produces machine tools; D produces breakfast cereal.

7. True or false?

   a. Many foreign stock markets are much more volatile than the U.S. market.

   b. The betas of foreign stock markets (calculated relative to the U.S. market) are usually greater than 1.0.

   c. Investors concentrate their holdings in their home countries. This means that companies domiciled in different countries may calculate different discount rates for the same project.

8. A project has a forecasted cash flow of $110 in year 1 and $121 in year 2. The interest rate is 5%, the estimated risk premium on the market is 10%, and the project has a beta of .5. If you use a constant risk-adjusted discount rate, what is

   a. The PV of the project?

   b. The certainty-equivalent cash flow in year 1 and year 2?

   c. The ratio of the certainty-equivalent cash flows to the expected cash flows in years 1 and 2?

PRACTICE QUESTIONS

9. The total market value of the common stock of the Okefenokee Real Estate Company is $6 million, and the total value of its debt is $4 million. The treasurer estimates that the beta of the stock is currently 1.5 and that the expected risk premium on the market is 6%. The Treasury bill rate is 4%. Assume for simplicity that Okefenokee debt is risk-free and the company does not pay tax.

   a. What is the required return on Okefenokee stock?

   b. Estimate the company cost of capital.

   c. What is the discount rate for an expansion of the company's present business?

   d. Suppose the company wants to diversify into the manufacture of rose-colored spectacles. The beta of unleveraged optical manufacturers is 1.2. Estimate the required return on Okefenokee's new venture.

10. Nero Violins has the following capital structure:

Security	Beta	Total Market Value ($ millions)
Debt	0	$100
Preferred stock	.20	40
Common stock	1.20	299

   a. What is the firm's asset beta? (*Hint:* What is the beta of a portfolio of all the firm's securities?)

   b. Assume that the CAPM is correct. What discount rate should Nero set for investments that expand the scale of its operations without changing its asset beta? Assume a risk-free interest rate of 5% and a market risk premium of 6%.

11. Look again at the companies listed in Table 9.2. Monthly rates of return for most of these companies can be found either on **finance.yahoo.com** or on the Standard & Poor's Market Insight Web site (**www.mhhe.com/edumarketinsight**)—see the "Monthly Adjusted Prices" spreadsheet. This spreadsheet also shows monthly returns for the Standard & Poor's 500 market index. What percentage of the variance of each company's return is explained by the index? Use the Excel function RSQ, which calculates R^2.

STANDARD &POOR'S

12. Pick at least five of the companies identified in Practice Question 11 (**finance.yahoo. com** or **www.mhhe.com/edumarketinsight**). The "Monthly Adjusted Prices" spreadsheets should contain about four years of monthly rates of return for the companies' stocks and for the Standard & Poor's 500 index.

STANDARD &POOR'S

   a. Split the rates of return into two consecutive two-year periods. Calculate betas for each period using the Excel SLOPE function. How stable was each company's beta?

   b. Suppose you had used these betas to estimate expected rates of return from the CAPM. Would your estimates have changed significantly from period to period?

   c. You may find it interesting to repeat your analysis using weekly returns from the "Weekly Adjusted Prices" spreadsheets. This will give more than 100 weekly rates of return for each two-year period.

13. The following table shows estimates of the risk of two well-known Canadian stocks:

	Standard Deviation, %	R^2	Beta	Standard Error of Beta
Alcan	29	.37	1.58	.27
Canadian Pacific	22	.15	.75	.23

   a. What proportion of each stock's risk was market risk, and what proportion was unique risk?

   b. What is the variance of Alcan? What is the unique variance?

   c. What is the confidence level on Canadian Pacific's beta?

   d. If the CAPM is correct, what is the expected return on Alcan? Assume a risk-free interest rate of 5% and an expected market return of 12%.

   e. Suppose that next year the market provides a zero return. Knowing this, what return would you expect from Alcan?

Visit us at www.mhhe.com/bma1e

STANDARD
&POOR'S

14. Identify a sample of food companies on **finance.yahoo.com** or on the Standard & Poor's Market Insight Web site (**www.mhhe.com/edumarketinsight**). For example, you could try Campbell Soup (CPB), General Mills (GIS), Kellogg (K), Kraft Foods (KFT), and Sara Lee (SLE).

a. Estimate beta and R^2 for each company. The Excel functions are SLOPE and RSQ.

b. Calculate an industry beta. Here is the best procedure: First calculate the monthly returns on an equally weighted portfolio of the stocks in your sample. Then calculate the industry beta using these portfolio returns. How does the R^2 of this portfolio compare to the average R^2 for the individual stocks?

c. Use the CAPM to calculate an average cost of equity (r_{equity}) for the food industry. Use current interest rates—take a look at the end of section 10.2—and a reasonable estimate of the market risk premium.

15. You are given the following information for Golden Fleece Financial:

Long-term debt outstanding:	$300,000
Current yield to maturity (r_{debt}):	8%
Number of shares of common stock:	10,000
Price per share:	$50
Book value per share:	$25
Expected rate of return on stock (r_{equity}):	15%

Calculate Golden Fleece's company cost of capital. Ignore taxes.

16. Look again at Table 10.1. This time we will concentrate on Burlington Northern.

a. Calculate Burlington's cost of equity from the CAPM using its own beta estimate and the industry beta estimate. How different are your answers? Assume a risk-free rate of 5% and a market risk premium of 7%.

b. Can you be confident that Burlington's true beta is *not* the industry average?

c. Under what circumstances might you advise Burlington to calculate its cost of equity based on its own beta estimate?

17. You run a perpetual encabulator machine, which generates revenues averaging $20 million per year. Raw material costs are 50% of revenues. These costs are variable—they are always proportional to revenues. There are no other operating costs. The cost of capital is 9%. Your firm's long-term borrowing rate is 6%.

Now you are approached by Studebaker Capital Corp., which proposes a fixed-price contract to supply raw materials at $10 million per year for 10 years.

a. What happens to the operating leverage and business risk of the encabulator machine if you agree to this fixed-price contract?

b. Calculate the present value of the encabulator machine with and without the fixed-price contract.

18. Mom and Pop Groceries has just dispatched a year's supply of groceries to the government of the Central Antarctic Republic. Payment of $250,000 will be made one year hence after the shipment arrives by snow train. Unfortunately there is a good chance of a coup d'état, in which case the new government will not pay. Mom and Pop's controller therefore decides to discount the payment at 40%, rather than at the company's 12% cost of capital.

a. What's wrong with using a 40% rate to offset political risk?

b. How much is the $250,000 payment really worth if the odds of a coup d'état are 25%?

19. An oil company is drilling a series of new wells on the perimeter of a producing oil field. About 20% of the new wells will be dry holes. Even if a new well strikes oil, there is still uncertainty about the amount of oil produced: 40% of new wells that strike oil produce only 1,000 barrels a day; 60% produce 5,000 barrels per day.

   a. Forecast the annual cash revenues from a new perimeter well. Use a future oil price of $15 per barrel.

   b. A geologist proposes to discount the cash flows of the new wells at 30% to offset the risk of dry holes. The oil company's normal cost of capital is 10%. Does this proposal make sense? Briefly explain why or why not.

20. Look back at project A in Section 10.4. Now assume that

   a. Expected cash flow is $150 per year for five years.

   b. The risk-free rate of interest is 5%.

   c. The market risk premium is 6%.

   d. The estimated beta is 1.2.

   Recalculate the certainty-equivalent cash flows, and show that the ratio of these certainty-equivalent cash flows to the risky cash flows declines by a constant proportion each year.

21. A project has the following forecasted cash flows:

Cash Flows, $ Thousands			
C_0	C_1	C_2	C_3
−100	+40	+60	+50

   The estimated project beta is 1.5. The market return r_m is 16%, and the risk-free rate r_f is 7%.

   a. Estimate the opportunity cost of capital and the project's PV (using the same rate to discount each cash flow).

   b. What are the certainty-equivalent cash flows in each year?

   c. What is the ratio of the certainty-equivalent cash flow to the expected cash flow in each year?

   d. Explain why this ratio declines.

22. The McGregor Whisky Company is proposing to market diet scotch. The product will first be test-marketed for two years in southern California at an initial cost of $500,000. This test launch is not expected to produce any profits but should reveal consumer preferences. There is a 60% chance that demand will be satisfactory. In this case McGregor will spend $5 million to launch the scotch nationwide and will receive an expected annual profit of $700,000 in perpetuity. If demand is not satisfactory, diet scotch will be withdrawn.

   Once consumer preferences are known, the product will be subject to an average degree of risk, and, therefore, McGregor requires a return of 12% on its investment. However, the initial test-market phase is viewed as much riskier, and McGregor demands a return of 40% on this initial expenditure.

   What is the NPV of the diet scotch project?

23. Look at Table 10.2. What would the nine countries' betas be if the correlation coefficient for each was 0.5? Do the calculation and explain.

24. Consider the beta estimates for the country indexes shown in Table 10.2. Could this information be helpful to a U.S. company considering capital investment projects in these countries? Would a German company find this information useful? Explain.

Visit us at
www.mhhe.com/bma1e.

25. Go to **quote.yahoo.com/m2?u.** Download monthly returns on the Taiwanese market index and the U.S. S&P 500 market index for the same period as in Table 10.2. Calculate the ratio of the standard deviation of the Taiwanese market to the standard deviation of the S&P 500 market index, the correlation of the two indexes, and the beta of the Taiwanese market relative to the S&P 500 market index.

CHALLENGE QUESTIONS

26. Suppose you are valuing a future stream of high-risk (high-beta) cash *outflows*. High risk means a high discount rate. But the higher the discount rate, the less the present value. This seems to say that the higher the risk of cash outflows, the less you should worry about them! Can that be right? Should the sign of the cash flow affect the appropriate discount rate? Explain.

27. An oil company executive is considering investing $10 million in one or both of two wells: Well 1 is expected to produce oil worth $3 million a year for 10 years; well 2 is expected to produce $2 million for 15 years. These are *real* (inflation-adjusted) cash flows.

    The beta for *producing wells* is .9. The market risk premium is 8%, the nominal risk-free interest rate is 6%, and expected inflation is 4%.

    The two wells are intended to develop a previously discovered oil field. Unfortunately there is still a 20% chance of a dry hole in each case. A dry hole means zero cash flows and a complete loss of the $10 million investment.

    Ignore taxes and make further assumptions as necessary.

    a. What is the correct real discount rate for cash flows from developed wells?

    b. The oil company executive proposes to add 20 percentage points to the real discount rate to offset the risk of a dry hole. Calculate the NPV of each well with this adjusted discount rate.

    c. What do *you* say the NPVs of the two wells are?

    d. Is there any *single* fudge factor that could be added to the discount rate for developed wells that would yield the correct NPV for both wells? Explain.

28. If you have access to "Data Analysis Tools" in Excel, use the "regression" functions to investigate the reliability of the betas estimated in Practice Problems 12 and 14.

    a. What are the standard errors of the betas from Practice Problems 12(a) and 12(c)? Given the standard errors, do you regard the different beta estimates obtained for each company as signficantly different? (Perhaps the differences are just "noise.") What would you propose as the most reliable *forecast* of beta for each company?

    b. How reliable are the beta estimates from Practice Problem 14(a)?

    c. Compare the standard error of the industry beta from Practice Problem 14(b) with the standard errors for individual-company betas. Given these standard errors, would you rely on the industry beta or betas for individual companies?

STANDARD
&POOR'S

MINI-CASE

The Jones Family, Incorporated

The Scene: Early evening in an ordinary family room in Manhattan. Modern furniture, with old copies of *The Wall Street Journal* and the *Financial Times* scattered around. Autographed photos of Alan Greenspan and George Soros are prominently displayed. A picture window reveals a distant view of lights on the Hudson River. John Jones sits at a computer terminal, glumly sipping a glass of chardonnay and putting on a carry trade in Japanese yen over the Internet. His wife Marsha enters.

Marsha: Hi, honey. Glad to be home. Lousy day on the trading floor, though. Dullsville. No volume. But I did manage to hedge next year's production from our copper mine. I couldn't get a good quote on the right package of futures contracts, so I arranged a commodity swap.

John doesn't reply.

Marsha: John, what's wrong? Have you been selling yen again? That's been a losing trade for weeks.

John: Well, yes. I shouldn't have gone to Goldman Sachs's foreign exchange brunch. But I've got to get out of the house somehow. I'm cooped up here all day calculating covariances and efficient risk-return trade-offs while you're out trading commodity futures. You get all the glamour and excitement.

Marsha: Don't worry dear, it will be over soon. We only recalculate our most efficient common stock portfolio once a quarter. Then you can go back to leveraged leases.

John: You trade, and I do all the worrying. Now there's a rumor that our leasing company is going to get a hostile takeover bid. I knew the debt ratio was too low, and you forgot to put on the poison pill. And now you've made a negative-NPV investment!

Marsha: What investment?

John: That wildcat oil well. Another well in that old Sourdough field. It's going to cost $5 million! Is there any oil down there?

Marsha: That Sourdough field has been good to us, John. Where do you think we got the capital for your yen trades? I bet we'll find oil. Our geologists say there's only a 30% chance of a dry hole.

John: Even if we hit oil, I bet we'll only get 300 barrels of crude oil per day.

Marsha: That's 300 barrels day in, day out. There are 365 days in a year, Dear.

John and Marsha's teenage son Johnny bursts into the room.

Johnny: Hi, Dad! Hi, Mom! Guess what? I've made the junior varsity derivatives team! That means I can go on the field trip to the Chicago Board Options Exchange. (*Pauses.*) What's wrong?

John: Your mother has made another negative-NPV investment. A wildcat oil well, way up on the North Slope of Alaska.

Johnny: That's OK, Dad. Mom told me about it. I was going to do an NPV calculation yesterday, but I had to finish calculating the junk-bond default probabilities for my corporate finance homework. (*Grabs a financial calculator from his backpack.*) Let's see: 300 barrels a day times 365 days per year times $25 per barrel when delivered in Los Angeles . . . that's $2.7 million per year.

John: That's $2.7 million *next* year, assuming that we find any oil at all. The production will start declining by 5% every year. And we still have to pay $10 per barrel in pipeline and tanker charges to ship the oil from the North Slope to Los Angeles. We've got some serious operating leverage here.

Marsha: On the other hand, our energy consultants project increasing oil prices. If they increase with inflation, price per barrel should increase by roughly 2.5% per year. The wells ought to be able to keep pumping for at least 15 years.

Johnny: I'll calculate NPV after I finish with the default probabilities. The interest rate is 6%. Is it OK if I work with the beta of .8 and our usual figure of 7% for the market risk premium?

Marsha: I guess so, Johnny. But I am concerned about the fixed shipping costs.

John: (*Takes a deep breath and stands up.*) Anyway, how about a nice family dinner? I've reserved our usual table at the Four Seasons.

Everyone exits.

Announcer: Is the wildcat well really negative-NPV? Will John and Marsha have to fight a hostile takeover? Will Johnny's derivatives team use Black–Scholes or the binomial method? Find out in the next episode of The Jones Family, Incorporated.

You may not aspire to the Jones family's way of life, but you will learn about all their activities, from futures contracts to binomial option pricing, later in this book. Meanwhile, you may wish to replicate Johnny's NPV analysis.

QUESTIONS

1. Calculate the NPV of the wildcat oil well, taking account of the probability of a dry hole, the shipping costs, the decline in production, and the forecasted increase in oil prices. How long does production have to continue for the well to be a positive-NPV investment? Ignore taxes and other possible complications.

2. Now consider operating leverage. How should the shipping costs be valued, assuming that output is known and the costs are fixed? How would your answer change if the shipping costs are proportional to output? Assume that unexpected fluctuations in output are zero-beta and diversifiable. (*Hint:* The Jones's oil company has an excellent credit rating. Its long-term borrowing rate is only 7%.)

PART THREE

BEST PRACTICES IN CAPITAL BUDGETING

EUROTUNNEL'S CONSTRUCTION OF a tunnel between England and France cost a record $15 billion. Before proceeding, the company developed cash-flow forecasts that indicated a satisfactory 14% return. Unfortunately, meticulous DCF calculations do not guarantee success. The tunnel proved more costly and took longer to build than anticipated. Also revenues were disappointing; 10 years after opening the tunnel, the company was still unable to earn enough to pay the interest on its debt. In exasperation a large group of shareholders rose up in revolt and sacked the entire board.

Eurotunnel's misfortunes serve as a reminder that a facility in discounted cash flow analysis does not automatically lead to good investment decisions. To be confident that a project truly has a positive NPV, you also need to ask some fundamental questions about the project. Does the firm have a strate-gic advantage or headstart over other firms? How will competitors react? Will their responses erode the project's profitability? For example, it seems likely that Eurotunnel's management understimated just how sharply existing operators of channel ferries would cut their prices.

In Part 3 we look at three prerequisites for making such judgments. We begin by looking at how firms organize the capital budgeting process to ensure that they get the information they need. Second, managements need to understand what a project's success or failure depends on. We therefore review some of the techniques that managers used to identify the factors that could put a project below water. Finally, we show how firms build flexibility into their investments, so that they can cut back if disaster threatens and to expand if things go right.

Web sites related to this Part appear at www.mhhe.com/bma1e.

11

PROJECT ANALYSIS

HAVING READ OUR earlier chapters on capital budgeting, you may have concluded that the choice of which projects to accept or reject is a simple one. You just need to draw up a set of cash-flow forecasts, choose the right discount rate, and crank out net present value. But finding projects that create value for the shareholders can never be reduced to a mechanical exercise. We therefore devote the next three chapters to ways in which companies can stack the odds in their favor when making investment decisions.

Investment proposals may emerge from many different parts of the organization. Companies therefore need procedures to ensure that every project is assessed consistently. Our first task in this chapter is to review how firms develop plans and budgets for capital investments, how they authorize specific projects, and how they check whether projects perform as promised.

When managers are presented with investment proposals, they do not accept the cash flow forecasts at face value. Instead, they try to understand what makes a project tick and what could go wrong with it. Remember Murphy's law, "if anything can go wrong, it will," and O'Reilly's corollary, "at the worst possible time."

Once you know what makes a project tick, you may be able to reconfigure it to improve its chance of success. And if you understand why the venture could fail, you can decide whether it is worth trying to rule out the possible causes of failure. Maybe further expenditure on market research would clear up those doubts about acceptance by consumers, maybe another drill hole would give you a better idea of the size of the ore body, and maybe some further work on the test bed would confirm the durability of those welds.

If the project really has a negative NPV, the sooner you can identify it, the better. And even if you decide that it is worth going ahead without further analysis, you do not want to be caught by surprise if things go wrong later. You want to know the danger signals and the actions that you might take.

Our second task in this chapter is to show how managers use *sensitivity analysis*, *break-even analysis*, and *Monte Carlo simulation* to identify the crucial assumptions in investment proposals and to explore what can go wrong. There is no magic in these techniques, just computer-assisted common sense. You do not need a license to use them.

Discounted-cash-flow analysis commonly assumes that companies hold assets passively, and it ignores the opportunities to expand the project if it is successful or to bail out if it is not. However, wise managers recognize these opportunities when considering whether to invest. They look for ways to capitalize on success and to reduce the costs of failure, and they are prepared to pay up for projects that give them this flexibility. Opportunities to modify projects as the future unfolds are known as *real options.* In the final section of the chapter we describe several important real options, and we show how to use *decision trees* to set out the possible future choices.

11.1 THE CAPITAL INVESTMENT PROCESS

Senior management needs some forewarning of future investment outlays. So for most large firms, the investment process starts with the preparation of an annual **capital budget,** which is a list of investment projects planned for the coming year.

Most firms let project proposals bubble up from plants for review by divisional management and then from divisions for review by senior management and their planning staff. Of course middle managers cannot identify all worthwhile projects. For example, the managers of plants A and B cannot be expected to see the potential economies of closing their plants and consolidating production at a new plant C. Divisional managers would propose plant C. But the managers of divisions 1 and 2 may not be eager to give up their own computers to a corporation-wide information system. That proposal would come from senior management, for example, the company's chief information officer.

Inconsistent assumptions often creep into expenditure plans. For example, suppose the manager of your furniture division is bullish on housing starts, but the manager of your appliance division is bearish. The furniture division may push for a major investment in new facilities, while the appliance division may propose a plan for retrenchment. It would be better if both managers could agree on a common estimate of housing starts and base their investment proposals on it. That is why many firms begin the capital budgeting process by establishing consensus forecasts of economic indicators, such as inflation and growth in gross national product, as well as forecasts of particular items that are important to the firm's business, such as housing starts or the prices of raw materials. These forecasts are then used as the basis for the capital budget.

Preparation of the capital budget is not a rigid, bureaucratic exercise. There is plenty of give-and-take and back-and-forth. Divisional managers negotiate with plant managers and fine-tune the division's list of projects. The final capital budget must also reflect the corporation's strategic planning. Strategic planning takes a top-down view of the company. It attempts to identify businesses where the company has a competitive advantage. It also attempts to identify businesses to sell or that should be allowed to run down.

A firm's capital investment choices should reflect both bottom-up and top-down views of the business—capital budgeting and strategic planning, respectively. Plant and division managers, who do most of the work in bottom-up capital budgeting, may not see the forest for the trees. Strategic planners may have a mistaken view of the forest because they do not look at the trees one by one.

Project Authorizations—and the Problem of Biased Forecasts

Once the capital budget has been approved by top management and the board of directors, it is the official plan for the ensuing year. However, it is not the final sign-off for specific projects. Most companies require **appropriation requests** for each proposal. These requests include detailed forecasts, discounted-cash-flow analyses, and back-up information.

Many investment projects carry a high price tag; they also determine the shape of the firm's business 10 or 20 years in the future. Hence final approval of appropriation requests tends to be reserved for top management. Companies set ceilings on the size of projects that divisional managers can authorize. Often these ceilings are surprisingly low. For example, a large company, investing $400 million per year, might require top management to approve all projects over $500,000.

This centralized decision making brings its problems: Senior management can't process detailed information about hundreds of projects and must rely on forecasts put together by project sponsors. A smart manager quickly learns to worry whether these forecasts are realistic.

Even when the forecasts are not consciously inflated, errors creep in. For example, most people tend to be overconfident when they forecast. Events they think are almost certain to occur may actually happen only 80% of the time, and events they believe are impossible may happen 20% of the time. Therefore project risks are understated. Anyone who is keen to get a project accepted is also likely to look on the bright side when forecasting the project's cash flows. Such overoptimism seems to be a common feature in financial forecasts. Overoptimism afflicts governments too, probably more than private businesses. How often have you heard of a new dam, highway, or military aircraft that actually cost *less* than was originally forecasted?

You can expect plant or divisional managers to look on the bright side when putting forward investment proposals. That is not altogether bad. Psychologists stress that optimism and confidence are likely to increase effort, commitment, and persistence. The problem is that hundreds of appropriation requests may reach senior management each year, all essentially sales documents presented by united fronts and designed to persuade. Alternative schemes have been filtered out at earlier stages.

It is probably impossible to eliminate bias completely, but senior managers should take care not to encourage it. For example, if managers believe that success depends on having the largest division rather than the most profitable one, they will propose large expansion projects that they do not truly believe have positive NPVs. Or if new plant managers are pushed to generate increased earnings right away, they will be tempted to propose quick-payback projects even when NPV is sacrificed.

Sometimes senior managers try to offset bias by increasing the hurdle rate for capital expenditure. Suppose the true cost of capital is 10%, but the CFO is frustrated by the large fraction of projects that don't earn 10%. She therefore directs project sponsors to use a 15% discount rate. In other words, she adds a 5% fudge factor in an attempt to offset forecast bias. But it doesn't work; it *never* works. Brealey, Myers, and Allen's Second Law[1] explains why. The law states: *The proportion of proposed projects having positive NPVs at the corporate hurdle rate is independent of the hurdle rate.*

---

[1] There is no First Law. We think "Second Law" sounds better. There is a Third Law, but that is for another chapter.

The law is not a facetious conjecture. It was tested in a large oil company where staff kept careful statistics on capital investment projects. About 85% of projects had positive NPVs. (The remaining 15% were proposed for other reasons, for example, to meet environmental standards.) One year, after several quarters of disappointing earnings, top management decided that more financial discipline was called for and increased the corporate hurdle rate by several percentage points. But in the following year the fraction of projects with positive NPVs stayed rock-steady at 85%.

If you're worried about bias in forecasted cash flows, the only remedy is careful analysis of the forecasts. *Do not add fudge factors to the cost of capital.*[2]

Postaudits

Most firms keep a check on the progress of large projects by conducting **postaudits** shortly after the projects have begun to operate. Postaudits identify problems that need fixing, check the accuracy of forecasts, and suggest questions that should have been asked before the project was undertaken. Postaudits pay off mainly by helping managers to do a better job when it comes to the next round of investments. After a postaudit the controller may say, "We should have anticipated the extra training required for production workers." When the next proposal arrives, training will get the attention it deserves.

Postaudits may not be able to measure all of a project's costs and benefits. It may be impossible to split the project away from the rest of the business. Suppose that you have just taken over a trucking firm that operates a delivery service for local stores. You decide to improve service by installing custom software to keep track of packages and to schedule trucks. You also construct a dispatching center and buy five new diesel trucks. A year later you try a postaudit of the investment in software. You verify that it is working properly and check actual costs of purchase, installation, and operation against projections. But how do you identify the incremental cash inflows? No one has kept records of the extra diesel fuel that *would have been* used or the extra shipments that *would have been* lost absent the software. You may be able to verify that service is better, but how much of the improvement comes from the new trucks, how much from the dispatching center, and how much from the software? The only meaningful measures of success are for the delivery business as a whole.

11.2   SENSITIVITY ANALYSIS

Uncertainty means that more things can happen than will happen. Whenever you are confronted with a cash-flow forecast, you should try to discover what else can happen.

Put yourself in the well-heeled shoes of the treasurer of the Otobai Company in Osaka, Japan. You are considering the introduction of an electrically powered

---

[2] Adding a fudge factor to the cost of capital also favors quick-payback projects and penalizes longer-lived projects, which tend to have lower rates of return but higher NPVs. Adding a 5% fudge factor to the discount rate is roughly equivalent to reducing the forecast and present value of the first project cash flow by 5%. The impact on the present value of a cash flow 10 years in the future is much greater, because the fudge factor is compounded in the discount rate. The fudge factor is not too much of a burden for a 2- or 3-year project, but an enormous burden for a 10- or 20-year project.

TABLE 11.1

Preliminary cash-flow forecasts for Otobai's electric scooter project (figures in ¥ billions).

Assumptions:
1. Investment is depreciated over 10 years straight-line.
2. Income is taxed at a rate of 50%.

"Live" Excel versions of Tables 11.1 to 11.5 are available on the book's Web site, **www.mhhe.com/bma1e**.

Visit us at
www.mhhe.com/bma1e.

		Year 0	Years 1-10
1	Investment	15	
2	Revenue		37.5
3	Variable cost		30
4	Fixed cost		3
5	Depreciation		1.5
6	Pretax profit		3
7	Tax		1.5
8	Net profit		1.5
	Operating cash flow		3
	Net cash flow	−15	3

motor scooter for city use. Your staff members have prepared the cash-flow forecasts shown in Table 11.1. Since NPV is positive at the 10% opportunity cost of capital, it appears to be worth going ahead.

$$\text{NPV} = -15 + \sum_{t=1}^{10} \frac{3}{(1.10)^t} = +\text{¥}3.43 \text{ billion}$$

Before you decide, you want to delve into these forecasts and identify the key variables that determine whether the project succeeds or fails. It turns out that the marketing department has estimated revenue as follows:

Unit sales = new product's share of market × size of scooter market
= .1 × 1 million = 100,000 scooters

Revenue = unit sales × price per unit
= 100,000 × 375,000 = ¥37.5 billion

The production department has estimated variable costs per unit as ¥300,000. Since projected volume is 100,000 scooters per year, total variable cost is ¥30 billion. Fixed costs are ¥3 billion per year. The initial investment can be depreciated on a straight-line basis over the 10-year period, and profits are taxed at a rate of 50%.

These seem to be the important things you need to know, but look out for unidentified variables. Perhaps there are patent problems, or perhaps you will need to invest in service stations that will recharge the scooter batteries. The greatest dangers often lie in these *unknown* unknowns, or "unk-unks," as scientists call them.

Having found no unk-unks (no doubt you will find them later), you conduct a **sensitivity analysis** with respect to market size, market share, and so on. To do this, the marketing and production staffs are asked to give optimistic and pessimistic estimates for the underlying variables. These are set out in the left-hand columns of Table 11.2. The right-hand side shows what happens to the project's net present value if the variables are set *one at a time* to their optimistic and pessimistic values. Your project appears to be by no means a sure thing. The most dangerous variables are market share and unit variable cost. If market share is only .04 (and all other variables are as expected), then the project has an NPV of −¥10.4 billion. If unit variable cost is ¥360,000 (and all other variables are as expected), then the project has an NPV of −¥15 billion.

Variable	Range			NPV, ¥ billions		
	Pessimistic	Expected	Optimistic	Pessimistic	Expected	Optimistic
Market size, million	0.9	1	1.1	1.1	3.4	5.7
Market share	0.04	0.10	0.16	−10.4	3.4	17.3
Unit price, yen	350,000	375,000	380,000	−4.2	3.4	5.0
Unit variable cost, yen	360,000	300,000	275,000	−15.0	3.4	11.1
Fixed cost, ¥ billions	4	3	2	0.4	3.4	6.5

TABLE 11.2

To undertake a sensitivity analysis of the electric scooter project, we set each variable in turn at its most pessimistic or optimistic value and recalculate the NPV of the project.

Value of Information

Now you can check whether you could resolve some of the uncertainty *before* your company parts with the ¥15 billion investment. Suppose that the pessimistic value for unit variable cost partly reflects the production department's worry that a particular machine will not work as designed and that the operation will have to be performed by other methods at an extra cost of ¥20,000 per unit. The chance that this will occur is only 1 in 10. But, if it does occur, the extra ¥20,000 unit cost will reduce after-tax cash flow by

$$\text{Unit sales} \times \text{additional unit cost} \times (1 - \text{tax rate})$$
$$= 100,000 \times 20,000 \times .50 = ¥1 \text{ billion}$$

It would reduce the NPV of your project by

$$\sum_{t=1}^{10}\frac{1}{(1.10)^t} = ¥6.14 \text{ billion,}$$

putting the NPV of the scooter project underwater at +3.43 − 6.14 = −¥2.71 billion. It is possible that a relatively small change in the scooter's design would remove the need for the new machine. Or perhaps a ¥10 million pretest of the machine will reveal whether it will work and allow you to clear up the problem. It clearly pays to invest ¥10 million to avoid a 10% probability of a ¥6.14 billion fall in NPV. You are ahead by −10 + .10 × 6,140 = +¥604 million.

On the other hand, the value of additional information about market size is small. Because the project is acceptable even under pessimistic assumptions about market size, you are unlikely to be in trouble if you have misestimated that variable.

Limits to Sensitivity Analysis

Sensitivity analysis boils down to expressing cash flows in terms of key project variables and then calculating the consequences of misestimating the variables. It forces the manager to identify the underlying variables, indicates where additional information would be most useful, and helps to expose confused or inappropriate forecasts.

One drawback to sensitivity analysis is that it always gives somewhat ambiguous results. For example, what exactly does *optimistic* or *pessimistic* mean? The marketing department may be interpreting the terms in a different way from the production department. Ten years from now, after hundreds of projects, hindsight may show that the marketing department's pessimistic limit was exceeded twice as often as the production department's; but what you may discover 10 years hence is no help now. Of course, you could specify that, when you use the terms "pessimistic" and "optimistic," you mean that there is only a 10% chance that the actual value will prove to be worse than the pessimistic figure or better than the optimistic one. However, it is far from easy to extract a forecaster's notion of the true probabilities of possible outcomes.[3]

Another problem with sensitivity analysis is that the underlying variables are likely to be interrelated. What sense does it make to look at the effect in isolation of an increase in market size? If market size exceeds expectations, it is likely that demand will be stronger than you anticipated and unit prices will be higher. And why look in isolation at the effect of an increase in price? If inflation pushes prices to the upper end of your range, it is quite probable that costs will also be inflated.

Sometimes the analyst can get around these problems by defining underlying variables so that they are roughly independent. But you cannot push *one-at-a-time* sensitivity analysis too far. It is impossible to obtain expected, optimistic, and pessimistic values for total *project* cash flows from the information in Table 11.2.

Scenario Analysis

If the variables are interrelated, it may help to consider some alternative plausible scenarios. For example, perhaps the company economist is worried about the possibility of another sharp rise in world oil prices. The direct effect of this would be to encourage the use of electrically powered transportation. The popularity of compact cars after the oil price increases in 2006 leads you to estimate that an immediate 20% rise in the price of oil would enable you to capture an extra 3% of the scooter market. On the other hand, the economist also believes that higher oil prices would prompt a world recession and at the same time stimulate inflation. In that case, market size might be in the region of .8 million scooters and both prices and cost might be 15% higher than your initial estimates. Table 11.3 shows that this scenario of higher oil prices and recession would on balance help your new venture. Its NPV would increase to ¥6.4 billion.

Managers often find **scenario analysis** helpful. It allows them to look at different but *consistent* combinations of variables. Forecasters generally prefer to give an estimate of revenues or costs under a particular scenario than to give some absolute optimistic or pessimistic value.

Break-Even Analysis

When we undertake a sensitivity analysis of a project or when we look at alternative scenarios, we are asking how serious it would be if sales or costs turned out to be worse than we forecasted. Managers sometimes prefer to rephrase this question and ask how bad sales can get before the project begins to lose money. This exercise is known as **break-even analysis.**

---

[3] If you doubt this, try some simple experiments. Ask the person who repairs your television to state a numerical probability that your set will work for at least one more year. Or construct your own subjective probability distribution of the number of telephone calls you will receive next week. That ought to be easy. Try it.

		Cash Flows, Years 1-10, ¥ billions	
		Base Case	High Oil Prices and Recession Case
1	Revenue	37.5	44.9
2	Variable cost	30	35.9
3	Fixed cost	3	3.5
4	Depreciation	1.5	1.5
5	Pretax profit	3	4.0
6	Tax	1.5	2.0
7	Net profit	1.5	2.0
8	Net cash flow	3	3.5
	PV of cash flows	18.4	21.4
	NPV	3.4	6.4
		Assumptions	
		Base Case	High Oil Prices and Recession Case
	Market size, million	1	0.8
	Market share	0.10	0.13
	Unit price, yen	375,000	431,300
	Unit variable cost, yen	300,000	345,000
	Fixed cost, ¥ billions	3	3.5

TABLE 11.3

How the NPV of the electric scooter project would be affected by higher oil prices and a world recession.

Visit us at
www.mhhe.com/bma1e.

	Inflows	Outflows						
		Year 0	Years 1-10					
Unit Sales,	Revenues,		Variable	Fixed		PV	PV	
Thousands	Years 1-10	Investment	Costs	Costs	Taxes	Inflows	Outflows	NPV
0	0	15	0	3	−2.25	0	19.6	−19.6
100	37.5	15	30	3	1.5	230.4	227.0	3.4
200	75.0	15	60	3	5.25	460.8	434.4	26.5

TABLE 11.4

NPV of electric scooter project under different assumptions about unit sales (figures in ¥ billions except as noted).

Visit us at
www.mhhe.com/bma1e.

In the left-hand portion of Table 11.4 we set out the revenues and costs of the electric scooter project under different assumptions about annual sales.[4] In the right-hand portion of the table we discount these revenues and costs to give the *present value* of the inflows and the *present value* of the outflows. Net present value is of course the difference between these numbers.

You can see that NPV is strongly negative if the company does not produce a single scooter. It is just positive if (as expected) the company sells 100,000 scooters and is strongly positive if it sells 200,000. Clearly the *zero*-NPV point occurs at a little under 100,000 scooters.

---

[4] Notice that if the project makes a loss, this loss can be used to reduce the tax bill on the rest of the company's business. In this case the project produces a tax saving—the tax outflow is negative.

FIGURE 11.1

A break-even chart showing the present values of Otobai's cash inflows and outflows under different assumptions about unit sales. NPV is zero when sales are 85,000.

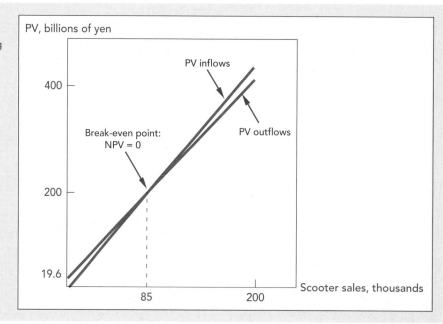

TABLE 11.5

The electric scooter project's accounting profit under different assumptions about unit sales (figures in ¥ billions except as noted).

Unit Sales, Thousands	Revenues Years 1-10	Variable Costs	Fixed Costs	Depreciation	Taxes	Total Costs	Profit after Tax
0	0	0	3	1.5	−2.25	2.25	−2.25
100	37.5	30	3	1.5	1.5	36.0	1.5
200	75.0	60	3	1.5	5.25	69.75	5.25

In Figure 11.1 we have plotted the present value of the inflows and outflows under different assumptions about annual sales. The two lines cross when sales are 85,000 scooters. This is the point at which the project has zero NPV. As long as sales are greater than 85,000, the project has a positive NPV.[5]

Managers frequently calculate break-even points in terms of accounting profits rather than present values. Table 11.5 shows Otobai's after-tax profits at three levels of scooter sales. Figure 11.2 once again plots revenues and costs against sales. But the story this time is different. Figure 11.2, which is based on accounting profits, suggests a breakeven of 60,000 scooters. Figure 11.1, which is based on present values, shows a breakeven at 85,000 scooters. Why the difference?

When we work in terms of accounting profit, we deduct depreciation of ¥1.5 billion each year to cover the cost of the initial investment. If Otobai sells

---

[5] We could also calculate break-even sales by plotting equivalent annual costs and revenues. Of course, the break-even point would be identical at 85,000 scooters.

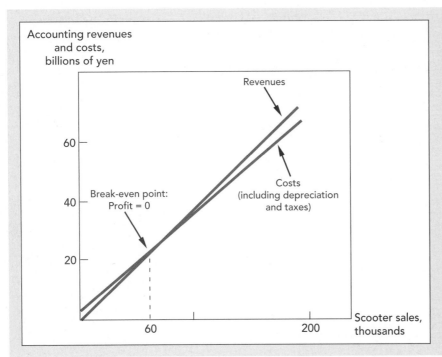

FIGURE 11.2

Sometimes break-even charts are constructed in terms of accounting numbers. After-tax profit is zero when sales are 60,000.

60,000 scooters a year, revenues will be sufficient both to pay operating costs and to recover the initial outlay of ¥15 billion. But they will *not* be sufficient to repay the *opportunity cost of capital* on that ¥15 billion. A project that breaks even in accounting terms will surely have a negative NPV.

Operating Leverage and Break-Even Points

Break-even charts like Figure 11.1 help managers appreciate *operating leverage*, that is, project exposure to fixed costs. High operating leverage means high risk, other things equal, of course.

The electric scooter project had low fixed costs, only ¥3 billion against projected revenues of ¥37.5 billion. But suppose Otobai now considers a different production technology with lower variable costs of only ¥120,000 per unit (versus ¥300,000 per unit) but higher fixed costs of ¥19 billion. Total forecasted production costs are lower (12 + 19 = ¥31 billion versus ¥33 billion), so profitability improves—compare Table 11.6 to Table 11.1. Project NPV apparently increases to ¥9.6 billion.

Figure 11.3 is the new break-even chart. Break-even sales have *increased* to 88,000 (that's bad), even though total production costs have *fallen*. A new sensitivity analysis would show that project NPV is much more exposed to changes in market size, market share, or unit price. All of these differences can be traced to the higher fixed costs of the alternative production technology.

Is the alternative technology better than the original one? The financial manager would have to consider the alternative technology's higher business risk, and perhaps recompute NPV at a higher discount rate, before making a final decision.[6]

---

[6] He or she could use the procedures outlined in Section 10.3 to recalculate beta and come up with a new discount rate.

TABLE 11.6

Cash-flow forecasts and NPV for the electric scooter project, here assuming a production technology with high fixed costs but low total costs (figures in ¥ billions). Compare Table 11.1.

	Year 0	Years 1–10
Investment	15	
1. Revenue		37.5
2. Variable cost		12.0
3. Fixed cost		19.0
4. Depreciation		1.5
5. Pretax profit (1 − 2 − 3 − 4)		5.0
6. Tax		2.5
7. Net profit (5 − 6)		2.5
8. Operating cash flow (4 + 7)		4.0
Net cash flow	−15	+4.0

$$NPV = -15 + \sum_{t=1}^{10} \frac{4.0}{(1.1)^t} = +¥9.6 \text{ billion}$$

FIGURE 11.3

Break-even chart for an alternative production technology with higher fixed costs. Notice that break-even sales increase to 88,000. Compare Figure 11.1.

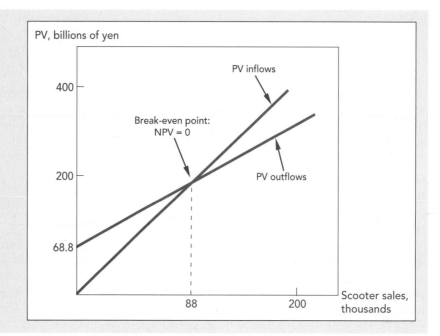

11.3   MONTE CARLO SIMULATION

Sensitivity analysis allows you to consider the effect of changing one variable at a time. By looking at the project under alternative scenarios, you can consider the effect of a *limited number* of plausible combinations of variables. **Monte Carlo simulation** is a tool for considering *all* possible combinations. It therefore enables you to inspect the entire distribution of project outcomes.

Imagine that you are a gambler at Monte Carlo. You know nothing about the laws of probability (few casual gamblers do), but a friend has suggested to you a complicated strategy for playing roulette. Your friend has not actually tested the strategy but is confident that it will *on the average* give you a 2½% return for every 50 spins of the wheel. Your friend's optimistic estimate for any series of 50 spins is a profit of 55%; your friend's pessimistic estimate is a loss of 50%. How can you find out whether these really are the odds? An easy but possibly expensive way is to start playing and record the outcome at the end of each series of 50 spins. After, say, 100 series of 50 spins each, plot a frequency distribution of the outcomes and calculate the average and upper and lower limits. If things look good, you can then get down to some serious gambling.

An alternative is to tell a computer to simulate the roulette wheel and the strategy. In other words, you could instruct the computer to draw numbers out of its hat to determine the outcome of each spin of the wheel and then to calculate how much you would make or lose from the particular gambling strategy.

That would be an example of Monte Carlo simulation. In capital budgeting we replace the gambling strategy with a model of the project, and the roulette wheel with a model of the world in which the project operates. Let us see how this might work with our project for an electrically powered scooter.

Simulating the Electric Scooter Project

Step 1: Modeling the Project   The first step in any simulation is to give the computer a precise model of the project. For example, the sensitivity analysis of the scooter project was based on the following implicit model of cash flow:

Cash flow = (revenues − costs − depreciation) × (1 − tax rate) + depreciation

Revenues = market size × market share × unit price

Costs = (market size × market share × variable unit cost) + fixed cost

This model of the project was all that you needed for the simpleminded sensitivity analysis that we described above. But if you wish to simulate the whole project, you need to think about how the variables are interrelated.

For example, consider the first variable—market size. The marketing department has estimated a market size of 1 million scooters in the first year of the project's life, but of course you do not know how things will work out. Actual market size will exceed or fall short of expectations by the amount of the department's forecast error:

Market size, year 1 = expected market size, year 1 × (1 + forecast error, year 1)

You *expect* the forecast error to be zero, but it could turn out to be positive or negative. Suppose, for example, that the actual market size turns out to be 1.1 million. That means a forecast error of 10%, or +.1:

Market size, year 1 = 1 × (1 + .1) = 1.1 million

You can write the market size in the second year in exactly the same way:

Market size, year 2 = expected market size, year 2 × (1 + forecast error, year 2)

But at this point you must consider how the expected market size in year 2 is affected by what happens in year 1. If scooter sales are below expectations in year 1, it is likely that they will continue to be below in subsequent years. Suppose that a shortfall in sales in year 1 would lead you to revise down your forecast of sales in year 2 by a like amount. Then

$$\text{Expected market size, year 2} = \text{actual market size, year 1}$$

Now you can rewrite the market size in year 2 in terms of the actual market size in the previous year plus a forecast error:

$$\text{Market size, year 2} = \text{market size, year 1} \times (1 + \text{forecast error, year 2})$$

In the same way you can describe the expected market size in year 3 in terms of market size in year 2 and so on.

This set of equations illustrates how you can describe interdependence between different *periods*. But you also need to allow for interdependence between different *variables*. For example, the price of electrically powered scooters is likely to increase with market size. Suppose that this is the only uncertainty and that a 10% addition to market size would lead you to predict a 3% increase in price. Then you could model the first year's price as follows:

$$\text{Price, year 1} = \text{expected price, year 1} \times (1 + .3 \times \text{error in market size forecast, year 1})$$

Then, if variations in market size exert a permanent effect on price, you can define the second year's price as

$$\text{Price, year 2} = \text{expected price, year 2} \times (1 + .3 \times \text{error in market size forecast, year 2})$$
$$= \text{actual price, year 1} \times (1 + .3 \times \text{error in market size forecast, year 2})$$

Notice how we have linked each period's selling price to the *actual* selling prices (including forecast error) in all previous periods. We used the same type of linkage for market size. These linkages mean that forecast errors accumulate; they do not cancel out over time. Thus, uncertainty *increases* with time: The farther out you look into the future, the more the actual price or market size may depart from your original forecast.

The complete model of your project would include a set of equations for each of the variables: market size, price, market share, unit variable cost, and fixed cost. Even if you allowed for only a few interdependencies between variables and across time, the result would be quite a complex list of equations.[7] Perhaps that is not a bad thing if it forces you to understand what the project is all about. Model building is like spinach: You may not like the taste, but it is good for you.

Step 2: Specifying Probabilities   Remember the procedure for simulating the gambling strategy? The first step was to specify the strategy, the second was to specify the numbers on the roulette wheel, and the third was to tell the computer to select these numbers at random and calculate the results of the strategy:

___

[7] Specifying the interdependencies is the hardest and most important part of a simulation. If all components of project cash flows were unrelated, simulation would rarely be necessary.

The steps are just the same for your scooter project:

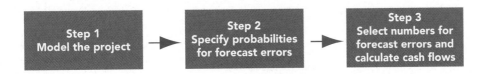

Think about how you might go about specifying your possible errors in forecasting market size. You *expect* market size to be 1 million scooters. You obviously don't think that you are underestimating or overestimating, so the expected forecast error is zero. On the other hand, the marketing department has given you a range of possible estimates. Market size could be as low as .85 million scooters or as high as 1.15 million scooters. Thus the forecast error has an expected value of 0 and a range of plus or minus 15%. If the marketing department has in fact given you the lowest and highest possible outcomes, actual market size should fall somewhere within this range with near certainty.[8]

That takes care of market size; now you need to draw up similar estimates of the possible forecast errors for each of the other variables that are in your model.

Step 3: Simulate the Cash Flows   The computer now *samples* from the distribution of the forecast errors, calculates the resulting cash flows for each period, and records them. After many iterations you begin to get accurate estimates of the probability distributions of the project cash flows—accurate, that is, only to the extent that your model and the probability distributions of the forecast errors are accurate. Remember the GIGO principle: "Garbage in, garbage out."

Figure 11.4 shows part of the output from an actual simulation of the electric scooter project.[9] Note the positive skewness of the outcomes—very large outcomes are more likely than very small ones. This is common when forecast errors accumulate over time. Because of the skewness the average cash flow is somewhat higher than the most likely outcome; in other words, a bit to the right of the peak of the distribution.[10]

Step 4: Calculate Present Value   The distributions of project cash flows should allow you to calculate the expected cash flows more accurately. In the final step you need to discount these expected cash flows to find present value.

---

[8] Suppose "near certainty" means "99% of the time." If forecast errors are normally distributed, this degree of certainty requires a range of plus or minus three standard deviations.

   Other distributions could, of course, be used. For example, the marketing department may view any market size between .85 and 1.15 million scooters as *equally likely*. In that case the simulation would require a uniform (rectangular) distribution of forecast errors.

[9] These are actual outputs from Crystal Ball™ software. The simulation assumed annual forecast errors were normally distributed and ran through 10,000 trials. We thank Christopher Howe for running the simulation. An Excel program to simulate the Otobai project was kindly provided by Marek Jochec, and is available on the Web site, **www.mhhe.com/bma1e.**

[10] When you are working with cash-flow forecasts, bear in mind the distinction between the expected value and the most likely (or modal) value. Present values are based on *expected* cash flows—that is, the probability-weighted average of the possible future cash flows. If the distribution of possible outcomes is skewed to the right as in Figure 11.4, the expected cash flow will be greater than the most likely cash flow.

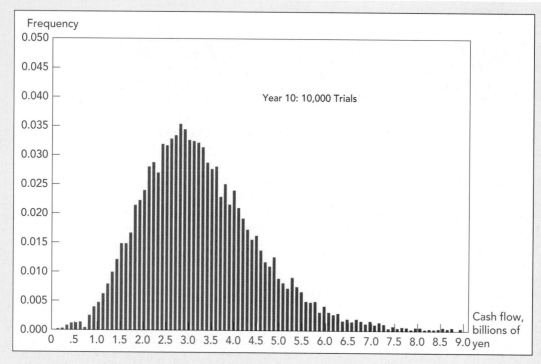

FIGURE 11.4

Simulation of cash flows for year 10 of the electric scooter project.

Simulation of Pharmaceutical Research and Development

Simulation, though sometimes costly and complicated, has the obvious merit of compelling the forecaster to face up to uncertainty and to interdependencies. Once you have set up your simulation model, it is a simple matter to analyze the principal sources of uncertainty in the cash flows and to see how much you could reduce this uncertainty by improving the forecasts of sales or costs. You may also be able to explore the effect of possible modifications to the project.

Several large pharmaceutical companies have used Monte Carlo simulation to analyze investments in research and development (R&D) of new drugs. Only a small fraction of drug candidates identified in basic research prove effective and achieve profitable production. At each phase of R&D, the company must decide whether to press on to the next phase or halt. The pharmaceutical companies face two kinds of uncertainty:

1. *Will the compound work?* Will it have harmful side effects? Will it ultimately gain FDA approval? (Most drugs do not: Of 10,000 promising compounds, only 1 or 2 may ever get to market. The 1 or 2 that are marketed have to generate enough cash flow to make up for the 9,999 or 9,998 that fail.)

2. *Market success.* FDA approval does not guarantee that a drug will sell. A competitor may be there first with a similar (or better) drug. The company may or may not be able to sell the drug worldwide. Selling prices and marketing costs are unknown.

Imagine that you are contemplating a research program that will investigate a promising class of compounds. Could you write down the expected cash inflows and outflows of the program up to 25 or 30 years in the future? We suggest that no mortal could do so without a model to help; simulation may provide the answer.[11]

Simulation may sound like a panacea for the world's ills, but, as usual, you pay for what you get. Sometimes you pay for more than you get. It is not just a matter of the time and money spent in building the model. It is extremely difficult to estimate interrelationships between variables and the underlying probability distributions, even when you are trying to be honest.[12] But in capital budgeting, forecasters are seldom completely impartial and the probability distributions on which simulations are based can be highly biased.

In practice, a simulation that attempts to be realistic will also be complex. Therefore the decision maker may delegate the task of constructing the model to management scientists or consultants. The danger here is that, even if the builders understand their creation, the decision maker cannot and therefore does not rely on it. This is a common but ironic experience.

11.4   REAL OPTIONS AND DECISION TREES

When you use discounted cash flow (DCF) to value a project, you implicitly assume that the firm will hold the assets passively. But managers are not paid to be dummies. After they have invested in a new project, they do not simply sit back and watch the future unfold. If things go well, the project may be expanded; if they go badly, the project may be cut back or abandoned altogether. Projects that can easily be modified in these ways are more valuable than those that do not provide such flexibility. The more uncertain the outlook, the more valuable this flexibility becomes.

That sounds obvious, but notice that sensitivity analysis and Monte Carlo simulation do not recognize the opportunity to modify projects.[13] For example, think back to the Otobai electric scooter project. In real life, if things go wrong with the project, Otobai would abandon to cut its losses. If so, the worst outcomes would not be as devastating as our sensitivity analysis and simulation suggested.

Options to modify projects are known as **real options.** Managers may not always use the term real option to describe these opportunities; for example, they may refer to "intangible advantages" of easy-to-modify projects. But when they review major investment proposals, these option intangibles are often the key to their decisions.

---

[11] N. A. Nichols, "Scientific Management at Merck: An Interview with CFO Judy Lewent," *Harvard Business Review* 72 (January–February 1994), p. 91.

[12] These difficulties are less severe for the pharmaceutical industry than for most other industries. Pharmaceutical companies have accumulated a great deal of information on the probabilities of scientific and clinical success and on the time and money required for clinical testing and FDA approval.

[13] Some simulation models *do* recognize the possibility of changing policy. For example, when a pharmaceutical company uses simulation to analyze its R&D decisions, it allows for the possibility that the company can abandon the development at each phase.

The Option to Expand

Long-haul airfreight businesses such as FedEx need to move a massive amount of goods each day. Therefore, when Airbus announced delays to its A380 superjumbo freighter, FedEx turned to Boeing and ordered 15 of its 777 freighters to be delivered between 2009 and 2011. If business continues to expand, FedEx will need more aircraft. But rather than placing additional firm orders in 2006, the company secured a place in Boeing's production line by acquiring *options* to buy a further 15 aircraft at a predetermined price. These options do not commit FedEx to expand but give it the flexibility to do so.

Figure 11.5 displays FedEx's expansion option as a simple **decision tree.** You can think of it as a game between FedEx and fate. Each square represents an action or decision by the company. Each circle represents an outcome revealed by fate. In this case there is only one outcome—when fate reveals the airfreight demand and FedEx's capacity needs. FedEx then decides whether to exercise its options and buy additional 777s. Here the future decision is easy: Buy the airplanes only if demand is high and the company can operate them profitably. If demand is low, FedEx walks away and leaves Boeing with the problem of finding another customer for the planes that were reserved for FedEx.

You can probably think of many other investments that take on added value because of the further options they provide. For example,

- When launching a new product, companies often start with a pilot program to iron out possible design problems and to test the market. The company can evaluate the pilot and then decide whether to expand to full-scale production.
- When designing a factory, it can make sense to provide extra land or floor space to reduce the future cost of a second production line.
- When building a four-lane highway, it may pay to build six-lane bridges so that the road can be converted later to six lanes if traffic volumes turn out to be higher than expected.

Such options to expand do not show up in the assets that the company lists in its balance sheet, but investors are very aware of their existence. If a company has

FIGURE 11.5

FedEx's expansion option expressed as a simple decision tree.

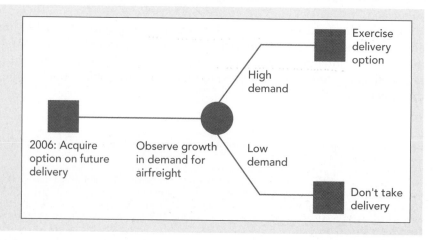

valuable real options that can allow it to invest in new profitable projects, its market value will be higher than the value of its physical assets now in place.

In Chapter 5 we showed how the present value of growth opportunities (PVGO) contributes to the value of a company's common stock. PVGO equals the forecasted total NPV of future investments. But it is better to think of PVGO as the value of the firm's *options* to invest and expand. The firm is not obliged to grow. It can invest more if the number of positive-NPV projects turns out high or slow down if that number turns out low. The flexibility to adapt investment to future opportunities is one of the factors that makes PVGO so valuable.

The Option to Abandon

If the option to expand has value, what about the decision to bail out? Projects do not just go on until assets expire of old age. The decision to terminate a project is usually taken by management, not by nature. Once the project is no longer profitable, the company will cut its losses and exercise its option to abandon the project.

Some assets are easier to bail out of than others. Tangible assets are usually easier to sell than intangible ones. It helps to have active secondhand markets, which really exist only for standardized items. Real estate, airplanes, trucks, and certain machine tools are likely to be relatively easy to sell. On the other hand, the knowledge accumulated by a software company's research and development program is a specialized intangible asset and probably would not have significant abandonment value. (Some assets, such as old mattresses, even have *negative* abandonment value; you have to pay to get rid of them. It is costly to decommission nuclear power plants or to reclaim land that has been strip-mined.)

Example   Managers should recognize the option to abandon when they make the initial investment in a new project or venture. For example, suppose you must choose between two technologies for production of a Wankel-engine outboard motor.

1. Technology A uses computer-controlled machinery custom-designed to produce the complex shapes required for Wankel engines in high volumes and at low cost. But if the Wankel outboard does not sell, this equipment will be worthless.
2. Technology B uses standard machine tools. Labor costs are much higher, but the machinery can be sold for $10 million if the engine does not sell.

Technology A looks better in a DCF analysis of the new product because it was designed to have the lowest possible cost at the planned production volume. Yet you can sense the advantage of technology B's flexibility if you are unsure about whether the new outboard will sink or swim in the marketplace.

We can make the value of this flexibility concrete by expressing it as a real option. Just for simplicity, assume that the initial capital outlays for technologies A and B are the same. Technology A, with its low-cost customized machinery, will provide a payoff of $18.5 million if the outboard is popular with boat owners and $8.5 million if it is not. Think of these payoffs as the project's cash flow in its first year of production plus the present value of all subsequent cash flows. The corresponding payoffs to technology B are $18 million and $8 million.

	Payoffs from Producing Outboard ($ millions)	
	Technology A	**Technology B**
Buoyant demand	$18.5	$18
Sluggish demand	8.5	8

If you are obliged to continue in production regardless of how unprofitable the project turns out to be, then technology A is clearly the superior choice. But remember that at year-end you can bail out of technology B for $10 million. If the outboard is not a success in the market, you are better off selling the plant and equipment for $10 million than continuing with a project that has a present value of only $8 million.

Figure 11.6 summarizes this example as a decision tree. The abandonment option occurs at the right-hand boxes for Technology B. The decisions are obvious: continue if demand is buoyant, abandon otherwise. Thus the payoffs to Technology B are:

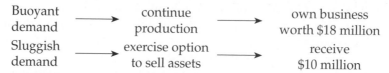

Technology B provides an insurance policy: If the outboard's sales are disappointing, you can abandon the project and recover $10 million. You can think of this abandonment option as an option to sell the assets for $10 million. The total value of the project using technology B is its DCF value, assuming that the company does not abandon, *plus* the value of the abandonment option. When you value this option, you are placing a value on flexibility.

Production Options

When companies undertake new investments, they generally think about the possibility that at a later stage they may wish to modify the project. After all, today everybody may be demanding round pegs, but, who knows, tomorrow square ones may be all the rage. In that case you need a plant that provides the flexibility to produce a variety of peg shapes. In just the same way, it may be worth paying up front for the flexibility to vary the inputs. For example, electric utilities often build in the option to switch between burning oil and burning natural gas. We refer to these opportunities as *production options*.

Timing Options

The fact that a project has a positive NPV does not mean that it is best undertaken now. It might be even more valuable if undertaken in the future.

Timing decisions are fairly straightforward under conditions of certainty. You first need to examine alternative dates (*t*) for making the investment and calculate its net future value at each of these dates. Then, to find which of the alternatives would add most to the firm's *current* value, you must discount these net future values back to the present:

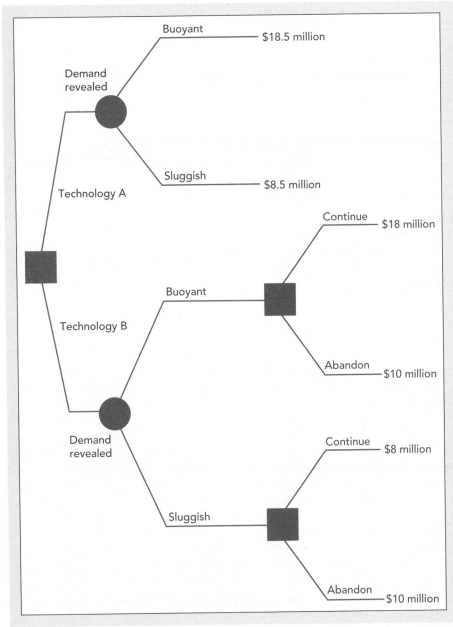

FIGURE 11.6

Decision tree for the Wankel outboard motor project. Technology B allows the firm to abandon the project and recover $10 million if demand is sluggish.

$$\text{Net present value of investment if undertaken at date } t = \frac{\text{Net future value at date } t}{(1 + r)^t}$$

Example   You own a large tract of inaccessible timber. To harvest it, you have to invest $75,000 in access roads and other facilities. The longer you wait, the higher the investment required. On the other hand, lumber prices will rise as you wait, and the trees will keep growing, although at a gradually decreasing rate.

Let us suppose that the net present value of the harvest at different *future* dates is as follows:

	Year of Harvest					
	0	**1**	**2**	**3**	**4**	**5**
Net *future* value ($ thousands)	50	64.4	77.5	89.4	100	109.4
Change in value from previous year (%)		+28.8	+20.3	+15.4	+11.9	+9.4

As you can see, the longer you defer cutting the timber, the more money you will make. However, your concern is with the date that maximizes the net *present* value of your investment, that is, its contribution to the value of your firm *today*. You therefore need to discount the net future value of the harvest back to the present. Suppose the appropriate discount rate is 10%. Then, if you harvest the timber in year 1, it has a net *present* value of $58,500:

$$\text{NPV if harvested in year 1} = \frac{64.4}{1.10} = 58.5, \text{ or } \$58,500$$

The net present value for other harvest dates is as follows:

	Year of Harvest					
	0	**1**	**2**	**3**	**4**	**5**
Net present value ($ thousands)	50	58.5	64.0	67.2	68.3	67.9

The optimal point to harvest the timber is year 4 because this is the point that maximizes NPV. Notice that before year 4 the net future value of the timber increases by more than 10% a year: The gain in value is greater than the cost of the capital tied up in the project. After year 4 the gain in value is still positive but less than the cost of capital. So delaying the harvest further just reduces shareholder wealth.[14]

In the timber-cutting example we assumed that there was no uncertainty about the cash flows, so that you knew the optimal time to exercise your option was in year 4. The timing option is much more complicated under uncertainty. An opportunity not taken at $t = 0$ might be more or less attractive at $t = 1$; there is rarely any way of knowing for sure. Perhaps it is better to strike while the iron is hot even if there is a chance it will become hotter. On the other hand, if you wait a bit you might obtain more information and avoid a bad mistake. That is why you often find that managers choose not to invest today in projects where the NPV is only marginally positive, and there is much to be learned by delay.

---

[14] Our timber-cutting example conveys the right idea about investment timing, but it misses an important practical point: The sooner you cut the first crop of trees, the sooner the second crop can start growing. Thus, the value of the second crop depends on when you cut the first. The more complex and realistic problem can be solved in one of two ways:

1. Find the cutting dates that maximize the present value of a series of harvests, taking into account the different growth rates of young and old trees.
2. Repeat our calculations, counting the future market value of cut-over land as part of the payoff to the first harvest. The value of cut-over land includes the present value of all subsequent harvests. The second solution is far simpler if you can figure out how much the cut-over land will be worth.

More on Decision Trees

In Chapters 17 and 18 we will return to the subject of options and show how to calculate their value. But we will close this chapter with a closer look at decision trees.

Decision trees are commonly used to describe the real options imbedded in capital investment projects. But decision trees were used in the analysis of projects years before real options were first explicitly identified. Decision trees can help to understand project risk and how future decisions will affect project cash flows. Even if you never learn or use option valuation theory, decision trees belong in your financial toolkit.

The best way to appreciate how decision trees can be used in project analysis is to work through a detailed example.

An Example: Magna Charter

Magna Charter is a new corporation formed by Agnes Magna to provide an executive flying service for the southeastern United States. The founder thinks there will be a ready demand from businesses that cannot justify a full-time company plane but nevertheless need one from time to time. However, the venture is not a sure thing. There is a 40% chance that demand in the first year will be low. If it is low, there is a 60% chance that it will remain low in subsequent years. On the other hand, if the initial demand is high, there is an 80% chance that it will stay high.

The immediate problem is to decide what kind of plane to buy. A turboprop costs $550,000. A piston-engine plane costs only $250,000 but has less capacity and customer appeal. Moreover, the piston-engine plane is an old design and likely to depreciate rapidly. Ms. Magna thinks that next year secondhand piston aircraft will be available for only $150,000.

That gives Ms. Magna an idea: Why not start out with one piston plane and buy another if demand is still high? It will cost only $150,000 to expand. If demand is low, Magna Charter can sit tight with one small, relatively inexpensive aircraft.

Figure 11.7 displays these choices. The square on the left marks the company's initial decision to purchase a turboprop for $550,000 or a piston aircraft for $250,000. After the company has made its decision, fate decides on the first year's demand. You can see in parentheses the probability that demand will be high or low. We also show the cash flow consequences of high or low demand. Since we would like to sidestep here the issue of risk, in Figure 11.7 we have converted the expected uncertain cash flows into their certainty equivalents.[15] This means that we can properly discount these certainty-equivalent flows at the risk-free rate of interest.

At the end of the year the company has a second decision to make if it has a piston-engine aircraft: It can either expand or sit tight. This decision point is marked by the second square. Finally fate takes over again and selects the level of demand for year 2. Again you can see in parentheses the probability of high or low demand. Notice that the probabilities for the second year depend on the first-period outcomes. For example, if demand is high in the first period, then there is an 80%

---

[15] Certainty-equivalent cash flows are the sure-fire cash flows that would have the same present value as the actual uncertain flows. We described certainty-equivalent flows in Chapter 10 and showed how they can be used to calculate present values. We will use them in Chapter 18, when we show how to value options.

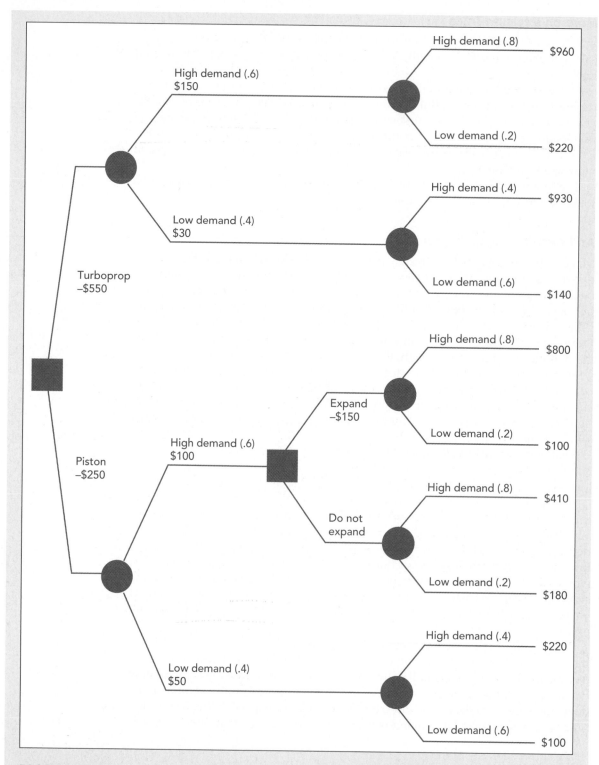

FIGURE 11.7

Decision tree for Magna Charter. Should it buy a turboprop or a smaller piston-engine plane? A second piston plane can be purchased in year 1 if demand turns out to be high. (All figures are in thousands. Probabilities are in parentheses.)

chance that it will also be high in the second. The chance of high demand in *both* the first and second periods is .6 × .8 = .48. After the parentheses we again show the profitability of the project for each combination of aircraft and demand level. You can interpret each of these figures as the present value at the end of year 2 of the cash flows for that and all subsequent years.

The problem for Ms. Magna is to decide what to do today. We solve that problem by thinking first what she would do next year. This means that we start at the right side of the tree and work backward to the beginning on the left.

The only decision that Ms. Magna needs to make next year is whether to expand if purchase of a piston-engine plane is succeeded by high demand. If she expands, she invests $150,000 and receives a payoff of $800,000 if demand continues to be high and $100,000 if demand falls. So her *expected* payoff is

(Probability high demand × payoff with high demand)
+ (probability low demand × payoff with low demand)
= (.8 × 800) + (.2 × 100) = +660, or $660,000

If the discount rate is 10%, then the net present value of expanding, computed as of year 1, is

$$NPV = -150 + \frac{660}{1.10} = +450, \text{ or } \$450,000$$

If Ms. Magna does *not* expand, the expected payoff is

(Probability high demand × payoff with high demand)
+ (probability low demand × payoff with low demand)
= (.8 × 410) + (.2 × 180) = +364, or $364,000

The net present value of *not* expanding, computed as of year 1, is

$$NPV = 0 + \frac{364}{1.10} = +331, \text{ or } \$331,000$$

Expansion obviously pays if market demand is high.

Now that we know what Magna Charter ought to do if faced with the expansion decision, we can roll back to today's decision. If the first piston-engine plane is bought, Magna can expect to receive cash worth $550,000 in year 1 if demand is high and cash worth $185,000 if it is low:

The net present value of the investment in the piston-engine plane is therefore $117,000:

$$NPV = -250 + \frac{.6(550) + .4(185)}{1.10} = +117, \text{ or } \$117,000$$

If Magna buys the turboprop, there are no future decisions to analyze, and so there is no need to roll back. We just calculate expected cash flows and discount:

$$\text{NPV} = -550 + \frac{.6(150) + .4(30)}{1.10}$$
$$+ \frac{.6[.8(960) + .2(220)] + .4[.4(930) + .6(140)]}{(1.10)^2}$$
$$= -550 + \frac{102}{1.10} + \frac{670}{(1.10)^2} = +96, \text{ or } \$96,000$$

Thus the investment in the piston-engine plane has an NPV of $117,000; the investment in the turboprop has an NPV of $96,000. The piston-engine plane is the better bet. Note, however, that the choice would be different if we forgot to take account of the option to expand. In that case the NPV of the piston-engine plane would drop from $117,000 to $52,000:

$$\text{NPV} = -250 + \frac{.6(100) + .4(50)}{1.10}$$
$$+ \frac{.6[.8(410) + .2(180)] + .4[.4(220) + .6(100)]}{(1.10)^2}$$
$$= +52, \text{ or } \$52,000$$

The value of the option to expand is, therefore,

$$117 - 52 = +65, \text{ or } \$65,000$$

The decision tree in Figure 11.7 recognizes that, if Ms. Magna buys one piston-engine plane, she is not stuck with that decision. She has the option to expand by buying an additional plane if demand turns out to be unexpectedly high. But Figure 11.7 also assumes that, if Ms. Magna goes for the big time by buying a turboprop, there is nothing that she can do if demand turns out to be unexpectedly *low*. That is unrealistic. If business in the first year is poor, it may pay for Ms. Magna to sell the turboprop and abandon the venture entirely. In Figure 11.7 we could represent this option to bail out by adding an extra decision point (a further square) if the company buys the turboprop and first-year demand is low. If that happens, Ms. Magna could decide either to sell the plane or to hold on and hope demand recovers. If the abandonment option is sufficiently valuable, it may make sense to take the turboprop and shoot for the big payoff.

Pro and Con Decision Trees

Any cash-flow forecast rests on some assumption about the firm's future investment and operating strategy. Often that assumption is implicit. Decision trees force the underlying strategy into the open. By displaying the links between today's and tomorrow's decisions, they help the financial manager to find the strategy with the highest net present value.

The trouble with decision trees is that they get so _____ complex so _____ quickly (insert your own expletives). What will Magna Charter do if demand is neither high nor low but just middling? In that event Ms. Magna might sell the turboprop and buy a piston-engine plane, or she might defer expansion and abandonment decisions until year 2. Perhaps middling demand requires a decision about a price cut or an intensified sales campaign.

We could draw a new decision tree covering this expanded set of events and decisions. Try it if you like: You will see how fast the circles, squares, and branches accumulate.

Life is complex, and there is very little we can do about it. It is therefore unfair to criticize decision trees because they can become complex. Our criticism is reserved for analysts who let the complexity become overwhelming. The point of decision trees is to allow explicit analysis of possible future events and decisions. They should be judged not on their comprehensiveness but on whether they show the most important links between today's and tomorrow's decisions. Decision trees used in real life will be more complex than Figure 11.7, but they will nevertheless display only a small fraction of possible future events and decisions. Decision trees are like grapevines: They are productive only if they are vigorously pruned.

Decision trees can help identify the future choices available to the manager and can give a clearer view of the cash flows and risks of a project. However, our analysis of the Magna Charter project begged an important question. The option to expand enlarged the spread of possible outcomes and therefore increased the risk of investing in a piston aircraft. Conversely, the option to bail out would narrow the spread of possible outcomes, reducing the risk of investment. We finessed this problem by interpreting all the cash-flow figures in Figure 11.7 as the certainty-equivalent cash flows, which could then be discounted at the risk-free interest rate. When we come to the issue of option pricing in Chapter 18, we will explain how investment options can be valued by calculating the certainty-equivalent cash flows.

Decision Trees and Monte Carlo Simulation

We have said that any cash-flow forecast rests on assumptions about future investment and operating strategy. Think back to the Monte Carlo simulation model that we constructed for Otobai's electric scooter project. What strategy was that based on? We don't know. Inevitably Otobai will face decisions about pricing, production, expansion, and abandonment, but the model builder's assumptions about these decisions are buried in the model's equations. The model builder may have implicitly identified a future strategy for Otobai, but it is clearly not the optimal one. There will be some runs of the model when nearly everything goes wrong and when in real life Otobai would abandon to cut its losses. Yet the model goes on period after period, heedless of the drain on Otobai's cash resources. The most unfavorable outcomes reported by the simulation model would never be encountered in real life.

On the other hand, the simulation model probably understates the project's potential value if nearly everything goes right: There is no provision for expanding to take advantage of good luck.

Most simulation models incorporate a business-as-usual strategy, which is fine as long as there are no major surprises. The greater the divergence from expected levels of market growth, market share, cost, etc., the less realistic is the simulation. Therefore the extreme high and low simulated values—the "tails" of the simulated distributions—should be treated with caution. Do not take the area under the tails as realistic probabilities of disaster or bonanza.

SUMMARY

Earlier chapters explained how companies calculate a project's NPV by forecasting the cash flows and discounting them at a rate that reflects project risk. The end result is the project's contribution to shareholder wealth. Understanding discounted-cash-flow analysis is important, but there is more to good capital budgeting practice than an ability to discount.

First, companies need to establish a set of capital budgeting procedures to ensure that decisions are made in an orderly manner. Most companies prepare an annual capital budget, which is a list of investment projects planned for the coming year. Inclusion of a project in the capital budget does not constitute final approval for the expenditure. Before the plant or division can go ahead with a proposal, it will usually need to submit an appropriation request that includes detailed forecasts, a discounted-cash-flow analysis, and back-up information.

Sponsors of capital investment projects often overstate future cash flows and understate risks. Therefore firms need procedures to ensure that projects fit in with the company's strategic plans, are developed on a consistent basis, and encourage honest and open discussion. (These procedures should *not* include fudge factors added to project hurdle rates in an attempt to offset optimistic forecasts.) Later, after a project has begun to operate, the firm can follow up with a postaudit. Postaudits identify problems that need fixing and help the firm learn from its mistakes.

Good capital budgeting practice also tries to identify the major uncertainties in project proposals. An awareness of these uncertainties may suggest ways that the project can be reconfigured to reduce the dangers, or it may point up some additional research that will confirm whether the project is worthwhile.

There are several ways in which companies try to identify and evaluate the threats to a project's success. The first is *sensitivity analysis*. Here the manager considers in turn each forecast or assumption that drives cash flows and recalculates NPV at optimistic and pessimistic values of that variable. The project is "sensitive to" that variable if the resulting range of NPVs is wide, particularly on the pessimistic side.

Sensitivity analysis often moves on to *break-even analysis,* which identifies break-even values of key variables. Suppose the manager is particularly concerned that competition will drive down prices and revenues. Then he or she can calculate the price level at which the project just breaks even (NPV = 0) and consider the odds that prices will fall that far. Break-even analysis is also done in terms of accounting income, although we do not recommend this application.

Sensitivity analysis and break-even analysis are easy, and they identify the forecasts and assumptions that really count for the project's success or might cause it to fail. The important variables do not change one at a time, however. For example, when raw material prices are higher than forecasted, it's a good bet that selling prices will be higher too. The logical response is *scenario analysis,* which examines the effects on NPV of changing several variables at a time.

Scenario analysis looks at a limited number of combinations of variables. If you want to go whole hog and look at all possible combinations, you will have to turn to *Monte Carlo simulation.* In that case, you must build a financial model of the project and specify the probability distribution of each variable that determines cash flow. Then you ask the computer to draw random numbers for each variable and work out the resulting cash flows. In fact you ask the computer to do this thousands of times, in order to generate complete distributions of future cash flows. With these distributions in hand, you can get a better handle on expected cash flows and project risks. You can also experiment to see how the distributions would be affected by altering project scope or the ranges for any of the variables.

Elementary treatises on capital budgeting sometimes create the impression that, once the manager has made an investment decision, there is nothing to do but sit back and watch the cash flows unfold. In practice, companies are constantly modifying their operations. If cash flows are better than anticipated, the project may be expanded; if they are worse, it may be contracted or abandoned altogether. Options to modify projects are known as *real options*. In this chapter we introduced the main categories of real options: *expansion* options, *abandonment* options, *timing* options, and options providing *flexibility in production*.

Good managers take account of real options when they value a project. One convenient way to summarize real options and their cash-flow consequences is to create a *decision tree*. You identify the things that could happen to the project and the main counteractions that you might take. Then, working back from the future to the present, you can consider which action you *should* take in each case.

Decision trees can help to identify the possible impact of real options on project cash flows, but we largely skirted the issue of how to value real options. In Chapter 18 we will give an example of how option valuation techniques can be used to value real options.

Merck's use of Monte Carlo simulation is discussed in:

N. A. Nichols, "Scientific Management at Merck: An Interview with Judy Lewent," *Harvard Business Review* 72 (January–February 1994), pp. 89–99.

Three not-too-technical references on real options are listed below:

A. Dixit and R. Pindyck, "The Options Approach to Capital Investment," *Harvard Business Review* 73 (May–June 1995), pp. 105–115.

W. C. Kester, "Today's Options for Tomorrow's Growth," *Harvard Business Review* 62 (March–April 1984), pp. 153–160.

A. Triantis and A. Borison, "Real Options: State of the Practice," *Journal of Applied Corporate Finance* 14 (Summer 2001), pp. 8–24.

FURTHER READING

1. Explain what is involved in (a) construction of the capital budget, (b) submitting an authorization request, (c) conducting a postaudit. (pages 269–271)

2. There are three ways a manager can try to identify the principal threats to a project's success—sensitivity analysis, scenario analysis, and Monte Carlo simulation. Briefly describe how you would use each technique. (pages 271–279)

3. Can you derive optimistic and pessimistic values for total project flows from sensitivity analysis? Why or why not? (pages 273–274)

CONCEPT REVIEW QUESTIONS

For a complete listing of your chapter Concept Review Questions, please visit us at www.mhhe.com/bma1e.

1. True or false?
   a. The approval of a capital budget allows managers to go ahead with any project included in the budget.
   b. Capital budgets and project authorizations are mostly developed "bottom up." Strategic planning is a "top-down" process.

QUIZ

Visit us at www.mhhe.com/bma1e

    c. Project sponsors are likely to be overoptimistic.

    d. Investments in marketing (for new products) and R&D are not capital outlays.

    e. Many capital investments are not included in the company's capital budget. (If true, give some examples.)

    f. Postaudits are typically undertaken about five years after project completion.

2. Explain how each of the following actions or problems can distort or disrupt the capital budgeting process.

    a. Overoptimism by project sponsors.

    b. Inconsistent forecasts of industry and macroeconomic variables.

    c. Capital budgeting organized solely as a bottom-up process.

3. Define and briefly explain each of the following terms or procedures:

    a. Sensitivity analysis

    b. Scenario analysis

    c. Break-even analysis

    d. Monte Carlo simulation

    e. Decision tree

    f. Real option

    g. Abandonment value

    h. Expansion value

4. True or false?

    a. Sensitivity analysis is unnecessary for projects with asset betas that are equal to 0.

    b. Sensitivity analysis can be used to identify the variables most crucial to a project's success.

    c. If only one variable is uncertain, sensitivity analysis gives "optimistic" and "pessimistic" values for project cash flow and NPV.

    d. The break-even sales level of a project is higher when *breakeven* is defined in terms of NPV rather than accounting income.

    e. Monte Carlo simulation can be used to help forecast cash flows.

5. Suppose a manager has already estimated a project's cash flows, calculated its NPV, and done a sensitivity analysis like the one shown in Table 11.2. List the additional steps required to carry out a Monte Carlo simulation of project cash flows.

6. True or false?

    a. Decision trees can help identify and describe real options.

    b. The option to expand increases NPV.

    c. High abandonment value decreases NPV.

    d. If a project has positive NPV, the firm should always invest immediately.

7. Explain why setting a higher discount rate is not a cure for upward-biased cash-flow forecasts.

PRACTICE QUESTIONS

8. Draw up an outline or flowchart tracing the capital budgeting process from the initial idea for a new investment project to the completion of the project and the start of operations. Assume the idea for a new obfuscator machine comes from a plant manager in the Deconstruction Division of the Modern Language Corporation.

    Here are some questions your outline or flowchart should consider: Who will prepare the original proposal? What information will the proposal contain? Who will evaluate it? What approvals will be needed, and who will give them? What happens if the machine costs 40% more to purchase and install than originally forecasted? What will happen when the machine is finally up and running?

9. Look back to the cash flows for projects F and G in Section 6.3. The cost of capital was assumed to be 10%. Assume that the forecasted cash flows for projects of this type are overstated by 8% on average. That is, the forecast for each cash flow from each project should be reduced by 8%. But a lazy financial manager, unwilling to take the time to argue with the projects' sponsors, instructs them to use a discount rate of 18%.

    a. What are the projects' true NPVs?

    b. What are the NPVs at the 18% discount rate.

    c. Are there any circumstances in which the 18% discount rate would give the correct NPVs? (*Hint:* Could upward bias be more severe for more-distant cash flows?)

10. What is the NPV of the electric scooter project under the following scenario?

Market size	1.1 million
Market share	.1
Unit price	¥400,000
Unit variable cost	¥360,000
Fixed cost	¥2 billion

11. Otobai's staff has come up with the following revised estimates for the electric scooter project:

	Pessimistic	Expected	Optimistic
Market size	.8 million	1.0 million	1.2 million
Market share	.04	.1	.16
Unit price	¥300,000	¥375,000	¥400,000
Unit variable cost	¥350,000	¥300,000	¥275,000
Fixed cost	¥5 billion	¥3 billion	¥1 billion

Conduct a sensitivity analysis using the "live" spreadsheets (available at **www.mhhe.com/bma1e**). What are the principal uncertainties in the project?

12. Otobai is considering still another production method for its electric scooter. It would require an additional investment of ¥15 billion but would reduce variable costs by ¥40,000 per unit. Other assumptions follow Table 11.1.

    a. What is the NPV of this alternative scheme?

    b. Draw break-even charts for this alternative scheme along the lines of Figure 11.1.

    c. Explain how you would interpret the break-even figure.

    d. Now suppose Otobai's management would like to know the figure for variable cost per unit at which the electric scooter project in Section 11.1 would break even. Calculate the level of costs at which the project would earn zero profit and at which it would have zero NPV. Assume that the initial investment is ¥15 billion.

13. The Rustic Welt Company is proposing to replace its old welt-making machinery with more modern equipment. The new equipment costs $9 million (the existing equipment has zero salvage value). The attraction of the new machinery is that it is expected to cut manufacturing costs from their current level of $8 a welt to $4. However, as

the following table shows, there is some uncertainty both about future sales and about the performance of the new machinery:

	Pessimistic	Expected	Optimistic
Sales, millions of welts	.4	.5	.7
Manufacturing cost with new machinery, dollars per welt	6	4	3
Economic life of new machinery, years	7	10	13

Conduct a sensitivity analysis of the replacement decision, assuming a discount rate of 12%. Rustic Welt does not pay taxes.

14. Rustic Welt could commission engineering tests to determine the actual improvement in manufacturing costs generated by the proposed new welt machines. (See Practice Problem 13 above.) The study would cost $450,000. Would you advise the company to go ahead with the study?

15. Operating leverage is often measured as the percentage increase in pretax profits after depreciation for a 1% increase in sales.

   a. Calculate the operating leverage for the electric scooter project assuming unit sales are 100,000 (see Section 11.2).

   b. Now show that this figure is equal to 1 + (fixed costs including depreciation divided by pretax profits).

   c. Would operating leverage be higher or lower if sales were 200,000 scooters?

16. Look back at the Vegetron electric mop project in Section 10.4. Assume that if tests fail and Vegetron continues to go ahead with the project, the $1 million investment would generate only $75,000 a year. Display Vegetron's problem as a decision tree.

17. Our Web site (**www.mhhe.com/bma1e**) contains an Excel program for simulating the cash flows from the Otobai project. Use this program to examine which are the principal uncertainties surrounding the project. Suppose that some more analysis could effectively remove uncertainty about *one* of the variables. Suggest where it could be most usefully applied.

18. Describe the real option in each of the following cases:

   a. Deutsche Metall postpones a major plant expansion. The expansion has positive NPV on a discounted-cash-flow basis but top management wants to get a better fix on product demand before proceeding.

   b. Western Telecom commits to production of digital switching equipment specially designed for the European market. The project has a negative NPV, but it is justified on strategic grounds by the need for a strong market position in the rapidly growing, and potentially very profitable, market.

   c. Western Telecom vetoes a fully integrated, automated production line for the new digital switches. It relies on standard, less-expensive equipment. The automated production line is more efficient overall, according to a discounted-cash-flow calculation.

   d. Mount Fuji Airways buys a jumbo jet with special equipment that allows the plane to be switched quickly from freight to passenger use or vice versa.

   e. The British–French treaty giving a concession to build a railroad link under the English Channel also required the concessionaire to propose by the year 2000 to build a "drive-through link" if "technical and economic conditions permit . . . and the increase in traffic shall justify it without undermining the expected return on the first [rail] link." Other companies will not be permitted to build a link before the year 2020.

19. An auto plant that costs $100 million to build can produce a new line of cars that will generate cash flows with a present value of $140 million if the line is successful, but only $50 million if it is unsuccessful. You believe that the probability of success is only about 50%.

   a. Would you build the plant?

   b. Suppose that the plant can be sold for $90 million to another automaker if the line is not successful. Now would you build the plant?

   c. Illustrate this option to abandon using a decision tree.

20. Agnes Magna has found some errors in her data (see Section 11.4). The corrected figures are as follows:

Price of turbo, year 0	$350,000
Price of piston, year 0	$180,000
Discount rate	8%

   Redraw the decision tree with the changed data. Calculate the value of the option to expand. Which plane should Ms. Magna buy?

21. Following discovery of the errors in her data (see Practice Problem 20), Ms. Magna has thought of another possibility. She could abandon the venture entirely by selling the plane at the end of the first year. Suppose that the piston-engine plane can be sold for $150,000 and the turboprop can be sold for $500,000.

   a. In what circumstances would it pay for Ms. Magna to sell either plane?

   b. Redraw the decision tree in Figure 11.7 to recognize that there will be circumstances in which Ms. Magna will choose to take the money and bail out.

   c. Recalculate the value of the project recognizing the abandonment option.

   d. How much does the option to abandon add to the value of the piston-engine project? How much does it add to the value of the turboprop project?

CHALLENGE QUESTIONS

22. You own an unused gold mine that will cost $100,000 to reopen. If you open the mine, you expect to be able to extract 1,000 ounces of gold a year for each of three years. After that, the deposit will be exhausted. The gold price is currently $500 an ounce, and each year the price is equally likely to rise or fall by $50 from its level at the start of the year. The extraction cost is $460 an ounce and the discount rate is 10%.

   a. Should you open the mine now or delay one year in the hope of a rise in the gold price?

   b. What difference would it make to your decision if you could costlessly (but irreversibly) shut down the mine at any stage?

23. Look back at the guano project in Section 7.2. Use the Crystal Ball™ software to simulate how uncertainty about inflation could affect the project's cash flows.

MINI-CASE

Waldo County

Waldo County, the well-known real estate developer, worked long hours, and he expected his staff to do the same. So George Chavez was not surprised to receive a call from the boss just as George was about to leave for a long summer's weekend.

	Year					
	0	1	2	3	4	5–17
Investment:						
Land	30					
Construction	20	30	10			
Operations:						
Rentals				12	12	12
Share of retail sales				24	24	24
Operating and maintenance costs	2	4	4	10	10	10
Real estate taxes	2	2	3	4	4	4

TABLE 11.7

Projected revenues and costs in real terms for the Downeast Tourist Mall (figures in $ millions).

Mr. County's success had been built on a remarkable instinct for a good site. He would exclaim "Location! Location! Location!" at some point in every planning meeting. Yet finance was not his strong suit. On this occasion he wanted George to go over the figures for a new $90 million outlet mall designed to intercept tourists heading downeast toward Maine. "First thing Monday will do just fine," he said as he handed George the file. "I'll be in my house in Bar Harbor if you need me."

George's first task was to draw up a summary of the projected revenues and costs. The results are shown in Table 11.7. Note that the mall's revenues would come from two sources: The company would charge retailers an annual rent for the space they occupied and in addition it would receive 5% of each store's gross sales.

Construction of the mall was likely to take three years. The construction costs could be depreciated straight-line over 15 years starting in year 3. As in the case of the company's other developments, the mall would be built to the highest specifications and would not need to be rebuilt until year 17. The land was expected to retain its value, but could not be depreciated for tax purposes.

Construction costs, revenues, operating and maintenance costs, and real estate taxes were all likely to rise in line with inflation, which was forecasted at 2% a year. The company's tax rate was 35% and the cost of capital was 9% in nominal terms.

George decided first to check that the project made financial sense. He then proposed to look at some of the things that might go wrong. His boss certainly had a nose for a good retail project, but he was not infallible. The Salome project had been a disaster because store sales had turned out to be 40% below forecast. What if that happened here? George wondered just how far sales could fall short of forecast before the project would be underwater.

Inflation was another source of uncertainty. Some people were talking about a zero long-term inflation rate, but George also wondered what would happen if inflation jumped to, say, 10%.

A third concern was possible construction cost overruns and delays due to required zoning changes and environmental approvals. George had seen cases of 25% construction cost overruns and delays up to 12 months between purchase of the land and the start of construction. He decided that he should examine the effect that this scenario would have on the project's profitability.

"Hey, this might be fun," George exclaimed to Mr. Waldo's secretary, Fifi, who was heading for Old Orchard Beach for the weekend. "I might even try Monte Carlo."

"Waldo went to Monte Carlo once," Fifi replied. "Lost a bundle at the roulette table. I wouldn't remind him. Just show him the bottom line. Will it make money or lose money? That's the bottom line."

"OK, no Monte Carlo," George agreed. But he realized that building a spreadsheet and running scenarios was not enough. He had to figure out how to summarize and present his results to Mr. County.

QUESTIONS

1. What is the project's NPV, given the projections in Table 11.7?
2. Conduct a sensitivity and a scenario analysis of the project. What do these analyses reveal about the project's risks and potential value?

PART FOUR 4

FINANCING DECISIONS AND MARKET EFFICIENCY

SO FAR OUR focus has been on the investment decision. Now we turn to the problem of paying for these investments. This can be a challenging task. For example, suppose that you are the finance director of BP. You need to ensure that there is cash to pay for capital expenditures of $13 billion a year. These investments are scattered across the world, including major developments in Angola, Azerbaijan, and Russia. BP has a variety of possible financing choices. For example, it can plow back part of its earnings, borrow from the banks, or make a public issue of stock or long-term bonds.

Later chapters will describe in detail the principal sources of finance, but Part 4 sets the scene. We begin in Chapter 12 with a fundamental question: Can managers be confident that investors will pay a fair price for the firm's securities? Many scholars believe that securities are competitively priced, but we will also encounter some conflicting evidence.

Web sites related to this Part appear at www.mhhe.com/bma1e.

CHAPTER TWELVE

EFFICIENT MARKETS AND BEHAVIORAL FINANCE

UP TO THIS point we have concentrated almost exclusively on the left-hand side of the balance sheet—the firm's capital expenditure decision. Now we move to the right-hand side and to the problems involved in financing the capital expenditures. To put it crudely, you've learned how to spend money, now learn how to raise it.

Of course, we haven't totally ignored financing in our discussion of capital budgeting. But we made the simplest possible assumption: all-equity financing. That means we assumed the firm raises its money by selling stock and then invests the proceeds in real assets. Later, when those assets generate cash flows, the cash is returned to the stockholders. Stockholders supply all the firm's capital, bear all the business risks, and receive all the rewards.

Now we are turning the problem around. We take the firm's present portfolio of real assets and its future investment strategy as given, and then we determine the best financing strategy. For example,

- Should the firm reinvest most of its earnings in the business, or distribute the cash to shareholders?
- If the firm needs more money, should it issue more stock or should it borrow?

- Should it borrow short term or long term?
- Should it borrow by issuing a normal long-term bond or a convertible bond (i.e., a bond which can be exchanged for stock by the bondholders)?

There are countless other financing trade-offs, as you will see.

The purpose of holding the firm's capital budgeting decision constant is to separate that decision from the financing decision. Strictly speaking, this assumes that capital budgeting and financing decisions are *independent*. In many circumstances this is a reasonable assumption. The firm is generally free to change its capital structure by repurchasing one security and issuing another. In that case there is no need to associate a particular investment project with a particular source of cash. The firm can think, first, about which projects to accept and, second, about how they should be financed.

Sometimes decisions about capital structure depend on project choice or vice versa, and in those cases the investment and financing decisions have to be considered jointly. However, we defer discussion of such interactions of financing and investment decisions until later in the book.

We start this chapter by contrasting investment and financing decisions. The objective in each case is the same—to maximize NPV. However, it may be harder to find positive-NPV financing opportunities. The reason it is difficult to add value by clever financing decisions is that capital markets are efficient. By this we mean that fierce competition between investors eliminates profit opportunities and causes debt and equity issues to be fairly priced. If you think that sounds like a sweeping statement, you are right. That is why we have devoted this chapter to explaining and evaluating the efficient-market hypothesis.

You may ask why we start our discussion of financing issues with this conceptual point, before you have even the most basic knowledge about securities and issue procedures. We do it this way because financing decisions seem overwhelmingly complex if you don't learn to ask the right questions. We are afraid you might flee from confusion to the myths that often dominate popular discussion of corporate financing. You need to understand the efficient-market hypothesis not because it is *universally* true but because it leads you to ask the right questions.

We define the efficient-market hypothesis more carefully in Section 12.2. The hypothesis comes in different strengths, depending on the information available to investors. Sections 12.2–12.4 review the evidence for and against efficient markets. The evidence "for" is considerable, but over the years a number of puzzling anomalies have accumulated. Many also believe that the notion of rational markets is inconsistent with the overblown prices that characterized the stock market bubbles in Japan during the 1980s and in the U.S. and elsewhere during the 1990s. To explain these anomalies and bubbles, scholars have turned to evidence of irrational behavior that has been well documented by behavioral psychologists. We describe the main features of behavioral finance and of the challenge that it poses to the efficient-market hypothesis.

The chapter closes with the *six lessons of market efficiency*.

12.1   WE ALWAYS COME BACK TO NPV

Although it is helpful to separate investment and financing decisions, there are basic similarities in the criteria for making them. The decisions to purchase a machine tool and to sell a bond each involve valuation of a risky asset. The fact that one asset is real and the other is financial doesn't matter. In both cases we end up computing net present value.

The phrase *net present value of borrowing* may seem odd to you. But the following example should help to explain what we mean: As part of its policy of encouraging small business, the government offers to lend your firm $100,000 for 10 years at 3%. This means that the firm is liable for interest payments of $3,000 in each of the years 1 through 10 and that it is responsible for repaying the $100,000 in the final year. Should you accept this offer?

We can compute the NPV of the loan agreement in the usual way. The one difference is that the first cash flow is *positive* and the subsequent flows are *negative:*

$$\text{NPV} = \text{amount borrowed} - \text{present value of interest payments}$$
$$- \text{present value of loan repayment}$$
$$= +100,000 - \sum_{t=1}^{10} \frac{3,000}{(1+r)^t} - \frac{100,000}{(1+r)^{10}}$$

The only missing variable is r, the opportunity cost of capital. You need that to value the liability created by the loan. We reason this way: The government's loan to you is a financial asset: a piece of paper representing your promise to pay $3,000 per year plus the final repayment of $100,000. How much would that paper sell for if freely traded in the capital market? It would sell for the present value of those cash flows, discounted at r, the rate of return offered by other securities issued by your firm. All you have to do to determine r is to answer the question, What interest rate would my firm have to pay to borrow money directly from the capital markets rather than from the government?

Suppose that this rate is 10%. Then

$$\text{NPV} = +100{,}000 - \sum_{t=1}^{10} \frac{3{,}000}{(1.10)^t} - \frac{100{,}000}{(1.10)^{10}}$$
$$= +100{,}000 - 56{,}988 = +\$43{,}012$$

Of course, you don't need any arithmetic to tell you that borrowing at 3% is a good deal when the fair rate is 10%. But the NPV calculations tell you just how much that opportunity is worth ($43,012).[1] It also brings out the essential similarity of investment and financing decisions.

Differences between Investment and Financing Decisions

In some ways investment decisions are simpler than financing decisions. The number of different securities and financing strategies is well into the hundreds (we have stopped counting). You will have to learn the major families, genera, and species. You will also need to become familiar with the vocabulary of financing. You will learn about such matters as strips, swaps, greenshoes, and bookrunners; behind each of these terms lies an interesting story.

There are also ways in which financing decisions are much easier than investment decisions. First, financing decisions do not have the same degree of finality as investment decisions. They are easier to reverse. That is, their abandonment value is higher. Second, it's harder to make money by smart financing strategies. The reason is that financial markets are more competitive than product markets. This means it is more difficult to find positive-NPV financing strategies than positive-NPV investment strategies.

When the firm looks at capital investment decisions, it does *not* assume that it is facing perfect, competitive markets. It may have only a few competitors that specialize in the same line of business in the same geographical area. And it may own some unique assets that give it an edge over its competitors. Often these assets are intangible, such as patents, expertise, or reputation. All this opens up the opportunity to make superior profits and find projects with positive NPVs.

In financial markets your competition is all other corporations seeking funds, to say nothing of the state, local, and federal governments that go to New York, London, and other financial centers to raise money. The investors who supply financing are comparably numerous, and they are smart: Money attracts brains. The financial amateur often views capital markets as *segmented*, that is, broken down into distinct sectors. But money moves between those sectors, and it moves fast. In general, as we shall see, firms should assume that the securities they issue are fairly priced. That takes us into the main topic of this chapter: efficient capital markets.

---

[1] We ignore here any tax consequences of borrowing. These are discussed in Chapter 15.

12.2   WHAT IS AN EFFICIENT MARKET?

A Startling Discovery: Price Changes Are Random

As is so often the case with important ideas, the concept of efficient capital markets stemmed from a chance discovery. In 1953 Maurice Kendall, a British statistician, presented a controversial paper to the Royal Statistical Society on the behavior of stock and commodity prices.[2] Kendall had expected to find regular price cycles, but to his surprise they did not seem to exist. Each series appeared to be "a 'wandering' one, almost as if once a week the Demon of Chance drew a random number . . . and added it to the current price to determine the next week's price." In other words, the prices of stocks and commodities seemed to follow a *random walk*.

If you are not sure what we mean by "random walk," you might like to think of the following example: You are given $100 to play a game. At the end of each week a coin is tossed. If it comes up heads, you win 3% of your investment; if it is tails, you lose 2.5%. Therefore, your capital at the end of the first week is either $103.00 or $97.50. At the end of the second week the coin is tossed again. Now the possible outcomes are:

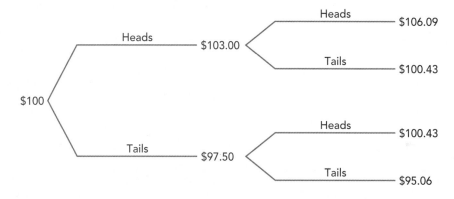

This process is a random walk with a positive drift of .25% per week.[3] It is a random walk because successive changes in value are independent. That is, the odds each week are the same, regardless of the value at the start of the week or of the pattern of heads and tails in the previous weeks.

If you find it difficult to believe that there are no patterns in share price changes, look at the two charts in Figure 12.1. One of these charts shows the outcome from playing our game for five years; the other shows the actual performance of the Standard and Poor's Index for a five-year period. Can you tell which one is which?[4]

---

[2] See M. G. Kendall, "The Analysis of Economic Time Series, Part I. Prices," *Journal of the Royal Statistical Society* 96 (1953), pp. 11–25. Kendall's idea was not wholly new. It had been proposed in an almost forgotten thesis written 53 years earlier by a French doctoral student, Louis Bachelier. Bachelier's accompanying development of the mathematical theory of random processes anticipated by five years Einstein's famous work on the random Brownian motion of colliding gas molecules. See L. Bachelier, *Theorie de la Speculation* (Paris: Gauthiers-Villars, 1900). Reprinted in English (A. J. Boness, trans.) in P. H. Cootner (ed.), *The Random Character of Stock Market Prices* (Cambridge, MA: MIT Press, 1964), pp. 17–78.

[3] The drift is equal to the expected outcome: $(1/2)(3) + (1/2)(-2.5) = .25\%$.

[4] The bottom chart in Figure 12.1 shows the actual Standard and Poor's Index for February 2002 to February 2007; the top chart is a series of cumulated random numbers. Of course, 50% of you are likely to have guessed right, but we bet it was just a guess.

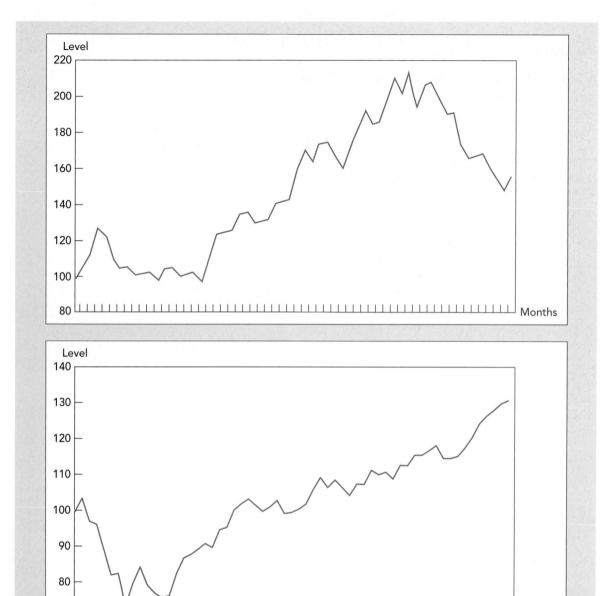

FIGURE 12.1

One of these charts shows the Standard and Poor's Index for a five-year period. The other shows the results of playing our coin-tossing game for five years. Can you tell which is which?

When Maurice Kendall suggested that stock prices follow a random walk, he was implying that the price changes are independent of one another just as the gains and losses in our coin-tossing game were independent. Figure 12.2 illustrates this for four stocks, Microsoft, BP, Fiat, and Sony. Each panel shows the change in price of the stock on successive days. The circled dot in the southeast

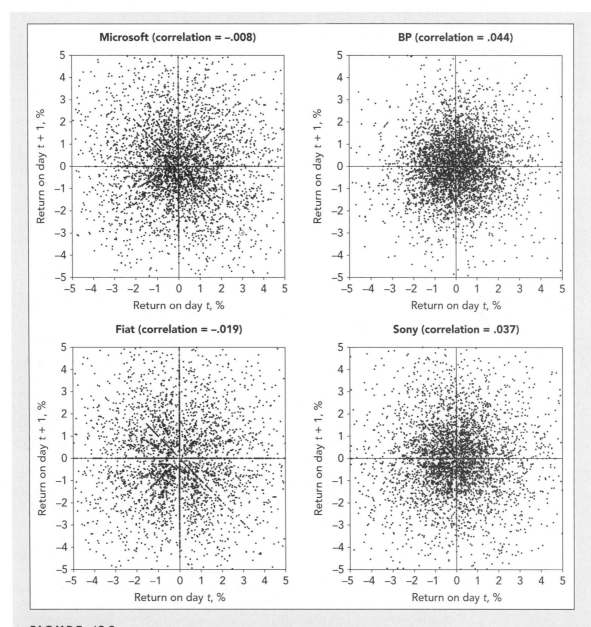

FIGURE 12.2

Each dot shows a pair of returns for a stock on two successive days between January 1990 and February 2007. The circled dot for Microsoft records a daily return of +3% and then −3% on the next day. The scatter diagram shows no significant relationship between returns on successive days.

quadrant of the Microsoft panel refers to a pair of days in which a 3% increase was followed by a 3% decrease. If there was a systematic tendency for increases to be followed by decreases, there would be many dots in the southeast quadrant and few in the northeast quadrant. It is obvious from a glance that there is very little pattern in these price movements, but we can test this more precisely by calculating

FIGURE 12.3

Cycles self-destruct as soon as they are recognized by investors. The stock price instantaneously jumps to the present value of the expected future price.

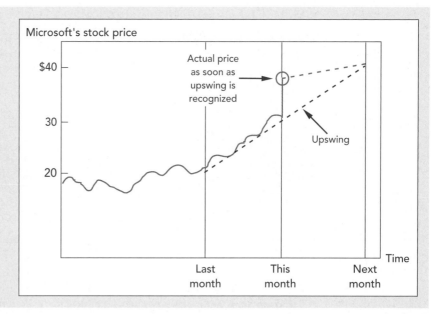

the coefficient of correlation between each day's price change and the next. If price movements persisted, the correlation would be positive; if there was no relationship, it would be 0. In our example, the correlation between successive price changes in Microsoft stock was −.008; there was a negligible tendency for price rises to be followed by price falls.[5] For Fiat this correlation was also negative at −.019. However, for BP and Sony the correlations were positive at +.044 and +.037, respectively. In these cases there was a negligible tendency for price rises to be followed by further price rises.

Figure 12.2 suggests that successive price changes of all four stocks were effectively uncorrelated. Today's price change gave investors almost no clue as to the likely change tomorrow. Does that surprise you? If so, imagine that it were not the case and that changes in Microsoft's stock price were expected to persist for several months. Figure 12.3 provides an example of such a predictable cycle. You can see that an upswing in Microsoft's stock price started last month, when the price was $20, and it is expected to carry the price to $40 next month. What will happen when investors perceive this bonanza? It will self-destruct. Since Microsoft stock is a bargain at $30, investors will rush to buy. They will stop buying only when the stock offers a normal rate of return. Therefore, as soon as a cycle becomes apparent to investors, they immediately eliminate it by their trading.

Three Forms of Market Efficiency

You should see now why prices in competitive markets must follow a random walk. If past price changes could be used to predict future price changes, investors could make easy profits. But in competitive markets easy profits don't last. As investors try to take advantage of the information in past prices, prices adjust

---

[5] The correlation coefficient between successive observations is known as the *autocorrelation coefficient*. An autocorrelation of −.008 implies that, if Microsoft's stock price rose by 1% more than the average yesterday, your best forecast of today's change would be −.008% *less* than the average.

immediately until the superior profits from studying past price movements disappear. As a result, all the information in past prices will be reflected in *today's* stock price, not tomorrow's. Patterns in prices will no longer exist and price changes in one period will be independent of changes in the next. In other words, the share price will follow a random walk.

In competitive markets today's stock price must already reflect the information in past prices. But why stop there? If markets are competitive, shouldn't today's stock price reflect *all* the information that is available to investors? If so, securities will be fairly priced and security returns will be unpredictable. No one earns superior returns in such a market. Collecting more information won't help, because all available information is already impounded in today's stock prices.

Economists often define three levels of market efficiency, which are distinguished by the degree of information reflected in security prices. In the first level, prices reflect the information contained in the record of past prices. This is called the *weak* form of efficiency. If markets are efficient in the weak sense, then it is impossible to make consistently superior profits by studying past returns. Prices will follow a random walk.

The second level of efficiency requires that prices reflect not just past prices but all other published information, such as you might get from reading the financial press. This is known as the *semistrong* form of market efficiency. If markets are efficient in this sense, then prices will adjust immediately to public information such as the announcement of the last quarter's earnings, a new issue of stock, a proposal to merge two companies, and so on.

Finally, we might envisage a *strong* form of efficiency, in which prices reflect all the information that can be acquired by painstaking analysis of the company and the economy. In such a market we would observe lucky and unlucky investors, but we wouldn't find any superior investment managers who can consistently beat the market.

Efficient Markets: The Evidence

In the years that followed Maurice Kendall's discovery, financial journals were packed with tests of the efficient-market hypothesis. To test the weak form of the hypothesis, researchers measured the profitability of some of the trading rules used by those investors who claim to find patterns in security prices. They also employed statistical tests such as the one that we described when looking for patterns in the returns on Microsoft, BP, Fiat, and Sony stock. It appears that throughout the world there are few patterns in day-to-day returns.

To analyze the semistrong form of the efficient-market hypothesis, researchers have measured how rapidly security prices respond to different items of news, such as earnings or dividend announcements, news of a takeover, or macroeconomic information.

Before we describe what they found, we should explain how to isolate the effect of an announcement on the price of a stock. Suppose, for example, that you need to understand how stock prices of takeover targets respond when the takeovers are first announced. As a first stab, you could simply calculate the average return on target-company stocks in the days leading up to the announcement and immediately after it. With daily returns on a large sample of targets, the average announcement effect should be clear. There won't be too much contamination from movements in the overall market around the announcement dates, because daily market returns average out to a very small number.[6] The potential contamination increases for weekly or monthly returns, however. Thus you will usually want to adjust for market movements. For example, you can simply subtract out the return on the market:

Adjusted stock return = return on stock − return on market index

Chapter 9 suggests a refined adjustment based on betas. (Just subtracting the market return assumes that target-firm betas equal 1.0.) This adjustment is called the *market model:*

Expected stock return = $\alpha + \beta \times$ return on market index

Alpha (α) states how much on average the stock price changed when the market index was unchanged. Beta (β) tells us how much *extra* the stock price moved for each 1% change in the market index.[7] Suppose that subsequently the stock price provides a return of $\tilde{r}$ in a month when the market return is $\tilde{r}_m$. In that case we would conclude that the *abnormal return* for that month is

Abnormal stock return = actual stock return − expected stock return

$$= \tilde{r} - (\alpha + \beta\tilde{r}_m)$$

This abnormal return abstracts from the fluctuations in the stock price that result from marketwide influences.[8]

Figure 12.4 illustrates how the release of news affects abnormal returns. The graph shows the abnormal return on a sample of nearly 17,000 firms that were targets of takeover attempts. In most takeovers, the acquiring firm is willing to pay a large premium over the current market price of the acquired firm; therefore when a firm becomes the target of a takeover attempt, its stock price increases in anticipation of the takeover premium. Figure 12.4 shows that on the day the public become aware of a takeover attempt (Day 0 in the graph), the stock price of the typical target takes a big upward jump. The adjustment in stock price is immediate: After the big price move on the public announcement day, the run-up is over, and there is no further drift in the stock price, either upward or downward.[9] Thus within the day, the new stock prices apparently reflect (at least on average) the magnitude of the takeover premium.

A study by Patell and Wolfson shows just how fast prices move when new information becomes available.[10] They found that, when a firm publishes its latest earnings or announces a dividend change, the major part of the adjustment in price occurs within 5 to 10 minutes of the announcement.

---

[6] Suppose, for example, that the market return is 12% per year. With 250 trading days in the year, the average daily return is $(1.12)^{1/250} - 1 = .00045$, or .045%.

[7] It is important when estimating α and β that you choose a period in which you believe that the stock behaved normally. If its performance was abnormal, then estimates of α and β cannot be used to measure the returns that investors expected. As a precaution, ask yourself whether your estimates of expected returns look sensible. Methods for estimating abnormal returns are analyzed in A. C. MacKinlay, "Event Studies in Economics and Finance," *Journal of Economic Literature* 35 (1997), pp. 13–39; and also S. P. Kothari and J. B. Warner, "Econometrics of Event Studies," in B. E. Eckbo (ed.), *The Handbook of Empirical Corporate Finance* (Amsterdam: Elsevier/North-Holland, 2007), Chapter 1.

[8] The market is not the only common influence on stock prices. For example, in Section 9.4 we described the Fama–French three-factor model, which states that a stock's return is influenced by three common factors—the market factor, a size factor, and a book-to-market factor. In this case we would calculate the expected stock return as $a + b_{market}(\tilde{r}_{market\ factor}) + b_{size}(\tilde{r}_{size\ factor}) + b_{book\text{-}to\text{-}market}(\tilde{r}_{book\text{-}to\text{-}market\ factor})$.

[9] See A. Keown and J. Pinkerton, "Merger Announcements and Insider Trading Activity," *Journal of Finance* 36 (September 1981), pp. 855–869. Note that prices on the days *before* the public announcement do show evidence of a sustained upward drift. This is evidence of a gradual leakage of information about a possible takeover attempt.

[10] See J. M. Patell and M. A. Wolfson, "The Intraday Speed of Adjustment of Stock Prices to Earnings and Dividend Announcements," *Journal of Financial Economics* 13 (June 1984), pp. 223–252.

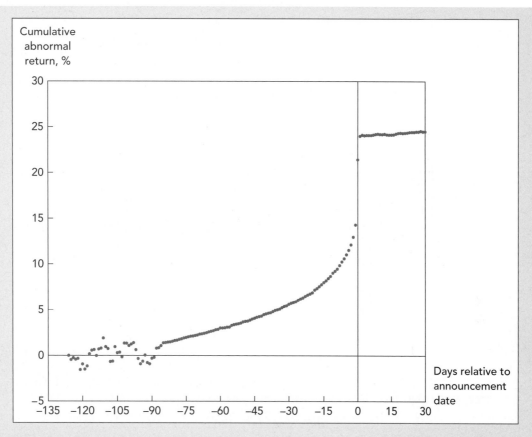

FIGURE 12.4

The performance of the stocks of target companies compared with that of the market. The prices of target stocks jump up on the announcement day, but from then on, there are no unusual price movements. The announcement of the takeover attempt seems to be fully reflected in the stock price on the announcement day.

Source: A. Keown and J. Pinkerton, "Merger Announcements and Insider Trading Activity," *Journal of Finance* 36 (September 1981), pp. 855–869. © 1981. Reprinted with permission of Blackwell Publishers Journal Rights. We are grateful to Jinghua Yan for updating the calculations to the period 1979–2004.

Tests of the strong form of the hypothesis have examined the recommendations of professional security analysts and have looked for mutual funds or pension funds that could predictably outperform the market. Some researchers have found a slight persistent outperformance, but just as many have concluded that professionally managed funds fail to recoup the costs of management. Look, for example, at Figure 12.5, which is an updated version of a study by Mark Carhart of the average return on a large sample of U.S. mutual funds. You can see that in some years the mutual funds beat the market, but roughly two-thirds of the time it was the other way around. Figure 12.5 provides a fairly crude comparison, for mutual funds have tended to specialize in particular sectors of the market, such as low-beta stocks or large-firm stocks, that may have given below-average returns. To control for such differences, each fund needs to be compared with a benchmark portfolio of similar securities. The study by Mark Carhart did this, but the message was unchanged: The funds earned a lower return than the benchmark portfolios *after* expenses and roughly matched the benchmarks *before* expenses.

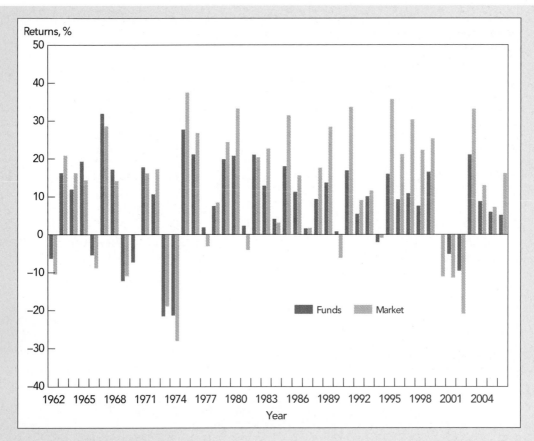

FIGURE 12.5

Average annual returns on a large sample of U.S. mutual funds and the market index, 1962–2006. Notice that mutual funds underperform the market in approximately two-thirds of the years.

Source: M. M. Carhart, "On Persistence in Mutual Fund Performance," *Journal of Finance* 52 (March 1997), pp. 57–82. © 1997 Blackwell Publishers. We are grateful to Jinghua Yan for updating the calculations.

It would be surprising if some managers were not smarter than others and could earn superior returns. But it seems difficult to spot the smart ones, and the top-performing managers one year have about an average chance of falling on their face the next year.[11]

Such evidence on strong-form efficiency has proved to be sufficiently convincing that many professionally managed funds have given up the pursuit of superior performance. They simply "buy the index," which maximizes diversification and minimizes the costs of managing the portfolio. Corporate pension plans now invest over a quarter of their U.S. equity holdings in index funds.

[11] See, for example, B. G. Malkiel, "Returns from Investing in Equity Mutual Funds 1971 to 1991," *Journal of Finance* 50 (June 1995), pp. 549–572. Some contrary evidence that good performance does persist is provided in R. Kosowski, A. Timmerman, R. Wermers, and H. White, "Can Mutual Fund 'Stars' Really Pick Stocks? New Evidence from a Bootstrap Analysis," *Journal of Finance* 61 (December 2006), pp. 2551–2595.

How far could indexing go? Not to 100%: If all investors hold index funds then nobody will be collecting information and prices will not respond to new information when it arrives. An efficient market needs some smart investors who gather information and attempt to profit from it. To provide incentives to gather costly information, prices cannot reflect *all* information.[12] There must be some profits available to allow the costs of information to be recouped.

<h2>12.3   THE EVIDENCE AGAINST MARKET EFFICIENCY</h2>

Almost without exception, early researchers concluded that the efficient-market hypothesis was a remarkably good description of reality. So powerful was the evidence that any dissenting research was regarded with suspicion. But eventually the readers of finance journals grew weary of hearing the same message. The interesting articles became those that turned up some puzzle. Soon the journals were packed with evidence of anomalies that investors have apparently failed to exploit.

What exactly is an anomaly? So far we have connected market efficiency to the absence of opportunities to make money. Let's be more precise: in an efficient market it is not possible to find expected returns greater (or less) than the risk-adjusted opportunity cost of capital. This implies that every security trades at its fundamental value, based on future cash flows (C_t) and the opportunity cost of capital (r):

$$P = \sum_{t=1}^{\infty} \frac{C_t}{(1 + r)^t}$$

If price equals fundamental value, the expected rate of return is the opportunity cost of capital, no more and no less. If price differs from fundamental value, then investors can earn more than the cost of capital, by selling if the price is too high and buying when it is too low.

You will recall these principles from our discussion of common stock values in Chapter 5. Here the principles tell us that you can't identify a superior return unless you know what the normal expected return is. Therefore, if you try to determine whether a market is efficient, you usually have to adopt an asset pricing model that specifies the relationship between risk and expected return. Any test of market efficiency is then a combined test of efficiency and the asset pricing model. Any test of an asset pricing model is also a combined test of the model and market efficiency.

The most commonly used asset pricing model is the CAPM. Chapter 9 pointed to some apparent violations of the CAPM, including the abnormally high returns on the stocks of small firms. For example, look back at Figure 9.10, which shows the cumulative difference between the returns on small-firm stocks and large-firm stocks. You can see that since 1926 the stocks of the firms with the lowest market capitalizations have performed substantially better than those with the highest capitalizations.

---

[12] See S. J. Grossman and J. E. Stiglitz, "On the Impossibility of Informationally Efficient Markets," *American Economic Review* 70 (June 1980), pp. 393–408.

Now this may mean one (or more) of several things. First, it could be that investors have demanded a higher expected return from small firms to compensate for some extra risk factor that is not captured in the simple capital asset pricing model. That is why we asked in Chapter 9 whether the small-firm effect is evidence against the CAPM.

Second, the superior performance of small firms could simply be a coincidence, a finding that stems from the efforts of many researchers to find interesting patterns in the data. There is evidence for and against the coincidence theory. Those who believe that the small-firm effect is a pervasive phenomenon can point to the fact that small-firm stocks have provided a higher return in many other countries. On the other hand, you can see from Figure 9.10 that the small-firm effect seems to have disappeared as soon as it was first documented in 1981.[13]

Third, the small-firm effect could be an important exception to the efficient-market theory, an exception that gave investors the opportunity for consistently superior returns over a period of two decades. If such anomalies offer easy pickings, you would expect to find a number of investors eager to take advantage of them. It turns out that, while many investors do try to exploit such anomalies, it is surprisingly difficult to get rich by doing so. For example, Professor Richard Roll, who probably knows as much as anyone about market anomalies, confesses

> Over the past decade, I have attempted to exploit many of the seemingly most promising "inefficiencies" by actually trading significant amounts of money according to a trading rule suggested by the "inefficiencies" . . . I have never yet found one that worked in practice, in the sense that it returned more after cost than a buy-and-hold strategy.[14]

Do Investors Respond Slowly to New Information?

We have dwelt on the small-firm effect, but there is no shortage of other puzzles and anomalies. Some of them relate to the short-term behavior of stock prices. For example, returns appear to be higher in January than in other months, they seem to be lower on a Monday than on other days of the week, and most of the daily return comes at the beginning and end of the day.

To have any chance of making money from such short-term patterns, you need to be a professional trader, with one eye on the computer screen and the other on your annual bonus. If you are a corporate financial manager, these short-term patterns in stock prices may be intriguing conundrums, but they are unlikely to change the major financial decisions about which projects to invest in and how they should be financed. The more troubling concern for the corporate financial manager is the possibility that it may be several years before investors fully appreciate the significance of new information. The studies of daily and hourly price movements that we referred to above may not pick up any long-term mispricing, but here are two examples of an apparent long-term delay in the reaction to news.

---

[13] This might also imply that investors *did* underestimate the attractions of small-firm stocks before 1981, but as soon as the mispricing was documented, practitioners moved to eliminate the profit opportunities.

[14] R. Roll, "What Every CFO Should Know about Scientific Progress in Financial Economics: What Is Known and What Remains to Be Resolved," *Financial Management* 23 (Summer 1994), pp. 69–75.

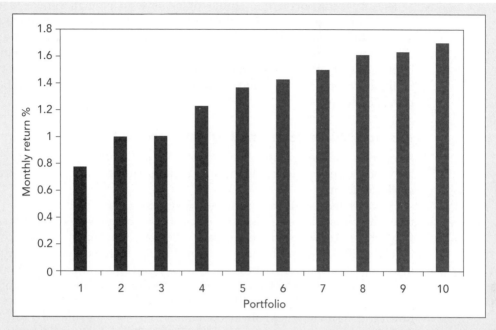

FIGURE 12.6

The average return 1972–2001 on stocks of firms over the six months following an announcement of quarterly earnings. The 10% of stocks with the best earnings news (portfolio 10) outperformed those with the worst news (portfolio1) by about 1% per month.

Source: T. Chordia and L. Shivakumar, "Inflation Illusion and the Post-earnings Announcement Drift," *Journal of Accounting Research* 43 (2005), pp. 521–556.

The Earnings Announcement Puzzle   The earnings announcement puzzle is summarized in Figure 12.6, which shows stock performance following the announcement of unexpectedly good or bad earnings during the years 1972 to 2001.[15] The 10% of the stocks of firms with the best earnings news outperform those with the worst news by about 1% per month over the six-month period following the announcement. It seems that investors underreact to the earnings announcement and become aware of the full significance only as further information arrives.

The New-Issue Puzzle   When firms issue stock to the public, investors typically rush to buy. On average those lucky enough to receive stock receive an immediate capital gain. However, researchers have found that these early gains often turn into losses. For example, suppose that you bought stock immediately following each initial public offering and then held that stock for five years. Over the period 1970–2003 your average annual return would have been 4.1% less than the return on a portfolio of similar-sized stocks.

[15] T. Chordia and L. Shivakumar, "Inflation Illusion and the Post-earnings Announcement Drift," *Journal of Accounting Research* 43 (2005) (4), pp. 521–556.

The jury is still out on these studies of longer-term anomalies. Take, for example, the new-issue puzzle. Most new issues during the past 30 years have involved growth stocks with high market values and limited book assets. When the long-run performance of new issues is compared with a portfolio that is matched in terms of both size and market-to-book ratios, the difference in performance almost halves.[16] So the new-issue puzzle could well turn out to be just the market-to-book ratio puzzle in disguise.[17]

Are Stock Prices Determined by Fundamentals?

Anomalies like the new-issue puzzle could be explained by inadequate asset pricing models. For many people the anomalies are not convincing evidence against market efficiency.

However, there are some examples of inefficiency that can't be dismissed so easily. One example is "Siamese twins," two securities with claims on exactly the same cash flows that nevertheless trade separately. Before Shell merged the two companies in July of 2005, the Dutch company Royal Dutch Petroleum and the British company Shell Transport & Trading (T&T) were Siamese twins that shared in the profits of the oil giant. Royal Dutch got 60% of the dividends and earnings of the joint company and Shell T&T got 40%. So you would expect that the market value of Royal Dutch shares would always be equal to 60/40 = 1.5 times the value of Shell T&T. But, as you can see from Figure 12.7, in practice the two shares often traded away from parity of 1.5 to 1 for long periods.

Bubbles are also evidence that prices can disconnect from fundamentals. Bubbles can occur when asset prices rise rapidly and more and more investors jump into the game on the assumption that prices will *continue* to rise. Bubbles can be self-sustaining for a while. It can be rational to join a bubble as long as you are sure that there will be greater fools to follow that you can sell out to. But remember that lots of money will be lost, maybe by you, when the bubble finally bursts.[18]

In the most notorious bubbles asset prices rose so high before collapsing that it is difficult to believe that the prices were determined by discounted cash flows. These include the Dutch Tulipmania of 1635, the Mississippi Land bubble of 1718–1720, and the South Sea bubble of 1720. More recent examples are the Japanese stock and real estate markets in the 1980s and technology stocks in the U.S. and other countries in the late 1990s.

The Japanese bubble is a good example. The Nikkei 225 Index rose about 300% between the start of 1985 until December 1989. After a sharp increase in interest rates at the beginning of 1990, stock prices began to fall. By October 1, 1990, the Nikkei had sunk to about half its peak. At its low in April 2003 it had fallen 80%. In March 2007 it was still less than half its level 17 years before.

---

[16] The long-run underperformance of new issues was described in R. Loughran and J. R. Ritter, "The New Issues Puzzle," *Journal of Finance* 50 (1995), pp. 23–51. The figures are updated on Jay Ritter's Web site and the returns compared with those of a portfolio that is matched in terms of size and market-to-book ratio. (See **bear.cba.ufl.edu/ritter.**)

[17] There may be still other forces at work, for example, tax effects. IPO stocks are very risky. Many IPOs crash a few years later, but a few do exceptionally well. An investor in a portfolio of IPOs could generate tax benefits by selling the losers and deducting the losses against other income. The investor would delay taxes on the winners, simply by holding on to them and deferring realization of capital gains. These tax benefits could offset the lower average pretax return on IPOs.

[18] However, mispricings and bubbles are not necessarily irrational. See F. Allen, "Do Financial Institutions Matter?" *Journal of Finance* 56 (August 2001) for a discussion of some of these issues and M. Brunnermeier, *Asset Pricing under Asymmetric Information: Bubbles, Crashes, Technical Analysis, and Herding* (Oxford: Oxford University Press, 2001) for a survey.

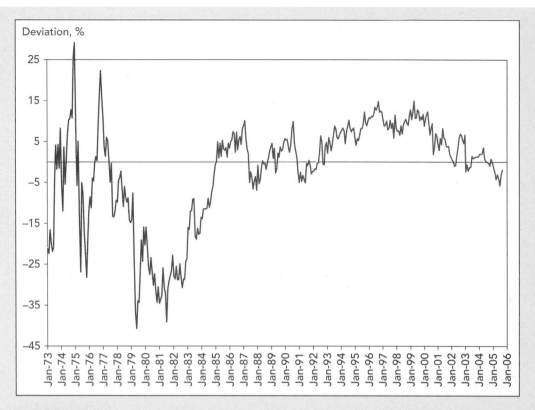

FIGURE 12.7

Log deviations from Royal Dutch Shell/Shell T&T parity.

Source: The plot extends and updates the original plot in K. Froot and E. Dabora, "How Are Stock Prices Affected by the Location of Trade," *Journal of Financial Economics* 53 (1999), pp. 189–216. © 1999 Elsevier Science, used with permission.

Land prices in Japan rose with few interruptions from 1955 until 1990. At the peak the price of real estate reached astronomical levels. Ziemba and Schwartz document that the few hundred acres of land under the Emperor's Palace in Tokyo, evaluated at neighborhood land prices, was worth as much as all the land in Canada or California![19]

In the 1990s investors in technology stocks in the U.S. and other countries also saw a remarkable run-up in the value of their holdings. The Nasdaq Composite Index, which has a heavy weighting in high-tech stocks, rose 580% from the start of 1995 to its high in March 2000. Then, as rapidly as it began, the boom ended, and by October 2002 the Nasdaq index had fallen 78% from its peak.

Some of the largest gains and losses were experienced by dot.com stocks. For example, Yahoo! shares, which began trading in April 1996, appreciated by 1,400% in four years. At this point the stock was valued at $124 billion, more than market value of GM, Heinz, and Boeing combined. In these heady days some companies

---

[19] See W. T. Ziemba and S. L. Schwartz, *Invest Japan* (Chicago, IL: Probus Publishing Co., 1992), p. 109.

found that they could boost their stock price simply by adding "dot.com" to the company name.[20]

What caused the extraordinary boom in these stocks? It is difficult to believe that future earnings growth would ever be sufficient to provide investors with a reasonable return.[21]

The Dot.com Boom and Relative Efficiency

The dot.com boom and crash remind us how exceptionally difficult it is to value common stocks. For example, imagine that at the market peak in 2000 you wanted to check whether the stocks forming Standard & Poor's Composite Index were fairly valued. As a first stab you might use the constant-growth formula that we introduced in Chapter 5.[22] In 2000 the annual dividends paid by the companies in the index totaled about $154.6 million. Suppose that these dividends were expected to grow at a steady rate of 8% a year and that investors required a return of 9.2%. Then the constant-growth formula gives a value for the common stocks of

$$\text{PV(common stocks)} = \frac{\text{DIV}}{r - g} = \frac{154.6}{.092 - .08} = \$12,883 \text{ million}$$

which was roughly their total value in March 2000. But how confident could anyone have been about these figures? Perhaps the likely dividend growth was only 7.4% per year. In that case the value of the common stocks would decline to

$$\text{PV(common stocks)} = \frac{\text{DIV}}{r - g} = \frac{154.6}{.092 - .074} = \$8,589 \text{ million}$$

which was the value of these stocks in October 2002. In other words, the 33% decline in the S&P Index could have been caused simply by investors revising their forecast of dividend growth by .6 percentage points.

The extreme difficulty of valuing common stocks from scratch has two important consequences. First, investors find it easier to price a common stock relative to yesterday's price or relative to today's price of comparable securities. In other words, they generally take yesterday's price as correct, adjusting upward or downward on the basis of today's information. If information arrives smoothly, then as time passes, investors become increasingly confident that today's price level is correct. But, when investors lose confidence in the benchmark of yesterday's price, there may be a period of confused trading and volatile prices before a new benchmark is established.

Second, most of the tests of market efficiency are concerned with *relative* prices and focus on whether there are easy profits to be made. It is almost impossible to test whether stocks are *correctly valued*, because no one can measure true value with any precision. Take, for example, Hershey stock, which sold for $55 in April 2007. Could we prove that this was its true value? Of course not, but we could be more confident that the price of Hershey should not be very different from that of Smucker ($55), since both companies had similar earnings and dividends per share and both had similar growth prospects.

---

[20] P. R. Rau, O. Dimitrov, and M. Cooper, "A Rose.com by Any Other Name," *Journal of Finance* 56 (2001), pp. 2371–2388.

[21] See, for example, E. Ofek and M. Richardson, "The Valuation and Market Rationality of Internet Stock Prices," *Oxford Review of Economic Policy* 18 (Autumn 2002), pp. 265–287.

[22] You would not want to use the formula to value a dot.com start-up. But most of the companies represented in the S&P index are mature firms for which the assumption of constant growth is more plausible.

12.4   BEHAVIORAL FINANCE

Let's assume for the moment that markets are often *inefficient*. How could the inefficiencies survive in a world where lots of rational and energetic investors stand ready to chase after any unusual profit opportunities? The first explanation is that there are *limits to arbitrage,* that is, limits on the ability of the rational investors to exploit inefficient markets. Limits to arbitrage open the door for studies of *behavioral finance,* which argue that individual investors have built-in biases and misperceptions that can push prices away from fundamental values.

Limits to Arbitrage

Strictly speaking, *arbitrage* means an investment strategy that guarantees superior returns without any risk. In practice, arbitrage is defined more casually as a strategy that exploits market inefficiency and generates superior returns if and when prices return to fundamental values. Such strategies can be very rewarding, but they are rarely risk-free.

In an efficient market, if prices get out of line, then arbitrage forces them back in line. The arbitrageur buys the underpriced securities (pushing up their prices) and sells the overpriced securities (pushing their prices down). The arbitrageur earns a profit by buying low and selling high and waiting for prices to converge to fundamentals. Thus arbitrage trading is often called *convergence trading.*

In practice arbitrage is harder than it looks. Trading costs can be significant and some trades are difficult to execute. For example, suppose that you identify an overpriced security that is *not* in your existing portfolio. You want to "sell high," but how do you sell a stock that you don't own? It can be done, but you have to *sell short.*

To sell a stock short, you borrow shares from an investor's portfolio, sell them, and then wait hopefully until the price falls and you can buy the stock back for less than you sold it for. If you're wrong and the stock price increases, then sooner or later you will be forced to repurchase the stock at a higher price (therefore at a loss) to return the borrowed shares to the lender. But if you're right and the price does fall, you repurchase, pocket the difference between the sale and repurchase prices, and return the borrowed shares. Sounds easy, once you see how short selling works, but there are costs and fees to be paid, and in some cases you will not be able to find shares to borrow.[23]

The most important limit to arbitrage is the risk that prices will diverge even further before they converge. Thus an arbitrageur has to have the guts and resources to hold on to a position that may get much worse before it gets better. Take another look at Royal Dutch and Shell T&T in Figure 12.7. Recall that Royal Dutch should trade at parity. Suppose that you were a professional money manager in 1977, when Royal Dutch was about 10% below parity. Therefore you bought Royal Dutch, sold Shell T&T short, and waited confidently for prices to converge to parity. It was a long wait. The first time you could have seen any

---

[23] Investment and brokerage firms identify shares eligible for lending and arrange to make them available to short-sellers. The supply of shares that can be borrowed is limited. You will be charged a fee for borrowing the stock, and you will be required to put up collateral to protect the lender in case the share price rises and the short-seller is unable to repurchase and return the shares. Putting up collateral is costless if the short-seller gets a market interest rate, but sometimes only lower interest rates are offered.

profit on your position was in 1983. In the meantime the mispricing got worse, not better. Royal Dutch fell to 35% below parity in early 1979. Therefore you had to report a substantial loss on your "arbitrage" strategy in that year. You were fired and took up a new career as a used-car salesman.[24]

We are joking about your dismissal, of course. But the demise in 1998 of Long Term Capital Management (LTCM) provides a dramatic example of the perils of convergence trades. LTCM, one of the largest and most profitable *hedge funds* of the 1990s, believed that interest rates in the different euro zone countries would converge when the euro replaced the countries' previous currencies. LTCM had taken massive positions to profit from this convergence, as well as massive positions designed to exploit other pricing discrepancies. After the Russian government announced a moratorium on some of its debt payments in August 1998, there was great turbulence in the financial markets, and many of the discrepancies that LTCM was betting on suddenly got much larger. LTCM was losing hundreds of millions of dollars daily. The fund's capital was nearly gone when the Federal Reserve Bank of New York arranged for a group of LTCM's creditor banks to take over LTCM's remaining assets and shut down what was left in an orderly fashion.

LTCM's sudden meltdown has not prevented rapid growth in the hedge-fund industry in the 2000s. If hedge funds can push back the limits to arbitrage and avoid the kinds of problems that LTCM ran into, markets will be more efficient going forward. But asking for complete efficiency is probably asking too much. Prices can get out of line and stay out of line if the risks of an arbitrage strategy outweigh the expected returns.

Behavioral Finance and Market Efficiency

Arbitrage is not powerful enough to drive all prices to fundamental values. This opens the door for mispricing. What determines the nature and direction of mispricing? Advocates of behavioral finance say that mispricing is driven by investor psychology. People are not 100% rational 100% of the time. This shows up in investors' attitudes to risk and the way they assess probabilities.

1. *Attitudes toward risk.* Psychologists have observed that, when making risky decisions, people are particularly loath to incur losses. It seems that investors do not focus solely on the current value of their holdings, but look back at whether their investments are showing a profit or a loss. For example, if I sell my holding of IBM stock for $10,000, I may feel on top of the world if the stock only cost me $5,000, but I will be much less happy if it had cost $11,000. This observation is the basis for *prospect theory*.[25] Prospect theory states that (a) the value investors place on a particular outcome is determined by the gains or losses that they have made since the asset was acquired or the holding last reviewed and (b) investors are particularly averse to the possibility of even a very small loss and need a high return to compensate for it.

---

[24] Deviations from parity for the two Shell companies are analyzed in K. A. Froot and E. M. Dabora, "How Are Stock Prices Affected by the Location of Trade?" *Journal of Financial Economics* 53 (August 1999), pp. 189–216. See also A. Shleifer and R. W. Vishny, "The Limits to Arbitrage," *Journal of Finance* 52 (March 1997), pp. 35–55.

[25] Prospect theory was first set out in D. Kahneman and A. Tversky, "Prospect Theory: An Analysis of Decision under Risk," *Econometrica* 47 (1979), pp. 263–291.

The pain of loss seems also to depend on whether it comes on the heels of earlier losses. Once investors have suffered a loss, they may be even more concerned not to risk a further loss. Conversely, just as gamblers are known to be more willing to make large bets when they are ahead, so investors may be more prepared to run the risk of a stock market dip after they have enjoyed a run of unexpectedly high returns.[26] If they do then suffer a small loss, they at least have the consolation of still being ahead on the year.

When we discussed portfolio theory in Chapters 8 and 9, we pictured the investor as forward-looking only. Past gains or losses were not mentioned. All that mattered was the investor's current wealth and the expectation and risk of future wealth. We did not allow for the possibility that Nicholas would be elated because his investment is in the black, while Nicola with an equal amount of wealth would be despondent because hers is in the red.

2. *Beliefs about probabilities.* Most investors do not have a PhD in probability theory and may make systematic errors in assessing the probability of uncertain events. Psychologists have found that, when judging possible future outcomes, individuals tend to look back at what happened in a few similar situations. As a result, they are led to place too much weight on a small number of recent events. For example, an investor might judge that an investment manager is particularly skilled because he has "beaten the market" for three years in a row or that three years of rapidly rising prices are a good indication of future profits from investing in the stock market. The investor may not stop to reflect on how little one can learn about expected returns from three years' experience.

   Most individuals are also too *conservative*, that is, too slow to update their beliefs in the face of new evidence. People tend to update their beliefs in the correct direction but the magnitude of the change is less than rationality would require.

   Another systematic bias is *overconfidence*. Most of us believe that we are better-than-average drivers and most investors think they are better-than-average stock pickers. Two speculators who trade with each other cannot both make money, but may be prepared to continue trading because each is confident that the other is the patsy. Overconfidence also shows up in the certainty that people express about their judgments. They consistently overestimate the odds that the future will turn out as they say and underestimate the chances of unlikely events.

Advocates of behavioral finance suggest that these patterns of behavior can explain why markets are not always efficient. Perhaps the underreaction of investors to earnings announcements is due to conservatism, manifested as a sluggish response to the new information contained in the announcements. The tendency to place too much emphasis on recent events, and therefore to overreact to recent news, could explain the prolonged underperformance of IPOs. It looks as if investors observe the hot new issues, get carried away by the

---

[26] The effect is described in R. H. Thaler and E. J. Johnson, "Gambling with the House Money and Trying to Break Even: The Effects of Prior Outcomes on Risky Choice," *Management Science* 36 (1990), pp. 643–660. The implications of prospect theory for stock returns are explored in N. Barberis, M. Huang, and T. Santos, "Prospect Theory and Asset Prices," *Quarterly Journal of Economics* 116 (February 2001), pp. 1–53.

apparent profits just waiting for them, and then spend the next few years regretting their enthusiasm.

Thus behavioral finance offers new interpretations of some long-standing puzzles and anomalies. On the other hand, perhaps it is too easy to reach for a psychology text every time we observe phenomena that we cannot explain. There are many quirks in investor behavior, and on the list of quirks there will usually be one that works with hindsight. At the end of the day the usefulness of behavioral finance will depend on whether it can *predict* mispricing before it is actually observed.

12.5   THE SIX LESSONS OF MARKET EFFICIENCY

The efficient-market hypothesis emphasizes that arbitrage will rapidly eliminate any profit opportunities and drive market prices back to fair value. Behavioral-finance specialists may concede that there are no easy profits, but argue that arbitrage is costly and sometimes slow-working, so that deviations from fair value may persist.

Sorting out the puzzles will take time, but we suggest that financial managers should assume, at least as a starting point, that there are no free lunches to be had on Wall Street.

The "no free lunch" principle gives us the following six lessons of market efficiency. After reviewing these lessons, we will consider what market *in*efficiency can mean for the financial manager.

Lesson 1: Markets Have No Memory

The weak form of the efficient-market hypothesis states that the sequence of past price changes contains no information about future changes. Economists express the same idea more concisely when they say that the market has no memory. Sometimes financial managers *seem* to act as if this were not the case. For example, after an abnormal market rise, managers prefer to issue equity rather than debt.[27] The idea is to catch the market while it is high. Similarly, they are often reluctant to issue stock after a fall in price. They are inclined to wait for a rebound. But we know that the market has no memory and the cycles that financial managers seem to rely on do not exist.[28]

Sometimes a financial manager will have inside information indicating that the firm's stock is overpriced or underpriced.[29] Suppose, for example, that there is some good news that the market does not know but you do. The stock price will rise sharply when the news is revealed. Therefore, if the company sold shares at the current price, it would be offering a bargain to new investors at the expense of present stockholders.

---

[27] See, for example, P. Asquith and D. W. Mullins, Jr., "Equity Issues and Offering Dilution," *Journal of Financial Economics* 15 (January–February 1986), pp. 16–89; and (for the U.K.) P. R. Marsh, "The Choice between Debt and Equity: An Empirical Study," *Journal of Finance* 37 (March 1982), pp. 121–144.

[28] If high stock prices signal expanded investment opportunities and the need to finance these new investments, we would expect to see firms raise more money *in total* when stock prices are historically high. But this does not explain why firms prefer to raise the extra cash at these times by an issue of equity rather than debt.

[29] For evidence that managers do successfully time equity issues, see M. Baker and J. Wurgler, "The Equity Share in New Issues and Aggregate Stock Returns," *Journal of Finance* 55 (October 2000), pp. 2219–2257.

Naturally, managers are reluctant to sell new shares when they have favorable inside information. But such information has nothing to do with the history of the stock price. Your firm's stock could be selling at half its price of a year ago, and yet you could have special information suggesting that it is *still* grossly overvalued. Or it may be undervalued at twice last year's price.

Lesson 2: Trust Market Prices

In an efficient market you can trust prices, for they impound all available information about the value of each security. This means that in an efficient market, there is no way for most investors to achieve consistently superior rates of return. To do so, you not only need to know more than *anyone* else; you also need to know more than *everyone* else. This message is important for the financial manager who is responsible for the firm's exchange-rate policy or for its purchases and sales of debt. If you operate on the basis that you are smarter than others at predicting currency changes or interest-rate moves, you will trade a consistent financial policy for an elusive will-o'-the-wisp.

The company's assets may also be directly affected by management's faith in its investment skills. For example, one company may purchase another simply because its management thinks that the stock is undervalued. On approximately half the occasions the stock of the acquired firm will with hindsight turn out to be undervalued. But on the other half it will be overvalued. On average the value will be correct, so the acquiring company is playing a fair game except for the costs of the acquisition.

Lesson 3: Read the Entrails

If the market is efficient, prices impound all available information. Therefore, if we can only learn to read the entrails, security prices can tell us a lot about the future. For example, information in a company's financial statements can help the financial manager to estimate the probability of bankruptcy. But the market's assessment of the company's securities can also provide important information about the firm's prospects. Thus, if the company's bonds are offering a much higher yield than the average, you can deduce that the firm is probably in trouble.

Here is another example: Suppose that investors are confident that interest rates are set to rise over the next year. In that case, they will prefer to wait before they make long-term loans, and any firm that wants to borrow long-term money today will have to offer the inducement of a higher rate of interest. In other words, the long-term rate of interest will have to be higher than the one-year rate. Differences between the long-term interest rate and the short-term rate tell you something about what investors expect to happen to short-term rates in the future.[30]

Example—Hewlett-Packard Proposes to Merge with Compaq On September 3, 2001, two computer companies, Hewlett-Packard and Compaq, revealed plans to merge. Announcing the proposal, Carly Fiorina, the chief executive of Hewlett-Packard, stated: "This combination vaults us into a leadership role" and creates

---

[30] We discussed the relationship between short-term and long-term interest rates in Chapter 4. Notice, however, that in an efficient market the difference between the prices of *any* short-term and long-term contracts always says something about how participants expect prices to move.

FIGURE 12.8

Cumulative abnormal returns on Hewlett-Packard and Compaq stocks during four-month period surrounding the announcement on September 3, 2001, of a proposed merger. Hewlett-Packard stock recovered after the Hewlett family announced on November 6 that it would vote against the merger.

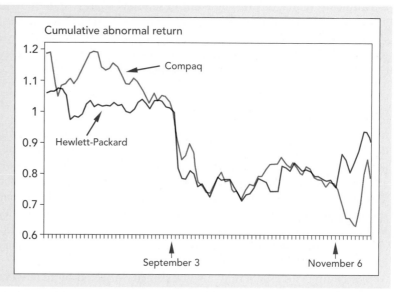

"substantial shareowner value through significant cost structure improvements and access to new growth opportunities." But investors and analysts gave the proposal a big thumbs-down. Figure 12.8 shows that over the following two days the shares of Hewlett-Packard underperformed the market by 21%, while Compaq shares underperformed by 16%. Investors, it seems, believed that the merger had a negative net present value of $13 billion. When on November 6 the Hewlett family announced that it would vote against the proposal, investors took heart, and the next day Hewlett-Packard shares gained 16%.[31] We do not wish to imply that investor concerns about the merger were justified, for management may have had important information that investors lacked. Our point is simply that the price reaction of the two stocks provided a potentially valuable summary of investor opinion about the effect of the merger on firm value.

Lesson 4: There Are No Financial Illusions

In an efficient market there are no financial illusions. Investors are unromantically concerned with the firm's cash flows and the portion of those cash flows to which they are entitled. However, there are occasions on which managers seem to assume that investors suffer from financial illusion.

Example—Accounting Changes Some firms devote considerable ingenuity to the task of manipulating earnings reported to stockholders. This is done by "creative accounting," that is, by choosing accounting methods that stabilize and increase reported earnings. Presumably firms go to this trouble because management believes that stockholders take the figures at face value.[32]

---

[31] The stock of Compaq, which was thought to be less badly affected by the merger, fell on the news, before also rising.

[32] For a discussion of the evidence that investors are not fooled by earnings manipulation, see R. Watts, "Does It Pay to Manipulate EPS?" in J. M. Stern and D. H. Chew, Jr. (eds.), *The Revolution in Corporate Finance* (Oxford: Basil Blackwell, 1992).

One way that companies can affect their reported earnings is through the way that they cost the goods taken out of inventory. Companies can choose between two methods. Under the FIFO (first-in, first-out) method, the firm deducts the cost of the first goods to have been placed in inventory. Under the LIFO (last-in, first-out) method companies deduct the cost of the latest goods to arrive in the warehouse. When inflation is high, the cost of the goods that were bought first is likely to be lower than the cost of those that were bought last. So earnings calculated under FIFO appear higher than those calculated under LIFO.

Now, if it were just a matter of presentation, there would be no harm in switching from LIFO to FIFO. But the IRS insists that the same method that is used to report to shareholders also be used to calculate the firm's taxes. So the lower apparent earnings from using the LIFO method also bring lower immediate tax payments.

If markets are efficient, investors should welcome a change to LIFO accounting, even though it reduces earnings. Biddle and Lindahl, who studied the matter, concluded that this is exactly what happens, so that the move to LIFO is associated with an abnormal rise in the stock price.[33] It seems that shareholders look behind the figures and focus on the amount of the tax savings.

Lesson 5: The Do-It-Yourself Alternative

In an efficient market investors will not pay others for what they can do equally well themselves. As we shall see, many of the controversies in corporate financing center on how well individuals can replicate corporate financial decisions. For example, companies often justify mergers on the grounds that they produce a more diversified and hence more stable firm. But if investors can hold the stocks of both companies why should they thank the companies for diversifying? It is much easier and cheaper for them to diversify than it is for the firm.

The financial manager needs to ask the same question when considering whether it is better to issue debt or common stock. If the firm issues debt, it will create financial leverage. As a result, the stock will be more risky and it will offer a higher expected return. But stockholders can obtain financial leverage without the firm's issuing debt; they can borrow on their own accounts. The problem for the financial manager is, therefore, to decide whether the company can issue debt more cheaply than the individual shareholder.

Lesson 6: Seen One Stock, Seen Them All

The elasticity of demand for any article measures the percentage change in the quantity demanded for each percentage addition to the price. If the article has close substitutes, the elasticity will be strongly negative; if not, it will be near zero. For example, coffee, which is a staple commodity, has a demand elasticity of about $-.2$. This means that a 5% increase in the price of coffee changes sales by $-.2 \times .05 = -.01$; in other words, it reduces demand by only 1%. Consumers are likely to regard different *brands* of coffee as much closer substitutes for each other. Therefore, the demand elasticity for a particular brand could be in the region of, say, -2.0. A 5% increase in the price of Maxwell House relative to that of Folgers would in this case reduce demand by 10%.

---

[33] G. C. Biddle and F. W. Lindahl, "Stock Price Reactions to LIFO Adoptions: The Association between Excess Returns and LIFO Tax Savings," *Journal of Accounting Research* 20 (Autumn 1982, Part 2), pp. 551–588.

Investors don't buy a stock for its unique qualities; they buy it because it offers the prospect of a fair return for its risk. This means that stocks should be like *very* similar brands of coffee, almost perfect substitutes. Therefore, the demand for a company's stock should be highly elastic. If its prospective return is too low relative to its risk, *nobody* will want to hold that stock. If the reverse is true, *everybody* will scramble to buy.

Suppose that you want to sell a large block of stock. Since demand is elastic, you naturally conclude that you need to cut the offering price only very slightly to sell your stock. Unfortunately, that doesn't necessarily follow. When you come to sell your stock, other investors may suspect that you want to get rid of it because you know something they don't. Therefore, they will revise their assessment of the stock's value downward. Demand is still elastic, but the whole demand curve moves down. Elastic demand does not imply that stock prices never change when a large sale or purchase occurs; it *does* imply that you can sell large blocks of stock at close to the market price *as long as you can convince other investors that you have no private information.*

Here again we encounter an apparent contradiction with practice. Many corporations seem to believe not only that the demand elasticity is low but also that it varies with the stock price, so that when the price is relatively low, new stock can be sold only at a substantial discount. State and federal regulatory commissions, which set the prices charged by local telephone companies, electric companies, and other utilities, have sometimes allowed significantly higher earnings to compensate the firm for price "pressure." This pressure is the decline in the firm's stock price that is supposed to occur when new shares are offered to investors. Yet Paul Asquith and David Mullins, who searched for evidence of pressure, found that new stock issues by utilities drove down their stock prices on average by only .9%.[34]

What If Markets Are Not Efficient? Implications for the Financial Manager

Our six lessons depend on efficient markets. What should financial managers do when markets are *not* efficient? The answer depends on the nature of the inefficiency.

Trading Opportunities—Are They Really There for Nonfinancial Corporations?

Suppose that the treasurer's staff in your firm notices mispricing in fixed-income or commodities markets, the kind of mispricing that a hedge fund would attempt to exploit in a convergence trade. Should the treasurer authorize the staff to undertake a similar convergence trade? In most cases, the answer should be *no*. First, the corporation faces the same limits to arbitrage that afflict hedge funds and other investors. Second, the corporation probably has no competitive edge in the convergence-trade business.

Procter & Gamble (P&G) supplied a costly example of this point in early 1994, when it lost $102 million in short order. It seems that in 1993 P&G's treasury staff believed that interest rates would be stable and decided to act on this belief to reduce P&G's borrowing costs. They committed P&G to deals with Bankers Trust

---

[34] See P. Asquith and D. W. Mullins, "Equity Issues and Offering Dilution," *Journal of Financial Economics* 15 (January–February 1986), pp. 61–89.

designed to do just that. Of course there was no free lunch. In exchange for a re-duced interest rate, P&G agreed to compensate Bankers Trust if interest rates rose sharply. Rates did increase dramatically in early 1994, and P&G was on the hook.

Then P&G accused Bankers Trust of misrepresenting the transactions—an em-barrassing allegation, since P&G was hardly investing as a widow or orphan—and sued Bankers Trust.

We take no stand on the merits of this litigation, which was eventually settled. But think of P&G's competition when it traded in the fixed-income markets. Its competition included the trading desks of all the major investment banks, hedge funds like LTCM, and fixed-income portfolio managers. P&G had no special in-sights or competitive advantages on the fixed-income playing field. There was no evident reason to expect positive NPV on the trades it committed to. Why was it trading at all? P&G would never invest to enter a new consumer market if it had no competitive advantage in that market.

A corporation should not invest unless it can identify a competitive advan-tage and a source of economic rents. Market inefficiencies may offer economic rents from convergence trades, but few corporations have a competitive edge in pursuing these rents. As a general rule, nonfinancial corporations gain nothing, on average, by speculation in financial markets. They should not try to imitate hedge funds.[35]

What If Your Company's Shares Are Mispriced?   The financial manager may not have special information about future interest rates, but definitely has special information about the value of his or her own company's shares. The strong form of market efficiency does not always hold, so the financial manager will often have information that outside investors do not have. Or investors may have the same information as management, but be slow in reacting to that information or may be infected with behavioral biases.

Sometimes you hear managers thinking out loud like this:

> Great! Our stock is clearly overpriced. This means we can raise capital cheaply and invest in Project X. Our high stock price gives us a big advantage over our com-petitors who could not possibly justify investing in Project X.

But that doesn't make sense. If your stock is truly overpriced, you can help your current shareholders by selling additional stock and using the cash to invest in other capital market securities. But you should *never* issue stock to invest in a proj-ect that offers a lower rate of return than you could earn elsewhere in the capital market. Such a project would have a negative NPV. You can always do better than investing in a negative-NPV project: Your company can go out and buy common stocks. In an efficient market, such purchases are always *zero* NPV.

What about the reverse? Suppose you know that your stock is *underpriced*. In that case, it certainly would not help your current shareholders to sell additional "cheap" stock to invest in other fairly priced stocks. If your stock is sufficiently underpriced, it may even pay to forego an opportunity to invest in a positive-NPV project rather than to allow new investors to buy into your firm at a low price. Financial managers who believe that their firm's stock is underpriced may

---

[35] There are of course some likely exceptions. Hershey and Nestlé are credible traders in cocoa futures markets. The major oil companies probably have special skills and knowledge relevant to energy markets.

be justifiably reluctant to issue more stock, but they may instead be able to finance their investment program by an issue of debt. In this case the market inefficiency would affect the firm's choice of financing but not its real investment decisions.

What If Your Firm Is Caught in a Bubble?   True bubbles are rare and hard to detect, except in extreme cases. But once in a lifetime, your company's stock price may be swept up in a bubble like the dot.com boom of the late 1990s. Bubbles can be exhilarating. It's hard not to join in the enthusiasm of the crowds of investors bidding up your firm's stock price. On the other hand, financial management *inside* a bubble poses difficult personal and ethical challenges. Managers don't want to "talk down" a high-flying stock price, especially when bonuses and stock-option payoffs depend on it. The temptation to cover up bad news or manufacture good news can be very strong. But the longer a bubble lasts, the greater the damage when it finally bursts. When it does burst, there will be lawsuits and possibly jail time for managers who have resorted to tricky accounting or misleading public statements in an attempt to sustain the inflated stock price.

SUMMARY

The patron saint of the Bolsa (stock exchange) in Barcelona, Spain, is Nuestra Señora de la Esperanza—Our Lady of Hope. She is the perfect patroness, for we all hope for superior returns when we invest. But competition between investors will tend to produce an efficient market. In such a market, prices will rapidly impound any new information, and it will be difficult to make consistently superior returns. We may indeed hope, but all we can rationally *expect* in an efficient market is a return just sufficient to compensate us for the time value of money and for the risks we bear.

The efficient-market hypothesis comes in three different flavors. The weak form of the hypothesis states that prices efficiently reflect all the information in the past series of stock prices. In this case it is impossible to earn superior returns simply by looking for patterns in stock prices; in other words, price changes are random. The semistrong form of the hypothesis states that prices reflect all published information. That means it is impossible to make consistently superior returns just by reading the newspaper, looking at the company's annual accounts, and so on. The strong form of the hypothesis states that stock prices effectively impound all available information. It tells us that superior information is hard to find because in pursuing it you are in competition with thousands, perhaps millions, of active, intelligent, and greedy investors. The best you can do in this case is to assume that securities are fairly priced and to hope that one day Nuestra Señora will reward your humility.

During the 1960s and 1970s every article on the topic seemed to provide additional evidence that markets are efficient. But then readers became tired of hearing the same message and wanted to read about possible exceptions. During the 1980s and 1990s more and more anomalies and puzzles were uncovered. Also the 1980s stock market and real estate bubble in Japan and the 1990s technology bubble cast doubt on whether markets were always and everywhere efficient.

Limits to arbitrage can explain why asset prices get out of line with fundamental values. Behavioral finance, which relies on psychological evidence to interpret investor behavior, is consistent with many of the deviations from market efficiency. Behavioral finance says that investors are averse to even small losses, especially when recent investment returns have been disappointing. Investors may rely too much on a few recent events in predicting the future. They may be overconfident in their predictions and may be sluggish in reacting to new information.

There are plenty of quirks and biases in human behavior, so behavioral finance has plenty of raw material. But if any puzzle or anomaly can be explained by some recipe of quirks, biases, and hindsight, what have we learned? Research in behavioral finance literature is informative and intriguing, but not yet at the stage where a few parsimonious models can account for most of the deviations from market efficiency.

For the corporate treasurer who is concerned with issuing or purchasing securities, the efficient-market theory has obvious implications. In one sense, however, it raises more questions than it answers. The existence of efficient markets does not mean that the financial manager can let financing take care of itself. It provides only a starting point for analysis.

FURTHER READING

Malkiel's book is an-easy-to-read book on market efficiency, while Fama has written two classic review articles on the topic:

B. G. Malkiel, *A Random Walk Down Wall Street,* 8th ed. (New York: W.W. Norton, 2004).

E. F. Fama, "Efficient Capital Markets: A Review of Theory and Empirical Work," *Journal of Finance* 25 (May 1970), pp. 383–417.

E. F. Fama, "Efficient Capital Markets: II," *Journal of Finance* 46 (December 1991), pp. 1575–1617.

There are a number of useful works on behavioral finance, including excellent surveys by Barberis and Thaler, and Baker, Ruback, and Wurgler:

N. Barberis and R. H. Thaler, "A Survey of Behavioral Finance," in G. M. Constantinides, M. Harris, and R. M. Stulz (eds.), *Handbook of the Economics of Finance* (Amsterdam: Elsevier Science, 2003).

M. Baker, R. S. Ruback, and J. Wurgler, "Behavioral Corporate Finance," in B. E. Eckbo (ed.), *The Handbook of Empirical Corporate Finance* (Amsterdam: Elsevier/North-Holland, 2007), chapter 4.

R. J. Shiller, "Human Behavior and the Efficiency of the Financial System," in J. B. Taylor and M. Woodford (eds.), *Handbook of Macroeconomics,* (Amsterdam: North-Holland, 1999).

A. Shleifer, *Inefficient Markets: An Introduction to Behavioral Finance* (Oxford: Oxford University Press, 2000).

R. H. Thaler (ed.), *Advances in Behavioral Finance,* (New York: Russell Sage Foundation, 1993).

Some conflicting views on market efficiency are provided by:

G. W. Schwert, "Anomalies and Market Efficiency," in G. M. Constantinides, M. Harris, and R. M. Stulz (eds.), *Handbook of the Economics of Finance* (Amsterdam: Elsevier Science, 2003).

M. Rubinstein, "Rational Markets: Yes or No? The Affirmative Case?" *Financial Analysts Journal* 57 (May–June 2001), pp. 15–29.

B. G. Malkiel, "The Efficient Market Hypothesis and Its Critics," *Journal of Economic Perspectives* 17 (Winter 2003), pp. 59–82.

R. J. Shiller, "From Efficient Markets Theory to Behavioral Finance," *Journal of Economic Perspectives* 17 (Winter 2003), pp. 83–104.

Bubbles are discussed in:

M. Brunnermeier, *Asset Pricing under Asymmetric Information: Bubbles, Crashes, Technical Analysis, and Herding* (Oxford: Oxford University Press, 2001).

R. J. Shiller, *Irrational Exuberance,* 2nd ed. (Princeton, NJ: Princeton University Press, 2005).

For a discussion of the implications of inefficient financial markets for financial managers, see:

J. C. Stein, "Rational Capital Budgeting in an Irrational World," *Journal of Business* 69 (October 1996), pp. 429–455.

CONCEPT REVIEW QUESTIONS

1. What is meant by a "random walk"? Explain why prices in an efficient market should follow something like a random walk. (pages 307–310)

2. Describe the three forms of the efficient-market hypothesis and give an example of the evidence for each. (pages 310–311)

3. Give three examples of apparent exceptions to the efficient-market hypothesis. (pages 316–317)

For a complete listing of your chapter Concept Review Questions, please visit us at www.mhhe.com/bma1e.

QUIZ

1. Which (if any) of these statements are true? Stock prices appear to behave as though successive values **(a)** are random numbers, **(b)** follow regular cycles, **(c)** differ by a random number.

2. Supply the missing words:

   "There are three forms of the efficient-market hypothesis. Tests of randomness in stock returns provide evidence for the _____ form of the hypothesis. Tests of stock price reaction to well-publicized news provide evidence for the _____ form, and tests of the performance of professionally managed funds provide evidence for the _____ form. Market efficiency results from competition between investors. Many investors search for new information about the company's business that would help them to value the stock more accurately. Such research helps to ensure that prices reflect all available information; in other words, it helps to keep the market efficient in the _____ form. Other investors study past stock prices for recurrent patterns that would allow them to make superior profits. Such research helps to ensure that prices reflect all the information contained in past stock prices; in other words, it helps to keep the market efficient in the _____ form."

3. True or false? The efficient-market hypothesis assumes that

   a. There are no taxes.

   b. There is perfect foresight.

   c. Successive price changes are independent.

   d. Investors are irrational.

   e. There are no transaction costs.

   f. Forecasts are unbiased.

4. True or false?

   a. Financing decisions are less easily reversed than investment decisions.

   b. Tests have shown that there is almost perfect negative correlation between successive price changes.

   c. The semistrong form of the efficient-market hypothesis states that prices reflect all publicly available information.

   d. In efficient markets the expected return on each stock is the same.

5. Analysis of 60 monthly rates of return on United Futon common stock indicates a beta of 1.45 and an alpha of $-.2\%$ per month. A month later, the market is up by 5%, and United Futon is up by 6%. What is Futon's abnormal rate of return?

6. True or false?

   a. Analysis by security analysts and investors helps keep markets efficient.

   b. Psychologists have found that, once people have suffered a loss, they are more relaxed about the possibility of incurring further losses.

   c. Psychologists have observed that people tend to regard recent events as representative of what might happen in the future.

   d. If the efficient-market hypothesis is correct, managers will not be able to increase stock prices by creative accounting that boosts reported earnings.

7. Geothermal Corporation has just received good news: its earnings increased by 20% from last year's value. Most investors are anticipating an increase of 25%. Will Geothermal's stock price increase or decrease when the announcement is made?

8. Here again are the six lessons of market efficiency. For each lesson give an example showing the lesson's relevance to financial managers.

   a. Markets have no memory.

   b. Trust market prices.

   c. Read the entrails.

   d. There are no financial illusions.

   e. The do-it-yourself alternative.

   f. Seen one stock, seen them all.

PRACTICE QUESTIONS

9. How would you respond to the following comments?

   a. "Efficient market, my eye! I know lots of investors who do crazy things."

   b. "Efficient market? Balderdash! I know at least a dozen people who have made a bundle in the stock market."

   c. "The trouble with the efficient-market theory is that it ignores investors' psychology."

   d. "Despite all the limitations, the best guide to a company's value is its written-down book value. It is much more stable than market value, which depends on temporary fashions."

10. Respond to the following comments:

   a. "The random-walk theory, with its implication that investing in stocks is like playing roulette, is a powerful indictment of our capital markets."

   b. "If everyone believes you can make money by charting stock prices, then price changes won't be random."

   c. "The random-walk theory implies that events are random, but many events are not random. If it rains today, there's a fair bet that it will rain again tomorrow."

11. Which of the following observations *appear* to indicate market inefficiency? Explain whether the observation appears to contradict the weak, semistrong, or strong form of the efficient-market hypothesis.

   a. Tax-exempt municipal bonds offer lower pretax returns than taxable government bonds.

b. Managers make superior returns on their purchases of their company's stock.

c. There is a positive relationship between the return on the market in one quarter and the change in aggregate profits in the next quarter.

d. There is disputed evidence that stocks that have appreciated unusually in the recent past continue to do so in the future.

e. The stock of an acquired firm tends to appreciate in the period before the merger announcement.

f. Stocks of companies with unexpectedly high earnings *appear* to offer high returns for several months after the earnings announcement.

g. Very risky stocks on average give higher returns than safe stocks.

12. Here are alphas and betas for Intel and Conagra for the 60 months ending February 2007. Alpha is expressed as a percent per month.

	Alpha	Beta
Intel	−.87	2.02
Conagra	.40	.40

Explain how these estimates would be used to calculate an abnormal return.

13. It is sometimes suggested that stocks with low price–earnings ratios tend to be under-priced. Describe a possible test of this view. Be as precise as possible.

14. "If the efficient-market hypothesis is true, the pension fund manager might as well select a portfolio with a pin." Explain why this is not so.

15. Two financial managers, Alpha and Beta, are contemplating a chart showing the actual performance of the Standard and Poor's Composite Index over a five-year period. Each manager's company needs to issue new shares of common stock sometime in the next year.

   Alpha: My company's going to issue right away. The stock market cycle has obviously topped out, and the next move is almost surely down. Better to issue now and get a decent price for the shares.

   Beta: You're too nervous; we're waiting. It's true that the market's been going nowhere for the past year or so, but the figure clearly shows a basic upward trend. The market's on the way up to a new plateau.

   What would you say to Alpha and Beta?

16. What does the efficient-market hypothesis have to say about these two statements?

   a. "I notice that short-term interest rates are about 1% below long-term rates. We should borrow short-term."

   b. "I notice that interest rates in Japan are lower than rates in the United States. We would do better to borrow Japanese yen rather than U.S. dollars."

17. We suggested that there are three possible interpretations of the small-firm effect: a required return for some unidentified risk factor, a coincidence, or market inefficiency. Write three brief memos, arguing each point of view.

Visit us at
www.mhhe.com/bma1e.

18. Column (A) in Table 12.1 shows the monthly return on the British FTSE 100 index from May 2005 through February 2007. Columns (B) and (C) show returns on the stocks of two firms—Executive Cheese and Paddington Beer. Both firms announced their earnings in February 2007. Calculate the average abnormal return of the two stocks during the month of the earnings announcement.

19. On May 15, 1997, the government of Kuwait offered to sell 170 million BP shares, worth about $2 billion. Goldman Sachs was contacted after the stock market closed in London and given one hour to decide whether to bid on the stock. They decided to

Month	(A) Market Return	(B) Executive Cheese Return	(C) Paddington Beer Return
2005:			
May	3.4	−1.9	−.5
June	3.0	−10.1	−17.2
July	3.3	8.1	9.8
Aug.	.3	7.5	16.5
Sep.	3.4	4.3	6.7
Oct.	−2.9	−5.3	−11.1
Nov.	2.0	5.7	−7.3
Dec.	3.6	−9.7	4.5
2006:			
Jan.	2.5	−4.7	23.0
Feb.	.5	−10.0	−1.1
Mar.	3.0	−2.7	−1.2
Apr.	1.0	.1	6.2
May	−4.9	3.4	12.4
June	1.9	5.6	−7.9
July	1.6	−2.2	11.5
Aug.	−.4	−6.5	4.3
Sep.	.9	−.2	3.4
Oct.	2.8	−3.7	4.1
Nov.	−1.3	−9.0	−14.1
Dec.	2.8	7.3	−6.5
2007:			
Jan.	−.3	4.7	12.6
Feb.	−.5	−7.1	−14.1

TABLE 12.1

See Practice Problem 18. Rates of return in percent per month:

Visit us at www.mhhe.com/bma1e

offer 710.5 pence ($11.59) per share, and Kuwait accepted. Then Goldman Sachs went looking for buyers. They lined up 500 institutional and individual investors worldwide, and resold all the shares at 716 pence ($11.70). The resale was complete before the London Stock Exchange opened the next morning. Goldman Sachs made $15 million overnight.[36]

What does this deal say about market efficiency? Discuss.

CHALLENGE QUESTIONS

20. "The strong-form of the efficient-market hypothesis is nonsense. Look at mutual fund X; it has had superior performance for each of the last 10 years." Does the speaker have a point? Suppose that there is a 50% probability that X will obtain superior performance in any year simply by chance.

   a. If X is the only fund, calculate the probability that it will have achieved superior performance for each of the past 10 years.

   b. Now recognize that there are over 10,000 mutual funds in the United States. What is the probability that by chance there is at least 1 out of 10,000 funds that obtained 10 successive years of superior performance?

---

[36] "Goldman Sachs Earns a Quick $15 Million Sale of BP Shares," *The Wall Street Journal*, May 16, 1997, p. A4.

21. "An analysis of the behavior of exchange rates and bond prices around the time of international assistance for countries in balance-of-payments difficulties suggests that on average prices decline sharply for a number of months before the announcement of the assistance and are largely stable after the announcement. This suggests that the assistance is effective but comes too late." Does this follow?

STANDARD
&POOR'S

22. Use either **finance.yahoo.com** or the Market Insight database (**www.mhhe.com/ edumarketinsight**) to download daily prices for five U.S. stocks for a recent 12-month period. For each stock construct a scatter diagram of successive returns as in Figure 12.2. Then calculate the correlation between the returns on successive days. Do you find any consistent patterns?

PART FIVE

PAYOUT POLICY
AND CAPITAL STRUCTURE

MANY ENERGY COMPANIES have been large borrowers and for many years Westar Energy, the Kansas utility company, was no exception. However, in 2003 Westar set about reducing its large mountain of debt and regaining an investment-grade rating for its bonds. It sold off some unwanted businesses, cut its dividend from $1.20 a share to $.76, and issued $250 million of common stock. By 2006, Westar had halved its burden of debt.

Westar's managers faced two basic financing decisions. One was how much cash should be distributed to shareholders. In cutting the dividend, the company stated that it planned to pay out in the future 60–75% of earnings. But the company could have chosen instead to maintain the dividend and to raise the cash by making a larger issue of common stock. Chapter 13 discusses the choice of how much a company should pay out.

Westar's second decision was to reduce its borrowing and to substitute equity. A company's mix of debt and equity is termed its *capital structure*. Chapters 14 through 16 examine the choice of capital structure and its implications for the cost of capital.

There are no simple answers to the dividend or capital structure decisions; for example, more debt can be good or bad, depending on the circumstances. But Part 5 will supply the concepts and facts needed for assessing how much the company should pay out to its shareholders and what is a sensible capital structure.

Web sites related to this Part appear at www.mhhe.com/bma1e.

CHAPTER THIRTEEN

PAYOUT POLICY

COMPANIES CAN RETURN cash to their shareholders either by paying a dividend or by buying back their stock. In this chapter we explain how companies decide on the amount and form of this payout, and we discuss the controversial question of how payout policy affects the value of the firm.

The first step toward understanding payout policy is to recognize that the phrase means different things to different people. Therefore, we must start by defining what we mean by it.

A firm's decision about how much cash to distribute is often mixed up with other financing and investment decisions. Some firms pay out little cash because management is optimistic about the firm's future and wishes to retain earnings for expansion. Suppose, however, that the future investment opportunities evaporate, that a dividend increase is announced, and the stock price falls. How do we separate the impact of the dividend increase from the impact of investor's disappointment at the lost growth opportunities?

Another firm might finance capital expenditures largely by borrowing. This releases cash that can be distributed to shareholders. In this case the payout is a by-product of the borrowing decision.

We must isolate payout policy from other financial decisions. The precise question we should ask is, What is the effect of a change in payout policy, *given the firm's capital budgeting and borrowing decisions?* Suppose that the firm proposes to increase its dividend. The cash for that payment must come from somewhere. If we fix the firm's investment outlays and borrowing, there is only one possible source—an issue of stock. What if the firm decides to *reduce* its dividend? In that case it will have extra cash. If investment outlays and borrowing are fixed, there is only one possible way that this cash can be used—to repurchase stock. Thus payout policy implies a trade-off between higher or lower cash dividends and the issue or repurchase of common stock.

We start the chapter with some basic institutional material on dividends and stock repurchases. We then look at how companies decide on the level and method of payment and we show how both dividends and stock repurchases provide information to investors about company prospects. We then come to the central question, How does the decision to pay a dividend or repurchase stock affect firm value?

13.1 THE CHOICE OF PAYOUT POLICY

Companies can pay out cash to their shareholders in two ways. They can pay a dividend or they can buy back some of the outstanding shares. Figure 13.1 shows that, taken together, dividend payments and stock repurchases amount to a high proportion of earnings. For example, between 2001 and 2005 dividend payments by U.S. companies averaged 49% of earnings, while repurchases came to a further 47%.

Although dividends remain the principal way that corporations return cash to their shareholders, in many countries the *proportion* of companies paying a dividend has declined. In the United States 64% of firms paid a dividend in 1980; by 2005 the figure had fallen to 41%.[1] Some of the non–dividend payers did pay a dividend in the past but then fell on hard times and were forced to conserve cash. But a large number of new growth companies have gone public in recent years and do not pay a dividend. In the United States these include such household names as Sun Microsystems, Cisco, Oracle, Amazon, and Google, as well as many small, rapidly growing firms that have not yet reached full profitability.

Figure 13.1 shows that before 1983 stock repurchases were fairly rare, but since then they have become increasingly common. In 2005, a record year for stock repurchases, 11 U.S. companies each bought back more than $5 billion of

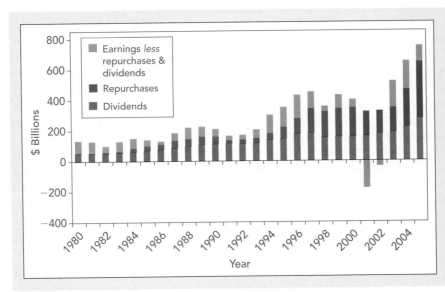

FIGURE 13.1

Dividends and stock repurchases in the United States, 1980–2005 (figures in $ billions).

Source: Standard & Poor's Compustat.

---

[1] The proportion of dividend payers among U.S. industrial companies is even lower. See E. Fama and K. French, "Disappearing Dividends: Changing Firm Characteristics or Lower Propensity to Pay?" *Journal of Financial Economics* 60 (2001), pp. 3–43. In Europe the decline in the proportion of dividend payers has been particularly marked in Germany. See D. J. Denis and I. Osobov, "Why Do Firms Pay Dividends? International Evidence on the Determinants of Dividend Policy," unpublished paper, Purdue University, August 2006.

stock. Among them were the veteran repurchaser, ExxonMobil,[2] with repurchases of $18.2 billion, Citi with $12.8 billion, Intel with $10.6 billion, and Cisco with $10.2 billion.

What was the reason for the sudden growth in repurchase? One explanation is that in 1982 the SEC adopted Rule 10b-18.[3] Before the adoption of this rule firms that repurchased their own shares ran the risk of being prosecuted for manipulating their share price. Rule 10b-18 laid out provisions that would protect firms against prosecution.

13.2   HOW FIRMS PAY DIVIDENDS AND REPURCHASE STOCK

Before we look at the choice between dividends and stock repurchases, we need to review how these payments to shareholders take place.

A company's dividend is set by the board of directors. The announcement of the dividend states that the payment will be made to all stockholders who are registered on a particular *record date.* Then a week or so later dividend checks are mailed to stockholders. Stocks are normally bought or sold *with dividend* (or *cum dividend*) until two business days before the record date, and then they trade *ex dividend.* If you buy stock on the ex-dividend date, your purchase will not be entered on the company's books before the record date and you will not be entitled to the dividend.

Figure 13.2 illustrates this sequence of events. On January 31, 2007, Exxon-Mobil declared a quarterly dividend of $.32 per share. The dividend was paid on March 9 to all shareholders who were registered on the company's books on February 9. Two days earlier on February 7 the shares began to trade ex dividend. Any investor who bought shares on that date would not have had his purchase registered by the record date and would not have been entitled to the dividend.

The company is not free to declare whatever dividend it chooses. In some countries, such as Brazil and Chile, companies are obliged by law to pay out a *minimum* proportion of their earnings. Some restrictions may be imposed by lenders, who are concerned that excessive dividend payments would not leave enough in the kitty to repay their loans. In the United States, state law also helps to protect the firm's creditors against excessive dividend payments. For example, companies are not allowed to pay a dividend out of legal capital, which is generally defined as the par value of outstanding shares.[4]

Most U.S. companies pay a *regular cash dividend* each quarter, but occasionally this is supplemented by a one-off *extra* or *special dividend.* Many companies offer shareholders automatic dividend reinvestment plans (DRIPs). Often the new

---

[2] Over the 10 years to 2005 ExxonMobil bought back $54 billion of stock.

[3] See G. Grullon and R. Michaely, "Dividends, Share Repurchases and the Substitution Hypothesis," *Journal of Finance* 57 (August 2001), pp. 1649–1684.

[4] Where there is no par value, legal capital is defined as part or all of the receipts from the issue of shares. Companies with wasting assets, such as mining companies, are sometimes permitted to pay out legal capital.

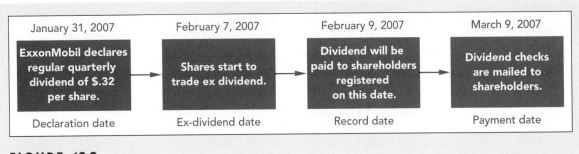

January 31, 2007	February 7, 2007	February 9, 2007	March 9, 2007
ExxonMobil declares regular quarterly dividend of $.32 per share.	**Shares start to trade ex dividend.**	**Dividend will be paid to shareholders registered on this date.**	**Dividend checks are mailed to shareholders.**
Declaration date	Ex-dividend date	Record date	Payment date

FIGURE 13.2

An illustration of how dividends are paid.

shares are issued at a 5% discount from the market price. Sometimes 10% or more of total dividends will be reinvested under such plans.[5]

Dividends are not always in the form of cash. Frequently companies also declare *stock dividends.* For example, if the firm pays a stock dividend of 5%, it sends each shareholder 5 extra shares for every 100 shares currently owned. A stock dividend is essentially the same as a stock split. Both increase the number of shares but do not affect the company's assets, profits, or total value. So both reduce value *per share.*[6] Our focus in this chapter will be on *cash* dividends.

How Firms Repurchase Stock

Instead of paying a dividend to its stockholders, the firm can use the cash to re-purchase stock. The reacquired shares may be kept in the company's treasury and resold if the company needs money. There are four main ways to repurchase stock. By far the most common method is for the firm to announce that it plans to buy its stock in the open market, just like any other investor. However, companies sometimes use a tender offer where they offer to buy back a stated number of shares at a fixed price, which is typically set at about 20% above the current market level. Shareholders can then choose whether to accept this offer. A third proce-dure is to employ a *Dutch auction.* In this case the firm states a series of prices at which it is prepared to repurchase stock. Shareholders submit offers declaring how many shares they wish to sell at each price and the company calculates the lowest price at which it can buy the desired number of shares. Finally, repurchase may take place by direct negotiation with a major shareholder. The most notorious instances are *greenmail* transactions, in which the target of an attempted takeover buys off the hostile bidder by repurchasing any shares that it has acquired. "Green-mail" means that these shares are repurchased at a price that makes the bidder happy to leave the target alone. This price does not always make the target's shareholders happy.

---

[5] Sometimes companies not only allow shareholders to reinvest dividends but also allow them to buy additional shares at a discount. For an amusing and true rags-to-riches story, see M. S. Scholes and M. A. Wolfson, "Decentral-ized Investment Banking: The Case of Dividend-Reinvestment and Stock-Purchase Plans," *Journal of Financial Economics* 24 (September 1989), pp. 7–36.

[6] The distinction between a stock dividend and a stock split is technical. A stock dividend is shown in the accounts as a transfer from retained earnings to equity capital, whereas a split is shown as a reduction in the par value of each share.

13.3   HOW DO COMPANIES DECIDE ON THE PAYOUT?

In 2004 a number of senior executives were asked about their firms' dividend policies.[7] Figure 13.3 paraphrases the executives' responses. Three features stand out:

1. Managers are reluctant to make dividend changes that may have to be reversed. They are particularly worried about having to rescind a dividend increase and, if necessary, would choose to raise new funds to maintain the payout.

2. To avoid the risk of a reduction in payout, managers "smooth" dividends. Consequently, dividend changes follow shifts in long-run sustainable earnings. Transitory earnings changes are unlikely to affect dividend payouts.

3. Managers focus more on dividend changes than on absolute levels. Thus paying a $2.00 dividend is an important financial decision if last year's dividend was $1.00, but no big deal if last year's dividend was $2.00.

While stock repurchases are like bumper dividends, they do not typically *substitute* for dividends. Over two-thirds of the companies that paid a dividend in 2005 also repurchased stock. Firms are likely to buy back stock when they have accumulated a large amount of unwanted cash or wish to change their capital structure by replacing equity with debt. Therefore, a firm may be willing to repurchase a large amount of stock one year and none the next.

Companies that pay a dividend often cite stock repurchase as a possible alternative way to distribute sustainable earnings. But the converse in less true. Unlike a stock repurchase, dividends are not regarded as an appropriate way to pay out transitory earnings. Therefore, many firms that repurchase stock would not contemplate using the cash to raise the dividend and so incur a commitment to maintain the payout.[8]

Given these differences in the way that dividends and repurchases are used, it is not surprising to find that repurchases are much more volatile than dividends. Repurchases generally mushroom during boom times as firms accumulate excess cash but wither in recessions. You can see this from Figure 13.1, which shows that repurchases fell sharply during the early 1990s and then again between 2000 and 2002.

Until recently many countries banned or severely restricted the use of stock repurchases. As a result, firms that had amassed large amounts of cash were tempted to invest it at very low rates of return rather than hand it back to shareholders, who could have reinvested it in firms that were short of cash. But many of these limitations have now been removed. For example, Japan permitted repurchases in 1995 and Sweden in 2000, while Germany relaxed its restrictions in 1998.[9] Many multinational giants now repurchase huge amounts of stock. In 2005 BP, Vodafone, Nokia, Royal Dutch Shell, and Total together bought back stock worth $36 billion.

---

[7] See A. Brav, J. R. Graham, C. R. Harvey, and R. Michaely, "Payout Policy in the 21st Century," *Journal of Financial Economics* 77 (September 2005), pp. 483–527. This paper revisits an earlier classic series of interviews on dividend policy described in J. Lintner, "Distribution of Incomes of Corporations among Dividends, Retained Earnings, and Taxes," *American Economic Review* 46 (May 1956), pp. 97–113.

[8] See, for example, R. Dittmar and A. Dittmar, "Stock Repurchase Waves: An Examination of the Trends in Aggregate Corporate Payout Policy," working paper, University of Michigan at Ann Arbor, February 2004.

[9] For a survey of repurchase practices in different countries, see International Organization of Securities Commissions (IOSCO), "Report on Stock Repurchase Programs," February 2004, **www.iosco.org**.

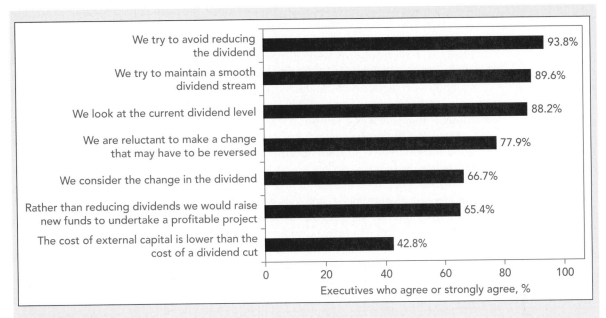

FIGURE 13.3

A 2004 survey of financial executives suggested that their firms were reluctant to cut the dividend and tried to maintain a smooth series of payments.

Source: A. Brav, J. R. Graham, C. R. Harvey, and R. Michaely, "Payout Policy in the 21st Century," *Journal of Financial Economics* 77 (September 2005), pp. 483–527. © 2005 Elsevier Science, with permission.

13.4 THE INFORMATION IN DIVIDENDS AND STOCK REPURCHASES

In some countries you cannot rely on the information that companies provide. Passion for secrecy and a tendency to construct multilayered corporate organizations produce asset and earnings figures that are next to meaningless. Some people say that, thanks to creative accounting, the situation is little better for some companies in the United States.

How does an investor in such a world separate marginally profitable firms from the real money makers? One clue is dividends. Investors can't read managers' minds, but they can learn from managers' actions. They know that a firm that reports good earnings and pays a generous dividend is putting its money where its mouth is. We can understand, therefore, why investors would value the information content of dividends and would refuse to believe a firm's reported earnings unless they were backed up by an appropriate dividend policy.

Of course, firms can cheat in the short run by overstating earnings and scraping up cash to pay a generous dividend. But it is hard to cheat in the long run, for a firm that is not making enough money will not have enough cash to pay out. If a firm chooses a high dividend payout without the cash flow to back it up, that firm will ultimately have to reduce its investment plans or turn to investors for additional debt or equity financing. All of these consequences are costly. Therefore, most managers don't increase dividends until they are confident that sufficient cash will flow in to pay them.

Researchers, who have attempted to measure the information in dividend changes, have come up with mixed evidence. Some have found that dividend changes have little or no ability to predict future earnings. However, Healy and Palepu, who focus on companies that paid a dividend for the first time, find that on average earnings jumped 43% in the year a dividend was paid. If managers thought that this was a temporary windfall, they might have been cautious about committing themselves to paying out cash. But it looks as if these managers had good reason to be confident about prospects, for earnings continued to rise in the following years.[10]

Investors certainly appear to take comfort from an increase in dividends. When the increase is announced, analysts generally up their forecast of the current year's earnings.[11] It is no surprise, therefore, to find that a higher dividend prompts a rise in the stock price, whereas a dividend cut results in a fall in price. For example, in the case of the dividend initiations studied by Healy and Palepu, the dividend announcement resulted in an abnormal rise of 4% in the stock price.[12]

Notice that investors do not get excited about the *level* of a company's dividend; they worry about the *change*, which they view as an important indicator of the sustainability of earnings. In Finance in the News we illustrate how an unexpected change in dividends can cause the stock price to bounce back and forth as investors struggle to interpret the significance of the change.

It seems that in some other countries investors are less preoccupied with dividend changes. For example, in Japan there is a much closer relationship between corporations and major stockholders, and therefore information may be more easily shared with investors. Consequently, Japanese corporations are more prone to cut their dividends when there is a drop in earnings, but investors do not mark the stocks down as sharply as in the United States.[13]

The Information Content of Share Repurchase

Share repurchases, like dividends, are a way to hand cash back to shareholders. But unlike dividends, share repurchases are frequently a one-off event. So a company that announces a repurchase program is not making a long-term commitment to earn and distribute more cash. The information in the announcement of a share repurchase program is therefore likely to be different from the information in a dividend payment.

Companies repurchase shares when they have accumulated more cash than they can invest profitably or when they wish to increase their debt levels. Neither circumstance is good news in itself, but shareholders are frequently relieved to see

---

[10] See P. Healy and K. Palepu, "Earnings Information Conveyed by Dividend Initiations and Omissions," *Journal of Financial Economics* 21 (1988), pp. 149–175. For an example of a study that finds no information in the announcement, see G. Grullon, R. Michaely, and B. Swaminathan, "Are Dividend Changes a Sign of Firm Maturity?" *Journal of Business* 75 (July 2002), pp. 387–424.

[11] A. R. Ofer and D. R. Siegel, "Corporate Financial Policy, Information, and Market Expectations: An Empirical Investigation of Dividends," *Journal of Finance* 42 (September 1987), pp. 889–911.

[12] Healy and Palepu also looked at companies that *stopped* paying a dividend. In this case the stock price on average declined by an abnormal 9.5% on the announcement and earnings fell over the next four quarters.

[13] The dividend policies of Japanese *keiretsus* are analyzed in K. L. Dewenter and V. A. Warther, "Dividends, Asymmetric Information, and Agency Conflicts: Evidence from a Comparison of the Dividend Policies of Japanese and U.S. Firms," *Journal of Finance* 53 (June 1998), pp. 879–904.

THE DIVIDEND CUT HEARD 'ROUND THE WORLD

On May 9, 1994, FPL Group, the parent company of Florida Power & Light Company, announced a 32% reduction in its quarterly dividend payout, from 62 cents per share to 42 cents. In its announcement, FPL did its best to spell out to investors why it had taken such an unusual step. It stressed that it had studied the situation carefully and that, given the prospect of increased competition in the electric utility industry, the company's high dividend payout ratio (which had averaged 90% in the past 4 years) was no longer in the shareholders' best interests. The new policy resulted in a payout of about 60% of the previous year's earnings. Management also announced that, starting in 1995, the dividend payout would be reviewed in February instead of May to reinforce the linkage between dividends and annual earnings. In doing so, the company wanted to minimize unintended "signaling effects" from any future changes in dividends.

At the same time that it announced this change in dividend policy, FPL Group's board authorized the repurchase of up to 10 million shares of common stock over the next three years. In adopting this strategy, the company noted that changes in the U.S. tax code since 1990 had made capital gains more attractive than dividends to shareholders.

Besides providing a more tax-efficient means of distributing excess cash to its stockholders, FPL's substitution of stock repurchases for dividends was also designed to increase the company's financial flexibility in preparation for a new era of heightened competition among utilities. Although much of the cash savings from the dividend cut would be returned to shareholders in the form of stock repurchases, the rest would be used to retire debt and so reduce the company's leverage ratio. This deleveraging was intended to prepare the company for the likely increase in business risk and to provide some slack that would allow the company to take advantage of future business opportunities.

All this sounded logical, but investors' first reaction was dismay. On the day of the announcement, the stock price fell nearly 14%. But, as analysts digested the news and considered the reasons for the reduction, they concluded that the action was not a signal of financial distress but a well-considered strategic decision. This view spread throughout the financial community, and FPL's stock price began to recover. By the middle of the following month at least 15 major brokerage houses had placed FPL's common stock on their "buy" lists and the price had largely recovered from its earlier fall.

Source: Modified from D. Soter, E. Brigham, and P. Evanson, "The Dividend Cut 'Heard 'Round the World': The Case of FPL," *Journal of Applied Corporate Finance* 9 (Spring 1996), pp. 4–15. © 1996 Blackwell Publishers.

companies paying out the excess cash rather than frittering it away on unprofitable investments. Shareholders also know that firms with large quantities of debt to service are less likely to squander cash. A study by Comment and Jarrell, who looked at the announcements of open-market repurchase programs, found that on average they resulted in an abnormal price rise of 2%.[14]

Stock repurchases may also be used to signal a manager's confidence in the future. Suppose that you, the manager, believe that your stock is substantially undervalued. You announce that the company is prepared to buy back a fifth of its

---

[14] See R. Comment and G. Jarrell, "The Relative Signalling Power of Dutch-Auction and Fixed Price Self-Tender Offers and Open-Market Share Repurchases," *Journal of Finance* 46 (September 1991), pp. 1243–1271. There is also evidence of continuing superior performance during the years following a repurchase announcement. See D. Ikenberry, J. Lakonishok, and T. Vermaelen, "Market Underreaction to Open Market Share Repurchases," *Journal of Financial Economics* 39 (October 1995), pp. 181–208.

stock at a price that is 20% above the current market price. But (you say) you are certainly not going to sell any of your own stock at that price. Investors jump to the obvious conclusion—you must believe that the stock is good value even at 20% above the current price.

When companies offer to repurchase their stock at a premium, senior management and directors usually commit to hold on to their stock.[15] So it is not surprising that researchers have found that announcements of offers to buy back shares above the market price have prompted a larger rise in the stock price, averaging about 11%.[16]

13.5   THE PAYOUT CONTROVERSY

We have seen that a change in payout may provide information about management's confidence in the future and so affect the stock price. But eventually this change in the stock price would happen anyway as information about future earnings seeps out through other channels. But does the payout policy *change* the value of the stock, rather than simply providing a signal of its value?

On this issue economists fall into three groups. On the right, there is a conservative group that believes an increase in the dividend payment increases firm value. On the left, there is a radical group that believes a higher dividend payout reduces value. And in the center, there is a middle-of-the-road party that claims that payout policy makes no difference.

The middle-of-the-road party was founded in 1961 by Miller and Modigliani (always referred to as "MM" or "M and M"), when they published a theoretical paper showing the irrelevance of dividend policy in a world without taxes, transaction costs, or other market imperfections.[17] By the standards of 1961 MM were leftist radicals, because at that time most people believed that even under idealized assumptions increased dividends made shareholders better off.[18] But now MM's proof is generally accepted as correct, and the argument has shifted to whether taxes or other market imperfections alter the situation. In the process MM have been pushed toward the center by a new leftist party that argues for *low* dividends. The leftists' position is based on MM's argument modified to take account of taxes and costs of issuing securities. The conservatives are still with us, relying on essentially the same arguments as in 1961.

Why should you care about this debate? Of course, if you help to decide your company's dividend payment or stock repurchase, you will want to know how it affects value. But there is a more general reason than that. We have up to this point assumed that the company's investment decision is independent of its financing

---

[15] Not only do managers hold on to their stock; on average they also add to their holdings *before* the announcement of a repurchase. See D. S. Lee, W. Mikkelson, and M. M. Partch, "Managers' Trading around Stock Repurchases," *Journal of Finance* 47 (December 1992), pp. 1947–1961.

[16] See R. Comment and G. Jarrell, *op. cit.*

[17] M. H. Miller and F. Modigliani: "Dividend Policy, Growth and the Valuation of Shares," *Journal of Business* 34 (October 1961), pp. 411–433.

[18] Not *everybody* believed dividends make shareholders better off. MM's arguments were anticipated in 1938 in J. B. Williams, *The Theory of Investment Value* (Cambridge, MA: Harvard University Press, 1938). Also, a proof very similar to MM's was developed by J. Lintner in "Dividends, Earnings, Leverage, Stock Prices and the Supply of Capital to Corporations," *Review of Economics and Statistics* 44 (August 1962), pp. 243–269.

policy. In that case a good project is a good project is a good project, no matter who undertakes it or how it is ultimately financed. If dividend policy does not affect value, that is still true. But perhaps it *does* affect value. In that case the attractiveness of a new project may depend on where the money is coming from. For example, if investors prefer companies with high payouts, companies might be reluctant to take on investments financed by retained earnings.

We begin our discussion of dividend policy with a presentation of MM's original argument. Then we will undertake a critical appraisal of the positions of the three parties. Perhaps we should warn you before we start that our own position is mostly middle-of-the-road but sometimes marginally leftist. (As investors we prefer low dividends because we don't like paying taxes!)

Dividend Policy Is Irrelevant in Perfect Capital Markets

In their classic 1961 article MM argued as follows: Suppose your firm has settled on its investment program. You have worked out how much of this program can be financed from borrowing, and you plan to meet the remaining funds requirement from retained earnings. Any surplus money is to be paid out as dividends.

Now think what happens if you want to increase the total payout by upping the dividend without also changing the investment and borrowing policy. The extra money must come from somewhere. If the firm fixes its borrowing, the only way it can finance the extra dividend is to print some more shares and sell them. The new stockholders are going to part with their money only if you can offer them shares that are worth as much as they cost. But how can the firm do this when its assets, earnings, investment opportunities, and, therefore, market value are all unchanged? The answer is that there must be a *transfer of value* from the old to the new stockholders. The new ones get the newly printed shares, each one worth less than before the dividend change was announced, and the old ones suffer a capital loss on their shares. The capital loss borne by the old shareholders just offsets the extra cash dividend they receive.

Figure 13.4 shows how this transfer of value occurs. Our hypothetical company pays out a third of its total value as a dividend and it raises the money to do so by selling new shares. The capital loss suffered by the old stockholders is represented by the reduction in the size of the maroon boxes. But that capital loss is exactly offset by the fact that the new money raised (the blue boxes) is paid over to them as dividends.

Does it make any difference to the old stockholders that they receive an extra dividend payment plus an offsetting capital loss? It might if that were the only way they could get their hands on cash. But as long as there are efficient capital markets, they can raise the cash by selling shares. Thus the old shareholders can cash in either by persuading the management to pay a higher dividend or by selling some of their shares. In either case there will be a transfer of value from old to new shareholders. The only difference is that in the former case this transfer is caused by a dilution in the value of each of the firm's shares, and in the latter case it is caused by a reduction in the number of shares held by the old shareholders. The two alternatives are compared in Figure 13.5.

Because investors do not need dividends to get their hands on cash, they will not pay higher prices for the shares of firms with high payouts. Therefore firms ought not to worry about dividend policy. They can let dividends fluctuate as a by-product of their investment and financing decisions.

FIGURE 13.4

This firm pays out a third of its worth as a dividend and raises the money by selling new shares. The transfer of value to the new stockholders is equal to the dividend payment. The total value of the firm is unaffected.

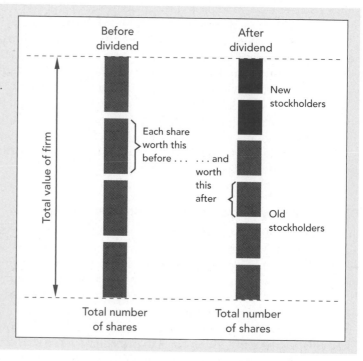

FIGURE 13.5

Two ways of raising cash for the firm's original shareholders. In each case the cash received is offset by a decline in the value of the old stockholders' claim on the firm. If the firm pays a dividend, each share is worth less because more shares have to be issued against the firm's assets. If the old stockholders sell some of their shares, each share is worth the same but the old stockholders have fewer shares.

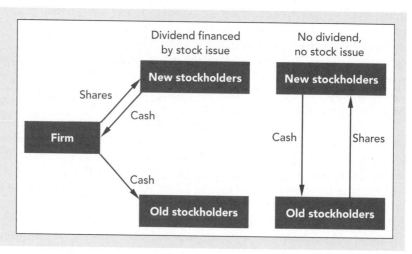

Dividend Irrelevance—An Illustration

Consider the case of Rational Demiconductor, which at this moment has the following balance sheet:

Rational Demiconductor's Balance Sheet (Market Values)

Cash ($1,000 held for investment)	1,000	0	Debt
Fixed assets	9,000	10,000 + NPV	Equity
Investment opportunity ($1,000 investment required)	NPV		
Total asset value	$10,000 + NPV	$10,000 + NPV	Value of firm

Rational Demiconductor has $1,000 cash earmarked for a project requiring a $1,000 investment. We do not know how attractive the project is, and so we enter it at NPV; after the project is undertaken it will be worth $1,000 + NPV. Note that the balance sheet is constructed with market values; equity equals the market value of the firm's outstanding shares (price per share times number of shares outstanding). It is not necessarily equal to their book value.

Now Rational Demiconductor uses the cash to pay a $1,000 dividend to its stockholders. The benefit to them is obvious: $1,000 of spendable cash. It is also obvious that there must be a cost. The cash is not free.

Where does the money for the dividend come from? Of course, the immediate source of funds is Rational Demiconductor's cash account. But this cash was earmarked for the investment project. Since we want to isolate the effects of dividend policy on shareholders' wealth, we assume that the company *continues* with the investment project. That means that $1,000 in cash must be raised by new financing. This could consist of an issue of either debt or stock. Again, we just want to look at dividend policy for now, and we defer discussion of the debt-equity choice until Chapters 14 and 15. Thus Rational Demiconductor ends up financing the dividend with a $1,000 stock issue.

Now we examine the balance sheet after the dividend is paid, the new stock is sold, and the investment is undertaken. Because Rational Demiconductor's investment and borrowing policies are unaffected by the dividend payment, its *overall* market value must be unchanged at $10,000 + NPV.[19] We know also that if the new stockholders pay a fair price, their stock is worth $1,000. That leaves us with only one missing number—the value of the stock held by the original stockholders. It is easy to see that this must be

$$\text{Value of original stockholders' shares} = \text{value of company} - \text{value of new shares}$$
$$= (10,000 + NPV) - 1,000$$
$$= \$9,000 + NPV$$

The old shareholders have received a $1,000 cash dividend and incurred a $1,000 capital loss. Dividend policy doesn't matter.

By paying out $1,000 with one hand and taking it back with the other, Rational Demiconductor is recycling cash. To suggest that this makes shareholders better off is like advising a cook to cool the kitchen by leaving the refrigerator door open.

Of course, our proof ignores taxes, issue costs, and a variety of other complications. We will turn to those items in a moment. The really crucial assumption in our proof is that the new shares are sold at a fair price. The shares sold to raise $1,000 must actually be *worth* $1,000.[20] In other words, we have assumed efficient capital markets.

Calculating Share Price

We have assumed that Rational Demiconductor's new shares can be sold at a fair price, but what is that price and how many new shares are issued?

Suppose that before this dividend payout the company had 1,000 shares outstanding and that the project had an NPV of $2,000. Then the old stock was worth

---

[19] All other factors that might affect Rational Demiconductor's value are assumed constant. This is not a necessary assumption, but it simplifies the proof of MM's theory.

[20] The "old" shareholders get all the benefit of the positive-NPV project. The new shareholders require only a fair rate of return. They are making a zero-NPV investment.

in total $10,000 + NPV = $12,000, which works out at $12,000/1,000 = $12 per share. After the company has paid the dividend and completed the financing, this old stock is worth $9,000 + NPV = $11,000. That works out at $11,000/1,000 = $11 per share. In other words, the price of the old stock falls by the amount of the $1 per share dividend payment.

Now let us look at the new stock. Clearly, after the issue this must sell at the same price as the rest of the stock. In other words, it must be valued at $11. If the new stockholders get fair value, the company must issue $1,000/$11 or 91 new shares in order to raise the $1,000 that it needs.

Stock Repurchase

We have seen that any increased cash dividend payment must be offset by a stock issue if the firm's investment and borrowing policies are held constant. In effect the stockholders finance the extra dividend by selling off part of their ownership of the firm. Consequently, the stock price falls by just enough to offset the extra dividend.

This process can also be run backward. With investment and borrowing policy given, any *reduction* in dividends must be balanced by a reduction in the number of shares issued or by repurchase of previously outstanding stock. But if the process has no effect on stockholders' wealth when run forward, it must likewise have no effect when run in reverse. We will confirm this by another numerical example.

Suppose that a technical discovery reveals that Rational Demiconductor's new project is not a positive-NPV venture but a sure loser. Management announces that the project is to be discarded and that the $1,000 earmarked for it will be paid out as an extra dividend of $1 per share. After the dividend payout, the balance sheet is

Rational Demiconductor's Balance Sheet (Market Values)

Cash	$ 0	$ 0	Debt
Existing fixed assets	9,000	9,000	Equity
New project	0		
Total asset value	$ 9,000	$ 9,000	Total firm value

Since there are 1,000 shares outstanding, the stock price is $10,000/1,000 = $10 before the dividend payment and $9,000/1,000 = $9 *after* the payment.

What if Rational Demiconductor uses the $1,000 to repurchase stock instead? As long as the company pays a fair price for the stock, the $1,000 buys $1,000/$10 = 100 shares. That leaves 900 shares worth 900 × $10 = $9,000.

As expected, we find that switching from cash dividends to share repurchase has no effect on shareholders' wealth. They forgo a $1 cash dividend but end up holding shares worth $10 instead of $9.

Note that when shares are repurchased the transfer of value is in favor of those stockholders who do not sell. They forgo any cash dividend but end up owning a larger slice of the firm. In effect they are using their share of Rational Demiconductor's $1,000 distribution to buy out some of their fellow shareholders.

Stock Repurchase and Valuation

Valuing the equity of a firm that repurchases its own stock can be confusing. Let's work through a simple example.

Company X has 100 shares outstanding. It earns $1,000 a year, all of which is paid out as a dividend. The dividend per share is, therefore, $1,000/100 = $10. Suppose that investors expect the dividend to be maintained indefinitely and that they require a return of 10%. In this case the value of each share is $PV_{share} = \$10/.10 = \$100$. Since there are 100 shares outstanding, the *total* market value of the equity is $PV_{equity} = 100 \times \$100 = \$10,000$. Note that we could reach the same conclusion by discounting the *total* dividend payments to shareholders ($PV_{equity} = \$1,000/.10 = \$10,000$).[21]

Now suppose the company announces that instead of paying a cash dividend in year 1, it will spend the same money repurchasing its shares in the open market. The total expected cash flows to shareholders (dividends and cash from stock repurchase) are unchanged at $1,000. So the total value of the equity also remains at $1,000/.10 = $10,000. This is made up of the value of the $1,000 received from the stock repurchase in year 1 ($PV_{repurchase} = \$1,000/1.1 = \$909.1$) and the value of the $1,000-a-year dividend starting in year 2 [$PV_{dividends} = \$1,000/(.10 \times 1.1) = \$9,091$]. Each share continues to be worth $10,000/100 = $100 just as before.

Think now about those shareholders who plan to sell their stock back to the company. They will demand a 10% return on their investment. So the expected price at which the firm buys back shares must be 10% higher than today's price, or $110. The company spends $1,000 buying back its stock, which is sufficient to buy $1,000/$110 = 9.09 shares.

The company starts with 100 shares, it buys back 9.09, and therefore 90.91 shares remain outstanding. Each of these shares can look forward to a dividend stream of $1,000/90.91 = $11 per share. So after the repurchase shareholders have 10% fewer shares, but earnings and dividends per share are 10% higher. An investor who owns one share today that is not repurchased will receive no dividends in year 1 but can look forward to $11 a year thereafter. The value of each share is therefore $11/(.1 \times 1.1) = \$100$.

Our example illustrates several points. First, other things equal, company value is unaffected by the decision to repurchase stock rather than to pay a cash dividend. Second, when valuing the entire equity you need to include both the cash that is paid out as dividends and the cash that is used to repurchase stock. Third, when calculating the cash flow *per share*, it is double counting to include both the forecasted dividends per share *and* the cash received from repurchase (if you sell back your share, you don't get any subsequent dividends). Fourth, a firm that repurchases stock instead of paying dividends reduces the number of shares outstanding but produces an offsetting increase in subsequent earnings and dividends per share.

13.6   THE RIGHTISTS

MM's argument implies that the value of the company is determined by the company's assets and the cash flows that they generate. If the company increases the total amount of the payout, the extra cash must be clawed back from the shareholders by a new issue of stock. And if the company chooses to hold the total

---

[21] When valuing the entire equity, remember that if the company is expected to issue additional shares in the future, we should include the dividend payments on these shares only if we also include the amount that investors pay for them.

payout constant, any increase in the dividend payment must be offset by a corresponding reduction in the cash that shareholders receive by a repurchase of their shares. Hence MM's conclusion that firm value cannot be increased by changing the amount or the form of the distribution.

Before MM published their paper, much of the finance literature had advocated high payout ratios. Here, for example, is a statement of the rightist position made by Graham and Dodd in 1951:

> The considered and continuous verdict of the stock market is overwhelmingly in favor of liberal dividends as against niggardly ones. The common stock investor must take this judgment into account in the valuation of common stock for purchase. It is now becoming standard practice to evaluate common stock by applying one multiplier to that portion of earnings paid out in dividends and a much smaller multiplier to the undistributed balance.[22]

Those who favor large payouts point out that there is a natural clientele for high-payout stocks. For example, some financial institutions are legally restricted from holding stocks lacking established dividend records.[23] Trusts and endowment funds may prefer high-dividend stocks because dividends are regarded as spendable "income," whereas capital gains are "additions to principal."

There is also a natural clientele of investors, such as the elderly, who look to their stock portfolios for a steady source of cash to live on.[24] In principle, this cash could be easily generated from stocks paying no dividends at all; the investor could just sell off a small fraction of his or her holdings from time to time. But it is simpler and cheaper for the company to send a quarterly check than for its shareholders to sell, say, one share every three months. Regular dividends relieve many of its shareholders of transaction costs and considerable inconvenience.[25]

Some observers have appealed to behavioral psychology to explain why we may prefer to receive those regular dividends rather than sell small amounts of stock.[26] We are all, they point out, liable to succumb to temptation. Some of us may hanker after fattening foods, while others may be dying for a drink. We could seek to control these cravings by willpower, but that can be a painful struggle. Instead, it may be easier to set simple rules for ourselves ("cut out chocolate," or "wine with meals only"). In just the same way, we may welcome the self-discipline that comes from spending only dividend income, and thereby sidestep the difficult decision of how much we should dip into capital.

---

[22] These authors later qualified this statement, recognizing the willingness of investors to pay high price–earnings multiples for growth stocks. But otherwise they stuck to their position. We quoted their 1951 statement because of its historical importance. Compare B. Graham and D. L. Dodd, *Security Analysis: Principles and Techniques*, 3rd ed. (New York: McGraw-Hill, 1951), p. 432, with B. Graham, D. L. Dodd, and S. Cottle, *Security Analysis: Principles and Techniques*, 4th ed. (New York: McGraw-Hill, 1962), p. 480.

[23] Most colleges and universities are legally free to spend capital gains from their endowments, but they usually restrict spending to a moderate percentage that can be covered by dividends and interest receipts.

[24] See, for example, J. R. Graham and A. Kumar, "Do Dividend Clienteles Exist? Evidence on Dividend Preferences of Retail Investors," *Journal of Finance* 61 (June 2006), pp. 1305–1336.

[25] Those advocating generous dividends might go on to argue that a regular cash dividend relieves stockholders of the risk of having to sell shares at "temporarily depressed" prices. Of course, the firm will have to issue shares eventually to finance the dividend, but (the argument goes) the firm can pick the *right time* to sell. If firms really try to do this and if they are successful—two big *ifs*—then stockholders of high-payout firms might indeed get something for nothing.

[26] See H. Shefrin and M. Statman, "Explaining Investor Preference for Cash Dividends," *Journal of Financial Economics* 13 (June 1984), pp. 253–282.

MICROSOFT'S PAYOUT BONANZA

There is a point at which hoarding money becomes embarrassing. . . . Microsoft, which grew into the world's largest software company . . . and which has been generating cash at the rate of $1 billion a month passed that point years ago. On July 20th, it finally addressed the issue.

Its solution was to give back to its shareholders, in various forms, an unprecedented $75 billion. One dollop, to the tune of $32 billion, will be a one-time dividend to be paid in December. Another will be share buy-backs worth $30 billion over four years. The third will be a doubling of Microsoft's ongoing dividend to 32 cents a share annually, payable in quarterly instalments. Not bad for a company that has not even turned 30 yet, and that only declared its first dividend in January 2003.

The decision is impressive for the mature analysis by Microsoft of its role in the industry and the prospects for the future that it implies.

Source: "An End to Growth?" *The Economist*, July 24, 2004, p. 61. © 2004 The Economist Newspaper Group, Inc. Reprinted with permission. Further reproduction prohibited (**www.economist.com**).

Payout Policy, Investment Policy, and Management Incentives

There is another reason that shareholders often clamor for more generous payouts. Suppose a company has plenty of free cash flow but few profitable investment opportunities. Shareholders may not trust the managers to spend retained earnings wisely and may fear that the money will be plowed back into building a larger empire rather than a more profitable one. In such cases investors may demand higher dividends or a stock repurchase not because these are valuable in themselves, but because they encourage a more careful, value-oriented investment policy.[27]

The nearby box describes how Microsoft announced the largest cash distribution in corporate history. By 2004 the company's investment opportunities had diminished, and investors were, therefore, happy to see Microsoft distribute its cash mountain rather than invest it in negative-NPV projects.

13.7 TAXES AND THE RADICAL LEFT

The left-wing dividend creed is simple: Whenever dividends are taxed more heavily than capital gains, firms should pay the lowest cash dividend they can get away with. Available cash should be retained or used to repurchase shares.

By shifting their distribution policies in this way, corporations can transmute dividends into capital gains. If this financial alchemy results in lower taxes, it should be welcomed by any taxpaying investor. That is the basic point made by the leftist party when it argues for low-dividend payout.

If dividends are taxed more heavily than capital gains, investors should pay more for stocks with low dividend yields. In other words, they should accept a lower *pretax* rate of return from securities offering returns in the form of capital

---

[27] La Porta et al. argue that in countries such as the United States shareholders are able to pressure companies to disgorge cash and this prevents managers from using too high a proportion of earnings to benefit themselves. By contrast, companies pay out a smaller proportion of earnings in those countries where the law is more relaxed about overinvestment and empire building. See R. La Porta, F. Lopez-de-Silanes, A. Shleifer, and R. W. Vishny, "Agency Problems and Dividend Policies around the World," *Journal of Finance* 55 (February 2000), pp. 1–34.

	Firm A (No Dividend)	Firm B (High Dividend)
Next year's price	$112.50	$102.50
Dividend	$0	$10.00
Total pretax payoff	$112.50	$112.50
Today's stock price	$100	$97.78
Capital gain	$12.50	$4.72
Before-tax rate of return	$100 \times \left(\frac{12.5}{100}\right) = 12.5\%$	$100 \times \left(\frac{14.72}{97.78}\right) = 15.05\%$
Tax on dividend at 40%	$0	$.40 \times 10 = \$4.00$
Tax on capital gains at 20%	$.20 \times 12.50 = \$2.50$	$.20 \times 4.72 = \$.94$
Total after-tax income (dividends plus capital gains less taxes)	$(0 + 12.50) - 2.50 = \$10.00$	$(10.00 + 4.72) - (4.00 + .94) = \$9.78$
After-tax rate of return	$100 \times \left(\frac{10}{100}\right) = 10.0\%$	$100 \times \left(\frac{9.78}{97.78}\right) = 10.0\%$

TABLE 13.1

Effects of a shift in dividend policy when dividends are taxed more heavily than capital gains. The high-payout stock (firm B) must sell at a lower price to provide the same after-tax return.

gains rather than dividends. Table 13.1 illustrates this. The stocks of firms A and B are equally risky. Investors expect A to be worth $112.50 per share next year. The share price of B is expected to be only $102.50, but a $10 dividend is also forecasted, and so the total pretax payoff is the same, $112.50.

Yet we find B's stock selling for less than A's and therefore offering a higher pretax rate of return. The reason is obvious: Investors prefer A because its return comes in the form of capital gains. Table 13.1 shows that A and B are equally attractive to investors who, we assume, pay a 40% tax on dividends and a 20% tax on capital gains. Each offers a 10% return after all taxes. The difference between the stock prices of A and B is exactly the present value of the extra taxes the investors face if they buy B.[28]

The management of B could save these extra taxes by eliminating the $10 dividend and using the released funds to repurchase stock instead. Its stock price should rise to $100 as soon as the new policy is announced.

Why Pay Any Dividends at All?

It is true that when companies make very large one-off distributions of cash to shareholders, they generally choose to do so by share repurchase than by a large temporary hike in dividends. But if dividends attract more tax than capital gains, why should any firm ever pay a cash dividend? If cash is to be distributed to stockholders, isn't share repurchase always the best channel for doing so? The

---

[28] Michael Brennan has modeled what happens when you introduce taxes into an otherwise perfect market. He found that the capital asset pricing model continues to hold, but on an *after-tax* basis. Thus, if A and B have the same beta, they should offer the same after-tax rate of return. The spread between pretax and post-tax returns is determined by a weighted average of investors' tax rates. See M. J. Brennan, "Taxes, Market Valuation and Corporate Financial Policy," *National Tax Journal* 23 (December 1970), pp. 417–427.

leftist position seems to call not just for low payouts but for *zero* payouts whenever capital gains have a tax advantage.

Few leftists would go quite that far. A firm that eliminates dividends and starts repurchasing stock on a regular basis may find that the Internal Revenue Service recognizes the repurchase program for what it really is and taxes the payments accordingly. That is why financial managers do not usually announce that they are repurchasing shares to save stockholders taxes; they give some other reason.[29]

The low-payout party has nevertheless maintained that the market rewards firms that have low-payout policies. They have claimed that firms that paid dividends and as a result had to issue shares from time to time were making a serious mistake. Any such firm was essentially financing its dividends by issuing stock; it should have cut its dividends at least to the point at which stock issues were unnecessary. This would not only have saved taxes for shareholders but it would also have avoided the transaction costs of the stock issues.[30]

Empirical Evidence on Dividends and Taxes

It is hard to deny that taxes are important to investors. You can see that in the bond market. Interest on municipal bonds is not taxed, and so municipals sell at low pretax yields. Interest on federal government bonds is taxed, and so these bonds sell at higher pretax yields. It does not seem likely that investors in bonds just forget about taxes when they enter the stock market.

There is some evidence that in the past taxes have affected U.S. investors' choice of stocks.[31] Lightly taxed institutional investors have tended to hold high-yield stocks and retail investors have preferred low-yield stocks. Moreover, this preference for low-yield stocks has been somewhat more marked for high-income individuals. Nevertheless, it seems that taxes have been only a secondary consideration with these investors, and have not deterred individuals in high-tax brackets from holding substantial amounts of dividend-paying stocks.

If investors are concerned about taxes, we might also expect that, when the tax penalty on dividends is high, companies would think twice about increasing the payout. Only about a fifth of U.S. financial managers cite investor taxes as an important influence when the firm makes its dividend decision. On the other hand, firms have sometimes responded to major shifts in the way that investors are taxed. For example, when Australia introduced a tax change in 1987 that effectively eliminated the tax penalty on dividends for Australian investors, firms became more willing to increase their payout.[32]

If tax considerations are important, we would expect to find a historical tendency for high-dividend stocks to sell at lower prices and therefore to offer higher returns, just as in Table 13.1. Unfortunately, there are difficulties in measuring this effect. For example, suppose that stock A is priced at $100 and is expected to pay a $5 dividend. The *expected* yield is, therefore, $5/100 = .05$, or 5%. The company now

---

[29] They might say, "Our stock is a good investment," or, "We want to have the shares available to finance acquisitions of other companies." What do you think of these rationales?

[30] These costs can be substantial.

[31] See, for example, Y. Grinstein and R. Michaely, "Institutional Holdings and Payout Policy," *Journal of Finance* 60 (June 2005), pp. 1389–1426; and J. R. Graham and A. Kumar, "Do Dividend Clienteles Exist? Evidence on Dividend Preferences of Retail Investors," *Journal of Finance* 61 (June 2006), pp. 1305–1336.

[32] K. Pattenden and G. Twite, "Taxes and Dividend Policy under Alternative Tax Regimes," Australian Graduate School of Management, January 2006.

announces bumper earnings and a $10 dividend. Thus with the benefit of hindsight, A's *actual* dividend yield is $10/100 = .10$, or 10%. If the unexpected increase in earnings causes a rise in A's stock price, we will observe that a high actual yield is accompanied by a high actual return. But that would not tell us anything about whether a high *expected* yield was accompanied by a high *expected* return. To measure the effect of dividend policy, we need to estimate the dividends that investors expected.

A second problem is that nobody is quite sure what is meant by high dividend yield. For example, utility stocks have generally offered high yields. But did they have a high yield all year, or only in months or on days that dividends were paid? Perhaps for most of the year, they had zero yields and were perfect holdings for the highly taxed individuals.[33] Of course, high-tax investors did not want to hold a stock on the days dividends were paid, but they could sell their stock temporarily to a security dealer. Dealers are taxed equally on dividends and capital gains and therefore should not have demanded any extra return for holding stocks over the dividend period.[34] If shareholders could pass stocks freely between each other at the time of the dividend payment, we should not observe any tax effects at all.

A number of researchers have attempted to tackle these problems and to measure whether investors demand a higher return from high-yielding stocks. Their findings offer some limited comfort to the dividends-are-bad school, for most of the researchers have suggested that high-yielding stocks have provided higher returns. However, the estimated tax rates differ substantially from one study to another. For example, while Litzenberger and Ramaswamy concluded that investors have priced stocks as if dividend income attracted an extra 14% to 23% rate of tax, Miller and Scholes using a different methodology came up with a negligible 4% difference in the rate of tax.[35]

The Taxation of Dividends and Capital Gains

Many of these attempts to measure the effect of dividends are of more historical than current interest, for they look back at the years before 1986 when there was a dramatic difference between the taxation of dividends and capital gains.[36] As we write this in 2007, the top rate of tax on both dividends and capital gains is 15%.[37]

There is, however, one way that tax law continues to favor capital gains. Taxes on dividends have to be paid immediately, but taxes on capital gains can be deferred until shares are sold and the capital gains are realized. Stockholders can

---

[33] Suppose there are 250 trading days in a year. Think of a stock paying quarterly dividends. We could say that the stock offers a high dividend yield on 4 days but a zero dividend yield on the remaining 246 days.

[34] The stock could also be sold to a corporation, which could "capture" the dividend and then resell the shares. Corporations are natural buyers of dividends, because they pay tax only on 30% of dividends received from other corporations. (We say more on the taxation of intercorporate dividends later in this section.)

[35] See R. H. Litzenberger and K. Ramaswamy, "The Effects of Dividends on Common Stock Prices: Tax Effects or Information Effects," *Journal of Finance* 37 (May 1982), pp. 429–443; and M. H. Miller and M. Scholes, "Dividends and Taxes: Some Empirical Evidence," *Journal of Political Economy* 90 (1982), pp. 1118–1141. Merton Miller provides a broad review of the empirical literature in "Behavioral Rationality in Finance: The Case of Dividends," *Journal of Business* 59 (October 1986), pp. S451–S468.

[36] The Tax Reform Act of 1986 equalized the tax rates on dividends and capital gains. A gap began to open up again in 1992.

[37] These rates were established by the *Jobs and Growth Tax Relief Reconciliation Act* of 2003 and have been extended to 2010. Note that capital gains realized within a year of purchase and dividends on stocks held for less than 61 days are taxed as ordinary income.

choose when to sell their shares and thus when to pay the capital gains tax. The longer they wait, the less the present value of the capital gains tax liability.[38]

The distinction between dividends and capital gains is not important for many financial institutions, which operate free of all taxes and therefore have no reason to prefer capital gains to dividends or vice versa. For example, pension funds are untaxed. These funds hold more than $4 trillion in common stocks, so they have enormous clout in the U.S. stock market. Only corporations have a tax reason to *prefer* dividends. They pay corporate income tax on only 30% of any dividends received. Thus the effective tax rate on dividends received by large corporations is 30% of 35% (the marginal corporate tax rate), or 10.5%. But they have to pay a 35% tax on the full amount of any realized capital gain.

The implications of these tax rules for dividend policy are pretty simple. Capital gains have advantages to many investors, but they are far less advantageous than they were 20 or 30 years ago.[39] Thus, the leftist case for minimizing cash dividends is weaker than it used to be. At the same time, the middle-of-the-road party has increased its share of the vote.

13.8 THE MIDDLE-OF-THE-ROADERS

The middle-of-the-road party, which is principally represented by Miller, Black, and Scholes,[40] maintains that a company's value is not affected by its dividend policy. Unlike the other two parties, they emphasize that the supply of dividends is free to adjust to the demand. Therefore, if companies could increase their stock price by changing their dividend payout, they would surely have done so. Presumably, dividends are where they are because no company believes that it could add value simply by upping or reducing its dividend payout.

This "supply argument" is not inconsistent with the existence of a clientele of investors who prefer low-payout stocks. If necessary, these investors would be prepared to pay a premium for low-payout stocks. But perhaps they do not have to. Enough firms may have already noticed the existence of this clientele and switched to low-payout policies. If so, there is no incentive for *additional* firms to switch to low-payout policies. Similarly, there may well be some investors who prefer high dividends, but these investors too already have a wide

---

[38] When securities are sold capital gains tax is paid on the difference between the selling price and the initial purchase price or *basis*. Thus, shares purchased in 2002 for $20 (the basis) and sold for $30 in 2007 would generate $10 per share in capital gains and a tax of $1.50 at a 15% tax rate.

Suppose the investor now decides to defer sale for one year. Then, if the interest rate is 5%, the present value of the tax, viewed from 2007, falls to 1.50/1.05 = $1.43. That is, the *effective* capital gains rate is 14.3%. The longer sale is deferred, the lower the effective rate will be.

The effective rate falls to zero if the investor dies before selling, because the investor's heirs get to "step up" the basis without recognizing any taxable gain. Suppose the price is still $30 when the investor dies. The heirs could sell for $30 and pay no tax, because they could claim a $30 basis. The $10 capital gain would escape tax entirely.

[39] We described above how Microsoft in 2004 declared a special dividend of $32 billion. Would the company have done so if there had still been a substantial tax disadvantage to dividend payments? We doubt it.

[40] F. Black and M. S. Scholes, "The Effects of Dividend Yield and Dividend Policy on Common Stock Prices and Returns," *Journal of Financial Economics* 1 (May 1974), pp. 1–22; M. H. Miller and M. S. Scholes, "Dividends and Taxes," *Journal of Financial Economics* 6 (December 1978), pp. 333–364; and M. H. Miller, "Behavioral Rationality in Finance: The Case of Dividends," *Journal of Business* 59 (October 1986), pp. S451–S468.

choice of suitable stocks. A third group of investors, such as pension funds and other tax-exempt institutions, may have no reason to prefer dividends to capital gains. These investors will be happy to hold both low- and high-payout stocks, and the value that they place on each stock will be unaffected by the company's dividend policy. In that case we are back in an MM world where dividend policy does not affect value.[41]

The middle-of-the-roaders stress that companies would not supply such a large quantity of dividends unless they believed that this was what investors wanted. But that still leaves a puzzle. Even in the days when there was a large tax disadvantage to dividends, many investors were apparently happy to hold high-payout stocks. Why? The response of the middle-of-the-roaders has been to argue that there are always plenty of wrinkles in the tax system that shareholders can use to avoid paying taxes on dividends. For example, instead of investing directly in common stocks, they can do so through a pension fund or insurance company, which receives more favorable tax treatment. However, it is not clear that this is the whole story, for a high proportion of dividends are regularly paid out to wealthy individuals and included in their taxable income.[42]

There is another possible reason that U.S. companies may pay dividends even when these dividends result in higher tax bills. Companies that pay *low* dividends will be more attractive to highly taxed individuals; those that pay *high* dividends will have a greater proportion of pension funds or other tax-exempt institutions as their stockholders. These financial institutions are sophisticated investors; they monitor carefully the companies that they invest in and they bring pressure on poor managers to perform. Successful, well-managed companies are happy to have financial institutions as investors, but their poorly managed brethren would prefer unsophisticated and more docile stockholders.

You can probably see now where the argument is heading. Well-managed companies want to signal their worth. They can do so by having a high proportion of demanding institutions among their stockholders. How do they achieve this? By paying high dividends. Those shareholders who pay tax do not object to these high dividends as long as the effect is to encourage institutional investors who are prepared to put the time and effort into monitoring the management.[43]

Alternative Tax Systems

In the United States shareholders' returns are taxed twice. They are taxed at the corporate level (corporate tax) and in the hands of the shareholder (income tax or capital gains tax). These two tiers of tax are illustrated in Table 13.2, which shows the after-tax return to the shareholder if the company distributes all its income as dividends. We assume the company earns $100 a share before tax and therefore pays corporate tax of $.35 \times 100 = \$35$. This leaves $65 a share to be paid out as a

---

[41] Baker and Wurgler argue that the demand for dividends may change. When this is reflected in stock prices, firms adjust their dividend policy to cater for the shift in demand. Thus a shift in clienteles shows up in a change in firms' propensity to pay dividends. See M. Baker and J. Wurgler, "A Catering Theory of Dividends," *Journal of Finance* 59 (June 2004), pp. 1125–1165.

[42] See, for example, F. Allen and R. Michaely, "Payout Policy," in G. Constantinides, M. Harris, and R. Stulz (eds.), *Handbook of the Economics of Finance: Corporate Finance* (Amsterdam: North-Holland, 2003).

[43] This signaling argument is developed in F. Allen, A. E. Bernardo, and I. Welch, "A Theory of Dividends Based on Tax Clienteles," *Journal of Finance* 55 (December 2000), pp. 2499–2536.

Operating income	100	
Corporate tax at 35%	35	◄—— Corporate tax
After-tax income (paid out as dividends)	65	
Income tax paid by investor at 15%	9.75	◄—— Second tax paid by investor
Net income to shareholder	55.25	

TABLE 13.2

In the United States returns to shareholders are taxed twice. This example assumes that all income after corporate taxes is paid out as cash dividends to an investor in the top income tax bracket (figures in dollars per share).

| | Rate of Income Tax | | |
	15%	30%	47%
Operating income	100	100	100
Corporate tax ($T_c = .30$)	30	30	30
After-tax income	70	70	70
Grossed-up dividend	100	100	100
Income tax	15	30	47
Tax credit for corporate payment	−30	−30	−30
Tax due from shareholder	−15	0	17
Available to shareholder	85	70	53

TABLE 13.3

Under imputation tax systems, such as that in Australia, shareholders receive a tax credit for the corporate tax that the firm has paid (figures in Australian dollars per share).

dividend, which is then subject to a second layer of tax. For example, a shareholder who is taxed at 15% pays tax on this dividend of .15 × 65 = $9.75. Only a tax-exempt pension fund or charity would retain the full $65.

Of course, dividends are regularly paid by companies that operate under very different tax systems. For example, Germany partly compensates for the corporate layer of tax by levying income tax on only half an individual's dividend income.

In some other countries, such as Australia and New Zealand, shareholders' returns are not taxed twice. For example, in Australia shareholders are taxed on dividends, but they may deduct from this tax bill their share of the corporate tax that the company has paid. This is known as an *imputation tax system*. Table 13.3 shows how the imputation system works. Suppose that an Australian company earns pretax profits of $A100 a share. After it pays corporate tax at 30%, the profit is $A70 a share. The company now declares a net dividend of $A70 and sends each shareholder a check for this amount. This dividend is accompanied by a tax credit saying that the company has already paid $A30 of tax on the shareholder's behalf. Thus shareholders are treated as if each received a total, or gross, dividend of 70 + 30 = $A100 and paid tax of $A30. If the shareholder's tax rate is 30%, there is no more tax to pay and the shareholder retains the net dividend of $A70. If the shareholder pays tax at the top personal rate of 47%, then he or she is required to pay an additional $17 of tax; if the tax rate is 15%

(the rate at which Australian pension funds are taxed), then the shareholder receives a *refund* of 30 − 15 = $A15.[44]

Under an imputation tax system, millionaires have to cough up the extra personal tax on dividends. If this is more than the tax that they would pay on capital gains, then millionaires would prefer that the company does not distribute earnings. If it is the other way around, they would prefer dividends.[45] Investors with low tax rates have no doubts about the matter. If the company pays a dividend, these investors receive a check from the revenue service for the excess tax that the company has paid, and therefore they prefer high payout rates.

Look once again at Table 13.3 and think what would happen if the corporate tax rate was zero. The shareholder with a 15% tax rate would still end up with $A85, and the shareholder with the 47% rate would still receive $A53. Thus, under an imputation tax system, when a company pays out all its earnings, there is effectively only one layer of tax—the tax on the shareholder. The revenue service collects this tax through the company and then sends a demand to the shareholder for any excess tax or makes a refund for any overpayment.[46]

---

[44] In Australia, shareholders receive a credit for the full amount of corporate tax that has been paid on their behalf. In other countries the tax credit is less than the corporate tax rate. You can think of the tax system in these countries as lying between the Australian and U.S. systems.

[45] In the case of Australia the tax rate on capital gains is the same as the tax rate on dividends. However, for securities that are held for more than 12 months only half of the gain is taxed.

[46] This is only true for earnings that are paid out as dividends. Retained earnings are subject to corporate tax. Shareholders get the benefit of retained earnings in the form of capital gains.

SUMMARY

When managers decide on the dividend, their primary concern seems to be to give shareholders a "fair" payment on their investment. However, most managers are very reluctant to reduce dividends and will not increase the payout unless they are confident it can be maintained.

As an alternative to dividend payments, the company can repurchase its own stock. In recent years companies have bought back their stock in large quantities, but repurchases do not generally substitute for dividends. Instead they are used to return unwanted cash to shareholders or to retire equity and replace it with debt. Investors usually interpret stock repurchases as an indication of managers' optimism.

If we hold the company's investment decision and capital structure constant, then payout policy is a trade-off between cash dividends and the issue or repurchase of common stock. Should firms retain whatever earnings are necessary to finance growth and pay out any residual as cash dividends? Or should they increase dividends and then (sooner or later) issue stock to make up the shortfall of equity capital? Or should they reduce dividends and use the released cash to repurchase stock?

If we lived in an ideally simple and perfect world, there would be no problem, for the choice would have no effect on market value. The controversy centers on the effects of dividend policy in our flawed world. Many investors believe that a high dividend payout enhances share price. Perhaps they welcome the self-discipline that comes from spending only dividend income rather than having to decide whether they should dip into capital. We suspect also that investors often pressure companies to increase dividends when they do not trust management to spend free cash flow wisely. In this case a dividend increase may lead to a rise in the stock price not because investors like dividends as such but because they want managers to run a tighter ship.

The most obvious and serious market imperfection has been the different tax treatment of dividends and capital gains. In the past, dividends in the United States have often been much more heavily taxed than capital gains. In 2003 the maximum tax rate was set at 15% on both dividends and gains, though capital gains continued to enjoy one advantage—the tax payment is not due until any gain was realized. If dividends are more heavily taxed, highly taxed investors should hold mostly low-payout stocks, and we would expect high-payout stocks to offer investors the compensation of greater pretax returns.

This view has a respectable theoretical basis. It is supported by some evidence that, when dividends were at a significant tax disadvantage in the United States, gross returns did reflect the tax differential. The weak link is the theory's silence on the question of why companies continued to distribute such large dividends when they landed investors with such large tax bills.

The third view of dividend policy starts with the notion that the actions of companies do reflect investors' preferences; thus the fact that companies pay substantial dividends is the best evidence that investors want them. If the supply of dividends exactly meets the demand, no single company could improve its market value by changing its payout policy.

It is difficult to be dogmatic over these controversies. If investment policy and borrowing are held constant, then the arguments over payout policy are largely about shuffling money from one pocket to another. Unless there are substantial tax consequences to these shuffles, it is unlikely that firm value is greatly affected either by the total amount of the payout or the choice between dividends and repurchase. Investors' concern with payout decisions seems to stem mainly from the information that they read into managers' actions.

If dividend policy doesn't affect firm value, then you don't need to worry about it when estimating the cost of capital. But if (say) you believe that tax effects are important, then in principle you should recognize that investors demand higher returns from high-payout stocks. Some financial managers do take dividend policy into account when estimating the cost of capital, but most become de facto middle-of-the-roaders. It seems that the effects of dividend policy are too uncertain to justify fine-tuning such estimates.

FURTHER READING

The classic paper on payout policy is:
M. H. Miller and F. Modigliani, "Dividend Policy, Growth, and the Valuation of Shares," *Journal of Business* 34 (October 1961), pp. 411–433.

For a comprehensive review of the literature on payout policy, see:
F. Allen and R. Michaely, "Payout Policy," in G. Constantinides, M. Harris, and R. Stulz, (eds.), *Handbook of the Economics of Finance: Corporate Finance* (Amsterdam: North-Holland, 2003).

For a recent survey of managers' attitudes to the payout decision, see:
A. Brav, J. R. Graham, C. R. Harvey, and R. Michaely, "Payout Policy in the 21st Century," *Journal of Financial Economics* 77 (September 2005), pp. 483–527.

CONCEPT REVIEW QUESTIONS

1. What are the two ways that firms pay out cash to shareholders? Which method has grown most rapidly in popularity? (page 339)

2. Are companies free to declare whatever dividends they choose? Why or why not? (page 340)

3. What are the four main ways to repurchase stock? (page 341)

For a complete listing of your chapter Concept Review Questions, please visit us at www.mhhe.com/bma1e.

QUIZ

1. In 2007 PepsiCo paid a regular quarterly dividend of $.30 a share.

   a. Match each of the following sets of dates:

(A1) 2 February 2007	(B1) Record date
(A2) 6 March 2007	(B2) Payment date
(A3) 7 March 2007	(B3) Ex-dividend date
(A4) 9 March 2007	(B4) Last with-dividend date
(A5) 30 March 2007	(B5) Declaration date

   b. On one of these dates the stock price is likely to fall by about the value of the dividend. Which date? Why?

   c. PepsiCo's stock price at the end of February was $63.15. What was the dividend yield?

   d. If earnings per share for 2007 are $3.32, what is the percentage payout rate?

   e. Suppose that in 2007 the company paid a 10% stock dividend. What would be the expected fall in price?

2. Here are several "facts" about typical corporate dividend policies. Which are true and which false?

   a. Companies decide each year's dividend by looking at their capital expenditure requirements and then distributing whatever cash is left over.

   b. Managers and investors seem more concerned with dividend changes than with dividend levels.

   c. Managers often increase dividends temporarily when earnings are unexpectedly high for a year or two.

   d. Companies undertaking substantial share repurchases usually finance them with an offsetting reduction in cash dividends.

3. a. Wotan owns 1,000 shares of a firm that has just announced an increase in its dividend from $2.00 to $2.50 a share. The share price is currently $150. If Wotan does not wish to spend the extra cash, what should he do to offset the dividend increase?

   b. Brunhilde owns 1,000 shares of a firm that has just announced a dividend cut from $8.00 a share to $5.00. The share price is currently $200. If Brunhilde wishes to maintain her consumption, what should she do to offset the dividend cut?

4. Patriot Games has 5 million shares outstanding. The president has proposed that, given the firm's large cash holdings, the annual dividend should be increased from $6.00 a share to $8.00. If you agree with the president's plans for investment and capital structure, what else must the company do as a consequence of the dividend increase?

5. House of Haddock has 5,000 shares outstanding and the stock price is $140. The company is expected to pay a dividend of $20 per share next year and thereafter the

dividend is expected to grow indefinitely by 5% a year. The President, George Mullet, now makes a surprise announcement: He says that the company will henceforth distribute half the cash in the form of dividends and the remainder will be used to repurchase stock.

a. What is the total value of the company before and after the announcement? What is the value of one share?

b. What is the expected stream of dividends per share for an investor who plans to retain his shares rather than sell them back to the company? Check your estimate of share value by discounting this stream of dividends per share.

6. Here are key financial data for House of Herring, Inc.:

Earnings per share for 2015	$5.50
Number of shares outstanding	40 million
Target payout ratio	50%
Planned dividend per share	$2.75
Stock price, year-end 2015	$130

House of Herring plans to pay the entire dividend early in January 2016. All corporate and personal taxes were repealed in 2014.

a. Other things equal, what will be House of Herring's stock price after the planned dividend payout?

b. Suppose the company cancels the dividend and announces that it will use the money saved to repurchase shares. What happens to the stock price on the announcement date? Assume that investors learn nothing about the company's prospects from the announcement. How many shares will the company need to repurchase?

c. Suppose the company increases dividends to $5.50 per share and then issues new shares to recoup the extra cash paid out as dividends. What happens to the with- and ex-dividend share prices? How many shares will need to be issued? Again, assume investors learn nothing from the announcement about House of Herring's prospects.

7. Answer the following question twice, once assuming current tax law and once assuming zero tax on capital gains.

Suppose all investments offered the same expected return *before* tax. Consider two equally risky shares, Hi and Lo. Hi shares pay a generous dividend and offer low expected capital gains. Lo shares pay low dividends and offer high expected capital gains. Which of the following investors would prefer the Lo shares? Which would prefer the Hi shares? Which should not care? (*Hint:* Assume that any stock purchased will be sold after one year.)

a. A pension fund.

b. An individual.

c. A corporation.

d. A charitable endowment.

e. A security dealer.

8. Look in a recent issue of *The Wall Street Journal* at "Dividend News" and choose a company reporting a regular dividend.

a. How frequently does the company pay a regular dividend?

b. What is the amount of the dividend?

c. By what date must your stock be registered for you to receive the dividend?

PRACTICE QUESTIONS

    d. How much later is the dividend paid?

    e. Look up the stock price and calculate the annual yield on the stock.

9. Which types of companies would you expect to distribute a relatively high or low proportion of current earnings? Which would you expect to have a relatively high or low price–earnings ratio?

    a. High-risk companies.

    b. Companies that have experienced an unexpected decline in profits.

    c. Companies that *expect* to experience a decline in profits.

    d. Growth companies with valuable future investment opportunities.

10. Little Oil has outstanding 1 million shares with a total market value of $20 million. The firm is expected to pay $1 million of dividends next year, and thereafter the amount paid out is expected to grow by 5% a year in perpetuity. Thus the expected dividend is $1.05 million in year 2, $1.105 million in year 3, and so on. However, the company has heard that the value of a share depends on the flow of dividends, and therefore it announces that next year's dividend will be increased to $2 million and that the extra cash will be raised immediately by an issue of shares. After that, the total amount paid out each year will be as previously forecasted, that is, $1.05 million in year 2 and increasing by 5% in each subsequent year.

    a. At what price will the new shares be issued in year 1?

    b. How many shares will the firm need to issue?

    c. What will be the expected dividend payments on these new shares, and what therefore will be paid out to the *old* shareholders after year 1?

    d. Show that the present value of the cash flows to current shareholders remains $20 million.

11. We stated in Section 13.5 that MM's proof of dividend irrelevance assumes that new shares are sold at a fair price. Look back at Practice Problem 10. Assume that new shares are issued in year 1 at $10 a share. Show who gains and who loses. Is dividend policy still irrelevant? Why or why not?

12. Respond to the following comment: "It's all very well saying that I can sell shares to cover cash needs, but that may mean selling at the bottom of the market. If the company pays a regular cash dividend, investors avoid that risk."

13. Refer to the first balance sheet prepared for Rational Demiconductor in Section 13.5. Again it uses cash to pay a $1,000 cash dividend, planning to issue stock to recover the cash required for investment. But this time catastrophe hits before the stock can be issued. A new pollution control regulation increases manufacturing costs to the extent that the value of Rational Demiconductor's existing business is cut in half, to $4,500. The NPV of the new investment opportunity is unaffected, however. Show that dividend policy is still irrelevant.

14. "Many companies use stock repurchases to increase earnings per share. For example, suppose that a company is in the following position:

Net profit	$10 million
Number of shares before repurchase	1 million
Earnings per share	$10
Price–earnings ratio	20
Share price	$200

The company now repurchases 200,000 shares at $200 a share. The number of shares declines to 800,000 shares and earnings per share increase to $12.50. Assuming the price–earnings ratio stays at 20, the share price must rise to $250." Discuss.

15. Hors d'Age Cheeseworks has been paying a regular cash dividend of $4 per share each year for over a decade. The company is paying out all its earnings as dividends and is not expected to grow. There are 100,000 shares outstanding selling for $80 per share. The company has sufficient cash on hand to pay the next annual dividend.

Suppose that Hors d'Age decides to cut its cash dividend to zero and announces that it will repurchase shares instead.

   a. What is the immediate stock price reaction? Ignore taxes, and assume that the repurchase program conveys no information about operating profitability or business risk.

   b. How many shares will Hors d'Age purchase?

   c. Project and compare future stock prices for the old and new policies. Do this for at least years 1, 2, and 3.

16. An article on stock repurchase in the *Los Angeles Times* noted: "An increasing number of companies are finding that the best investment they can make these days is in themselves." Discuss this view. How is the desirability of repurchase affected by company prospects and the price of its stock?

17. Comment briefly on each of the following statements:

   a. "Unlike American firms, which are always being pressured by their shareholders to increase dividends, Japanese companies pay out a much smaller proportion of earnings and so enjoy a lower cost of capital."

   b. "Unlike new capital, which needs a stream of new dividends to service it, retained earnings have zero cost."

   c. "If a company repurchases stock instead of paying a dividend, the number of shares falls and earnings per share rise. Thus stock repurchase must always be preferred to paying dividends."

18. Formaggio Vecchio has just announced its regular quarterly cash dividend of $1 per share.

   a. When will the stock price fall to reflect this dividend payment—on the record date, the ex-dividend date, or the payment date?

   b. Assume that there are no taxes. By how much is the stock price likely to fall?

   c. Now assume that *all* investors pay tax of 30% on dividends and nothing on capital gains. What is the likely fall in the stock price?

   d. Suppose, finally, that everything is the same as in part (c), except that security dealers pay tax on *both* dividends and capital gains. How would you expect your answer to (c) to change? Explain.

19. Refer back to Practice Problem 18. Assume no taxes and a stock price immediately after the dividend announcement of $100.

   a. If you own 100 shares, what is the value of your investment? How does the dividend payment affect your wealth?

   b. Now suppose that Formaggio Vecchio cancels the dividend payment and announces that it will repurchase 1% of its stock at $100. Do you rejoice or yawn? Explain.

20. The shares of A and B both sell for $100 and offer a pretax return of 10%. However, in the case of company A the return is entirely in the form of dividend yield (the company pays a regular annual dividend of $10 a share), while in the case of B the return comes entirely as capital gain (the shares appreciate by 10% a year). Suppose that dividends and capital gains are both taxed at 30%. What is the after-tax return on share A? What is the after-tax return on share B to an investor who sells after two years? What about an investor who sells after 10 years?

21. **a.** The Horner Pie Company pays a quarterly dividend of $1. Suppose that the stock price is expected to fall on the ex-dividend date by $.90. Would you prefer to buy on the with-dividend date or the ex-dividend date if you were (i) a tax-free investor, (ii) an investor with a marginal tax rate of 40% on income and 16% on capital gains?

b. In a study of ex-dividend behavior, Elton and Gruber[48] estimated that the stock price fell on the average by 85% of the dividend. Assuming that the tax rate on capital gains was 40% of the rate on income tax, what did Elton and Gruber's result imply about investors' marginal rate of income tax?

c. Elton and Gruber also observed that the ex-dividend price fall was different for high-payout stocks and for low-payout stocks. Which group would you expect to show the larger price fall as a proportion of the dividend?

d. Would the fact that investors can trade stocks freely around the ex-dividend date alter your interpretation of Elton and Gruber's study?

e. Suppose Elton and Gruber repeat their tests for 2007, when the tax rate was the same on dividends and capital gains. How would you expect their results to change?

22. The middle-of-the-road party holds that dividend policy doesn't matter because the *supply* of high-, medium-, and low-payout stocks has already adjusted to satisfy investors' demands. Investors who like generous dividends hold stocks that give them all the dividends that they want. Investors who want capital gains see ample low-payout stocks to choose from. Thus, high-payout firms cannot gain by transforming to low-payout firms, or vice versa.

Suppose the government reduces the tax rate on dividends but not on capital gains. Suppose that before this change the supply of dividends matched investor needs. How would you expect the tax change to affect the total cash dividends paid by U.S. corporations and the proportion of high- versus low-payout companies? Would dividend policy still be irrelevant after any dividend supply adjustments are completed? Explain.

CHALLENGE QUESTIONS

23. Consider the following two statements: "Dividend policy is irrelevant," and "Stock price is the present value of expected future dividends." (See Chapter 5.) They *sound* contradictory. This question is designed to show that they are fully consistent.

The current price of the shares of Charles River Mining Corporation is $50. Next year's earnings and dividends per share are $4 and $2, respectively. Investors expect perpetual growth at 8% per year. The expected rate of return demanded by investors is $r = 12\%$.

We can use the perpetual-growth model to calculate stock price:

$$P_0 = \frac{DIV}{r - g} = \frac{2}{.12 - .08} = 50$$

Suppose that Charles River Mining announces that it will switch to a 100% payout policy, issuing shares as necessary to finance growth. Use the perpetual-growth model to show that current stock price is unchanged.

---

[48] E. J. Elton and M. J. Gruber, "Marginal Stockholders' Tax Rates and the Clientele Effect," *Review of Economics and Statistics* 52 (1970), pp. 68–74.

24. "If a company pays a dividend, the investor is liable for tax on the total value of the dividend. If instead the company distributes the cash by stock repurchase, the investor is liable for tax only on any capital gain rather than on the entire amount. Therefore, even if the tax rates on dividend income and capital gains are the same, stock repurchase is always preferable to a dividend payment." Explain with a simple example why this is not the case. (*Hint:* Ignore the fact that capital gains may be postponed.)

25. Adherents of the "dividends-are-good" school sometimes point to the fact that stocks with high yields tend to have above-average price–earnings multiples. Is this evidence convincing? Discuss.

26. Suppose that there are just three types of investors with the following tax rates:

	Individuals	Corporations	Institutions
Dividends	50%	5%	0%
Capital gains	15	35	0

Individuals invest a total of $80 billion in stock and corporations invest $10 billion. The remaining stock is held by the institutions. All three groups simply seek to maximize their after-tax income.

These investors can choose from three types of stock offering the following pretax payouts:

	Low Payout	Medium Payout	High Payout
Dividends	$ 5	$5	$30
Capital gains	15	5	0

These payoffs are expected to persist in perpetuity. The low-payout stocks have a total market value of $100 billion, the medium-payout stocks have a value of $50 billion, and the high-payout stocks have a value of $120 billion.

a. Who are the marginal investors that determine the prices of the stocks?

b. Suppose that this marginal group of investors requires a 12% after-tax return. What are the prices of the low-, medium-, and high-payout stocks?

c. Calculate the after-tax returns of the three types of stock for each investor group.

d. What are the dollar amounts of the three types of stock held by each investor group?

CHAPTER FOURTEEN

DOES DEBT POLICY MATTER?

A FIRM'S BASIC resource is the stream of cash flows produced by its assets. When the firm is financed entirely by common stock, all those cash flows belong to the stockholders. When it issues both debt and equity securities, it splits the cash flows into two streams, a relatively safe stream that goes to the debtholders and a riskier stream that goes to the stockholders.

The firm's mix of debt and equity financing is called its **capital structure.** Of course capital structure is not just "debt versus equity." There are many different flavors of debt, at least two flavors of equity (common versus preferred), plus hybrids such as convertible bonds. The firm can issue dozens of distinct securities in countless combinations. It attempts to find the particular combination that maximizes the overall market value of the firm.

Are such attempts worthwhile? We must consider the possibility that *no* combination has any greater appeal than any other. Perhaps the really important decisions concern the company's assets, and decisions about capital structure are mere details—matters to be attended to but not worried about.

Modigliani and Miller (MM), who showed that payout policy doesn't matter in perfect capital markets, also showed that financing decisions don't matter in perfect markets. Their famous "proposi-

tion 1" states that a firm cannot change the total value of its securities just by splitting its cash flows into different streams: The firm's value is determined by its real assets, not by the securities it issues. Thus capital structure is irrelevant as long as the firm's investment decisions are taken as given.

MM's proposition 1 allows complete separation of investment and financing decisions. It implies that any firm could use the capital budgeting procedures presented in Chapters 6 through 11 without worrying about where the money for capital expenditures comes from. In those chapters, we assumed all-equity financing without really thinking about it. If MM are right, that is exactly the right approach. If the firm uses a mix of debt and equity financing, its overall cost of capital will be exactly the same as its cost of equity with all-equity financing.

We believe that in practice capital structure does matter, but we nevertheless devote all of this chapter to MM's argument. If you don't fully understand the conditions under which MM's theory holds, you won't fully understand why one capital structure is better than another. The financial manager needs to know what kinds of market imperfection to look for.

For example, the firm may invent some new security that a particular clientele of investors is willing to buy at a premium price, thereby increasing the overall market value of the firm. (We will argue, however, that such financial innovations are easily copied and that any gains in value will be confined to the first few issuers.)

In Chapter 15 we undertake a detailed analysis of the imperfections that are most likely to make a difference, including taxes, the costs of bankruptcy and financial distress, the costs of writing and enforcing complicated debt contracts, differences created by imperfect information, and the effects of debt on incentives for management. In Chapter 16 we show how such imperfections (especially taxes) affect the weighted-average cost of capital and the value of the firm.

14.1 THE EFFECT OF FINANCIAL LEVERAGE IN A COMPETITIVE TAX-FREE ECONOMY

Financial managers try to find the combination of securities that has the greatest overall appeal to investors—the combination that maximizes the market value of the firm. Before tackling this problem, we should check whether a policy that maximizes firm value also maximizes the wealth of the shareholders.

Let D and E denote the market values of the outstanding debt and equity of the Wapshot Mining Company. Wapshot's 1,000 shares sell for $50 apiece. Thus

$$E = 1,000 \times 50 = \$50,000$$

Wapshot has also borrowed $25,000, and so V, the aggregate market value of all Wapshot's outstanding securities, is

$$V = D + E = \$75,000$$

Wapshot's stock is known as *levered equity.* Its stockholders face the benefits and costs of **financial leverage,** or *gearing.* Suppose that Wapshot "levers up" still further by borrowing an additional $10,000 and paying the proceeds out to shareholders as a special dividend of $10 per share. This substitutes debt for equity capital with no impact on Wapshot's assets.

What will Wapshot's equity be worth after the special dividend is paid? We have two unknowns, E and V:

Old debt	$25,000	$35,000 = D
New debt	$10,000	
Equity		? = E
Firm value		? = V

If V is $75,000 as before, then E must be $V - D = 75,000 - 35,000 = \$40,000$. Stockholders have suffered a capital loss that exactly offsets the $10,000 special dividend. But if V *increases* to, say, $80,000 as a result of the change in capital structure, then $E = \$45,000$ and the stockholders are $5,000 ahead. In general, any increase or decrease in V caused by a shift in capital structure accrues to the firm's stockholders. We conclude that a policy that maximizes the market value of the firm is also best for the firm's stockholders.

This conclusion rests on two important assumptions: first, that Wapshot can ignore payout policy and, second, that after the change in capital structure the old and new debt is *worth* $35,000.

Payout policy may or may not be relevant, but there is no need to repeat the discussion of Chapter 13. We need only note that shifts in capital structure sometimes force important decisions about payout policy. Perhaps Wapshot's cash dividend has costs or benefits that should be considered in addition to any benefits achieved by its increased financial leverage.

Our second assumption that old and new debt ends up worth $35,000 seems innocuous. But it could be wrong. Perhaps the new borrowing has increased the risk of the old bonds. If the holders of old bonds cannot demand a higher rate of interest to compensate for the increased risk, the value of their investment is reduced. In this case Wapshot's stockholders gain at the expense of the holders of old bonds even though the overall value of the firm is unchanged.

But this anticipates issues better left to Chapter 15. In this chapter we will assume that any issue of debt has no effect on the market value of existing debt.

Enter Modigliani and Miller

Let us accept that the financial manager would like to find the combination of securities that maximizes the value of the firm. How is this done? MM's answer is that the financial manager should stop worrying: In a perfect market any combination of securities is as good as another. The value of the firm is unaffected by its choice of capital structure.[1]

You can see this by imagining two firms that generate the same stream of operating income and differ only in their capital structure. Firm U is unlevered. Therefore the total value of its equity E_U is the same as the total value of the firm V_U. Firm, L, on the other hand, is levered. The value of its stock is, therefore, equal to the value of the firm less the value of the debt: $E_L = V_L - D_L$.

Now think which of these firms you would prefer to invest in. If you don't want to take much risk, you can buy common stock in the unlevered firm U. For example, if you buy 1% of firm U's shares, your investment is $.01V_U$ and you are entitled to 1% of the gross profits:

Dollar Investment	Dollar Return
$.01V_U$	$.01 \times$ Profits

Now compare this with an alternative strategy. This is to purchase the same fraction of *both* the debt and the equity of firm L. Your investment and return would then be as follows:

	Dollar Investment	Dollar Return
Debt	$.01D_L$	$.01 \times$ Interest
Equity	$.01E_L$	$.01 \times$ (Profits $-$ interest)
Total	$.01(D_L + E_L)$	$.01 \times$ Profits
	$= .01V_L$	

[1] F. Modigliani and M. H. Miller, "The Cost of Capital, Corporation Finance and the Theory of Investment," *American Economic Review* 48 (June 1958), pp. 261–297. MM's basic argument was anticipated in 1938 by J. B. Williams and to some extent by David Durand. See J. B. Williams, *The Theory of Investment Value* (Cambridge, MA: Harvard University Press, 1938) and D. Durand, "Cost of Debt and Equity Funds for Business: Trends and Problems of Measurement," in *Conference on Research in Business Finance,* National Bureau of Economic Research, New York, 1952.

Both strategies offer the same payoff: 1% of the firm's profits. The law of one price tells us that in well-functioning markets two investments that offer the same payoff must have the same price. Therefore, $.01V_U$ must equal $.01V_L$: The value of the unlevered firm must equal the value of the levered firm.

Suppose that you are willing to run a little more risk. You decide to buy 1% of the outstanding shares in the *levered* firm. Your investment and return are now as follows:

Dollar Investment	Dollar Return
$.01E_L$ $= .01(V_L - D_L)$	$.01 \times (\text{Profits} - \text{interest})$

But there is an alternative strategy. This is to borrow $.01D_L$ on your own account and purchase 1% of the stock of the *unlevered* firm. In this case, your borrowing gives you an immediate cash *inflow* of $.01D_L$, but you have to pay interest on your loan equal to 1% of the interest that is paid by firm L. Your total investment and return are, therefore, as follows:

	Dollar Investment	Dollar Return
Borrowing	$-.01D_L$	$-.01 \times \text{Interest}$
Equity	$.01V_U$	$.01 \times \text{Profits}$
Total	$.01(V_U - D_L)$	$.01 \times (\text{Profits} - \text{interest})$

Again both strategies offer the same payoff: 1% of profits after interest. Therefore, both investments must have the same cost. The payoff $.01(V_U - D_L)$ must equal $.01(V_L - D_L)$ and V_U must equal V_L.

It does not matter whether the world is full of risk-averse chickens or venturesome lions. All would agree that the value of the unlevered firm U must be equal to the value of the levered firm L. As long as investors can borrow or lend on their own account on the same terms as the firm, they can "undo" the effect of any changes in the firm's capital structure. This is the basis for MM's famous proposition 1: "The market value of any firm is independent of its capital structure."

The Law of Conservation of Value

MM's argument that debt policy is irrelevant is an application of an astonishingly simple idea. If we have two streams of cash flow, A and B, then the present value of A + B is equal to the present value of A plus the present value of B. We met this principle of *value additivity* in our discussion of capital budgeting, where we saw that the present value of two assets combined is equal to the sum of their present values considered separately.

In the present context we are not combining assets but splitting them up. But value additivity works just as well in reverse. We can slice a cash flow into as many parts as we like; the values of the parts will always sum back to the value of the unsliced stream. (Of course, we have to make sure that none of the stream is lost in the slicing. We cannot say, "The value of a pie is independent of how it is sliced," if the slicer is also a nibbler.)

This is really a *law of conservation of value.* The value of an asset is preserved regardless of the nature of the claims against it. Thus proposition 1: Firm value is determined on the *left-hand* side of the balance sheet by real assets—not by the proportions of debt and equity securities issued to buy the assets.

The simplest ideas often have the widest application. For example, we could apply the law of conservation of value to the choice between issuing preferred stock, common stock, or some combination. The law implies that the choice is irrelevant, assuming perfect capital markets and providing that the choice does not affect the firm's investment, borrowing, and operating policies. If the total value of the equity "pie" (preferred and common combined) is fixed, the firm's owners (its common stockholders) do not care how this pie is sliced.

The law also applies to the *mix* of debt securities issued by the firm. The choices of long-term versus short-term, secured versus unsecured, senior versus subordinated, and convertible versus nonconvertible debt all should have no effect on the overall value of the firm.

Combining assets and splitting them up will not affect values as long as they do not affect an investor's choice. When we showed that capital structure does not affect choice, we implicitly assumed that both companies and individuals can borrow and lend at the same risk-free rate of interest. As long as this is so, individuals can undo the effect of any changes in the firm's capital structure.

In practice corporate debt is not risk-free and firms cannot escape with rates of interest appropriate to a government security. Some people's initial reaction is that this alone invalidates MM's proposition. It is a natural mistake, but capital structure can be irrelevant even when debt is risky.

If a company borrows money, it does not *guarantee* repayment: It repays the debt in full only if its assets are worth more than the debt obligation. The shareholders in the company, therefore, have limited liability.

Many individuals would like to borrow with limited liability. They might, therefore, be prepared to pay a small premium for levered shares *if the supply of levered shares were insufficient to meet their needs.*[2] But there are literally thousands of common stocks of companies that borrow. Therefore it is unlikely that an issue of debt would induce them to pay a premium for *your* shares.[3]

An Example of Proposition 1

Macbeth Spot Removers is reviewing its capital structure. Table 14.1 shows its current position. The company has no leverage and all the operating income is paid as dividends to the common stockholders (we assume still that there are no taxes). The expected earnings and dividends per share are $1.50, but this figure is by no means certain—it could turn out to be more or less than $1.50. The price of each share is $10. Since the firm expects to produce a level stream of earnings in perpetuity, the expected return on the share is equal to the earnings–price ratio, $1.50/10.00 = .15$, or 15%.

---

[2] Of course, individuals could *create* limited liability if they chose. In other words, the lender could agree that borrowers need repay their debt in full only if the assets of company X are worth more than a certain amount. Presumably individuals don't enter into such arrangements because they can obtain limited liability more simply by investing in the stocks of levered companies.

[3] Capital structure is also irrelevant if each investor holds a fully diversified portfolio. In that case he or she owns *all* the risky securities offered by a company (both debt and equity). But anybody who owns *all* the risky securities doesn't care about how the cash flows are divided among different securities.

Data				
Number of shares	1,000			
Price per share	$10			
Market value of shares	$10,000			
			Outcomes	
Operating income ($)	500	1,000	**1,500**	2,000
Earnings per share ($)	.50	1.00	**1.50**	2.00
Return on shares (%)	5	10	**15**	20
			Expected outcome	

TABLE 14.1

Macbeth Spot Removers is entirely equity-financed. Although it expects to have an income of $1,500 a year in perpetuity, this income is not certain. This table shows the return to the stockholder under different assumptions about operating income. We assume no taxes.

Data				
Number of shares	500			
Price per share	$10			
Market value of shares	$5,000			
Market value of debt	$5,000			
Interest at 10%	$500			
			Outcomes	
Operating income ($)	500	1,000	**1,500**	2,000
Interest ($)	500	500	**500**	500
Equity earnings ($)	0	500	**1,000**	1,500
Earnings per share ($)	0	1	**2**	3
Return on shares (%)	0	10	**20**	30
			Expected outcome	

TABLE 14.2

Macbeth Spot Removers is wondering whether to issue $5,000 of debt at an interest rate of 10% and repurchase 500 shares. This table shows the return to the shareholder under different assumptions about operating income.

Ms. Macbeth, the firm's president, has come to the conclusion that shareholders would be better off if the company had equal proportions of debt and equity. She therefore proposes to issue $5,000 of debt at an interest rate of 10% and use the proceeds to repurchase 500 shares. To support her proposal, Ms. Macbeth has analyzed the situation under different assumptions about operating income. The results of her calculations are shown in Table 14.2.

In order to see more clearly how leverage would affect earnings per share, Ms. Macbeth has also produced Figure 14.1. The maroon line shows how earnings per share would vary with operating income under the firm's current all-equity financing. It is, therefore, simply a plot of the data in Table 14.1. The blue line shows how earnings per share would vary given equal proportions of debt and equity. It is, therefore, a plot of the data in Table 14.2.

Ms. Macbeth reasons as follows: "It is clear that the effect of leverage depends on the company's income. If income is greater than $1,000, the return to the equity-holder is *increased* by leverage. If it is less than $1,000, the return is *reduced* by leverage. The return is unaffected when operating income is exactly $1,000. At this point the return on the market value of the assets is 10%, which is exactly equal to the interest rate on the debt. Our capital structure decision, therefore, boils down

FIGURE 14.1

Borrowing increases Macbeth's EPS (earnings per share) when operating income is greater than $1,000 and reduces EPS when operating income is less than $1,000. Expected EPS rises from $1.50 to $2.

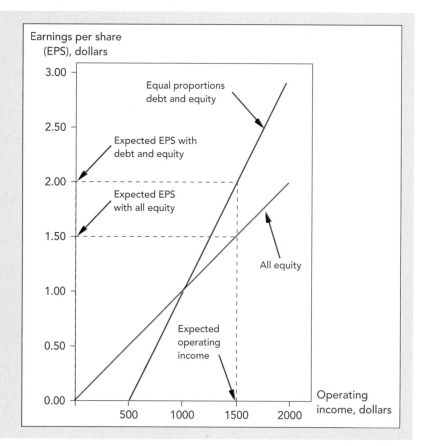

TABLE 14.3

Individual investors can replicate Macbeth's leverage.

	Operating Income ($)			
	500	**1,000**	**1,500**	**2,000**
Earnings on two shares ($)	1	2	**3**	4
Less interest at 10% ($)	1	1	**1**	1
Net earnings on investment ($)	0	1	**2**	3
Return on $10 investment (%)	0	10	**20**	30
			Expected outcome	

to what we think about income prospects. Since we expect operating income to be above the $1,000 break-even point, I believe we can best help our shareholders by going ahead with the $5,000 debt issue."

As financial manager of Macbeth Spot Removers, you reply as follows: "I agree that leverage will help the shareholder as long as our income is greater than $1,000. But your argument ignores the fact that Macbeth's shareholders have the alternative of borrowing on their own account. For example, suppose that an investor borrows $10 and then invests $20 in two unlevered Macbeth shares. This person has to put up only $10 of his or her own money. The payoff on the investment varies with Macbeth's operating income, as shown in Table 14.3. This is exactly the same set of payoffs as the investor would get by buying one share in the levered company. (Compare the last two lines of Tables 14.2 and 14.3.) Therefore, a share in the levered company must also sell for $10. If Macbeth goes ahead and borrows, it will not allow investors to do anything that they could not do already, and so it will not increase value."

The argument that you are using is exactly the same as the one MM used to prove proposition 1.

14.2 FINANCIAL RISK AND EXPECTED RETURNS

Consider now the implications of MM's proposition 1 for the expected returns on Macbeth stock:

	Current Structure: All Equity	Proposed Structure: Equal Debt and Equity
Expected earnings per share ($)	1.50	2.00
Price per share ($)	10	10
Expected return on share (%)	15	20

Leverage increases the expected stream of earnings per share but *not* the share price. The reason is that the change in the expected earnings stream is exactly offset by a change in the rate at which the earnings are discounted. The expected return on the share (which for a perpetuity is equal to the earnings–price ratio) increases from 15% to 20%. We now show how this comes about.

The expected return on Macbeth's assets r_A is equal to the expected operating income divided by the total market value of the firm's securities:

$$\text{Expected return on assets} = r_A = \frac{\text{expected operating income}}{\text{market value of all securities}}$$

We have seen that in perfect capital markets the company's borrowing decision does not affect *either* the firm's operating income *or* the total market value of its securities. Therefore the borrowing decision also does not affect the expected return on the firm's assets r_A.

Suppose that an investor holds all of a company's debt and all of its equity. This investor is entitled to all the firm's operating income; therefore, the expected return on the portfolio is just r_A.

The expected return on a portfolio is equal to a weighted average of the expected returns on the individual holdings. Therefore the expected return on a portfolio consisting of *all* the firm's securities is

Expected return on assets = (proportion in debt × expected return on debt)
   + (proportion in equity × expected return on equity)

$$r_A = \left(\frac{D}{D+E} \times r_D\right) + \left(\frac{E}{D+E} \times r_E\right)$$

This formula is of course an old friend from Chapter 10. The overall expected return r_A is called the *company cost of capital* or the *weighted-average cost of capital* (WACC).

We can turn the formula around to solve for r_E, the expected return to equity for a levered firm:

Expected return on equity = expected return on assets
$$+ \text{(expected return on assets} - \text{expected return on debt)}$$
$$\times \text{debt–equity ratio}$$

$$r_E = r_A + (r_A - r_D)\frac{D}{E}$$

Proposition 2

This is MM's proposition 2: The expected rate of return on the common stock of a levered firm increases in proportion to the debt–equity ratio (D/E), expressed in market values; the rate of increase depends on the spread between r_A, the expected rate of return on a portfolio of all the firm's securities, and r_D, the expected return on the debt. Note that $r_E = r_A$ if the firm has no debt.

We can check out this formula for Macbeth Spot Removers. Before the decision to borrow

$$r_E = r_A = \frac{\text{expected operating income}}{\text{market value of all securities}}$$

$$= \frac{1,500}{10,000} = .15, \text{ or } 15\%$$

If the firm goes ahead with its plan to borrow, the expected return on assets r_A is still 15%. The expected return on equity is

$$r_E = r_A + (r_A - r_D)\frac{D}{E}$$

$$= .15 + (.15 - .10)\frac{5,000}{5,000} = .20, \text{ or } 20\%$$

MM's proposition 1 says that financial leverage has no effect on shareholders' wealth. Proposition 2 says that the rate of return they can expect to receive on their shares increases as the firm's debt–equity ratio increases. How can shareholders be indifferent to increased leverage when it increases expected return? The answer is that any increase in expected return is exactly offset by an increase in risk and therefore in shareholders' *required* rate of return.

Look at what happens to the risk of Macbeth shares if it moves to equal debt–equity proportions. Table 14.4 shows how a shortfall in operating income affects the payoff to the shareholders.

TABLE 14.4

Financial leverage increases the risk of Macbeth shares. A $1,000 drop in operating income reduces earnings per share by $1 with all-equity financing, but by $2 with 50% debt.

If operating income falls from		$1,500	to	$500	Change
No debt:	Earnings per share	$1.50		$.50	−$1.00
	Return	15%		5%	−10%
50% debt:	Earnings per share	$2.00		0	−$2.00
	Return	20%		0	−20%

The debt–equity proportion does not affect the *dollar* risk borne by equity-holders. Suppose operating income drops from $1,500 to $500. Under all-equity financing, equity earnings drop by $1 per share. There are 1,000 outstanding shares, and so *total* equity earnings fall by $1 × 1,000 = $1,000. With 50% debt, the same drop in operating income reduces earnings per share by $2. But there are only 500 shares outstanding, and so total equity income drops by $2 × 500 = $1,000, just as in the all-equity case.

However, the debt–equity choice does amplify the spread of *percentage* returns. If the firm is all-equity-financed, a decline of $1,000 in the operating income reduces the return on the shares by 10%. If the firm issues risk-free debt with a fixed interest payment of $500 a year, then a decline of $1,000 in the operating income reduces the return on the shares by 20%. In other words, the effect of the proposed leverage is to double the amplitude of the swings in Macbeth's shares. Whatever the beta of the firm's shares before the refinancing, it would be twice as high afterward.

Now you can see why investors require higher returns on levered equity. The required return simply rises to match the increased risk.

Example Let us revisit a numerical example from Chapter 10. We looked at a company with the following market-value balance sheet:

Asset value	100	Debt (D)	30 at r_D = 7.5%
		Equity (E)	70 at r_E = 15%
Asset value	100	Firm value (V)	100

and an overall cost of capital of:

$$r_A = r_D \frac{D}{V} + r_E \frac{E}{V}$$

$$= \left(7.5 \times \frac{30}{100}\right) + \left(15 \times \frac{70}{100}\right) = 12.75\%$$

If the firm is contemplating investment in a project that has the same risk as the firm's existing business, the opportunity cost of capital for this project is the same as the firm's cost of capital; in other words, it is 12.75%.

What would happen if the firm issued an additional 10 of debt and used the cash to repurchase 10 of its equity? The revised market-value balance sheet is

Asset value	100	Debt value (D)	40
		Equity value (E)	60
Asset value	100	Firm value (V)	100

The change in financial structure does not affect the amount or risk of the cash flows on the total package of debt and equity. Therefore, if investors required a return of 12.75% on the total package before the refinancing, they must require a 12.75% return on the firm's assets afterward.

Although the required return on the *package* of debt and equity is unaffected, the change in financial structure does affect the required return on the individual securities. Since the company has more debt than before, the debtholders are likely to demand a higher interest rate. We will suppose that the expected return on the debt rises to 7.875%. Now you can write down the basic equation for the return on assets.

$$r_A = r_D \frac{D}{V} + r_E \frac{E}{V}$$

$$= \left(7.875 \times \frac{40}{100}\right) + \left(r_E \times \frac{60}{100}\right) = 12.75\%$$

and solve for the return on equity $r_E = 16.0\%$.

Increasing the amount of debt increased debtholder risk and led to a rise in the return that debtholders required (r_{debt} rose from 7.5 to 7.875%). The higher leverage also made the equity riskier and increased the return that shareholders required (r_E rose from 15% to 16%). The weighted-average return on debt and equity remained at 12.75%:

$$r_A = (r_D \times .4) + (r_E \times .6)$$

$$= (7.875 \times .4) + (16 \times .6) = 12.75\%$$

Suppose that the company decided instead to repay all its debt and to replace it with equity. In that case all the cash flows would go to the equityholders. The company cost of capital, r_A, would stay at 12.75%, and r_E would also be 12.75%.

How Changing Capital Structure Affects Beta

We have looked at how changes in financial structure affect expected return. Let us now look at the effect on beta.

The stockholders and debtholders both receive a share of the firm's cash flows, and both bear part of the risk. For example, if the firm's assets turn out to be worthless, there will be no cash to pay stockholders or debtholders. But debtholders usually bear much less risk than stockholders. Debt betas of large blue-chip firms are typically in the range of .1 to .3.

If you owned a portfolio of all the firm's securities, you wouldn't share the cash flows with anyone. You wouldn't share the risks with anyone either; you would bear them all. Thus the firm's asset beta is equal to the beta of a portfolio of all the firm's debt and its equity.

The beta of this hypothetical portfolio is just a weighted average of the debt and equity betas:

$$\beta_A = \beta_{\text{portfolio}} = \beta_D \frac{D}{V} + \beta_E \frac{E}{V}$$

Think back to our example. If the debt before the refinancing has a beta of .1 and the equity has a beta of 1.1, then

$$\beta_A = (.1 \times .3) + (1.1 \times .7) = .8$$

What happens after the refinancing? The risk of the total package is unaffected, but both the debt and the equity are now more risky. Suppose that the debt beta increases to .2. We can work out the new equity beta:

$$\beta_A = \beta_{\text{portfolio}} = \beta_D \frac{D}{V} + \beta_E \frac{E}{V}$$

$$.8 = (.2 \times .4) + (\beta_E \times .6)$$

$$\beta_E = 1.2$$

You can see why borrowing is said to create financial leverage or gearing. Financial leverage does not affect the risk or the expected return on the firm's assets, but it does push up the risk of the common stock. Shareholders demand a correspondingly higher return because of this *financial risk*.

Now you can see how to *unlever* betas, that is, how to go from an observed β_E to β_A. You have the equity beta, say, 1.2. You also need the debt beta, say, .2, and the relative market values of debt (D/V) and equity (E/V). If debt accounts for 40% of overall value V,

$$\beta_A = (.2 \times .4) + (1.2 \times .6) = .8$$

This runs the previous example in reverse. Just remember the basic relationship:

$$\beta_A = \beta_{\text{portfolio}} = \beta_D\left(\frac{D}{V}\right) + \beta_E\left(\frac{E}{V}\right)$$

MM's propositions warn us that higher leverage increases both expected equity returns and equity risk. It does *not* increase shareholder value. Having worked through the example of Macbeth, this much should now seem obvious. But watch out for hidden changes in leverage, such as a decision to lease new equipment or to underfund the pension scheme. Do not interpret any resultant increase in the expected equity return as creating additional shareholder value.

14.3 THE WEIGHTED-AVERAGE COST OF CAPITAL

What did financial experts think about debt policy before MM? It is not easy to say because with hindsight we see that they did not think too clearly.[4] However, a "traditional" position emerged in response to MM. In order to understand it, we have to return to the weighted-average cost of capital.

Figure 14.2 sums up the implications of MM's propositions for the costs of debt and equity and the weighted-average cost of capital. The figure assumes that the firm's bonds are essentially risk-free at low debt levels. Thus r_D is independent of D/E, and r_E increases linearly as D/E increases. As the firm borrows more, the risk of default increases and the firm is required to pay higher rates of interest. Proposition 2 predicts that when this occurs the rate of increase in r_E slows down. This is also shown in Figure 14.2. The more debt the firm has, the less sensitive r_E is to further borrowing.

Why does the slope of the r_E line in Figure 14.2 taper off as D/E increases? Essentially because holders of risky debt bear some of the firm's business risk. As the firm borrows more, more of that risk is transferred from stockholders to bondholders.

Two Warnings

Sometimes the objective in financing decisions is stated not as "maximize overall market value" but as "minimize the weighted-average cost of capital." If MM's proposition 1 holds, then these are equivalent objectives. If MM's proposition 1 does *not* hold, then the capital structure that maximizes the value of the firm also minimizes

---

[4] Financial economists in 20 years may remark on Brealey, Myers, and Allen's blind spots and clumsy reasoning. On the other hand, they may not remember us at all.

FIGURE 14.2

MM's proposition 2. The expected return on equity r_E increases linearly with the debt–equity ratio so long as debt is risk-free. But if leverage increases the risk of the debt, debtholders demand a higher return on the debt. This causes the rate of increase in r_E to slow down.

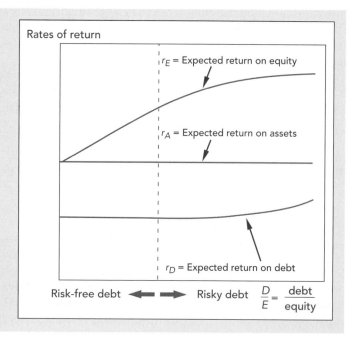

the weighted-average cost of capital, *provided* that operating income is independent of capital structure. Remember that the weighted-average cost of capital is the expected rate of return on the market value of all of the firm's securities. Anything that increases the value of the firm reduces the weighted-average cost of capital if operating income is constant. But if operating income is varying too, all bets are off.

In Chapter 15 we will show that financial leverage can affect operating income in several ways. Therefore maximizing the value of the firm is *not* always equivalent to minimizing the weighted-average cost of capital.

Warning 1   Shareholders want management to increase the firm's value. They are more interested in being rich than in owning a firm with a low weighted-average cost of capital.

Warning 2   Trying to minimize the weighted-average cost of capital seems to encourage logical short circuits like the following. Suppose that someone says, "Shareholders demand—and deserve—higher expected rates of return than bondholders do. Therefore debt is the cheaper capital source. We can reduce the weighted-average cost of capital by borrowing more." But this doesn't follow if the extra borrowing leads stockholders to demand a still higher expected rate of return. According to MM's proposition 2 the cost of equity capital r_E increases by just enough to keep the weighted-average cost of capital constant.

This is not the only logical short circuit you are likely to encounter. We have cited two more in Practice Problem 15 at the end of this chapter.

Rates of Return on Levered Equity—The Traditional Position

You may ask why we have even mentioned the aim of minimizing the weighted-average cost of capital if it is often wrong or confusing. We had to because the traditionalists accept this objective and argue their case in terms of it.

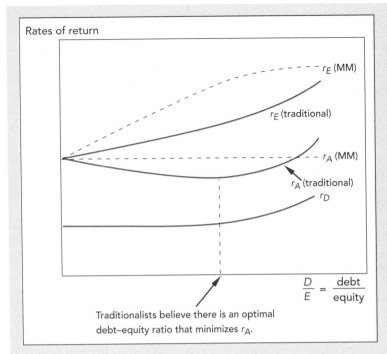

FIGURE 14.3

The dashed lines show MM's view of the effect of leverage on the expected return on equity r_E and the weighted-average cost of capital r_A. (See Figure 14.2.) The solid lines show the traditional view. Traditionalists say that borrowing at first increases r_E more slowly than MM predict but that r_E shoots up with excessive borrowing. If so, the weighted-average cost of capital can be minimized if you use just the right amount of debt.

The logical short circuit we just described rested on the assumption that r_E, the expected rate of return demanded by stockholders, does not rise, or rises very slowly, as the firm borrows more. Suppose, just for the sake of argument, that this is true. Then r_A, the weighted-average cost of capital, must decline as the debt–equity ratio rises.

The traditionalists' position is shown in Figure 14.3. They say that a moderate degree of financial leverage may increase the expected equity return r_E, but not as much as predicted by MM's proposition 2. But irresponsible firms that borrow *excessively* find r_E shooting up *faster* than MM predict. Therefore the weighted-average cost of capital declines at first, then rises. It reaches a minimum at some intermediate debt ratio. Remember that minimizing the weighted-average cost of capital is equivalent to maximizing firm value if operating income is not affected by borrowing.

Two arguments could be advanced in support of this position. First, perhaps investors do not notice or appreciate the financial risk created by moderate borrowing, although they wake up when debt is "excessive." If so, stockholders in moderately leveraged firms may accept a lower rate of return than they really should.

That seems naive.[5] The second argument is better. It accepts MM's reasoning as applied to perfect capital markets but holds that actual markets are imperfect. Imperfections may allow firms that borrow to provide a valuable service for investors. If so, levered shares might trade at premium prices compared to their theoretical values in perfect markets.

---

[5] This first argument may reflect a confusion between financial risk and the risk of default. Default is not a serious threat when borrowing is moderate; stockholders worry about it only when the firm goes "too far." But stockholders bear financial risk—in the form of increased volatility of rate of return and higher beta—even when the chance of default is nil.

Suppose that corporations can borrow more cheaply than individuals. Then it would pay investors who want to borrow to do so indirectly by holding the stock of levered firms. They would be willing to live with expected rates of return that do not fully compensate them for the business and financial risk they bear.

Is corporate borrowing really cheaper? It's hard to say. Interest rates on home mortgages are not too different from rates on high-grade corporate bonds.[6] Rates on margin debt (borrowing from a stockbroker with the investor's shares tendered as security) are not too different from the rates firms pay banks for short-term loans.

There are some individuals who face relatively high interest rates, largely because of the costs lenders incur in making and servicing small loans. There are economies of scale in borrowing. A group of small investors could do better by borrowing via a corporation, in effect pooling their loans and saving transaction costs.[7]

But suppose that this class of investors is large, both in number and in the aggregate wealth it brings to capital markets. That creates a clientele for whom corporate borrowing is better than personal borrowing. That clientele would, in principle, be willing to pay a premium for the shares of a levered firm.

But maybe it doesn't *have* to pay a premium. Perhaps smart financial managers long ago recognized this clientele and shifted the capital structures of their firms to meet its needs. The shifts would not have been difficult or costly to make. But if the clientele is now satisfied, it no longer needs to pay a premium for levered shares. Only the financial managers who *first* recognized the clientele extracted any advantage from it.

Maybe the market for corporate leverage is like the market for automobiles. Americans need millions of automobiles and are willing to pay thousands of dollars apiece for them. But that doesn't mean that you could strike it rich by going into the automobile business. You're at least 80 years too late.

Today's Unsatisfied Clienteles Are Probably Interested in Exotic Securities

So far we have made little progress in identifying cases where firm value might plausibly depend on financing. But our examples illustrate what smart financial managers look for. They look for an *unsatisfied* clientele, investors who want a particular kind of financial instrument but because of market imperfections can't get it or can't get it cheaply.

MM's proposition 1 is violated when the firm, by imaginative design of its capital structure, can offer some *financial service* that meets the needs of such a clientele. Either the service must be new and unique or the firm must find a way to provide some old service more cheaply than other firms or financial intermediaries can.

Now, is there an unsatisfied clientele for garden-variety debt or levered equity? We doubt it. But perhaps you can invent an exotic security and uncover a latent demand for it.

In the next several chapters we will encounter a number of new securities that have been invented by companies and advisers. These securities take the company's

---

[6] One of the authors once obtained a home mortgage at a rate 1/2 percentage point *less* than the contemporaneous yield on long-term AAA bonds.

[7] Even here there are alternatives to borrowing on personal account. Investors can draw down their savings accounts or sell a portion of their investment in bonds. The impact of reductions in lending on the investor's balance sheet and risk position is exactly the same as increases in borrowing.

basic cash flows and repackage them in ways that are thought to be more attractive to investors. However, while inventing these new securities is easy, it is more difficult to find investors who will rush to buy them.

Imperfections and Opportunities

The most serious capital market imperfections are often those created by government. An imperfection that supports a violation of MM's proposition 1 *also* creates a money-making opportunity. Firms and intermediaries will find some way to reach the clientele of investors frustrated by the imperfection.

For many years the U.S. government imposed a limit on the rate of interest that could be paid on savings accounts. It did so to protect savings institutions by limiting competition for their depositors' money. The fear was that depositors would run off in search of higher yields, causing a cash drain that savings institutions would not be able to meet.

These regulations created an opportunity for firms and financial institutions to design new savings schemes that were not subject to the interest-rate ceilings. One invention was the *floating-rate note*, first issued in 1974 by Citicorp, and with terms designed to appeal to individual investors. Floating-rate notes are medium-term debt securities whose interest payments "float" with short-term interest rates. On the Citicorp issue, for example, the coupon rate used to calculate each semiannual interest payment was set at 1 percentage point above the contemporaneous yield on Treasury bills. The holder of the Citicorp note was therefore protected against fluctuating interest rates, because Citicorp sent a larger check when interest rates rose (and, of course, a smaller check when rates fell).

Citicorp evidently found an untapped clientele of investors, for it was able to raise $650 million in the first offering. The success of the issue suggests that Citicorp was able to add value by changing its capital structure. However, other companies were quick to jump on Citicorp's bandwagon, and within five months an additional $650 million of floating-rate notes were issued by other companies. By the mid-1980s about $43 billion of floating-rate securities were outstanding, and now floating-rate debt securities seem ubiquitous.

Interest-rate regulation also provided financial institutions with an opportunity to create value by offering money-market funds. These are mutual funds invested in Treasury bills, commercial paper, and other high-grade, short-term debt instruments. Any saver with a few thousand dollars to invest can gain access to these instruments through a money-market fund and can withdraw money at any time by writing a check against his or her fund balance. Thus the fund resembles a checking or savings account that pays close to market interest rates.[8] These money-market funds have become enormously popular. By 2006, their assets had increased to $2 trillion.

Long before interest-rate ceilings were finally removed, most of the gains had gone out of issuing the new securities to individual investors. Once the clientele was finally satisfied, MM's proposition 1 was restored (until the government creates a new imperfection). The moral of the story is this: If you ever find an unsatisfied clientele, do something right away, or capital markets will evolve and steal it from you.

---

[8] Money-market funds offer rates slightly lower than those on the securities they invest in. This spread covers the fund's operating costs and profits.

This is actually an encouraging message for the economy as a whole. If MM are right, investors' demands for different types of securities are satisfied at minimal cost. The cost of capital will reflect only business risk. Capital will flow to companies with positive-NPV investments, regardless of the companies' capital structures. This is the efficient outcome.

14.4   A FINAL WORD ON THE AFTER-TAX WEIGHTED-AVERAGE COST OF CAPITAL

MM left us a simple message. When the firm changes its mix of debt and equity securities, the risk and expected returns of these securities change, but the company's overall cost of capital does not change.

Now if you think that message is too neat and simple, you're right. The complications are spelled out in the next two chapters. But we must note one complication here: Interest paid on a firm's borrowing can be deducted from taxable income. Thus the *after-tax* cost of debt is $r_D(1 - T_c)$, where T_c is the marginal corporate tax rate. When companies discount an average-risk project, they do not use the company cost of capital as we have computed it. They use the after-tax cost of debt to compute the after-tax weighted-average cost of capital or WACC:

$$\text{After-tax WACC} = r_D(1 - T_c)\frac{D}{V} + r_E\frac{E}{V}$$

Union Pacific's WACC

We already have two estimates of Union Pacific's cost of equity: a discounted-cash-flow estimate of 14.6% from Section 5.3, and an estimate from the capital asset pricing model of 9.9% from Section 10.2. Let's compromise with $r_E = 12\%$.[9] Union Pacific's long-term borrowing rate was $r_D = 6\%$. The company's capital structure, using market values of debt and equity, was:[10]

Debt (D)	$ 6.7 billion	at $r_D = $ 6.0%
Equity (E)	26.2	at $r_E = $ 12.0%
Firm value (V)	$32.9 billion	

The market-value debt ratio is $D/V = 6.7/32.9 = .20$ and the equity ratio is $E/V = .80$. We will assume that Union Pacific's marginal tax rate is the statutory rate of $T_C = .35$. Therefore the after-tax cost of debt is $.06 \times (1 - .35) = .039$, and the after-tax WACC is

$$\text{After-tax WACC} = .06 \times (1 - .35) \times .20 + .12 \times .80 = .104, \text{ or } 10.4\%$$

---

[9] The difference between the DCF and CAPM estimates is, admittedly, unusually large. We noted in Section 5.3 that the DCF figure may be an overestimate because of the high growth rates in cash flows assumed in the calculations.

[10] U.S. Surface Transportation Board, "Railroad Cost of Capital – 2002," June 19, 2003. Union Pacific issued several different types of debt, plus long-term lease financing and preferred stock. For simplicity we have lumped all these sources of financing into one number for total debt. Chapter 16 explains how to calculate WACC when preferred stock or other financing sources are treated separately.

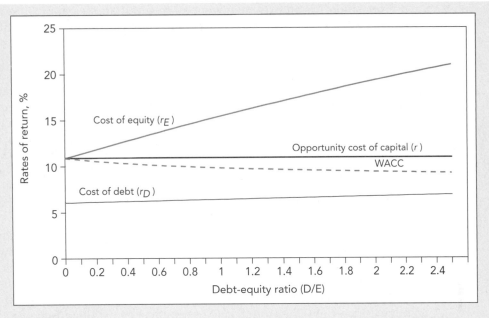

FIGURE 14.4

Estimated after-tax WACC for Union Pacific at different debt–equity ratios. The figure assumes $r_E = 12.0\%$ at a 20% debt ratio and a borrowing rate of $r_D = 6.0\%$. Notice that the debt interest rate is assumed to increase with the debt–equity ratio.

Figure 14.4 shows how the after-tax WACC falls as debt increases. In this example it falls *only* because debt interest is tax-deductible. Note that the opportunity cost of capital r is still plotted as a straight horizontal line.

SUMMARY

Think of the financial manager as taking all of the firm's real assets and selling them to investors as a package of securities. Some financial managers choose the simplest package possible: all-equity financing. Some end up issuing dozens of debt and equity securities. The problem is to find the particular combination that maximizes the market value of the firm.

Modigliani and Miller's (MM's) famous proposition 1 states that no combination is better than any other—that the firm's overall market value (the value of all its securities) is independent of capital structure. Firms that borrow do offer investors a more complex menu of securities, but investors yawn in response. The menu is redundant. Any shift in capital structure can be duplicated or "undone" by investors. Why should they pay extra for borrowing indirectly (by holding shares in a levered firm) when they can borrow just as easily and cheaply on their own accounts?

MM agree that borrowing increases the expected rate of return on shareholders' investments. But it also increases the risk of the firm's shares. MM show that the risk increase exactly offsets the increase in expected return, leaving stockholders no better or worse off.

Proposition 1 is an extremely general result. It applies not just to the debt–equity trade-off but to *any* choice of financing instruments. For example, MM would say that the choice between long-term and short-term debt has no effect on firm value.

The formal proofs of proposition 1 all depend on the assumption of perfect capital markets. MM's opponents, the "traditionalists," argue that market imperfections make personal borrowing excessively costly, risky, and inconvenient for some investors. This creates a natural clientele willing to pay a premium for shares of levered firms. The traditionalists say that firms should borrow to realize the premium.

But this argument is incomplete. There may be a clientele for levered equity, but that is not enough; the clientele has to be *unsatisfied.* There are already thousands of levered firms available for investment. Is there still an unsatiated clientele for garden-variety debt and equity? We doubt it.

Proposition 1 is violated when financial managers find an untapped demand and satisfy it by issuing something new and different. The argument between MM and the traditionalists finally boils down to whether this is difficult or easy. We lean toward MM's view: Finding unsatisfied clienteles and designing exotic securities to meet their needs is a game that's fun to play but hard to win.

If MM are right, the overall cost of capital—the expected rate of return on a portfolio of all the firm's outstanding securities—is the same regardless of the mix of securities issued to finance the firm. The overall cost of capital is usually called the company cost of capital or the weighted-average cost of capital (WACC). MM say that WACC doesn't depend on capital structure. But MM assume away lots of complications. The first complication is taxes. When we recognize that debt interest is tax-deductible, and compute WACC with the after-tax interest rate, WACC declines as the debt ratio increases. There is more—lots more—on taxes and other complications in the next two chapters.

FURTHER READING

The pioneering work on the theory of capital structure is:

F. Modigliani and M. H. Miller, "The Cost of Capital, Corporation Finance and the Theory of Investment," *American Economic Review* 48 (June 1958), pp. 261–297.

The fall 1988 issue of the Journal of Economic Perspectives *contains an anniversary collection of articles, including one by Modigliani and Miller, which review and assess the MM propositions. The summer 1989 issue of* Financial Management *contains three more articles under the heading "Reflections on the MM Propositions 30 Years Later."*

The Winter 1992 edition of the Journal of Applied Corporate Finance *contains several interesting surveys of financial innovation. Other articles include:*

K. A. Karow, G. R. Erwin, and J. J. McConnell, "Survey of U.S. Corporate Financing Innovations: 1970–1997," *Journal of Applied Corporate Finance* 12 (Spring 1999), pp. 55–69.

P. Tufano, "Financial Innovation," in G. M. Constantinides, M. Harris, and R. Stulz (eds.), *Handbook of the Economics of Finance,* Vol 1A (Amsterdam: Elsevier/North-Holland, 2003).

Miller reviews the MM propositions in:

M. H. Miller, "The Modigliani-Miller Propositions after Thirty Years," *Journal of Applied Corporate Finance* 2 (Spring 1989), pp. 6–18.

For a skeptic's view of MM's arguments see:

S. Titman, "The Modigliani-Miller Theorem and the Integration of Financial Markets," *Financial Management* 31 (Spring 2002), pp. 101–115.

CONCEPT REVIEW QUESTIONS

1. "Financial managers try to find the combination of securities…that maximizes the market value of the firm." Why does pursuit of this goal benefit *shareholders*? (page 369)

2. MM's proposition 1 says that financing with debt instead of equity does *not* affect:

   a. The price–earnings ratio for the firm's stock.

   b. The total market value of the firm's shares (price per share × number of shares outstanding).

   c. The total market value of the firm.

   d. The beta of the firm's stock.

   e. The interest rate on the firm's debt.

   f. The cost of equity.

   g. The firm's overall (weighted-average) cost of capital.

   Which statements are correct? (pages 371–379)

3. What is *financial risk*? How does it depend on the firm's capital structure? (pages 376–379)

> **For a complete listing of your chapter Concept Review Questions, please visit us at www.mhhe.com/bma1e.**

QUIZ

1. Ms. Kraft owns 50,000 shares of the common stock of Copperhead Corporation with a market value of $2 per share, or $100,000 overall. The company is currently financed as follows:

	Book Value
Common stock (8 million shares)	$2 million
Short-term loans	$2 million

Copperhead now announces that it is replacing $1 million of short-term debt with an issue of common stock. What action can Ms. Kraft take to ensure that she is entitled to exactly the same proportion of profits as before?

2. Spam Corp. is financed entirely by common stock and has a beta of 1.0. The firm is expected to generate a level, perpetual stream of earnings and dividends. The stock has a price–earnings ratio of 8 and a cost of equity of 12.5%. The company's stock is selling for $50. Now the firm decides to repurchase half of its shares and substitute an equal value of debt. The debt is risk-free, with a 5% interest rate. The company is exempt from corporate income taxes. Assuming MM are correct, calculate the following items after the refinancing:

   a. The cost of equity.

   b. The overall cost of capital (WACC).

   c. The price–earnings ratio.

   d. The stock price.

   e. The stock's beta.

3. The common stock and debt of Northern Sludge are valued at $50 million and $30 million, respectively. Investors currently require a 16% return on the common stock and an 8% return on the debt. If Northern Sludge issues an additional $10 million of common stock and uses this money to retire debt, what happens to the expected return on the stock? Assume that the change in capital structure does not affect the risk of the debt and that there are no taxes.

4. Suppose that Macbeth Spot Removers issues only $2,500 of debt and uses the proceeds to repurchase 250 shares.

   a. Rework Table 14.2 to show how earnings per share and share return now vary with operating income.

   b. If the beta of Macbeth's assets is .8 and its debt is risk-free, what would be the beta of the equity after the debt issue?

5. True or false?

   a. MM's propositions assume perfect financial markets, with no distorting taxes or other imperfections.

   b. MM's proposition 1 says that corporate borrowing increases earnings per share but reduces the price–earnings ratio.

   c. MM's proposition 2 says that the cost of equity increases with borrowing and that the increase is proportional to D/V, the ratio of debt to firm value.

   d. MM's proposition 2 assumes that increased borrowing does not affect the interest rate on the firm's debt.

   e. Borrowing does not increase financial risk and the cost of equity if there is no risk of bankruptcy.

   f. Borrowing increases firm value if there is a clientele of investors with a reason to prefer debt.

6. Look back to Section 14.1. Suppose that Ms. Macbeth's investment bankers have informed her that since the new issue of debt is risky, debtholders will demand a return of 12.5%, which is 2.5% above the risk-free interest rate.

   a. What are r_A and r_E?

   b. Suppose that the beta of the unlevered stock was .6. What will β_A, β_E, and β_D be after the change to the capital structure?

7. Note the two blank graphs in Figure 14.5. On graph (a), assume MM are right, and plot the relationship between financial leverage (debt-equity ratio) and (i) the rates of return on debt and equity and (ii) the weighted-average cost of capital. Then fill in graph (b), assuming the traditionalists are right.

FIGURE 14.5

See Quiz Question 7.

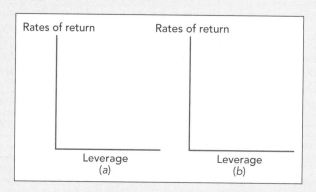

8. Gaucho Services starts life with all-equity financing and a cost of equity of 14%. Suppose it refinances to the following market-value capital structure:

Debt (D)	45%	at $r_D = 9.5\%$
Equity (E)	55%	

Use MM's proposition 2 to calculate the new cost of equity. Gaucho pays taxes at a marginal rate of $T_C = 40\%$. Calculate Gaucho's after-tax weighted-average cost of capital.

PRACTICE
QUESTIONS

9. Companies A and B differ only in their capital structure. A is financed 30% debt and 70% equity; B is financed 10% debt and 90% equity. The debt of both companies is risk-free.

   a. Rosencrantz owns 1% of the common stock of A. What other investment package would produce identical cash flows for Rosencrantz?

   b. Guildenstern owns 2% of the common stock of B. What other investment package would produce identical cash flows for Guildenstern?

   c. Show that neither Rosencrantz nor Guildenstern would invest in the common stock of B if the *total* value of company A were less than that of B.

10. Here is a limerick:

    There once was a man named Carruthers,
    Who kept cows with miraculous udders.
    He said, "Isn't this neat?
    They give cream from one teat,
    And skim milk from each of the others!"

    What is the analogy between Mr. Carruthers's cows and firms' financing decisions? What would MM's proposition 1, suitably adapted, say about the value of Mr. Carruthers's cows? Explain.

11. Executive Chalk is financed solely by common stock and has outstanding 25 million shares with a market price of $10 a share. It now announces that it intends to issue $160 million of debt and to use the proceeds to buy back common stock.

    a. How is the market price of the stock affected by the announcement?

    b. How many shares can the company buy back with the $160 million of new debt that it issues?

    c. What is the market value of the firm (equity plus debt) after the change in capital structure?

    d. What is the debt ratio after the change in structure?

    e. Who (if anyone) gains or loses?

    Now try the next question.

12. Executive Cheese has issued debt with a market value of $100 million and has outstanding 15 million shares with a market price of $10 a share. It now announces that it intends to issue a further $60 million of debt and to use the proceeds to buy back common stock. Debtholders, seeing the extra risk, mark the value of the existing debt down to $70 million.

    a. How is the market price of the stock affected by the announcement?

    b. How many shares can the company buy back with the $60 million of new debt that it issues?

c. What is the market value of the firm (equity plus debt) after the change in capital structure?

d. What is the debt ratio after the change in structure?

e. Who (if anyone) gains or loses?

13. Hubbard's Pet Foods is financed 80% by common stock and 20% by bonds. The expected return on the common stock is 12% and the rate of interest on the bonds is 6%. Assuming that the bonds are default-risk free, draw a graph that shows the expected return of Hubbard's common stock (r_E) and the expected return on the package of common stock and bonds (r_A) for different debt–equity ratios.

14. "MM totally ignore the fact that as you borrow more, you have to pay higher rates of interest." Explain carefully whether this is a valid objection.

15. Indicate what's wrong with the following arguments:

a. "As the firm borrows more and debt becomes risky, both stockholders and bond-holders demand higher rates of return. Thus by *reducing* the debt ratio we can reduce *both* the cost of debt and the cost of equity, making everybody better off."

b. "Moderate borrowing doesn't significantly affect the probability of financial distress or bankruptcy. Consequently moderate borrowing won't increase the expected rate of return demanded by stockholders."

16. Each of the following statements is false or at least misleading. Explain why in each case.

a. "A capital investment opportunity offering a 10% DCF rate of return is an attractive project if it can be 100% debt-financed at an 8% interest rate."

b. "The more debt the firm issues, the higher the interest rate it must pay. That is one important reason why firms should operate at conservative debt levels."

17. Can you invent any new kinds of debt that might be attractive to investors? Why do you think they have not been issued?

18. Imagine a firm that is expected to produce a level stream of operating profits. As leverage is increased, what happens to

a. The ratio of the market value of the equity to income after interest?

b. The ratio of the market value of the *firm* to income before interest if (i) MM are right and (ii) the traditionalists are right?

19. Archimedes Levers is financed by a mixture of debt and equity. You have the following information about its cost of capital:

$r_E =$ __	$r_D = 12\%$	$r_A =$ __
$\beta_E = 1.5$	$\beta_D =$ __	$\beta_A =$ __
$r_f = 10\%$	$r_m = 18\%$	$D/V = .5$

Can you fill in the blanks?

20. Look back to Practice Problem 19. Suppose now that Archimedes repurchases debt and issues equity so that $D/V = .3$. The reduced borrowing causes r_D to fall to 11%. How do the other variables change?

21. Omega Corporation has 10 million shares outstanding, now trading at $55 per share. The firm has estimated the expected rate of return to shareholders at about 12%. It has also issued long-term bonds at an interest rate of 7%. It pays tax at a marginal rate of 35%.

a. What is Omega's after-tax WACC?

b. How much higher would WACC be if Omega used no debt at all? (*Hint:* For this problem you can assume that the firm's overall beta (β_A) is not affected by its capital structure or the taxes saved because debt interest is tax-deductible.)

22. Gamma Airlines has an asset beta of 1.5. The risk-free interest rate is 6%, and the market risk premium is 8%. Assume the capital asset pricing model is correct. Gamma pays taxes at a marginal rate of 35%. Draw a graph plotting Gamma's cost of equity and after-tax WACC as a function of its debt-to-equity ratio D/E, from no debt to $D/E = 1.0$. Assume that Gamma's debt is risk-free up to $D/E = .25$. Then the interest rate increases to 6.5% at $D/E = .5$, 7% at $D/E = .8$, and 8% at $D/E = 1.0$. As in Practice Problem 21, you can assume that the firm's overall beta (β_A) is not affected by its capital structure or the taxes saved because debt interest is tax-deductible.

CHALLENGE QUESTIONS

23. Consider the following three tickets: ticket A pays $10 if _____ is elected as president, ticket B pays $10 if _____ is elected, and ticket C pays $10 if neither is elected. (Fill in the blanks yourself.) Could the three tickets sell for less than the present value of $10? Could they sell for more? Try auctioning off the tickets. What are the implications for MM's proposition 1?

24. People often convey the idea behind MM's proposition 1 by various supermarket analogies, for example, "The value of a pie should not depend on how it is sliced," or, "The cost of a whole chicken should equal the cost of assembling one by buying two drumsticks, two wings, two breasts, and so on."

    Actually proposition 1 doesn't work in the supermarket. You'll pay less for an uncut whole pie than for a pie assembled from pieces purchased separately. Supermarkets charge more for chickens after they are cut up. Why? What costs or imperfections cause proposition 1 to fail in the supermarket? Are these costs or imperfections likely to be important for corporations issuing securities on the U.S. or world capital markets? Explain.

25. Suppose that new security designs could be patented.[11] The patent holder could restrict use of the new design or charge other firms royalties for using it. What effect would such patents have on MM's capital-structure irrelevance theory?

---

[11] So far security designs cannot be patented, but other financial applications have received patent protection. See J. Lerner, "Where Does State Street Lead? A First Look at Finance Patents," *Journal of Finance* 57 (April 2002), pp. 901–930.

CHAPTER FIFTEEN

HOW MUCH SHOULD A FIRM BORROW?

IN CHAPTER 14 we found that debt policy rarely matters in well-functioning capital markets with no frictions or imperfections. Few financial managers would accept that conclusion as a practical guideline. If debt policy doesn't matter, then they shouldn't worry about it—financing decisions should be delegated to underlings. Yet financial managers do worry about debt policy. This chapter explains why.

If debt policy were completely irrelevant, then actual debt ratios should vary randomly from firm to firm and industry to industry. Yet almost all airlines, utilities, banks, and real estate development companies rely heavily on debt. And so do many firms in capital-intensive industries like steel, aluminum, chemicals, petroleum, and mining. On the other hand, it is rare to find a pharmaceutical company or advertising agency that is not predominantly equity-financed. Glamorous growth companies rarely use much debt despite rapid expansion and often heavy requirements for capital.

The explanation of these patterns lies partly in the things we left out of the last chapter. We mostly ignored taxes. We assumed bankruptcy was cheap, quick, and painless. It isn't, and there are costs associated with financial distress even if legal bankruptcy is ultimately avoided. We ignored potential conflicts of interest between the firm's security holders. For example, we did not consider what happens to the firm's "old" creditors when new debt is issued or when a shift in investment strategy takes the firm into a riskier business. We ignored the information problems that favor debt over equity when cash must be raised from new security issues. We ignored the incentive effects of financial leverage on management's investment and payout decisions.

Now we will put all these things back in: taxes first, then the costs of bankruptcy and financial distress. This will lead us to conflicts of interest and to information and incentive problems. In the end we will have to admit that debt policy does matter.

However, we will not throw away the MM theory we developed so carefully in Chapter 14. We're shooting for a theory combining MM's insights plus the effects of taxes, costs of bankruptcy and financial distress, and various other complications. We're not dropping back to a theory based on inefficiencies in the capital market. Instead, we want to see how well-functioning capital markets respond to taxes and the other things covered in this chapter.

15.1   CORPORATE TAXES

Debt financing has one important advantage under the corporate income tax system in the United States. The interest that the company pays is a tax-deductible expense. Thus the return to bondholders escapes taxation at the corporate level.

Table 15.1 shows simple income statements for firm U, which has no debt, and firm L, which has borrowed $1,000 at 8%. L's tax bill is $28 less than U's. This is the *tax shield* provided by the debt of L. In effect the government pays 35% of the interest expense of L. The total income that L can pay out to its bondholders and stockholders increases by that amount.

Tax shields can be valuable assets. Suppose that the debt of L is fixed and permanent. (That is, the company commits to refinance its present debt obligations when they mature and to keep rolling over its debt obligations indefinitely.) Then L can look forward to a permanent stream of cash flows of $28 per year. The risk of these flows is likely to be less than the risk of the operating assets of L. The tax shields depend only on the corporate tax rate[1] and on the ability of L to earn enough to cover interest payments. The corporate tax rate has been pretty stable. And the ability of L to earn its interest payments must be reasonably sure; otherwise it could not have borrowed at 8%. Therefore we should discount the interest tax shields at a relatively low rate.

But what rate? One common assumption is that the risk of the tax shields is the same as that of the interest payments generating them. Thus we discount at 8%, the expected rate of return demanded by investors who are holding the firm's debt:

$$PV(\text{tax shield}) = \frac{28}{.08} = \$350$$

In effect the government itself assumes 35% of the $1,000 debt obligation of L.

Under these assumptions, the present value of the tax shield is independent of the return on the debt r_D. It equals the corporate tax rate T_c times the amount borrowed D:

$$\text{Interest payment} = \text{return on debt} \times \text{amount borrowed}$$
$$= r_D \times D$$

$$PV(\text{tax shield}) = \frac{\text{corporate tax rate} \times \text{interest payment}}{\text{expected return on debt}}$$

$$= \frac{T_c(r_D D)}{r_D} = T_c D$$

Of course, PV(tax shield) is less if the firm does not plan to borrow a permanent fixed amount,[2] or if it may not have enough taxable income to use the interest tax shields.[3]

---

[1] Always use the marginal corporate tax rate, not the average rate. Average rates are often much lower than marginal rates because of accelerated depreciation and other tax adjustments. For large corporations, the marginal rate is usually taken as the statutory rate, which was 35% when this chapter was written (2007). However, effective marginal rates can be less than the statutory rate, especially for smaller, riskier companies that cannot be sure that they will earn taxable income in the future.

[2] In this example, we assume that the amount of debt is fixed and stable over time. The natural alternative assumption is a fixed *ratio* of debt to firm value. If the ratio is fixed, then the level of debt and the amount of interest tax shields will fluctuate as firm value fluctuates. In that case projected interest tax shields can't be discounted at the cost of debt. We cover this point in detail in the next chapter.

[3] If the income of L does not cover interest in some future year, the tax shield is not necessarily lost. L can carry back the loss and receive a tax refund up to the amount of taxes paid in the previous two years. If L has a string of losses, and thus no prior tax payments that can be refunded, then losses can be carried forward and used to shield income in subsequent years.

TABLE 15.1

The tax deductibility of interest increases the total income that can be paid out to bondholders and stockholders.

	Income Statement of Firm U	Income Statement of Firm L
Earnings before interest and taxes	$1,000	$1,000
Interest paid to bondholders	0	80
Pretax income	1,000	920
Tax at 35%	350	322
Net income to stockholders	$ 650	$ 598
Total income to both bondholders and stockholders	$0 + 650 = $650	$80 + 598 = $678
Interest tax shield (.35 × interest)	$0	$28

TABLE 15.2

Normal and expanded market value balance sheets. In a normal balance sheet, assets are valued after tax. In the expanded balance sheet, assets are valued pretax, and the value of the government's tax claim is recognized on the right-hand side. Interest tax shields are valuable because they reduce the government's claim.

Normal Balance Sheet (Market Values)	
Asset value (present value of after-tax cash flows)	Debt
	Equity
Total assets	Total value

Expanded Balance Sheet (Market Values)	
Pretax asset value (present value of pretax cash flows)	Debt
	Government's claim (present value of future taxes)
	Equity
Total pretax assets	Total pretax value

How Do Interest Tax Shields Contribute to the Value of Stockholders' Equity?

MM's proposition 1 amounts to saying that the value of a pie does not depend on how it is sliced. The pie is the firm's assets, and the slices are the debt and equity claims. If we hold the pie constant, then a dollar more of debt means a dollar less of equity value.

But there is really a third slice, the government's. Look at Table 15.2. It shows an *expanded* balance sheet with *pretax* asset value on the left and the value of the government's tax claim recognized as a liability on the right. MM would still say that the value of the pie—in this case *pretax* asset value—is not changed by slicing. But anything the firm can do to reduce the size of the government's slice obviously makes stockholders better off. One thing it can do is borrow money, which reduces its tax bill and, as we saw in Table 15.1, increases the cash flows to debt and equity investors. The *after-tax* value of the firm (the sum of its debt and equity values as shown in a normal market value balance sheet) goes up by PV(tax shield).

Recasting Merck's Capital Structure

Merck is a large, successful firm that uses relatively little long-term debt. Table 15.3(*a*) shows simplified book and market value balance sheets for Merck in December 2005.

Book Values			
Net working capital	$ 7,746	$ 5,126	Long-term debt
		8,500	Other long-term liabilities
Long-term assets	23,796	17,916	Equity
Total assets	$31,542	$31,542	Total value
Market Values			
Net working capital	$ 7,746	$ 5,126	Long-term debt
PV interest tax shield	1,974	8,500	Other long-term liabilities
Long-term assets	73,315	69,409	Equity
Total assets	$83,035	$83,035	Total value

TABLE 15.3(a)

Simplified balance sheets for Merck, December 2005 (figures in millions).

Notes:
1. Market value is equal to book value for net working capital, long-term debt, and other long-term liabilities. Market value of equity = number of shares times closing price for December 2005. The difference between the market and book values of long-term assets is equal to the difference between the market and book values of equity.
2. PV interest tax shield assumes fixed, perpetual debt, with a 35% tax rate.

Book Values			
Net working capital	$ 7,746	$ 6,126	Long-term debt
		8,500	Other long-term liabilities
Long-term assets	23,796	16,916	Equity
Total assets	$31,542	$31,542	Total value
Market Values			
Net working capital	$ 7,746	$ 6,126	Long-term debt
PV interest tax shield	2,324	8,500	Other long-term liabilities
Long-term assets	73,315	68,759	Equity
Total assets	$83,385	$83,385	Total value

TABLE 15.3(b)

Balance sheets for Merck with additional $1 billion of long-term debt substituted for stockholders' equity (figures in millions).

Suppose that you were Merck's financial manager with complete responsibility for its capital structure. You decide to borrow an additional $1 billion on a permanent basis and use the proceeds to repurchase shares.

Table 15.3(b) shows the new balance sheets. The book version simply has $1,000 million more long-term debt and $1,000 million less equity. But we know that Merck's assets must be worth more because its tax bill has been reduced by 35% of the interest on the new debt. In other words, Merck has an increase in PV(tax shield), which is worth $T_cD = .35 \times \$1,000$ million = $350 million. If the MM theory holds *except* for taxes, firm value must increase by $350 million to $83,385 million. Merck's equity ends up worth $68,759 million.

Now you have repurchased $1,000 million worth of shares, but Merck's equity value has dropped by only $650 million. Therefore Merck's stockholders must be $350 million ahead. Not a bad day's work.[4]

---

[4] Notice that as long as the bonds are sold at a fair price, all the benefits from the tax shield go to the shareholders.

MM and Taxes

We have just developed a version of MM's proposition 1 as corrected by them to reflect corporate income taxes.[5] The new proposition is

$$\text{Value of firm} = \text{value if all-equity-financed} + \text{PV(tax shield)}$$

In the special case of permanent debt,

$$\text{Value of firm} = \text{value if all-equity-financed} + T_c D$$

Our imaginary financial surgery on Merck provides the perfect illustration of the problems inherent in this "corrected" theory. That $350 million came too easily; it seems to violate the law that there is no such thing as a money machine. And if Merck's stockholders would be richer with $6,126 million of corporate debt, why not $7,126 or $17,216 million? At what debt level should Merck stop borrowing? Our formula implies that firm value and stockholders' wealth continue to go up as D increases. The optimal debt policy appears to be embarrassingly extreme. All firms should be 100% debt-financed.

MM were not that fanatical about it. No one would expect the formula to apply at extreme debt ratios. There are several reasons why our calculations overstate the value of interest tax shields. First, it's wrong to think of debt as fixed and perpetual; a firm's ability to carry debt changes over time as profits and firm value fluctuate. Second, many firms face marginal tax rates less than 35%. Third, you can't use interest tax shields unless there will be future profits to shield—and no firm can be absolutely sure of that.

But none of these qualifications explains why companies like Merck survive and thrive at low debt ratios. It's hard to believe that Merck's financial managers are simply missing the boat.

A conservative debt policy can of course be great comfort when a company suffers a sudden adverse shock. For Merck, that shock came in September 2004, when it became clear that its blockbuster painkiller Vioxx increased the risk of heart attacks in some patients. When Merck withdrew Vioxx from the market, it lost billions of dollars in future revenues and had to spend or set aside nearly $1 billion for legal costs. Yet the company's credit rating was not harmed, and it retained ample cash flow to fund all its investments, including research and development, and to maintain its regular dividend. But if Merck was that strong financially *after* the loss of Vioxx, was its debt policy before the loss excessively conservative? Why did it pass up the opportunity to borrow a few billion more (as in Table 15.3(*b*)), thus substituting tax-deductible interest for taxable income to shareholders?

We seem to have argued ourselves into a blind alley. But there may be two ways out:

1. Perhaps a fuller examination of the U.S. system of corporate *and personal* taxation will uncover a tax disadvantage of corporate borrowing, offsetting the present value of the interest tax shield.

2. Perhaps firms that borrow incur other costs—bankruptcy costs, for example.

We will now explore these two escape routes.

---

[5] Interest tax shields are recognized in MM's original article, F. Modigliani and M. H. Miller, "The Cost of Capital, Corporation Finance and the Theory of Investment," *American Economic Review* 48 (June 1958), pp. 261–296. The valuation procedure used in Table 15.3(*b*) is presented in their 1963 article "Corporate Income Taxes and the Cost of Capital: A Correction," *American Economic Review* 53 (June 1963), pp. 433–443.

15.2   CORPORATE AND PERSONAL TAXES

When personal taxes are introduced, the firm's objective is no longer to minimize the *corporate* tax bill; the firm should try to minimize the present value of *all* taxes paid on corporate income. "All taxes" include *personal* taxes paid by bondholders and stockholders.

Figure 15.1 illustrates how corporate and personal taxes are affected by leverage. Depending on the firm's capital structure, a dollar of operating income will accrue to investors either as debt interest or equity income (dividends or capital gains). That is, the dollar can go down either branch of Figure 15.1.

Notice that Figure 15.1 distinguishes between T_p, the personal tax rate on interest, and T_{pE}, the effective personal tax rate on equity income. This rate can be well below T_p, depending on the mix of dividends and capital gains realized by shareholders. The top marginal rate on dividends and capital gains is now (2007) only 15% while the top rate on other income, including interest income, is 35%. Also capital gains taxes can be deferred until shares are sold, so the top *effective* capital gains rate is usually less than 15%.

The firm's objective should be to arrange its capital structure to maximize after-tax income. You can see from Figure 15.1 that corporate borrowing is better if $(1 - T_p)$ is more than $(1 - T_{pE}) \times (1 - T_c)$; otherwise it is worse. The *relative tax advantage of debt* over equity is

$$\text{Relative tax advantage of debt} = \frac{1 - T_p}{(1 - T_{pE})(1 - T_c)}$$

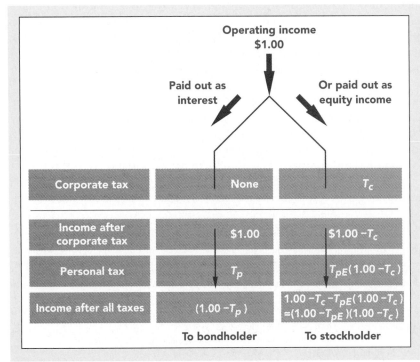

FIGURE 15.1

The firm's capital structure determines whether operating income is paid out as interest or equity income. Interest is taxed only at the personal level. Equity income is taxed at both the corporate and the personal levels. However, T_{pE}, the personal tax rate on equity income, can be less than T_p, the personal tax rate on interest income.

This suggests two special cases. First, suppose that debt and equity income were taxed at the same effective personal rate. But with $T_{pE} = T_p$, the relative advantage depends only on the *corporate rate:*

$$\text{Relative advantage} = \frac{1 - T_p}{(1 - T_{pE})(1 - T_c)} = \frac{1}{1 - T_c}$$

In this case, we can forget about personal taxes. The tax advantage of corporate borrowing is exactly as MM calculated it.[6] They do not have to assume away personal taxes. Their theory of debt and taxes requires only that debt and equity be taxed at the same rate.

The second special case occurs when corporate and personal taxes cancel to make debt policy irrelevant. This requires

$$1 - T_p = (1 - T_{pE})(1 - T_c)$$

This case can happen only if T_c, the corporate rate, is less than the personal rate T_p and if T_{pE}, the effective rate on equity income, is small. Merton Miller explored this situation at a time when U.S. tax rates on interest and dividends were much higher than now, but we won't go into the details of his analysis here.[7]

In any event we seem to have a simple, practical decision rule. Arrange the firm's capital structure to shunt operating income down that branch of Figure 15.1 where the tax is least. Unfortunately that is not as simple as it sounds. What's T_{pE}, for example? The shareholder roster of any large corporation is likely to include tax-exempt investors (such as pension funds or university endowments) as well as millionaires. All possible tax brackets will be mixed together. And it's the same with T_p, the personal tax rate on interest. The large corporation's "typical" bondholder might be a tax-exempt pension fund, but many taxpaying investors also hold corporate debt.

Some investors may be much happier to buy your debt than others. For example, you should have no problems inducing pension funds to lend; they don't have to worry about personal tax. But taxpaying investors may be more reluctant to hold debt and will be prepared to do so only if they are compensated by a high rate of interest. Investors paying tax on interest at the top rate of 35% may be particularly reluctant to hold debt. They will prefer to hold common stock or tax-exempt bonds issued by states and municipalities.

To determine the net tax advantage of debt, companies would need to know the tax rates faced by the marginal investor—that is, an investor who is equally happy to hold debt or equity. This makes it hard to put a precise figure on the tax benefit, but we can nevertheless provide a back-of-the-envelope calculation. Let's consider a large, dividend-paying company like Merck. Merck's dividend payout ratio has averaged about 65%, so for each $1.00 of income, $.65 is received as dividends and $.35 as capital gains. Suppose the marginal investor is in the top tax bracket,

---

[6] Of course, personal taxes reduce the dollar amount of corporate interest tax shields, but the appropriate discount rate for cash flows after personal tax is also lower. If investors are willing to lend at a prospective return *before* personal taxes of r_D, then they must also be willing to accept a return *after* personal taxes of $r_D(1 - T_p)$, where T_p is the marginal rate of personal tax. Thus we can compute the value after personal taxes of the tax shield on permanent debt:

$$PV(\text{tax shield}) = \frac{T_c \times r_D D \times (1 - T_p)}{r_D \times (1 - T_p)} = T_c D$$

This brings us back to our previous formula for firm value:

$$\text{Value of firm} = \text{value if all-equity-financed} + T_c D$$

[7] See M. H. Miller, "Debt and Taxes," *Journal of Finance* 32 (May 1977), pp. 261–276.

paying 35% on interest and 15% on dividends and capital gains. Let's assume that deferred realization of capital gains cuts the effective capital gains rate in half, to $15/2 = 7.5\%$. Therefore, if the investor invests in Merck common stock, the tax on each \$1.00 of equity income is $T_{pE} = (.65 \times 15) + (.35 \times 7.5) = 12.4\%$.

Now we can calculate the effect of shunting a dollar of income down each of the two branches in Figure 15.1:

	Interest	Equity Income
Income before tax	\$1.00	\$1.00
Less corporate tax at $T_c = .35$	0	.35
Income after corporate tax	1.00	.65
Personal tax at $T_p = .35$ and $T_{pE} = .124$	.35	.081
Income after all taxes	\$ .65	\$ .569
	Advantage to debt = \$.081	

The advantage to debt financing appears to be about \$.08 on the dollar.

We should emphasize that our back-of-the-envelope calculation is just that. But it's interesting to see how debt's tax advantage shrinks when we account for the relatively low personal tax rate on equity income.

Most financial managers believe that there is a moderate tax advantage to corporate borrowing, at least for companies that are reasonably sure they can use the corporate tax shields. For companies that cannot benefit from corporate tax shields there is probably a moderate tax disadvantage.

Do companies make full use of interest tax shields? John Graham argues that they don't. His estimates suggest that a typical tax-paying corporation could add 7.5% to firm value by levering up to a still-conservative debt ratio.[8] This is hardly spare change. Therefore it still appears that financial managers have passed by some easy tax savings. Perhaps they saw some offsetting disadvantage to increased borrowing. We will now explore this second escape route.

15.3   COSTS OF FINANCIAL DISTRESS

Financial distress occurs when promises to creditors are broken or honored with difficulty. Sometimes financial distress leads to bankruptcy. Sometimes it only means skating on thin ice.

As we will see, financial distress is costly. Investors know that levered firms may fall into financial distress, and they worry about it. That worry is reflected in the current market value of the levered firm's securities. Thus, the value of the firm can be broken down into three parts:

$$\text{Value of firm} = \text{value if all-equity-financed} + \text{PV(tax shield)} - \text{PV(costs of financial distress)}$$

---

[8] Graham's estimates for individual firms recognize both the uncertainty in future profits and the existence of non-interest tax shields. See J. R. Graham, "How Big Are the Tax Benefits of Debt?" *Journal of Finance* 55 (October 2000), pp. 1901–1941.

FIGURE 15.2

The value of the firm is equal to its value if all-equity-financed plus PV tax shield minus PV costs of financial distress. According to the trade-off theory of capital structure, the manager should choose the debt ratio that maximizes firm value.

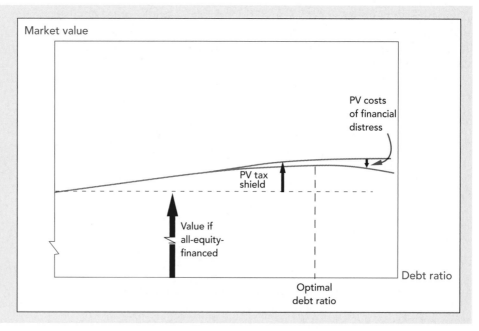

The costs of financial distress depend on the probability of distress and the magnitude of costs encountered if distress occurs.

Figure 15.2 shows how the trade-off between the tax benefits and the costs of distress determines optimal capital structure. PV(tax shield) initially increases as the firm borrows more. At moderate debt levels the probability of financial distress is trivial, and so PV(cost of financial distress) is small and tax advantages dominate. But at some point the probability of financial distress increases rapidly with additional borrowing; the costs of distress begin to take a substantial bite out of firm value. Also, if the firm can't be sure of profiting from the corporate tax shield, the tax advantage of additional debt is likely to dwindle and eventually disappear. The theoretical optimum is reached when the present value of tax savings due to further borrowing is just offset by increases in the present value of costs of distress. This is called the *trade-off theory* of capital structure.

Costs of financial distress cover several specific items. Now we identify these costs and try to understand what causes them.

Bankruptcy Costs

You rarely hear anything nice said about corporate bankruptcy. But there is some good in almost everything. Corporate bankruptcies occur when stockholders exercise their *right to default.* That right is valuable; when a firm gets into trouble, limited liability allows stockholders simply to walk away from it, leaving all its troubles to its creditors. The former creditors become the new stockholders, and the old stockholders are left with nothing.

In our legal system all stockholders in corporations automatically enjoy limited liability. But suppose that this were not so. Suppose that there are two firms with identical assets and operations. Each firm has debt outstanding, and each has promised to repay $1,000 (principal and interest) next year. But only one of the

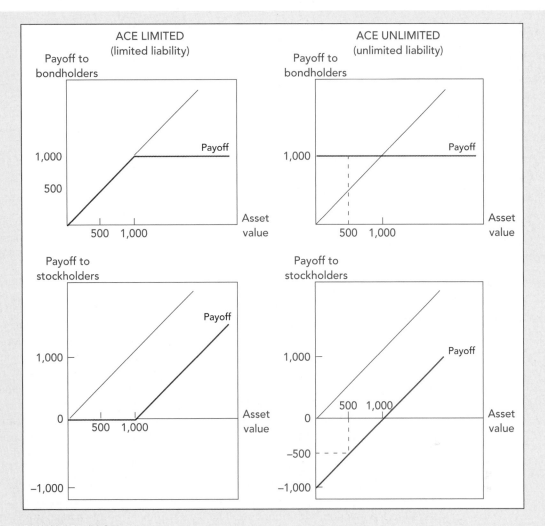

FIGURE 15.3

Comparison of limited and unlimited liability for two otherwise identical firms. If the two firms' asset values are less than $1,000, Ace Limited stockholders default and its bondholders take over the assets. Ace Unlimited stockholders keep the assets, but they must reach into their own pockets to pay off its bondholders. The total payoff to both stockholders and bondholders is the same for the two firms.

firms, Ace Limited, enjoys limited liability. The other firm, Ace Unlimited, does not; its stockholders are personally liable for its debt.[9]

Figure 15.3 compares next year's possible payoffs to the creditors and stockholders of these two firms. The only differences occur when next year's asset value turns out to be less than $1,000. Suppose that next year the assets of each company are worth only $500. In this case Ace Limited defaults. Its stockholders walk away; their payoff is zero. Bondholders get the assets worth $500. But Ace Unlimited's

---

[9] Ace Unlimited could be a partnership or sole proprietorship.

FIGURE 15.4

Total payoff to Ace Limited security holders. There is a $200 bankruptcy cost in the event of default (shaded area).

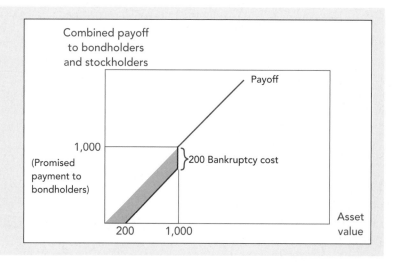

stockholders can't walk away. They have to cough up $500, the difference between asset value and the bondholders' claim. The debt is paid whatever happens.

Suppose that Ace Limited does go bankrupt. Of course, its stockholders are disappointed that their firm is worth so little, but that is an operating problem having nothing to do with financing. Given poor operating performance, the right to go bankrupt—the right to default—is a valuable privilege. As Figure 15.3 shows, Ace Limited's stockholders are in better shape than Unlimited's are.

The example illuminates a mistake people often make in thinking about the costs of bankruptcy. Bankruptcies are thought of as corporate funerals. The mourners (creditors and especially shareholders) look at their firm's present sad state. They think of how valuable their securities used to be and how little is left. Moreover, they think of the lost value as a cost of bankruptcy. That is the mistake. The decline in the value of assets is what the mourning is really about. That has no necessary connection with financing. The bankruptcy is merely a legal mechanism for allowing creditors to take over when the decline in the value of assets triggers a default. Bankruptcy is not the *cause* of the decline in value. It is the result.

Be careful not to get cause and effect reversed. When a person dies, we do not cite the implementation of his or her will as the cause of death.

We said that bankruptcy is a legal mechanism allowing creditors to take over when a firm defaults. *Bankruptcy costs* are the costs of using this mechanism. There are no bankruptcy costs at all shown in Figure 15.3. Note that only Ace Limited can default and go bankrupt. But, regardless of what happens to asset value, the *combined* payoff to the bondholders and stockholders of Ace Limited is always the same as the *combined* payoff to the bondholders and stockholders of Ace Unlimited. Thus the overall market values of the two firms now (this year) must be identical. Of course, Ace Limited's stock is worth more than Ace Unlimited's stock because of Ace Limited's right to default. Ace Limited's debt is worth correspondingly less.

Our example was not intended to be strictly realistic. Anything involving courts and lawyers cannot be free. Suppose that court and legal fees are $200 if Ace Limited defaults. The fees are paid out of the remaining value of Ace's assets. Thus if asset value turns out to be $500, creditors end up with only $300. Figure 15.4 shows next year's *total* payoff to bondholders and stockholders net of this bankruptcy cost. Ace Limited, by issuing risky debt, has given lawyers and the court system a claim on the firm if it defaults. The market value of the firm is reduced by the present value of this claim.

It is easy to see how increased leverage affects the present value of the costs of financial distress. If Ace Limited borrows more, it increases the probability of default and the value of the lawyers' claim. It increases PV (costs of financial distress) and reduces Ace's present market value.

The costs of bankruptcy come out of stockholders' pockets. Creditors foresee the costs and foresee that *they* will pay them if default occurs. For this they demand compensation in advance in the form of higher payoffs when the firm does *not* default; that is, they demand a higher promised interest rate. This reduces the possible payoffs to stockholders and reduces the present market value of their shares.

Evidence on Bankruptcy Costs

Bankruptcy costs can add up fast. While United Airlines was in bankruptcy, it paid over $350 million to lawyers, accountants, and consultants.[10] Enron set a record with legal, accounting, and other professional costs of nearly $1 billion. Professional fees for another distressed energy company, Mirant Corp., were a bit more moderate. The "burn rate" of fees for the first year of Mirant's bankruptcy proceedings was $120 to $140 million.[11]

Daunting as such numbers may seem, they are not a large fraction of the companies' asset values. For example, the fees incurred by Eastern Airlines amounted to only 3.5% of its assets when it entered bankruptcy, or about the equivalent of one jumbo jet. Lawrence Weiss, who studied 31 firms that went bankrupt between 1980 and 1986, found average costs of about 3% of total book assets and 20% of the market value of equity in the year prior to bankruptcy. A study by Edward Altman found that costs were similar for retail companies but higher for industrial companies. Also, bankruptcy eats up a larger fraction of asset value for small companies than for large ones. There are significant economies of scale in going bankrupt.[12] A study by Andrade and Kaplan of a sample of troubled and highly leveraged firms estimated costs of financial distress amounting to 10% to 20% of predistress market value, although they found it hard to decide whether these costs were caused by financial distress or by the business setbacks that led to distress.[13]

Direct versus Indirect Costs of Bankruptcy

So far we have discussed the *direct* (that is, legal and administrative) costs of bankruptcy. There are indirect costs too, which are nearly impossible to measure. But we have circumstantial evidence indicating their importance.

---

[10] "Bankruptcy Lawyers Flying High; Airlines' Woes Mean Big Paydays For Consultants and Law Firms; Partner's $177,000 Bill for August," *The Wall Street Journal,* October 21, 2005, p. C.1.

[11] "Enron Bankruptcy Specialist to File for Additional Payment; On Top of $63.4 Million, 'Success Fee' to Be Sought of Additional $25 Million," *The Wall Street Journal,* September 3, 2004, p. A.2; and "Mirant Bankruptcy Legal Fees Seen Topping $120 Million," Reuters, January 20, 2004.

[12] The pioneering study of bankruptcy costs is J. B. Warner, "Bankruptcy Costs: Some Evidence," *Journal of Finance* 26 (May 1977), pp. 337–348. The Weiss and Altman papers are L. A. Weiss, "Bankruptcy Resolution: Direct Costs and Violation of Priority of Claims," *Journal of Financial Economics* 27 (October 1990), pp. 285–314; and E. I. Altman, "A Further Investigation of the Bankruptcy Cost Question," *Journal of Finance* 39 (September 1984), pp. 1067–1089.

[13] G. Andrade and S. N. Kaplan, "How Costly Is Financial (not Economic) Distress? Evidence from Highly Leveraged Transactions That Became Distressed," *Journal of Finance* 53 (October 1998), pp. 1443–1493.

Managing a bankrupt firm is not easy. Consent of the bankruptcy court is required for many routine business decisions, such as the sale of assets or investment in new equipment. At best this involves time and effort; at worst the proposals are thwarted by the firm's creditors, who have little interest in the firm's long-term prosperity and would prefer the cash to be paid out to them.

Sometimes the problem is reversed: The bankruptcy court is so anxious to maintain the firm as a going concern that it allows the firm to engage in negative-NPV activities. When Eastern Airlines entered the "protection" of the bankruptcy court in 1989, it still had some valuable, profit-making routes and saleable assets such as planes and terminal facilities. The creditors would have been best served by a prompt liquidation, which probably would have generated enough cash to pay off all debt and preferred stockholders. But the bankruptcy judge was keen to keep Eastern's planes flying at all costs, so he allowed the company to sell many of its assets to fund hefty operating losses. When Eastern finally closed down after two years, it was not just bankrupt, but *administratively* insolvent: There was almost nothing for creditors, and the company was running out of cash to pay legal expenses.[14]

We do not know what the sum of direct and indirect costs of bankruptcy amounts to. We suspect it is a significant number, particularly for large firms for which proceedings would be lengthy and complex. Perhaps the best evidence is the reluctance of creditors to force bankruptcy. In principle, they would be better off to end the agony and seize the assets as soon as possible. Instead, creditors often overlook defaults in the hope of nursing the firm over a difficult period. They do this in part to avoid costs of bankruptcy.[15] There is an old financial saying, "Borrow $1,000 and you've got a banker. Borrow $10,000,000 and you've got a partner."

Financial Distress without Bankruptcy

Not every firm that gets into trouble goes bankrupt. As long as the firm can scrape up enough cash to pay the interest on its debt, it may be able to postpone bankruptcy for many years. Eventually the firm may recover, pay off its debt, and escape bankruptcy altogether.

But the mere threat of financial distress can be costly to the threatened firm. Customers and suppliers are extra cautious about doing business with a firm that may not be around for long. Customers worry about resale value and the availability of service and replacement parts. (Would you buy a new car from a manufacturer that is driving down the road to bankruptcy?) Suppliers are disinclined to put effort into servicing the distressed firm's account and may demand cash on the nail for their products. Potential employees are unwilling to sign on and existing staff keep slipping away from their desks for job interviews.

---

[14] See L. A. Weiss and K. H. Wruck, "Information Problems, Conflicts of Interest, and Asset Stripping: Chapter 11's Failure in the Case of Eastern Airlines," *Journal of Financial Economics* 48 (1998), pp. 55–97.

[15] There is another reason. Creditors are not always given absolute priority in bankruptcy. *Absolute priority* means that creditors must be paid in full before stockholders receive a cent. Sometimes reorganizations are negotiated that provide something for everyone, even though creditors are *not* paid in full. Thus creditors can never be sure how they will fare in bankruptcy.

High debt, and thus high financial risk, also appears to reduce firms' appetites for business risk. For example, Luigi Zingales looked at the fortunes of U.S. trucking companies after the trucking industry was deregulated in the late 1970s.[16] The deregulation sparked a wave of competition and restructuring. Survival required new investment and improvements in operating efficiency. Zingales found that conservatively financed trucking companies were more likely to survive in the new competitive environment. High-debt firms were more likely to drop out of the game.

Debt and Incentives

When a firm is in trouble, both bondholders and stockholders want it to recover, but in other respects their interests may be in conflict. In times of financial distress the security holders are like many political parties—united on generalities but threatened by squabbling on any specific issue.

Financial distress is costly when these conflicts of interest get in the way of proper operating, investment, and financing decisions. Stockholders are tempted to forsake the usual objective of maximizing the overall market value of the firm and to pursue narrower self-interest instead. They are tempted to play games at the expense of their creditors. We will now illustrate how such games can lead to costs of financial distress.

Here is the Circular File Company's book balance sheet:

Circular File Company (Book Values)

Net working capital	$ 20	$ 50	Bonds outstanding
Fixed assets	80	50	Common stock
Total assets	$100	$100	Total value

We will assume there is only one share and one bond outstanding. The stockholder is also the manager. The bondholder is somebody else.

Here is its balance sheet in market values—a clear case of financial distress, since the face value of Circular's debt ($50) exceeds the firm's total market value ($30):

Circular File Company (Market Values)

Net working capital	$20	$25	Bonds outstanding
Fixed assets	10	5	Common stock
Total assets	$30	$30	Total value

If the debt matured today, Circular's owner would default, leaving the firm bankrupt. But suppose that the bond actually matures one year hence, that there is enough cash for Circular to limp along for one year, and that the bondholder cannot "call the question" and force bankruptcy before then.

The one-year grace period explains why the Circular share still has value. Its owner is betting on a stroke of luck that will rescue the firm, allowing it to pay off the debt with something left over. The bet is a long shot—the owner wins only if firm value increases from $30 to more than $50.[17] But the owner has a secret weapon: He controls investment and operating strategy.

---

[16] L. Zingales, "Survival of the Fittest or the Fattest? Exit and Financing in the Trucking Industry," *Journal of Finance* 53 (June 1998), pp. 905–938.

[17] We are not concerned here with how to work out whether $5 is a fair price for stockholders to pay for the bet.

Risk Shifting: The First Game

Suppose that Circular has $10 cash. The following investment opportunity comes up:

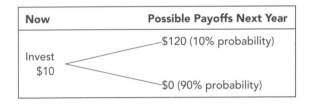

Now	Possible Payoffs Next Year
Invest $10	$120 (10% probability)
	$0 (90% probability)

This is a wild gamble and probably a lousy project. But you can see why the owner would be tempted to take it anyway. Why not go for broke? Circular will probably go under anyway, so the owner is essentially betting with the bondholder's money. But the owner gets most of the loot if the project pays off.

Suppose that the project's NPV is −$2 but that it is undertaken anyway, thus depressing firm value by $2. Circular's new balance sheet might look like this:

Circular File Company (Market Values)

Net working capital	$10	$20	Bonds outstanding
Fixed assets	18	8	Common stock
Total assets	$28	$28	Total value

Firm value falls by $2, but the owner is $3 ahead because the bond's value has fallen by $5.[18] The $10 cash that used to stand behind the bond has been replaced by a very risky asset worth only $8.

Thus a game has been played at the expense of Circular's bondholder. The game illustrates the following general point: Stockholders of levered firms gain when business risk increases. Financial managers who act strictly in their shareholders' interests (and *against* the interests of creditors) will favor risky projects over safe ones. They may even take risky projects with negative NPVs.

This warped strategy for capital budgeting clearly is costly to the firm and to the economy as a whole. Why do we associate the costs with financial distress? Because the temptation to play is strongest when the odds of default are high. A blue-chip company like ExxonMobil would never invest in our negative-NPV gamble. Its creditors are not vulnerable to one risky project.

Refusing to Contribute Equity Capital: The Second Game

We have seen how stockholders, acting in their immediate, narrow self-interest, may take projects that reduce the overall market value of their firm. These are errors of commission. Conflicts of interest may also lead to errors of omission.

Assume that Circular cannot scrape up any cash, and therefore cannot take that wild gamble. Instead a *good* opportunity comes up: a relatively safe asset costing $10 with a present value of $15 and NPV = +$5.

This project will not in itself rescue Circular, but it is a step in the right direction. We might therefore expect Circular to issue $10 of new stock and to go ahead

---

[18] We are not calculating this $5 drop. We are simply using it as a plausible assumption.

with the investment. Suppose that two new shares are issued to the original owner for $10 cash. The project is taken. The new balance sheet might look like this:

Circular File Company (Market Values)

Net working capital	$20	$33	Bonds outstanding
Fixed assets	25	12	Common stock
Total assets	$45	$45	Total value

The total value of the firm goes up by $15 ($10 of new capital and $5 NPV). Notice that the Circular bond is no longer worth $25, but $33. The bondholder receives a capital gain of $8 because the firm's assets include a new, safe asset worth $15. The probability of default is less, and the payoff to the bondholder if default occurs is larger.

The stockholder loses what the bondholder gains. Equity value goes up not by $15 but by $15 − $8 = $7. The owner puts in $10 of fresh equity capital but gains only $7 in market value. Going ahead is in the firm's interest but not the owner's.

Again, our example illustrates a general point. If we hold business risk constant, any increase in firm value is shared among bondholders and stockholders. The value of any investment opportunity to the firm's *stockholders* is reduced because project benefits must be shared with bondholders. Thus it may not be in the stockholders' self-interest to contribute fresh equity capital even if that means forgoing positive-NPV investment opportunities.

This problem theoretically affects all levered firms, but it is most serious when firms land in financial distress. The greater the probability of default, the more bondholders have to gain from investments that increase firm value.

And Three More Games, Briefly

As with other games, the temptation to play the next three games is particularly strong in financial distress.

Cash In and Run   Stockholders may be reluctant to put money into a firm in financial distress, but they are happy to take the money out—in the form of a cash dividend, for example. The market value of the firm's stock goes down by less than the amount of the dividend paid, because the decline in *firm* value is shared with creditors. This game is just "refusing to contribute equity capital" run in reverse.

Playing for Time   When the firm is in financial distress, creditors would like to salvage what they can by forcing the firm to settle up. Naturally, stockholders want to delay this as long as they can. There are various devious ways of doing this, for example, through accounting changes designed to conceal the true extent of trouble, by encouraging false hopes of spontaneous recovery, or by cutting corners on maintenance, research and development, and so on, in order to make this year's operating performance look better.

Bait and Switch   This game is not always played in financial distress, but it is a quick way to get *into* distress. You start with a conservative policy, issuing a limited amount of relatively safe debt. Then you suddenly switch and issue a lot more. That makes all your debt risky, imposing a capital loss on the "old" bondholders. Their capital loss is the stockholders' gain.

The most dramatic example of bait and switch occurred in October 1988, when the management of RJR Nabisco announced its intention to acquire the company in a *leveraged buy-out* (LBO). This put the company "in play" for a transaction in which existing shareholders would be bought out and the company would be "taken private." The cost of the buy-out would be almost entirely debt-financed. The new private company would start life with an extremely high debt ratio.

RJR Nabisco had debt outstanding with a market value of about $2.4 billion. The announcement of the coming LBO drove down this market value by $298 million.[19]

What the Games Cost

Why should anyone object to these games so long as they are played by consenting adults? Because playing them means poor decisions about investments and operations. These poor decisions are *agency costs* of borrowing.

The more the firm borrows, the greater is the temptation to play the games (assuming the financial manager acts in the stockholders' interest). The increased odds of poor decisions in the future prompt investors to mark down the present market value of the firm. The fall in value comes out of the shareholders' pockets. Therefore it is ultimately in their interest to avoid temptation. The easiest way to do this is to limit borrowing to levels at which the firm's debt is safe or close to it.

Banks and other corporate lenders are also not financial innocents. They realize that games may be played at their expense and so protect themselves by rationing the amount that they will lend or by imposing restrictions on the company's actions. For example, consider the case of Henrietta Ketchup, a budding entrepreneur with two possible investment projects that offer the following payoffs:

	Investment	Payoff	Probability of Payoff
Project 1	−12	+15	1.0
Project 2	−12	+24	.5
		0	.5

Project 1 is surefire and very profitable; project 2 is risky and a rotten project. Ms. Ketchup now approaches her bank and asks to borrow the present value of $10 (she will find the remaining money out of her own purse). The bank calculates that the payoff will be split as follows:

	Expected Payoff to Bank	Expected Payoff to Ms. Ketchup
Project 1	+10	+5
Project 2	(.5 × 10) + (.5 × 0) = +5	.5 × (24 − 10) = +7

If Ms. Ketchup accepts project 1, the bank's debt is certain to be paid in full; if she accepts project 2, there is only a 50% chance of payment and the expected payoff to the bank is only $5. Unfortunately, Ms. Ketchup will prefer to take

---

[19] We thank Paul Asquith for these figures. RJR Nabisco was finally taken private not by its management but by another LBO partnership.

project 2, for if things go well, she gets most of the profit, and if they go badly, the bank bears most of the loss. Unless Ms. Ketchup can convince the bank that she will not gamble with its money, the bank will limit the amount that it is prepared to lend.[20]

How can Ms. Ketchup reassure the bank of her intentions? The obvious answer is to give it veto power over potentially dangerous decisions. There we have the ultimate economic rationale for all that fine print backing up corporate debt. Debt contracts frequently limit dividends or equivalent transfers of wealth to stockholders; the firm may not be allowed to pay out more than it earns, for example. Additional borrowing is almost always limited. For example, many companies are prevented by existing bond indentures from issuing any additional long-term debt unless their ratio of earnings to interest charges exceeds 2.0.

Sometimes firms are restricted from selling assets or making major investment outlays except with the lenders' consent. The risks of playing for time are reduced by specifying accounting procedures and by giving lenders access to the firm's books and its financial forecasts.

Of course, fine print cannot be a complete solution for firms that insist on issuing risky debt. The fine print has its own costs; you have to spend money to save money. Obviously a complex debt contract costs more to negotiate than a simple one. Afterward it costs the lender more to monitor the firm's performance. Lenders anticipate monitoring costs and demand compensation in the form of higher interest rates; thus the monitoring costs—another agency cost of debt—are ultimately paid by stockholders.

Perhaps the most severe costs of the fine print stem from the constraints it places on operating and investment decisions. For example, an attempt to prevent the risk-shifting game may also prevent the firm from pursuing *good* investment opportunities. At the minimum there are delays in clearing major investments with lenders. In some cases lenders may veto high-risk investments even if net present value is positive. The lenders are tempted to play a game of their own, forcing the firm to stay in cash or low-risk assets even if good projects are forgone.

Debt contracts cannot cover every possible manifestation of the games we have just discussed. Any attempt to do so would be hopelessly expensive and doomed to failure in any event. Human imagination is insufficient to conceive of all the possible things that could go wrong. Therefore contracts are always *incomplete.* We will always find surprises coming at us on dimensions we never thought to think about.

We hope we have not left the impression that managers and stockholders always succumb to temptation unless restrained. Usually they refrain voluntarily, not only from a sense of fair play but also on pragmatic grounds: A firm or individual that makes a killing today at the expense of a creditor will be coldly received when the time comes to borrow again. Aggressive game playing is done only by out-and-out crooks and by firms in extreme financial distress. Firms limit borrowing precisely because they don't wish to land in distress and be exposed to the temptation to play.

---

[20] You might think that, if the bank suspects Ms. Ketchup will undertake project 2, it should just raise the interest rate on its loan. In this case Ms. Ketchup will not want to take on project 2 (they can't both be happy with a lousy project). But Ms. Ketchup also would not want to pay a high rate of interest if she is going to take on project 1 (she would do better to borrow less money at the risk-free rate). So simply raising the interest rate is not the answer.

Costs of Distress Vary with Type of Asset

Suppose your firm's only asset is a large downtown hotel, mortgaged to the hilt. The recession hits, occupancy rates fall, and the mortgage payments cannot be met. The lender takes over and sells the hotel to a new owner and operator. You use your firm's stock certificates for wallpaper.

What is the cost of bankruptcy? In this example, probably very little. The value of the hotel is, of course, much less than you hoped, but that is due to the lack of guests, not to the bankruptcy. Bankruptcy doesn't damage the hotel itself. The direct bankruptcy costs are restricted to items such as legal and court fees, real estate commissions, and the time the lender spends sorting things out.

Suppose we repeat the story of Heartbreak Hotel for Fledgling Electronics. Everything is the same, except for the underlying real assets—not real estate but a high-tech going concern, a growth company whose most valuable assets are technology, investment opportunities, and its employees' human capital.

If Fledgling gets into trouble, the stockholders may be reluctant to put up money to cash in on its growth opportunities. Failure to invest is likely to be much more serious for Fledgling than for the Heartbreak Hotel.

If Fledgling finally defaults on its debt, the lender will find it much more difficult to cash in by selling off the assets. Many of them are intangibles that have value only as a part of a going concern.

Could Fledgling be kept as a going concern through default and reorganization? It may not be as hopeless as putting a wedding cake through a car wash, but there are a number of serious difficulties. First, the odds of defections by key employees are higher than they would be if the firm had never gotten into financial trouble. Special guarantees may have to be given to customers who have doubts about whether the firm will be around to service its products. Aggressive investment in new products and technology will be difficult; each class of creditors will have to be convinced that it is in its interest for the firm to invest new money in risky ventures.

Some assets, like good commercial real estate, can pass through bankruptcy and reorganization largely unscathed;[21] the values of other assets are likely to be considerably diminished. The losses are greatest for the intangible assets that are linked to the health of the firm as a going concern—for example, technology, human capital, and brand image. That may be why debt ratios are low in the pharmaceutical industry, where value depends on continued success in research and development, and in many service industries where value depends on human capital. We can also understand why highly profitable growth companies, such as Microsoft or Pfizer, use mostly equity finance.

The moral of these examples is this: *Do not think only about the probability that borrowing will bring trouble. Think also of the value that may be lost if trouble comes.*

Heartbreak Hotel for Enron?   Enron was one of the most glamorous, fast-growing, and (apparently) profitable companies of the 1990s. It played a lead role in the

---

[21] In 1989 the Rockefeller family sold 80% of Rockefeller Center—several acres of extremely valuable Manhattan real estate—to Mitsubishi Estate Company for $1.4 billion. A REIT, Rockefeller Center Properties, held a $1.3 billion mortgage loan (the REIT's only asset) secured by this real estate. But rents and occupancy rates did not meet forecasts, and by 1995 Mitsubishi had incurred losses of about $600 million. Then Mitsubishi quit, and Rockefeller Center was bankrupt. That triggered a complicated series of maneuvers and negotiations. But did this damage the value of the Rockefeller Center properties? Was Radio City Music Hall, one of the properties, any less valuable because of the bankruptcy? We doubt it.

deregulation of electric power markets, both in the United States and internationally. It invested in electric power generation and distribution, gas pipelines, telecommunications networks, and various other ventures. It also built up an active energy trading business. At its peak the aggregate market value of Enron's common stock exceeded $60 billion. By the end of 2001, Enron was in bankruptcy and its shares were worthless.

With hindsight we see that Enron was playing many of the games that we described earlier in this section. It was borrowing aggressively and hiding the debt in "special purpose entities" (SPEs). The SPEs also allowed it to pump up its reported earnings, playing for time while making more and more risky investments. When the bubble burst, there was hardly any value left.

The collapse of Enron didn't really destroy $60 billion in value, because that $60 billion wasn't there in the first place. But there were genuine costs of financial distress. Let's focus on Enron's energy trading business. That business was not as profitable as it appeared, but it was nevertheless a valuable asset. It provided an important service for wholesale energy customers and suppliers who wanted to buy or sell contracts that locked in the future prices and quantities of electricity, natural gas, and other commodities.

What happened to this business when it became clear that Enron was in financial distress and probably headed for bankruptcy? It disappeared. Trading volume went to zero immediately. None of its customers were willing to make a new trade with Enron, because it was far from clear that Enron would be around to honor its side of the bargain. With no trading volume, there was no trading business. As it turned out, Enron's trading business more resembled Fledgling Electronics than a tangible asset like Heartbreak Hotel.

The value of Enron's trading business depended on Enron's creditworthiness. The value should have been protected by conservative financing. Most of the lost value can be traced back to Enron's aggressive borrowing. This loss of value was therefore a cost of financial distress.

The Trade-off Theory of Capital Structure

Financial managers often think of the firm's debt–equity decision as a trade-off between interest tax shields and the costs of financial distress. Of course, there is controversy about how valuable interest tax shields are and what kinds of financial trouble are most threatening, but these disagreements are only variations on a theme. Thus, Figure 15.2 illustrates the debt–equity trade-off.

This *trade-off theory* of capital structure recognizes that target debt ratios may vary from firm to firm. Companies with safe, tangible assets and plenty of taxable income to shield ought to have high target ratios. Unprofitable companies with risky, intangible assets ought to rely primarily on equity financing.

If there were no costs of adjusting capital structure, then each firm should always be at its target debt ratio. However, there are costs, and therefore delays, in adjusting to the optimum. Firms cannot immediately offset the random events that bump them away from their capital structure targets, so we should see random differences in actual debt ratios among firms having the same target debt ratio.

All in all, this trade-off theory of capital structure choice tells a comforting story. Unlike MM's theory, which seemed to say that firms should take on as much debt as possible, it avoids extreme predictions and rationalizes moderate debt ratios. Also, if you ask financial managers whether their firms have target debt ratios, they will usually say yes.[22] This is consistent with the trade-off theory.

But what are the facts? Can the trade-off theory of capital structure explain how companies actually behave?

The answer is "yes and no." On the "yes" side, the trade-off theory successfully explains many industry differences in capital structure. High-tech growth companies, for example, whose assets are risky and mostly intangible, normally use relatively little debt. Airlines can and do borrow heavily because their assets are tangible and relatively safe.[23]

On the "no" side, there are a few things the trade-off theory cannot explain. It cannot explain why some of the most successful companies thrive with little debt. Think of Merck, which as Table 15.3(*a*) shows is basically all-equity-financed. Granted, Merck's most valuable assets are intangible, the fruits of its pharmaceutical research and development. We know that intangible assets and conservative capital structures go together. But Merck also has a very large corporate income tax bill (about $2.7 billion in 2005) and the highest possible credit rating. It could borrow enough to save tens of millions of dollars without raising a whisker of concern about possible financial distress.

Merck illustrates an odd fact about real-life capital structures: The most profitable companies commonly borrow the least.[24] Here the trade-off theory fails, for it predicts exactly the reverse. Under the trade-off theory, high profits should mean more debt-servicing capacity and more taxable income to shield and so should give a *higher* target debt ratio.[25]

In general it appears that public companies rarely make major shifts in capital structure just because of taxes,[26] and it is hard to detect the present value of interest tax shields in firms' market values.[27]

A final point on the "no" side for the trade-off theory: Debt ratios today are no higher than they were in the early 1900s, when income tax rates were low (or

[22] See J. Graham and C. Harvey, "The Theory and Practice of Corporate Finance: Evidence from the Field," *Journal of Financial Economics* 60 (May/June 2001), pp. 187–244.

[23] We are not suggesting that all airline companies are safe; many are not. But air*craft* can support debt where air*lines* cannot. If Fly-by-Night Airlines fails, its planes retain their value in another airline's operations. There's a good secondary market in used aircraft, so a loan secured by aircraft can be well protected even if made to an airline flying on thin ice (and in the dark).

[24] For example, in an international comparison Wald found that profitability was the single largest determinant of firm capital structure. See J. K. Wald, "How Firm Characteristics Affect Capital Structure: An International Comparison," *Journal of Financial Research* 22 (Summer 1999), pp. 161–187.

[25] Here we mean debt as a fraction of the book or replacement value of the company's assets. Profitable companies might not borrow a greater fraction of their market value. Higher profits imply higher market value as well as stronger incentives to borrow.

[26] Mackie-Mason found that taxpaying companies are more likely to issue debt (vs. equity) than nontaxpaying companies. This shows that taxes do affect financing choices. However, it is not necessarily evidence for the trade-off theory. Look back to Section 15.2, and note the special case where corporate and personal taxes cancel to make debt policy irrelevant. In that case, taxpaying firms would see no net tax advantage to debt: corporate interest tax shields would be offset by the taxes paid by investors in the firm's debt. But the balance would tip in favor of equity for a firm that was losing money and reaping no benefits from interest tax shields. See J. Mackie-Mason, "Do Taxes Affect Corporate Financing Decisions?" *Journal of Finance* 45 (December 1990), pp. 1471–1493.

[27] A study by E. F. Fama and K. R. French, covering over 2,000 firms from 1965 to 1992, failed to find any evidence that interest tax shields contributed to firm value. See "Taxes, Financing Decisions and Firm Value," *Journal of Finance* 53 (June 1998), pp. 819–843.

zero). Debt ratios in other industrialized countries are equal to or higher than those in the United States. Many of these countries have imputation tax systems, which should eliminate the value of the interest tax shields.[28]

None of this disproves the trade-off theory. As George Stigler emphasized, theories are not rejected by circumstantial evidence; it takes a theory to beat a theory. So we now turn to a completely different theory of financing.

15.4 THE PECKING ORDER OF FINANCING CHOICES

The pecking-order theory starts with *asymmetric information*—a fancy term indicating that managers know more about their companies' prospects, risks, and values than do outside investors.

Managers obviously know more than investors. We can prove that by observing stock price changes caused by announcements by managers. For example, when a company announces an increased regular dividend, stock price typically rises, because investors interpret the increase as a sign of management's confidence in future earnings. In other words, the dividend increase transfers information from managers to investors. This can happen only if managers know more in the first place.

Asymmetric information affects the choice between internal and external financing and between new issues of debt and equity securities. This leads to a *pecking order,* in which investment is financed first with internal funds, reinvested earnings primarily; then by new issues of debt; and finally with new issues of equity. New equity issues are a last resort when the company runs out of debt capacity, that is, when the threat of costs of financial distress brings regular insomnia to existing creditors and to the financial manager.

We will take a closer look at the pecking order in a moment. First, you must appreciate how asymmetric information can force the financial manager to issue debt rather than common stock.

Debt and Equity Issues with Asymmetric Information

To the outside world Smith & Company and Jones, Inc., our two example companies, are identical. Each runs a successful business with good growth opportunities. The two businesses are risky, however, and investors have learned from experience that current expectations are frequently bettered or disappointed.

---

[28] We described the Australian imputation tax system in Section 13.8. Look again at Table 13.3, supposing that an Australian corporation pays $A10 of interest. This reduces the corporate tax by $A3.00; it also reduces the tax credit taken by the shareholders by $A3.00. The final tax does not depend on whether the corporation or the shareholder borrows.

You can check this by redrawing Figure 15.1 for the Australian system. The corporate tax rate T_c will cancel out. Since income after all taxes depends only on investors' tax rates, there is no special advantage to corporate borrowing.

Current expectations price each company's stock at $100 per share, but the true values could be higher or lower:

	Smith & Co.	Jones, Inc.
True value could be higher, say	$120	$120
Best current estimate	100	100
True value could be lower, say	80	80

Now suppose that both companies need to raise new money from investors to fund capital investment. They can do this either by issuing bonds or by issuing new shares of common stock. How would the choice be made? One financial manager—we will not tell you which one—might reason as follows:

> Sell stock for $100 per share? Ridiculous! It's worth at least $120. A stock issue now would hand a free gift to new investors. I just wish those skeptical shareholders would appreciate the true value of this company. Our new factories will make us the world's lowest-cost producer. We've painted a rosy picture for the press and security analysts, but it just doesn't seem to be working. Oh well, the decision is obvious: we'll issue debt, not underpriced equity. A debt issue will save underwriting fees too.

The other financial manager is in a different mood:

> Beefalo burgers were a hit for a while, but it looks like the fad is fading. The fast-food division's gotta find some good new products or it's all downhill from here. Export markets are OK for now, but how are we going to compete with those new Siberian ranches? Fortunately the stock price has held up pretty well—we've had some good short-run news for the press and security analysts. Now's the time to issue stock. We have major investments underway, and why add increased debt service to my other worries?

Of course, outside investors can't read the financial managers' minds. If they could, one stock might trade at $120 and the other at $80.

Why doesn't the optimistic financial manager simply educate investors? Then the company could sell stock on fair terms, and there would be no reason to favor debt over equity or vice versa.

This is not so easy. (Note that both companies are issuing upbeat press releases.) Investors can't be told what to think; they have to be convinced. That takes a detailed layout of the company's plans and prospects, including the inside scoop on new technology, product design, marketing plans, and so on. Getting this across is expensive for the company and also valuable to its competitors. Why go to the trouble? Investors will learn soon enough, as revenues and earnings evolve. In the meantime the optimistic financial manager can finance growth by issuing debt.

Now suppose there are two press releases:

> Jones, Inc., will issue $120 million of five-year senior notes.

> Smith & Co. announced plans today to issue 1.2 million new shares of common stock. The company expects to raise $120 million.

As a rational investor, you immediately learn two things. First, Jones's financial manager is optimistic and Smith's is pessimistic. Second, Smith's financial manager is also naive to think that investors would pay $100 per share. The *attempt* to sell stock shows that it must be worth less. Smith might sell stock at $80 per share, but certainly not at $100.[29]

Smart financial managers think this through ahead of time. The end result? Both Smith and Jones end up issuing debt. Jones, Inc., issues debt because its financial manager is optimistic and doesn't want to issue undervalued equity. A smart, but pessimistic, financial manager at Smith issues debt because an attempt to issue equity would force the stock price down and eliminate any advantage from doing so. (Issuing equity also reveals the manager's pessimism immediately. Most managers prefer to wait. A debt issue lets bad news come out later through other channels.)

The story of Smith and Jones illustrates how asymmetric information favors debt issues over equity issues. If managers are better informed than investors and both groups are rational, then any company that can borrow will do so rather than issuing fresh equity. In other words, debt issues will be higher in the pecking order.

Taken literally this reasoning seems to rule out any issue of equity. That's not right, because asymmetric information is not always important and there are other forces at work. For example, if Smith had already borrowed heavily, and would risk financial distress by borrowing more, then it would have a good reason to issue common stock. In this case announcement of a stock issue would not be entirely bad news. The announcement would still depress the stock price—it would highlight managers' concerns about financial distress—but the fall in price would not necessarily make the issue unwise or infeasible.

High-tech, high-growth companies can also be credible issuers of common stock. Such companies' assets are mostly intangible, and bankruptcy or financial distress would be especially costly. This calls for conservative financing. The only way to grow rapidly and keep a conservative debt ratio is to issue equity. If investors see equity issued for these reasons, problems of the sort encountered by Smith's financial manager become much less serious.

With such exceptions noted, asymmetric information can explain the dominance of debt financing over new equity issues in practice. Debt issues are frequent; equity issues, rare. The bulk of external financing comes from debt, even in the United States, where equity markets are highly information-efficient. Equity issues are even more difficult in countries with less well developed stock markets.

None of this says that firms ought to strive for high debt ratios—just that it's better to raise equity by plowing back earnings than issuing stock. In fact, a firm with ample internally generated funds doesn't have to sell any kind of security and thus avoids issue costs and information problems completely.[30]

Implications of the Pecking Order

The pecking-order theory of corporate financing goes like this.

1. Firms prefer internal finance.
2. They adapt their target dividend payout ratios to their investment opportunities, while trying to avoid sudden changes in dividends.

---

[29] A Smith stock issue might not succeed even at $80. Persistence in trying to sell at $80 could convince investors that the stock is worth even less!

[30] Even debt issues can create information problems if the odds of default are significant. A pessimistic manager may try to issue debt quickly, before bad news gets out. An optimistic manager will delay pending good news, perhaps arranging a short-term bank loan in the meantime. Rational investors will take this behavior into account in pricing the risky debt issue.

3. Sticky dividend policies, plus unpredictable fluctuations in profitability and investment opportunities, mean that internally generated cash flow is sometimes more than capital expenditures and other times less. If it is more, the firm pays off debt or invests in marketable securities. If it is less, the firm first draws down its cash balance or sells its marketable securities.

4. If external finance is required, firms issue the safest security first. That is, they start with debt, then possibly hybrid securities such as convertible bonds, then perhaps equity as a last resort.

In this theory, there is no well-defined target debt–equity mix, because there are two kinds of equity, internal and external, one at the top of the pecking order and one at the bottom. Each firm's observed debt ratio reflects its cumulative requirements for external finance.

The pecking order explains why the most profitable firms generally borrow less—not because they have low target debt ratios but because they don't need outside money. Less profitable firms issue debt because they do not have internal funds sufficient for their capital investment programs and because debt financing is first on the pecking order of *external* financing.

In the pecking-order theory, the attraction of interest tax shields is assumed to be second-order. Debt ratios change when there is an imbalance of internal cash flow, net of dividends, and real investment opportunities. Highly profitable firms with limited investment opportunities work down to low debt ratios. Firms whose investment opportunities outrun internally generated funds are driven to borrow more and more.

This theory explains the inverse intraindustry relationship between profitability and financial leverage. Suppose firms generally invest to keep up with the growth of their industries. Then rates of investment will be similar within an industry. Given sticky dividend payouts, the least profitable firms will have less internal funds and will end up borrowing more.

The Trade-off Theory vs. the Pecking-Order Theory—Some Recent Tests

In 1995 Rajan and Zingales published a study of debt versus equity choices by large firms in Canada, France, Germany, Italy, Japan, the United Kingdom, and the United States. Rajan and Zingales found that the debt ratios of individual companies seemed to depend on four main factors:[31]

1. *Size.* Large firms tend to have higher debt ratios.

2. *Tangible assets.* Firms with high ratios of fixed assets to total assets have higher debt ratios.

3. *Profitability.* More profitable firms have lower debt ratios.

4. *Market to book.* Firms with higher ratios of market-to-book value have lower debt ratios.

These results convey good news for both the trade-off and pecking-order theories. Trade-off enthusiasts note that large companies with tangible assets are less exposed

---

[31] R. G. Rajan and L. Zingales, "What Do We Know about Capital Structure? Some Evidence from International Data," *Journal of Finance* 50 (December 1995), pp. 1421–1460. The same four factors seem to work in developing economies. See L. Booth, V. Aivazian, A. Demirguc-Kunt, and V. Maksimovic, "Capital Structure in Developing Countries," *Journal of Finance* 56 (February 2001), pp. 87–130.

to costs of financial distress and would be expected to borrow more. They interpret the market-to-book ratio as a measure of growth opportunities and argue that growth companies could face high costs of financial distress and would be expected to borrow less. Pecking-order advocates stress the importance of profitability, arguing that profitable firms use less debt because they can rely on internal financing. They interpret the market-to-book ratio as just another measure of profitability.

It seems that we have two competing theories, and they're both right! That's not a comfortable conclusion. So recent research has tried to run horse races between the two theories in order to find the circumstances in which one or the other wins. It seems that the pecking order works best for large, mature firms that have access to public bond markets. These firms rarely issue equity. They prefer internal financing, but turn to debt markets if needed to finance investment. Smaller, younger, growth firms are more likely to rely on equity issues when external financing is required.[32]

There is also some evidence that debt ratios incorporate the cumulative effects of *market timing*.[33] Market timing is an example of behavioral corporate finance. Suppose that investors are sometimes irrationally exuberant (as in the late 1990s) and sometimes irrationally despondent. If the financial manager's views are more stable than investors', then he or she can take advantage by issuing shares when the stock price is too high and switching to debt when the price is too low. Thus lucky companies with a history of buoyant stock prices will issue less debt and more shares, ending up with low debt ratios. Unfortunate and unpopular companies will avoid share issues and end up with high debt ratios.

Market timing can explain why companies tend to issue shares after run-ups in stock prices and also why aggregate stock issues are concentrated in bull markets and fall sharply in bear markets.

The Bright Side and the Dark Side of Financial Slack

Other things equal, it's better to be at the top of the pecking order than at the bottom. Firms that have worked down the pecking order and need external equity may end up living with excessive debt or passing by good investments because shares can't be sold at what managers consider a fair price.

In other words, *financial slack* is valuable. Having financial slack means having cash, marketable securities, readily salable real assets, and ready access to debt markets or to bank financing. Ready access basically requires conservative financing so that potential lenders see the company's debt as a safe investment.

In the long run, a company's value rests more on its capital investment and operating decisions than on financing. Therefore, you want to make sure your firm has sufficient financial slack so that financing is quickly available for good investments. Financial slack is most valuable to firms with plenty of positive-NPV growth opportunities. That is another reason why growth companies usually aspire to conservative capital structures.

---

[32] L. Shyam-Sunder and S. C. Myers found that the pecking-order hypothesis outperformed the trade-off hypothesis for a sample of large companies in the 1980s. See "Testing Static Trade-off against Pecking-Order Theories of Capital Structure," *Journal of Financial Economics* 51 (February 1999), pp. 219–244. M. Frank and V. Goyal found that the performance of the pecking-order hypothesis deteriorated in the 1990s, especially for small growth firms. See "Testing the Pecking Order Theory of Capital Structure," *Journal of Financial Economics* 67 (February 2003), pp. 217–248. See also E. Fama and K. French, "Testing Trade-off and Pecking Order Predictions about Dividends and Debt," *Review of Financial Studies* 15 (Spring 2002), pp. 1–33.

[33] M. Baker and J. Wurgler, "Market Timing and Capital Structure," *Journal of Finance* 57 (February 2002), pp. 1–32.

There is also a dark side to financial slack. Too much of it may encourage managers to take it easy, expand their perks, or empire-build with cash that should be paid back to stockholders. In other words, slack can make agency problems worse.

Michael Jensen has stressed the tendency of managers with ample free cash flow (or unnecessary financial slack) to plow too much cash into mature businesses or ill-advised acquisitions. "The problem," Jensen says, "is how to motivate managers to disgorge the cash rather than investing it below the cost of capital or wasting it in organizational inefficiencies."[34]

If that's the problem, then maybe debt is an answer. Scheduled interest and principal payments are contractual obligations of the firm. Debt forces the firm to pay out cash. Perhaps the best debt level would leave just enough cash in the bank, after debt service, to finance all positive-NPV projects, with not a penny left over.

We do not recommend this degree of fine-tuning, but the idea is valid and important. Debt can discipline managers who are tempted to invest too much. It can also provide the pressure to force improvements in operating efficiency.

---

[34] M. C. Jensen, "Agency Costs of Free Cash Flow, Corporate Finance and Takeovers," *American Economic Review* 26 (May 1986), p. 323.

SUMMARY

Our task in this chapter was to show why capital structure matters. We did not throw away MM's proposition that capital structure is irrelevant; we added to it. However, we did not arrive at any simple, universal theory of optimal capital structure.

The trade-off theory emphasizes taxes and financial distress. The value of the firm is broken down as

Value if all-equity-financed + PV(tax shield) − PV(costs of financial distress)

According to this theory, the firm should increase debt until the value from PV(tax shield) is just offset, at the margin, by increases in PV(costs of financial distress).

The costs of financial distress are:

1. Bankruptcy costs
   a. Direct costs such as legal and accounting fees.
   b. Indirect costs reflecting the difficulty of managing a company undergoing liquidation or reorganization.
2. Costs of financial distress short of bankruptcy
   a. Doubts about a firm's creditworthiness can hobble its operations. Customers and suppliers will be reluctant to deal with a firm that may not be around next year. Key employees will be tempted to leave. We noted evidence that highly leveraged firms seem to be less vigorous product-market competitors.
   b. Conflicts of interest between bondholders and stockholders of firms in financial distress may lead to poor operating and investment decisions. Stockholders acting in their narrow self-interest can gain at the expense of creditors by playing "games" that reduce the overall value of the firm.
   c. The fine print in debt contracts is designed to prevent these games. But fine print increases the costs of writing, monitoring, and enforcing the debt contract.

The value of the tax shield is more controversial. It would be easy to compute if we had only corporate taxes to worry about. In that case the net tax saving from borrowing would be just the marginal corporate tax rate T_c times $r_D D$, the interest payment. If debt is fixed, the tax shield can be valued by discounting at the borrowing rate r_D. In the special case of fixed, permanent debt

$$\text{PV(tax shield)} = \frac{T_c(r_D D)}{r_D} = T_c D$$

However, corporate taxes are only part of the story. If investors pay higher taxes on interest income than on equity income (dividends and capital gains), then interest tax shields to the corporation will be partly offset by higher taxes paid by investors. The low (15% maximum) U.S. tax rates on dividends and capital gains have reduced the tax advantage to corporate borrowing.

The trade-off theory balances the tax advantages of borrowing against the costs of financial distress. Corporations are supposed to pick a target capital structure that maximizes firm value. Firms with safe, tangible assets and plenty of taxable income to shield ought to have high targets. Unprofitable companies with risky, intangible assets ought to rely more on equity financing.

This theory of capital structure successfully explains many industry differences in capital structure, but it does not explain why the most profitable firms *within* an industry generally have the most conservative capital structures. Under the trade-off theory, high profitability should mean high debt capacity *and* a strong corporate tax incentive to use that capacity.

There is a competing, pecking-order theory, which states that firms use internal financing when available and choose debt over equity when external financing is required. This explains why the less profitable firms in an industry borrow more—not because they have higher target debt ratios but because they need more external financing and because debt is next on the pecking order when internal funds are exhausted.

The pecking order is a consequence of asymmetric information. Managers know more about their firms than outside investors do, and they are reluctant to issue stock when they believe the price is too low. They try to time issues when shares are fairly priced or overpriced. Investors understand this, and interpret a decision to issue shares as bad news. That explains why stock price usually falls when a stock issue is announced.

Debt is better than equity when these information problems are important. Optimistic managers will prefer debt to undervalued equity, and pessimistic managers will be pressed to follow suit. The pecking-order theory says that equity will be issued only when debt capacity is running out and financial distress threatens.

The pecking-order theory stresses the value of financial slack. Without sufficient slack, the firm may be caught at the bottom of the pecking order and be forced to choose between issuing undervalued shares, borrowing and risking financial distress, or passing up positive-NPV investment opportunities.

There is, however, a dark side to financial slack. Surplus cash or credit tempts managers to overinvest or to indulge an easy and glamorous corporate lifestyle. When temptation wins, or threatens to win, a high debt ratio can help: It forces the company to disgorge cash and prods managers and organizations to try harder to be more efficient.

FURTHER READING

Modigliani and Miller's analysis of the present value of interest tax shields at the corporate level is in:

F. Modigliani and M. H. Miller, "Corporate Income Taxes and the Cost of Capital: A Correction," *American Economic Review* 53 (June 1963), pp. 433–443.

F. Modigliani and M. H. Miller, "Some Estimates of the Cost of Capital to the Electric Utility Industry, 1954–57," *American Economic Review* 56 (June 1966), pp. 333–391.

Miller extends the MM model to personal as well as corporate taxes. Graham's estimates of the tax benefits of debt recognize the possibility that firms will not earn taxable profits in the future:

M. H. Miller, "Debt and Taxes," *Journal of Finance* 32 (May 1977), pp. 261–276.

J. R. Graham, "How Big Are the Tax Benefits of Debt?" *Journal of Finance* 55 (October 2000), pp. 1901–1941.

The following articles analyze the conflicts of interest between bondholders and stockholders and their implications for financing policy:

M. C. Jensen and W. H. Meckling, "Theory of the Firm: Managerial Behavior, Agency Costs and Ownership Structure," *Journal of Financial Economics* 3 (October 1976), pp. 305–360.

S. C. Myers, "Determinants of Corporate Borrowing," *Journal of Financial Economics* 5 (1977), pp. 146–175.

Myers's 1984 paper describes the pecking-order theory:

S. C. Myers, "The Capital Structure Puzzle," *Journal of Finance* 39 (July 1984), pp. 575–592.

The following paper surveys chief financial officers' views about capital structure:

J. Graham and C. Harvey, "How Do CFOs Make Capital Budgeting and Capital Structure Decisions?" *Journal of Applied Corporate Finance* 15 (Spring 2002), pp. 8–23.

Finally, here are two review articles on capital structure:

M. Harris and A. Raviv, "The Theory of Capital Structure," *Journal of Finance* 46 (March 1991), pp. 297–355.

S. C. Myers, "Financing of Corporations," in G. M. Constantinides, M. Harris, and R. Stulz (eds.), *Handbook of the Economics of Finance* (Amsterdam: Elsevier North-Holland, 2003).

The Winter 2005 issue of the Journal of Applied Corporate Finance *contains several articles on capital structure decisions in practice.*

CONCEPT REVIEW QUESTIONS

1. Suppose a company borrows $1 million at an interest rate of 6% and the corporate tax rate is 30%. What is the annual interest tax shield? If the debt is permanent, what is the value of the tax shield? (page 393)

2. Why might the existence of personal taxes partly offset the benefit of the corporate tax shield on interest payments? (page 397)

3. List the direct and indirect costs of bankruptcy. Would you expect the indirect costs to be above or below average for firms with lots of intangible assets? (pages 403–404 and 410)

For a complete listing of your chapter Concept Review Questions, please visit us at www.mhhe.com/bma1e.

QUIZ

1. The present value of interest tax shields is often written as T_cD, where D is the amount of debt and T_c is the marginal corporate tax rate. Under what assumptions is this present value correct?

2. Here are book and market value balance sheets of the United Frypan Company (UF):

Book					Market				
Net working capital	$ 20	Debt	$ 40		Net working capital	$ 20	Debt	$ 40	
Long-term assets	80	Equity	60		Long-term assets	140	Equity	120	
	$100		$100			$160		$160	

Assume that MM's theory holds with taxes. There is no growth, and the $40 of debt is expected to be permanent. Assume a 40% corporate tax rate.

a. How much of the firm's value is accounted for by the debt-generated tax shield?

b. How much better off will UF's shareholders be if the firm borrows $20 more and uses it to repurchase stock?

3. What is the relative tax advantage of corporate debt if the corporate tax rate is $T_c = .35$, the personal tax rate is $T_p = .35$, but all equity income is received as capital gains and escapes tax entirely ($T_{pE} = 0$)? How does the relative tax advantage change if the company decides to pay out all equity income as cash dividends that are taxed at 15%?

4. "The firm can't use interest tax shields unless it has (taxable) income to shield." What does this statement imply for debt policy? Explain briefly.

5. This question tests your understanding of financial distress.

a. What are the costs of going bankrupt? Define these costs carefully.

b. "A company can incur costs of financial distress without ever going bankrupt." Explain how this can happen.

c. Explain how conflicts of interest between bondholders and stockholders can lead to costs of financial distress.

6. On February 29, 2009, when PDQ Computers announced bankruptcy, its share price fell from $3.00 to $.50 per share. There were 10 million shares outstanding. Does that imply bankruptcy costs of $10 \times (3.00 - .50) = \$25$ million? Explain.

7. The traditional theory of optimal capital structure states that firms trade off corporate interest tax shields against the possible costs of financial distress due to borrowing. What does this theory predict about the relationship between book profitability and target book debt ratios? Is the theory's prediction consistent with the facts?

8. Rajan and Zingales identified four variables that seemed to explain differences in debt ratios in several countries. What are the four variables?

9. Why does asymmetric information push companies to raise external funds by borrowing rather than by issuing common stock?

10. Fill in the blanks: According to the pecking-order theory,

(a) The firm's debt ratio is determined by _____.

(b) Debt ratios depend on past profitability, because _____.

11. For what kinds of companies is financial slack most valuable? Are there situations in which financial slack should be reduced by borrowing and paying out the proceeds to the stockholders? Explain.

12. Compute the present value of interest tax shields generated by these three debt issues. Consider corporate taxes only. The marginal tax rate is $T_c = .35$.

a. A $1,000, one-year loan at 8%.

b. A five-year loan of $1,000 at 8%. Assume no principal is repaid until maturity.

c. A $1,000 perpetuity at 7%.

PRACTICE QUESTIONS

13. Suppose that, in an effort to reduce the federal deficit, Congress increases the top personal tax rate on interest and dividends to 35% but retains a 15% tax rate on realized capital gains. The corporate tax rate stays at 35%. Compute the total corporate plus personal taxes paid on debt versus equity income if (**a**) all capital gains are realized immediately and (**b**) capital gains are deferred forever. Assume capital gains are half of equity income.

14. "The trouble with MM's argument is that it ignores the fact that individuals can deduct interest for personal income tax." Show why this is not an objection if personal tax rates on interest and equity income are the same.

15. Look back at the Merck example in Section 15.1. Suppose Merck increases its long-term debt to $10 billion. It uses the additional debt to repurchase shares. Reconstruct Table 15.3(*b*) with the new capital structure. How much additional value is added for Merck shareholders if the table's assumptions are correct?

STANDARD &POOR'S

16. Look up Merck on the Market Insight database (**www.mhhe.com/edumarketinsight**).

   a. Recalculate book- and market-value balance sheets using the most recent available financial information. Use the same format as for Table 15.3.

   b. Track Merck's long-term debt and debt ratio over the last five years. How have they changed? Does it appear that Merck has a stable target debt ratio? Do you see any evidence of pecking-order financing?

   c. How much has Merck spent to repurchase its own shares? Would the trade-off theory predict share repurchases for a conservatively financed company like Merck?

17. In Section 15.3, we briefly referred to three games: cash in and run, playing for time, and bait and switch.

   For each game, construct a simple numerical example (like the example for the risk-shifting game) showing how shareholders can gain at the expense of creditors. Then explain how the temptation to play these games could lead to costs of financial distress.

18. Look at some real companies with different types of assets. What operating problems would each encounter in the event of financial distress? How well would the assets keep their value?

19. Let us go back to Circular File's market value balance sheet:

Net working capital	$20	$25	Bonds outstanding
Fixed assets	10	5	Common stock
Total assets	$30	$30	Total value

Who gains and who loses from the following maneuvers?

   a. Circular scrapes up $5 in cash and pays a cash dividend.

   b. Circular halts operations, sells its fixed assets, and converts net working capital into $20 cash. Unfortunately the fixed assets fetch only $6 on the secondhand market. The $26 cash is invested in Treasury bills.

   c. Circular encounters an acceptable investment opportunity, NPV = 0, requiring an investment of $10. The firm borrows to finance the project. The new debt has the same security, seniority, etc., as the old.

   d. Suppose that the new project has NPV = +$2 and is financed by an issue of preferred stock.

   e. The lenders agree to extend the maturity of their loan from one year to two in order to give Circular a chance to recover.

20. The Salad Oil Storage (SOS) Company has financed a large part of its facilities with long-term debt. There is a significant risk of default, but the company is not on the ropes yet. Explain:

  a. Why SOS stockholders could lose by investing in a positive-NPV project financed by an equity issue.

  b. Why SOS stockholders could gain by investing in a negative-NPV project financed by cash.

  c. Why SOS stockholders could gain from paying out a large cash dividend.

21. a. Who benefits from the fine print in bond contracts when the firm gets into financial trouble? Give a one-sentence answer.

  b. Who benefits from the fine print when the bonds are issued? Suppose the firm is offered the choice of issuing (i) a bond with standard restrictions on dividend payout, additional borrowing, etc., and (ii) a bond with minimal restrictions but a much higher interest rate? Suppose the interest rates on both (i) and (ii) are fair from the viewpoint of lenders. Which bond would you expect the firm to issue? Why?

22. "I was amazed to find that the announcement of a stock issue drives down the value of the issuing firm by 30%, on average, of the proceeds of the issue. That issue cost dwarfs the underwriter's spread and the administrative costs of the issue. It makes common stock issues prohibitively expensive."

  a. You are contemplating a $100 million stock issue. On past evidence, you anticipate that announcement of this issue will drive down stock price by 3% and that the market value of your firm will fall by 30% of the amount to be raised. On the other hand, additional equity funds are necessary to fund an investment project that you believe has a positive NPV of $40 million. Should you proceed with the issue?

  b. Is the fall in market value on announcement of a stock issue an *issue cost* in the same sense as an underwriter's spread? Respond to the quote that begins this question.

  Use your answer to (a) as a numerical example to explain your response to (b).

23. Ronald Masulis[35] has analyzed the stock price impact of *exchange offers* of debt for equity or vice versa. In an exchange offer, the firm offers to trade freshly issued securities for seasoned securities in the hands of investors. Thus, a firm that wanted to move to a higher debt ratio could offer to trade new debt for outstanding shares. A firm that wanted to move to a more conservative capital structure could offer to trade new shares for outstanding debt securities.

  Masulis found that debt for equity exchanges were good news (stock price increased on announcement) and equity for debt exchanges were bad news.

  a. Are these results consistent with the trade-off theory of capital structure?

  b. Are the results consistent with the evidence that investors regard announcements of (i) stock issues as bad news, (ii) stock repurchases as good news, and (iii) debt issues as no news, or at most trifling disappointments?

  c. How could Masulis's results be explained?

24. The possible payoffs from Ms. Ketchup's projects (see Section 15.3) have not changed but there is now a 40% chance that project 2 will pay off $24 and a 60% chance that it will pay off $0.

---

[35] R. W. Masulis, "The Effects of Capital Structure Change on Security Prices: A Study of Exchange Offers," *Journal of Financial Economics* 8 (June 1980), pp. 139–177, and "The Impact of Capital Structure Change on Firm Value," *Journal of Finance* 38 (March 1983), pp. 107–126.

Visit us at www.mhhe.com/bma1e

a. Recalculate the expected payoffs to the bank and Ms. Ketchup if the bank lends the present value of $10. Which project would Ms. Ketchup undertake?

b. What is the maximum amount the bank could lend that would induce Ms. Ketchup to take project 1?

STANDARD &POOR'S

25. Select a dozen companies from the Market Insight database (**www.mhhe.com/edumarketinsight**). Estimate how much more these companies could borrow before they would exhaust taxable profits.

STANDARD &POOR'S

26. The Market Insight database (**www.mhhe.com/edumarketinsight**) gives access to dozens of industry surveys. Check out the financial tables at the end of these surveys for several different industries. We suggest that you start with Autos and Auto Parts, Broadcasting and Cable TV, Department Stores and Trucking, plus a couple more industries that interest you. Write down the debt-to-capital ratios for a few of the largest companies in each industry, and average within the industry. Can you explain the differences between these industry-average ratios?

CHALLENGE QUESTIONS

27. Most financial managers measure debt ratios from their companies' book balance sheets. Financial economists tend to emphasize ratios from market-value balance sheets. Which is the right measure in principle? Does the trade-off theory propose to explain book or market leverage? How about the pecking-order theory?

STANDARD &POOR'S

28. Use the Market Insight database (**www.mhhe.com/edumarketinsight**) to see how well differences in company leverage seem to support the trade-off theory and the pecking-order theory.

CHAPTER SIXTEEN

16

FINANCING AND VALUATION

IN CHAPTERS 6 and 7 we showed how to value a capital investment project by a four-step procedure:

1. Forecast after-tax cash flows, assuming all-equity financing.
2. Assess the project's risk.
3. Estimate the opportunity cost of capital.
4. Calculate NPV, using the opportunity cost of capital as the discount rate.

There's nothing wrong with this procedure, but now we're going to extend it to include value contributed by financing decisions. There are two ways to do this:

1. *Adjust the discount rate.* The adjustment is typically downward, to account for the value of interest tax shields. This is the most common approach, which is usually implemented via the after-tax weighted-average cost of capital (WACC). We introduced the after-tax WACC in Chapters 10 and 14, but here we will provide a lot more guidance on how it is calculated and used.

2. *Adjust the present value.* That is, start by estimating the firm or project's base-case value, assuming it is all-equity-financed, and then adjust this base-case value to account for financing.

Adjusted present value (APV)
= base-case value + value of financing side effects

Once you identify and value the financing side effects, calculating APV is no more than addition or subtraction.

This is a how-to-do-it chapter. In the first section, we explain and derive the after-tax WACC and use it to value a project and business. Then in Section 16.2 we work through a more complex and realistic valuation problem. Section 16.3 covers some tricks of the trade: helpful hints on how to estimate inputs and on how to adjust WACC when business risk or capital structure changes. Section 16.4 turns to the APV method. The idea behind APV is simple enough, but tracing through all the financing side effects can be tricky. We conclude the chapter with a question-and-answer section designed to clarify points that managers and students often find confusing. The Appendix covers an important special case, namely, the after-tax valuation of safe cash flows.

16.1   THE AFTER-TAX WEIGHTED-AVERAGE COST OF CAPITAL

We first addressed problems of valuation and capital budgeting in Chapters 2 to 7. In those early chapters we said hardly a word about financing decisions. In fact we proceeded under the simplest possible financing assumption, namely, all-equity financing. We were really assuming a Modigliani–Miller (MM) world in which all financing decisions are irrelevant. In a strict MM world, firms can analyze real investments as if they are all-equity-financed; the actual financing plan is a mere detail to be worked out later.

Under MM assumptions, decisions to spend money can be separated from decisions to raise money. Now we reconsider the capital budgeting decision when investment and financing decisions interact and cannot be wholly separated.

One reason that financing and investment decisions interact is taxes. Interest is a tax-deductible expense. Think back to Chapters 10 and 14 where we introduced the *after-tax* weighted-average cost of capital:

$$\text{WACC} = r_D(1 - T_c)\frac{D}{V} + r_E\frac{E}{V}$$

Here D and E are the market values of the firm's debt and equity, $V = D + E$ is the total market value of the firm, r_D and r_E are the costs of debt and equity, and T_c is the marginal corporate tax rate.

Notice that the WACC formula uses the *after-tax* cost of debt $r_D (1 - T_c)$. That is how the after-tax WACC captures the value of interest tax shields. Notice too that all the variables in the WACC formula refer to the firm as a whole. As a result, the formula gives the right discount rate only for projects that are just like the firm undertaking them. The formula works for the "average" project. It is incorrect for projects that are safer or riskier than the average of the firm's existing assets. It is incorrect for projects whose acceptance would lead to an increase or decrease in the firm's target debt ratio.

The WACC is based on the firm's *current* characteristics, but managers use it to discount *future* cash flows. That's fine as long as the firm's business risk and debt ratio are expected to remain constant, but when the business risk and debt ratio are expected to change, discounting cash flows by the WACC is only approximately correct.

Example: Sangria Corporation

Sangria is a U.S.-based company whose products aim to promote happy, low-stress lifestyles. Let's calculate Sangria's WACC. Its book and market-value balance sheets are:

Sangria Corporation (Book Values, $ millions)

Asset value	$1,000	$ 500	Debt
		500	Equity
	$1,000	$1,000	

Sangria Corporation (Market Values, $ millions)

Asset value	$1,250	$ 500	Debt
		750	Equity
	$1,250	$1,250	

We calculated the market value of equity on Sangria's balance sheet by multiplying its current stock price ($7.50) by 100 million, the number of its outstanding shares. The company's future prospects are good, so the stock is trading above book value ($7.50 vs. $5.00 per share). However, interest rates have been stable since the firm's debt was issued and the book and market values of debt are in this case equal.

Sangria's cost of debt (the market interest rate on its existing debt and on any new borrowing[1]) is 6%. Its cost of equity (the expected rate of return demanded by investors in Sangria's stock) is 12.4%.

The market-value balance sheet shows assets worth $1,250 million. Of course we can't observe this value directly, because the assets themselves are not traded. But we know what they are worth to debt and equity investors ($500 + 750 = $1,250 million). This value is entered on the left of the market-value balance sheet.

Why did we show the book balance sheet? Only so you could draw a big X through it. Do so now.

When estimating the weighted-average cost of capital, you are not interested in past investments but in current values and expectations for the future. Sangria's true debt ratio is not 50%, the book ratio, but 40%, because its assets are worth $1,250 million. The cost of equity, $r_E = .124$, is the expected rate of return from purchase of stock at $7.50 per share, the current market price. It is not the return on book value per share. You can't buy shares in Sangria for $5 anymore.

Sangria is consistently profitable and pays taxes at the marginal rate of 35%. This tax rate is the final input for Sangria's WACC. The inputs are summarized here:

Cost of debt (r_D)	.06
Cost of equity (r_E)	.124
Marginal tax rate (T_c)	.35
Debt ratio (D/V)	500/1,250 = .4
Equity ratio (E/V)	750/1,250 = .6

The company's after-tax WACC is

$$\text{WACC} = .06 \times (1 - .35) \times .4 + .124 \times .6 = .090, \text{ or } 9.0\%$$

That's how you calculate the weighted-average cost of capital. Now let's see how Sangria would *use* it.

Example   Sangria's enologists have proposed investing $12.5 million in the construction of a perpetual crushing machine, which (conveniently for us) never depreciates and generates a perpetual stream of earnings and cash flow of $1.731 million per year pretax. The project is average risk, so we can use WACC. The after-tax cash flow is:

Pretax cash flow	$1.731 million
Tax at 35%	.606
After-tax cash flow	$C = $1.125 million

---

[1] Always use an up-to-date interest rate (yield to maturity), not the interest rate when the firm's debt was first issued and not the coupon rate on the debt's book value.

Notice: This after-tax cash flow takes no account of interest tax shields on debt supported by the perpetual crusher project. As we explained in Chapter 7, standard capital budgeting practice calculates after-tax cash flows as if the project were all-equity-financed. However, the interest tax shields will not be ignored: We are about to discount the project's cash flows by Sangria's WACC, in which the cost of debt is entered after tax. The value of interest tax shields is picked up not as higher after-tax cash flows, but in a lower discount rate.

The crusher generates a perpetual after-tax cash flow of $C = \$1.125$ million, so NPV is

$$NPV = -12.5 + \frac{1.125}{0.09} = 0$$

NPV = 0 means a barely acceptable investment. The annual cash flow of $1.125 million per year amounts to a 9% rate of return on investment ($1.125/12.5 = .09$), exactly equal to Sangria's WACC.

If project NPV is exactly zero, the return to equity investors must exactly equal the cost of equity, 12.4%. Let's confirm that Sangria shareholders can actually look forward to a 12.4% return on their investment in the perpetual crusher project.

Suppose Sangria sets up this project as a mini-firm. Its market-value balance sheet looks like this:

Perpetual Crusher (Market Values, $ millions)

Asset value	$ 12.5	$ 5.0	Debt
		7.5	Equity
	$ 12.5	$ 12.5	

Calculate the expected dollar return to shareholders:

$$\text{After-tax interest} = r_D(1 - T_c)D = 0.06 \times (1 - .35) \times 5 = .195$$
$$\text{Expected equity income} = C - r_D(1 - T_c)D = 1.125 - .195 = 0.93$$

The project's earnings are level and perpetual, so the expected rate of return on equity is equal to the expected equity income divided by the equity value:

$$\text{Expected equity return} = r_E = \frac{\text{expected equity income}}{\text{equity value}}$$
$$= \frac{0.93}{7.5} = .124, \text{ or } 12.4\%$$

The expected return on equity equals the cost of equity, so it makes sense that the project's NPV is zero.

Review of Assumptions

When discounting the perpetual crusher's cash flows at Sangria's WACC, we assume that:

- The project's business risks are the same as those of Sangria's other assets and remain so for the life of the project.
- The project supports the same fraction of debt to value as in Sangria's overall capital structure, which remains constant for the life of the project.

You can see the importance of these two assumptions: If the perpetual crusher had greater business risk than Sangria's other assets, or if the acceptance of the project would lead to a permanent, material change in Sangria's debt ratio,[2] then Sangria's shareholders would not be content with a 12.4% expected return on their equity investment in the project.

We have illustrated the WACC formula only for a project offering perpetual cash flows. But the formula works for any cash-flow pattern if the firm adjusts its borrowing to maintain a constant debt ratio over time.[3] When the firm departs from this borrowing policy, WACC is only approximately correct.

16.2   VALUING BUSINESSES

On most workdays the financial manager concentrates on valuing projects, arranging financing, and helping run the firm more effectively. The valuation of the business as a whole is left to investors and financial markets. But on some days the financial manager has to take a stand on what an entire business is worth. When this happens, a *big* decision is typically in the offing. For example:

- If firm A is about to make a takeover offer for firm B, then A's financial managers have to decide how much the combined business A + B is worth under A's management. This task is particularly difficult if B is a private company with no observable share price.

- If firm C is considering the sale of one of its divisions, it has to decide what the division is worth in order to negotiate with potential buyers.

- When a firm goes public, the investment bank must evaluate how much the firm is worth in order to set the issue price.

---

[2] Users of WACC need not worry about small or temporary fluctuations in debt-to-value ratios. Suppose that Sangria management decides for convenience to borrow $12.5 million to allow immediate construction of the crusher. This does not necessarily change Sangria's long-term financing policy. If the crusher supports only $5.0 million of debt, Sangria would have to pay down debt to restore its overall debt ratio to 40%. For example, it could fund later projects with less debt and more equity.

[3] We can prove this statement as follows. Denote expected after-tax cash flows (assuming all-equity financing) as $C_1, C_2, \ldots, C_T$. With all-equity financing, these flows would be discounted at the opportunity cost of capital r. But we need to value the cash flows for a firm that is financed partly with debt.

Start with value in the next to last period: $V_{T-1} = D_{T-1} + E_{T-1}$. The total cash payoff to debt and equity investors is the cash flow plus the interest tax shield. The expected total return to debt and equity investors is:

$$\text{Expected cash payoff in } T = C_T + T_c\, r_D D_{T-1} \qquad (1)$$

$$= V_{T-1}\left(1 + r_D \frac{D_{T-1}}{V_{T-1}} + r_E \frac{E_{T-1}}{V_{T-1}}\right) \qquad (2)$$

Assume the debt ratio is constant at $L = D/V$. Equate (1) and (2) and solve for V_{T-1}:

$$V_{T-1} = \frac{C_T}{1 + (1 - T_c)r_D L + r_E(1 - L)} = \frac{C_T}{1 + \text{WACC}}$$

The logic repeats for V_{T-2}. Note that the next period's payoff includes V_{T-1}:

$$\text{Expected cash payoff in } T - 1 = C_{T-1} + T_c r_D D_{T-2} + V_{T-1}$$

$$= V_{T-2}\left(1 + r_D \frac{D_{T-2}}{V_{T-2}} + r_E \frac{E_{T-2}}{V_{T-2}}\right)$$

$$V_{T-2} = \frac{C_{T-1} + V_{T-1}}{1 + (1 - T_c)r_D L + r_E(1 - L)} = \frac{C_{T-1} + V_{T-1}}{1 + \text{WACC}} = \frac{C_{T-1}}{1 + \text{WACC}} + \frac{C_T}{(1 + \text{WACC})^2}$$

We can continue all the way back to date 0:

$$V_0 = \sum_{t=1}^{T} \frac{C_t}{(1 + \text{WACC})^t}$$

In addition, thousands of analysts in stockbrokers' offices and investment firms spend every workday burrowing away in the hope of finding undervalued firms. Many of these analysts use the valuation tools we are about to cover.

In Chapter 5 we took a first pass at valuing an entire business. We assumed then that the business was financed solely by equity. Now we will show how WACC can be used to value a company that is financed by a mixture of debt and equity as long as the debt ratio is expected to remain approximately constant. You just treat the company as if it were one big project. You forecast the company's cash flows (the hardest part of the exercise) and discount back to present value. But be sure to remember three important points:

1. If you discount at WACC, cash flows have to be projected just as you would for a capital investment project. Do not deduct interest. Calculate taxes as if the company were all-equity-financed. (The value of interest tax shields is not ignored, because the after-tax cost of debt is used in the WACC formula.)

2. Unlike most projects, companies are potentially immortal. But that does not mean that you need to forecast every year's cash flow from now to eternity. Financial managers usually forecast to a medium-term horizon and add a terminal value to the cash flows in the horizon year. The terminal value is the present value at the horizon of all subsequent cash flows. Estimating the terminal value requires careful attention because it often accounts for the majority of the company's value.

3. Discounting at WACC values the assets and operations of the company. If the object is to value the company's equity, that is, its common stock, don't forget to subtract the value of the company's outstanding debt.

Here's an example.

Valuing Rio Corporation

Sangria is tempted to acquire the Rio Corporation, which is also in the business of promoting relaxed, happy lifestyles. Rio has developed a special weight-loss program called the Brazil Diet, based on barbecues, red wine, and sunshine. The firm guarantees that within three months you will have a figure that will allow you to fit right in at Ipanema or Copacabana beach in Rio de Janeiro. But before you head for the beach, you've got the job of working out how much Sangria should pay for Rio.

Rio is a U.S. company. It is privately held, so Sangria has no stock-market price to rely on. Rio has 1.5 million shares outstanding and debt with a market and book value of $36 million. Rio is in the same line of business as Sangria, so we will assume that it has the same business risk as Sangria and can support the same proportion of debt. Therefore we can use Sangria's WACC.

Your first task is to forecast Rio's *free cash flow* (FCF). Free cash flow is the amount of cash that the firm can pay out to investors after making all investments necessary for growth. Free cash flow is calculated assuming the firm is all-equity-financed. Discounting the free cash flows at the after-tax WACC gives the total value of Rio (debt *plus* equity). To find the value of its equity, you will need to subtract the $36 million of debt.

We will forecast each year's free cash flow out to a *valuation horizon* (H) and predict the business's value at that horizon (PV_H). The cash flows and horizon value are then discounted back to the present:

$$PV = \underbrace{\frac{FCF_1}{1 + WACC} + \frac{FCF_2}{(1 + WACC)^2} + \cdots + \frac{FCF_H}{(1 + WACC)^H}}_{PV(\text{free cash flow})} + \underbrace{\frac{PV_H}{(1 + WACC)^H}}_{PV(\text{horizon value})}$$

Of course, the business will continue after the horizon, but it's not practical to forecast free cash flow year by year to infinity. PV_H stands in for the value in year H of free cash flow in periods $H + 1, H + 2$, etc.

Free cash flow and net income are not the same. They differ in several important ways:

- Income is the return to shareholders, calculated after interest expense. Free cash flow is calculated before interest.
- Income is calculated after various noncash expenses, including depreciation. Therefore we will add back depreciation when we calculate free cash flow.
- Capital expenditures and investments in working capital do not appear as expenses on the income statement, but they do reduce free cash flow.

Free cash flow can be negative for rapidly growing firms, even if the firms are profitable, because investment exceeds cash flow from operations. Negative free cash flow is normally temporary, fortunately for the firm and its stockholders. Free cash flow turns positive as growth slows down and the payoffs from prior investments start to roll in.

Table 16.1 sets out the information that you need to forecast Rio's free cash flows. We will follow common practice and start with a projection of sales. In the year just ended Rio had sales of $83.6 million. In recent years sales have grown by between 5% and 8% a year. You forecast that sales will grow by about 7% a year for the next three years. Growth will then slow to 4% for years 4 to 6 and to 3% starting in year 7.

The other components of cash flow in Table 16.1 are driven by these sales forecasts. For example, you can see that costs are forecasted at 74% of sales in the first year with a gradual increase to 76% of sales in later years, reflecting increased marketing costs as Rio's competitors gradually catch up.

Increasing sales are likely to require further investment in fixed assets and working capital. Rio's net fixed assets are currently about $0.79 for each dollar of sales. Unless Rio has surplus capacity or can squeeze more output from its existing plant and equipment, its investment in fixed assets will need to grow along with sales. Therefore we assume that every dollar of sales growth requires an increase of $0.79 in net fixed assets. We also assume that working capital grows in proportion to sales.

Rio's free cash flow is calculated in Table 16.1 as profit after tax, plus depreciation, minus investment. Investment is the change in the stock of (gross) fixed assets and working capital from the previous year. For example, in year 1:

Free cash flow = Profit after tax + depreciation − investment in fixed assets
$$\qquad\qquad - \text{ investment in working capital}$$
$$= 8.7 + 9.9 - (109.6 - 95.0) - (11.6 - 11.1) = \$3.5 \text{ million}$$

	Latest year	Forecast						
	0	**1**	**2**	**3**	**4**	**5**	**6**	**7**
1. Sales	83.6	89.5	95.8	102.5	106.6	110.8	115.2	118.7
2. Cost of goods sold	63.1	66.2	71.3	76.3	79.9	83.1	87.0	90.2
3. EBITDA (1 - 2)	20.5	23.3	24.4	26.1	26.6	27.7	28.2	28.5
4. Depreciation	3.3	9.9	10.6	11.3	11.8	12.3	12.7	13.1
5. Profit before tax (EBIT) (3 - 4)	17.2	13.4	13.8	14.8	14.9	15.4	15.5	15.4
6. Tax	6.0	4.7	4.8	5.2	5.2	5.4	5.4	5.4
7. Profit after tax (5 - 6)	11.2	8.7	9.0	9.6	9.7	10.0	10.1	10.0
8. Investment in fixed assets	11.0	14.6	15.5	16.6	15.0	15.6	16.2	15.9
9. Investment in working capital	1.0	0.5	0.8	0.9	0.5	0.6	0.6	0.4
10. Free cash flow (7 + 4 - 8 - 9)	2.5	3.5	3.2	3.4	5.9	6.1	6.0	6.8
PV Free cash flow, years 1-6	**20.3**							
PV Horizon value	**67.6**			(Horizon value in year 6)			113.4	
PV of company	**87.9**							
Assumptions:								
Sales growth, %	6.7	7.0	7.0	7.0	4.0	4.0	4.0	3.0
Costs (percent of sales)	75.5	74.0	74.5	74.5	75.0	75.0	75.5	76.0
Working capital (percent of sales)	13.3	13.0	13.0	13.0	13.0	13.0	13.0	13.0
Net fixed assets (percent of sales)	79.2	79.0	79.0	79.0	79.0	79.0	79.0	79.0
Depreciation (percent of net fixed assets)	5.0	14.0	14.0	14.0	14.0	14.0	14.0	14.0
Tax rate, %	35.0							
WACC, %	9.0							
Long-term growth forecast, %	3.0							
Fixed assets and working capital								
Gross fixed assets	95.0	109.6	125.1	141.8	156.8	172.4	188.6	204.5
Less accumulated depreciation	29.0	38.9	49.5	60.8	72.6	84.9	97.6	110.7
Net fixed assets	66.0	70.7	75.6	80.9	84.2	87.5	91.0	93.8
Net working capital	11.1	11.6	12.4	13.3	13.9	14.4	15.0	15.4

TABLE 16.1

Free-cash-flow projections and company value for Rio Corporation ($ millions).

Estimating Horizon Value

Valuation horizons are often chosen arbitrarily. Sometimes the boss tells everybody to use 10 years because that's a round number. We will use year 6, because Rio's sales are expected to settle down to stable, long-term growth starting in year 7. To find the present value of the cash flows in years 1 to 6, we discount at the 9% WACC:

$$PV = \frac{3.5}{1.09} + \frac{3.2}{1.09^2} + \frac{3.4}{1.09^3} + \frac{5.9}{1.09^4} + \frac{6.1}{1.09^5} + \frac{6.0}{1.09^6} = \$20.3 \text{ million}$$

Now we need to find the value of the cash flows from year 7 onward.

There are several formulas or rules of thumb for estimating horizon value. First let's try the constant-growth DCF formula. This requires a forecast of the free cash flow for year 7, which we have worked out in the final column of Table 16.1, assuming a long-run growth rate of 3% per year.[4] The free cash flow is $6.8 million, so

$$PV_H = \frac{FCF_{H+1}}{WACC - g} = \frac{6.8}{.09 - .03} = \$113.4 \text{ million}$$

$$PV \text{ at year } 0 = \frac{1}{1.09^6} \times 113.4 = \$67.6 \text{ million}$$

We now have all we need to value the business:

$$PV(\text{company}) = PV(\text{cash flow years } 1\text{--}6) + PV(\text{horizon value})$$
$$= \$20.3 + 67.6 = \$87.9 \text{ million}$$

This is the total value of Rio. To find the value of the equity, we simply subtract the value of the debt:

$$\text{Total value of equity} = \$87.9 - 36.0 = \$51.9 \text{ million}$$

And to find the value per share, we divide by the total number of shares outstanding:

$$\text{Value per share} = 51.9/1.5 = \$34.60$$

Thus Sangria could afford to pay up to $34.60 per share for Rio.

You now have an estimate of the value of Rio Corporation. But how confident can you be in this figure? Notice that less than a quarter of Rio's value comes from cash flows in the first six years. The rest comes from the horizon value. Moreover, this horizon value can change in response to only minor changes in assumptions. For example, if the long-run growth rate is 4% rather than 3%, Rio needs to invest more to support this higher growth, but firm value increases from $87.9 million to $89.9 million.

In Chapter 5 we stressed that wise managers won't stop at this point. They will check their calculations by identifying comparable companies and comparing their price–earnings multiples and ratios of market to book value.[5]

When you forecast cash flows, it is easy to become mesmerized by the numbers and just do it mechanically. But it is important to think critically about the assumptions that are built into your cash-flow forecasts. Are the revenue figures consistent with what you expect your competitors to do? Are the costs you have predicted realistic? Probe the assumptions behind the numbers to make sure they are sensible. Be particularly careful about the growth rates and profitability assumptions that drive horizon values. Don't assume that the business you are valuing will grow and earn more than the cost of capital in perpetuity.[6] This would be a nice outcome for the business, but not an outcome that competition will tolerate.

---

[4] Notice that expected free cash flow increases by about 14% from year 6 to year 7 because the transition from 4% to 3% sales growth reduces required investment. But sales, investment, and free cash flow will all increase at 3% once the company settles into stable growth. Recall that the first cash flow in the constant-growth DCF formula occurs in the next year, year 7 in this case. Growth progresses at a steady-state 3% from year 7 onward. Therefore it's OK to use the 3% growth rate in the horizon-value formula.

[5] See Section 5.5.

[6] Table 16.1 is too optimistic in this respect, because the horizon value increases with the assumed long-run growth rate. This implies that Rio has valuable growth opportunities (PVGO) even after the horizon in year 6. A more sophisticated spreadsheet would add an intermediate growth stage, say from years 7 through 10, and gradually reduce profitability to competitive levels. See Challenge Question 29 at the end of this chapter.

You should also check whether the business is worth more dead than alive. Sometimes a company's *liquidation value* exceeds its value as a going concern. Smart financial analysts sometimes ferret out idle or underexploited assets that would be worth much more if sold to someone else. You may end up counting these assets at their likely sale price and valuing the rest of the business without them.

WACC vs. the Flow-to-Equity Method

When valuing Rio we forecast the cash flows assuming all-equity financing and we used the WACC to discount these cash flows. The WACC formula picked up the value of the interest tax shields. Then to find equity value, we subtracted the value of debt from the total value of the firm.

If our task is to value a firm's equity, there's an obvious alternative to discounting company cash flows at the firm's WACC: Discount cash flows to *equity*, after interest and after taxes, at the cost of equity capital. This is called the *flow-to-equity method*. If the company's debt ratio is constant over time, the flow-to equity method should give the same answer as discounting cash flows at the WACC and then subtracting debt.

The flow-to-equity method seems simple, and it is simple if the proportions of debt and equity financing stay reasonably close to constant for the life of the company. But the cost of equity depends on financial leverage; in other words, it depends on financial risk as well as business risk. If financial leverage is expected to change significantly, discounting flows to equity at today's cost of equity will not give the right answer.

16.3   USING WACC IN PRACTICE

Some Tricks of the Trade

Sangria had just one asset and two sources of financing. A real company's market-value balance sheet has many more entries, for example:[7]

Current assets, including cash, inventory, and accounts receivable	Current liabilities, including accounts payable and short-term debt
Property, plant, and equipment	Long-term debt (D)
	Preferred stock (P)
Growth opportunities	Equity (E)
Total assets	Total liabilities plus equity

---

[7] This balance sheet is for exposition and should not be confused with a real company's books. It includes the value of growth opportunities, which accountants do not recognize, though investors do. It excludes certain accounting entries, for example, deferred taxes.

Deferred taxes arise when a company uses faster depreciation for tax purposes than it uses in reports to investors. That means the company reports more in taxes than it pays. The difference is accumulated as a liability for deferred taxes. In a sense there is a liability, because the Internal Revenue Service "catches up," collecting extra taxes, as assets age. But this is irrelevant in capital investment analysis, which focuses on actual after-tax cash flows and uses accelerated tax depreciation.

Deferred taxes should not be regarded as a source of financing or an element of the weighted-average cost of capital formula. The liability for deferred taxes is not a security held by investors. It is a balance sheet entry created for accounting purposes.

Deferred taxes can be important in regulated industries, however. Regulators take deferred taxes into account in calculating allowed rates of return and the time patterns of revenues and consumer prices.

Several questions immediately arise:

How does the formula change when there are more than two sources of financing? Easy: There is one cost for each element. The weight for each element is proportional to its market value. For example, if the capital structure includes both preferred and common shares,[8]

$$\text{WACC} = r_D(1 - T_c)\frac{D}{V} + r_P\frac{P}{V} + r_E\frac{E}{V}$$

where r_p is investors' expected rate of return on the preferred stock, P is the amount of preferred stock outstanding, and $V = D + P + E$.

What about short-term debt? Many companies consider only long-term financing when calculating WACC. They leave out the cost of short-term debt. In principle this is incorrect. The lenders who hold short-term debt are investors who can claim their share of operating earnings. A company that ignores this claim will misstate the required return on capital investments.

But "zeroing out" short-term debt is not a serious error if the debt is only temporary, seasonal, or incidental financing or if it is offset by holdings of cash and marketable securities. Suppose, for example, that one of your foreign subsidiaries takes out a six-month loan to finance its inventory and accounts receivable. The dollar equivalent of this loan will show up as a short-term debt. At the same time headquarters may be lending money by investing surplus dollars in short-term securities. If this lending and borrowing offset, there is no point in including the cost of short-term debt in the weighted-average cost of capital, because the company is not a *net* short-term borrower.

What about other current liabilities? Current liabilities are usually "netted out" by subtracting them from current assets. The difference is entered as net working capital on the left-hand side of the balance sheet. The sum of long-term financing on the right is called *total capitalization*.

Net working capital
   = current assets
   − current liabilities
Property, plant, and equipment
Growth opportunities
	Long-term debt (D)
	
	Preferred stock (P)
	
	Equity (E)
	Total capitalization (V)

When net working capital is treated as an asset, forecasts of cash flows for capital investment projects must treat increases in net working capital as a cash outflow and decreases as an inflow. This is standard practice, which we followed in Section 7.2. We also did so when we estimated the future investments that Rio would need to make in working capital.

Since current liabilities include short-term debt, netting them out against current assets excludes the cost of short-term debt from the weighted-average cost of capital. We have just explained why this can be an acceptable approximation. But when short-term debt is an important, permanent source of financing—as is common for small firms and firms outside the United States—it should be shown

---

[8] Preferred stock promises a fixed dividend. Payment is within the discretion of the Board, but the company may not pay a dividend on the common stock unless the dividend on the preferred has been paid.

explicitly on the right-hand side of the balance sheet, not netted out against current assets.[9] The interest cost of short-term debt is then one element of the weighted-average cost of capital.

How are the costs of financing calculated? You can often use stock market data to get an estimate of r_E, the expected rate of return demanded by investors in the company's stock. With that estimate, WACC is not too hard to calculate, because the borrowing rate r_D and the debt and equity ratios D/V and E/V can be directly observed or estimated without too much trouble.[10] Estimating the value and required return for preferred shares is likewise usually not too complicated.

Estimating the required return on other security types can be troublesome. Convertible debt, where the investors' return comes partly from an option to exchange the debt for the company's stock, is one example.

Low grade (or *junk*) debt, where the risk of default is high, is likewise difficult. The higher the odds of default, the lower the market price of the debt, and the higher is the *promised* rate of interest. But the weighted-average cost of capital is an *expected*, that is, average, rate of return, not a promised one. For example, in June 2004, Delta Airline bonds maturing in 2016 sold at only 42% of face value and offered a 24% promised yield, about 19 percentage points above yields on the highest-quality debt issues maturing at the same time. The price and yield on the Delta bond demonstrated investors' concern about the company's chronic financial ill-health. But the 24% yield was not an expected return, because it did not average in the losses to be incurred if Delta were to default. Including 24% as a "cost of debt" in a calculation of WACC would therefore have overstated Delta's true cost of capital.

This is bad news: There is no easy or tractable way of estimating the expected rate of return on most junk debt issues.[11] The good news is that for most debt the odds of default are small. That means the promised and expected rates of return are close, and the promised rate can be used as an approximation in the weighted-average cost of capital.

Company vs. Industry WACCs   Of course you want to know what your company's WACC is. Yet industry WACCs are sometimes more useful. Here's an example. Kansas City Southern used to be a portfolio of (1) the Kansas City Southern Railroad, with operations running from the U.S. Midwest south to Texas and Mexico, and (2) Stillwell Financial, an investment-management business that included the Janus mutual funds. It's hard to think of two more dissimilar businesses. Kansas City Southern's overall WACC was not right for either of them. The company would have been well advised to use a railroad industry WACC for its railroad operations and an investment management WACC for Stillwell.

---

[9] Financial practitioners have rules of thumb for deciding whether short-term debt is worth including in WACC. One rule checks whether short-term debt is at least 10% of total liabilities and net working capital is negative. If so, then short-term debt is almost surely being used to finance long-term assets and is explicitly included in WACC.

[10] Most corporate debt is not actively traded, so its market value cannot be observed directly. But you can usually value a nontraded debt security by looking to securities that *are* traded and that have approximately the same default risk and maturity.

For healthy firms the market value of debt is usually not too far from book value, so many managers and analysts use book value for D in the weighted-average cost of capital formula. However, be sure to use *market*, not book, values for E.

[11] When betas can be estimated for the junk issue or for a sample of similar issues, the expected return can be calculated from the capital asset pricing model. Otherwise the yield should be adjusted for the probability of default.

KSU spun off Stillwell in 2000 and is now a pure-play railroad. But even now the company would be wise to check its WACC against a railroad industry WACC. Industry WACCs are less exposed to random noise and estimation errors. Fortunately for Kansas City Southern, there are several large, pure-play U.S. railroads from which a railroad industry WACC can be estimated.[12] Of course, use of an industry WACC for a particular company's investments assumes that the company and industry have approximately the same business risk and financing.

Mistakes People Make in Using the Weighted-Average Formula

The weighted-average formula is very useful but also dangerous. It tempts people to make logical errors. For example, manager Q, who is campaigning for a pet project, might look at the formula

$$\text{WACC} = r_D(1 - T_c)\frac{D}{V} + r_E\frac{E}{V}$$

and think, "Aha! My firm has a good credit rating. It could borrow, say, 90% of the project's cost if it likes. That means $D/V = .9$ and $E/V = .1$. My firm's borrowing rate r_D is 8%, and the required return on equity, r_E, is 15%. Therefore

$$\text{WACC} = .08(1 - .35)(.9) + .15(.1) = .062$$

or 6.2%. When I discount at that rate, my project looks great."

Manager Q is wrong on several counts. First, the weighted-average formula works only for projects that are carbon copies of the firm. The firm isn't 90% debt-financed.

Second, the immediate source of funds for a project has no necessary connection with the hurdle rate for the project. What matters is the project's overall contribution to the firm's borrowing power. A dollar invested in Q's pet project will not increase the firm's debt capacity by $.90. If the firm borrows 90% of the project's cost, it is really borrowing in part against its *existing* assets. Any advantage from financing the new project with more debt than normal should be attributed to the old projects, not to the new one.

Third, even if the firm were willing and able to lever up to 90% debt, its cost of capital would not decline to 6.2% (as Q's naive calculation predicts). You cannot increase the debt ratio without creating financial risk for stockholders and thereby increasing r_E, the expected rate of return they demand from the firm's common stock. Going to 90% debt would certainly increase the borrowing rate, too.

Adjusting WACC when Debt Ratios and Business Risks Differ

The WACC formula assumes that the project or business to be valued will be financed in the same debt–equity proportions as the company (or industry) as a whole. What if that is not true? For example, what if Sangria's perpetual crusher project supports only 20% debt, versus 40% for Sangria overall?

---

[12] See Tables 5.3 and 10.1.

FIGURE 16.1

This plot shows WACC for the Sangria Corporation at debt-to-equity ratios of 25% and 67%. The corresponding debt-to-value ratios are 20% and 40%.

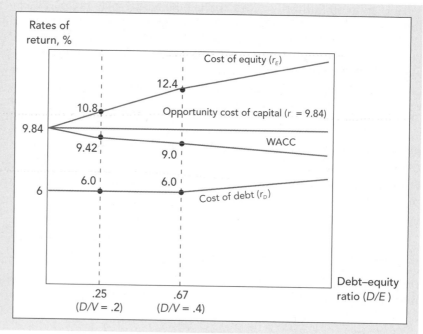

Moving from 40% to 20% debt may change all the inputs to the WACC formula.[13] Obviously the financing weights change. But the cost of equity r_E is less, because financial risk is reduced. The cost of debt may be lower too.

Take another look at Figure 14.4 on page 385, which plots WACC and the costs of debt and equity as a function of the debt–equity ratio. The flat line is r, the opportunity cost of capital. Remember, this is the expected rate of return that investors would want from the project if it were all-equity-financed. The opportunity cost of capital depends only on business risk and is the natural reference point.

Suppose Sangria or the perpetual crusher project were all-equity-financed ($D/V = 0$). At that point WACC equals cost of equity, and both equal the opportunity cost of capital. Start from that point in Figure 16.1. As the debt ratio increases, the cost of equity increases, because of financial risk, but notice that WACC declines. The decline is *not* caused by use of "cheap" debt in place of "expensive" equity. It falls because of the tax shields on debt interest payments. If there were no corporate income taxes, the weighted-average cost of capital would be constant, and equal to the opportunity cost of capital, at all debt ratios. We showed this in Chapter 14.

Figure 16.1 shows the *shape* of the relationship between financing and WACC, but initially we have numbers only for Sangria's current 40% debt ratio. We want to recalculate WACC at a 20% ratio.

---

[13] Even the tax rate could change. For example, Sangria might have enough taxable income to cover interest payments at 20% debt but not at 40% debt. In that case the effective marginal tax rate would be higher at 20% than 40% debt.

Here is the simplest way to do it. There are three steps.

Step 1   Calculate the opportunity cost of capital. In other words, calculate WACC and the cost of equity at zero debt. This step is called *unlevering* the WACC. The simplest unlevering formula is

$$\text{Opportunity cost of capital} = r = r_D D/V + r_E E/V$$

This formula comes directly from Modigliani and Miller's proposition 1 (see Section 14.1). If taxes are left out, the weighted-average cost of capital equals the opportunity cost of capital and is independent of leverage.

Step 2   Estimate the cost of debt, r_D, at the new debt ratio, and calculate the new cost of equity.

$$r_E = r + (r - r_D)D/E$$

This formula is Modigliani and Miller's proposition 2 (see Section 14.2). It calls for D/E, the ratio of debt to *equity*, not debt to value.

Step 3   Recalculate the weighted-average cost of capital at the new financing weights.

Let's do the numbers for Sangria at $D/V = .20$, or 20%.

Step 1. Sangria's current debt ratio is $D/V = .4$. So

$$r = .06(.4) + .124(.6) = .0984, \text{ or } 9.84\%$$

Step 2. We will assume that the debt cost stays at 6% when the debt ratio is 20%. Then

$$r_E = .0984 + (.0984 - .06)(.25) = .108, \text{ or } 10.8\%$$

Note that the debt–*equity* ratio is $.2/.8 = .25$.

Step 3. Recalculate WACC.

$$\text{WACC} = .06(1 - .35)(.2) + .108(.8) = .0942, \text{ or } 9.42\%$$

Figure 16.1 enters these numbers on the plot of WACC versus the debt–equity ratio.

Unlevering and Relevering Betas

Our three-step procedure (1) unlevers and then (2) relevers the cost of equity. Some financial managers find it convenient to (1) unlever and then (2) relever the equity beta. Given the beta of equity at the new debt ratio, the cost of equity is determined from the capital asset pricing model. Then WACC is recalculated.

The formula for unlevering beta was given in Section 14.2.

$$\beta_A = \beta_D (D/V) + \beta_E (E/V)$$

This equation says that the beta of a firm's assets is revealed by the beta of a portfolio of all of the firm's outstanding debt and equity securities. An investor who bought such a portfolio would own the assets free and clear and absorb only business risks.

The formula for relevering beta closely resembles MM's proposition 2, except that betas are substituted for rates of return:

$$\beta_E = \beta_A + (\beta_A - \beta_D) D/E$$

Use this formula to recalculate β_E when D/E changes.

The Importance of Rebalancing

The formulas for WACC and for unlevering and relevering expected returns are simple, but we must be careful to remember underlying assumptions. The most important point is _rebalancing_.

Calculating WACC for a company at its existing capital structure requires that the capital structure _not_ change; in other words, the company must rebalance its capital structure to maintain the same market-value debt ratio for the relevant future. Take Sangria Corporation as an example. It starts with a debt-to-value ratio of 40% and a market value of $1,250 million. Suppose that Sangria's products do unexpectedly well in the marketplace and that market value increases to $1,500 million. Rebalancing means that it will then increase debt to .4 × 1,500 = $600 million,[14] thus regaining a 40% ratio. If market value instead falls, Sangria would have to pay down debt proportionally.

Of course real companies do not rebalance capital structure in such a mechanical and compulsive way. For practical purposes, it's sufficient to assume gradual but steady adjustment toward a long-run target. But if the firm plans significant changes in capital structure (for example, if it plans to pay off its debt), the WACC formula won't work. In such cases, you should turn to the APV method, which we describe in the next section.

Our three-step procedure for recalculating WACC makes a similar rebalancing assumption.[15] Whatever the starting debt ratio, the firm is assumed to rebalance to maintain that ratio in the future.[16]

---

[14] The proceeds of the additional borrowing would be paid out to shareholders or used, along with additional equity investment, to finance Sangria's growth.

[15] Similar, but not identical. The basic WACC formula is correct whether rebalancing occurs at the end of each period or continuously. The unlevering and relevering formulas used in steps 1 and 2 of our three-step procedure are exact only if rebalancing is continuous so that the debt ratio stays constant day-to-day and week-to-week. However, the errors introduced from annual rebalancing are very small and can be ignored for practical purposes.

[16] Here's why the formulas work with continuous rebalancing. Think of a market-value balance sheet with assets and interest tax shields on the left and debt and equity on the right, with $D + E = PV(\text{assets}) + PV(\text{tax shield})$. The total risk (beta) of the firm's debt and equity equals the blended risk of PV(assets) and PV(tax shield)

$$\beta_D \frac{D}{V} + \beta_E \frac{E}{V} = \alpha\beta_A + (1 - \alpha)\beta_{\text{tax shield}} \tag{1}$$

where α is the proportion of the total firm value from its assets and $1 - \alpha$ is the proportion from interest tax shields. If the firm readjusts its capital structure to keep D/V constant, then the beta of the tax shield must be the same as the beta of the assets. With rebalancing, an x% change in firm value V changes debt D by x% the interest tax shield $T_c r_D D$ will change by x% as well. Thus the risk of the tax shield must be the same as the risk of the firm as a whole:

$$\beta_{\text{tax shield}} = \beta_A = \beta_D \frac{D}{V} + \beta_E \frac{E}{V} \tag{2}$$

This is our unlevering formula expressed in terms of beta. Since expected returns depend on beta:

$$r_A = r_D \frac{D}{V} + r_E \frac{E}{V} \tag{3}$$

Rearrange formulas (2) and (3) to get the relevering formulas for β_E and r_E:

$$\beta_E = \beta_A + (\beta_A - \beta_D)D/E$$
$$r_E = r_A + (r_A - r_D)D/E$$

All this assumes continuous rebalancing. Suppose instead that the firm rebalances once a year, so that the next year's interest tax shield, which depends on this year's debt, is known. Then you can use a formula developed by Miles and Ezzell:

$$r_{\text{Miles-Ezzell}} = r_A - (D/V)r_D T_c \left(\frac{1 + r_A}{1 + r_D} \right)$$

See J. Miles and J. Ezzell, "The Weighted Average Cost of Capital, Perfect Capital Markets, and Project Life: A Clarification," _Journal of Financial and Quantitative Analysis_ 15 (September 1980), pp. 719–730.

The Modigliani–Miller Formula, Plus Some Final Advice

What if the firm does not rebalance to keep its debt ratio constant? In this case the only general approach is adjusted present value, which we cover in the next section. But sometimes financial managers turn to other discount-rate formulas, including one derived by Modigliani and Miller (MM). MM considered a company or project generating a level, perpetual stream of cash flows financed with fixed, perpetual debt, and derived a simple after-tax discount rate:[17]

$$r_{MM} = r(1 - T_c D/V)$$

Here it's easy to unlever: just set the debt-capacity parameter (D/V) equal to zero.[18]

MM's formula is still used in practice, but the formula is exact only in the special case where there is a level, perpetual stream of cash flows and fixed, perpetual debt. However, the formula is not a bad approximation for shorter-lived projects when debt is issued in a fixed amount.[19]

So which team do you want to play with, the fixed-debt team or the rebalancers? If you join the fixed-debt team you will be outnumbered. Most financial managers use the plain, after-tax WACC, which assumes constant market-value debt ratios and therefore assumes rebalancing. That makes sense, because the debt *capacity* of a firm or project must depend on its future value, which will fluctuate.

At the same time, we must admit that the typical financial manager doesn't care much if his or her firm's debt ratio drifts up or down within a reasonable range of moderate financial leverage. The typical financial manager acts as if a plot of WACC against the debt ratio is "flat" (constant) over this range. This too makes sense, if we just remember that interest tax shields are the *only* reason why the after-tax WACC declines in Figure 14.4 or 16.1. The WACC formula doesn't explicitly capture costs of financial distress or any of the other nontax complications discussed in Chapter 15.[20] All these complications may roughly cancel the value added by interest tax shields (within a range of moderate leverage). If so, the financial manager is wise to focus on the firm's operating and investment decisions, rather than on fine-tuning its debt ratio.

---

[17] The formula first appeared in F. Modigliani and M. H. Miller, "Corporate Income Taxes and the Cost of Capital: A Correction," *American Economic Review* 53 (June 1963) pp. 433–443. It is explained more fully in M. H. Miller and F. Modigliani: "Some Estimates of the Cost of Capital to the Electric Utility Industry: 1954–1957," *American Economic Review* 56 (June 1966), pp. 333–391.

Given perpetual fixed debt,

$$V = \frac{C}{r} + T_c D$$

$$V = \frac{C}{r(1 - T_c D/V)} = \frac{C}{r_{MM}}$$

[18] In this case the relevering formula for the cost of equity is:

$$r_E = r_A + (1 - T_c)(r_A - r_D)D/E$$

The unlevering and relevering formulas for betas are

$$\beta_A = \frac{\beta_D(1 - T_c)D/E + \beta_E}{1 + (1 - T_c)D/E}$$

and

$$\beta_E = \beta_A + (1 - T_c)(\beta_A - \beta_D)D/E$$

See R. Hamada: "The Effect of a Firm's Capital Structure on the Systematic Risk of Common Stocks," *Journal of Finance* 27 (May 1972), pp. 435–452.

[19] See S. C. Myers, "Interactions of Corporate Financing and Investment Decisions—Implications for Capital Budgeting," *Journal of Finance* 29 (March 1974), pp. 1–25.

[20] Costs of financial distress can show up as rapidly increasing costs of debt and equity, especially at high debt ratios. The costs of financial distress could "flatten out" the WACC curve in Figures 14.4 and 16.1, and finally increase WACC as leverage climbs. Thus some practitioners calculate an industry WACC and take it as constant, at least within the range of debt ratios observed for healthy companies in the industry.

Personal taxes could also generate a flatter curve for after-tax WACC as a function of leverage. See Section 15.2.

16.4 ADJUSTED PRESENT VALUE

The idea behind **adjusted present value (APV)** is to divide and conquer. APV does not attempt to capture taxes or other effects of financing in a WACC or adjusted discount rate. A series of present value calculations is made instead. The first establishes a base-case value for the project or firm: its value as a separate, all-equity-financed venture. The discount rate for the base-case value is just the opportunity cost of capital. Once the base-case value is set, then each financing side effect is traced out, and the present value of its cost or benefit to the firm is calculated. Finally, all the present values are added together to estimate the project's total contribution to the value of the firm:

$$\text{APV} = \text{base-case NPV} + \text{sum of PVs of financing side effects}$$

The most important financing side effect is the interest tax shield on the debt supported by the project (a plus). Other possible side effects are the issue costs of securities (a minus) or financing packages subsidized by a supplier or government (a plus).

APV gives the financial manager an explicit view of the factors that are adding or subtracting value. APV can prompt the manager to ask the right follow-up questions. For example, suppose that base-case NPV is positive but less than the costs of issuing shares to finance the project. That should prompt the manager to look around to see if the project can be rescued by an alternative financing plan.

APV for the Perpetual Crusher

APV is easiest to understand in simple numerical examples. Let's apply it to Sangria's perpetual crusher project. We start by showing that APV is equivalent to discounting at WACC if we make the same assumptions about debt policy.

We used Sangria's WACC (9%) as the discount rate for the crusher's projected cash flows. The WACC calculation assumed that debt will be maintained at a constant 40% of the future value of the project or firm. In this case, the risk of interest tax shields is the same as the risk of the project.[21] Therefore we will discount the tax shields at the opportunity cost of capital (r). We calculated the opportunity cost of capital in the last section by unlevering Sangria's WACC to obtain $r = 9.84\%$.

The first step is to calculate base-case NPV. We discount after-tax project cash flows of $1.125 million at the opportunity cost of capital of 9.84% and subtract the $12.5 million outlay. The cash flows are perpetual, so

$$\text{Base-case NPV} = -12.5 + \frac{1.125}{.0984} = -\$1.067 \text{ million}$$

Thus the project would not be worthwhile with all-equity financing. But it actually supports debt of $5 million. At a 6% borrowing rate ($r_D = .06$) and a 35% tax rate ($T_c = .35$), annual tax shields are $.35 \times .06 \times 5 = .105$, or $105,000.

What are those tax shields worth? If the firm is constantly rebalancing its debt, we discount at $r = 9.84\%$:

$$\text{PV(interest tax shields, debt rebalanced)} = \frac{105,000}{.0984} = \$1.067 \text{ million}$$

---

[21] That is, $\beta_A = \beta_{\text{tax shields}}$. See footnote 16.

APV is the sum of base-case value and PV(interest tax shields)

$$APV = -1.067 \text{ million} + 1.067 \text{ million} = 0$$

This is exactly the same as we obtained by one-step discounting with WACC. The perpetual crusher is a break-even project by either valuation method.

But with APV, we don't have to hold debt at a constant proportion of value. Suppose Sangria plans to keep project debt fixed at $5 million. In this case we assume the risk of the tax shields is the same as the risk of the debt and we discount at the 6% rate on debt:

$$PV(\text{tax shields, debt fixed}) = \frac{105,000}{.06} = \$1.75 \text{ million}$$

$$APV = -1.067 + 1.75 = \$.683 \text{ million}$$

Now the project is more attractive. With fixed debt, the interest tax shields are safe and therefore worth more. (Whether the fixed debt is safer for Sangria is another matter. If the perpetual crusher project fails, the $5 million of fixed debt may end up as a burden on Sangria's other assets.)

Other Financing Side Effects

Suppose Sangria has to finance the perpetual crusher by issuing debt and equity. It issues $7.5 million of equity with issue costs of 7% ($525,000) and $5 million of debt with issue costs of 2% ($100,000). Assume the debt is fixed once issued, so that interest tax shields are worth $1.75 million. Now we can recalculate APV, taking care to subtract the issue costs:

$$APV = -1.067 + 1.75 - .525 - .100 = .058 \text{ million, or } \$58,000$$

The issue costs would reduce APV to nearly zero.

Sometimes there are favorable financing side effects that have nothing to do with taxes. For example, suppose that a potential manufacturer of crusher machinery offers to sweeten the deal by leasing it to Sangria on favorable terms. Then you could calculate APV as the sum of base-case NPV plus the NPV of the lease. Or suppose that a local government offers to lend Sangria $5 million at a very low interest rate if the crusher is built and operated locally. The NPV of the subsidized loan could be added in to APV. (We cover subsidized loans in the Appendix to this chapter.)

APV for Businesses

APV can also be used to value businesses. Let's take another look at the valuation of Rio. In Table 16.1, we assumed a constant 40% debt ratio and discounted free cash flow at Sangria's WACC. Table 16.2 runs the same analysis, but with a fixed debt schedule.

We'll suppose that Sangria has decided to make an offer for Rio. If successful, it plans to finance the purchase with $51 million of debt. It intends to pay down the debt to $45 million in year 6. Recall Rio's horizon value of $113.4 million, which is calculated in Table 16.1 and shown again in Table 16.2. The debt ratio at the horizon is therefore projected at $45/113.4 = .397$, about 40%. Thus Sangria plans to take Rio back to a normal 40% debt ratio at the horizon.[22] But Rio will be carrying

---

[22] Therefore we still calculate the horizon value in year 6 by discounting subsequent free cash flows at WACC. The horizon value in year 6 is discounted back to year 0 at the opportunity cost of capital, however.

	Latest year	Forecast						
	0	**1**	**2**	**3**	**4**	**5**	**6**	**7**
Free cash flow	2.5	3.5	3.2	3.4	5.9	6.1	6.0	6.8
PV Free cash flow, years 1-6	**19.7**							
PV Horizon value	**64.6**			(Horizon value in year 6)			113.4	
Base-Case PV of company	**84.3**							
Debt	51.0	50.0	49.0	48.0	47.0	46.0	45.0	
Interest		3.06	3.00	2.94	2.88	2.82	2.76	
Interest tax shield		1.07	1.05	1.03	1.01	0.99	0.97	
PV Interest tax shields	**5.0**							
APV	**89.3**							
Tax rate, %	35.0							
Opportunity cost of capital, %	9.84							
WACC, % (to discount horizon value to year 6)	9.0							
Long-term growth forecast, %	3.0							
Interest rate, % (years 1-6)	6.0							
After-tax debt service		2.99	2.95	2.91	2.87	2.83	2.79	

TABLE 16.2

APV valuation of Rio Corporation ($ millions).

Visit us at
www.mhhe.com/bma1e.

a heavier debt load before the horizon. For example, the $51 million of initial debt is about 58% of company value as calculated in Table 16.1.

Let's see how Rio's APV is affected by this more aggressive borrowing schedule. Table 16.2 shows projections of free cash flows from Table 16.1.[23] Now we need Rio's base-case value, so we discount these flows at the opportunity cost of capital (9.84%), not at WACC. The resulting base-case value for Rio is $84.3 million. Table 16.2 also projects debt levels, interest, and interest tax shields. If the debt levels are taken as fixed, then the tax shields should be discounted back at the 6% borrowing rate. The resulting PV of interest tax shields is $5.0 million. Thus,

$$\text{APV} = \text{base-case NPV} + \text{PV(interest tax shields)}$$
$$= \$84.3 + 5.0 = \$89.3 \text{ million}$$

an increase of $1.4 million from NPV in Table 16.1. The increase can be traced to the higher early debt levels and to the assumption that the debt levels and interest tax shields are fixed and relatively safe.[24]

---

[23] Many of the assumptions and calculations in Table 16.1 have been hidden in Table 16.2. The hidden rows can be re-called in the "live" version of Table 16.2, which is available on this book's Web site (**www.mhhe.com/bma1e**).

[24] But will Rio really *support* debt at the levels shown in Table 16.2? If not, then the debt must be partly supported by Sangria's other assets, and only part of the $5 million in PV(interest tax shields) can be attributed to Rio itself.

Now a difference of $1.4 million is not a big deal, considering all the lurking risks and pitfalls in forecasting Rio's free cash flows. But you can see the advantage of the flexibility that APV provides. The APV spreadsheet allows you to explore the implications of different financing strategies without locking into a fixed debt ratio or having to calculate a new WACC for every scenario.

APV is particularly useful when the debt for a project or business is tied to book value or has to be repaid on a fixed schedule. For example, Kaplan and Ruback used APV to analyze the prices paid for a sample of leveraged buyouts (LBOs). LBOs are takeovers, typically of mature companies, financed almost entirely with debt. However, the new debt is not intended to be permanent. LBO business plans call for generating extra cash by selling assets, shaving costs, and improving profit margins. The extra cash is used to pay down the LBO debt. Therefore you can't use WACC as a discount rate to evaluate an LBO because its debt ratio will not be constant.

APV works fine for LBOs. The company is first evaluated as if it were all-equity-financed. That means that cash flows are projected after tax, but without any interest tax shields generated by the LBO's debt. The tax shields are then valued separately and added to the all-equity value. Any other financing side effects are added also. The result is an APV valuation for the company.[25] Kaplan and Ruback found that APV did a pretty good job explaining prices paid in these hotly contested takeovers, considering that not all the information available to bidders had percolated into the public domain. Kaplan and Ruback were restricted to publicly available data.

APV for International Investments

APV is most useful when financing side effects are numerous and important. This is frequently the case for large international investments, which may have custom-tailored *project financing* and special contracts with suppliers, customers, and governments. Here are a few examples of financing side effects encountered in international finance.

Large stand-alone investments are often separately funded with *project finance*. Project finance typically means very high debt ratios to start, with most or all of a project's early cash flows committed to debt service. Equity investors have to wait. Since the debt ratio will not be constant, you have to turn to APV.

Project financing may include debt available at favorable interest rates. Most governments subsidize exports by making special financing packages available, and manufacturers of industrial equipment may stand ready to lend money to help close a sale. Suppose, for example, that your project requires construction of an on-site electricity generating plant. You solicit bids from suppliers in various countries. Don't be surprised if the competing suppliers sweeten their bids with offers of low interest rate project loans or if they offer to lease the plant on favorable terms. You should then calculate the NPVs of these loans or leases and include them in your project analysis.

Sometimes international projects are supported by contracts with suppliers or customers. Suppose a manufacturer wants to line up a reliable supply of a

---

[25] Kaplan and Ruback actually used "compressed" APV, in which all cash flows, including interest tax shields, are discounted at the opportunity cost of capital. S. N. Kaplan and R. S. Ruback, "The Valuation of Cash Flow Forecasts: An Empirical Analysis," *Journal of Finance* 50 (September 1995), pp. 1059–1093.

crucial raw material—powdered magnoosium, say. The manufacturer could subsidize a new magnoosium smelter by agreeing to buy 75% of production and guaranteeing a minimum purchase price. The guarantee is clearly a valuable addition to project APV: If the world price of powdered magnoosium falls below the minimum, the project doesn't suffer. You would calculate the value of this guarantee (by the methods explained in Chapters 17 and 18) and add it to APV.

Sometimes local governments impose costs or restrictions on investment or disinvestment. For example, Chile, in an attempt to slow down a flood of short-term capital inflows in the 1990s, required investors to "park" part of their incoming money in non-interest-bearing accounts for a period of two years. An investor in Chile during this period would calculate the cost of this requirement and subtract it from APV.

16.5   YOUR QUESTIONS ANSWERED

Question: All these cost of capital formulas—which ones do financial managers actually use?

Answer: The after-tax weighted-average cost of capital, most of the time. WACC is estimated for the company, or sometimes for an industry. We recommend industry WACCs when data are available for firms with similar assets, operations, business risks, and growth opportunities.

Of course, conglomerate companies, with divisions operating in two or more unrelated industries, should not use a single company or industry WACC. Such firms should try to estimate a different industry WACC for each operating division.

Question: But WACC is the correct discount rate only for "average" projects. What if the project's financing differs from the company's or industry's?

Answer: Remember, investment projects are usually not separately financed. Even when they are, you should focus on the project's contribution to the firm's overall debt capacity, not on its immediate financing. (Suppose it's convenient to raise all the money for a particular project with a bank loan. That doesn't mean the project itself supports 100% debt financing. The company is borrowing against its existing assets as well as the project.)

But if the project's debt capacity is materially different from the company's existing assets, or if the company's overall debt policy changes, WACC should be adjusted. The adjustment can be done by the three-step procedure explained in Section 16.3.

Question: Could we do one more numerical example?

Answer: Sure. Suppose that WACC has been estimated as follows at a 30% debt ratio:

$$\text{WACC} = r_D(1 - T_c)\frac{D}{V} + r_E\frac{E}{V}$$

$$= .09(1 - .35)(.3) + .15(.7) = .1226, \text{ or } 12.26\%$$

What is the correct discount rate at a 50% debt ratio?

Step 1. Calculate the opportunity cost of capital.

$$r = r_D D/V + r_E E/V$$
$$= .09(.3) + .15(.7) = .132, \text{ or } 13.2\%$$

Step 2. Calculate the new costs of debt and equity. The cost of debt will be higher at 50% debt than 30%. Say it is $r_D = .095$. The new cost of equity is

$$r_E = r + (r - r_D)D/E$$
$$= .132 + (.132 - .095)\ 50/50$$
$$= .169, \text{ or } 16.9\%$$

Step 3. Recalculate WACC.

$$\text{WACC} = r_D(1 - T_c)D/V + r_E E/V$$
$$= .095(1 - .35)(0.5) + .169(.5) = .1154, \text{ or about } 11.5\%$$

Question: How do I use the capital asset pricing model to calculate the after-tax weighted-average cost of capital?

Answer: First plug the equity beta into the capital asset pricing formula to calculate r_E, the expected return to equity. Then use this figure, along with the after-tax cost of debt and the debt-to-value and equity-to-value ratios, in the WACC formula.

Of course the CAPM is not the only way to estimate the cost of equity. For example, you might be able to use the dividend-discount model (see Section 5.3).

Question: But suppose I do use the CAPM? What if I have to recalculate the equity beta for a different debt ratio?

Answer: The formula for the equity beta is

$$\beta_E = \beta_A + (\beta_A - \beta_D)\ D/E$$

where β_E is the equity beta, β_A is the asset beta, and β_D is the beta of the company's debt. The asset beta is a weighted average of the debt and equity betas:

$$\beta_A = \beta_D (D/V) + \beta_E (E/V)$$

Suppose you needed the opportunity cost of capital r. You could calculate β_A and then r from the capital asset pricing model.

Question: I think I understand how to adjust for differences in debt capacity or debt policy. How about differences in business risk?

Answer: If business risk is different, then r, the opportunity cost of capital, is different.

Figuring out the right r for an unusually safe or risky project is never easy. Sometimes the financial manager can use estimates of risk and expected return for companies similar to the project. Suppose, for example, that a traditional pharmaceutical company is considering a major commitment to biotech research. The financial manager could pick a sample of biotech companies, estimate their average beta and cost of capital, and use these estimates as benchmarks for the biotech investment.

But in many cases it's difficult to find a good sample of matching companies for an unusually safe or risky project. Then the financial manager has to adjust the opportunity cost of capital by judgment. Section 10.3 may be helpful in such cases.

Question: When do I need adjusted present value (APV)?

Answer: The WACC formula picks up only one financing side effect: the value of interest tax shields on debt supported by a project. If there are other side effects—subsidized financing tied to a project, for example—you should use APV.

You can also use APV to break out the value of interest tax shields:

$$APV = \text{base-case NPV} + PV(\text{tax shield})$$

Suppose, for example, that you are analyzing a company just after a leveraged buyout. The company has a very high initial debt level but plans to pay down the debt as rapidly as possible. APV could be used to obtain an accurate valuation.

Question: When should personal taxes be incorporated into the analysis?

Answer: Always use T_c, the marginal corporate tax rate, when calculating WACC as a weighted average of the costs of debt and equity. The discount rate is adjusted *only* for corporate taxes.

In principle, APV can be adjusted for personal taxes by replacing the marginal corporate rate T_c with an effective tax rate that combines corporate and personal taxes and reflects the net tax advantage per dollar of interest paid by the firm. We provided back-of-the-envelope calculations of this advantage in Section 15.2. The effective tax rate is almost surely less than T_c, but it is very difficult to pin down the numerical difference. Therefore, in practice T_c is almost always used as an approximation.

Question: Are taxes really that important? Do financial managers really fine-tune the debt ratio to minimize WACC?

Answer: As we saw in Chapter 15, financing decisions reflect many forces beyond taxes, including costs of financial distress, differences in information, and incentives for managers. There may not be a sharply defined optimal capital structure. Therefore most financial managers don't fine-tune their companies' debt ratios, and they don't rebalance financing to keep debt ratios strictly constant. In effect they assume that a plot of WACC for different debt ratios is "flat" over a reasonable range of moderate leverage.

SUMMARY

In this chapter we considered how financing can be incorporated into the valuation of projects and ongoing businesses. There are two ways to take financing into account. The first is to calculate NPV by discounting at an adjusted discount rate, usually the after-tax weighted-average cost of capital (WACC). The second approach discounts at the opportunity cost of capital and then adds or subtracts the present values of financing side effects. The second approach is called adjusted present value, or APV.

The formula for the after-tax WACC is:

$$WACC = r_D(1 - T_c)\frac{D}{V} + r_E\frac{E}{V}$$

where r_D and r_E are the expected rates of return demanded by investors in the firm's debt and equity securities, D and E are the current *market values* of debt and equity, and V is the total market value of the firm ($V = D + E$). Of course, the WACC formula expands if there are other sources of financing, for example, preferred stock.

Strictly speaking, discounting at WACC works only for projects that are carbon copies of the existing firm—projects with the same business risk that will be financed to maintain the firm's current, market debt ratio. But firms can use WACC as a benchmark rate to be adjusted for differences in business risk or financing. We gave a three-step procedure for adjusting WACC for different debt ratios.

Discounting cash flows at the WACC assumes that debt is rebalanced to keep a constant ratio of debt to market value. The amount of debt supported by a project is assumed to rise or fall with the project's after-the-fact success or failure. The WACC formula also assumes that financing matters *only* because of interest tax shields. When this or other assumptions are violated, only APV will give an absolutely correct answer.

APV is, in concept at least, simple. First calculate the base-case NPV of the project or business on the assumption that financing *doesn't* matter. (The discount rate is not WACC, but the opportunity cost of capital.) Then calculate the present values of any relevant financing side effects and add or subtract from base-case value. A capital investment project is worthwhile if

$$APV = \text{base-case NPV} + PV(\text{financing side effects})$$

is positive. Common financing side effects include interest tax shields, issue costs, and special financing packages offered by suppliers or governments.

For firms or going-concern businesses, value depends on free cash flow. Free cash flow is the amount of cash that can be paid out to all investors, debt as well as equity, after deducting cash needed for new investment or increases in working capital. Free cash flow does not include the value of interest tax shields, however. The WACC formula accounts for interest tax shields by using the after-tax cost of debt. APV adds PV(interest tax shields) to base-case value.

Businesses are usually valued in two steps. First free cash flow is forecasted out to a valuation horizon and discounted back to present value. Then a horizon value is calculated and also discounted back. The horizon value is usually estimated by using the perpetual-growth DCF formula or by multiplying forecasted EBIT or EBITDA[26] by multiples observed for similar firms. Be particularly careful to avoid unrealistically high horizon values. By the time the horizon arrives, competitors will have had several years to catch up. Also, when you are done valuing the business, don't forget to subtract its debt to get the value of the firm's equity.

All of this chapter's examples reflect assumptions about the amount of debt supported by a project or business. Remember not to confuse "supported by" with the immediate source of funds for investment. For example, a firm might, as a matter of convenience, borrow $1 million for a $1 million research program. But the research is unlikely to contribute $1 million in debt capacity; a large part of the $1 million new debt would be supported by the firm's other assets.

Also remember that *debt capacity* is not meant to imply an absolute limit on how much the firm *can* borrow. The phrase refers to how much it *chooses* to borrow against a project or ongoing business.

---

[26] Recall that EBIT = earnings before interest and taxes and EBITDA = EBIT plus depreciation and amortization.

FURTHER READING

The adjusted-present-value rule was developed in:

S. C. Myers, "Interactions of Corporate Financing and Investment Decisions—Implications for Capital Budgeting," *Journal of Finance* 29 (March 1974), pp. 1–25.

The Harvard Business Review has published a popular account of APV:

T. A. Luehrman, "Using APV: A Better Tool for Valuing Operations," *Harvard Business Review* 75 (May–June 1997), pp. 145–154.

There have been dozens of articles on the weighted-average cost of capital and other issues discussed in this chapter. Here are three:

J. Miles and R. Ezzell, "The Weighted Average Cost of Capital, Perfect Capital Markets, and Project Life: A Clarification," *Journal of Financial and Quantitative Analysis* 15 (September 1980), pp. 719–730.

R. A. Taggart, Jr., "Consistent Valuation and Cost of Capital Expressions with Corporate and Personal Taxes," *Financial Management* 20 (Autumn 1991), pp. 8–20.

R. S. Ruback, "Capital Cash Flows: A Simple Approach to Valuing Risky Cash Flows," *Financial Management* 31 (Summer 2002), pp. 85–103.

Two books that provide detailed explanations of how to value companies are:

T. Koller, M. Goedhart, and D. Wessels, *Valuation: Measuring and Managing the Value of Companies*, 4th ed. (New York: Wiley, 2005).

S. P. Pratt and A.V. Niculita, *Valuing a Business: The Analysis and Appraisal of Closely Held Companies*, 5th ed. (New York: McGraw-Hill, 2007).

The valuation rule for safe, nominal cash flows is developed in:

R. S. Ruback, "Calculating the Market Value of Risk-Free Cash Flows," *Journal of Financial Economics* 15 (March 1986), pp. 323–339.

CONCEPT REVIEW QUESTIONS

1. Write down the formula for the after-tax WACC. Why is WACC usually less than the opportunity cost of capital? (page 426)

2. What assumptions does WACC rely on? (pages 428–429)

3. **a.** In the Sangria example in Section 16.1, how would the WACC change if the *book* values were $300 million debt and $700 million equity?

   b. How would the WACC change if instead the *market* values were $300 million debt and $950 million equity? (pages 426–428)

For a complete listing of your Concept Review Questions, please visit us at www.mhhe.com/bma1e.

QUIZ

1. Calculate the weighted-average cost of capital (WACC) for Federated Junkyards of America, using the following information:

   - Debt: $75,000,000 book value outstanding. The debt is trading at 90% of book value. The yield to maturity is 9%.

   - Equity: 2,500,000 shares selling at $42 per share. Assume the expected rate of return on Federated's stock is 18%.

   - Taxes: Federated's marginal tax rate is $T_c = .35$.

2. Suppose Federated Junkyards decides to move to a more conservative debt policy. A year later its debt ratio is down to 15% ($D/V = .15$). The interest rate has dropped to 8.6%. Recalculate Federated's WACC under these new assumptions. The company's business risk, opportunity cost of capital, and tax rate have not changed. Use the three-step procedure explained in Section 16.3.

3. True or false? Use of the WACC formula assumes

   a. A project supports a fixed amount of debt over the project's economic life.

   b. The *ratio* of the debt supported by a project to project value is constant over the project's economic life.

   c. The firm rebalances debt each period, keeping the debt-to-value ratio constant.

4. What is meant by the flow-to-equity valuation method? What discount rate is used in this method? What assumptions are necessary for this method to give an accurate valuation?

5. True or false? The APV method

   a. Starts with a base-case value for the project.

   b. Calculates the base-case value by discounting project cash flows, forecasted assuming all-equity financing, at the WACC for the project.

   c. Is especially useful when debt is to be paid down on a fixed schedule.

6. A project costs $1 million and has a base-case NPV of exactly zero (NPV = 0). What is the project's APV in the following cases?

   a. If the firm invests, it has to raise $500,000 by a stock issue. Issue costs are 15% of *net* proceeds.

   b. If the firm invests, its debt capacity increases by $500,000. The present value of interest tax shields on this debt is $76,000.

7. Whispering Pines, Inc., is all-equity-financed. The expected rate of return on the company's shares is 12%.

   a. What is the opportunity cost of capital for an average-risk Whispering Pines investment?

   b. Suppose the company issues debt, repurchases shares, and moves to a 30% debt-to-value ratio ($D/V = .30$). What will the company's weighted-average cost of capital be at the new capital structure? The borrowing rate is 7.5% and the tax rate is 35%.

8. Consider a project lasting one year only. The initial outlay is $1,000 and the expected inflow is $1,200. The opportunity cost of capital is $r = .20$. The borrowing rate is $r_D = .10$, and the tax shield per dollar of interest is $T_c = .35$.

   a. What is the project's base-case NPV?

   b. What is its APV if the firm borrows 30% of the project's required investment?

9. The WACC formula seems to imply that debt is "cheaper" than equity—that is, that a firm with more debt could use a lower discount rate. Does this make sense? Explain briefly.

10. Suppose KCS Corp. buys out Patagonia Trucking, a privately owned business, for $50 million. KCS has only $5 million cash in hand, so it arranges a $45 million bank loan. A normal debt-to-value ratio for a trucking company would be 50% at most, but the bank is satisfied with KCS's credit rating.

    Suppose you were valuing Patagonia by APV in the same format as Table 16.2. How much debt would you include? Explain briefly.

PRACTICE QUESTIONS

11. Table 16.3 shows a *book* balance sheet for the Wishing Well Motel chain. The company's long-term debt is secured by its real estate assets, but it also uses short-term bank financing. It pays 10% interest on the bank debt and 9% interest on the secured debt. Wishing Well has 10 million shares of stock outstanding, trading at $90 per share. The expected return on Wishing Well's common stock is 18%.

    Calculate Wishing Well's WACC. Assume that the book and market values of Wishing Well's debt are the same. The marginal tax rate is 35%.

TABLE 16.3

Balance sheet for Wishing Well, Inc. (figures in $ millions).

Cash and marketable securities	100	Bank loan	280
Inventory	50	Accounts payable	120
Accounts receivable	200	Current liabilities	400
Current assets	350		
Real estate	2,100	Long-term debt	1,800
Other assets	150	Equity	400
Total	2,600	Total	2,600

TABLE 16.4

Simplified book balance sheet for Rensselaer Felt (figures in $ thousands).

Cash and marketable securities	1,500	Short-term debt	75,600
Accounts receivable	120,000	Accounts payable	62,000
Inventories	125,000	Current liabilities	137,600
Current assets	246,500		
Property, plant, and equipment	302,000	Long-term debt	208,600
Other assets	89,000	Deferred taxes	45,000
		Shareholders' equity	246,300
Total	637,500	Total	637,500

12. Suppose Wishing Well is evaluating a new motel and resort on a romantic site in Madison County, Wisconsin. Explain how you would forecast the after-tax cash flows for this project. (*Hints:* How would you treat taxes? Interest expense? Changes in working capital?)

13. To finance the Madison County project, Wishing Well will have to arrange an additional $80 million of long-term debt and make a $20 million equity issue. The costs of this financing will total $4 million. How would you take this into account in valuing the proposed investment?

14. Table 16.4 shows a simplified balance sheet for Rensselaer Felt. Calculate this company's weighted-average cost of capital. The debt has just been refinanced at an interest rate of 6% (short term) and 8% (long term). The expected rate of return on the company's shares is 15%. There are 7.46 million shares outstanding, and the shares are trading at $46. The tax rate is 35%.

15. How will Rensselaer Felt's WACC and cost of equity change if it issues $50 million in new equity and uses the proceeds to retire long-term debt? Assume the company's borrowing rates are unchanged. Use the three-step procedure from Section 16.3.

16. Digital Organics (DO) has the opportunity to invest $1 million now ($t = 0$) and expects after-tax returns of $600,000 in $t = 1$ and $700,000 in $t = 2$. The project will last for two years only. The appropriate cost of capital is 12% with all-equity financing, the borrowing rate is 8%, and DO will borrow $300,000 against the project. This debt must be repaid in two equal installments. Assume debt tax shields have a net value of $.30 per dollar of interest paid. Calculate the project's APV using the procedure followed in Table 16.2.

17. Consider another perpetual project like the crusher described in Section 16.1. Its initial investment is $1,000,000, and the expected cash inflow is $95,000 a year in perpetuity. The opportunity cost of capital with all-equity financing is 10%, and the project allows the firm to borrow at 7%. The tax rate is 35%.
    Use APV to calculate this project's value.
    a. Assume first that the project will be partly financed with $400,000 of debt and that the debt amount is to be fixed and perpetual.
    b. Then assume that the initial borrowing will be increased or reduced in proportion to changes in the future market value of this project.
    Explain the difference between your answers to (a) and (b).

18. Suppose the project described in Practice Problem 17 is to be undertaken by a university. Funds for the project will be withdrawn from the university's endowment, which is

invested in a widely diversified portfolio of stocks and bonds. However, the university can also borrow at 7%. The university is tax exempt.

The university treasurer proposes to finance the project by issuing $400,000 of perpetual bonds at 7% and by selling $600,000 worth of common stocks from the endowment. The expected return on the common stocks is 10%. He therefore proposes to evaluate the project by discounting at a weighted-average cost of capital, calculated as

$$r = r_D \frac{D}{V} + r_E \frac{E}{V}$$

$$= .07 \left(\frac{400,000}{1,000,000} \right) + .10 \left(\frac{600,000}{1,000,000} \right)$$

$$= .088, \text{ or } 8.8\%$$

What's right or wrong with the treasurer's approach? Should the university invest? Should it borrow? Would the project's value to the university change if the treasurer financed the project entirely by selling common stocks from the endowment?

19. Consider a project to produce solar water heaters. It requires a $10 million investment and offers a level after-tax cash flow of $1.75 million per year for 10 years. The opportunity cost of capital is 12%, which reflects the project's business risk.

    a. Suppose the project is financed with $5 million of debt and $5 million of equity. The interest rate is 8% and the marginal tax rate is 35%. The debt will be paid off in equal annual installments over the project's 10-year life. Calculate APV.

    b. How does APV change if the firm incurs issue costs of $400,000 to raise the $5 million of required equity?

20. Take another look at the valuations of Rio in Tables 16.1 and 16.2. Now use the live spreadsheets on this book's Web site (**www.mhhe.com/bma1e**) to show how the valuations depend on:

Visit us at
www.mhhe.com/bma1e.

    a. The forecasted long-term growth rate.

    b. The required amounts of investment in fixed assets and working capital.

    c. The opportunity cost of capital. Note you can also vary the opportunity cost of capital in Table 16.1.

    d. Profitability, that is, cost of goods sold as a percentage of sales.

    e. The assumed amount of debt financing.

21. The Bunsen Chemical Company is currently at its target debt ratio of 40%. It is contemplating a $1 million expansion of its existing business. This expansion is expected to produce a cash inflow of $130,000 a year in perpetuity.

The company is uncertain whether to undertake this expansion and how to finance it. The two options are a $1 million issue of common stock or a $1 million issue of 20-year debt. The flotation costs of a stock issue would be around 5% of the amount raised, and the flotation costs of a debt issue would be around 1½%.

Bunsen's financial manager, Miss Polly Ethylene, estimates that the required return on the company's equity is 14%, but she argues that the flotation costs increase the cost of new equity to 19%. On this basis, the project does not appear viable.

On the other hand, she points out that the company can raise new debt on a 7% yield, which would make the cost of new debt 8½%. She therefore recommends that Bunsen should go ahead with the project and finance it with an issue of long-term debt.

Is Miss Ethylene right? How would you evaluate the project?

22. Nevada Hydro is 40% debt-financed and has a weighted-average cost of capital of 9.7%:

$$\text{WACC} = (1 - T_c) r_D \frac{D}{V} + r_E \frac{E}{V}$$

$$= (1 - .35)(.085)(.40) + .125(.60) = .097$$

Goldensacks Company is advising Nevada Hydro to issue $75 million of preferred stock at a dividend yield of 9%. The proceeds would be used to repurchase and retire common stock. The preferred issue would account for 10% of the preissue market value of the firm.

Goldensacks argues that these transactions would reduce Nevada Hydro's WACC to 9.4%:

$$\text{WACC} = (1 - .35)(.085)(.40) + .09(.10) + .125(.50)$$
$$= .094, \text{ or } 9.4\%$$

Do you agree with this calculation? Explain.

23. Table 16.5 is a simplified book balance sheet for Apache Corp. at year-end 2006. Here is some further information:

Number of outstanding shares (N)	330.7 million
Price per share (P)	$66.51
Beta	.98
Treasury bill rate	4.7%
20-year Treasury bond rate	4.8%
Cost of debt (r_D)	6.3%
Marginal tax rate	35%

a. Calculate Apache's WACC. Use the capital asset pricing model and the additional information given above. Make additional assumptions and approximations as necessary.

b. What is Apache's opportunity cost of capital?

c. Now go to the Standard & Poor's Market Insight Web site (**www.mhhe.com/ edumarketinsight**) and update your answers to questions (a) and (b).

24. Chiara Company's management has made the projections shown in Table 16.6. Use this Excel spreadsheet as a starting point to value the company as a whole. The WACC for Chiara is 12% and the long-run growth rate after year 5 is 4%. The company has $5 million debt and 865,000 shares outstanding. What is the value per share?

The following problems refer to the Appendix to this chapter, see pages 455–458.

25. The U.S. government has settled a dispute with your company for $16 million. It is committed to pay this amount in exactly 12 months. However, your company will have to pay tax on the award at a marginal tax rate of 35%. What is the award worth? The one-year Treasury rate is 5.5%.

26. You are considering a five-year lease of office space for R&D personnel. Once signed, the lease cannot be canceled. It would commit your firm to six annual $100,000 payments, with the first payment due immediately. What is the present value of the lease if your company's borrowing rate is 9% and its tax rate is 35%? (*Note:* The lease payments would be tax-deductible.)

TABLE 16.5

Simplified book balance sheet for Apache, year–end 2006 (figures in $ millions).

Current assets	2,490.3	Current liabilities	3,811.6
Net property, plant, and equipment	21,346.3	Long-term debt	2,019.8
Investments and other assets	471.7	Deferred taxes	3,619.0
		Other liabilities	1,666.9
		Shareholders' equity	13,191.0
Total	24,308.3	Total	24,308.3

		Historical			Forecast				
Year:		−2	−1	0	1	2	3	4	5
1. Sales		35,348	39,357	40,123	36,351	30,155	28,345	29,982	30,450
2. Cost of goods sold		17,834	18,564	22,879	21,678	17,560	16,459	15,631	14,987
3. Other costs		6,968	7,645	8,025	6,797	5,078	4,678	4,987	5,134
4. EBITDA (1 - 2 - 3)		10,546	13,148	9,219	7,876	7,517	7,208	9,364	10,329
5. Depreciation		5,671	5,745	5,678	5,890	5,670	5,908	6,107	5,908
6. EBIT (Pretax profit) (4 - 5)		4,875	7,403	3,541	1,986	1,847	1,300	3,257	4,421
7. Tax at 35%		1,706	2,591	1,239	695	646	455	1,140	1,547
8. Profit after tax (6 - 7)		3,169	4,812	2,302	1,291	1,201	845	2,117	2,874
9. Change in working capital		325	566	784	−54	−342	−245	127	235
10. Investment (change in gross fixed assets)		5,235	6,467	6,547	7,345	5,398	5,470	6,420	6,598

TABLE 16.6

Cash flow projections for Chiara Corp. ($ thousands).

CHALLENGE QUESTIONS

27. In footnote 16 we referred to the Miles–Ezzell discount rate formula, which assumes that debt is not rebalanced continuously, but at one-year intervals. Derive this formula. Then use it to unlever Sangria's WACC and calculate Sangria's opportunity cost of capital. Your answer will be slightly different from the opportunity cost that we calculated in Section 16.3. Can you explain why?

28. The WACC formula assumes that debt is rebalanced to maintain a constant debt ratio D/V. Rebalancing ties the level of future interest tax shields to the future value of the company. This makes the tax shields risky. Does that mean that fixed debt levels (no rebalancing) are better for stockholders?

29. Modify Table 16.1 on the assumption that competition eliminates any opportunities to earn more than WACC on new investment after year 7 (PVGO = 0). How does the valuation of Rio change?

APPENDIX

Discounting Safe, Nominal Cash Flows

Suppose you're considering purchase of a $100,000 machine. The manufacturer sweetens the deal by offering to finance the purchase by lending you $100,000 for five years, with annual interest payments of 5%. You would have to pay 13% to borrow from a bank. Your marginal tax rate is 35% ($T_c = .35$).

How much is this loan worth? If you take it, the cash flows, in thousands of dollars, are

		Period				
	0	1	2	3	4	5
Cash flow	100	−5	−5	−5	−5	−105
Tax shield		+1.75	+1.75	+1.75	+1.75	+1.75
After-tax cash flow	100	−3.25	−3.25	−3.25	−3.25	−103.25

What is the right discount rate?

Here you are discounting *safe, nominal* cash flows—safe because your company must commit to pay if it takes the loan,[27] and nominal because the payments would be fixed regardless of future inflation. Now, the correct discount rate for safe, nominal cash flows is your company's *after-tax*, unsubsidized borrowing rate,[28] which is $r_D(1 - T_c) = .13(1 - .35) = .0845$. Therefore

$$\text{NPV} = +100 - \frac{3.25}{1.0845} - \frac{3.25}{(1.0845)^2} - \frac{3.25}{(1.0845)^3} - \frac{3.25}{(1.0845)^4} - \frac{103.25}{(1.0845)^5}$$

$$= +20.52, \text{ or } \$20{,}520$$

The manufacturer has effectively cut the machine's purchase price from \$100,000 to \$100,000 − \$20,520 = \$79,480. You can now go back and recalculate the machine's NPV using this fire-sale price, or you can use the NPV of the subsidized loan as one element of the machine's adjusted present value.

A General Rule

Clearly, we owe an explanation of why $r_D(1 - T_c)$ is the right discount rate for safe, nominal cash flows. It's no surprise that the rate depends on r_D, the unsubsidized borrowing rate, for that is investors' opportunity cost of capital, the rate they would demand from your company's debt. But why should r_D be converted to an *after-tax* figure?

Let's simplify by taking a *one-year* subsidized loan of \$100,000 at 5%. The cash flows, in thousands of dollars, are

	Period 0	Period 1
Cash flow	100	−105
Tax shield		+1.75
After-tax cash flow	100	−103.25

Now ask, What is the maximum amount X that could be borrowed for one year through regular channels if \$103,250 is set aside to service the loan?

"Regular channels" means borrowing at 13% pretax and 8.45% after tax. Therefore you will need 108.45% of the amount borrowed to pay back principal plus after-tax interest charges. If $1.0845X = 103{,}250$, then $X = 95{,}205$. Now if you can borrow \$100,000 by a subsidized loan, but only \$95,205 through normal channels, the difference (\$4,795) is money in the bank. Therefore, it must also be the NPV of this one-period subsidized loan.

When you discount a safe, nominal cash flow at an after-tax borrowing rate, you are implicitly calculating the *equivalent loan*, the amount you could borrow through normal channels, using the cash flow as debt service. Note that

$$\text{Equivalent loan} = \text{PV(cash flow available for debt service)} = \frac{103{,}250}{1.0845} = 95{,}205$$

In some cases, it may be easier to think of taking the lender's side of the equivalent loan rather than the borrower's. For example, you could ask, How much would my company have to invest today in order to cover next year's debt service on the

---

[27] In theory, *safe* means literally "risk-free," like the cash returns on a Treasury bond. In practice, it means that the risk of not paying or receiving a cash flow is small.

[28] In Section 12.1 we calculated the NPV of subsidized financing using the *pretax* borrowing rate. Now you can see that was a mistake. Using the pretax rate implicitly defines the loan in terms of its pretax cash flows, violating a rule promulgated way back in Section 7.1: *Always* estimate cash flows on an after-tax basis.

subsidized loan? The answer is $95,205: If you lend that amount at 13%, you will earn 8.45% after tax, and therefore have 95,205(1.0845) = $103,250. By this transaction, you can in effect cancel, or "zero out," the future obligation. If you can borrow $100,000 and then set aside only $95,205 to cover all the required debt service, you clearly have $4,795 to spend as you please. That amount is the NPV of the subsidized loan.

Therefore, regardless of whether it's easier to think of borrowing or lending, the correct discount rate for safe, nominal cash flows is an after-tax interest rate.[29]

In some ways, this is an obvious result once you think about it. Companies are free to borrow or lend money. If they *lend*, they receive the after-tax interest rate on their investment; if they *borrow* in the capital market, they pay the after-tax interest rate. Thus, the opportunity cost to companies of investing in debt-equivalent cash flows is the after-tax interest rate. This is the adjusted cost of capital for debt-equivalent cash flows.[30]

Some Further Examples

Here are some further examples of debt-equivalent cash flows.

Payout Fixed by Contract   Suppose you sign a maintenance contract with a truck leasing firm, which agrees to keep your leased trucks in good working order for the next two years in exchange for 24 fixed monthly payments. These payments are debt-equivalent flows.

Depreciation Tax Shields   Capital projects are normally valued by discounting the total after-tax cash flows they are expected to generate. Depreciation tax shields contribute to project cash flow, but they are not valued separately; they are just folded into project cash flows along with dozens, or hundreds, of other specific inflows and outflows. The project's opportunity cost of capital reflects the average risk of the resulting aggregate.

However, suppose we ask what depreciation tax shields are worth *by themselves.* For a firm that's sure to pay taxes, depreciation tax shields are a safe, nominal flow. Therefore, they should be discounted at the firm's after-tax borrowing rate.

Suppose we buy an asset with a depreciable basis of $200,000, which can be depreciated by the five-year tax depreciation schedule (see Table 7.4). The resulting tax shields are

	Period					
	1	2	3	4	5	6
Percentage deductions	20	32	19.2	11.5	11.5	5.8
Dollar deductions (thousands)	$40	$64	$38.4	$23	$23	$11.6
Tax shields at $T_c = .35$ (thousands)	$14	$22.4	$13.4	$8.1	$8.1	$4.0

[29] Borrowing and lending rates should not differ by much if the cash flows are truly safe, that is, if the chance of default is small. Usually your decision will not hinge on the rate used. If it does, ask which offsetting transaction—borrowing or lending—seems most natural and reasonable for the problem at hand. Then use the corresponding interest rate.

[30] All the examples in this section are forward-looking; they call for the value today of a stream of future debt-equivalent cash flows. But similar issues arise in legal and contractual disputes when a *past* cash flow has to be brought forward in time to a present value today. Suppose it's determined that company A should have paid B $1 million 10 years ago. B clearly deserves more than $1 million today, because it has lost the time value of money. The time value of money should be expressed as an after-tax borrowing or lending rate, or if no risk enters, as the after-tax risk-free rate. The time value of money is *not* equal to B's overall cost of capital. Allowing B to "earn" its overall cost of capital on the payment allows it to earn a risk premium without bearing risk. For a broader discussion of these issues, see F. Fisher and C. Romaine, "Janis Joplin's Yearbook and Theory of Damages," *Journal of Accounting, Auditing & Finance* 5 (Winter/Spring 1990), pp. 145–157.

The after-tax discount rate is $r_D(1 - T_c) = .13(1 - .35) = .0845$. (We continue to assume a 13% pretax borrowing rate and a 35% marginal tax rate.) The present value of these shields is

$$PV = \frac{14}{1.0845} + \frac{22.4}{(1.0845)^2} + \frac{13.4}{(1.0845)^3} + \frac{8.1}{(1.0845)^4} + \frac{8.1}{(1.0845)^5} + \frac{4.0}{(1.0845)^6}$$
$$= +56.2, \text{ or } \$56,200$$

A Consistency Check

You may have wondered whether our procedure for valuing debt-equivalent cash flows is consistent with the WACC and APV approaches presented earlier in this chapter. Yes, it is consistent, as we will now illustrate.

Let's look at another very simple numerical example. You are asked to value a $1 million payment to be received from a blue-chip company one year hence. After taxes at 35%, the cash inflow is $650,000. The payment is fixed by contract.

Since the contract generates a debt-equivalent flow, the opportunity cost of capital is the rate investors would demand on a one-year note issued by the blue-chip company, which happens to be 8%. For simplicity, we'll assume this is your company's borrowing rate too. Our valuation rule for debt-equivalent flows is therefore to discount at $r_D(1 - T_c) = .08(1 - .35) = .052$:

$$PV = \frac{650,000}{1.052} = \$617,900$$

What is the *debt capacity* of this $650,000 payment? Exactly $617,900. Your company could borrow that amount and pay off the loan completely—principal and after-tax interest—with the $650,000 cash inflow. The debt capacity is 100% of the PV of the debt-equivalent cash flow.

If you think of it that way, our discount rate $r_D(1 - T_c)$ is just a special case of WACC with a 100% debt ratio ($D/V = 1$).

$$WACC = r_D(1 - T_c)D/V + r_E E/V$$
$$= r_D(1 - T_c) \text{ if } D/V = 1 \text{ and } E/V = 0$$

Now let's try an APV calculation. This is a two-part valuation. First, the $650,000 inflow is discounted at the opportunity cost of capital, 8%. Second, we add the present value of interest tax shields on debt supported by the project. Since the firm can borrow 100% of the cash flow's value, the tax shield is $r_D T_c$ APV, and APV is

$$APV = \frac{650,000}{1.08} + \frac{.08(.35)APV}{1.08}$$

Solving for APV, we get $617,900, the same answer we obtained by discounting at the after-tax borrowing rate. Thus our valuation rule for debt-equivalent flows is a special case of APV.

PART SIX

OPTIONS

POP QUIZ: What do the following events have in common?

- Flatiron offers its president a bonus if the company's stock price exceeds $120.
- Kindred Healthcare reaches an agreement with its junior debtholders to pay them off with a mixture of common stock and warrants. The warrants give the debtholders a five-year option to buy the common stock at prices of $30 and $33.33 a share.
- The French telecom company, Iliad, issues a €2.88 billion convertible bond that can be exchanged in the future for common stock.
- Blitzen Computer dips a toe in the water and enters a new market.
- Malted Herring postpones investment in a positive-NPV plant.
- Hewlett-Packard exports partially assembled printers even though it would be cheaper to ship the finished product.
- Dominion installs a dual-fired unit at its Possum Point power station that can use either fuel oil or natural gas.

Answers: (1) each of these events involves an option, and (2) the understanding that you need for analyzing each of these options is provided in subsequent chapters. But you must walk before you can run. Therefore we start by focusing on a simple option to buy the stock of Genentech. Chapter 17 examines the payoffs from this option and Chapter 18 shows how it is valued.

Web sites related to this Part appear at www.mhhe.com/bma1e.

CHAPTER SEVENTEEN

UNDERSTANDING OPTIONS

THIS AND THE following chapter are concerned with options. But why should the financial manager of an industrial company be interested in such an exotic subject? There are several reasons. First, companies regularly use commodity, currency, and interest-rate options to reduce risk. For example, a meatpacking company that wishes to put a ceiling on the cost of beef might take out an option to buy live cattle at a fixed price. A company that wishes to limit its future borrowing costs might take out an option to sell long-term bonds at a fixed price. And so on.

Second, many capital investments include an embedded option to expand in the future. For instance, the company may invest in a patent that allows it to exploit a new technology or it may purchase adjoining land that gives it the option in the future to increase capacity. In each case the company is paying money today for the opportunity to make a further investment. To put it another way, the company is acquiring *growth opportunities.*

Here is another disguised option to invest: You are considering the purchase of a tract of desert land that is known to contain gold deposits. Unfortunately, the cost of extraction is higher than the current price of gold. Does this mean the land is almost worthless? Not at all. You are not obliged to

mine the gold, but ownership of the land gives you the option to do so. Of course, if you know that the gold price will remain below the extraction cost, then the option is worthless. But if there is uncertainty about future gold prices, you could be lucky and make a killing.

If the option to expand has value, what about the option to bail out? Projects don't usually go on until the equipment disintegrates. The decision to terminate a project is usually taken by management, not by nature. Once the project is no longer profitable, the company will cut its losses and exercise its option to abandon the project. Some projects have higher abandonment value than others. Those that use standardized equipment may offer a valuable abandonment option. Others may actually cost money to discontinue. For example, it is very costly to decommission an offshore oil platform.

We took a peek at investment options in Chapter 11, and we showed there how to use decision trees to analyze Magna Charter's options to expand its airline operation or abandon it. In Chapter 18 we will practice valuing a real option.

The other important reason why financial managers need to understand options is that they are often tacked on to an issue of corporate securities and so provide the investor or the company with the flexibility to change the terms of the issue.

In fact, whenever a company borrows, it gains an option. It can choose to walk away from its debts and surrender its assets to the bondholders. If the value of the company's assets is less than the amount of the debt, the company will choose to default on the payment and the bondholders will get to keep the company's assets. Thus, when the firm borrows, the lender effectively acquires the company and the shareholders obtain the option to buy it back by paying off the debt. This is an extremely important insight. It means that anything that we can learn about traded options applies equally to corporate liabilities.

In this chapter we use traded stock options to explain how options work, but we hope that our brief survey has convinced you that the interest of

financial managers in options goes far beyond traded stock options. That is why we are asking you to invest here to acquire several important ideas for use later.

If you are unfamiliar with the wonderful world of options, it may seem baffling on first encounter. We will therefore divide this chapter into three bite-sized pieces. Our first task is to introduce you to call and put options and to show you how the payoff on these options depends on the price of the underlying asset. We will then show how financial alchemists can combine options to produce a variety of interesting strategies.

We conclude the chapter by identifying the variables that determine option values. Here you will encounter some surprising and counterintuitive effects. For example, investors are used to thinking that increased risk reduces present value. But for options it is the other way around.

17.1   CALLS, PUTS, AND SHARES

Investors regularly trade options on common stocks.[1] For example, Table 17.1 reproduces quotes from the Chicago Board Options Exchange (CBOE) for options on the stock of the biotech company, Genentech. You can see that there are two types of option—calls and puts. We will explain each in turn.

Call Options and Position Diagrams

A **call option** gives its owner the right to buy stock at a specified *exercise* or *strike price* on or before a specified exercise date. If the option can be exercised only on one particular day, it is conventionally known as a *European call;* in other cases (such as the Genentech options shown in Table 17.1), the option can be exercised on or at any time before that day, and it is then known as an *American call.*

The third column of Table 17.1 sets out the prices of Genentech call options with different exercise prices and exercise dates. Look at the quotes for options maturing in December 2006. The first entry says that for $14.30 you could acquire an option

---

[1] The two principal options exchanges in the United States are the International Securities Exchange and the Chicago Board Options Exchange (CBOE).

TABLE 17.1

Selected prices of put and call options on Genentech stock in September 2006, when the closing stock price was about $82.50.

* Long-term options are called "LEAPS."

Source: Yahoo! Finance, **finance.yahoo.com.** Reproduced with permission of Yahoo! Inc. © 2007 by Yahoo! Inc. Yahoo! and the Yahoo! logo are trademarks of Yahoo! Inc.

Exercise Date	Exercise Price	Price of Call Option	Price of Put Option
December 2006	$ 70	$14.30	$ 0.75
	75	9.90	1.40
	80	6.50	2.75
	85	3.70	5.10
	90	1.90	8.70
March 2007	$ 70	$15.10	$ 2.20
	75	12.20	2.65
	80	**9.00**	**4.60**
	85	6.20	7.70
	90	4.10	9.46
January 2008*	$ 70	$20.50	$ 4.30
	75	18.00	5.70
	80	14.90	7.30
	85	12.00	10.40
	90	9.90	12.70

to buy one share[2] of Genentech stock for $70 on or before December 2006. Moving down to the next row, you can see that an option to buy for $5 more ($75 vs. $70) costs $4.40 less, that is $9.90. In general, the value of a call option goes down as the exercise price goes up.

Now look at the quotes for options maturing in March 2007 and January 2008. Notice how the option price increases as option maturity is extended. For example, at an exercise price of $80, the December 2006 call option costs $6.50, the March 2007 option costs $9.00, and the January 2008 option costs $14.90.

In Chapter 12 we met Louis Bachelier, who in 1900 first suggested that security prices follow a random walk. Bachelier also devised a very convenient shorthand to illustrate the effects of investing in different options. We will use this shorthand to compare a call option and a put option on Genentech stock.

The *position diagram* in Figure 17.1(*a*) shows the possible consequences of investing in Genentech March 2007 call options with an exercise price of $80 (boldfaced in Table 17.1). The outcome from investing in Genentech calls depends on what happens to the stock price. If the stock price at the end of this six-month period turns out to be less than the $80 exercise price, nobody will pay $80 to obtain the share via the call option. Your call will in that case be valueless, and you will throw it away. On the other hand, if the stock price turns out to be greater than $80, it will pay to exercise your option to buy the share. In this case the call will be worth the market price of the share minus the $80 that you must pay to acquire it. For example, suppose that the price of Genentech stock rises to $120. Your call will then be worth $120 − $80 = $40. That is your payoff, but of course it is not all profit. Table 17.1 shows that you had to pay $9.00 to buy the call.

---

[2] You can't actually buy an option on a single share. Trades are in multiples of 100. The minimum order would be for 100 options on 100 Genentech shares.

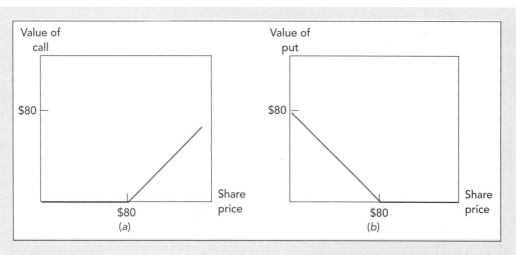

FIGURE 17.1

Position diagrams show how payoffs to owners of Genentech calls and puts (shown by the colored lines) depend on the share price. (*a*) Result of buying Genentech call exercisable at $80. (*b*) Result of buying Genentech put exercisable at $80.

Put Options

Now let us look at the Genentech **put options** in the right-hand column of Table 17.1. Whereas the call option gives you the right to *buy* a share for a specified exercise price, the comparable put gives you the right to *sell* the share. For example, the boldfaced entry in the right-hand column of Table 17.1 shows that for $4.60 you could acquire an option to sell Genentech stock for a price of $80 anytime before March 2007. The circumstances in which the put turns out to be profitable are just the opposite of those in which the call is profitable. You can see this from the position diagram in Figure 17.1(*b*). If Genentech's share price immediately before expiration turns out to be *greater* than $80, you won't want to sell stock at that price. You would do better to sell the share in the market, and your put option will be worthless. Conversely, if the share price turns out to be *less* than $80, it will pay to buy stock at the low price and then take advantage of the option to sell it for $80. In this case, the value of the put option on the exercise date is the difference between the $80 proceeds of the sale and the market price of the share. For example, if the share is worth $60, the put is worth $20:

$$\text{Value of put option at expiration} = \text{exercise price} - \text{market price of the share}$$
$$= \$80 - \$60 = \$20$$

Selling Calls, Puts, and Shares

Let us now look at the position of an investor who *sells* these investments. If you sell, or "write," a call, you promise to deliver shares if asked to do so by the call buyer. In other words, the buyer's asset is the seller's liability. If the share price is below the exercise price when the option matures, the buyer will not exercise the call and the seller's liability will be zero. If it rises above the exercise price, the buyer will exercise and the seller must give up the shares. The seller loses the

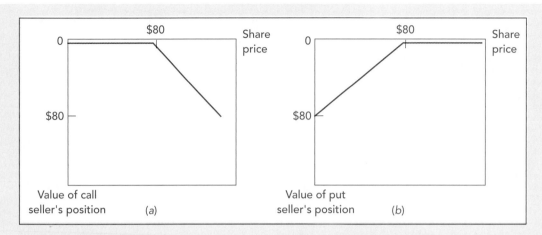

FIGURE 17.2

Payoffs to *sellers* of Genentech calls and puts (shown by the colored lines) depend on the share price. (*a*) Result of selling Genentech call exercisable at $80. (*b*) Result of selling Genentech put exercisable at $80.

difference between the share price and the exercise price received from the buyer. Notice that it is the buyer who always has the option to exercise; option sellers simply do as they are told.

Suppose that the price of Genentech stock turns out to be $100, which is above the option's exercise price of $80. In this case the buyer will exercise the call. The seller is forced to sell stock worth $100 for only $80 and so has a payoff of −$20.[3] Of course, that $20 loss is the buyer's gain. Figure 17.2(*a*) shows how the payoffs to the seller of the Genentech call option vary with the stock price. Notice that for every dollar the buyer makes, the seller loses a dollar. Figure 17.2(*a*) is just Figure 17.1(*a*) drawn upside down.

In just the same way we can depict the position of an investor who sells, or writes, a put by standing Figure 17.1(*b*) on its head. The seller of the put has agreed to pay $80 for the share if the buyer of the put should request it. Clearly the seller will be safe as long as the share price remains above $80 but will lose money if the share price falls below this figure. The worst thing that can happen is that the stock becomes worthless. The seller would then be obliged to pay $80 for a stock worth $0. The "value" of the option position would be −$80.

Position Diagrams Are Not Profit Diagrams

Position diagrams show *only* the payoffs at option exercise; they do not account for the initial cost of buying the option or the initial proceeds from selling it.

This is a common point of confusion. For example, the position diagram in Figure 17.1(*a*) makes purchase of a call *look* like a sure thing—the payoff is at worst zero, with plenty of "upside" if Genentech's stock price goes above $80 by March 2007. But compare the *profit diagram* in Figure 17.3(*a*), which subtracts the $9.00 *cost* of the call in September 2006 from the payoff at maturity. The call buyer

---

[3] The seller has some consolation, for he or she was paid $9.00 in September for selling the call.

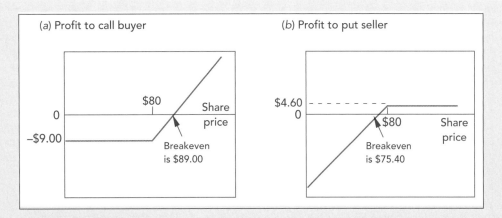

FIGURE 17.3

Profit diagrams incorporate the costs of buying an option or the proceeds from selling one. In panel (a), we subtract the $9.00 cost of the Genentech call from the payoffs plotted in Figure 17.1(a). In panel (b), we add the $4.60 proceeds from selling the Genentech put to the payoffs in Figure 17.2(b).

loses money at all share prices less than $80 + 9.00 = $89.00. Take another example: The position diagram in Figure 17.2(b) makes selling a put *look* like a sure loss—the *best* payoff is zero. But the profit diagram in Figure 17.3(b), which recognizes the $4.60 received by the seller, shows that the seller gains at all prices above $80 − 4.60 = $75.40.[4]

Profit diagrams like those in Figure 17.3 may be helpful to the options beginner, but options experts rarely draw them.[5] Now that you've graduated from the first options class we won't draw them either. We will stick to position diagrams, because you have to focus on payoffs at exercise to understand options and to value them properly.

17.2 FINANCIAL ALCHEMY WITH OPTIONS

Look now at Figure 17.4(a), which shows the payoff if you buy Genentech stock at $80. You gain dollar-for-dollar if the stock price goes up and you lose dollar-for-dollar if it falls. That's trite; it doesn't take a genius to draw a 45-degree line.

Look now at panel (b), which shows the payoffs from an investment strategy that retains the upside potential of Genentech stock but gives complete downside protection. In this case your payoff stays at $80 even if the Genentech stock price falls to $70, $60, or zero. Panel (b)'s payoffs are clearly better than panel (a)'s. If a financial alchemist could turn panel (a) into panel (b), you'd be willing to pay for the service.

Of course alchemy has its dark side. Panel (c) shows an investment strategy for masochists. You lose if the stock price falls, but you give up any chance of profiting

[4] The fact that you have made a profit on your position is not necessarily a cause for rejoicing. The profit needs to compensate you for the time value of money and the risk that you took.
[5] Profit diagrams such as Figure 17.3 deduct the initial cost of the option from the final payoff. They therefore ignore the first lesson of finance—"A dollar today is worth more than a dollar in the future."

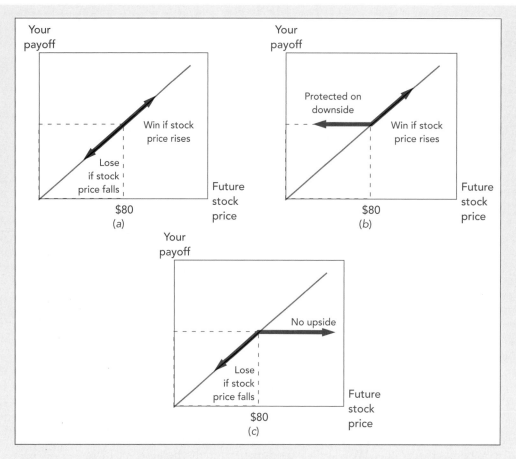

FIGURE 17.4

Payoffs at the end of 6 months to three investment strategies for Genentech stock. (*a*) You buy one share for $80. (*b*) No downside. If stock price falls, your payoff stays at $80. (*c*) A strategy for masochists? You lose if stock price falls, but you don't gain if it rises.

from a rise in the stock price. If you *like* to lose, or if someone pays you enough to take the strategy on, this is the investment for you.

Now, as you have probably suspected, all this financial alchemy is for real. You can do both the transmutations shown in Figure 17.4. You do them with options, and we will show you how.

Consider first the strategy for masochists. The first diagram in Figure 17.5 shows the payoffs from buying a share of Genentech stock, while the second shows the payoffs from *selling* a call option with an $80 exercise price. The third diagram shows what happens if you combine these two positions. The result is the no-win strategy that we depicted in panel (*c*) of Figure 17.4. You lose if the stock price declines below $80, but, if the stock price rises above $80, the owner of the call will demand that you hand over your stock for the $80 exercise price. So you lose on the downside and give up any chance of a profit. That's the bad news. The good news is that you get paid for taking on this liability. In September 2006 you would have been paid $9.00, the price of a six-month call option.

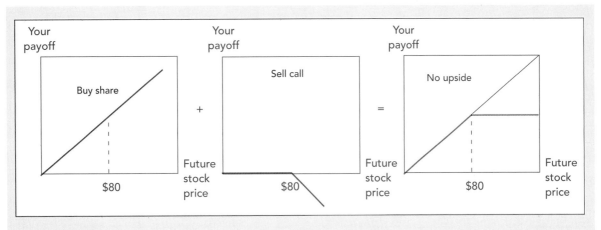

FIGURE 17.5

Options you can use to create a strategy where you lose if the stock price falls but do not gain if it rises [strategy (c) in Figure 17.4].

Now, we'll create the downside protection shown in Figure 17.4(*b*). Look at row 1 of Figure 17.6. The first diagram again shows the payoff from buying a share of Genentech stock, while the next diagram in row 1 shows the payoffs from buying a Genentech put option with an exercise price of $80. The third diagram shows the effect of combining these two positions. You can see that, if Genentech's stock price rises above $80, your put option is valueless, so you simply receive the gains from your investment in the share. However, if the stock price falls below $80, you can exercise your put option and sell your stock for $80. Thus, by adding a put option to your investment in the stock, you have protected yourself against loss.[6] This is the strategy that we depicted in panel (*b*) of Figure 17.4. Of course, there is no gain without pain. The *cost* of insuring yourself against loss is the amount that you pay for a put option on Genentech stock with an exercise price of $80. In September 2006 the price of this put was $4.60. This was the going rate for financial alchemists.

We have just seen how put options can be used to provide downside protection. We will now show you how call options can be used to get the same result. This is illustrated in row 2 of Figure 17.6. The first diagram shows the payoff from placing the present value of $80 in a bank deposit. Regardless of what happens to the price of Genentech stock, your bank deposit will pay off $80. The second diagram in row 2 shows the payoff from a call option on Genentech stock with an exercise price of $80, and the third diagram shows the effect of combining these two positions. Notice that, if the price of Genentech stock falls, your call is worthless, but you still have your $80 in the bank. For every dollar that Genentech stock price rises above $80, your investment in the call option pays off an extra dollar. For example, if the stock price rises to $120, you will have $80 in the bank and a call worth $40. Thus you participate fully in any rise in the price of the stock, while being fully protected against any fall. So we have just found another way to provide the downside protection depicted in panel (*b*) of Figure 17.4.

---

[6] This combination of a stock and a put option is known as a *protective put*.

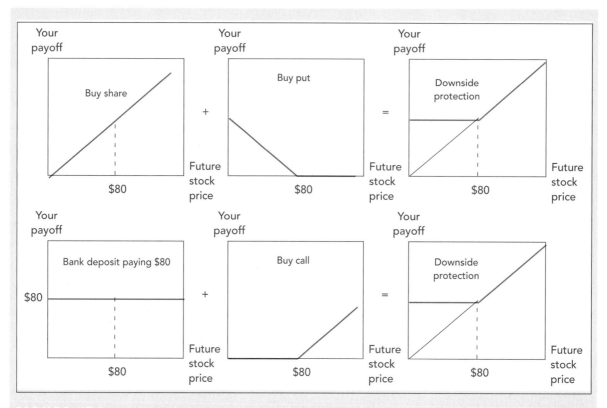

FIGURE 17.6

Each row in the figure shows a different way to create a strategy where you gain if the stock price rises but are protected on the downside [strategy (b) in Figure 17.4].

These last two rows of Figure 17.6 tell us something about the relationship between a call option and a put option. Regardless of the future stock price, both investment strategies provide identical payoffs. In other words, if you buy the share and a put option to sell it for $80, you receive the same payoff as from buying a call option and setting enough money aside to pay the $80 exercise price. Therefore, if you are committed to holding the two packages until the options expire, the two packages should sell for the same price today. This gives us a fundamental relationship for European options:

Value of call + present value of exercise price = value of put + share price

To repeat, this relationship holds because the payoff of

Buy call, invest present value of exercise price in safe asset[7]

is identical to the payoff from

Buy put, buy share

---

[7] The present value is calculated at the *risk-free* rate of interest. It is the amount that you would have to invest today in a bank deposit or Treasury bills to realize the exercise price on the option's expiration date.

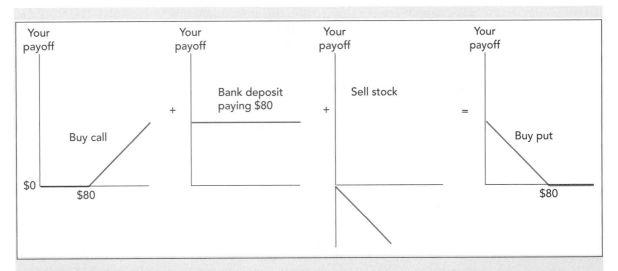

FIGURE 17.7

A strategy of buying a call, depositing the present value of the exercise price in the bank, and selling the stock is equivalent to buying a put.

This basic relationship among share price, call and put values, and the present value of the exercise price is called **put–call parity.**[8]

Put–call parity can be expressed in several ways. Each expression implies two investment strategies that give identical results. For example, suppose that you want to solve for the value of a put. You simply need to twist the put–call parity formula around to give

Value of put = value of call + present value of exercise price − share price

From this expression you can deduce that

Buy put

is identical to

Buy call, invest present value of exercise price in safe asset, sell share

In other words, if puts are not available, you can get exactly the same payoff by buying calls, putting cash in the bank, and selling shares.

If you find this difficult to believe, look at Figure 17.7, which shows the possible payoffs from each position. The diagram on the left shows the payoffs from a call option on Genentech stock with an exercise price of $80. The second diagram shows the payoffs from placing the present value of $80 in the bank. Regardless of

---

[8] Put–call parity holds only if you are committed to holding the options until the final exercise date. It therefore does not hold for American options, which you can exercise *before* the final date. We discuss possible reasons for early exercise in Chapter 18. Also if the stock makes a dividend payment before the final exercise date, you need to recognize that the investor who buys the call misses out on this dividend. In this case the relationship is

Value of call + present value of exercise price = value of put + share price − present value of dividend

what happens to the share price, this investment will pay off $80. The third dia-gram shows the payoffs from selling Genentech stock. When you sell a share that you don't own, you have a liability—you must sometime buy it back. As they say on Wall Street:

> He who sells what isn't his'n
> Buys it back or goes to pris'n

Therefore the best that can happen to you is that the share price falls to zero. In that case it costs you nothing to buy the share back. But for every extra dollar on the future share price, you will need to spend an extra dollar to buy the share. The final diagram in Figure 17.7 shows that the *total* payoff from these three po-sitions is the same as if you had bought a put option. For example, suppose that when the option matures the stock price is $50. Your call will be worthless, your bank deposit will be worth $80, and it will cost you $50 to repurchase the share. Your total payoff is $0 + 80 - 50 = \$30$, exactly the same as the payoff from the put.

If two investments offer identical payoffs, then they should sell for the same price today. If the law of one price is violated, you have a potential arbitrage op-portunity. So let's check whether there are any arbitrage profits to be made from our Genentech calls and puts. In September 2006 the price of a six-month call with an $80 exercise price was $9.00, the interest rate was about 5%, and the price of Genentech stock was $82.50. Therefore the cost of a homemade put was

$$\text{Buy call} + \text{present value of exercise price} - \text{share price} = \text{cost of homemade put}$$
$$9.00 \quad + \quad 80/1.05^{.5} \quad - \quad 82.50 \quad = \quad \$4.57$$

This is exactly the same (except for a 3¢ rounding error) as it would have cost you to buy a put directly.

Spotting the Option

Options rarely come with a large label attached. Often the trickiest part of the problem is to identify the option. When you are not sure whether you are dealing with a put or a call or a complicated blend of the two, it is a good precaution to draw a position diagram. Here is an example.

The Flatiron and Mangle Corporation has offered its president, Ms. Higden, the following incentive scheme: At the end of the year Ms. Higden will be paid a bonus of $50,000 for every dollar that the price of Flatiron stock exceeds its cur-rent figure of $120. However, the maximum bonus that she can receive is set at $2 million.

You can think of Ms. Higden as owning 50,000 tickets, each of which pays noth-ing if the stock price fails to beat $120. The value of each ticket then rises by $1 for each dollar rise in the stock price up to the maximum of $2,000,000/50,000 = \$40$. Figure 17.8 shows the payoffs from just one of these tickets. The payoffs are not the same as those of the simple put and call options that we drew in Figure 17.1, but it is possible to find a combination of options that exactly replicates Figure 17.8. Be-fore going on to read the answer, see if you can spot it yourself. (If you are some-one who enjoys puzzles of the make-a-triangle-from-just-two-matchsticks type, this one should be a walkover.)

The answer is in Figure 17.9. The solid black line represents the purchase of a call option with an exercise price of $120, and the dotted line shows the sale of another call option with an exercise price of $160. The colored line shows the

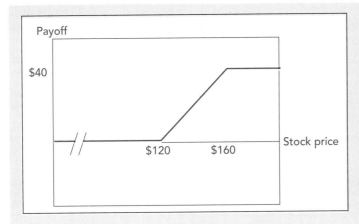

FIGURE 17.8

The payoff from one of Ms. Higden's "tickets" depends on Flatiron's stock price.

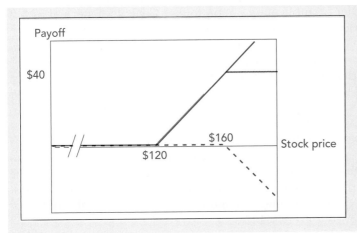

FIGURE 17.9

The solid black line shows the payoff from buying a call with an exercise price of $120. The dotted line shows the sale of a call with an exercise price of $160. The combined purchase and sale (shown by the colored line) is identical to one of Ms. Higden's "tickets."

payoffs from a combination of the purchase and the sale—exactly the same as the payoffs from one of Ms. Higden's tickets.

Thus, if we wish to know how much the incentive scheme is costing the company, we need to calculate the difference between the value of 50,000 call options with an exercise price of $120 and the value of 50,000 calls with an exercise price of $160.

We could have made the incentive scheme depend in a much more complicated way on the stock price. For example, the bonus could peak at $2 million and then fall steadily back to zero as the stock price climbs above $160.[9] You could still have represented this scheme as a combination of options. In fact, we can state a general theorem:

> Any set of contingent payoffs—that is, payoffs that depend on the value of some other asset—can be constructed with a mixture of simple options on that asset.

---

[9] This is not as nutty a bonus scheme as it may sound. Maybe Ms. Higden's hard work can lift the value of the stock by so much and the only way she can hope to increase it further is by taking on extra risk. You can deter her from doing this by making her bonus start to decline beyond some point. We are reminded here of a senior investment banker, who commented that the first time a trader made unusually large profits he would be warned; the second time, he would be fired. It was a good bet that such a trader was taking excessive risks.

In other words, you can create any position diagram—with as many ups and downs or peaks and valleys as your imagination allows—by buying or selling the right combinations of puts and calls with different exercise prices.[10]

Finance pros often talk about **financial engineering,** which is the practice of packaging different investments to create new tailor-made instruments. Perhaps a German company would like to set a minimum and maximum cost at which it can buy dollars in six-months' time. Or perhaps an oil company would like to pay a lower rate of interest on its debt if the price of oil falls. Options provide the building blocks that financial engineers use to create these interesting payoff structures.

17.3   WHAT DETERMINES OPTION VALUES?

So far we have said nothing about how the market value of an option is determined. We do know what an option is worth when it matures, however. Consider, for instance, our earlier example of an option to buy Genentech stock at $80. If Genentech's stock price is below $80 on the exercise date, the call will be worthless; if the stock price is above $80, the call will be worth $80 less than the value of the stock. This relationship is depicted by the heavy, lower line in Figure 17.10.

Even before maturity the price of the option can never remain *below* the heavy, lower-bound line in Figure 17.10. For example, if our option were priced at $5 and the stock were priced at $95, it would pay any investor to sell the stock and then buy it back by purchasing the option and exercising it for an additional $80. That would give an arbitrage opportunity with a profit of $10. The demand for options from investors seeking to exploit this opportunity would quickly force the option price up, at least to the heavy line in the figure. For options that still have some time to run, the heavy line is therefore a *lower bound* on the market price of the option. Option geeks express the same idea more concisely when they say Lower bound = Max(stock price − exercise price, 0).

The diagonal line in Figure 17.10 is the *upper bound* to the option price. Why? Because the option cannot give a higher ultimate payoff than the stock. If at the option's expiration the stock price ends up *above* the exercise price, the option is worth the stock price *less* the exercise price. If the stock price ends up *below* the exercise price, the option is worthless, but the stock's owner still has a valuable security. For example, if the option's exercise price is $80, then the extra dollar returns realized by stockholders are shown in the following table:

	Stock Payoff	Option Payoff	Extra Payoff from Holding Stock Instead of Option
Option exercised (stock price greater than $80)	Stock price	Stock price − 80	$80
Option expires unexercised (stock price less than or equal to $80)	Stock price	0	Stock price

---

[10] In some cases you may also have to borrow or lend money to generate a position diagram with your desired pattern. Lending raises the payoff line in position diagrams, as in the bottom row of Figure 17.6. Borrowing lowers the payoff line.

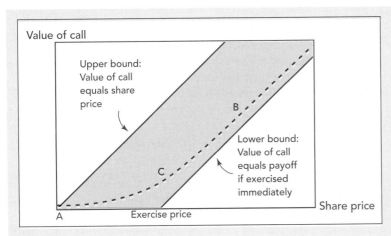

FIGURE 17.10

Value of a call before its expiration date (dashed line). The value depends on the stock price. It is always worth more than its value if exercised now (heavy line). It is never worth more than the stock price itself.

If the stock and the option have the same price, everyone will rush to sell the option and buy the stock. Therefore, the option price must be somewhere in the shaded region of Figure 17.10. In fact, it will lie on a curved, upward-sloping line like the dashed curve shown in the figure. This line begins its travels where the upper and lower bounds meet (at zero). Then it rises, gradually becoming parallel to the upward-sloping part of the lower bound.

But let us look more carefully at the shape and location of the dashed line. Three points, *A*, *B*, and *C*, are marked on the dashed line. As we explain each point you will see why the option price has to behave as the dashed line predicts.

Point A *When the stock is worthless, the option is worthless:* A stock price of zero means that there is no possibility the stock will ever have any future value.[11] If so, the option is sure to expire unexercised and worthless, and it is worthless today.

That brings us to our first important point about option value:

The value of an option increases as stock price increases, if the exercise price is held constant.

That should be no surprise. Owners of call options clearly hope for the stock price to rise and are happy when it does.

Point B *When the stock price becomes large, the option price approaches the stock price less the present value of the exercise price:* Notice that the dashed line representing the option price in Figure 17.10 eventually becomes parallel to the ascending heavy line representing the lower bound on the option price. The reason is as follows: The higher the stock price, the higher is the probability that the option will eventually be exercised. If the stock price is high enough, exercise becomes a virtual certainty; the probability that the stock price will fall below the exercise price before the option expires becomes trivially small.

If you own an option that you *know* will be exchanged for a share of stock, you effectively own the stock now. The only difference is that you don't have to pay for

---

[11] If a stock *can* be worth something in the future, then investors will pay *something* for it today, although possibly a very small amount.

the stock (by handing over the exercise price) until later, when formal exercise occurs. In these circumstances, buying the call is equivalent to buying the stock but financing part of the purchase by borrowing. The amount implicitly borrowed is the present value of the exercise price. The value of the call is therefore equal to the stock price less the present value of the exercise price.

This brings us to another important point about options. Investors who acquire stock by way of a call option are buying on credit. They pay the purchase price of the option today, but they do not pay the exercise price until they actually take up the option. The delay in payment is particularly valuable if interest rates are high and the option has a long maturity.

Thus, the value of an option increases with both the rate of interest and the time to maturity.

<u>Point C</u>   *The option price always exceeds its minimum value* (except when stock price is zero): We have seen that the dashed and heavy lines in Figure 17.10 coincide when stock price is zero (point *A*), but elsewhere the lines diverge; that is, the option price must exceed the minimum value given by the heavy line. The reason for this can be understood by examining point *C*.

At point *C*, the stock price exactly equals the exercise price. The option is therefore worthless if exercised today. However, suppose that the option will not expire until three months hence. Of course we do not know what the stock price will be at the expiration date. There is roughly a 50% chance that it will be higher than the exercise price and a 50% chance that it will be lower. The possible payoffs to the option are therefore

Outcome	Payoff
Stock price rises (50% probability)	Stock price less exercise price (option is exercised)
Stock price falls (50% probability)	Zero (option expires worthless)

If there is a positive probability of a positive payoff, and if the worst payoff is zero, then the option must be valuable. That means the option price at point *C* exceeds its lower bound, which at point *C* is zero. In general, the option prices will exceed their lower-bound values as long as there is time left before expiration.

One of the most important determinants of the *height* of the dashed curve (i.e., of the difference between actual and lower-bound value) is the likelihood of substantial movements in the stock price. An option on a stock whose price is unlikely to change by more than 1% or 2% is not worth much; an option on a stock whose price may halve or double is very valuable.

As an option holder, you gain from volatility because the payoffs are not symmetric. If the stock price falls *below* the exercise price, your call option will be worthless, regardless of whether the shortfall is a few cents or many dollars. On the other hand, for every dollar that the stock price rises *above* the exercise price, your call will be worth an extra dollar. Therefore, the option holder gains from the increased volatility on the upside, but does not lose on the downside.

A simple example may help to illustrate the point. Consider two stocks, X and Y, each of which is priced at $100. The only difference is that the outlook for Y is much less easy to predict. There is a 50% chance that the price of Y will rise to $150

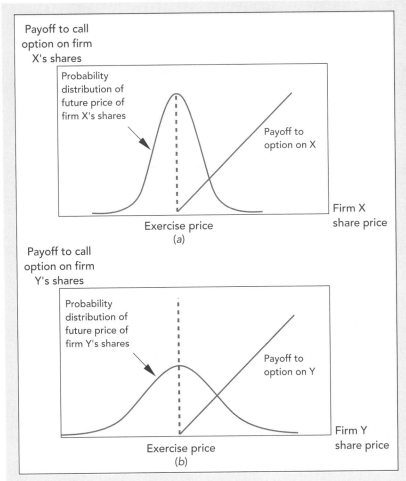

FIGURE 17.11

Call options on the shares of (a) firm X and (b) firm Y. In each case, the current share price equals the exercise price, so each option has a 50% chance of ending up worthless (if the share price falls) and a 50% chance of ending up "in the money" (if the share price rises). However, the chance of a large payoff is greater for the option on firm Y's shares because Y's stock price is more volatile and therefore has more upside potential.

and a similar chance that it will fall to $70. By contrast, there is a 50-50 chance that the price of X will either rise to $130 or fall to $90.

Suppose that you are offered a call option on each of these stocks with an exercise price of $100. The following table compares the possible payoffs from these options:

	Stock Price Falls	Stock Price Rises
Payoff from option on X	$0	$130 − $100 = $30
Payoff from option on Y	$0	$150 − $100 = $50

In both cases there is a 50% chance that the stock price will decline and make the option worthless but, if the stock price rises, the option on Y will give the larger payoff. Since the chance of a zero payoff is the same, the option on Y is worth more than the option on X.

Of course, in practice future stock prices may take on a range of different values. We have recognized this in Figure 17.11, where the uncertain outlook for Y's

FIGURE 17.12

How the value of the Genentech call option increases with the volatility of the stock price. Each of the curved lines shows the value of the option for different initial stock prices. The only difference is that the upper line assumes a much higher level of uncertainty about Genentech's future stock price.

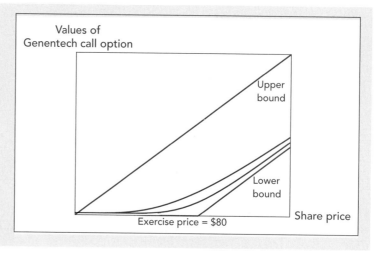

stock price shows up in the wider probability distribution of future prices.[12] The greater spread of outcomes for stock Y again provides more upside potential and therefore increases the chance of a large payoff on the option.

Figure 17.12 shows how volatility affects the value of an option. The upper curved line depicts the value of the Genentech call option assuming that Genentech's stock price, like that of stock Y, is highly variable. The lower curved line assumes a lower (and more realistic) degree of volatility.[13]

The probability of large stock price changes during the remaining life of an option depends on two things: (1) the variance (i.e., volatility) of the stock price *per period* and (2) the number of periods until the option expires. If there are t remaining periods, and the variance per period is σ^2, the value of the option should depend on cumulative variability $\sigma^2 t$.[14] Other things equal, you would like to hold an option on a volatile stock (high σ^2). Given volatility, you would like to hold an option with a long life ahead of it (large t).

Thus the value of an option increases with both the volatility of the share price and the time to maturity.

It's a rare person who can keep all these properties straight at first reading. Therefore, we have summed them up in Table 17.2.

---

[12] Figure 17.11 continues to assume that the exercise price on both options is equal to the current stock price. This is not a necessary assumption. Also in drawing Figure 17.11 we have assumed that the distribution of stock prices is symmetric. This also is not a necessary assumption, and we will look more carefully at the distribution of stock prices in the next chapter.

[13] The option values shown in Figure 17.12 were calculated by using the Black-Scholes option-valuation model. We explain this model in Chapter 18 and use it to value the Genentech option.

[14] Here is an intuitive explanation: If the stock price follows a random walk (see Section 12.2), successive price changes are statistically independent. The cumulative price change before expiration is the sum of t random variables. The variance of a sum of independent random variables is the sum of the variances of those variables. Thus, if σ^2 is the variance of the daily price change, and there are t days until expiration, the variance of the cumulative price change is $\sigma^2 t$.

TABLE 17.2

What the price of a call option depends on.

1. If there is an *increase* in:	The change in the call option price is:
Stock price (P)	Positive
Exercise price (EX)	Negative
Interest rate (r_f)	Positive*
Time to expiration (t)	Positive
Volatility of stock price (σ)	Positive*

2. Other properties of call options:
   a. *Upper bound.* The option price is always less than the stock price.
   b. *Lower bound.* The call price never falls below the payoff to immediate exercise (P − EX or zero, whichever is larger).
   c. If the stock is worthless, the call is worthless.
   d. As the stock price becomes very large, the call price approaches the stock price less the present value of the exercise price.

* The direct effect of increases in r_f or σ on option price, *given* the stock price. There may also be *indirect* effects. For example, an increase in r_f could reduce stock price P. This in turn could affect option price.

TABLE 17.3

Which package of executive stock options would you choose? The package offered by Digital Organics is more valuable, because the volatility of that company's stock is higher.

	Establishment Industries	Digital Organics
Number of options	100,000	100,000
Exercise price	$25	$25
Maturity	5 years	5 years
Current stock price	$22	$22
Stock price volatility (standard deviation of return)	24%	36%

Risk and Option Values

In most financial settings, risk is a bad thing; you have to be paid to bear it. Investors in risky (high-beta) stocks demand higher expected rates of return. High-risk capital investment projects have correspondingly high costs of capital and have to beat higher hurdle rates to achieve positive NPV.

For options it's the other way around. As we have just seen, options written on volatile assets are worth *more* than options written on safe assets. If you can understand and remember that one fact about options, you've come a long way.

Example. Suppose you have to choose between two job offers, as CFO of either Establishment Industries or Digital Organics. Establishment Industries' compensation package includes a grant of the stock options described on the left side of Table 17.3. You demand a similar package from Digital Organics, and they comply. In fact they match the Establishment Industries options in every respect, as you can see on the right side of Table 17.3. (The two companies' current stock prices just happen to be the same.) The only difference is that Digital Organics' stock is 50% more volatile than Establishment Industries' stock (36% annual standard deviation vs. 24% for Establishment Industries).

If your job choice hinges on the value of the executive stock options, you should take the Digital Organics offer. The Digital Organics options are written on the more volatile asset and therefore are worth more. We will value the two stock-option packages in the next chapter.

SUMMARY

If you have managed to reach this point, you are probably in need of a rest and a stiff gin and tonic. So we will summarize what we have learned so far and take up the subject of options again in the next chapter when you are rested (or drunk).

There are two types of option. An American call is an option to buy an asset at a specified exercise price on or before a specified exercise date. Similarly, an American put is an option to sell the asset at a specified price on or before a specified date. European calls and puts are exactly the same except that they cannot be exercised before the specified exercise date. Calls and puts are the basic building blocks that can be combined to give any pattern of payoffs.

What determines the value of a call option? Common sense tells us that it ought to depend on three things:

1. To exercise an option you have to pay the exercise price. Other things being equal, the less you are obliged to pay, the better. Therefore, the value of a call option increases with the ratio of the asset price to the exercise price.

2. You do not have to pay the exercise price until you decide to exercise the option. Therefore, a call option gives you a free loan. The higher the rate of interest and the longer the time to maturity, the more this free loan is worth. So the value of a call option increases with the interest rate and time to maturity.

3. If the price of the asset falls short of the exercise price, you won't exercise the call option. You will, therefore, lose 100% of your investment in the option no matter how far the asset depreciates below the exercise price. On the other hand, the more the price rises *above* the exercise price, the more profit you will make. Therefore the option holder does not lose from increased volatility if things go wrong, but gains if they go right. The value of an option increases with the variance per period of the stock return multiplied by the number of periods to maturity.

Always remember that an option written on a risky (high-variance) asset is worth more than an option on a safe asset. It's easy to forget, because in most other financial contexts increases in risk reduce present value.

FURTHER READING

See Further Readings for Chapter 18.

CONCEPT REVIEW QUESTIONS

1. Explain the difference between an American and a European option. (page 461)

2. "Someone who sells an option can only lose money." True or false? (pages 464–465)

3. Draw the position diagram for the buyer of a put option. What is the maximum possible payoff? (page 463)

For a complete listing of your chapter Concept Review Questions, please visit us at www.mhhe.com/bma1e.

QUIZ

1. Complete the following passage:

   A _____ option gives its owner the opportunity to buy a stock at a specified price that is generally called the _____ price. A _____ option gives its owner the opportunity to sell stock at a specified price. Options that can be exercised only at maturity are called _____ options.

2. Note Figure 17.13. Match each diagram, (*a*) and (*b*), with one of the following positions:
   - Call buyer
   - Call seller
   - Put buyer
   - Put seller

3. Suppose that you hold a share of stock and a put option on that share. What is the payoff when the option expires if (**a**) the stock price is below the exercise price? (**b**) the stock price is above the exercise price?

4. What is put–call parity and why does it hold? Could you apply the parity formula to a call and put with different exercise prices?

5. There is another strategy involving calls and borrowing or lending that gives the same payoffs as the strategy described in Quiz Question 3. What is the alternative strategy?

6. Dr. Livingstone I. Presume holds £600,000 in East African gold stocks. Bullish as he is on gold mining, he requires absolute assurance that at least £500,000 will be available in six months to fund an expedition. Describe two ways for Dr. Presume to achieve this goal. There is an active market for puts and calls on East African gold stocks, and the rate of interest is 6% per year.

7. Suppose you buy a one-year European call option on Wombat stock with an exercise price of $100 and sell a one-year European put option with the same exercise price. The current stock price is $100, and the interest rate is 10%.

   a. Draw a position diagram showing the payoffs from your investments.

   b. How much will the combined position cost you? Explain.

8. Look again at Figure 17.13. It appears that the investor in panel (*b*) can't lose and the investor in panel (*a*) can't win. Is that correct? Explain. (*Hint:* Draw a profit diagram for each panel.)

9. What is a call option worth if (**a**) the stock price is zero? (**b**) the stock price is extremely high relative to the exercise price?

FIGURE 17.13

See Quiz Question 2.

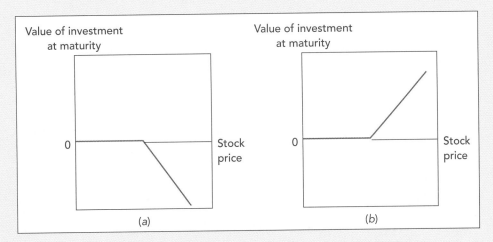
(a)   (b)

10. How does the price of a call option respond to the following changes, other things equal? Does the call price go up or down?

   a. Stock price increases.

   b. Exercise price is increased.

   c. Risk-free rate increases.

   d. Expiration date of the option is extended.

   e. Volatility of the stock price falls.

   f. Time passes, so the option's expiration date comes closer.

11. Respond to the following statements.

   a. "I'm a conservative investor. I'd much rather hold a call option on a safe stock like ExxonMobil than a volatile stock like Genentech."

   b. "I bought an American call option on Fava Farms stock, with an exercise price of $45 per share and three more months to maturity. Fava Farms' stock has skyrocketed from $35 to $55 per share, but I'm afraid it will fall back below $45. I'm going to lock in my gain and exercise my call right now."

PRACTICE QUESTIONS

12. Discuss briefly the risks and payoffs of the following positions:

   a. Buy stock and a put option on the stock.

   b. Buy stock.

   c. Buy call.

   d. Buy stock and sell call option on the stock.

   e. Buy bond.

   f. Buy stock, buy put, and sell call.

   g. Sell put.

13. "The buyer of the call and the seller of the put both hope that the stock price will rise. Therefore the two positions are identical." Is the speaker correct? Illustrate with a position diagram.

14. Pintail's stock price is currently $200. A one-year *American* call option has an exercise price of $50 and is priced at $75. How would you take advantage of this great opportunity? Now suppose the option is a *European* call. What would you do?

15. It is possible to buy three-month call options and three-month puts on stock Q. Both options have an exercise price of $60 and both are worth $10. If the interest rate is 5% a year, what is the stock price? (*Hint:* Use put–call parity.)

16. In March 2007, a four-month call on the stock of Amazon.com, with an exercise price of $40.00, sold for $2.85. The stock price was $39. The risk-free interest rate was 5.3%. How much would you be willing to pay for a put on Amazon stock with the same maturity and exercise price? Assume that the Amazon options are European options. (*Note:* Amazon does not pay a dividend.)

17. Go to **finance.yahoo.com**. Check out the delayed quotes for Genentech for different exercise prices and maturities.

   a. Confirm that higher exercise prices mean lower call prices and higher put prices.

   b. Confirm that longer maturity means higher prices for both puts and calls.

   c. Choose a Genentech put and call with the same exercise price and maturity. Confirm that put–call parity holds (approximately). (*Note:* You will have to use an up-to-date risk-free interest rate.)

18. FX Bank has succeeded in hiring ace foreign exchange trader, Lucinda Cable. Her remuneration package reportedly includes an annual bonus of 20% of the profits that

she generates in excess of $100 million. Does Ms. Cable have an option? Does it provide her with the appropriate incentives?

19. Suppose that Mr. Colleoni borrows the present value of $100, buys a six-month put option on stock Y with an exercise price of $150, and sells a six-month put option on Y with an exercise price of $50.

    a. Draw a position diagram showing the payoffs when the options expire.

    b. Suggest two other combinations of loans, options, and the underlying stock that would give Mr. Colleoni the same payoffs.

20. Which *one* of the following statements is correct?

    a. Value of put + present value of exercise price = value of call + share price.

    b. Value of put + share price = value of call + present value of exercise price.

    c. Value of put − share price = present value of exercise price − value of call.

    d. Value of put + value of call = share price − present value of exercise price.

    The correct statement equates the value of two investment strategies. Plot the payoffs to each strategy as a function of the stock price. Show that the two strategies give identical payoffs.

21. Test the formula linking put and call prices by using it to explain the relative prices of actual traded puts and calls. (*Note:* The formula is exact only for European options. Most traded puts and calls are American.)

22. a. If you can't sell a share short, you can achieve exactly the same final payoff by a combination of options and borrowing or lending. What is this combination?

    b. Now work out the mixture of stock and options that gives the same final payoff as investment in a risk-free loan.

23. The common stock of Triangular File Company is selling at $90. A 26-week call option written on Triangular File's stock is selling for $8. The call's exercise price is $100. The risk-free interest rate is 10% per year.

    a. Suppose that puts on Triangular stock are not traded, but you want to buy one. How would you do it?

    b. Suppose that puts *are* traded. What should a 26-week put with an exercise price of $100 sell for?

24. Ms. Higden has been offered yet another incentive scheme (see Section 17.2). She will receive a bonus of $500,000 if the stock price at the end of the year is $120 or more; otherwise she will receive nothing. (Don't ask why anyone should want to offer such an arrangement. Maybe there's some tax angle.)

    a. Draw a position diagram illustrating the payoffs from such a scheme.

    b. What combination of options would provide these payoffs? (*Hint:* You need to buy a large number of options with one exercise price and sell a similar number with a different exercise price.)

25. Option traders often refer to "straddles" and "butterflies." Here is an example of each:

    • *Straddle:* Buy call with exercise price of $100 and simultaneously buy put with exercise price of $100.

    • *Butterfly:* Simultaneously buy one call with exercise price of $100, sell two calls with exercise price of $110, and buy one call with exercise price of $120.

    Draw position diagrams for the straddle and butterfly, showing the payoffs from the investor's net position. Each strategy is a bet on variability. Explain briefly the nature of each bet.

26. Look at actual trading prices of call options on stocks to check whether they behave as the theory presented in this chapter predicts. For example,

    a. Follow several options as they approach maturity. How would you expect their prices to behave? Do they actually behave that way?

TABLE 17.4

Prices of options on common stocks (in dollars). See Practice Problem 28.

Stock	Time to Exercise (months)	Exercise Price	Stock Price	Put Price	Call Price
Drongo Corp.	6	$ 50	$80	$20	$52
Ragwort, Inc.	6	100	80	10	15
Wombat Corp.	3	40	50	7	18
	6	40	50	5	17
	6	50	50	8	10

    b. Compare two call options written on the same stock with the same maturity but different exercise prices.

    c. Compare two call options written on the same stock with the same exercise price but different maturities.

27. Is it more valuable to own an option to buy a portfolio of stocks or to own a portfolio of options to buy each of the individual stocks? Say briefly why.

28. Table 17.4 lists some prices of options on common stocks (prices are quoted to the nearest dollar). The interest rate is 10% a year. Can you spot any mispricing? What would you do to take advantage of it?

29. You've just completed a month-long study of energy markets and conclude that energy prices will be *much* more volatile in the next year than historically. Assuming you're right, what types of option strategies should you undertake? (*Note:* You can buy or sell options on oil-company stocks or on the price of future deliveries of crude oil, natural gas, fuel oil, etc.)

CHALLENGE QUESTIONS

30. Figure 17.14 shows some complicated position diagrams. Work out the combination of stocks, bonds, and options that produces each of these positions.

31. In 1988 the Australian firm Bond Corporation sold a share in some land that it owned near Rome for $110 million and as a result boosted its 1988 earnings by $74 million. In 1989 a television program revealed that the buyer was given a put option to sell its share in the land back to Bond for $110 million and that Bond had paid $20 million for a call option to repurchase the share in the land for the same price.[15]

    a. What happens if the land is worth more than $110 million when the options expire? What if it is worth less than $110 million?

    b. Use position diagrams to show the net effect of the land sale and the option transactions.

    c. Assume a one-year maturity on the options. Can you deduce the interest rate?

    d. The television program argued that it was misleading to record a profit on the sale of land. What do you think?

32. Three six-month call options are traded on Hogswill stock:

Exercise Price	Call Option Price
$ 90	$ 5
100	11
110	15

---

[15] See *Sydney Morning Herald*, March 14, 1989, p. 27. The options were subsequently renegotiated.

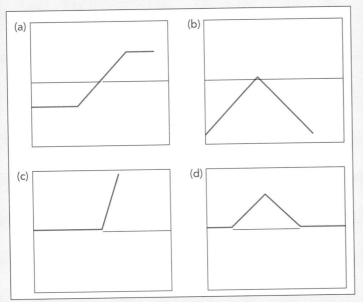

FIGURE 17.14

Some complicated position diagrams. See Challenge Question 30.

How would you make money by trading in Hogswill options? (*Hint:* Draw a graph with the option price on the vertical axis and the ratio of stock price to exercise price on the horizontal axis. Plot the three Hogswill options on your graph. Does this fit with what you know about how option prices should vary with the ratio of stock price to exercise price?) Now look in the newspaper at options with the same maturity but different exercise prices. Can you find any money-making opportunities?

33. Digital Organics has 10 million outstanding shares trading at $25 per share. It also has a large amount of debt outstanding, all coming due in one year. The debt pays interest at 8%. It has a par (face) value of $350 million, but is trading at a market value of only $280 million. The one-year risk-free interest rate is 6%.

   a. Write out the put–call parity formula for Digital Organics' stock, debt, and assets.

   b. What is the value of the default put given up by Digital Organics' creditors?

CHAPTER EIGHTEEN

VALUING OPTIONS

IN THE LAST chapter we introduced you to call and put options. Call options give the owner the right to buy an asset at a specified exercise price; put options give the right to sell. We also took the first step toward understanding how options are valued. The value of a call option depends on five variables:

1. The higher the price of the asset, the more valuable an option to buy it.
2. The lower the price that you must pay to exercise the call, the more valuable the option.
3. You do not need to pay the exercise price until the option expires. This delay is most valuable when the interest rate is high.
4. If the stock price is below the exercise price at maturity, the call is valueless regardless of whether the price is $1 below or $100 below. However, for every dollar that the stock price rises above the exercise price, the option holder gains an additional dollar. Thus, the value of the call option increases with the volatility of the stock price.
5. Finally, a long-term option is more valuable than a short-term option. A distant maturity delays the point at which the holder needs to pay the exercise price and increases the chance of a large jump in the stock price before the option matures.

In this chapter we show how these variables can be combined into an exact option-valuation model—a formula we can plug numbers into to get a definite answer. We first describe a simple way to value options, known as the binomial model. We then introduce the Black–Scholes formula for valuing options. Finally, we provide a checklist showing how these two methods can be used to solve a number of practical option problems.

The most efficient way to value most options is to use a computer. But in this chapter we will work through some simple examples by hand. We do so because unless you understand the basic principles behind option valuation, you are likely to make mistakes in setting up an option problem and you won't know how to interpret the computer's answer and explain it to others.

In the last chapter we introduced you to the put and call options on Genentech stock. In this chapter we will stick with that example and show you how to value the Genentech options. But remember *why* you need to understand option valuation. It is not to make a quick buck trading on an options exchange. It is because many capital budgeting and financing decisions have options embedded in them.

18.1   A SIMPLE OPTION-VALUATION MODEL

Why Discounted Cash Flow Won't Work for Options

For many years economists searched for a practical formula to value options until Fischer Black and Myron Scholes finally hit upon the solution. Later we will show you what they found, but first we should explain why the search was so difficult.

Our standard procedure for valuing an asset is to (1) figure out expected cash flows and (2) discount them at the opportunity cost of capital. Unfortunately, this is not practical for options. The first step is messy but feasible, but finding *the* opportunity cost of capital is impossible, because the risk of an option changes every time the stock price moves.

When you buy a call, you are taking a position in the stock but putting up less of your own money than if you had bought the stock directly. Thus, an option is always riskier than the underlying stock. It has a higher beta and a higher standard deviation of return.

How much riskier the option is depends on the stock price relative to the exercise price. A call option that is in the money (stock price greater than exercise price) is safer than one that is out of the money (stock price less than exercise price). Thus a stock price increase raises the option's price *and* reduces its risk. When the stock price falls, the option's price falls *and* its risk increases. That is why the expected rate of return investors demand from an option changes day by day, or hour by hour, every time the stock price moves.

We repeat the general rule: The higher the stock price is relative to the exercise price, the safer is the call option, although the option is always riskier than the stock. The option's risk changes every time the stock price changes.

Constructing Option Equivalents from Common Stocks and Borrowing

If you've digested what we've said so far, you can appreciate why options are hard to value by standard discounted-cash-flow formulas and why a rigorous option-valuation technique eluded economists for many years. The breakthrough came when Black and Scholes exclaimed, "Eureka! We have found it![1] The trick is to set up an *option equivalent* by combining common stock investment and borrowing. The net cost of buying the option equivalent must equal the value of the option."

We'll show you how this works with a simple numerical example. We'll travel back to September 2006 and consider a six-month call option on Genentech stock with an exercise price of $80. We'll pick a day when Genentech stock was also trading at $80, so that this option is *at the money*. The short-term, risk-free interest rate was 5% per year, or about 2.5% for six months.

To keep the example as simple as possible, we assume that Genentech stock can do only two things over the option's six-month life: either the price will fall by a quarter to $60 or rise by one-third to $106.67.

---

[1] We do not know whether Black and Scholes, like Archimedes, were sitting in bathtubs at the time.

If Genentech's stock price falls to $60, the call option will be worthless, but if the price rises to $106.67, the option will be worth $106.67 − 80 = $26.67. The possible payoffs to the option are therefore

	Stock Price = $60	Stock Price = $106.67
1 call option	$0	$26.67

Now compare these payoffs with what you would get if you bought 4/7 Genentech shares and borrowed $33.45 from the bank:[2]

	Stock Price = $60	Stock Price = $106.67
4/7 shares	$34.29	$60.95
Repayment of loan + interest	−34.29	−34.29
Total payoff	$ 0	$26.67

Notice that the payoffs from the levered investment in the stock are identical to the payoffs from the call option. Therefore, the law of one price tells us that both investments must have the same value:

$$\text{Value of call} = \text{value of } (4/7) \text{ shares} - \$33.45 \text{ bank loan}$$
$$= 80 \times (4/7) - 33.45 = 12.26$$

Presto! You've valued a call option.

To value the Genentech option, we borrowed money and bought stock in such a way that we exactly replicated the payoff from a call option. This is called a **replicating portfolio.** The number of shares needed to replicate one call is called the **hedge ratio** or **option delta.** In our Genentech example one call is replicated by a levered position in 4/7 shares. The option delta is, therefore, 4/7, or about .571.

How did we know that Genentech's call option was equivalent to a levered position in 4/7 shares? We used a simple formula that says

$$\text{Option delta} = \frac{\text{spread of possible option prices}}{\text{spread of possible share prices}} = \frac{26.67 - 0}{106.67 - 60} = \frac{26.67}{46.67} = \frac{4}{7}$$

You have learned not only to value a simple option but also that you can replicate an investment in the option by a levered investment in the underlying asset. Thus, if you can't buy or sell a call option on an asset, you can create a homemade option by a replicating strategy—that is, you buy or sell delta shares and borrow or lend the balance.

Risk-Neutral Valuation   Notice why the Genentech call option should sell for $12.26. If the option price is higher than $12.26, you could make a certain profit by buying 4/7 shares of stock, selling a call option, and borrowing $33.45. Similarly, if the option price is less than $12.26, you could make an equally certain profit by

---

[2] The amount that you need to borrow from the bank is simply the present value of the difference between the payoffs from the option and the payoffs from 4/7 shares. In our example, amount borrowed = ((4/7) × 60 − 0)/1.025 = ((4/7) × 106.67 − 26.67)/1.025 = $33.45.

selling 4/7 shares, buying a call, and lending the balance. In either case there would be an arbitrage opportunity.[3]

If there's a possible arbitrage profit, everyone scurries to take advantage of it. So when we said that the option price had to be $12.26 or there would be an arbitrage opportunity, we did not have to know anything about investor attitudes to risk. The option price cannot depend on whether investors detest risk or do not care a jot.

This suggests an alternative way to value the option. We can *pretend* that all investors are *indifferent* about risk, work out the expected future value of the option in such a world, and discount it back at the risk-free interest rate to give the current value. Let us check that this method gives the same answer.

If investors are indifferent to risk, the expected return on the stock must be equal to the risk-free rate of interest:

$$\text{Expected return on Genentech stock} = 2.5\% \text{ per six months}$$

We know that Genentech stock can either rise by 33.3% to $106.67 or fall by 25% to $60. We can, therefore, calculate the probability of a price rise in our hypothetical risk-neutral world:

$$\begin{aligned} \text{Expected return} = &[\text{probability of rise} \times 33.3] \\ &+ [(1 - \text{probability of rise}) \times (-25)] \\ = &\ 2.5\% \end{aligned}$$

Therefore,

$$\text{Probability of rise} = .471, \text{ or } 47.1\%$$

Notice that this is *not* the *true* probability that Genentech stock will rise. Since investors dislike risk, they will almost surely require a higher expected return than the risk-free interest rate from Genentech stock. Therefore the true probability is greater than .471.

The general formula for calculating the risk-neutral probability of a rise in value is

$$p = \frac{\text{interest rate} - \text{downside change}}{\text{upside change} - \text{downside change}}$$

In the case of Genentech stock

$$p = \frac{.025 - (-.25)}{.333 - (-.25)} = .471$$

We know that if the stock price rises, the call option will be worth $26.67; if it falls, the call will be worth nothing. Therefore, if investors are risk-neutral, the expected value of the call option is

$$\begin{aligned} [\text{Probability of rise} \times 26.67] &+ [(1 - \text{probability of rise}) \times 0] \\ &= (.471 \times 26.67) + (.529 \times 0) \\ &= \$12.57 \end{aligned}$$

---

[3] Of course, you don't get seriously rich by dealing in 4/7 shares. But if you multiply each of our transactions by a million, it begins to look like real money.

And the *current* value of the call is

$$\frac{\text{Expected future value}}{1 + \text{interest rate}} = \frac{12.57}{1.025} = \$12.26$$

Exactly the same answer that we got earlier!

We now have two ways to calculate the value of an option:

1. Find the combination of stock and loan that replicates an investment in the option. Since the two strategies give identical payoffs in the future, they must sell for the same price today.

2. Pretend that investors do not care about risk, so that the expected return on the stock is equal to the interest rate. Calculate the expected future value of the option in this hypothetical *risk-neutral* world and discount it at the risk-free interest rate. This idea may seem familiar to you. In Chapter 10 we showed how you can value an investment either by discounting the expected cash flows at a risk-adjusted discount rate or by adjusting the expected cash flows for risk and then discounting these *certainty-equivalent* flows at the risk-free interest rate. We have just used this second method to value the Genentech option. The certainty-equivalent cash flows on the stock and option are the cash flows that would be expected in a risk-neutral world.

Valuing the Genentech Put Option

Valuing the Genentech call option may well have seemed like pulling a rabbit out of a hat. To give you a second chance to watch how it is done, we will use the same method to value another option—this time, the six-month Genentech put option with an $80 exercise price.[4] We continue to assume that the stock price will either rise to $106.67 or fall to $60.

If Genentech's stock price rises to $106.67, the option to sell for $80 will be worthless. If the price falls to $60, the put option will be worth $80 − 60 = $20. Thus the payoffs to the put are

	Stock Price = $60	Stock Price = $106.67
1 put option	$20	$0

We start by calculating the option delta using the formula that we presented above:[5]

$$\text{Option delta} = \frac{\text{spread of possible option prices}}{\text{spread of possible stock prices}} = \frac{0 - 20}{106.67 - 60}$$

$$= -\frac{3}{7}, \text{ or about } -.429$$

Notice that the delta of a put option is always negative; that is, you need to *sell* delta shares of stock to replicate the put. In the case of the Genentech put you can replicate

---

[4] When valuing *American* put options, you need to recognize the possibility that it will pay to exercise early. We discuss this complication later in the chapter, but it is unimportant for valuing the Genentech put and we ignore it here.
[5] The delta of a put option is always equal to the delta of a call option with the same exercise price minus one. In our example, delta of put = (4/7) − 1 = −(3/7).

the option payoffs by *selling* 3/7 Genentech shares and *lending* $44.60. Since you have sold the share short, you will need to lay out money at the end of six months to buy it back, but you will have money coming in from the loan. Your net payoffs are exactly the same as the payoffs you would get if you bought the put option:

	Stock Price = $60	Stock Price = $106.67
Sale of 3/7 shares	−$25.71	−$45.71
Repayment of loan + interest	+45.71	+45.71
Total payoff	$20	$ 0

Since the two investments have the same payoffs, they must have the same value:

$$\text{Value of put} = -(3/7) \text{ shares} + \$44.60 \text{ bank loan}$$
$$= -(3/7) \times 80 + \$44.60 = 10.31$$

Valuing the Put Option by the Risk-Neutral Method   Valuing the Genentech put option with the risk-neutral method is a cinch. We already know that the probability of a rise in the stock price is .471. Therefore the expected value of the put option in a risk-neutral world is

$$[\text{Probability of rise} \times 0] + [(1 - \text{probability of rise}) \times 20]$$
$$= (.471 \times 0) + (.529 \times 20)$$
$$= \$10.57$$

And therefore the *current* value of the put is

$$\frac{\text{Expected future value}}{1 + \text{interest rate}} = \frac{10.57}{1.025} = \$10.31$$

The Relationship between Call and Put Prices   We pointed out earlier that for European options there is a simple relationship between the value of the call and that of the put.[6]

Value of put = value of call + present value of exercise price − share price

Since we had already calculated the value of the Genentech call, we could also have used this relationship to find the value of the put:

$$\text{Value of put} = 12.26 + \frac{80}{1.025} - 80 = \$10.31$$

Everything checks.

18.2   THE BINOMIAL METHOD FOR VALUING OPTIONS

The essential trick in pricing any option is to set up a package of investments in the stock and the loan that will exactly replicate the payoffs from the option. If we can price the stock and the loan, then we can also price the option. Equivalently,

---

[6] *Reminder:* This formula applies only when the two options have the same exercise price and exercise date.

we can pretend that investors are risk-neutral, calculate the expected payoff on the option in this fictitious risk-neutral world, and discount by the rate of interest to find the option's present value.

These *concepts* are completely general, but there are several ways to find the replicating package of investments. The example in the last section used a simplified version of what is known as the **binomial method.** The method starts by reducing the possible changes in next period's stock price to two, an "up" move and a "down" move. This assumption that there are just two possible prices for Genentech stock at the end of six months is clearly fanciful.

We could make the Genentech problem a trifle more realistic by assuming that there are two possible price changes in each three-month period. This would give a wider variety of six-month prices. And there is no reason to stop at three-month periods. We could go on to take shorter and shorter intervals, with each interval showing two possible changes in Genentech's stock price and giving an even wider selection of six-month prices.

This is illustrated in Figure 18.1. The left-hand diagram shows our starting assumption: just two possible prices at the end of six months. Moving to the right, you can see what happens when there are two possible price changes every three months. This gives three possible stock prices when the option matures. In Figure 18.1(c) we have gone on to divide the six-month period into 26 weekly periods, in each of which the price can make one of two small moves. The distribution of prices at the end of six months is now looking much more realistic.

We could continue in this way to chop the period into shorter and shorter intervals, until eventually we would reach a situation in which the stock price is changing continuously and there is a continuum of possible future stock prices.

Example: The Two-Stage Binomial Method

Dividing the period into shorter intervals doesn't alter the basic method for valuing a call option. We can still replicate the call by a levered investment in the stock, but we need to adjust the degree of leverage at each stage. We will demonstrate first with our simple two-stage case in Figure 18.1(b). Then we will work up to the situation where the stock price is changing continuously.

Figure 18.2 is taken from Figure 18.1(b) and shows the possible prices of Genentech stock, assuming that in each three-month period the price will either rise by 22.6% or fall by 18.4%.[7] We show in parentheses the possible values at maturity of a six-month call option with an exercise price of $80. For example, if Genentech's stock price turns out to be $53.26 in month 6, the call option will be worthless; at the other extreme, if the stock value is $120.16, the call will be worth $120.16 − $80 = $40.16. We haven't worked out yet what the option will be worth *before* maturity, so we just put question marks there for now.

Option Value in Month 3   To find the value of Genentech's option today, we start by working out its possible values in month 3 and then work back to the present. Suppose that at the end of three months the stock price is $98.05. In this case investors know that, when the option finally matures in month 6, the stock price will be

[7] We will explain shortly why we picked these figures.

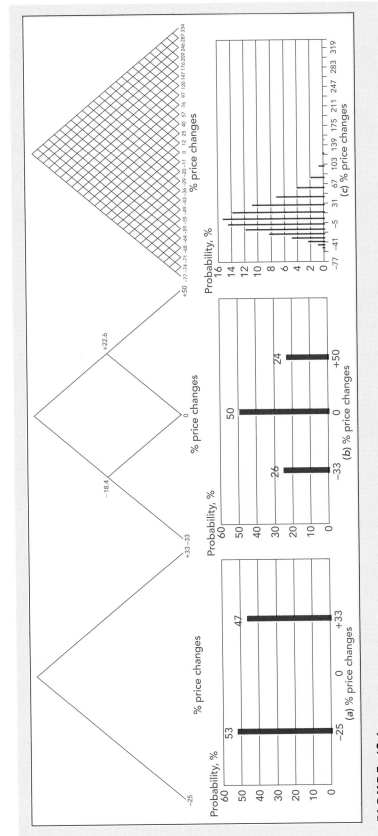

FIGURE 18.1

This figure shows the possible six-month price changes for Genentech stock assuming that the stock makes a single up or down move each six months [Fig. 18.1(a)], two moves, one every three months [Fig. 18.1(b)], or 26 moves, one every week [Fig. 18.1(c)]. Beneath each tree we show a histogram of the possible six-month price changes, assuming investors are risk-neutral.

FIGURE 18.2

Present and possible future prices of Genentech stock assuming that in each three-month period the price will either rise by 22.6% or fall by 18.4%. Figures in parentheses show the corresponding values of a six-month call option with an exercise price of $80.

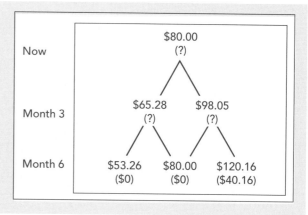

either $80 or $120.16, and the corresponding option price will be $0 or $40.16. We can therefore use our simple formula to find how many shares we need to buy in month 3 to replicate the option:

$$\text{Option delta} = \frac{\text{spread of possible option prices}}{\text{spread of possible stock prices}} = \frac{40.16 - 0}{120.16 - 80} = 1.0$$

Now we can construct a leveraged position in delta shares that would give identical payoffs to the option:

	Month 6 Stock Price = **$80**	Month 6 Stock Price = **$120.16**
Buy 1.0 shares	$80	$120.16
Borrow PV(80)	−80	−80
Total payoff	$ 0	$40.16

Since this portfolio provides identical payoffs to the option, we know that the value of the option in month 3 must be equal to the price of 1 share less the $80 loan discounted for 3 months at 5% per year, about 1.25% for 3 months:

$$\text{Value of call in month 3} = \$98.05 - \$80/1.0125 = \$19.04$$

Therefore, if the share price rises in the first three months, the option will be worth $19.04. But what if the share price falls to $65.28? In that case the most that you can hope for is that the share price will recover to $80. Therefore the option is bound to be worthless when it matures and must be worthless at month 3.

Option Value Today   We can now get rid of two of the question marks in Figure 18.2. Figure 18.3 shows that if the stock price in month 3 is $98.05, the option value is $19.04 and, if the stock price is $65.28, the option value is zero. It only remains to work back to the option value today.

We again begin by calculating the option delta:

$$\text{Option delta} = \frac{\text{spread of possible option prices}}{\text{spread of possible stock prices}} = \frac{19.04 - 0}{98.05 - 65.28} = .581$$

FIGURE 18.3

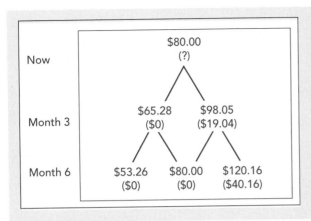

Present and possible future prices of Genentech stock. Figures in parentheses show the corresponding values of a six-month call option with an exercise price of $80.

We can now find the leveraged position in delta shares that would give identical payoffs to the option:

	Month 3 Stock Price = $65.28	Month 3 Stock Price = $98.05
Buy .581 shares	$37.93	$56.97
Borrow PV(37.93)	−37.93	−37.93
Total payoff	$ 0	$19.04

The value of the Genentech option today is equal to the value of this leveraged position:

$$\text{PV option} = \text{PV(.581 shares)} - \text{PV(\$37.93)}$$
$$= .581 \times \$80 - \$37.93/1.0125 = \$9.02$$

The General Binomial Method

Moving to two steps when valuing the Genentech call probably added extra realism. But there is no reason to stop there. We could go on, as in Figure 18.1, to chop the period into smaller and smaller intervals. We could still use the binomial method to work back from the final date to the present. Of course, it would be tedious to do the calculations by hand, but simple to do so with a computer.

Since a stock can usually take on an almost limitless number of future values, the binomial method gives a more realistic and accurate measure of the option's value if we work with a large number of subperiods. But that raises an important question. How do we pick sensible figures for the up and down changes in value? For example, why did we pick figures of +22.6% and −18.4% when we revalued Genentech's option with two subperiods? Fortunately, there is a neat little formula that relates the up and down changes to the standard deviation of stock returns:

$$1 + \text{upside change } = u = e^{\sigma\sqrt{h}}$$
$$1 + \text{downside change} = d = 1/u$$

where

e = base for natural logarithms = 2.718

σ = standard deviation of (continuously compounded) stock returns

h = interval as fraction of a year

TABLE 18.1

As the number of steps is increased, you must adjust the range of possible changes in the value of the asset to keep the same standard deviation. But you will get increasingly close to the Black–Scholes value of the Genentech call option.

Note: The standard deviation is $\sigma = .4068$

Number of Steps	Change per Interval (%)		Estimated Option Value
	Upside	**Downside**	
1	+33.3	−25.0	$12.26
2	+22.6	−18.4	9.02
6	+12.5	−11.1	9.68
26	+5.8	−5.5	9.96
		Black–Scholes value = 10.05	

When we said that Genentech's stock could either rise by 33.3% or fall by 25% over six months ($h = .5$), our figures were consistent with a figure of 40.68% for the standard deviation of annual returns:[8]

$$1 + \text{upside change (6-month interval)} = u = e^{.4068\sqrt{.5}} = 1.333$$
$$1 + \text{downside change} = d = 1/u = 1/1.333 = .75$$

To work out the equivalent upside and downside changes when we divide the period into two three-month intervals ($h = .25$), we use the same formula:

$$1 + \text{upside change (3-month interval)} = u = e^{.4068\sqrt{.25}} = 1.226$$
$$1 + \text{downside change} = d = 1/u = 1/1.226 = .816$$

The center columns in Table 18.1 show the equivalent up and down moves in the value of the firm if we chop the period into six monthly or 26 weekly periods, and the final column shows the effect on the estimated option value. (We will explain the Black–Scholes value shortly.)

The Binomial Method and Decision Trees

Calculating option values by the binomial method is basically a process of solving decision trees. You start at some future date and work back through the tree to the present. Eventually the possible cash flows generated by future events and actions are folded back to a present value.

Is the binomial method *merely* another application of decision trees, a tool of analysis that you learned about in Chapter 11? The answer is no, for at least two reasons. First, option pricing theory is absolutely essential for discounting within decision trees. Discounting expected cash flows doesn't work within decision trees for the same reason that it doesn't work for puts and calls. As we pointed out in Section 18.1, there is no single, constant discount rate for options because the risk of the option changes as time and the price of the underlying asset change. There is no single discount rate inside a decision tree, because if the tree contains meaningful future decisions, it also contains options. The market value of the future cash flows described by the decision tree has to be calculated by option pricing methods.

---

[8] To find the standard deviation given u, we turn the formula around:

$$\sigma = \log(u)/\sqrt{h}$$

where log = natural logarithm. In our example:

$$\sigma = \log(1.333)/\sqrt{.5} = .2877/\sqrt{.5} = .4068$$

Second, option theory gives a simple, powerful framework for describing complex decision trees. For example, suppose that you have the option to abandon an investment. The complete decision tree would overflow the largest classroom chalkboard. But now that you know about options, the opportunity to abandon might be summarized as "an American put." Of course, not all real problems have such easy option analogies, but we can often approximate complex decision trees by some simple package of assets and options. A custom decision tree may get closer to reality, but the time and expense may not be worth it. Most men buy their suits off the rack even though a custom-made Armani suit would fit better and look nicer.

18.3   THE BLACK–SCHOLES FORMULA

Look back at Figure 18.1, which showed what happens to the distribution of possible Genentech stock price changes as we divide the option's life into a larger and larger number of increasingly small subperiods. You can see that the distribution of price changes becomes increasingly smooth.

If we continued to chop up the option's life in this way, we would eventually reach the situation shown in Figure 18.4, where there is a continuum of possible stock price changes at maturity. Figure 18.4 is an example of a lognormal distribution. The lognormal distribution is often used to summarize the probability of different stock price changes.[9] It has a number of good commonsense features. For example, it recognizes the fact that the stock price can never fall by more than 100%, but that there is some, perhaps small, chance that it could rise by much more than 100%.

Subdividing the option life into indefinitely small slices does not affect the principle of option valuation. We could still replicate the call option by a levered

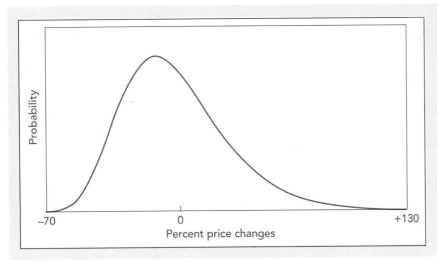

FIGURE 18.4

As the option's life is divided into more and more subperiods, the distribution of possible stock price changes approaches a lognormal distribution.

---

[9] When we first looked at the distribution of stock price changes in Chapter 9, we depicted these changes as normally distributed. We pointed out at the time that this is an acceptable approximation for very short intervals, but the distribution of changes over longer intervals is better approximated by the lognormal.

investment in the stock, but we would need to adjust the degree of leverage continuously as time went by. Calculating option value when there is an infinite number of subperiods may sound a hopeless task. Fortunately, Black and Scholes derived a formula that does the trick.[10] It is an unpleasant-looking formula, but on closer acquaintance you will find it exceptionally elegant and useful. The formula is

$$\text{Value of call option} = [\text{delta} \times \text{share price}] - [\text{bank loan}]$$

$$[N(d_1) \quad \times \quad P] \quad - \quad [N(d_2) \times \text{PV(EX)}]$$

where

$$d_1 = \frac{\log[P/\text{PV(EX)}]}{\sigma\sqrt{t}} + \frac{\sigma\sqrt{t}}{2}$$

$$d_2 = d_1 - \sigma\sqrt{t}$$

$N(d)$ = cumulative normal probability density function[11]

EX = exercise price of option; PV(EX) is calculated by discounting at the risk-free interest rate r_f

t = number of periods to exercise date

P = price of stock now

σ = standard deviation per period of (continuously compounded) rate of return on stock

Notice that the value of the call in the Black–Scholes formula has the same properties that we identified earlier. It increases with the level of the stock price P and decreases with the present value of the exercise price PV(EX), which in turn depends on the interest rate and time to maturity. It also increases with the time to maturity and the stock's variability ($\sigma\sqrt{t}$).

To derive their formula Black and Scholes assumed that there is a continuum of stock prices, and therefore to replicate an option investors must continuously adjust their holding in the stock. Of course this is not literally possible, but even so the formula performs remarkably well in the real world, where stocks trade only intermittently and prices jump from one level to another. The Black–Scholes model has also proved very flexible; it can be adapted to value options on a variety of assets such as foreign currencies, bonds, and commodities. It is not surprising, therefore, that it has been extremely influential and has become the standard model for valuing options. Every day dealers on the options exchanges use this formula to make huge trades. These dealers are not for the most part trained in the formula's mathematical derivation; they just use a computer or a specially programmed calculator to find the value of the option.

Using the Black–Scholes Formula

The Black–Scholes formula may look difficult, but it is very straightforward to apply. Let us practice using it to value the Genentech call.

---

[10] The important assumptions of the Black–Scholes formula are that (a) the price of the underlying asset follows a lognormal random walk, (b) investors can adjust their hedge continuously and costlessly, (c) the risk-free rate is known, and (d) the underlying asset does not pay dividends.

[11] That is, $N(d)$ is the probability that a normally distributed random variable $\tilde{x}$ will be less than or equal to d. $N(d_1)$ in the Black–Scholes formula is the option delta. Thus the formula tells us that the value of a call is equal to an investment of $N(d_1)$ in the common stock less borrowing of $N(d_2) \times \text{PV(EX)}$.

Here are the data that you need:

- Price of stock now $= P = 80$
- Exercise price $= EX = 80$
- Standard deviation of continuously compounded annual returns $= \sigma = .4068$
- Years to maturity $= t = .5$
- Interest rate per annum $= r_f = 5\%$ (or about 2.5% for six months).[12]

Remember that the Black–Scholes formula for the value of a call is

$$[N(d_1) \times P] - [N(d_2) \times PV(EX)]$$

where

$$d_1 = \log[P/PV(EX)]/\sigma\sqrt{t} + \sigma\sqrt{t}/2$$
$$d_2 = d_1 - \sigma\sqrt{t}$$

$N(d)$ = cumulative normal probability function

There are three steps to using the formula to value the Genentech call:

Step 1 Calculate d_1 and d_2. This is just a matter of plugging numbers into the formula (noting that "log" means *natural* log):

$$
\begin{aligned}
d_1 &= \log[P/PV(EX)]/\sigma\sqrt{t} + \sigma\sqrt{t}/2 \\
&= \log[80/(80/1.025)]/(.4068 \times \sqrt{.5}) + .4068 \times \sqrt{.5}/2 \\
&= .2297
\end{aligned}
$$

$$d_2 = d_1 - \sigma\sqrt{t} = .2297 - .4068 \times \sqrt{.5} = -.0580$$

Step 2 Find $N(d_1)$ and $N(d_2)$. $N(d_1)$ is the probability that a normally distributed variable will be less than d_1 standard deviations above the mean. If d_1 is large, $N(d_1)$ is close to 1.0 (i.e., you can be almost certain that the variable will be less than d_1 standard deviations above the mean). If d_1 is zero, $N(d_1)$ is .5 (i.e., there is a 50% chance that a normally distributed variable will be below the average).

The simplest way to find $N(d_1)$ is to use the Excel function NORMSDIST. For example, if you enter NORMSDIST(.2297) into an Excel spreadsheet, you will see that there is a .5908 probability that a normally distributed variable will be less than .2297 standard deviations above the mean. Alternatively, you can use a set of normal probability tables such as those in Appendix Table 6 (on page A-5). You can see that if $d_1 = .23$, then $N(d_1) = .5910$, quite close to the value that you need.

Again you can use the Excel function to find $N(d_2)$. If you enter NORMS-DIST(−.0580) into an Excel spreadsheet, you should get the answer .4769. In other words, there is a probability of .4769 that a normally distributed variable will be less than .0580 standard deviations *below* the mean. Alternatively, if you

---

[12] In our binomial example, we assumed an interest rate of 2.5% for six months, equivalent to $1.025^2 - 1 = .05063$, or 5.063% annually compounded. Thus $PV(EX) = 80/1.05063^{.5} = 80/1.025 = \$78.05$.

When valuing options, it is more common to use continuously compounded rates (see Section 3.4). If the annual rate is 5.063%, the equivalent continuously compounded rate is 4.939%. (The natural log of 1.05063 is .04939 and $e^{.04939} = 1.05063$.) Using continuous compounding, $PV(EX) = 80 \times e^{-.5 \times .04939} = \$78.05$. Both methods give the same answer.

There is only one trick here. If you are using a spreadsheet or computer program that calls for a continuously compounded rate, make sure that this is what you enter. The error if you use the wrong rate will usually be small, but you can waste a lot of time trying to trace it.

FIGURE 18.5

The curved line shows how the value of the Genentech call option changes as the price of Genentech stock changes.

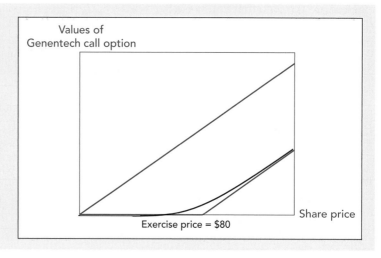

use Appendix Table 6 (on page A-5), you need to look up the value for $+.0580$ and subtract it from 1.0:

$$N(d_2) = N(-.0580) = 1 - N(+.0580)$$
$$= 1 - .5231 = .4769$$

Step 3   Plug these numbers into the Black–Scholes formula. You can now calculate the value of the Genentech call:

$$[\text{Delta} \times \text{price}] - [\text{bank loan}]$$
$$= [N(d_1) \times P] - [N(d_2) \times \text{PV(EX)}]$$
$$= [.5908 \times 80] - [.4769 \times 80/1.025] = 10.05$$

Some More Practice   Suppose you repeat the calculations for the Genentech call for a wide range of stock prices. The result is shown in Figure 18.5. You can see that the option values lie along an upward-sloping curve that starts its travels in the bottom left-hand corner of the diagram. As the stock price increases, the option value rises and gradually becomes parallel to the lower bound for the option value. This is exactly the shape we deduced in Chapter 17 (see Figure 17.10).

The height of this curve of course depends on risk and time to maturity. For example, if the risk of Genentech stock had suddenly decreased, the curve shown in Figure 18.5 would drop at every possible stock price.

The Black–Scholes Formula and the Binomial Method

Look back at Table 18.1 where we used the binomial method to calculate the value of the Genentech call. Notice that, as the number of intervals is increased, the values that you obtain from the binomial method begin to snuggle up to the Black–Scholes value of $10.05.

The Black–Scholes formula recognizes a continuum of possible outcomes. This is usually more realistic than the limited number of outcomes assumed in the binomial method. The formula is also more accurate and quicker to use than the binomial method. So why use the binomial method at all? The answer is that there are many circumstances in which you cannot use the Black–Scholes formula but the binomial method will still give you a good measure of the option's value. We will look at several such cases in Section 18.5.

18.4 BLACK–SCHOLES IN ACTION

To illustrate the principles of option valuation, we focused on the example of Genentech's options. But financial managers turn to the Black–Scholes model to estimate the value of a variety of different options. Here are four examples.

Executive Stock Options

In 2005 the CEO of Capital One Financial did not receive any salary. Does that mean he was condemned to a life of poverty? Not really. In the same year he exercised stock options on shares worth about $250 million that were granted to him by the company.

The example highlights the fact that executive stock options are often an important part of compensation. For many years companies were able to avoid reporting the cost of these options in their financial statements. However, under new accounting rules firms must treat options as an expense just like salaries and wages, and therefore they need to estimate the value of all new options that they have granted. For example, Capital One's financial statements show that in 2005 the company issued a total of 2.2 million options with an average exercise price of $81 and a life of 5.3 years. These options were at, or close to, the money; in other words their exercise price was close to the current stock price. Capital One calculated that the average value of these options was $37.07. How did it come up with this figure? It just used the Black–Scholes model assuming a standard deviation of 46% and an interest rate of 4.26%.

In recent years companies have sometimes disguised how much their management is paid by backdating the grant of an option. Suppose, for example, that a firm's stock price has risen from $20 to $40. At that point the firm awards its CEO options exercisable at $20. That is generous but not illegal. However, if the firm pretends that the options were *actually* awarded when the stock price was $20 and values them on that basis, it will substantially understate the CEO's compensation.[13] The nearby box discusses the backdating scandal.

Speaking of executive stock options, we can now use the Black–Scholes formula to value the option packages you were offered in Section 17.3 (see Table 17.3). Table 18.2 calculates the value of the options from the safe-and-stodgy Establishment

	Establishment Industries	Digital Organics
Stock price (P)	$22	$22
Exercise price (EX)	$25	$25
Interest rate (r_f)	.04	.04
Maturity in years (t)	5	5
Standard deviation (σ)	.24	.36
d1 = log[P/PV(EX)]/$\sigma\sqrt{t}$ + $\sigma\sqrt{t}$/2	0.3955	0.4873
d2 = d1 − $\sigma\sqrt{t}$	−0.1411	−0.3177
Call value = [N(d1) x P] − [N(d2) x PV(EX)]	$5.26	$7.40

TABLE 18.2

Using the Black-Scholes formula to value the executive stock options for Establishment Industries and Digital Organics (see Table 17.3).

Visit us at www.mhhe.com/bma1e.

---

[13] Until 2005 companies were obliged to record as an expense any difference between the stock price when the options were granted and the exercise price. Thus, as long as the options were granted at-the-money (exercise price equals stock price), the company was not obliged to show any expense.

THE PERFECT PAYDAY

In the spring of 2007 the SEC was investigating over 120 instances where companies appeared to have backdated option grants to their executives. Evidence of this practice had appeared two years earlier in an academic paper,* and was subsequently highlighted in a Wall Street Journal *article entitled "The Perfect Payday." The following extracts are taken from this article.*

ON A SUMMER DAY IN 2002, shares of Affiliated Computer Services Inc. sank to their lowest level in a year. Oddly, that was good news for Chief Executive Jeffrey Rich.

His annual grant of stock options was dated that day, entitling him to buy stock at that price for years. Had they been dated a week later, when the stock was 27% higher, they'd have been far less rewarding. It was the same through much of Mr. Rich's tenure: In a striking pattern, all six of his stock-option grants from 1995 to 2002 were dated just before a rise in the stock price, often at the bottom of a steep drop.

Just lucky? A *Wall Street Journal* analysis suggests the odds of this happening by chance are extraordinarily remote—around one in 300 billion. The odds of winning the multistate Powerball lottery with a $1 ticket are one in 146 million.

Suspecting such patterns aren't due to chance, the Securities and Exchange Commission is examining whether some option grants carry favorable grant dates for a different reason: They were backdated.

Stock options give recipients a right to buy company stock at a set price, called the exercise price or strike price. The right usually doesn't vest for a year or more, but then it continues for several years. The exercise price is usually the stock's 4 P.M. price on the date of the grant, an average of the day's high and low, or the 4 P.M. price the day before. Naturally, the lower it is, the more money the recipient can potentially make someday by exercising the options.

Which day's price the options carry makes a big difference. Suppose an executive gets 100,000 options on a day when the stock is at $30. Exercising them after it has reached $50 would bring a profit of $20 times 100,000, or $2 million. But if the grant date was a month earlier and the stock then was at, say, $20, the options would bring in an extra $1 million.

A key purpose of stock options is to give recipients an incentive to improve their employer's performance, including its stock price. No stock gain, no profit on the options. Backdating them so they carry a lower price would run counter to this goal, by giving the recipient a paper gain right from the start.

Companies have a right to give executives lavish compensation if they choose to, but they can't mislead shareholders about it. Granting an option at a price below the current market value, while not illegal in itself, could result in false disclosure. That's because companies grant their options under a shareholder-approved "option plan" on file with the SEC. The plans typically say options will carry the stock price of the day the company awards them or the day before. If it turns out they carry some other price, the company could be in violation of its options plan, and potentially vulnerable to an allegation of securities fraud.

It could even face accounting issues. Options priced below the stock's fair market value when they're awarded bring the recipient an instant paper gain. Under accounting rules, that's equivalent to extra pay and thus is a cost to the company. A company that failed to include such a cost in its books may have overstated its profits, and might need to restate past financial results.

The *Journal's* analysis raises questions about one of the most lucrative stock-option grants ever. On Oct. 13, 1999, William W. McGuire, CEO of giant insurer UnitedHealth Group Inc., got an enormous grant in three parts that—after adjustment for later stock splits—came to 14.6 million options. So far, he has exercised about 5% of them, for a profit of about $39 million. As of late February he had 13.87 million unexercised options left from the October 1999 tranche. His profit on those, if he exercised them today, would be about $717 million more.

The 1999 grant was dated the very day United-Health stock hit its low for the year. Grants to Dr. McGuire in 1997 and 2000 were also dated on the day with those years' single lowest closing price. A grant in 2001 came near the bottom of a sharp stock dip. In all, the odds of such a favorable pattern occurring by chance would be one in 200 million or greater.

---

*E. Lie, "On the Timing of CEO Stock Option Awards," *Management Science* 51 (2005), pp. 802–812.

Source: C. Forelle and J. Bandler, "The Perfect Payday; Some CEOs Reap Millions by Landing Stock Options When They Are Most Valuable; Luck—or Something Else?" *The Wall Street Journal*, March 18, 2006, p. A1. © 2006 Dow Jones & Company, Inc.

Industries at $5.26 each. The options from risky-and-glamorous Digital Organics are worth $7.40 each. Congratulations.[14]

Warrants

In May 2004 the Texas communications company INX raised $8.3 million by selling 500,000 packages of securities. Each package contained two shares of common stock and a warrant that gave the holder the right to buy a share of common stock for $12.45 at any time before May 2009. The share price at the time was $8.30 and each package was sold for $16.60. So the warrants were effectively thrown in for free to tempt investors to apply for the issue. You can be sure that when it was decided to add this sweetener, INX's investment bankers calculated the value of the warrants under different assumptions about the stock's volatility. The Black–Scholes formula is tailor-made for this purpose.

Portfolio Insurance

Your company's pension fund owns an $800 million diversified portfolio of common stocks that moves closely in line with the market index. The pension fund is currently fully funded, but you are concerned that if it falls by more than 20% it will start to be underfunded. Suppose that your bank offers to insure you for one year against this possibility. What would you be prepared to pay for this insurance? Think back to Section 17.2 (Figure 17.6), where we showed that you can shield against a fall in asset prices by buying a protective put option. In the present case the bank would be selling you a one-year put option on U.S. stock prices with an exercise price 20% below their current level. You can get the value of that option in two steps. First use the Black-Scholes formula to value a call with the same exercise price and maturity. Then back out the put value from put-call parity. (You will have to adjust for dividends, but we'll leave that to the next section.)

Calculating Implied Volatilities

So far we have used our option pricing model to calculate the value of an option given the standard deviation of the asset's returns. Sometimes it is useful to turn the problem around and ask what the option price is telling us about the asset's variability. For example, the Chicago Board Options Exchange trades options on several market indexes. As we write this, the Standard and Poor's 500-share index is 1300, while a six-month at-the-money call on the index is priced at 63.00. If the Black–Scholes formula is correct, then an option value of 63.00 makes sense only if investors believe that the standard deviation of index returns is a little over 14% a year.[15]

The Chicago Board Options Exchange regularly publishes the implied volatility on the Standard and Poor's index, which it terms the VIX. There is an active market in the VIX. For example, suppose you feel that the implied volatility is implausibly low. Then you can "buy" the VIX at the current low price and hope to "sell" it at a profit when implied volatility has increased.

You may be interested to compare the current implied volatility that we calculated earlier with Figure 18.6, which shows past measures of implied volatility for the Standard and Poor's index and for the Nasdaq index (VXN). Notice the sharp

---

[14] The Black–Scholes formula tells us the *cost* of your options to the company. If the options oblige you to hold a less diversified portfolio than you would wish, you might place a lower value on them. Note also that for this reason you may wish to exercise your options earlier than you otherwise would.

[15] In calculating the implied volatility we need to allow for the dividends paid on the shares. We explain how to take these into account in the next section.

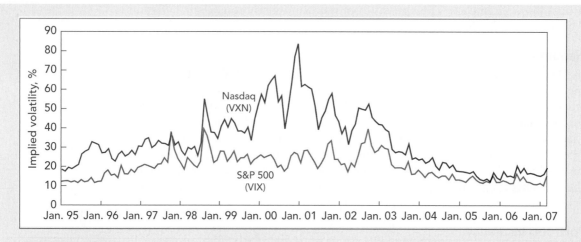

FIGURE 18.6

Standard deviations of market returns implied by prices of options on stock indexes.

Source: Data from the Chicago Board Options Exchange **www.cboe.com**.

increase in investor uncertainty about the value of Nasdaq stocks during the crash of the dot.com stocks in late 2000. This uncertainty showed up in the high price that investors were prepared to pay for options.

Valuing an Option to Expand

Real options, such as the option to expand or abandon a project, are often complex and can absorb a lot of analytical and computational horsepower. But to give you some feel for how option techniques can be used to evaluate these real options, we will take a step back in time and come to the aid of the chief financial officer (CFO) of Blitzen Computers.

It is 1982. You are assistant to the CFO of Blitzen Computers, an established computer manufacturer casting a profit-hungry eye on the rapidly developing personal computer market. You are helping the CFO evaluate the proposed introduction of the Blitzen Mark I Micro.

The Mark I would involve an investment of $450 million. Unfortunately it can't meet Blitzen's customary 20% hurdle rate and has a $46.5 million negative NPV, contrary to top managment's strong gut feeling that Blitzen ought to be in the personal computer market.

The CFO has called you in to discuss the project:

"The Mark I just can't make it on financial grounds," the CFO says, "But we've got to do it for strategic reasons. I'm recommending we go ahead."

"But you're missing the all-important financial advantage, Chief," you reply.

"Don't call me 'Chief.' What financial advantage?"

"If we don't launch the Mark I, it will probably be too expensive to enter the micro market later, when Apple, IBM, and others are firmly established. If we go ahead, we have the opportunity to make follow-on investments that could be extremely profitable. The Mark I provides not only its own cash flows but also a call option to go on with a Mark II micro. That call option is the real source of strategic value."

"So it's strategic value by another name. That doesn't tell me what the Mark II investment's worth. The Mark II could be a great investment or a lousy one—we haven't got a clue."

"That's exactly when a call option is worth the most," you point out perceptively. "The call lets us invest in the Mark II if it's great and walk away from it if it's lousy."

"So what's it worth?"

"Hard to say precisely, but I've done a back-of-the envelope calculation, which suggests that the value of the option to invest in the Mark II could more than offset the Mark I's $46 million negative NPV. If, as I estimate, the option to invest is worth $55 million, the total value of the Mark I is its own NPV, −$45 million, plus the $55 million option attached to it, or +$9 million."

"You're just overstimating the Mark II," the CFO says gruffly. "It's easy to be optimistic when an investment is three years away."

"No, no," you reply patiently. "The Mark II is expected to be no more profitable than the Mark I—just twice as big and therefore twice as bad in terms of discounted cash flow. I'm forecasting it to have a negative NPV of nearly $100 million. But there's a chance the Mark II could be extremely valuable. The call option allows Blitzen to cash in on those upside outcomes. The chance to cash in could be worth $55 million."

"Of course, the $55 million is only a trial calculation, but it illustrates how valuable follow-on investment opportunities can be, especially when uncertainty is high and the product market is growing rapidly. Moreover, the Mark II will give us a call on the Mark III, the Mark III on the Mark IV, and so on. My calculations don't take subsequent calls into account."

"I think I'm beginning to understand a little bit of corporate strategy," mumbles the CFO.

Tables 18.3 and 18.4 show how you arrived at your estimate of the value of the option to develop the Mark II. Table 18.3 shows that the project involves an initial outlay of $900 million in 1985. The cash inflows start in the following year and have a present value of $807 million in 1985, equivalent to $467 million 1982. So the real option to invest in the Mark II amounts to a three-year call on an underlying asset worth $467 million, with a $900 million exercise price.

TABLE 18.3

Cash flows of the Mark II microcomputer as forecasted from 1982 ($ millions). The Mark II requires double the investment of the Mark I and it is forecasted to be twice as unprofitable with an NPV of −$93 million vs. an NPV of −$46.5 for the Mark I.

| | **Year** | | | | | | |
	1982	1985	1986	1987	1988	1989	1990
After-tax operating cash flow			+220	+318	+590	+370	0
Increase in working capital			100	200	200	−250	−250
Net cash flow			+120	+118	+390	+620	+250
Present value at 20%	+467	← +807					
Investment		900					
Forecasted NPV in 1985		−93					

TABLE 18.4

Valuing the option to invest in the Mark II microcomputer.

Assumptions

1. The decision to invest in the Mark II must be made after 3 years in 1985.
2. The investment required for the Mark II is $900 million (the exercise price), which is taken as fixed.
3. Forecasted cash inflows of the Mark II have a present value of $807 million in 1985 and $807/(1.1)^3 = $467 million in 1982. With traded call options, you can see the value of the *underlying asset* that the call is written on. Here the option is to buy a nontraded real asset, the Mark II. We can't observe the Mark II's value; we have to use DCF to compute it.
4. The future value of the Mark II's cash flows is highly uncertain. This value evolves as a stock price does with a standard deviation of 35% per year. (Many high-technology stocks have standard deviations higher than 35%.)
5. The annual interest rate is 10%.

Interpretation

The opportunity to invest in the Mark II is a three-year call option ($t = 3$) on an asset worth $467 million ($P = 467$) with an exercise price of $900 million ($EX = 900$).

Valuation

$$PV(\text{exercise price}) = 9000/(1.1)^3 = 676$$
$$\text{Call value} = [N(d_1) \times P] - [N(d_2) \times PV(EX)]$$
$$d_1 = \log[P/PV(EX)]/\sigma\sqrt{t} + \sigma\sqrt{t}/2$$
$$= \log[.691]/.606 + .606/2 = -.3072$$
$$d_2 = d_1 - \sigma\sqrt{t} = -.3072 - .606 = -.9134$$
$$N(d_1) = .3793, \ N(d_2) = .1805$$
$$\text{Call value} = [.3793 \times .467] - [.1805 \times 676] = \$55.1 \text{ million}$$

Table 18.4 uses the Black–Scholes model to value this call. The option to invest in the Mark II is "out-of-the-money" because the Mark II's value is far less than the required investment. Nevertheless, the option is worth +$55 million. It is especially valuable because the Mark II is a risky project with lots of upside potential. Of course, it also has lots of downside potential, but this is irrelevant because Blitzen won't invest unless the Mark II's value turns out to be higher than the $900 million investment.

18.5   OPTION VALUES AT A GLANCE

So far our discussion of option values has assumed that investors hold the option until maturity. That is certainly the case with European options that *cannot* be exercised before maturity but may not be the case with American options that can be exercised at any time. Also, when we valued the Genentech call, we could ignore dividends, because Genentech did not pay any. Can the same valuation methods be extended to American options and to stocks that pay dividends?

American Calls—No Dividends   Unlike European options, American options can be exercised anytime. However, we know that in the absence of dividends the value of a call option increases with time to maturity. So, if you exercised an American call option early, you would needlessly reduce its value. Since an American call should not be exercised before maturity, its value is the same as that of a European call, and the Black–Scholes model applies to both options.

European Puts—No Dividends   If we wish to value a European put, we can use the put–call parity formula from Chapter 17:

$$\text{Value of put} = \text{value of call} - \text{value of stock} + \text{PV(exercise price)}$$

American Puts—No Dividends   It can sometimes pay to exercise an American put before maturity to reinvest the exercise price. For example, suppose that immediately after you buy an American put, the stock price falls to zero. In this case there is no advantage to holding onto the option since it *cannot* become more valuable. It is better to exercise the put and invest the exercise money. Thus an American put is always more valuable than a European put. In our extreme example, the difference is equal to the present value of the interest that you could earn on the exercise price. In all other cases the difference is less.

Because the Black–Scholes formula does not allow for early exercise, it cannot be used to value an American put exactly. But you can use the step-by-step binomial method as long as you check at each point whether the option is worth more dead than alive and then use the higher of the two values.

European Calls and Puts on Dividend-Paying Stocks   Part of the share value comprises the present value of dividends. The option holder is not entitled to dividends. Therefore, when using the Black–Scholes model to value a European option on a dividend-paying stock, you should reduce the price of the stock by the present value of the dividends paid before the option's maturity.

Dividends don't always come with a big label attached, so look out for instances where the asset holder gets a benefit and the option holder does not. For example, when you buy foreign currency, you can invest it to earn interest; but if you own an option to buy foreign currency, you miss out on this income. Therefore, when valuing an option to buy foreign currency, you need to deduct the present value of this foreign interest from the current price of the currency.[16]

American Calls on Dividend-Paying Stocks   We have seen that when the stock does not pay dividends, an American call option is *always* worth more alive than dead. By holding onto the option, you not only keep your option open but also earn interest on the exercise money. Even when there are dividends, you should never exercise early if the dividend you gain is less than the interest you lose by having to pay the exercise price early. However, if the dividend is sufficiently large, you might want to capture it by exercising the option just before the ex-dividend date.

The only general method for valuing an American call on a dividend-paying stock is to use the step-by-step binomial method. In this case you must check at each stage to see whether the option is more valuable if exercised just before the ex-dividend date than if held for at least one more period.

---

[16] For example, suppose that it currently costs $2 to buy £1 and that this pound can be invested to earn interest of 5%. The option holder misses out on interest of $.05 \times \$2 = \$.10$. So, before using the Black–Scholes formula to value an option to buy sterling, you must adjust the current price of sterling:

$$\text{Adjusted price of sterling} = \text{current price} - \text{PV(interest)}$$
$$= \$2 - .10/1.05 = \$1.905$$

18.6   THE OPTION MENAGERIE

Our focus in the past two chapters has been on plain-vanilla puts and calls or combinations of them. An understanding of these options and how they are valued will allow you to handle most of the option problems that you are likely to encounter in corporate finance. However, you may occasionally encounter some more unusual options. We are not going to be looking at them in this book, but just for fun and to help you hold your own in conversations with your investment banker friends, here is a crib sheet that summarizes a few of these exotic options:

Asian (or average) option	The exercise price is equal to the *average* of the asset's price during the life of the option.
Barrier option	Option where the payoff depends on whether the asset price reaches a specified level. A knock-in option (up-and-in call or down-and-in put) comes into existence only when the underlying asset reaches the barrier. Knock-out options (down-and-out call or up-and-out put) *cease* to exist if the asset price reaches the barrier.
Bermuda option	The option is exercisable on discrete dates before maturity.
Caput option	Call option on a put option.
Chooser (as-you-like-it) option	The holder must decide before maturity whether the option is a call or a put.
Compound option	An option on an option.
Digital (binary or cash-or-nothing) option	The option payoff is zero if the asset price is the wrong side of the exercise price and otherwise is a fixed sum.
Lookback option	The option holder chooses as the exercise price any of the asset prices that occurred before the final date.

SUMMARY

In this chapter we introduced the basic principles of option valuation by considering a call option on a stock that could take on one of two possible values at the option's maturity. We showed that it is possible to construct a package of the stock and a loan that would provide exactly the same payoff as the option *regardless* of whether the stock price rises or falls. Therefore the value of the option must be the same as the value of this replicating portfolio.

We arrived at the same answer by pretending that investors are risk-neutral, so that the expected return on every asset is equal to the interest rate. We calculated the expected future value of the option in this imaginary risk-neutral world and then discounted this figure at the interest rate to find the option's present value.

The general binomial method adds realism by dividing the option's life into a number of subperiods in each of which the stock price can make one of two possible moves. Chopping the period into these shorter intervals doesn't alter the basic method for valuing a call option. We can still replicate the call by a package of the stock and a loan, but the package changes at each stage.

Finally, we introduced the Black–Scholes formula. This calculates the option's value when the stock price is constantly changing and takes on a continuum of possible future values.

When valuing options in practical situations there are a number of features to look out for. For example, you may need to recognize that the option value is reduced by the fact that the holder is not entitled to any dividends.

FURTHER READING

The classic articles on option valuation are:

F. Black and M. Scholes, "The Pricing of Options and Corporate Liabilities," *Journal of Political Economy* 81 (May–June 1973), pp. 637–654.

R. C. Merton, "Theory of Rational Option Pricing," *Bell Journal of Economics and Management Science* 4 (Spring 1973), pp. 141–183.

Two readable articles about the Black–Scholes model are:

F. Black, "How We Came up with the Option Formula," *Journal of Portfolio Management* 15 (1989), pp. 4–8.

F. Black, "The Holes in Black–Scholes," *RISK* Magazine 1 (1988), pp. 27–29.

There are a number of good books on option valuation. They include:

J. Hull, *Options, Futures and Other Derivatives,* 6th ed. (Englewood Cliffs, NJ: Prentice-Hall, Inc., 2005).

R. Jarrow and S. Turnbull, *Derivative Securities,* 2nd ed. (Cincinnati, OH: South-Western 1999).

R. L. McDonald, *Derivatives Markets,* 2nd ed. (Reading, MA: Pearson Addison Wesley, 2005).

P. Wilmott, *Paul Wilmott on Quantitative Finance,* 2nd ed. (New York: John Wiley & Sons, 2006).

CONCEPT REVIEW QUESTIONS

1. Why won't discounted cash flow work for options? (page 485)

2. There are two equivalent ways to value an option. One is to create a replicating portfolio. What is the other? (pages 486–488)

3. Explain what is meant by an option's delta. (page 486)

For a complete listing of your chapter Concept Review Questions, please visit us at www.mhhe.com/bma1e.

QUIZ

1. The stock price of Heavy Metal (HM) changes only once a month: either it goes up by 20% or it falls by 16.7%. Its price now is $40. The interest rate is 12.7% per year, or about 1% per month.

   a. What is the value of a one-month call option with an exercise price of $40?

   b. What is the option delta?

   c. Show how the payoffs of this call option can be replicated by buying HM's stock and borrowing.

   d. What is the value of a two-month call option with an exercise price of $40?

   e. What is the option delta of the two-month call over the first one-month period?

Visit us at www.mhhe.com/bma1e

2. **a.** Can the delta of a call option be greater than 1.0? Explain.

    b. Can it be less than zero?

    c. How does the delta of a call change if the stock price rises?

    d. How does it change if the risk of the stock increases?

3. Take another look at our two-step binomial trees for Genentech, for example, in Figure 18.2. Use the replicating-portfolio or risk-neutral method to value six-month call and put options with an exercise price of $75. Assume the Genentech stock price is $80.

4. Imagine that Genentech's stock price will either rise by 25% or fall by 20% over the next six months (see Section 18.1). Recalculate the value of the call option (exercise price = $80) using (**a**) the replicating portfolio method and (**b**) the risk-neutral method. Explain intuitively why the option value falls from the value computed in Section 18.1.

5. Over the coming year Ragwort's stock price will halve to $50 from its current level of $100 or it will rise to $200. The one-year interest rate is 10%.

    a. What is the delta of a one-year call option on Ragwort stock with an exercise price of $100?

    b. Use the replicating-portfolio method to value this call.

    c. In a risk-neutral world what is the probability that Ragwort stock will rise in price?

    d. Use the risk-neutral method to check your valuation of the Ragwort option.

    e. If someone told you that in reality there is a 60% chance that Ragwort's stock price will rise to $200, would you change your view about the value of the option? Explain.

6. Use the Black–Scholes formula and Appendix A: Present Value Table 6 (page A-5) to value the following options:

    a. A call option written on a stock selling for $60 per share with a $60 exercise price. The stock's standard deviation is 6% per month. The option matures in three months. The risk-free interest rate is 1% per month.

    b. A put option written on the same stock at the same time, with the same exercise price and expiration date.

    Now for each of these options find the combination of stock and risk-free asset that would replicate the option.

7. "An option is always riskier than the stock it is written on." True or false? How does the risk of an option change when the stock price changes?

8. For which of the following options *might* it be rational to exercise before maturity? Explain briefly why or why not.

    a. American put on a non-dividend-paying stock.

    b. American call—the dividend payment is $5 per annum, the exercise price is $100 pesos, and the interest rate is 10%.

    c. American call—the interest rate is 10%, and the dividend payment is 5% of future stock price. (*Hint:* The dividend depends on the stock price, which could either rise or fall.)

PRACTICE QUESTIONS

9. Johnny Jones's high school derivatives homework asks for a binomial valuation of a 12-month call option on the common stock of the Overland Railroad. The stock is now selling for $45 per share and has an annual standard deviation of 24%. Johnny first constructs a binomial tree like Figure 18.2, in which stock price moves up or down every six months. Then he constructs a more realistic tree, assuming that the stock price moves up or down once every three months, or four times per year.

a. Construct these two binomial trees.

b. How would these trees change if Overland's standard deviation were 30%? (*Hint:* Make sure to specify the right up and down percentage changes.)

10. Suppose a stock price can go up by 15% or down by 13% over the next year. You own a one-year put on the stock. The interest rate is 10%, and the current stock price is $60.

a. What exercise price leaves you indifferent between holding the put or exercising it now?

b. How does this break-even exercise price change if the interest rate is increased?

11. The price of Moria Mining stock is $100. During each of the next two six-month periods the price may either rise by 25% or fall by 20% (equivalent to a standard deviation of 31.5% a year). At month 6 the company will pay a dividend of $20. The interest rate is 10% per six-month period. What is the value of a one-year American call option with an exercise price of $80? Now recalculate the option value, assuming that the dividend is equal to 20% of the with-dividend stock price.

12. Buffelhead's stock price is $220 and could halve or double in each six-month period (equivalent to a standard deviation of 98%). A one-year call option on Buffelhead has an exercise price of $165. The interest rate is 21% a year.

a. What is the value of the Buffelhead call?

b. Now calculate the option delta for the second six months if (i) the stock price rises to $440 and (ii) the stock price falls to $110.

c. How does the call option delta vary with the level of the stock price? Explain intuitively why.

d. Suppose that in month 6 the Buffelhead stock price is $110. How at that point could you replicate an investment in the stock by a combination of call options and risk-free lending? Show that your strategy does indeed produce the same returns as those from an investment in the stock.

13. Suppose that you own an American put option on Buffelhead stock (see Practice Problem 12) with an exercise price of $220.

a. Would you ever want to exercise the put early?

b. Calculate the value of the put.

c. Now compare the value with that of an equivalent European put option.

14. Recalculate the value of the Buffelhead call option (see Practice Problem 12), assuming that the option is American and that at the end of the first six months the company pays a dividend of $25. (Thus the price at the end of the year is either double or half the *ex*-dividend price in month 6.) How would your answer change if the option were European?

15. Suppose that you have an option that allows you to sell Buffelhead stock (see Practice Problem 12) in month 6 for $165 *or* to buy it in month 12 for $165. What is the value of this unusual option?

16. The current price of the stock of Mont Tremblant Air is C$100. During each six-month period it will either rise by 11.1% or fall by 10% (equivalent to an annual standard deviation of 14.9%). The interest rate is 5% per six-month period.

a. Calculate the value of a one-year European put option on Mont Tremblant's stock with an exercise price of C$102.

b. Recalculate the value of the Mont Tremblant put option, assuming that it is an American option.

17. The current price of United Carbon (UC) stock is $200. The standard deviation is 22.3% a year, and the interest rate is 21% a year. A one-year call option on UC has an exercise price of $180.

a. Use the Black–Scholes model to value the call option on UC. You may find it helpful to use the "live" spreadsheet in Table 18.2 on the book's Web site, **www.mhhe.com/bma1e.**

b. Use the formula given in Section 18.2 to calculate the up and down moves that you would use if you valued the UC option with the one-period binomial method. Now value the option by using that method.

c. Recalculate the up and down moves and revalue the option by using the two-period binomial method.

d. Use your answer to part (**c**) to calculate the option delta (i) today; (ii) next period if the stock price rises; and (iii) next period if the stock price falls. Show at each point how you would replicate a call option with a levered investment in the company's stock.

18. Suppose you construct an option hedge by buying a levered position in delta shares of stock and selling one call option. As the share price changes, the option delta changes, and you will need to adjust your hedge. You can minimize the cost of adjustments if changes in the stock price have only a small effect on the option delta. Construct an example to show whether the option delta is likely to vary more if you hedge with an in-the-money option, an at-the-money option, or an out-of-the-money option.

19. Other things equal, which of these American options are you most likely to want to exercise early?

a. A put option on a stock with a large dividend or a call on the same stock.

b. A put option on a stock that is selling below exercise price or a call on the same stock.

c. A put option when the interest rate is high or the same put option when the interest rate is low.

Illustrate your answer with examples.

20. Is it better to exercise a call option on the with-dividend date or on the ex-dividend date? How about a put option? Explain.

Visit us at
www.mhhe.com/bma1e.

21. Look back to the companies listed in Table 8.3. Most of these companies are covered in the Standard & Poor's Market Insight Web site (**www.mhhe.com/edumarketinsight**), and most will have traded options. Pick at least three companies. For each company, download "Monthly Adjusted Prices" as an Excel spreadsheet. Calculate each company's standard deviation from the monthly returns given on the spreadsheet. The Excel function is STDEV. Convert the standard deviations from monthly to annual units by multiplying by the square root of 12.

a. Use the Black–Scholes formula to value three-, six-, and nine-month call options on each stock. Assume the exercise price equals the current stock price, and use a current, risk-free, annual interest rate. To check your answer, you can use the "live" spreadsheet in Table 18.2 on the book's Web site, **www.mhhe.com/bma1e.**

b. For each stock, pick a traded option with an exercise price approximately equal to the current stock price. Use the Black–Scholes formula and your estimate of standard deviation to value the option. How close is your calculated value to the traded price of the option?

c. Your answer to part (**b**) will not exactly match the traded price. Experiment with different values for standard deviation until your calculations match the traded options prices as closely as possible. What are these implied volatilities? What do the implied volatilities say about investors' forecasts of future volatility?

22. Look again at Table 18.4. How does the value in 1982 of the option to invest in the Mark II change if:

    a. The investment required for the Mark II is $800 million (vs. $900 million)?

    b. The present value of the Mark II in 1982 is $500 million (vs. $467 million)?

    c. The standard deviation of the Mark II's present value is only 20% (vs. 35%)?

23. Use the "live" Black–Scholes program on this book's Web site, **www.mhhe.com/ bma1e,** to value the INX warrants described in Section 18.4. The standard deviation of INX stock was 87% a year and the interest rate when the warrants were issued was 2.8%. INX did not pay a dividend.

Visit us at www.mhhe.com/bma1e.

24. Use the "live" Black–Scholes program at **www.mhhe.com/bma1e** to estimate how much you should be prepared to pay to insure the value of your pension fund portfolio for the coming year. Make reasonable assumptions about the volatility of the market and use current interest rates. Remember to subtract the present value of likely dividend payments from the current level of the market index.

Visit us at www.mhhe.com/bma1e.

CHALLENGE QUESTIONS

25. Use the formula that relates the value of the call and the put (see Section 17.2) and the one-period binomial model to show that the option delta for a put option is equal to the option delta for a call option minus 1.

26. Show how the option delta changes as the stock price rises relative to the exercise price. Explain intuitively why this is the case. (*Hints:* What happens to the option delta if the exercise price of an option is zero? What happens if the exercise price becomes indefinitely large?)

27. Your company has just awarded you a generous stock option scheme. You suspect that the board will either decide to increase the dividend or announce a stock repurchase program. Which do you secretly hope they will decide? Explain. (You may find it helpful to refer back to Chapter 13.)

28. Some corporations have issued *perpetual* warrants. Warrants are call options issued by a firm, allowing the warrant holder to buy the firm's stock.

    a. What does the Black–Scholes formula predict for the value of an infinite-lived call option on a non-dividend-paying stock? Explain the value you obtain. (*Hint:* what happens to the present value of the exercise price of a long-maturity option?)

    b. Do you think this prediction is realistic? If not, explain carefully why. (*Hints:* What about dividends? What about bankruptcy?)

MINI-CASE

Bruce Honiball's Invention

It was another disappointing year for Bruce Honiball, the manager of retail services at the Gibb River Bank. Sure, the retail side of Gibb River was making money, but it didn't grow at all in 2006. Gibb River had plenty of loyal depositors, but few new ones. Bruce had to figure out some new product or financial service—something that would generate some excitement and attention.

Bruce had been musing on one idea for some time. How about making it easy *and safe* for Gibb River's customers to put money in the stock market? How about giving them the upside of investing in equities—at least *some* of the upside—but none of the downside?

Visit us at www.mhhe.com/bma1e

TABLE 18.5

Australian interest rates and equity returns, 1987–2006.

Year	Interest Rate	Market Return	End-Year Dividend Yield	Year	Interest Rate	Market Return	End-Year Dividend Yield
1987	14.1%	−7.9%	4.7%	1997	5.5%	12.2%	3.9%
1988	11.7	17.9	5.1	1998	5.0	11.6	3.5
1989	17.3	17.4	5.7	1999	4.9	16.1	3.2
1990	15.9	−17.5	6.8	2000	4.9	5.2	3.4
1991	11.1	34.2	3.8	2001	4.8	10.4	3.3
1992	6.8	−2.3	3.8	2002	4.8	−8.8	4.0
1993	5.3	45.4	3.0	2003	4.8	14.6	3.9
1994	5.4	−8.7	4.0	2004	5.4	28.0	3.5
1995	8.0	20.2	4.0	2005	5.6	22.8	3.7
1996	7.4	14.6	3.6	2006	5.9	24.2	3.7

Bruce could see the advertisements now:

How would you like to invest in Australian stocks completely risk-free? You can with the new Gibb River Bank *Equity-Linked Deposit*. You share in the good years; we take care of the bad ones.

Here's how it works. Deposit $A100 with us for one year. At the end of that period you get back your $A100 *plus* $A5 for every 10% rise in the value of the Australian All Ordinaries stock index. But, if the market index falls during this period, the Bank will still refund your $A100 deposit in full.

There's no risk of loss. Gibb River Bank is your safety net.

Bruce had floated the idea before and encountered immediate skepticism, even derision: "Heads they win, tails we lose—is that what you're proposing, Mr. Honiball?" Bruce had no ready answer. Could the bank really afford to make such an attractive offer? How should it invest the money that would come in from customers? The bank had no appetite for major new risks.

Bruce has puzzled over these questions for the past two weeks but has been unable to come up with a satisfactory answer. He believes that the Australian equity market is currently fully valued, but he realizes that some of his colleagues are more bullish than he is about equity prices.

Fortunately, the bank had just recruited a smart new MBA graduate, Sheila Liu. Sheila was sure that she could find the answers to Bruce Honiball's questions. First she collected data on the Australian market to get a preliminary idea of whether equity-linked deposits could work. These data are shown in Table 18.5. She was just about to undertake some quick calculations when she received the following further memo from Bruce:

Sheila, I've got another idea. A lot of our customers probably share my view that the market is overvalued. Why don't we also give them a chance to make some money by offering a "bear market deposit"? If the market goes up, they would just get back their $A100 deposit. If it goes down, they get their $A100 back plus $5 for each 10% that the market falls. Can you figure out whether we could do something like this? Bruce.

QUESTION

1. What kinds of options is Bruce proposing? How much would the options be worth? Would the equity-linked and bear-market deposits generate positive NPV for Gibb River Bank?

PART SEVEN

FINANCIAL PLANNING AND THE MANAGEMENT OF WORKING CAPITAL

IN 1994 39-YEAR-OLD JEAN-MARIE MESSIER became CEO of the French company Generale des Eaux. He immediately set out to transform it from a sleepy water and sewage business into a multinational media and telecommunications group. The company, now renamed Vivendi, entered into a series of major acquisitions, including a $42 billion purchase of Seagram, owner of Universal Studios. To finance its expansion Vivendi increased its borrowing to $35 billion, and it increased its leverage further by repurchasing 104 million shares for $6.3 billion. Confident that its share price would rise, the company raised the stakes even more by selling a large number of put options on its own stock.

Vivendi's strategy made it very vulnerable to any decline in operating cash flow. As profits began to evaporate, the company faced a severe cash shortage. Its banks were reluctant to extend further credit and its bonds were downgraded to junk status. By July 2002 the share price had fallen to less than 10% of its level two years earlier. With the company facing imminent bankruptcy, M. Messier was ousted and the new management set about slashing costs and selling assets to reduce the debt burden.[1]

Vivendi's problems were exacerbated by considerable waste and ostentatious extravagance, but its brush with bankruptcy was a result of a lack of financial planning. The company's goals for growth were unsustainable and it had few options for surviving a decline in operating cash flow. Part 7 shows how firms can check that their growth strategy is consistent with their financing plans. Chapter 19 explains how managers monitor the company's financial health and develop long-term financial plans. Chapter 20 focuses on short-term planning. We first show how managers forecast their cash needs and then look at how firms alleviate any short-term cash shortage and invest any cash surplus.

Web sites related to this Part appear at www.mhhe.com/bma1e.

[1] The rise and fall of Vivendi is chronicled in J. Johnson and M. Orange, *The Man Who Tried to Buy the World: Jean-Marie Messier and Vivendi Universal* (Portfolio, 2003).

CHAPTER NINETEEN

FINANCIAL ANALYSIS AND PLANNING

A CAMEL LOOKS like an animal designed by a committee. If a firm made all its financial decisions piecemeal, it would end up with a financial camel. Therefore, smart financial managers consider the overall effect of financing and investment decisions and ensure that they have the financial strategies in place to support the firm's plans for future growth.

Knowing where you stand today is a necessary prelude to contemplating where you might be in the future. Therefore we start the chapter with a brief review of a company's financial statements and we show how you can use these statements to assess the firm's overall performance and its current financial standing.

To produce order out of chaos, financial analysts calculate a few key financial ratios that summarize the company's financial strengths and weaknesses. These ratios are no substitute for a crystal ball, but they do help you to ask the right questions. For example, when the firm needs a loan from the bank,

the financial manager can expect some searching questions about the firm's debt ratio and the proportion of profits that is absorbed by interest. Likewise, financial ratios may alert senior management to potential problem areas. If a division is earning a low rate of return on its capital or its profit margins are under pressure, you can be sure that management will demand an explanation.

Growing firms need to invest in working capital, plant and equipment, product development, and so on. All this requires cash. We will, therefore, explain how firms use financial planning models to help them understand the financial implications of their business plans and to explore the consequences of alternative financial strategies.

Our focus in this chapter is on the long-term future. For example, firms may have a planning horizon of 5 or 10 years. In Chapter 20 we will look at how firms also develop more detailed strategies to ensure that they can get safely through the next few months.

19.1 FINANCIAL STATEMENTS

Public companies have a variety of stakeholders, such as shareholders, bondholders, bankers, suppliers, employees, and management. All these stakeholders need to monitor the firm and to ensure that their interests are being served. They rely on the company's financial statements to provide the necessary information.

When reviewing a company's financial statements, it is important to remember that accountants still have a fair degree of leeway in reporting earnings and book values. For example, accountants have discretion in the choice of depreciation method and the speed at which the firm's assets are written off.

Although accountants around the world are working toward common practices, there are considerable variations in the accounting rules of different countries. In Anglo-Saxon countries such as the United States or the U.K., which have large and active equity markets, the rules have been designed with the shareholder very much in mind. By contrast, in Germany the focus of accounting standards is to verify that the creditors are properly protected.

Another difference is the way that taxes are shown in the income statement. For example, in Germany taxes are paid on the published profits and the depreciation method must therefore be approved by the revenue service. That is not so in Anglo-Saxon countries, where the numbers shown in the published accounts are generally *not* the basis for calculating the company's tax payments. For instance, the depreciation method used to calculate the published profits may differ from the depreciation method used by the tax authorities.

Sometimes the effect of these differences in accounting rules can be substantial. When the German car manufacturer, Daimler-Benz, decided to list its shares on the New York Stock Exchange in 1993, it was required to revise its accounting practices to conform to U.S. standards. While it reported a modest profit in the first half of 1993 using German accounting rules, it reported a loss of $592 million under U.S. rules, primarily because of differences in the treatment of reserves.

For investors and multinational companies these variations in accounting rules can be irksome. Accounting bodies have therefore been getting together to see whether they can iron out some of the differences. It is not a simple task, as the nearby box illustrates.

19.2 EXECUTIVE PAPER'S FINANCIAL STATEMENTS

Your task is to assess the financial standing of the Executive Paper Corporation. Perhaps you are a financial analyst with Executive Paper and are helping to develop a five-year financial plan. Perhaps you are employed by a rival company that is contemplating a takeover bid for Executive Paper. Or perhaps you are a banker who needs to assess whether the bank should lend to the company. In each case your first step is to assess the company's *current* condition. You have before you the latest balance sheet, income statement, and sources and uses of funds.

SPEAKING IN TONGUES

Forget Esperanto. Too straightforward. The *lingua franca* that is increasingly spanning the globe is a tongue-twisting accounting-speak that is forcing even Americans to rethink some precious notions of financial sovereignty.

International Financial Reporting Standards (IFRS), which aim to harmonize financial reporting in a world of cross-border trade and investment, have made great strides since they were adopted by 7,000 or so listed companies in the European Union in 2005. To date, over 100 countries from Canada to China have adopted the rules or say they plan to adopt them. The London-based International Accounting Standards Board (IASB) expects that to swell to 150 in the next four years.

Even America, no ardent internationalist, is working with the IASB to narrow the gap between its own accounting standards and IFRS, which foreign companies listed in America could choose by 2009 or possibly sooner. Today such companies must "reconcile" their accounts with American rules—a costly exercise that some believe is driving foreign listings away from the United States.

In late April America's Securities and Exchange Commission (SEC) unexpectedly floated the idea of giving American, and not just foreign, companies the choice of using IFRS. Critics of the idea claim that this will give companies the option of shopping around for whichever regime best suits their business. Inevitably, however, by opening the door (if only a crack), America's own accounting regime would be in jeopardy.

Whether pure IFRS or not, all countries are prone to interpret the rules in ways that reflect their old accounting standards, according to KPMG, an accountancy firm. Regulators are working through IOSC, an international body of securities regulators, to attempt to whittle down these differences.

The task is further complicated by the fact that international accounting rules tend to be "principles based," which mean there are no hard-and-fast codes to follow. This is different from America, where accounting principles are accompanied by thousands of pages of prescriptive regulatory guidance and interpretations from auditors and accounting groups, some of it gleaned from SEC speeches. IFRS have no such baggage, leaving more room for judgment.

Source: Adapted from "Speaking in Tongues," *The Economist,* May 19, 2007, p. 83.

The Balance Sheet

Executive Paper's balance sheet in Table 19.1 provides a snapshot of the company's assets and the sources of the money used to buy those assets.

The items in the balance sheet are listed in declining order of liquidity. For example, you can see that the accountant lists first these assets that are most likely to be turned into cash in the near future. They include cash itself, marketable securities and receivables (that is, bills to be paid by the firm's customers), and inventories of raw materials, work in process, and finished goods. These assets are all known as *current assets.*

The remaining assets on the balance sheet consist of long-term, usually illiquid, assets such as pulp and paper mills, office buildings, and timberlands. The balance sheet does not show up-to-date market values of these long-term assets. Instead, the accountant records the amount that each asset originally cost and then, in the case of plant and equipment, deducts a fixed annual amount for

TABLE 19.1

The balance sheet of Executive Paper Corporation (figures in $ millions).

e**X**cel

Visit us at
www.mhhe.com/bma1e.

Assets	Dec 2004	Dec 2005	Change
Current assets:			
Cash and securities	75	110	+35
Receivables	433.1	440	+6.9
Inventory	339.9	350	+10.1
Total current assets	848	900	+52
Fixed assets:			
Property, plant, and equipment	929.5	1,000	+70.5
Less accumulated depreciation	396.7	450	+53.3
Net fixed assets	532.8	550	+17.2
Total assets	1,380.8	1,450	+69.2
Liabilities and Shareholders' Equity	**Dec 2004**	**Dec 2005**	**Change**
Current liabilities:			
Debt due within 1 year	96.6	100	+3.4
Payables	349.9	360	+10.1
Total current liabilities	446.5	460	+13.5
Long-term debt	425	450	+25
Shareholders' equity	509.3	540	+30.7
Total liabilities and shareholders' equity	1,380.8	1,450	+69.2
Other financial information:			
Market value of equity	598	708	
Average number of shares (millions)	14.16	14.16	
Share price ($)	42.25	50.00	

depreciation. The balance sheet does not include all the company's assets. Some of the most valuable ones are intangible, such as patents, reputation, a skilled management, and a well-trained labor force. Accountants are generally reluctant to record these assets in the balance sheet unless they can be readily identified and valued.

Now look at the right-hand portion of Executive Paper's balance sheet, which shows where the money to buy the assets came from.[2] The accountant starts by looking at the liabilities, that is, the money owed by the company. First come those liabilities that need to be paid off in the near future. These *current liabilities* include debts that are due to be repaid within the next year and payables (that is, amounts owed by the company to its suppliers).

The difference between the current assets and current liabilities is known as the *net current assets* or *net working capital*. It roughly measures the company's potential reservoir of cash. For Executive Paper in 2005

$$\text{Net working capital} = \text{current assets} - \text{current liabilities}$$
$$= 900 - 460 = \$440 \text{ million}$$

---

[2] The British and Americans can never agree whether to keep to the left or the right. British accountants list liabilities on the left and assets on the right. (The right side is actually plotted below in the table.)

TABLE 19.2

The 2005 income statement of Executive Paper Corporation (figures in $ millions).

Visit us at
www.mhhe.com/bma1e.

	$ millions
Revenues	2,200
Costs	1,980
Depreciation	53.3
EBIT	166.7
Interest	42.5
Tax	49.7
Net income	74.5
Dividends	43.8
Retained earnings	30.7
Earnings per share ($)	5.26
Dividend per share ($)	3.09

The bottom portion of the balance sheet shows the sources of the cash that was used to acquire the net working capital and fixed assets. Some of the cash has come from the issue of bonds and leases that will not be repaid for many years. After all these long-term liabilities have been paid off, the remaining assets belong to the common stockholders. The company's equity is simply the total value of the net working capital and fixed assets less the long-term liabilities. Part of this equity has come from the sale of shares to investors and the remainder has come from earnings that the company has retained and invested on behalf of the shareholders.

Table 19.1 provides some other financial information about Executive Paper. For example, it shows the market value of the common stock. It is often helpful to compare the *book value* of the equity (shown in the company's accounts) with the *market value* established in the capital markets.

The Income Statement

If Executive Paper's balance sheet resembles a snapshot of the firm at a particular point in time, its income statement is like a video. It shows how profitable the firm has been over the past year.

Look at the summary income statement in Table 19.2. You can see that during 2005 Executive Paper sold goods worth $2,200 million and that the total costs of producing and selling these goods were $1,980 million. In addition to these out-of-pocket expenses, Executive Paper also made a deduction of $53.3 million for the value of the fixed assets used up in producing the goods. Thus Executive Paper's earnings before interest and taxes (EBIT) were

$$\text{EBIT} = \text{Total revenues} - \text{costs} - \text{depreciation}$$
$$= 2{,}200 - 1{,}980 - 53.3 = \$166.7 \text{ million}$$

Of this sum $42.5 million went to pay the interest on the short- and long-term debt (remember debt interest is paid out of pretax income) and a further $49.7 million went to the government in the form of taxes. The $74.5 million that was left over belonged to the shareholders. Executive Paper paid out $43.8 million as dividends and reinvested the remaining $30.7 million in the business.

	$ millions	Notes:
Sources:		
Net income	74.5	See Table 19.2
Depreciation	53.3	See Table 19.2
Operating cash flow	127.8	
Issues of long-term debt	25.0	See Table 19.1: 450 – 425
Issues of equity	0.0	See Tables 19.1 and 19.2: 540 – 509.3 – (74.5 – 43.8)
Total sources	152.8	
Uses:		
Investment in net working capital	38.5	See Table 19.1: (900 – 460) – (848 – 446.5)
Investment in fixed assets	70.5	See Table 19.1: 1000 – 929.5
Dividends	43.8	See Table 19.2
Total uses	152.8	

TABLE 19.3

Sources and uses of funds for Executive Paper Corporation, 2005 (figures in $ millions).

Visit us at
www.mhhe.com/bma1e.

Sources and Uses of Funds

Table 19.3 shows where Executive Paper raised funds and how it spent them.[3] Beside each row in the table we have added a brief note on how the figure is calculated. We will explain each item in turn.

Look first at the uses of funds. The money that Executive Paper generates is either invested in net working capital and fixed assets or it is paid out to shareholders as dividends. Thus

$$\text{Total uses of funds} = \text{investment in net working capital}$$
$$+ \text{ investment in fixed assets}$$
$$+ \text{ dividends paid to shareholders}$$

Table 19.1 shows that in 2005 Executive Paper started the year with net working capital of 848 − 446.5 = $401.5 million. By the end of the year it had grown to 900 − 460 = $440 million. So the company invested an additional $38.5 million in working capital. Over the same period fixed assets rose from $929.5 million to $1,000 million, an increase of $70.5 million. Finally, the income statement in Table 19.2 shows that Executive Paper distributed $43.8 million as dividends. Thus, in total, Executive Paper invested or paid out as dividends 38.5 + 70.5 + 43.8 = $152.8 million.

Where did the funds come from? There are two sources—the cash generated from operations and new money raised from investors:

$$\text{Total sources of funds} = \text{operating cash flow} + \text{new issues of long-term debt}$$
$$+ \text{ new issues of equity}$$

---

[3] Notice that in a *Sources and Uses of Funds* table the different components of net working capital are not separated out. When we discuss short-term planning in Chapter 20, we will show how to draw up a *Sources and Uses of Cash* table, which separates out different items of net working capital.

The income statement shows that in 2005 the company generated $127.8 million from operations. This included $53.3 million of depreciation (remember depreciation is not a cash outflow) and $74.5 million of net income. This left a deficiency of 152.8 − 127.8 = $25 million that Executive Paper needed to raise from the capital market. You can see from the balance sheet that Executive Paper raised this $25 million by an issue of long-term debt (debt increased from $425 million to $450 million). Executive Paper did not issue new equity capital in 2005. So why does the balance sheet show an increase in equity of 540 − 509.3 = $30.7 million? The answer is that this increase in equity came from income that the company retained and plowed back on behalf of its shareholders (retained earnings = net income − dividends = 74.5 − 43.8 = $30.7 million).

19.3 MEASURING EXECUTIVE PAPER'S FINANCIAL CONDITION

Executive Paper's financial statements provide you with the basic information to assess its current financial standing. However, financial statements typically contain large amounts of data—far more than is contained in the simplified statements for Executive Paper. To condense these data into a convenient form, financial managers generally focus on a few key financial ratios.

Table 19.4 summarizes the key financial ratios for Executive Paper.[4] We will explain how to calculate these ratios and use them to shed light on five sets of questions:

- How much has the company borrowed? Is the amount of debt likely to result in financial distress?
- How liquid is the company? Can it easily lay its hands on cash if needed?
- How productively is the company using its assets? Are there any signs that the assets are not being used efficiently?
- How profitable is the company?
- How highly is the firm valued by investors? Are investors' expectations reasonable?

When you calculate a company's financial ratios, you need some criteria to decide whether they are a cause for concern or a matter for congratulation. Unfortunately, there is no "right" set of financial ratios to which all companies should aspire. Take, for example, the company's capital structure. Debt has both advantages and disadvantages, and, even if there were an optimal level of debt for company A, it would not be appropriate for company B.

How Much Has Executive Paper Borrowed?

When Executive Paper borrows, it promises to make a series of fixed payments. Because its shareholders get only what is left over after the debtholders have been

---

[4] In addition to the ratios that we describe below, Table 19.4 includes a few other ratios that you may well encounter. Some are simply alternative ways to express the same result; others are variations on a theme.

Leverage Ratios:		
Debt ratio	(Long-term debt + leases)/(long-term debt + leases + equity)	**0.45**
Debt ratio (incl. short-term debt)*	(Long-term debt + short-term debt + leases)/	
	(long-term debt + short-term debt + leases + equity)	0.50
Debt-equity ratio	(Long-term debt + leases)/equity	0.83
Times-interest-earned	(EBIT + depreciation)/interest	5.18
Liquidity Ratios:		
Net-working-capital to total-assets ratio*	(Current assets-current liabilities)/total assets	0.30
Current ratio	Current assets/current liabilities	1.96
Quick ratio	(Cash + short-term securities + receivables)/current liabilities	1.20
Cash ratio	(Cash + short-term securities)/current liabilities	0.24
Interval measure*	(Cash + short-term securities + receivables)/	
	(costs from operations/365)	101.39
Efficiency Ratios:		
Sales-to-assets ratio	Sales/average total assets	1.55
Sales-to-net-working-capital*	Sales/average net working capital	5.23
Days in inventory	Average inventory/(cost of goods sold/365)	63.59
Inventory turnover*	Cost of goods sold/average inventory	5.74
Average collection period (days)	Average receivables/(sales/365)	72.43
Receivables turnover*	Sales/average receivables	5.04
Profitability Ratios:		
Net profit margin, %	(EBIT – tax)/sales	5.32%
Return on assets % (ROA)	(EBIT – tax)/average total assets	8.27%
Return on equity % (ROE)	Earnings available for common stockholders/average equity	14.20%
Payout ratio	Dividend per share/earnings per share	0.59
Market-Value Ratios:		
Price-earnings ratio (P/E)	Stock price/earnings per share	9.50
Dividend Yield %	Dividend per share/stock price	6.19%
Market-to-book ratio	Stock price/book value per share	1.31

TABLE 19.4

Visit us at
www.mhhe.com/bma1e.

Financial ratios for Executive Paper, 2005.

* This ratio is an extra bonus not discussed in Section 19.3.

paid, the debt is said to create *financial leverage*. In extreme cases, if hard times come, a company may be unable to pay its debts.

The company's bankers and bondholders also want to make certain that Executive Paper does not borrow excessively. So, if Executive wishes to take out a new loan, the lenders will scrutinize several measures of whether the company is borrowing too much and will demand that it *keep* its debt within reasonable bounds. Such borrowing limits are stated in terms of financial ratios.

Debt Ratio   Financial leverage is usually measured by the ratio of long-term debt to total long-term capital. Since long-term lease agreements also commit the firm to a series of fixed payments, it makes sense to include the value of lease obligations with the long-term debt. For Executive Paper

$$\text{Debt ratio} = \frac{\text{(long-term debt + value of leases)}}{\text{(long-term debt + value of leases + equity)}}$$
$$= 450/(450 + 540) = .45$$

Another way to say the same thing is that Executive Paper has a debt-to-equity ratio of $450/540 = .83$:

$$\text{Debt-equity ratio} = \frac{\text{(long-term debt + value of leases)}}{\text{equity}}$$
$$= 450/540 = .83$$

Notice that this measure makes use of book (i.e., accounting) values rather than market values.[5] The market value of the company finally determines whether the debtholders get their money back, so you might expect analysts to look at the face amount of the debt as a proportion of the total market value of debt and equity. On the other hand, the market value includes the value of intangible assets generated by research and development, advertising, staff training, and so on. These assets are not readily salable, and if the company falls on hard times, their value may disappear altogether. For some purposes, it may be just as good to follow the accountant and ignore these intangible assets. This is what lenders do when they insist that the borrower should not allow the book debt ratio to exceed a specified limit.

Debt ratios are sometimes defined in other ways. For example, analysts may include short-term debt or other obligations such as payables. There is a general point here. There are a variety of ways to define most financial ratios and there is no law stating how they *should* be defined. So be warned: Don't accept a ratio at face value without understanding how it has been calculated.

Times-Interest-Earned (or Interest Cover)   Another measure of financial leverage is the extent to which interest is covered by earnings before interest and taxes (EBIT) plus depreciation. For Executive Paper,[6]

$$\text{Times-interest-earned} = \frac{\text{(EBIT + depreciation)}}{\text{interest}}$$
$$= \frac{(166.7 + 53.3)}{42.5} = 5.18$$

The regular interest payment is a hurdle that companies must keep jumping if they are to avoid default. The times-interest-earned ratio measures how much clear air there is between hurdle and hurdler.

---

[5] In the case of leased assets accountants try to estimate the present value of the lease commitments. In the case of long-term debt they simply show the face value. This can sometimes be very different from present value. For example, the present value of low-coupon debt may be only a fraction of its face value. The difference between the book value of equity and its market value can be even more dramatic.

[6] The numerator of times-interest-earned can be defined in several ways. Sometimes depreciation is excluded. Sometimes it is just earnings plus interest, that is, earnings before interest but *after* tax. This last definition seems nutty to us, because the point of times-interest-earned is to assess the risk that the firm won't have enough money to pay interest. If EBIT falls below interest obligations, the firm won't have to worry about taxes. Interest is paid before the firm pays taxes.

How Liquid Is Executive Paper?

If Executive Paper is borrowing for a short period or has some large bills coming up for payment, you want to make sure that it can lay its hands on the cash when it is needed. The company's bankers and suppliers also need to keep an eye on Executive's liquidity. They know that illiquid firms are more likely to fail and default on their debts.

Another reason that analysts focus on liquid assets is that the figures are often more reliable. The book value of Executive's newsprint mill may be a poor guide to its true value, but at least you know what its cash in the bank is worth. Liquidity ratios also have some *less* desirable characteristics. Because short-term assets and liabilities are easily changed, measures of liquidity can rapidly become out-of-date. You may not know what that newsprint mill is worth, but you can be fairly sure that it won't disappear overnight.

Current Ratio   Executive Paper's current assets consist of cash and assets that can readily be turned into cash. Its current liabilities consist of payments that the company expects to make in the near future. Thus the ratio of the current assets to the current liabilities measures the margin of liquidity. It is known as the *current ratio:*

$$\text{Current ratio} = \frac{\text{current assets}}{\text{current liabilities}} = \frac{900}{460} = 1.96$$

Rapid decreases in the current ratio sometimes signify trouble. However, they can also be misleading. For example, suppose that a company borrows a large sum from the bank and invests it in short-term securities. If nothing else happens, net working capital is unaffected, but the current ratio changes. For this reason it might be preferable to net off the short-term investments and the short-term debt when calculating the current ratio.

Quick (or Acid-Test) Ratio   Some assets are closer to cash than others. If trouble comes, inventories may not sell at anything above fire-sale prices. (Trouble typically comes *because* customers are not buying and the firm's warehouse is stuffed with unwanted goods.) Thus, managers often focus only on cash, short-term securities, and bills that customers have not yet paid:

$$\text{Quick ratio} = \frac{(\text{cash} + \text{short-term securities} + \text{receivables})}{\text{current liabilities}}$$

$$= \frac{110 + 440}{460} = 1.20$$

Cash Ratio   A company's most liquid assets are its holdings of cash and marketable securities. That is why analysts also look at the cash ratio:

$$\text{Cash ratio} = \frac{(\text{cash} + \text{short-term securities})}{\text{current liabilities}} = \frac{110}{460} = .24$$

Of course, these summary measures of liquidity are just that. They are no substitute for detailed plans to ensure that the company can pay its bills. In Chapter 20 we will describe how companies forecast their cash needs and draw up a short-term financial plan to deal with any cash shortage.

How Productively Is Executive Paper Using Its Assets?

Financial analysts employ another set of ratios to judge how efficiently the firm is using its investment in current and fixed assets. Later in the chapter we will look at the financial implications of Executive's ambitious plans to expand output, but understanding the investment in fixed assets and working capital that is needed to support Executive Paper's *current* output may help to uncover any inconsistencies in these plans for the future.

Sales-to-Assets (or Asset Turnover) Ratio   The sales-to-assets ratio shows how hard the firm's assets are being put to use:

$$\frac{\text{Sales}}{\text{average total assets}} = \frac{2{,}200}{(1{,}380.8 + 1{,}450)/2} = 1.55$$

Assets here are measured as the sum of current and fixed assets. Notice that since assets are likely to change over the course of a year, we use the *average* of the assets at the beginning and end of the year. Averages are commonly used whenever a *flow* figure (in this case, sales) is compared with a *stock* or snapshot figure (total assets).

A high sales-to-assets ratio may have several causes: (1) The company uses its assets efficiently; (2) it is working close to capacity, so that it may be difficult to increase sales without additional invested capital; or (3) the firm produces high volume, low margin products. You need to dig deeper to know which explanation is correct. Remember our earlier comment—financial ratios help you to *ask* the right questions, not to *answer* them.

Instead of looking at the ratio of sales to total assets, managers sometimes look at how hard particular types of capital are being put to use. For example, they might calculate Executive's ratio of sales to net working capital.

Days in Inventory   The speed with which a company turns over its inventory is measured by the number of days that it takes for the goods to be produced and sold. First convert the cost of goods sold to a daily basis by dividing by 365. Then express inventories as a multiple of the daily cost of goods sold:

$$\text{Days in inventory} = \frac{\text{average inventory}}{\text{cost of goods sold}/365}$$
$$= \frac{(339.9 + 350)/2}{1{,}980/365} = 63.6 \text{ days}$$

Average Collection Period   The average collection period measures how quickly customers pay their bills:

$$\text{Average collection period} = \frac{\text{average receivables}}{\text{sales}/365}$$
$$= \frac{(433.1 + 440)/2}{2{,}200/365} = 72.4 \text{ days}$$

The collection period for Executive Paper is longer than that of many paper companies. Perhaps Executive has a conscious policy of offering attractive credit terms to lure business, but it is worth looking at whether the credit manager is lax in chasing up the slow payers.

How Profitable Is Executive Paper?

Net Profit Margin   If you want to know the proportion of sales that finds its way into profits, you look at the profit margin. Thus[7]

$$\text{Net profit margin} = \frac{(\text{EBIT} - \text{tax})}{\text{sales}} = \frac{166.7 - 49.7}{2,200} = .053, \text{ or } 5.3\%$$

Return on Assets (ROA)   Managers often measure the performance of the firm by the ratio of income to total assets (income is usually defined as earnings before interest but after taxes). This is known as the firm's *return on assets* (ROA) or *return on investment* (ROI):[8]

$$\text{Return on assets} = \frac{(\text{EBIT} - \text{tax})}{(\text{average total assets})}$$

$$= \frac{(166.7 - 49.7)}{(1,380.8 + 1,450)/2} = .083, \text{ or } 8.3\%$$

Another measure focuses on the return on the firm's equity:

$$\text{Return on equity (ROE)} = \frac{(\text{earnings available for common stockholders})}{\text{average equity}}$$

$$= \frac{74.5}{(509.3 + 540)/2} = .142, \text{ or } 14.2\%$$

It is natural to compare the return earned by Executive Paper with the opportunity cost of capital. Of course, the assets in the financial statements are shown at *net book value,* that is, original cost less depreciation. So a low ROA does not necessarily imply that those assets could be better employed elsewhere. Nor would a high ROA necessarily mean that you could buy similar assets today and get a high return.

---

[7] Net profit margin is sometimes measured as net income ÷ sales. This ignores the profits that are paid out to debt-holders as interest and should therefore not be used to compare firms with different capital structures.

   When making comparisons between firms, it makes sense to recognize that firms that pay more interest pay less tax. We suggest that you calculate the tax that the company would pay if it were all-equity-financed. To do this you need to adjust taxes by adding back interest tax shields (interest payments × marginal tax rate). Using an assumed tax rate of 40%,

$$\text{Net profit margin} = \frac{\text{EBIT} - (\text{tax} + \text{interest tax shields})}{\text{sales}}$$

$$= \frac{166.7 - [49.7 + (.4 \times 42.5)]}{2,200} = 0.45, \text{ or } 4.5\%$$

[8] When comparing the returns on total assets of firms with different capital structures, it makes sense to add back interest tax shields to tax payments (see footnote 7). This adjusted ratio then measures the returns that the company would have earned if it were all-equity-financed.

   One other point about return on assets. Since profits are a flow figure and assets are a snapshot figure, analysts commonly divide profits by the average of assets at the start and end of the year. The reason that they do this is that the firm may raise large amounts of new capital during the year and then put it to work. Therefore part of the year's earnings is a return on this new capital.

   However, this measure is potentially misleading and should not be compared closely with the cost of capital. After all, when we defined the return that shareholders require from investing in the capital market, we divided expected profit by the initial outlay, not by an average of starting and ending values.

In a competitive industry, firms can expect to earn only their cost of capital. Therefore, managers whose businesses are earning more than the cost of capital are likely to earn a pat on the back, while those that are earning a low return may face some tough questions or worse. Although shareholders like to see their companies earn a high return on assets, consumers' groups or regulators often regard a high return as evidence that the firm is charging excessive prices. Naturally, such conclusions are seldom cut and dried. There is plenty of room for argument as to whether the return on assets is properly measured or whether it exceeds the cost of capital.

Payout Ratio   The payout ratio measures the proportion of earnings that is paid out as dividends. Thus

$$\text{Payout ratio} = \frac{\text{dividends}}{\text{earnings}} = \frac{43.8}{74.5} = .6$$

We saw in Section 13.3 that managers don't like to cut dividends if there is a shortfall in earnings. Therefore, if a company's earnings are particularly variable, management is likely to play it safe by setting a low average payout ratio. When earnings fall unexpectedly, the payout ratio will rise temporarily. Likewise, if earnings are expected to rise next year, management may feel that it can pay somewhat more generous dividends than it would otherwise have done.

How Highly Is Executive Paper Valued by Investors?

There is no law that prohibits you from introducing data that are not in the company accounts. For example, when you are assessing Executive Paper's efficiency, you might wish to look at the cost per ton of paper produced. Similarly, an airline might calculate revenue per passenger mile flown, and so on.

If you want to gauge how highly Executive Paper is valued by investors, then you will need to calculate ratios that combine accounting and stock market data. Here are three examples.

Price–Earnings Ratio   The price–earnings, or P/E, ratio measures the price that investors are prepared to pay for each dollar of earnings. In the case of Executive Paper

$$\text{P/E ratio} = \frac{\text{stock price}}{\text{earnings per share}} = \frac{50}{5.26} = 9.5$$

A high P/E ratio may indicate that investors think the firm has good growth opportunities or that its earnings are relatively safe and therefore more valuable. Of course, it may also mean that earnings are temporarily depressed. If a company just breaks even with zero earnings, its P/E ratio is infinite.

Dividend Yield   Executive's dividend yield is simply its dividend as a proportion of the stock price. Thus

$$\text{Dividend yield} = \frac{\text{dividend per share}}{\text{stock price}} = \frac{3.09}{50} = .062, \text{ or } 6.2\%$$

Remember that the return to an investor comes in two forms—dividend yield and capital appreciation. A high dividend yield may indicate that investors are demanding a relatively high rate of return or that they are not expecting rapid dividend growth with consequent capital gains.

Market-to-Book Ratio   The market-to-book ratio is the ratio of the stock price to book value per share. For Executive Paper

$$\text{Market-to-book ratio} = \frac{\text{stock price}}{\text{book value per share}} = \frac{50}{540/14.16} = 1.3$$

Book value per share is just stockholders' book equity divided by the number of shares outstanding. Book equity equals common stock plus retained earnings—the net amount that the firm has received from stockholders or reinvested on their behalf.[9] Thus Executive Paper's market-to-book ratio of 1.3 means that the firm is worth 30% more than past and present stockholders have put into it.

The Dupont System

Some of the profitability and efficiency ratios that we described above can be linked in useful ways. These relationships are often referred to as the **Dupont system,** in recognition of the chemical company that popularized them.

The first relationship links the return on assets (ROA) with the firm's sales-to-assets ratio and its profit margin:

$$\text{ROA} = \frac{\text{EBIT} - \text{tax}}{\text{assets}} = \underset{\underset{\substack{\text{sales-to-}\\\text{assets ratio}}}{\uparrow}}{\frac{\text{sales}}{\text{assets}}} \times \underset{\underset{\substack{\text{profit}\\\text{margin}}}{\uparrow}}{\frac{\text{EBIT} - \text{tax}}{\text{sales}}}$$

All firms would like to earn a higher return on assets but their ability to do so is limited by competition. If the expected return on assets is fixed by competition, firms face a trade-off between the sales-to-assets ratio and the profit margin. For example, fast-food chains, which turn over their capital frequently, also tend to operate on low profit margins. Classy hotels have relatively high margins, but this is offset by lower sales-to-assets ratios.

Firms often seek to increase their profit margins by becoming more vertically integrated; for example, they may acquire a supplier or one of their sales outlets. Unfortunately, unless they have some special skill in running these new businesses, they are likely to find that any gain in profit margin is offset by a decline in the sales-to-assets ratio.

The return on equity (ROE) can be broken down as follows:

$$\text{ROE} = \frac{\text{EBIT} - \text{tax} - \text{interest}}{\text{equity}}$$

$$= \underset{\underset{\substack{\text{leverage}\\\text{ratio}}}{\uparrow}}{\frac{\text{assets}}{\text{equity}}} \times \underset{\underset{\substack{\text{sales-to-}\\\text{assets}\\\text{ratio}}}{\uparrow}}{\frac{\text{sales}}{\text{assets}}} \times \underset{\underset{\substack{\text{profit}\\\text{margin}}}{\uparrow}}{\frac{\text{EBIT} - \text{tax}}{\text{sales}}} \times \underset{\underset{\substack{\text{"debt}\\\text{burden"}}}{\uparrow}}{\frac{\text{EBIT} - \text{tax} - \text{interest}}{(\text{EBIT} - \text{tax})}}$$

---

[9] Retained earnings are measured net of depreciation. They represent stockholders' new investment in the business over and above the amount needed to maintain the firm's existing stock of assets.

Notice that the product of the two middle terms is the return on assets. This depends on the firm's production and marketing skills and is unaffected by the financing mix. However, the first and fourth terms do depend on the debt–equity mix.[10] The first term measures the ratio of gross assets to equity, while the last term measures the extent to which profits are reduced by interest. If the firm is leveraged, the first term is greater than 1.0 (assets are greater than equity) and the fourth term is less than 1.0 (part of the profits are absorbed by interest). Thus, leverage can either increase or reduce the return on equity. In the case of Executive Paper

$$\text{ROE} = \text{leverage ratio} \times \text{sales-to-assets ratio} \times \text{profit margin} \times \text{debt burden}$$
$$= 2.70 \times 1.55 \times .053 \times .637 = .14$$

So, for Executive Paper the leverage ratio (2.70) more than offsets the debt burden (.637). Executive's leverage increases its return on equity.

Industry Comparisons

If you are analyzing Executive Paper's financial standing, it makes sense to look at how it stacks up against its competitors. A good starting point is to prepare *common-size financial statements* for each firm. In this case all items in the balance sheet are expressed as a percentage of total assets and all items in the income statement are expressed as a percentage of revenues.

We have not calculated here common-size statements for Executive Paper, but Tables 19.5 and 19.6 provide summary common-size statements for a sample of U.S. industries. Notice the large variations. For example, retail firms have a major investment in inventory; software companies have almost none. High-tech businesses, such as semiconductors, hold huge amounts of cash; utilities hold very little.[11] Oil companies and utilities invest principally in fixed assets; software companies and computer manufacturers have mainly current assets.

Table 19.7 lists some financial ratios for these companies. The variation between industries also shows up in many of these ratios. These differences arise partly from chance; in 2005 the sun shone more kindly on some industries than on others. But the differences also reflect more fundamental industry factors. For example, notice the high debt ratios of utilities. By contrast, semiconductor producers and software companies scarcely borrow at all. We pointed out earlier that some businesses are able to generate a high level of sales from relatively few assets. For example, you can see that the sales-to-assets ratio for retailers is more than three times that for pharmaceutical companies. But competition ensures that retailers earn a correspondingly lower margin on their sales. The net effect is that the return on assets is broadly similar for the two groups of companies.

---

[10] There is a complication here because the amount of tax paid does depend on the financing mix. We suggested in footnote 7 that it would be better to add back any interest tax shields to the tax payment when calculating the firm's profit margin.

[11] We return to this difference in Chapter 20.

TABLE 19.5

	Industrials	Paper	Oil	Chemicals	Metals	Machinery	Pharmaceuticals	Computers	Software	Semiconductors	Telecoms	Utilities	Food	Retail
Assets:														
Cash & securities	14	5	7	6	11	12	25	26	31	43	3	2	4	12
Receivables	12	14	11	15	15	18	10	17	13	11	5	7	11	7
Inventory	9	10	4	11	14	13	9	6	1	9	1	2	11	27
Other current assets	4	2	2	3	4	5	5	6	5	4	3	7	3	3
Total current assets	39	31	23	34	43	48	49	54	49	66	12	18	28	49
Fixed assets	54	78	104	90	63	38	33	25	20	43	121	88	58	61
Depreciation	25	41	39	55	35	21	13	14	11	25	73	31	30	25
Net fixed assets	29	37	65	36	27	17	20	11	9	19	49	57	28	36
Other long-term assets	32	32	12	30	30	35	31	35	43	16	40	25	44	16
Total assets	100	100	100	100	100	100	100	100	100	100	100	100	100	100
Liabilities:														
Short-term debt	3	5	1	6	2	5	5	2	1	1	3	5	6	2
Payables	8	8	12	7	9	7	3	13	3	9	3	4	7	16
Other current liabilities	13	11	8	10	11	12	13	19	22	11	8	10	11	13
Total current liabilities	24	24	21	23	22	24	21	34	26	21	14	19	24	31
Long-term debt	18	24	17	22	18	14	12	8	7	8	31	32	28	14
Other long-term liabilities	14	15	19	22	17	10	7	10	12	3	21	26	14	7
Equity	45	37	44	33	43	51	59	49	55	69	34	23	33	48
Total liabilities	100	100	100	100	100	100	100	100	100	100	100	100	100	100

Common-size balance sheets in 2005 for U.S. companies in Standard & Poor's Composite Index. Entries for each company are expressed as a percentage of total assets and then averaged by industry. Some columns do not add up because of rounding.

Source: Compustat.

	Indus-trials	Paper	Oil	Chem-icals	Metals	Machinery	Pharma-ceuticals	Computers	Soft-ware	Semicon-ductors	Tele-coms	Utilities	Food	Retail
Revenues	100	100	100	100	100	100	100	100	100	100	100	100	100	100
Costs	79.1	83.4	63.0	81.1	84.2	83.2	68.9	84.1	77.6	73.6	60.9	76.5	82.7	90.1
Depreciation	5.5	4.9	10.3	5.9	3.4	3.7	6.3	3.5	5.1	7.1	18.4	9.1	3.9	2.3
EBIT	15.4	11.7	26.7	13.0	12.4	13.0	24.8	12.4	17.3	19.2	20.7	14.4	13.4	7.5
Interest	2.0	2.0	3.0	2.0	1.2	1.2	1.1	0.7	0.5	0.5	6.2	6.8	2.0	0.6
Nonoperating income & special items	0.0	-0.3	-0.1	-0.9	-0.3	0.4	-1.2	0.1	0.6	0.2	0.8	2.7	0.0	0.2
Pretax income	13.4	9.3	23.6	10.1	11.0	12.2	22.5	11.8	20.3	18.9	15.2	10.2	11.4	7.1
Tax	4.4	2.5	8.6	3.0	2.8	3.3	6.5	3.2	6.8	5.2	5.1	3.3	3.5	2.4
Minority interests	0.1	0.1	0.1	0.2	0.5	0.0	0.2	0.0	0.1	-0.1	0.5	-0.2	0.1	0.0
Net income	8.9	6.7	14.9	6.9	7.7	8.8	15.8	8.5	13.4	13.8	9.5	7.0	7.8	4.7

TABLE 19.6

Common-size income statements in 2005 for U.S. companies in Standard & Poor's Composite Index. Entries for each company are expressed as a percentage of revenues and then averaged by industry. Some columns do not add up because of rounding.

Source: Compustat.

	Indus-trials	Paper	Oil	Chem-icals	Metals	Machinery	Pharma-ceuticals	Computers	Soft-ware	Semicon-ductors	Tele-coms	Utilities	Food	Retail
Debt ratio (%)	28.5	39.3	27.9	40.1	30.2	21.5	17.3	14.4	10.7	10.4	47.5	57.8	45.3	22.9
Current ratio	1.62	1.31	1.15	1.50	1.96	1.93	2.28	1.65	1.87	3.22	.86	.96	1.13	1.60
Quick ratio	1.08	.78	.86	.89	1.17	1.21	1.64	1.29	1.66	2.62	.63	.48	.59	.63
Cash ratio	.59	.19	.33	.25	.49	.48	1.18	.78	1.18	2.07	.25	.13	.16	.39
Sales-to-assets ratio	1.03	.95	1.21	.85	1.15	.96	.64	1.07	.72	.90	.45	.42	1.16	2.21
Sales to net working capital ratio	6.8	11.6	41.4	6.6	5.8	4.1	2.3	5.2	3.0	2.0	*	*	28.6	11.8
Inventory turnover	9.6	8.2	26.4	8.3	6.3	6.6	9.7	14.7	114.8	9.7	147.5	37.5	7.9	3.3
Receivables turnover	8.8	7.0	11.9	5.7	7.6	5.3	6.4	6.7	5.6	8.1	8.6	6.8	10.7	31.3
Net profit margin (%)	11.0	9.3	18.1	9.9	9.6	9.7	18.2	9.2	10.4	14.0	15.5	11.1	9.9	5.1
Return on assets (%)	12.6	11.0	20.1	10.4	13.5	12.4	15.1	10.5	13.9	12.5	9.2	6.1	13.7	14.4
Return on equity (%)	17.1	17.6	27.1	18.4	20.4	16.3	17.0	15.0	14.9	12.4	12.3	11.5	24.1	18.8

TABLE 19.7

Selected 2005 financial ratios for U.S. companies in Standard & Poor's Composite Index.

* Negative net working capital.

Source: Compustat.

19.4   FINANCIAL PLANNING

Financial statements not only help you to understand the past but they also provide the starting point for developing a financial plan for the future. Here is where finance and strategy need to come together. A coherent financial plan demands an understanding of how the firm can generate superior long-term returns by its choice of industry and by the way that it positions itself within that industry.

When companies prepare a financial plan, they don't look just at the most likely outcomes. They also plan for the unexpected. One way to do this is to work through the consequences of the plan under the most likely set of circumstances and then use *sensitivity analysis* to vary the assumptions one at a time. Another approach is to look at the implications of different plausible scenarios. For example, one scenario might envisage high interest rates leading to a slowdown in economic growth and lower commodity prices. Another scenario might involve a buoyant domestic economy, high inflation, and a weak currency. And so on.

19.5   FINANCIAL PLANNING MODELS

Back to Executive Paper. Suppose that the company management's analysis of the industry leads it to forecast a 20% annual growth in Executive Paper's sales and profits over the next five years. Can the company realistically expect to finance this out of retained earnings and borrowing, or should it plan for an issue of equity? Spreadsheet programs are tailor-made for such questions. Let's investigate.

The basic sources and uses relationship tells us that

External capital required = investment in net working capital
+ investment in fixed assets
+ dividends
− operating cash flow

Thus there are four steps to finding how much extra cash Executive Paper will need and the implications for its debt ratio:

Step 1   Project next year's operating cash flow (depreciation provision plus net income) assuming the planned 20% increase in revenues. This gives the total sources of funds in the absence of any new issue of securities. Look, for example, at the second column of Table 19.8, which provides a forecast of operating cash flow in year 2006 for Executive Paper.

Step 2   Project what additional investment in net working capital and fixed assets will be needed to support this increased activity and how much of the net income will be paid out as dividends. The sum of these expenditures gives you the total *uses* of funds. The second column of Table 19.9 provides a forecast of uses of funds for Executive Paper.

	2005	2006	2010
Revenues	2,200	2,640	5,474
Costs (90% of revenues)	1,980	2,376	4,927
Depreciation (10% of fixed assets at start of year)	53.3	55.0	114.0
EBIT	166.7	209.0	433.4
Interest (10% of long-term debt at start of year)	42.5	45.0	131.3
Tax (40% of pretax profit)	49.7	65.6	120.8
Net income	74.5	98.4	181.2
Operating cash flow	127.8	153.4	295.3

TABLE 19.8

Latest and pro forma income statements for Executive Paper (figures in $ millions).

Visit us at
www.mhhe.com/bma1e.

	2005	2006	2010
Increase in net working capital (NWC) assuming NWC = 20% of revenues	38.5	88.0	182.5
Investment in fixed assets (FA) assuming net FA = 25% of revenues	70.5	165.0	342.1
Dividend (60% of net income)	43.8	59.0	108.7
Total use of funds	152.8	312.0	633.4
External capital required = total uses of funds – operating cash flow	25.0	158.6	338.1

TABLE 19.9

Visit us at
www.mhhe.com/bma1e.

Latest and pro forma income statements of sources and uses of funds for Executive Paper (figures in $ millions).

	2005	2006	2010
Net working capital (20% of revenues)	440	528	1,095
Net fixed assets (25% of revenues)	550	660	1,369
Total net assets	990	1188	2,463
Long-term debt	450	609	1,651
Equity	540	579	812
Total long-term liabilities and equity	990	1,188	2,463

TABLE 19.10

Latest and pro forma balance sheets for Executive Paper (figures in $ millions).

Visit us at
www.mhhe.com/bma1e.

Step 3   Calculate the difference between the projected operating cash flow (from Step 1) and the projected uses (Step 2). This is the cash that will need to be raised from new sales of securities. For example, you can see from Table 19.9 that Executive Paper will need to issue $158.6 million of debt in 2006 if it is to expand at the planned rate and not sell more shares.

Step 4   Finally, construct a pro forma balance sheet that incorporates the additional assets and the increase in debt and equity. This is done in the second column of Table 19.10. Executive Paper's equity increases by the additional retained earnings (net income less dividends), while long-term debt is increased by the $158.6 million new issue.

Once you have set up the spreadsheet, it is easy to run out your projections for several years. The final columns in Tables 19.8–19.10 show the pro forma income statement, sources and uses of funds, and balance sheet for the year 2010, assuming

Executive Paper continues to fund a 20% annual growth rate solely from retained earnings and new debt issues. Over the five-year period Executive Paper would need to borrow an additional $1.2 billion and by year 2010 its debt ratio would have increased to 67%. Most financial managers would regard this as sailing much too close to the wind, and the debt ratio would probably be above the limit set by the company's banks and bondholders.

The obvious solution for Executive Paper is to issue a mix of debt and equity, but there are other possibilities that the financial manager may want to explore. One option may be to hold back dividends during this period of rapid growth. An alternative might be to investigate whether the company could cut back on net working capital. For example, we have seen that Executive Paper's customers take 72 days to pay their bills. Perhaps more careful control of credit collection could help to economize on capital.

We stated earlier that financial planning is not just about exploring how to cope with the most likely outcomes. It also needs to ensure that the firm is prepared for unlikely ones. For example, the paper industry is notoriously exposed to economic downturn. So you would certainly wish to check that Executive Paper could cope with a cyclical decline in sales and profit margins. Sensitivity analysis or scenario analysis can help you to do so.

Pitfalls in Model Design

The Executive Paper model that we have developed is too simple for practical application. You probably have already thought of several ways to improve it—by keeping track of the outstanding shares, for example, and printing out earnings and dividends per share. Or you might want to distinguish between short-term lending and borrowing opportunities, now buried in working capital.

The model that we developed for Executive Paper is known as a *percentage of sales model.* Almost all the forecasts for the company are proportional to the forecasted level of sales. However, in reality many variables will *not* be proportional to sales. For example, important components of working capital such as inventory and cash balances will generally rise less rapidly than sales. In addition, fixed assets such as plant and equipment are typically not added in small increments as sales increase. Executive Paper's plant may well be operating at less than full capacity, so that the company can initially increase output without *any* additions to capacity. Eventually, however, if sales continue to increase, the firm may need to make a large new investment in plant and equipment.

But beware of adding too much complexity: There is always the temptation to make a model bigger and more detailed. You may end up with an exhaustive model that is too cumbersome for routine use. The fascination of detail, if you give in to it, distracts attention from crucial decisions like stock issues and payout policy.

There Is No Finance in Financial Planning Models

Financial planning models help the manager to develop consistent forecasts of crucial financial variables. For example, if you wish to value Executive Paper, you need forecasts of future free cash flows. These are easily derived up to the end of the planning period from our financial planning model.[12]

---

[12] Look back at Table 16.1, where we set out the free cash flows for Rio Corporation. A financial planning model would be a natural tool for deriving these figures.

So why do we say that there is no finance in these planning models? The reason is that they produce no signposts pointing toward optimal decisions. They do not even tell us which alternatives are worth examining. For example, we saw that Executive Paper is planning for a rapid growth in sales and earnings per share. But is that good news for the shareholders? Well, not necessarily; it depends on the opportunity cost of the capital that Executive Paper needs to invest. If the new investment earns more than the cost of capital, it will have a positive NPV and add to shareholder wealth. If the investment earns less than the cost of capital, shareholders will be worse off, even though the company expects steady growth in earnings.

The capital that Executive Paper needs to raise depends on its decision to pay out two-thirds of its earnings as a dividend. But the financial planning model does not tell us whether this dividend payment makes sense or what mixture of equity or debt the company should issue. In the end the management has to decide. We would like to tell you exactly how to make the choice, but we can't. There is no model that encompasses all the complexities encountered in financial planning.

As a matter of fact, there never will be one. This bold statement is based on Brealey, Myers, and Allen's Third Law:[13]

- *Axiom:* The number of unsolved problems is infinite.
- *Axiom:* The number of unsolved problems that humans can hold in their minds is at any time limited to 10.
- *Law:* Therefore in any field there will always be 10 problems that can be addressed but that have no formal solution.

BMA's Third Law implies that no model can find the best of all financial strategies.[14]

19.6   GROWTH AND EXTERNAL FINANCING

We started this chapter by noting that financial plans force managers to be consistent in their goals for growth, investment, and financing. Before leaving the topic of financial planning, we should look at some general relationships between a firm's growth objectives and its financing needs.

Recall that Executive Paper ended 2005 with fixed assets and net working capital of $990 million. In 2006 it plans to plow back $39.4 million, so net assets will increase by 39.4/990, or 3.98%. Thus Executive Paper can grow by 3.98% without needing to raise additional capital. The growth rate that a company can achieve without external funds is known as the **internal growth rate.** For Executive Paper

$$\text{Internal growth rate} = \frac{\text{retained earnings}}{\text{net assets}} = 3.98\%$$

[13] The second law is presented in Section 11.1.
[14] It is possible to build linear programming models that help search for the best strategy subject to specified assumptions and constraints. These models can be more effective in screening alternative financial strategies.

We can gain more insight into what determines this growth rate by multiplying the top and bottom of the expression for internal growth rate by *net income* and *equity* as follows:

$$\text{Internal growth rate} = \frac{\text{retained earnings}}{\text{net income}} \times \frac{\text{net income}}{\text{equity}} \times \frac{\text{equity}}{\text{net assets}}$$

$$= \text{plowback ratio} \times \text{return on equity} \times \frac{\text{equity}}{\text{net assets}}$$

In 2006 Executive Paper expects to plow back 40% of net income and to earn a return of 18.22% on the equity with which it began the year. At the start of the year equity finances 54.55% of Executive Paper's net assets. Therefore

$$\text{Internal growth rate} = .40 \times .1822 \times .5455 = .0398, \text{ or } 3.98\%$$

Notice that if Executive Paper wishes to grow faster than this without raising equity capital, it would need to (1) plow back a higher proportion of its earnings, (2) earn a higher return on equity (ROE), or (3) have a lower debt-to-equity ratio.[15]

Instead of focusing on how rapidly the company can grow without *any* external financing, Executive Paper's financial manager may be interested in the growth rate that can be sustained without additional *equity* issues. Of course, if the firm is able to raise enough debt, virtually any growth rate can be financed. It makes more sense to assume that the firm has settled on an optimal capital structure that it will maintain as equity is increased by the retained earnings. Thus the firm issues only enough debt to keep the debt–equity ratio constant. The **sustainable growth rate** is the highest growth rate the firm can maintain without increasing its financial leverage. It turns out that the sustainable growth rate depends only on the plowback rate and the return on equity:

$$\text{Sustainable growth rate} = \text{plowback ratio} \times \text{return on equity}$$

For Executive Paper,

$$\text{Sustainable growth rate} = .40 \times .1822 = .0729, \text{ or } 7.29\%$$

We first encountered this formula in Chapter 5, where we used it to value common stocks.

These simple formulas remind us that financial plans need to be consistent. Firms may grow rapidly in the short term by relying on debt finance, but such growth cannot be maintained without incurring excessive debt levels.

---

[15] Notice, however, that if assets grow by only 3.98%, either the sales-to-assets ratio or the profit margin must increase to maintain an 18.22% return on equity.

SUMMARY

Managers use financial statements to monitor their own company's performance, to help understand the policies of a competitor, or to check on the health of a customer. But there is a danger of being overwhelmed by the sheer volume of data. That is why managers use a few salient ratios to summarize the firm's leverage, liquidity, efficiency, profitability, and market valuation. We have described some of the more popular financial ratios.

We offer the following general advice to users of these ratios:

1. Financial ratios seldom provide answers, but they do help you to ask the right questions.
2. There is no international standard for financial ratios. A little thought and common sense are worth far more than blind application of formulas.
3. You need a benchmark for assessing a company's financial position. Compare financial ratios with the company's ratios in earlier years and with the ratios of other firms in the same business.

Understanding the past is the first step to being prepared for the future. Most firms prepare a financial plan that describes the firm's strategy and projects its future consequences by means of pro forma balance sheets, income statements, and statements of sources and uses of funds. The plan establishes financial goals and is a benchmark for evaluating subsequent performance.

The plan is the end result, but the process that produces the plan is valuable in its own right. First, planning forces the financial manager to consider the combined effects of all the firm's investment and financing decisions. This is important because these decisions interact and should not be made independently. Second, planning requires the manager to consider events that could upset the firm's progress and to devise strategies to be held in reserve for counterattack when unhappy surprises occur.

There is no theory or model that leads straight to *the* optimal financial strategy. Consequently, financial planning proceeds by trial and error. Many different strategies may be projected under a range of assumptions about the future. The dozens of separate projections that may be made during this trial-and-error process generate a heavy load of arithmetic. Firms have responded by developing corporate financial planning models to forecast the financial consequences of different strategies. We showed how you can use a simple spreadsheet model to analyze Executive Paper's strategies. But remember there is no finance in these models. Their primary purpose is to produce accounting statements.

FURTHER READING

There are some good general texts on financial statement analysis. See, for example:

K. G. Palepu, V. L. Bernard, and P. M. Healy, *Business Analysis and Valuation,* 3rd ed. (Cincinnati, OH: South-Western College Publishing, 2003).

S. Penman, *Financial Statement Analysis and Security Valuation,* 3rd ed. (New York: McGraw-Hill/Irwin, 2006).

Corporate planning has an extensive literature of its own. Good books and articles include:

G. Donaldson, "Financial Goals and Strategic Consequences," *Harvard Business Review* 63 (May–June 1985), pp. 57–66.

G. Donaldson, *Strategy for Financial Mobility* (Boston: Harvard Business School Press, 1986).

A. C. Hax and N. S. Majluf, *The Strategy Concept and Process—A Pragmatic Approach,* 2nd ed. (Englewood Cliffs, NJ: Prentice-Hall, Inc., 1996).

The links between capital budgeting, strategy, and financial planning are discussed in:

S. C. Myers, "Finance Theory and Financial Strategy," *Interfaces* 14 (January–February, 1984), pp. 126–137.

Here are three references on corporate planning models:

W. T. Carleton, C. L. Dick, Jr., and D. H. Downes, "Financial Policy Models: Theory and Practice," *Journal of Financial and Quantitative Analysis* 8 (December 1973), pp. 691–709.

W. T. Carleton and J. M. McInnes, "Theory, Models and Implementation in Financial Management," *Management Science* 28 (September 1982), pp. 957–978.

S. C. Myers and G. A. Pogue, "A Programming Approach to Corporate Financial Management," *Journal of Finance* 29 (May 1974), pp. 579–599.

WEB PROJECTS

STANDARD &POOR'S

1. The Web site **edgarscan.pwcglobal.com** provides a very user-friendly way to compare financial ratios. Use the *Benchmarking Assistant* to enter the name of a large airline. Find and select some peer airlines and then graph their financial ratios. How does the company's financial strength stack up with that of other firms in the airline industry?

2. You can find financial ratios for different industries on the Market Insight database at **www.mhhe.com/edumarketinsight** or on **www.census.gov/csd/qfr.** Can you account for some of the differences between industries?

CONCEPT REVIEW QUESTIONS

1. We said that financial ratios are designed to shed light on five sets of questions. What are those questions? Give an example of each of the five categories of financial ratio. (page 520)

2. The Dupont system expresses the return on assets (ROA) in terms of the sales-to-assets ratio and the profit margin. What is this relationship? Would you expect firms with a high profit margin to have a high ratio of sales to assets? Why or why not? (page 527)

3. List the major elements of a completed financial plan. (pages 532–533)

For a complete listing of your chapter Concept Review Questions, please visit us at www.mhhe.com/bma1e.

QUIZ

1. Table 19.11 gives abbreviated balance sheets and income statements for H. J. Heinz Company. Calculate the following ratios:

   a. Debt ratio.

   b. Times-interest-earned ratio.

   c. Current ratio.

   d. Quick ratio.

   e. Net profit margin.

   f. Days in inventory.

   g. Return on equity.

   h. Payout ratio.

2. There are no universally accepted definitions of financial ratios, but five of the following ratios make no sense at all. Substitute the correct definitions.

   a. Debt–equity ratio = (long-term debt + value of leases)/(long-term debt + value of leases + equity)

   b. Return on equity = (EBIT − tax)/average equity

   c. Payout ratio = dividend/stock price

   d. Profit margin = (EBIT − tax)/sales

   e. Inventory turnover = sales/average inventory

   f. Current ratio = current liabilities/current assets

TABLE 19.11

Income statement and balance sheet for H. J. Heinz Company, 2006 (figures in millions).

Source: H. J. Heinz Company, *2006 Annual Report.*

Income Statement

Net sales	$ 8,643
Cost of goods sold	5,550
Other expenses	1,819
Depreciation	264
Earnings before interest and tax (EBIT)	1,010
Net interest	316
Tax	251
Earnings	$ 443
Dividends	408

Balance Sheet

	End of Year	Start of Year
Cash and short-term securities	$ 446	$ 1,085
Receivables	1,002	1,092
Inventories	1,074	1,257
Other current assets	183	213
Total current assets	2,704	3,646
Tangible fixed assets	1,901	2,164
Other long-term assets	5,133	4,767
Total assets	$ 9,738	$10,577
Short-term debt	$ 55	$ 573
Payables	1,963	1,958
Other current liabilities	0	55
Total current liabilities	2,018	2,587
Long-term debt and capital leases	4,357	4,122
Other long-term liabilities	1,314	1,267
Common shareholders' equity	2,049	2,603
Total liabilities	$ 9,738	$10,577

   g. Sales-to-net-working-capital = average sales/average net working capital

   h. Average collection period = sales/(average receivables/365)

   i. Quick ratio = (current assets − inventories)/current liabilities

3. True or false?

   a. A company's debt–equity ratio is always less than 1.

   b. The quick ratio is always less than the current ratio.

   c. The return on equity is always less than the return on assets.

   d. If a project is slow to reach full profitability, straight-line depreciation is likely to produce an overstatement of profits in the early years.

   e. A substantial new advertising campaign by a cosmetics company will tend to depress earnings and cause the stock to sell at a low price–earnings multiple.

4. A firm has $30,000 of inventory. If this represents 30 days' sales, what is the annual cost of goods sold? What is the inventory turnover ratio?

5. Keller Cosmetics maintains a profit margin of 4% and a sales-to-assets ratio of 3.

   a. What is its return on assets?

   b. If its debt–equity ratio is 1.0, its interest payments and taxes are each $10,000, and EBIT is $40,000, what is the return on equity?

6. A firm has a long-term debt–equity ratio of .4. Shareholders' equity is $1 million. Current assets are $200,000, and the current ratio is 2.0. Long-term assets total $1.5 million. What is the ratio of debt to total long-term capital?

7. Magic Flutes has total receivables of $3,000, which represent 20 days' sales. Average total assets are $75,000. The firm's profit margin is 5%. Find the firm's sales-to-assets ratio and return on assets.

8. Consider this simplified balance sheet for Geomorph Trading:

Current assets	$100	$ 60	Current liabilities
		280	Long-term debt
Long-term assets	500	70	Other liabilities
		190	Equity
	$600	$600	

   a. Calculate the ratio of debt to equity.

   b. What are Geomorph's net working capital and total long-term capital? Calculate the ratio of debt to total long-term capital.

9. Airlux Antarctica has current assets of $300 million, current liabilities of $200 million, and a crash—sorry—*cash* ratio of .05. How much cash and marketable securities does it hold?

10. On average, it takes Microlimp's customers 60 days to pay their bills. If Microlimp has annual sales of $500 million, what is the average value of unpaid bills?

11. True or false?

   a. Financial planning should attempt to minimize risk.

   b. The primary aim of financial planning is to obtain better forecasts of future cash flows and earnings.

   c. Financial planning is necessary because financing and investment decisions interact and should not be made independently.

   d. Firms' planning horizons rarely exceed three years.

   e. Financial planning requires accurate forecasting.

   f. Financial planning models should include as much detail as possible.

12. Table 19.12 summarizes the 2008 income statement and end-year balance sheet of Drake's Bowling Alleys. Drake's financial manager forecasts a 10% increase in sales and costs in 2009. The ratio of sales to *average* assets is expected to remain at .40. Interest is forecasted at 5% of debt at start of year.

   a. What is the implied level of assets at the end of 2009?

   b. If the company pays out 50% of net income as dividends, how much cash will Drake need to raise in the capital markets in 2009?

   c. If Drake is unwilling to make an equity issue, what will be the debt ratio at the end of 2009?

13. Abbreviated financial statements for Archimedes Levers are shown in Table 19.13. If sales increase by 10% in 2008 and all other items, including debt, increase correspondingly, what must be the balancing item? What will be its value?

14. What is the maximum possible growth rate for Archimedes (see Quiz Question 13) if the payout ratio is set at 50% and (a) no external debt or equity is to be issued? (b) the firm maintains a fixed debt ratio but issues no equity?

TABLE 19.12

Financial statement for Drake's Bowling Alleys, 2008 (figures in thousands).

* Assets at end-2007 were $2,400,000.
† Debt at end-2007 was $500,000.

Income Statement	
Sales	$1,000 (40% of average assets)*
Costs	750 (75% of sales)
Interest	25 (5% of debt at start of year)†
Pretax profit	225
Tax	90 (40% of pretax profit)
Net income	$ 135

Balance Sheet			
Assets	$2,600	Debt	$ 500
		Equity	2,100
Total	$2,600	Total	$2,600

TABLE 19.13

Financial statements for Archimedes Levers, 2007.

Income Statement	
Sales	$4,000
Costs, including interest	3,500
Net income	$ 500

Balance Sheet, Year-end						
	2007	2006			2007	2006
Assets	$3,200	$2,700		Debt	$1,200	$1,033
				Equity	2,000	1,667
Total	$3,200	$2,700		Total	$3,200	$2,700

PRACTICE QUESTIONS

15. Look up the latest financial statements for any company on the Market Insight database (**www.mhhe.com/edumarketinsight**) and calculate a sources and uses of funds table for the latest year. Don't be put off by the fact that actual financial statements are more complicated than the simplified ones we showed for Executive Paper.

16. Look up the latest financial statements for any company on **finance.yahoo.com** or the Market Insight database (**www.mhhe.com/edumarketinsight**) and calculate the following ratios for the latest year:

    a. Debt ratio.

    b. Times-interest-earned.

    c. Current ratio.

    d. Quick ratio.

    e. Net profit margin.

    f. Days in inventory.

    g. Return on equity.

    h. Payout ratio.

17. Select a sample of companies with financial statements on **finance.yahoo.com** or the Market Insight database (**www.mhhe.com/edumarketinsight**) and compare the days in inventory and the average collection period for receivables. Can you explain these differences?

18. This question reviews some of the difficulties encountered in interpreting accounting numbers.

   a. Give four examples of important assets, liabilities, or transactions that may not be shown on the company's books.

   b. How does investment in intangible assets, such as research and development, distort accounting ratios? Give at least two examples.

19. Discuss alternative measures of financial leverage. Should the market value of equity be used or the book value? Is it better to use the market value of debt, the book value, or the book value discounted at the risk-free interest rate? How should you treat off-balance-sheet obligations such as pension liabilities? How would you treat preferred stock, deferred tax reserves, and minority interest?

20. Suppose that at year-end 2005 Executive Paper had unused lines of credit that would have allowed it to borrow a further $300 million. Suppose also that it used this line of credit to raise short-term loans of $300 million and invested the proceeds in marketable securities. Would the company have appeared to be (a) more or less liquid? (b) more or less highly levered? Calculate the appropriate ratios.

21. How would the following actions affect a firm's current ratio?

   a. Inventory is sold.

   b. The firm takes out a bank loan to pay its suppliers.

   c. A customer pays its overdue bills.

   d. The firm uses cash to purchase additional inventories.

22. Sara Togas sells all its output to Federal Stores. The following table shows selected financial data, in millions, for the two firms:

	Sales	Profits	Assets
Federal Stores	$100	$10	$50
Sara Togas	20	4	20

Calculate the sales-to-assets ratio, the profit margin, and the return on the two firms. Now assume that the two companies merge. If Federal continues to sell goods worth $100 million, how will the three financial ratios change?

23. United Ratio's common stock has a dividend yield of 4%. Its dividend per share is $2, and it has 10 million shares outstanding. If the market-to-book ratio is 1.5, what is the total book value of the equity?

24. As you can see, someone has spilled ink over some of the entries in the balance sheet and income statement of Transylvania Railroad (Table 19.14). Can you use the following information to work out the missing entries?

   • Debt ratio: .4.

   • Times-interest-earned: 11.2.

   • Current ratio: 1.4.

   • Quick ratio: 1.0.

   • Cash ratio: .2.

   • Return on total assets: .18.

   • Return on equity: .41.

   • Inventory turnover: 5.0.

   • Receivables' collection period: 71.2 days.

	December 2007	December 2006
Balance Sheet		
Cash	■■■	20
Accounts receivable	■■■	34
Inventory	■■■	26
Total current assets	■■■	80
Fixed assets, net	■■■	25
Total	■■■	105
Notes payable	30	35
Accounts payable	25	20
Total current liabilities	■■■	55
Long-term debt	■■■	20
Equity	■■■	30
Total	115	105
Income Statement		
Sales	■■■	
Cost of goods sold	■■■	
Selling, general, and administrative expenses	10	
Depreciation	20	
EBIT	■■■	
Interest	■■■	
Earnings before tax	■■■	
Tax	■■■	
Earnings available for common stock	■■■	

TABLE 19.14

Balance sheet and income statement of Transylvania Railroad (figures in $ millions).

25. Here are some data for five companies in the same industry:

	Company Code				
	A	**B**	**C**	**D**	**E**
Net income (millions)	$ 10	$ .5	$ 6.67	−$ 1	$ 6.67
Total book assets (millions)	$300	$30	$120	$50	$120
Shares outstanding (millions)	3	4	2	5	10
Share price	$100	$ 5	$ 50	$ 8	$ 10

You have been asked to calculate a measure of the industry price–earnings ratio. Discuss the possible ways that you might calculate such a measure. Does changing the method of calculation make a significant difference to the end result?

26. How would rapid inflation affect the accuracy and relevance of a manufacturing company's balance sheet and income statement? Does your answer depend on how much debt the company has issued?

27. Suppose you wish to use financial ratios to estimate the risk of a company's stock. Which of those that we have described in this chapter are likely to be helpful? Can you think of other accounting measures of risk?

28. Look up some firms that have been in trouble. Plot the changes over the preceding years in the principal financial ratios. Are there any patterns?

29. Our model of Executive Paper is an example of a top-down planning model. Some firms use a bottom-up financial planning model, which incorporates forecasts of

revenues and costs for particular products, advertising plans, major investment projects, and so on. What sort of firms would you expect to use each type, and what would they use them for?

30. Corporate financial plans are often used as a basis for judging subsequent performance. What do you think can be learned from such comparisons? What problems are likely to arise, and how might you cope with these problems?

31. The balancing item in the Executive Paper model is borrowing. What is meant by *balancing item*? How would the model change if dividends were made the balancing item instead? In that case how would you suggest that planned borrowing be determined?

32. Construct a new model for Executive Paper based on your answer to Practice Question 31. Does your model generate a feasible financial plan for 2006? (*Hint:* If it doesn't, you may have to allow the firm to issue stock.)

33. **a.** Use the Executive Paper model (Tables 19.8–19.10) and the "live" spreadsheets on the book's Web site at **www.mhhe.com/bma1e** to produce pro forma income statements, balance sheets, and sources and uses of funds statements for 2006 and 2007. Assume business as usual except that now sales and costs are planned to expand by 30% per year, as are fixed assets and net working capital. The interest rate is forecasted to remain at 10% and stock issues are ruled out. Executive Paper also sticks to its 60% dividend payout ratio.

b. What are the firm's debt ratio and interest coverage under this plan?

c. Can the company continue to finance expansion by borrowing?

34. Table 19.15 shows the 2007 financial statements for the Executive Cheese Company. Annual depreciation is 10% of fixed assets at the beginning of the year, plus 10% of new investment. The company plans to invest a further $200 thousand per year in fixed assets for the next five years and net working capital is expected to remain a constant proportion of fixed assets. The company forecasts that the ratio of revenues to total assets at the start of each year will remain at 1.75. Fixed costs are expected to remain at $53, and variable costs at 80% of revenue. The company's policy is to pay out two-thirds of net income as dividends and to maintain a book debt ratio of 20%.

a. Construct a model for Executive Cheese like the one in Tables 19.8–19.10.

b. Use your model to produce a set of financial statements for 2008.

35. The financial statements of Eagle Sport Supply are shown in Table 19.16. For simplicity, "Costs" include interest. Assume that Eagle's assets are proportional to its sales.

a. Find Eagle's required external funds if it maintains a dividend payout ratio of 60% and plans a growth rate of 15% in 2009.

b. If Eagle chooses not to issue new shares of stock, what variable must be the balancing item? What will its value be?

c. Now suppose that the firm plans instead to increase long-term debt only to $1,100 and does not wish to issue any new shares of stock. Why must the dividend payment now be the balancing item? What will its value be?

36. **a.** What is the internal growth rate of Eagle Sport (see Practice Problem 35) if the dividend payout ratio is fixed at 60% and the equity-to-asset ratio is fixed at 2/3?

b. What is the sustainable growth rate?

37. Bio-Plasma Corp. is growing at 30% per year. It is all-equity-financed and has total assets of $1 million. Its return on equity is 20%. Its plowback ratio is 40%.

a. What is the internal growth rate?

b. What is the firm's need for external financing this year?

c. By how much would the firm increase its internal growth rate if it reduced its payout rate to zero?

Income Statement	
Revenue	$1,785
Fixed costs	53
Variable costs (80% of revenue)	1,428
Depreciation	80
Interest (at 11.8%)	24
Taxes (at 40%)	80
Net income	$ 120

Sources and Uses of Funds	
Sources:	
Operating cash flow	$ 200
Borrowing	36
Stock issues	104
Total sources	$ 340
Uses:	
Increase in net working capital	$ 60
Investment	200
Dividends	80
Total uses	$ 340

Balance Sheet, Year-end		
	2007	**2006**
Assets:		
Net working capital	$ 400	$ 340
Fixed assets	800	680
Total assets	$1,200	$1,020
Liabilities:		
Debt	$ 240	$ 204
Book equity	960	816
Total liabilities	$1,200	$1,020

TABLE 19.15

Financial statements for Executive Cheese Company, 2007 (figures in thousands).

Income Statement	
Sales	$950
Costs	250
EBIT	700
Taxes (tax rate = 28.6%)	200
Net income	$500

Balance Sheet, Year-end					
	2008	**2007**		**2008**	**2007**
Assets	$3,000	$2,700	Debt	$1,000	$ 900
			Equity	2,000	1,800
Total	$3,000	$2,700	Total	$3,000	$2,700

TABLE 19.16

Financial statements for Eagle Sport Supply, 2008.

d. By how much would such a move reduce the need for external financing? What do you conclude about the relationship between dividend policy and requirements for external financing?

CHALLENGE QUESTIONS

STANDARD &POOR'S

38. Take another look at Geomorph Trading's balance sheet in Quiz Question 8, and consider the following additional information:

Current Assets		Current Liabilities		Other Liabilities	
Cash	$ 15	Payables	$35	Deferred tax	$32
Inventories	35	Taxes due	10	Unfunded pensions	22
Receivables	50	Bank loan	15	R&R reserve	16
	$100		$60		$70

The "R&R reserve" covers the future costs of removal of an oil pipeline and environmental restoration of the pipeline route.

There are many ways to calculate a debt ratio for Geomorph. Suppose you are evaluating the safety of Geomorph's debt and want a debt ratio for comparison with the ratios of other companies in the same industry. Would you calculate the ratio in terms of total liabilities or total capitalization? What would you include in debt—the bank loan, the deferred tax account, the R&R reserve, the unfunded pension liability? Explain the pros and cons of these choices.

39. Take any firm whose financial statements are shown on the Market Insight database (**www.mhhe.com/edumarketinsight**) and make some plausible forecasts for future growth and the asset base needed to support that growth. Then use a spreadsheet program to develop a five-year financial plan. What financing is needed to support the planned growth? How vulnerable is the company to an error in your forecasts?

20

SHORT-TERM FINANCIAL PLANNING

IN THE LAST CHAPTER we looked at how firms develop financial plans for the next 5 or 10 years. Our focus in this chapter is on short-term planning. Short-term financial decisions differ in two ways from long-term decisions such as capital investment and the choice of capital structure. First, they generally involve short-lived assets and liabilities, and, second, they are usually easily reversed. Compare, for example, a 60-day bank loan for $50 million with a $50 million issue of 20-year bonds. The bank loan is clearly a short-term decision. The firm can repay it two months later and be right back where it started. A firm might conceivably issue a 20-year bond in January and retire it in March, but it would be extremely inconvenient and expensive to do so. In practice, such a bond issue is a long-term decision, not only because of the bond's 20-year maturity but also because the decision to issue it cannot be reversed on short notice.

A financial manager responsible for short-term financial decisions does not have to look far into the future. The decision to take the 60-day bank loan could properly be based on cash-flow forecasts for the next few months only. The bond issue decision will normally reflect forecasted cash requirements 5, 10, or more years into the future.

Managers concerned with short-term financial decisions can avoid many of the difficult conceptual issues encountered elsewhere in this book. In a sense, short-term decisions are easier than long-term decisions, but they are not less important. A firm can identify extremely valuable capital investment opportunities, find the precise optimal debt ratio, follow the perfect dividend policy, and yet founder because no one bothers to raise the cash to pay this year's bills. Hence the need for short-term planning.

We start the chapter by showing how long-term financing decisions affect the firm's short-term financial planning problem. We describe how financial managers trace changes in cash and working capital, and we look at how they forecast month-by-month cash requirements or surpluses and develop short-term financing strategies. We conclude by examining more closely the principal sources of short-term finance, and the possible parking places for any surplus cash.

20.1   LINKS BETWEEN LONG-TERM AND SHORT-TERM FINANCING DECISIONS

All businesses require capital, that is, money invested in plant, machinery, inventories, accounts receivable, and all the other assets it takes to run a business efficiently. Typically, these assets are not purchased all at once but obtained gradually over time. Let us call the total cost of these assets the firm's *cumulative capital requirement*.

For most firms the cumulative capital requirement grows irregularly, like the wavy line in Figure 20.1. This line shows a clear upward trend as the firm's business grows. But there is also seasonal variation around the trend: in the figure, the capital requirements peak late in each year. Finally, there would be unpredictable week-to-week and month-to-month fluctuations, but we have not attempted to show these in Figure 20.1.

The cumulative capital requirement can be met either from long-term or short-term financing. When long-term financing does not cover the cumulative capital requirement, the firm must raise short-term capital to make up the difference. When long-term financing *more* than covers the cumulative capital requirement, the firm has surplus cash available. Thus the amount of long-term financing raised, given the capital requirement, determines whether the firm is a short-term borrower or lender.

Lines *A*, *B*, and *C* in Figure 20.1 illustrate this. Each depicts a different long-term financing strategy. Strategy *A* always implies a cash surplus, which can be invested in short-term securities. Strategy *C* implies a permanent need for short-term borrowing. Under *B*, which is probably the most common strategy, the firm is a short-term lender during part of the year and a borrower during the rest.

What is the *best* level of long-term financing relative to the cumulative capital requirement? It is hard to say. There is no convincing theoretical analysis of this question. We can make practical observations, however. First, most financial managers attempt to "match maturities" of assets and liabilities.[1] That is, they largely finance long-lived assets like plant and machinery with long-term borrowing and equity. Second, most firms make a permanent investment in net working capital (current assets less current liabilities). This investment is financed from long-term sources.

Current assets can be converted into cash more easily than can long-term assets. So firms with large holdings of current assets enjoy greater liquidity. Of course, some of these assets are more liquid than others. Inventories are converted into cash only when the goods are produced, sold, and paid for. Receivables are more liquid; they become cash as customers pay their outstanding bills. Short-term securities can generally be sold if the firm needs cash on short notice and are therefore more liquid still.

Some firms choose to hold more liquidity than others. For example, many high-tech companies, such as Intel and Cisco, hold huge amounts of short-term securities. On the other hand, firms in old-line manufacturing industries—such

---

[1] A survey by Graham and Harvey found that managers considered that the desire to match the maturity of the debt with that of the assets was the single most important factor in their choice between short- and long-term debt. See J. R. Graham and C. R. Harvey, "The Theory and Practice of Finance: Evidence from the Field," *Journal of Financial Economics* 61 (May 2001), pp. 187–243. Stohs and Mauer confirm that firms with a preponderance of short-term assets do indeed tend to issue short-term debt. See M. H. Stohs and D. C. Mauer, "The Determinants of Corporate Debt Maturity Structure," *Journal of Business* 69 (July 1996), pp. 279–312.

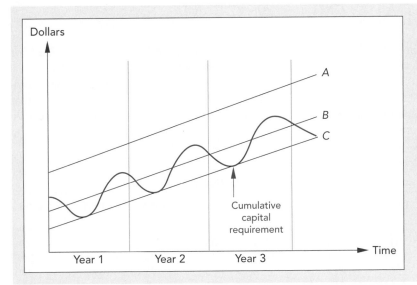

FIGURE 20.1

The firm's cumulative capital requirement (maroon line) is the cumulative investment in all the assets needed for the business. In this case the requirement grows year by year, but there is seasonal fluctuation within each year. The requirement for short-term financing is the difference between long-term financing (lines A, B, and C) and the cumulative capital requirement. If long-term financing follows line C, the firm always needs short-term financing. At line B, the need is seasonal. At line A, the firm never needs short-term financing. There is always extra cash to invest.

as chemicals, paper, or steel—manage with a far smaller reservoir of liquidity. Why is this? One reason is that companies with rapidly growing profits may generate cash faster than they can redeploy it in new positive-NPV investments. This produces a surplus of cash that can be invested in short-term securities. Of course, companies faced with a growing mountain of cash may eventually respond by adjusting their payout policies. In Chapter 13 we saw how Microsoft reduced its cash mountain by paying a special dividend and repurchasing its stock.

There are some advantages to holding a large reservoir of cash, particularly for smaller firms that face relatively high costs to raise funds on short notice. For example, biotech firms require large amounts of cash if their drugs succeed in gaining regulatory approval. Therefore, these firms generally have substantial cash holdings to fund their possible investment needs. A reservoir of cash can also help to protect the firm against a rainy day and give it the breathing space to make changes to operations. That is not always in shareholders' interests; sometimes it simply helps to postpone the day of reckoning. The nearby box describes how the fashion company L. A. Gear was able to use its cash to survive six years of large losses and to employ a variety of radical, though ultimately unsuccessful, new strategies.

If these precautionary reasons for holding liquid assets are important, we should find that small companies in relatively high-risk industries are more likely to hold large cash surpluses. A study by Tim Opler and others confirms that this is in fact the case.[2]

Financial managers of firms with a surplus of long-term financing and with cash in the bank don't have to worry about finding the money to pay next month's bills. But there are also costs to having surplus cash. Holdings of marketable securities are at best a zero-NPV investment for a taxpaying firm.[3] Also managers of firms

---

[2] T. Opler, L. Pinkowitz, R. Stulz, and R. Williamson, "The Determinants and Implications of Corporate Cash Holdings," *Journal of Financial Economics* 52 (April 1999), pp. 3–46.

[3] If there is a tax advantage to borrowing as most people believe, there must be a corresponding tax disadvantage to lending, since the firm must pay tax at the corporate rate on the interest that it receives from Treasury bills. In this case investment in Treasury bills has a negative NPV. See Section 15.1.

THE RISE AND FALL OF L. A. GEAR

Fashion company L. A. Gear was one of the stars of the 1980s. Teenie boppers loved its pink sequined sneakers and its silver and gold lamé workout shoes. Investors preferred the 1300% growth in the company's stock price in the space of four years. But as the company failed to react to changes in fashion during the 1990s, sales and profits fell away rapidly. In January 1998 L. A. Gear filed for Chapter 11 bankruptcy.

The decline of L. A. Gear illustrates how a company's liquid assets can provide the financial slack that allows it to evade market discipline and survive repeated losses. The following table summarizes the changes in L. A. Gear's profitability and its assets:

Sales, income, and assets of L. A. Gear 1989–1996 (figures in $ millions)								
	1989	**1990**	**1991**	**1992**	**1993**	**1994**	**1995**	**1996**
Sales	617	820	619	430	398	416	297	196
Net income	55	31	−66	−72	−33	−22	−51	−62
Cash & securities	0	3	1	84	28	50	36	34
Receivables	101	156	112	56	73	77	47	24
Inventory	140	161	141	62	110	58	52	33
Current assets	257	338	297	230	220	194	138	93
Total assets	267	364	326	250	255	225	160	101

The first two rows of the table show that after 1990 L. A. Gear's sales declined sharply and the firm produced losses for the rest of its life. The remaining rows show the company's assets. Since L. A. Gear farmed out shoe and clothing production, it had few fixed assets and owned largely cash, receivables, and inventory. As sales declined, two things happened. First, the company was able to reduce its inventory of finished goods. Second, customers paid off their outstanding bills. Thus, despite making steady losses, the company's holdings of cash and short-term securities initially increased.

The next table shows L. A. Gear's capital structure. Notice that after 1991 the company had almost no short-term bank debt, so that it was largely free from the discipline that is exerted whenever a company has to approach its bank for a loan to be renewed.[*] As losses cumulated, common equity dwindled and the debt ratio climbed to 92%. Yet even in 1996 the company's cash holdings were over eight times that year's interest payments.

	1989	**1990**	**1991**	**1992**	**1993**	**1994**	**1995**	**1996**
Bank debt	37	94	20	0	4	1	1	0
Long-term debt	0	0	0	0	50	50	50	50
Preferred stock	0	0	100	100	100	100	108	116
Common equity	168	206	132	88	47	18	−41	−111

Because the company could liquidate its inventories and receivables and had no maturing debt, it was able to survive six years of large losses and to try a variety of radical new strategies, including a new emphasis on performance athletic shoes and then on children's shoes. All these strategies were ultimately unsuccessful. A company with large fixed assets that are not so easily liquidated would have found it less easy to survive so long.

[*]L. A. Gear had a line of credit with the Bank of America. This was used to provide the company's suppliers with letters of credit that guaranteed they would receive payment. Although the bank progressively reduced this line of credit, L. A. Gear's sales also fell and therefore reduced the extent to which the line of credit was needed.

Source: The decline of L. A. Gear is chronicled in H. DeAngelo, L. DeAngelo, and K. H. Wruck, "Asset Liquidity, Debt Covenants, and Managerial Discretion in Financial Distress: The Collapse of L. A. Gear," *Journal of Financial Economics* 64 (2002), pp. 3–34.

with large cash surpluses may be tempted to run a less tight ship. If that is the case, firms with a permanent cash surplus should go on a diet and use the money to retire some of their long-term securities.

20.2   TRACING CHANGES IN CASH AND WORKING CAPITAL

Table 20.1 compares 2006 and 2007 year-end balance sheets for Dynamic Mattress Company. Table 20.2 shows the firm's income statement for 2007. Note that Dynamic's cash balance increased by $1 million during 2007. What caused this increase? Did the extra cash come from Dynamic Mattress Company's additional long-term borrowing, from reinvested earnings, from cash released by reducing inventory, or from extra credit extended by Dynamic's suppliers? (*Note:* The increase in accounts payable.)

	2006	2007
Current assets:		
Cash	4	5
Marketable securities	0	5
Inventory	26	25
Accounts receivable	25	30
Total current assets	55	65
Fixed assets:		
Gross investment	56	70
Less depreciation	−16	−20
Net fixed assets	40	50
Total assets	95	115
Current liabilities:		
Bank loans	5	0
Accounts payable	20	27
Total current liabilities	25	27
Long-term debt	5	12
Net worth (equity and retained earnings)	65	76
Total liabilities and net worth	95	115

TABLE 20.1

Year-end balance sheets for 2006 and 2007 for Dynamic Mattress Company (figures in $ millions).

Sales	350
Operating costs	−321
	29
Depreciation	−4
	25
Interest	−1
Pretax income	24
Tax at 50%	−12
Net income	12

TABLE 20.2

Income statement for Dynamic Mattress Company, 2007 (figures in $ millions).

Note: Dividend = $1 million; retained earnings = $11 million.

TABLE 20.3

Sources and uses of cash for Dynamic Mattress Company, 2007 (figures in $ millions).

Sources:	
Issued long-term debt	7
Reduced inventories	1
Increased accounts payable	7
Cash from operations:	
Net income	12
Depreciation	4
Total sources	31
Uses:	
Repaid short-term bank loan	5
Invested in fixed assets	14
Purchased marketable securities	5
Increased accounts receivable	5
Dividend	1
Total uses	30
Increase in cash balance	1

The correct answer is "all the above." Financial analysts often summarize sources and uses of cash in a statement like the one shown in Table 20.3. The statement shows that Dynamic *generated* cash from the following sources:

1. It issued $7 million of long-term debt.
2. It reduced inventory, releasing $1 million.
3. It increased its accounts payable, in effect borrowing an additional $7 million from its suppliers.
4. By far the largest source of cash was Dynamic's operations, which generated $16 million. See Table 20.2, and note that Income ($12 million) understates cash flow because depreciation is deducted in calculating income. Depreciation is *not* a cash outlay. Thus, it must be added back in order to obtain operating cash flow.

Dynamic *used* cash for the following purposes:

1. It paid a $1 million dividend. (*Note:* The $11 million increase in Dynamic's equity is due to retained earnings: $12 million of equity income, less the $1 million dividend.)
2. It repaid a $5 million short-term bank loan.[4]
3. It invested $14 million. This shows up as the increase in gross fixed assets in Table 20.1.
4. It purchased $5 million of marketable securities.
5. It allowed accounts receivable to expand by $5 million. In effect, it lent this additional amount to its customers.

---

[4] This is principal repayment, not interest. Sometimes interest payments are explicitly recognized as a use of funds. If so, operating cash flow would be defined *before* interest, that is, as net income plus interest plus depreciation.

	2006	2007
Net working capital	30	38
Fixed assets:		
Gross investment	56	70
Less depreciation	−16	−20
Net fixed assets	40	50
Total net assets	70	88
Long-term debt	5	12
Net worth (equity and retained earnings)	65	76
Long-term liabilities and net worth*	70	88

TABLE 20.4

Condensed year-end balance sheets for 2006 and 2007 for Dynamic Mattress Company (figures in $ millions).

* When only *net* working capital appears on a firm's balance sheet, this figure (the sum of long-term liabilities and net worth) is often referred to as *total capitalization*.

Tracing Changes in Net Working Capital

Financial analysts often find it useful to collapse all current assets and liabilities into a single figure for net working capital. Dynamic's net-working-capital balances were (in millions):

	Current Assets	Less	Current Liabilities	Equals	Net Working Capital
Year-end 2006	$55	−	$25	=	$30
Year-end 2007	$65	−	$27	=	$38

Table 20.4 gives balance sheets that report only net working capital, not individual current asset or liability items.

"Sources and uses" statements can likewise be simplified by defining *sources* as activities that contribute to net working capital and *uses* as activities that use up working capital. In this context working capital is usually referred to as *funds,* and a *sources and uses of funds statement* is presented.[5]

In 2006, Dynamic contributed to net working capital by

1. Issuing $7 million of long-term debt.
2. Generating $16 million from operations.

It used up net working capital by

1. Investing $14 million.
2. Paying a $1 million dividend.

The year's changes in net working capital are thus summarized by Dynamic Mattress Company's sources and uses of funds statement, given in Table 20.5.

Profits and Cash Flow

Now look back to Table 20.3, which shows sources and uses of *cash.* We want to register two warnings about the entry called *cash from operations.* It may not represent actual dollars—dollars you can buy beer with.

First, depreciation may not be the only noncash expense deducted in calculating income. For example, most firms use accounting procedures in their tax books

---

[5] We drew up a *sources and uses of funds* statement for Executive Paper in Section 19.2.

TABLE 20.5

Sources and uses of funds (net working capital) for Dynamic Mattress Company, 2007 (figures in $ millions).

Sources:	
Issued long-term debt	7
Cash from operations:	
Net income	12
Depreciation	4
	23
Uses:	
Invested in fixed assets	14
Dividend	1
	15
Increase in net working capital	8

different from those in their reports to shareholders. The point of special tax accounts is to minimize current taxable income. The effect is that the shareholder books overstate the firm's current cash tax liability,[6] and after-tax cash flow from operations is therefore understated.

Second, income statements record sales when made, not when the customer's payment is received. Think of what happens when Dynamic sells goods on credit. The company records a profit at the time of sale, but there is no cash inflow until the bills are paid. Since there is no cash inflow, there is no change in the company's cash balance, although there is an increase in working capital in the form of an increase in accounts receivable. No net addition to cash would be shown in a sources and uses statement like Table 20.3. The increase in cash from operations would be offset by an increase in accounts receivable.

Later, when the bills are paid, there is an increase in the cash balance. However, there is no further profit at this point and no increase in working capital. The increase in the cash balance is exactly matched by a decrease in accounts receivable.

That brings up an interesting characteristic of working capital. Imagine a company that conducts a very simple business. It buys raw materials for cash, processes them into finished goods, and then sells these goods on credit. The whole cycle of operations looks like this:

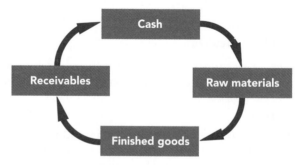

---

[6] The difference between taxes reported and paid to the Internal Revenue Service shows up on the balance sheet as a deferred tax liability. The reason that a liability is recognized is that accelerated depreciation and other devices used to reduce current taxable income do not eliminate taxes; they only delay them. Of course, this reduces the present value of the firm's tax liability, but still the ultimate liability has to be recognized. In the sources and uses statements an increase in deferred taxes would be treated as a source of funds. In the Dynamic Mattress example we ignore deferred taxes.

If you draw up a balance sheet at the beginning of the process, you see cash. If you delay a little, you find the cash replaced by inventories of raw materials and, still later, by inventories of finished goods. When the goods are sold, the inventories give way to accounts receivable, and finally, when the customers pay their bills, the firm draws out its profit and replenishes the cash balance.

There is only one constant in this process, namely, working capital. The components of working capital are constantly changing. That is one reason why (net) working capital is a useful summary measure of current assets and liabilities.

The strength of the working-capital measure is that it is unaffected by seasonal or other temporary movements between different current assets or liabilities. But the strength is also its weakness, for the working-capital figure hides a lot of interesting information. In our example cash was transformed into inventory, then into receivables, and back into cash again. But these assets have different degrees of risk and liquidity. You can't pay bills with inventory or with receivables, you must pay with cash.

20.3   CASH BUDGETING

The past is interesting for what one can learn from it. The financial manager's problem is to forecast *future* sources and uses of cash. These forecasts serve two purposes. First, they provide a standard, or budget, against which subsequent performance can be judged. Second, they alert the manager to future cash-flow needs. Cash, as we all know, has a habit of disappearing fast.

Preparing the Cash Budget: Inflow

We will illustrate the preparation of the capital budget by continuing the example of Dynamic Mattress.

Most of Dynamic's cash inflow comes from the sale of mattresses. We therefore start with a sales forecast by quarter[7] for 2008:

	First Quarter	Second Quarter	Third Quarter	Fourth Quarter
Sales ($ millions)	87.5	78.5	116	131

But sales become accounts receivable before they become cash. Cash flow comes from *collections* on accounts receivable.

Most firms keep track of the average time it takes customers to pay their bills. From this they can forecast what proportion of a quarter's sales is likely to be converted into cash in that quarter and what proportion is likely to be carried over to the next quarter as accounts receivable. Suppose that 80% of sales are "cashed in" in the immediate quarter and 20% are cashed in in the next. Table 20.6 shows forecasted collections under this assumption.

---

[7] Most firms would forecast by month instead of by quarter. Sometimes weekly or even daily forecasts are made. But presenting a monthly forecast would triple the number of entries in Table 20.6 and subsequent tables. We wanted to keep the examples as simple as possible.

TABLE 20.6

To forecast Dynamic Mattress's collections on accounts receivable, you have to forecast sales and collection rates (figures in $ millions).

[a] Sales in the fourth quarter of the previous year were $75 million.

Visit us at
www.mhhe.com/bma1e.

	First Quarter	Second Quarter	Third Quarter	Fourth Quarter
1. Receivables at start of period	30	32.5	30.7	38.2
2. Sales	87.5	78.5	116	131
3. Collections:				
Sales in current period (80%)	70	62.8	92.8	104.8
Sales in last period (20%)	15[a]	17.5	15.7	23.2
Total collections	85	80.3	108.5	128
4. Receivables at end of period 1 + 2 - 3	32.5	30.7	38.2	41.2

TABLE 20.7

Dynamic Mattress's cash budget for 2008 (figures in $ millions).

[a] Of course, firms cannot literally hold a negative amount of cash. This is the amount the firm will have to raise to pay its bills.
[b] A negative sign would indicate a cash *surplus*. But in this example the firm must raise cash for all quarters.

Visit us at
www.mhhe.com/bma1e.

	First Quarter	Second Quarter	Third Quarter	Fourth Quarter
Sources of cash:				
Collections on accounts receivable	85	80.3	108.5	128
Other	0	0	12.5	0
Total sources	85	80.3	121	128
Uses of cash:				
Payments on accounts payable	65	60	55	50
Labor and other expenses	30	30	30	30
Capital expenditures	32.5	1.3	5.5	8
Taxes, interest, and dividends	4	4	4.5	5
Total uses	131.5	95.3	95	93
Sources minus uses	-46.5	-15.0	+26.0	+35.0
Calculation of short-term financing requirement:				
1. Cash at start of period	5	-41.5	-56.5	-30.5
2. Change in cash balance (sources less uses)	-46.5	-15	+26.0	+35.0
3. Cash at end of period[a] 1 + 2	-41.5	-56.5	-30.5	+4.5
4. Minimum operating balance	5	5	5	5
5. Cumulative financing required[b] 4 - 3	46.5	61.5	35.5	.5

In the first quarter, for example, collections from current sales are 80% of $87.5, or $70 million. But the firm also collects 20% of the previous quarter's sales, or .2(75) = $15 million. Therefore total collections are $70 + $15 = $85 million.

Dynamic started the first quarter with $30 million of accounts receivable. The quarter's sales of $87.5 million were *added* to accounts receivable, but collections of $85 million were *subtracted*. Therefore, as Table 20.6 shows, Dynamic ended the quarter with accounts receivable of $30 + 87.5 − 85 = $32.5 million. The general formula is

Ending accounts receivable = beginning accounts receivable + sales − collections

The top section of Table 20.7 shows forecasted sources of cash for Dynamic Mattress. Collection of receivables is the main source, but it is not the only one. Perhaps the firm plans to dispose of some land or expects a tax refund or payment of an insurance claim. All such items are included as "other" sources. It is also possible that you may raise additional capital by borrowing or selling stock, but we don't want to prejudge that question. Therefore, for the moment we just assume that Dynamic will not raise further long-term finance.

Preparing the Cash Budget: Outflow

So much for the incoming cash. Now for the outgoing. There always seem to be many more uses for cash than there are sources. For simplicity, we have condensed the uses into four categories in Table 20.7.

1. *Payments on accounts payable.* You have to pay your bills for raw materials, parts, electricity, etc. The cash-flow forecast assumes all these bills are paid on time, although Dynamic could probably delay payment to some extent. Delaying payment is sometimes called *stretching payables.* Stretching is one source of short-term financing, but for most firms it is an expensive source, because by stretching they lose discounts given to firms that pay promptly.
2. *Labor, administrative, and other expenses.* This category includes all other regular business expenses.
3. *Capital expenditures.* Note that Dynamic Mattress plans a major capital outlay in the first quarter.
4. *Taxes, interest, and dividend payments.* This includes interest on presently outstanding long-term debt but does not include interest on any additional borrowing to meet cash requirements in 2008. At this stage in the analysis, Dynamic does not know how much it will have to borrow, or whether it will have to borrow at all.

The forecasted net inflow of cash (sources minus uses) is shown in the box in Table 20.7. Note the large negative figure for the first quarter: a $46.5 million forecasted *outflow.* There is a smaller forecasted outflow in the second quarter, and then substantial cash inflows in the second half of the year.

The bottom part of Table 20.7 calculates how much financing Dynamic will have to raise if its cash-flow forecasts are right. It starts the year with $5 million in cash. There is a $46.5 million cash outflow in the first quarter, and so Dynamic will have to obtain at least $46.5 − 5 = $41.5 million of additional financing. This would leave the firm with a forecasted cash balance of exactly zero at the start of the second quarter.

Most financial managers regard a planned cash balance of zero as driving too close to the edge of the cliff. They establish a *minimum operating cash balance* to absorb unexpected cash inflows and outflows. We will assume that Dynamic's minimum operating cash balance is $5 million. That means it will have to raise the full $46.5 million cash outflow in the first quarter and $15 million more in the second quarter. Thus its cumulative financing requirement is $61.5 million in the second quarter. This is the peak, fortunately: The cumulative requirement declines in the third quarter by $26 million to $35.5 million. In the final quarter Dynamic is almost out of the woods: Its cash balance is $4.5 million, just $.5 million shy of its minimum operating balance.

The next step is to develop a *short-term financing plan* that covers the forecasted requirements in the most economical way possible. We will move on to that topic after two general observations:

1. The large cash outflows in the first two quarters do not necessarily spell trouble for Dynamic Mattress. In part, they reflect the capital investment made in the first quarter: Dynamic is spending $32.5 million, but it should be acquiring an asset worth that much or more. In part, the cash outflows reflect low sales in the first half of the year; sales recover in the

second half.[8] If this is a predictable seasonal pattern, the firm should have no trouble borrowing to tide it over the slow months.

2. Table 20.7 is only a best guess about future cash flows. It is a good idea to think about the *uncertainty* in your estimates. For example, you could undertake a sensitivity analysis, in which you inspect how Dynamic's cash requirements would be affected by a shortfall in sales or by a delay in collections. The trouble with such sensitivity analyses is that you are changing only one item at a time, whereas in practice a downturn in the economy might affect, say, sales levels *and* collection rates. An alternative but more complicated solution is to build a model of the cash budget and then to simulate to determine the probability of cash requirements significantly above or below the forecasts shown in Table 20.7. If cash requirements are difficult to predict, you may wish to hold additional cash or marketable securities to cover a possible unexpected cash outflow.

20.4   THE SHORT-TERM FINANCING PLAN

Dynamic's cash budget defines its problem: Its financial manager must find short-term financing to cover the firm's forecasted cash requirements. There are dozens of sources of short-term financing, but for simplicity we assume that Dynamic has just two options.

Options for Short-Term Financing

1. *Bank loan:* Dynamic has an existing arrangement with its bank allowing it to borrow up to $38 million at an interest cost of 10% a year or 2.5% per quarter. The firm can borrow and repay whenever it wants to as long as it does not exceed its credit limit.

2. *Stretching payables:* Dynamic can also raise capital by putting off paying its bills. The financial manager believes that Dynamic can defer the following amounts in each quarter:

	First Quarter	Second Quarter	Third Quarter	Fourth Quarter
Amount deferrable ($ millions)	52	48	44	40

Thus, $52 million can be saved in the first quarter by *not* paying bills in that quarter. (*Note:* The cash-flow forecasts in Table 20.7 assumed that these bills *will* be paid in the first quarter.) If deferred, these payments *must* be made in the second quarter. Similarly, up to $48 million of the second quarter bills can be deferred to the third quarter, and so on.

Stretching payables is often costly, even if no ill will is incurred. The reason is that suppliers may offer discounts for prompt payment. Dynamic loses this discount

---

[8] Maybe people buy more mattresses late in the year when the nights are longer.

	First Quarter	Second Quarter	Third Quarter	Fourth Quarter
New borrowing:				
1. Bank loan	38.0	0.0	0.0	0.0
2. Stretching payables	3.5	19.7	0.0	0.0
3. Total	41.5	19.7	0.0	0.0
Repayments:				
4. Bank loan	0.0	0.0	4.2	33.8
5. Stretching payables	0.0	3.5	19.7	0.0
6. Total	0.0	3.5	24.0	33.8
7. Net new borrowing	41.5	16.2	-24.0	-33.8
8. Plus securities sold	5.0	0.0	0.0	0.0
9. Less securities bought	0.0	0.0	0.0	0.3
10. Total cash raised	46.5	16.2	-24.0	-34.1
Interest payments[a]				
11. Bank loan	0.0	1.0	1.0	0.8
12. Stretching payables	0.0	0.2	1.0	0.0
13. Interest on securities sold[b]	0.0	0.1	0.1	0.1
14. Net interest paid	0.0	1.2	2.0	0.9
15. Cash required for operations[c]	46.5	15.0	-26.0	-35.0
16. Total cash required	46.5	16.2	-24.0	-34.1

TABLE 20.8

Dynamic Mattress's financing plan (figures in $ millions).

[a] We assume that the first interest payment occurs one quarter after a loan is taken out.
[b] Dynamic sold $5 million of marketable securities in the first quarter. The yield is assumed to be 2% per quarter.
[c] From Table 20.7.

Visit us at
www.mhhe.com/bma1e.

if it pays late. In this example we assume the lost discount is 5% of the amount deferred. In other words, if a $100 payment is delayed, the firm must pay $105 in the next quarter.

Dynamic's Financing Plan

With these two options, the short-term financing strategy is obvious. Use the bank loan first, if necessary up to the $38 million limit. If there is still a shortage of cash, stretch payables.

Table 20.8 shows the resulting plan. In the first quarter the plan calls for borrowing the full amount available from the bank ($38 million) and stretching $3.5 million of payables (see lines 1 and 2 in the table). In addition the company sells the $5 million of marketable securities it held at the end of 2007 (line 8). Thus it raises 38 + 3.5 + 5 = $46.5 million of cash in the first quarter (line 10).

In the second quarter, the plan calls for Dynamic to continue to borrow $38 million from the bank and to stretch $19.7 million of payables. This raises a further $16.2 million after paying off the $3.5 million of bills deferred from the first quarter.

Why raise $16.2 million when Dynamic needs only an additional $15 million to finance its operations? The answer is that the company must pay interest on the borrowings that it undertook in the first quarter and it foregoes interest on the marketable securities that were sold.[9]

---

[9] The bank loan calls for quarterly interest of .025 × 38 = $.95 million; the lost discount on the stretched payables amounts to .05 × 3.5 = $.175 million; and the interest lost on the marketable securities is .02 × 5 = $.1 million.

In the third and fourth quarters the plan calls for Dynamic to pay off its debt and to make a small purchase of marketable securities.

Evaluating the Plan

Does the plan shown in Table 20.8 solve Dynamic's short-term financing problem? No: The plan is feasible, but Dynamic can probably do better. The most glaring weakness is its reliance on stretching payables, an extremely expensive financing device. Remember that it costs Dynamic 5% *per quarter* to delay paying bills—20% per year at simple interest. The first plan would merely stimulate the financial manager to search for cheaper sources of short-term borrowing.

The financial manager would ask several other questions as well. For example:

1. Does the plan yield satisfactory current and quick ratios?[10] Its bankers may be worried if these ratios deteriorate.[11]

2. Are there intangible costs of stretching payables? Will suppliers begin to doubt Dynamic's creditworthiness?

3. Does the plan for 2008 leave Dynamic in good financial shape for 2009? (Here the answer is yes, since Dynamic will have paid off all short-term borrowing by the end of the year.)

4. Should Dynamic try to arrange long-term financing for the major capital expenditure in the first quarter? This seems sensible, following the rule of thumb that long-term assets deserve long-term financing. It would also reduce the need for short-term borrowing dramatically. A counterargument is that Dynamic is financing the capital investment *only temporarily* by short-term borrowing. By year-end, the investment is paid for by cash from operations. Thus Dynamic's initial decision not to seek immediate long-term financing may reflect a preference for ultimately financing the investment with retained earnings.

5. Perhaps the firm's operating and investment plans can be adjusted to make the short-term financing problem easier. Is there any easy way of deferring the first quarter's large cash outflow? For example, suppose that the large capital investment in the first quarter is for new mattress-stuffing machines to be delivered and installed in the first half of the year. The new machines are not scheduled to be ready for full-scale use until August. Perhaps the machine manufacturer could be persuaded to accept 60% of the purchase price on delivery and 40% when the machines are installed and operating satisfactorily.

6. Dynamic may also be able to release cash by reducing the level of other current assets. For example, it could reduce receivables by getting tough with customers who are late paying their bills. (The cost is that in the future these customers may take their business elsewhere.) Or it may be able to get by with lower inventories of mattresses. (The cost is that it may lose business if there is a rush of orders that it cannot supply.)

Short-term financing plans are developed by trial and error. You lay out one plan, think about it, and then try again with different assumptions on financing and investment alternatives. You continue until you can think of no further improvements.

---

[10] These ratios are discussed in Chapter 19.

[11] We have not worked out these ratios explicitly, but you can infer from Table 20.8 that they would be fine at the end of the year but relatively low midyear, when Dynamic's borrowing is high.

Trial and error is important because it helps you understand the real nature of the problem the firm faces. Here we can draw a useful analogy between the *process* of planning and Chapter 11, "Project Analysis." In Chapter 11 we described sensitivity analysis and other tools used by firms to find out what makes capital investment projects tick and what can go wrong with them. Dynamic's financial manager faces the same kind of task: not just to choose a plan but to understand what can go wrong with it and what will be done if conditions change unexpectedly.[12]

A Note on Short-Term Financial Planning Models

Working out a consistent short-term plan requires burdensome calculations.[13] Fortunately much of the arithmetic can be delegated to a computer. Many large firms have built *short-term financial planning models* to do this. Smaller companies like Dynamic Mattress do not face so much detail and complexity and find it easier to work with a spreadsheet program on a personal computer. In either case the financial manager specifies forecasted cash requirements or surpluses, interest rates, credit limits, etc., and the model grinds out a plan like the one shown in Table 20.8. The computer also produces balance sheets, income statements, and whatever special reports the financial manager may require.

Smaller firms that do not want custom-built models can rent general-purpose models offered by banks, accounting firms, management consultants, or specialized computer software firms.

Most of these models are *simulation* programs.[14] They simply work out the consequences of the assumptions and policies specified by the financial manager. *Optimization* models for short-term financial planning are also available. These models are usually linear programming models. They search for the *best* plan from a range of alternative policies identified by the financial manager. Optimization helps when the firm faces complex problems with many interdependent alternatives and restrictions for which trial and error might never identify the *best* combination of alternatives.

Of course the best plan for one set of assumptions may prove disastrous if the assumptions are wrong. Thus the financial manager has to explore the implications of alternative assumptions about future cash flows, interest rates, and so on. Linear programming can help identify good strategies, but even with an optimization model the financial plan is still sought by trial and error.

20.5   SOURCES OF SHORT-TERM BORROWING

Dynamic solved the greater part of its cash shortage by borrowing from a bank. But banks are not the only source of short-term loans. Finance companies are also a major source of cash, particularly for financing receivables and inventories.[15] In

---

[12] This point is even more important in *long-term* financial planning. See Chapter 19.

[13] If you doubt that, look again at Table 20.8. Notice that the cash requirements in each quarter depend on borrowing in the previous quarter, because borrowing creates an obligation to pay interest. Moreover, the problem's complexity would have been tripled had we not simplified by forecasting per quarter rather than by month.

[14] The models are generally built and used in the same way as the long-term financial planning models described in Section 19.5.

[15] *Finance companies* are firms that specialize in lending to businesses or individuals. They include independent firms, such as CIT Group, as well as subsidiaries of nonfinancial corporations, such as General Motors Acceptance Corporation (GMAC). In their lending finance companies compete with banks. However, they raise funds not by attracting deposits, as banks do, but by issuing commercial paper and other longer-term securities.

addition to borrowing from an intermediary like a bank or finance company, firms also sell short-term commercial paper or medium-term notes directly to investors. It is time to look more closely at these sources of short-term funds.

Bank Loans

To finance its investment in current assets, a company may rely on a variety of short-term loans. Obviously, if you approach a bank for a loan, the bank's lending officer is likely to ask searching questions about your firm's financial position and its plans for the future. Also, the bank will want to monitor the firm's subsequent progress. There is, however, a good side to this. Other investors know that banks are hard to convince, and, therefore, when a company announces that it has arranged a large bank facility, the share price tends to rise.

Bank loans come in a variety of flavors. Here are a few of the ways that they differ.

Commitment   Companies sometimes wait until they need the money before they apply for a bank loan, but about 80% of commercial bank loans are made under commitment. In this case the company establishes a line of credit that allows it to borrow up to an established limit from the bank. This line of credit may be an **evergreen credit** with no fixed maturity, but more commonly it is a **revolving credit** (*revolver*) with a fixed maturity. For example, one common arrangement is a 364-day facility that allows the company over the next year to borrow, repay, and reborrow as its need for cash varies.

Unused lines of credit total 10% of corporate assets and therefore represent considerable borrowing power. But to borrow under a line of credit a company needs to satisfy a number of financial covenants, such as maintaining a specified level of cash flow and profitability. Credit lines are also relatively expensive, for in addition to paying interest on any borrowings, the company must pay a commitment fee of around .25% on the unused amount. In exchange for this extra cost, the firm receives a valuable option: It has guaranteed access to the bank's money at a fixed spread over the general level of interest rates.

The growth in the use of credit lines has changed the role of banks. They are no longer simply lenders; they are also in the business of providing companies with liquidity insurance. Many companies discovered the value of this insurance in 1998, when Russia stopped payments on part of its debt and created turmoil in the world's debt markets. Companies in the United States suddenly found it much more expensive to issue their own debt to investors. Those who had arranged lines of credit with their banks rushed to take advantage of them. As a result, new debt issues languished, while bank lending boomed.

Maturity   Many bank loans are for only a few months. For example, a company may need a short-term **bridge loan** to finance the purchase of new equipment or the acquisition of another firm. In this case the loan serves as interim financing until the purchase is completed and long-term financing arranged. Often a short-term loan is needed to finance a temporary increase in inventory. Such a loan is described as **self-liquidating;** in other words, the sale of goods provides the cash to repay the loan.

Banks also provide longer-maturity loans, known as **term loans.** A term loan typically has a maturity of four to five years. Usually the loan is repaid in level amounts over this period, though there is sometimes a large final *balloon* payment or just a single *bullet* payment at maturity. Banks can accommodate the repayment pattern to the anticipated cash flows of the borrower. For example, the first repayment might be delayed a year until the new factory is completed. Term loans are often renegotiated before maturity. Banks are willing to do this if the borrower is an established customer, remains creditworthy, and has a sound business reason for making the change.[16]

Rate of Interest Most short-term bank loans are made at a fixed rate of interest, which is often quoted as a discount. For example, if the interest rate on a one-year loan is stated as a discount of 5%, the borrower receives $100 - 5 = \$95$ and undertakes to pay $100 at the end of the year. The return on such a loan is not 5%, but $5/95 = .0526$, or 5.26%.

For longer-term bank loans the interest rate is usually linked to the general level of interest rates. The most common benchmarks are the London Interbank Offered Rate (LIBOR),[17] the federal funds rate,[18] or the bank's prime rate. Thus, if the rate is set at "1% over LIBOR," the borrower may pay 5% in the first three months when LIBOR is 4%, 6% in the next three months when LIBOR is 5%, and so on.

Syndicated Loans Some bank loans are too large for a single lender. In these cases the borrower may pay an arrangement fee to one or more lead banks, which then parcels out the loan or credit line among a syndicate of banks.[19] For example, when the German utility company, E.ON, needed to borrow €32 billion to help finance its unsuccessful bid for the Spanish power company Endesa, it engaged four banks to arrange a large syndicate of lenders to provide the cash. The loan came in two slices. The major portion had a one-year maturity with a one-year extension option at E.ON's discretion, and the remaining portion had a three-year maturity. The E.ON syndication is a reminder that for large bank loans, the market is an international one. HSBC, Citigroup, J. P. Morgan, and Deutsche Bank were the four arrangers, while other banks that were reportedly asked to participate in the loan included Barclays, Bank of Tokyo-Mitsubishi UFJ, HypoVereinsbank, BNP Paribas, Calyon, and Dresdner Kleinwort Wasserstein.

The syndicate arranger serves as underwriter to the loan. It prices the loan, markets it to other banks, and may also guarantee to take on any unsold portion. The arranger's first step is to prepare an *information memo* that provides potential lenders with information on the loan. The syndicate desk will then try to sound out the level of interest in the deal before the loan is finally priced and marketed to interested buyers. If the borrower is a good credit or if the arranging bank has a particularly good reputation, the majority of the loan is likely to be syndicated. In other cases the arranging bank may need to demonstrate its faith in the deal by keeping a high proportion of the loan on its own books.[20]

---

[16] Term loans typically allow the borrower to repay early, but in many cases the loan agreement specifies that the firm must pay a penalty for early repayment.

[17] LIBOR is the rate of interest that major international banks offer each other on eurodollar deposits.

[18] The federal funds rate is the rate at which banks lend excess reserves to each other.

[19] For a standard loan to a blue-chip company the fee for arranging a syndicated loan may be as low as 10 basis points, while a complex deal with a highly leveraged firm may carry a fee of up to 2.5%. For good reviews of the syndicated loan market see S. C. Miller, "A Guide to the Syndicated Loan Market," Standard & Poor's, September 2005 (**www.standardandpoors.com**); and B. Gadanecz, "The Syndicated Loan Market: Structure, Development and Implications," *BIS Quarterly Review*, December 2004, pp. 75–89 (**www.bis.org**).

[20] See A. Sufi, "Information Asymmetry and Financing Arrangements: Evidence from Syndicated Loans," *Journal of Finance* 62 (April 2007), pp. 629–668.

Loan Sales and Collateralized Loan Obligations   Bank loans used to be illiquid; once the bank had made a loan, it was stuck with it. This is no longer the case, so that banks with an excess demand for loans may solve the problem by selling a portion of their existing loans to other institutions. For example, about 20% of syndicated loans are subsequently resold, and these sales are reported weekly in *The Wall Street Journal*.

Loan sales generally take one of two forms: *assignments* or *participations*. In the former case a portion of the loan is transferred with the agreement of the borrower. In the second case the lead bank maintains its relationship with the borrower but agrees to pay over to the buyer a portion of the cash flows that it receives.

Participations carry an extra risk that buyers learned the hard way when Penn Square National Bank went belly-up in 1982. The problem was that Penn Square had sold more than $200 million of its loan portfolio to Chase Bank. Because these were participations, Chase did not have a claim against the original borrowers but only against the bankrupt Penn Square.

Loan sales often involve a single loan, but sometimes they can be huge deals involving a portfolio of several hundred loans. The buyer is then entitled to a share of the cash flows on this portfolio. In recent years many banks have repackaged the cash flows from a portfolio of loans and sold off separate slices (or *tranches*), known as *collateralized loan obligations* (or *CLOs*).[21] The senior tranches have first claim on the cash flows and are therefore attractive to conservative investors such as insurance companies or pension funds. The riskiest (or *equity*) tranche may be retained by the bank or bought by hedge funds or mutual funds that specialize in low-quality debt.

Example   In 2005 the British bank HSBC created a package of 250 dollar, euro, and sterling loans worth £2 billion. This package was then resold in five tranches. The senior tranche had first claim on the cash flows and received a AAA rating. It offered the lowest yield of 20–21 basis points (.20–.21%) above LIBOR. The middle tranches lined up behind the AAA tranche, while the most junior tranche received all the remaining cash flows. Because the holders of this tranche took the first hit from any defaults, it compensated them with a yield of 3.10% over LIBOR.

Security   If a bank is concerned about a firm's credit risk, it will ask the firm to provide security for the loan. This is most common for longer-term bank loans, over half of which are secured.[22] The collateral usually consists of liquid assets such as receivables, inventories, or securities. Sometimes the bank will take a *floating charge*.[23] This gives it a general claim if the firm defaults, but it does not specify the assets in detail, and it sets few restrictions on what the company can do with the assets.

More commonly, banks will require specific collateral. For example, suppose that there is a significant delay between the time that you ship your goods and when your customers pay you. If you need the money up front, you can borrow by using these receivables as collateral. First, you must send the bank a copy of

---

[21] CLOs, together with collateralized bond obligations (CBOs) and collateralized mortgage obligations (CMOs), are more broadly known as collateralized debt obligations (CDOs).

[22] The results of a survey of the terms of business lending by banks in the United States are published quarterly in the *Federal Reserve Bulletin* (see **www.federalreserve.gov/releases/E2**).

[23] Floating charges are more common outside the USA.

each invoice and provide it with a claim against the money that you receive from your customers. The bank will then lend up to 80% of the value of the receivables.

Each day, as you make more sales, your collateral increases and you can borrow more money. Each day also some customers pay their bills. This money is placed in a special collateral account under the bank's control and is periodically used to reduce the size of the loan. Therefore, as the firm's business fluctuates, so does the amount of the collateral and the size of the loan.[24]

You can also use inventories as security for a loan. For example, if your goods are stored in a warehouse, you need to arrange for an independent warehouse company to provide the bank with a receipt showing that the goods are held on the bank's behalf. The bank will generally be prepared to lend up to 50% of the value of the inventories. When the loan is repaid, the bank returns the warehouse receipt and you are free to remove the goods.[25]

Banks are naturally choosey about the security that they will accept. They want to make sure that they can identify and sell the collateral if you default. They may be happy to lend against a warehouse full of a standard nonperishable commodity, but they would turn up their nose at a warehouse of ripe Camemberts.

Banks also need to ensure that the collateral is safe and the borrower doesn't sell the assets and run off with the money. This is what happened in the great salad oil swindle. Fifty-one banks and companies made loans of nearly $200 million to the Allied Crude Vegetable Oil Refining Corporation. In return the company agreed to provide security in the form of storage tanks full of valuable salad oil. Unfortunately, cursory inspections failed to notice that the tanks contained seawater and sludge. When the fraud was discovered, the president of Allied went to jail and the 51 lenders were left out in the cold, looking for their $200 million. Lenders have been more careful since then, but Finance in the News shows that even old scams can still work.

Secured bank lending is most common for small firms with relatively poor credit, but it can also be used by major companies. For example, in 2007 Ford arranged to borrow up to $24.5 billion. Because Ford was generating huge losses, the banks demanded that the loans be secured by Ford's assets. These included most of Ford's U.S. manufacturing plants, its domestic accounts receivable, its inventory, and up to $4 billion in marketable securities. In addition, the loans were secured by 100% of the equity in Ford's subsidiaries including Ford Motor Credit Company. Thus almost every asset that Ford owned was swept up and used to secure the loan.

Commercial Paper

Banks borrow money from one group of firms or individuals and relend the money to another group. They make their profit by charging the borrowers a higher rate of interest than they offer the lender.

---

[24] Firms sometimes raise money by selling their receivables to a factor. The factor is responsible for collecting the debt and suffers any losses if the customers don't pay. When you pledge your receivables as collateral for a loan, *you* remain responsible for collecting the debt and *you* suffer if a customer is delinquent.

[25] It is not always practicable to keep inventory in a warehouse. For example, automobile dealers need to display their cars in a showroom. One solution is to enter into a floor-planning arrangement in which the finance company buys the cars and the dealer holds them in trust. When the cars are sold, the proceeds are used to redeem the cars from the finance company.

THE HAZARDS OF SECURED BANK LENDING

The National Safety Council of Australia's Victoria Division had been a sleepy outfit until John Friedrich took over. Under its new management, NSC members trained like commandos and were prepared to go anywhere and do anything. They saved people from drowning, they fought fires, found lost bushwalkers and went down mines. Their lavish equipment included 22 helicopters, 8 aircraft and a mini-submarine. Soon the NSC began selling its services internationally.

Unfortunately the NSC's paramilitary outfit cost millions of dollars to run—far more than it earned in revenue. Friedrich bridged the gap by borrowing $A236 million of debt. The banks were happy to lend because the NSC's debt appeared well secured. At one point the company showed $A107 million of receivables (that is, money owed by its customers), which it pledged as security for bank loans. Later checks revealed that many of these customers did not owe the NSC a cent. In other cases banks took comfort in the fact that their loans were secured by containers of valuable rescue gear. There were more than 100 containers stacked around the NSC's main base. Only a handful contained any equipment, but these were the ones that the bankers saw when they came to check that their loans were safe. Sometimes a suspicious banker would ask to inspect a particular container. Friedrich would then explain that it was away on exercise, fly the banker across the country in a light plane and point to a container well out in the bush. The container would of course be empty, but the banker had no way to know that.

Six years after Friedrich was appointed CEO, his massive fraud was uncovered. But a few days before a warrant could be issued, Friedrich disappeared. Although he was eventually caught and arrested, he shot himself before he could come to trial. Investigations revealed that Friedrich was operating under an assumed name, having fled from his native Germany, where he was wanted by the police. Many rumors continued to circulate about Friedrich. He was variously alleged to have been a plant of the CIA and the KGB and the NSC was said to have been behind an attempted counter-coup in Fiji. For the banks there was only one hard truth. Their loans to the NSC, which had appeared so well secured, would never be repaid.

Source: Adapted from Chapter 7 of T. Sykes, *The Bold Riders* (St. Leonards, NSW, Australia: Allen & Unwin, 1994).

Sometimes it is convenient to have a bank in the middle. It saves the lenders the trouble of looking for borrowers and assessing their creditworthiness, and it saves the borrowers the trouble of looking for lenders. Depositors do not care whom the bank lends to: They need only satisfy themselves that the bank as a whole is safe.

There are also occasions on which it is *not* worth paying an intermediary to perform these functions. Large well-known companies can bypass the banking system by issuing their own short-term unsecured notes. These notes are known as **commercial paper (CP).** Financial institutions, such as bank holding companies and finance companies,[26] also issue commercial paper, sometimes in very large quantities. For example, GE Capital Corporation has $88 billion of commercial paper in issue. The major issuers of commercial paper have set up their own marketing departments and sell their paper directly to investors, often using the Web to do so. Smaller companies sell through dealers who receive a fee for marketing the issue.

---

[26] A *bank holding company* is a firm that owns both a bank and nonbanking subsidiaries.

Commercial paper in the United States has a maximum maturity of nine months, though most paper is for 60 days or less. Buyers of commercial paper generally hold it to maturity, but the company or dealer that sells the paper is usually prepared to repurchase it earlier.

The majority of commercial paper is issued by high-grade, nationally known companies.[27] Issuers generally support their commercial paper by arranging a backup line of credit with a bank, which guarantees that they can find the money to repay the paper.[28] The risk of default is, therefore, small.

Because investors are reluctant to buy commercial paper that does not have the highest credit rating, companies cannot rely on the commercial paper market to provide them always with the short-term capital that they need. For example, when the rating services downgraded the commercial paper of Ford and General Motors, both companies were forced to reduce sharply their sales of paper. Ford Credit had $45 billion of unsecured commercial paper outstanding at the end of 2000; five years later it had cut the amount to $1.0 billion.[29]

Recent years have not been kind to the commercial paper market.[30] In addition to Ford and GM, a number of other major companies, such as AT&T, Lucent, Corning, Motorola, and Nortel Networks, have had their commercial paper downgraded. An even bigger shock occurred in 2001, when two large California utilities, Pacific Gas and Electric and Southern California Edison, became the first companies in 10 years to default on their nonfinancial commercial paper. These events dented investor enthusiasm for commercial paper and, as you can see from Figure 20.2, the earlier rapid growth in issuance went into reverse.

Medium-Term Notes

New issues of securities do not need to be registered with the SEC as long as they mature within 270 days. So by limiting the maturity of commercial paper issues, companies can avoid the delays and expense of registration. However, large blue-chip companies also make regular issues of unsecured **medium-term notes (MTNs).**

You can think of MTNs as a hybrid between corporate bonds and commercial paper. Like bonds they are relatively long-term instruments; their maturity is never less than 270 days, though it is typically less than 10 years.[31] On the other hand, like commercial paper, MTNs are not underwritten but are sold on a regular basis either through dealers or, occasionally, direct to investors. Dealers support a secondary market in these MTNs and are prepared to buy the notes back before maturity.

[27] Moody's, Standard and Poor's, and Fitch publish quality ratings for commercial paper. For example, Moody's provides three ratings, from P-1 (that is, Prime 1, the highest-grade paper) to P-3. Most investors are reluctant to buy low-rated paper. For example, money-market funds are largely limited to holding P-1 paper.

[28] For top-tier issuers the credit line is generally 75% of the amount of paper; for lower-grade issuers it is 100%. The company may not be able to draw on this line of credit if it does not satisfy bank covenants. Therefore, lower-rated companies may back their paper with an irrevocable line of credit.

[29] As the auto companies reduced their sales of unsecured commercial paper, they increasingly issued *asset-backed commercial paper*, secured by the firm's receivables. This is not really commercial paper but is essentially secured debt. As the firm's customers pay their bills, the cash is passed through to the commercial paper holders.

[30] For a discussion of the decline in commercial paper issuance, see P. Shen, "Why Has the Nonfinancial Commercial Paper Market Shrunk Recently?" *Economic Review*, Federal Reserve Bank of Kansas City, First Quarter 2003, pp. 55–76, at **www.kc.frb.org.**

[31] Occasionally, an MTN registration may be used to issue much longer term bonds. For example, Disney has even used its MTN program to issue a 100-year bond.

FIGURE 20.2

Commercial paper issuance by nonfarm, nonfinancial corporate business.

Source: Board of Governors of the Federal Reserve System, Division of Research and Statistics, Flow of Funds Accounts, Table L102 at **www.federalreserve. gov/releases/z1/ current.**

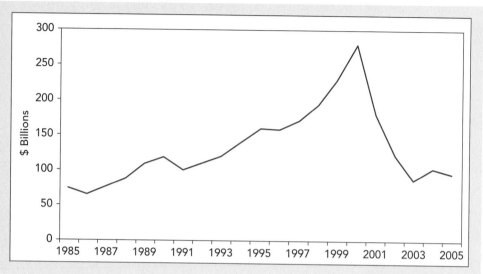

Borrowers such as finance companies, which always need cash, welcome the flexibility of MTNs. For example, a company may tell its dealers the amount of money that it needs to raise that week, the range of maturities that it can offer, and the maximum interest that it is prepared to pay. It is then up to the dealers to find the buyers. Investors may also suggest their own terms to one of the dealers, and, if these terms are acceptable, the deal is done.

20.6   MARKETABLE SECURITIES

In June 2006 Microsoft was sitting on a $34.8 billion mountain of cash and fixed income investments, amounting to 50% of the company's total assets.[32] The company kept $3.2 billion in the bank to support day-to-day operations and invested the surplus as follows:

Fixed Income Investments	Value at Cost
Money-market mutual funds	$ 723 million
Commercial paper	3,242
Certificates of deposit	364
U.S. government and agency securities	4,904
Foreign government bonds	6,034
Mortgage-backed securities	4,285
Corporate notes and bonds	7,605
Municipal securities	4,008
Other investments	383
Total	$31,548 million

[32] We described in Chapter 13 how Microsoft decided in July 2004 to pay out a large part of its surplus cash to shareholders.

Most companies do not have the luxury of such huge cash surpluses, but they also park any spare cash in short-term investments. The market for these investments is known as the **money market.** The money market has no physical marketplace. It consists of a loose collection of banks and dealers linked together by telephones or through the Web. But a huge volume of securities is regularly traded on the money market, and competition is vigorous.

Most large corporations manage their own money-market investments, but small companies sometimes find it more convenient to hire a professional investment management firm or to put their cash into a money-market fund. This is a mutual fund that invests only in low-risk, short-term securities.[33] Despite its large cash surplus, Microsoft invested a small proportion of its money in money-market funds.

Calculating the Yield on Money-Market Investments

Many money-market investments are pure discount securities. This means that they don't pay interest. The return consists of the difference between the amount you pay and the amount you receive at maturity. Unfortunately, it is no good trying to persuade the Internal Revenue Service that this difference represents capital gain. The IRS is wise to that one and will tax your return as ordinary income.

Interest rates on money-market investments are often quoted on a discount basis. For example, suppose that three-month bills are issued at a discount of 5%. This is a rather complicated way of saying that the price of a three-month bill is $100 - (3/12) \times 5 = 98.75$. Therefore, for every \$98.75 that you invest today, you receive \$100 at the end of three months. The return over three months is $1.25/98.75 = .0127$, or 1.27%. This is equivalent to an annual yield of 5.08% simple interest or 5.18% if interest is compounded annually. Note that the return is always higher than the discount. When you read that an investment is selling at a discount of 5%, it is very easy to slip into the mistake of thinking that this is its return.[34]

Yields on Money-Market Investments

When we value long-term debt, it is important to take account of default risk. Almost anything may happen in 30 years, and even today's most respectable company may get into trouble eventually. Therefore, corporate bonds offer higher yields than Treasury bonds.

Short-term debt is not risk-free either. When California was mired in the energy crisis of 2001, Southern California Edison and Pacific Gas and Electric were forced to suspend payments on nearly \$1 billion of maturing commercial paper. However, such examples are exceptions; in general, the danger of default is less for money-market securities issued by corporations than for corporate bonds. There are two reasons for this. First, the range of possible outcomes is smaller for short-term investments. Even though the distant future may be clouded, you can usually be confident that a particular company will survive for at least the next month. Second, for the most part only well-established companies can borrow in the money market. If you are going to lend money for just a few days, you can't afford to spend too much time in evaluating the loan. Thus, you will consider only blue-chip borrowers.

---

[33] We discussed money-market funds in Section 14.3.

[34] To confuse things even more, dealers in the money market often quote rates as if there were only 360 days in a year. So a discount of 5% on a bill maturing in 91 days translates into a price of $100 - 5 \times (91/360) = 98.74\%$.

Despite the high quality of money-market investments, there are often significant differences in yield between corporate and U.S. government securities. Why is this? One answer is the risk of default. Another is that the investments have different degrees of liquidity or "moneyness." Investors like Treasury bills because they are easily turned into cash on short notice. Securities that cannot be converted so quickly and cheaply into cash need to offer relatively high yields.

During times of market turmoil investors may place a higher value on having ready access to cash. On these occasions the yield on illiquid securities can increase dramatically. This happened in the fall of 1998 when a large hedge fund, Long Term Capital Management (LTCM), came close to collapse.[35] Fearful that LTCM would be forced to liquidate its huge positions, investors shrank from illiquid securities, and there was a "flight to quality." The spread between the yield on commercial paper and Treasury bills rose to about 120 basis points (1.20%), almost four times its level at the beginning of the year.

The International Money Market

In addition to the domestic money market, there is also an international market for short-term dollar investments, which is known as the *eurodollar* market.

Eurodollars have nothing to do with the euro, the currency of the European Monetary Union (EMU). They are simply dollars deposited in a bank in Europe. For example, suppose that an American oil company buys crude oil from an Arab sheik and pays for it with a $1 million check drawn on JP Morgan Chase. The sheik then deposits the check with his account at Barclays Bank in London. As a result, Barclays has an asset in the form of a $1 million credit in its account with JP Morgan Chase. It also has an offsetting liability in the form of a dollar deposit. Since that dollar deposit is placed in Europe, it is called a eurodollar deposit.[36]

Just as there is both a domestic U.S. money market and a eurodollar market, so there is both a domestic Japanese money market and a market in London for euro-yen. So, if a U.S. corporation wishes to make a short-term investment in yen, it can deposit the yen with a bank in Tokyo or it can make a euroyen deposit in London. Similarly, there is both a domestic money market in the euro area as well as a money market for euros in London.[37] And so on.

Major international banks in London lend dollars to one another at the *London interbank offered rate* (LIBOR). Similarly, they lend yen to each other at the yen LIBOR interest rate, and they lend euros at the **euro interbank offered rate,** or **Euribor.** These interest rates are used as a benchmark for pricing many types of short-term loans in the United States and in other countries. For example, a corporation in the United States may issue a floating-rate note with interest payments tied to dollar LIBOR.

If we lived in a world without regulation and taxes, the interest rate on a eurodollar loan would have to be the same as the rate on an equivalent domestic dollar loan. However, the international debt markets thrive because governments at-

---

[35] Hedge funds follow a variety of strategies including taking short positions in securities and currencies that they believe are overvalued. The story of LTCM is told in R. Lowenstein, *"When Genius Failed: The Rise and Fall of Long Term Capital Management* (New York: Random House, 2000); and N. Dunbar, *Inventing Money: The Story of Long Term Capital Management and the Legends behind It* (New York: John Wiley, 2000).

[36] The sheik could equally well deposit the check with the London branch of a U.S. bank or a Japanese bank. He would still have made a eurodollar deposit.

[37] Occasionally (but only occasionally) referred to as "euroeuros."

tempt to regulate domestic bank lending. When the U.S. government limited the rate of interest that banks in the United States could pay on domestic deposits, companies could earn a higher rate of interest by keeping their dollars on deposit in Europe. As these restrictions have been removed, differences in interest rates have largely disappeared.

In the late 1970s the U.S. government was concerned that its regulations were driving business overseas to foreign banks and the overseas branches of American banks. To attract some of this business back to the States, the government in 1981 allowed U.S. and foreign banks to establish **international banking facilities (IBFs)**. An IBF is the financial equivalent of a free-trade zone; it is physically located in the United States, but it is not required to maintain reserves with the Federal Reserve and depositors are not subject to any U.S. tax.[38] However, there are tight restrictions on what business an IBF can conduct. In particular, it cannot accept deposits from domestic U.S. corporations or make loans to them.

Money-Market Instruments

The principal money-market instruments are summarized in Table 20.9. We will describe each in turn.

U.S. Treasury Bills The first item in Table 20.9 is U.S. Treasury bills. These are usually issued weekly and mature in four weeks, three months, or six months.[39] Sales are by a single-price auction. This means that all successful bidders are allotted bills at the same price.[40] You don't have to participate in the auction to invest in Treasury bills. There is also an excellent secondary market in which billions of dollars of bills are bought and sold every week.

Federal Agency Securities Agencies of the federal government and government-sponsored enterprises, such as the Federal Home Loan Bank (FHLB) and the Federal National Mortgage Association ("Fannie Mae"), borrow both short and long term. The short-term debt consists of discount notes, which are similar to Treasury bills. They are very actively traded and are often held by corporations. The yields on these discount notes are slightly above those on comparable Treasury securities. One reason is that agency debt is not quite as marketable as Treasury issues. Another is that most agency debt is backed not by the "full faith and credit" of the U.S. government but only by the agency itself.[41] Most investors do not believe that the U.S. government would allow one of its agencies to default, but in 2000 their faith and the price of agency debt both took a knock when a senior Treasury official reminded Congress that the government did *not* guarantee the debt. Soothing noises from the Treasury subsequently helped to reassure investors.

Short-Term Tax-Exempts Short-term notes are also issued by municipalities, states, and agencies such as state universities and school districts.[42] These are

---

[38] For these reasons dollars held on deposit in an IBF are classed as eurodollars.

[39] A small proportion of bills is sold to *noncompetitive* bidders. Noncompetitive bids are filled at the same price as the successful competitive bids.

[40] Three-month bills actually mature 91 days after issue, and six-month bills mature 182 days after issue. For information on bill auctions, see **www.publicdebt.treas.gov.**

[41] The principal exception is Ginnie Mae, whose debts are guaranteed by the government.

[42] Some of these notes are *general obligations* of the issuer; others are *revenue securities,* and in these cases payments are made from rent receipts or other user charges.

somewhat more risky than Treasury bills and not as easy to buy or sell.[43] Nevertheless they have one particular attraction—the interest is not subject to federal tax.[44] Of course, this does not mean that companies should necessarily pile their surplus cash into "munis," for the tax advantage of municipal debt is recognized in its price. For example, as we write this, the yield on one-year AAA municipal debt is 3.7% compared with a yield of 5.3% on equivalent agency debt. Any investor with a tax rate of less than 30% would do better to buy the higher-yielding agency debt and pay the tax $((1 - .30) \times 5.3 = 3.7\%)$.

Variable-Rate Demand Bonds   There is no law preventing firms from making short-term investments in long-term securities. If a firm has $1 million set aside for an income tax payment, it could buy a long-term bond on January 1 and sell it on April 15, when the taxes must be paid. However, the danger with this strategy is obvious. What happens if bond prices fall by 10% between January and April? There you are with a $1 million liability to the Internal Revenue Service, bonds worth only $900,000, and a very red face. Of course, bond prices could also go up, but why take the chance? Corporate treasurers entrusted with excess funds for short-term investments are naturally averse to the price volatility of long-term bonds.

One solution is to buy municipal variable-rate demand bonds (VRDBs). These are long-term securities, whose interest payments are linked to the level of short-term interest rates. Whenever the interest rate is reset, investors have the right to sell the bonds back to the issuer for their face value. This ensures that on these reset dates the price of the bonds cannot be less than their face value. Therefore, although VRDBs are long-term bonds, their prices are very stable. In addition, the interest on municipal debt has the advantage of being tax-exempt. So a municipal variable-rate demand bond offers a safe, tax-free, short-term haven for your $1 million of cash.

Bank Time Deposits and Certificates of Deposit   If you make a time deposit with a bank, you are lending money to the bank for a fixed period. If you need the money before maturity, the bank will usually allow you to withdraw it but will exact a penalty in the form of a reduced rate of interest.

In the 1960s banks introduced the **negotiable certificate of deposit (CD)** for time deposits of $1 million or more. In this case, when a bank borrows, it issues a certificate of deposit, which is simply evidence of a time deposit with that bank. If a lender needs the money before maturity, it can sell the CD to another investor. When the loan matures, the new owner of the CD presents it to the bank and receives payment.[45]

Commercial Paper and Medium-Term Notes   These consist of unsecured, short- and medium-term debt issued by companies on a fairly regular basis. We described both in Section 20.5.

Bankers' Acceptances   Bankers' acceptances (BAs) may be used to finance exports or imports. An acceptance begins life as a written demand for the bank to

---

[43] Defaults on tax-exempts are rare but not unknown. For example, in 1983 Washington Public Power Supply System (unfortunately known as WPPSS or "WOOPS") defaulted on $2.25 billion of bonds. In 1994 Orange County in California also defaulted after losing $1.7 billion on its investment portfolio.

[44] This advantage is partly offset by the fact that Treasury securities are free of state and local taxes.

[45] Some CDs are not negotiable and are simply identical to time deposits. For example, banks may sell low-value non-negotiable CDs to individuals.

pay a given sum at a future date. Once the bank accepts this demand, it becomes a negotiable security that can be bought or sold through money-market dealers. Acceptances by the large U.S. banks generally mature in one to six months and involve very low credit risk.

Repurchase Agreements   Repurchase agreements, or *repos*, are effectively secured loans that are typically made to a government security dealer. They work as follows: The investor buys part of the dealer's holding of Treasury securities and simultaneously arranges to sell them back again at a later date at a specified higher price.[46] The borrower (the dealer) is said to have entered into a *repo;* the lender (who buys the securities) is said to have a *reverse repo.*

Repos sometimes run for several months, but more frequently they are just overnight (24-hour) agreements. No other domestic money-market investment offers such liquidity. Corporations can treat overnight repos almost as if they were interest-bearing demand deposits.

Suppose that you decide to invest cash in repos for several days or weeks. You don't want to keep renegotiating agreements every day. One solution is to enter into an *open repo* with a security dealer. In this case there is no fixed maturity to the agreement; either side is free to withdraw at one day's notice. Alternatively, you may arrange with your bank to transfer any excess cash automatically into repos.

Floating-Rate Preferred Stock   Common stock and preferred stock have an interesting tax advantage for corporations, since firms pay tax on only 30% of the dividends that they receive. So, for each $1 of dividends received, the firm gets to keep $1 - (.30 \times .35) = \$.895$. Thus the effective tax rate is only 10.5%. This is higher than the zero tax rate on the interest from municipal debt but much lower than the rate that the company pays on other debt interest.

Suppose that you consider investing your firm's spare cash in some other corporation's preferred stock. The 10.5% tax rate is very tempting. On the other hand, you worry that the price of the preferred shares may change if long-term interest rates change. You can reduce that worry by investing in preferred shares whose dividend payments are linked to the general level of interest rates.[47]

Varying the dividend payment on preferred stock doesn't quite do the trick, for the price of the preferred stock could still fall if the risk increases. So companies sometimes add another wrinkle to floating-rate preferred. Instead of being tied rigidly to interest rates, the dividend can be reset periodically by means of an auction that is open to all investors. Any investor can state the yield at which he or she would be prepared to buy the stock. Existing shareholders who require a higher yield simply sell their stock to the new investors at its face value. The result is similar to the variable-rate demand note. Because auction-rate preferred stock can be resold at regular intervals for its face value, its price cannot wander far in the interim.[48]

---

[46] To reduce the risk of repos, it is common to value the security at less than its market value. This difference is known as a *haircut*.

[47] The company *issuing* preferred stock must pay dividends out of after-tax income. So most tax-paying firms would prefer to issue debt rather than floating-rate preferred. However, there are plenty of firms that are not paying taxes and cannot make use of the interest tax shield. Moreover, they have been able to issue floating-rate preferred at yields *lower* than they would have to pay on a debt issue. The corporations buying the preferreds are happy with these lower yields because 70% of the dividends they receive escape tax.

[48] For a description of auction-rate preferred, see M. J. Alderson, K. C. Brown, and S. L. Lummer, "Dutch Auction Rate Preferred Stock," *Financial Management* 16 (Summer 1987), pp. 68–73.

Investment	Borrower	Maturities When Issued	Marketability	Basis for Calculating Interest	Comments
Treasury bills	U.S. government	4 weeks, 3 months, or 6 months	Excellent secondary market	Discount	Auctioned weekly
Federal agency benchmark bills and discount notes	FHLB, "Fannie Mae," "Sallie Mae," "Freddie Mac," etc.	Overnight to 360 days	Very good secondary market	Discount	Benchmark bills by regular auction; discount notes sold through dealers
Tax-exempt municipal notes	Municipalities, states, school districts, etc.	3 months to 1 year	Good secondary market	Usually interest-bearing with interest at maturity	Tax-anticipation notes (TANs), revenue anticipation notes (RANs), bond anticipation notes (BANs), etc.
Tax-exempt variable-rate demand bonds (VRDBs)	Municipalities, states, state universities, etc.	10 to 40 years	Good secondary market	Variable interest rate	Long-term bonds with put options to demand repayment
Nonnegotiable time deposits and negotiable certificates of deposit (CDs)	Commercial banks, savings and loans	Usually 1 to 3 months; also longer-maturity variable-rate CDs	Fair secondary market for negotiable CDs	Interest-bearing with interest at maturity	Receipt for time deposit
Commercial paper (CP)	Industrial firms, finance companies, and bank holding companies; also municipalities	Maximum 270 days; usually 60 days or less	Dealers or issuer will repurchase paper	Usually discount	Unsecured promissory note; may be placed through dealer or directly with investor
Medium-term notes (MTNs)	Largely finance companies and banks; also industrial firms	Minimum 270 days; usually less than 10 years	Dealers will repurchase notes	Interest-bearing; usually fixed rate	Unsecured promissory note placed through dealer
Bankers' acceptances (BAs)	Major commercial banks	1 to 6 months	Fair secondary market	Discount	Demand to pay that has been accepted by a bank
Repurchase agreements (repos)	Dealers in U.S. government securities	Overnight to about 3 months; also open repos (continuing contracts)	No secondary market	Repurchase price set higher than selling price; difference quoted as repo interest rate	Sales of government securities by dealer with simultaneous agreement to repurchase

TABLE 20.9

Money-market investments in the United States.

Short-term financial planning is concerned with the management of the firm's short-term, or current, assets and liabilities. The most important current assets are cash, marketable securities, inventory, and accounts receivable. The most important current liabilities are short-term loans and accounts payable. The difference between current assets and current liabilities is called (net) working capital.

SUMMARY

Current assets and liabilities are turned over much more rapidly than the other items on the balance sheet. Short-term financing and investment decisions are more quickly and easily reversed than long-term decisions. Consequently, the financial manager does not need to look so far into the future when making them.

The nature of the firm's short-term financial planning problem is determined by the amount of long-term capital it raises. A firm that issues large amounts of long-term debt or common stock, or that retains a large part of its earnings, may find it has permanent excess cash. In such cases there is never any problem paying bills, and short-term financial planning consists of managing the firm's portfolio of marketable securities. A firm holding a reservoir of cash is able to buy itself time to react to a short-term crisis. This may be important for risky firms that find it difficult to raise cash on short notice. However, large cash holdings can lead to complacency. We suggest that firms with permanent cash surpluses ought to return the excess cash to their stockholders.

Other firms raise relatively little long-term capital and end up as permanent short-term debtors. Most firms attempt to find a golden mean by financing all fixed assets and part of current assets with equity and long-term debt. Such firms may invest cash surpluses during part of the year and borrow during the rest of the year.

The starting point for short-term financial planning is an understanding of sources and uses of cash.[49] Firms forecast their net cash requirements by forecasting collections on accounts receivable, adding other cash inflows, and subtracting all cash outlays. If the forecasted cash balance is insufficient to cover day-to-day operations and to provide a buffer against contingencies, the company will need to find additional finance. The search for the best short-term financial plan inevitably proceeds by trial and error. The financial manager must explore the consequences of different assumptions about cash requirements, interest rates, sources of finance, and so on. Firms are increasingly using computerized financial models to help in this process. The models range from simple spreadsheet programs that merely help with the arithmetic to linear programming models that help to find the best financial plan.

If you foresee a large and permanent cash deficiency, the financial plan may involve raising long-term finance. If the shortage is temporary, you may be able to finance it by not paying your bills for a while or you can choose from a variety of short- and medium-term loans.

---

[49] We pointed out in Section 20.2 that sources and uses of *funds* are often analyzed rather than sources and uses of cash. Anything that contributes to working capital is called a *source of funds*; anything that diminishes working capital is called a *use of funds*. Sources and uses of funds statements are relatively simple because many sources and uses of cash are buried in changes in working capital. However, in forecasting, the emphasis is on cash flow. You pay bills with cash, not working capital.

Often firms arrange a *revolving line of credit* with a bank that allows them to borrow up to an agreed amount whenever they need financing. This is usually intended to tide the firm over a temporary shortage of cash and is therefore repaid in only a few months. However, banks also make *term loans* that sometimes extend for five years or more. In addition to borrowing from their domestic banks, companies may borrow dollars (or any other currency) from overseas banks or the foreign branches of U.S. banks. Very large bank loans are commonly *syndicated* among a group of major banks. Banks do not need to hold these loans until maturity, and they may later decide to sell their holdings to other banks or financial institutions. Banks may also package together a portfolio of loans for sale. Frequently this sale takes the form of a collateralized loan obligation (CLO). In this case the loan portfolio is sliced up into different tranches. The senior tranche has first claim on the cash flows, while the junior (or equity) claim is at the bottom of the pecking order.

Many bank loans are unsecured, but less-creditworthy borrowers may be asked to provide security. Sometimes this consists of a floating charge on receivables and inventories, but usually you will be asked to pledge specific assets. When you borrow against receivables, the bank is informed of all sales of goods and the resulting receivables are pledged to the bank. As the customers pay their bills, the money is paid into a special collateral account under the bank's control. Similarly, when you borrow against stocks of raw materials, the bank may insist that the goods are under the control of an independent warehouse company. As long as the bank holds the warehouse receipt for these goods, they cannot be released without the bank's permission.

The interest rate on very short-term bank loans is generally fixed for the life of the loan, but in other cases the rate floats with the general level of short-term interest rates. For example, it might be set at 1% over LIBOR (the London Interbank Offered Rate).

Of course, the interest rate that the bank charges must be sufficient to cover not only the opportunity cost of capital for the loan but also the costs of running the loan department. As a result, large regular borrowers have found it cheaper to bypass the banking system and issue their own short-term unsecured debt. This is called *commercial paper.* Longer-term loans that are marketed on a regular basis are known as *medium-term notes.*

If you have more cash than is currently needed, you can invest it in the money market. There is a wide choice of money-market investments, with different degrees of liquidity and risk. Remember that the interest rate on these investments is often quoted as a discount. The compound return is always higher than the rate of discount. The principal money-market investments in the United States are:

- U.S. Treasury bills
- Federal agency notes
- Short-term tax exempts
- Time deposits and certificates of deposit
- Repurchase agreements
- Commercial paper
- Bankers' acceptances

Figure 20.3 should give you some feel for which of these investments are the most popular homes for surplus cash.

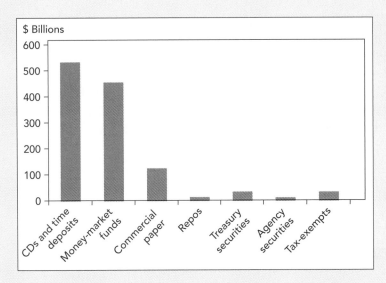

FIGURE 20.3

Short-term assets held by U.S. nonfinancial corporations, 2nd quarter, 2006.

Source: Federal Reserve System, Division of Research and Statistics, *Flow of Funds Accounts* (**www.federalreserve.gov/ releases/Z1/current/data.htm**).

FURTHER READING

Here are some general textbooks on working-capital management:

G. W. Gallinger and B. P. Healey, *Liquidity Analysis and Management,* 2nd. ed. (Reading, MA: Addison-Wesley 1991).

N. C. Hill and W. L. Sartoris, *Short-Term Financial Management: Text and Cases,* 3rd. ed. (Englewood Cliffs, NJ: Prentice-Hall, Inc. 1994).

K. V. Smith and G. W. Gallinger, *Readings on Short-Term Financial Management,* 3rd ed. (New York: West, 1988).

F. C. Scherr, *Modern Working Capital Management: Text and Cases* (Englewood Cliffs, NJ: Prentice-Hall, Inc. 1989).

F. J. Fabozzi (ed.), *Bank Loans: Secondary Market and Portfolio Management* (New Hope, PA: Frank J. Fabozzi Associates, 1998).

WEB PROJECT

The Federal Reserve Bulletin publishes the results of a quarterly survey of bank lending (see **www.federalreserve.gov/releases/E2**). Use the latest survey to describe the pattern of bank lending by domestic banks. Examine, for example, whether most loans are secured and whether they are made under commitment. What are the different characteristics of small and large loans? Now compare the results of this survey with an earlier one. Have there been any important changes?

CONCEPT REVIEW QUESTIONS

1. Growth firms commonly have relatively larger cash holdings than do old-line manufacturing firms. Why might this be so? (pages 548–549)

2. What are the advantages and disadvantages of holding a large reservoir of cash? (pages 549–551)

3. Why do we say that holdings of marketable securities are at best a zero-NPV investment for a taxpaying firm? (page 549)

For a complete listing of your chapter Concept Review Questions, please visit us at www.mhhe.com/bma1e.

Visit us at www.mhhe.com/bma1e

QUIZ

1. Listed below are six transactions that Dynamic Mattress might make. Indicate how each transaction would affect (a) cash and (b) working capital.
   The transactions are
   i. Pay out $2 million cash dividend.
   ii. Receive $2,500 from a customer who pays a bill resulting from a previous sale.
   iii. Pay $5,000 previously owed to one of its suppliers.
   iv. Borrow $1 million long term and invest the proceeds in inventory.
   v. Borrow $1 million short term and invest the proceeds in inventory.
   vi. Sell $5 million of marketable securities for cash.

2. State how each of the following events would affect the firm's balance sheet. State whether each change is a source or use of cash.
   a. An automobile manufacturer increases production in response to a forecasted increase in demand. Unfortunately, the demand does not increase.
   b. Competition forces the firm to give customers more time to pay for their purchases.
   c. Inflation increases the value of raw material inventories by 20%.
   d. The firm sells a parcel of land for $100,000. The land was purchased five years earlier for $200,000.
   e. The firm repurchases its own common stock.
   f. The firm doubles its quarterly dividend.
   g. The firm issues $1 million of long-term debt and uses the proceeds to repay a short-term bank loan.

3. Here is a forecast of sales by National Bromide for the first four months of 2009 (figures in $ thousands):

	Month 1	Month 2	Month 3	Month 4
Cash sales	15	24	18	14
Sales on credit	100	120	90	70

On the average 50% of credit sales are paid for in the current month, 30% are paid in the next month, and the remainder are paid in the month after that. What is the expected cash inflow from operations in months 3 and 4?

4. Dynamic Futon forecasts the following purchases from suppliers:

	Jan.	Feb.	Mar.	Apr.	May	Jun.
Value of goods ($ millions)	32	28	25	22	20	20

   a. Forty percent of goods are supplied cash on delivery. The remainder are paid with an average delay of one month. If Dynamic Futon starts the year with payables of $22 million, what is the forecasted level of payables for each month?
   b. Suppose that from the start of the year the company stretches payables by paying 40% after one month and 20% after two months. (The remainder continue to be paid cash on delivery.) Recalculate payables for each month assuming that there are no cash penalties for late payment.

5. Each of the following events affects one or more tables in the chapter. Show the effects of each event by adjusting the tables listed in parentheses:
   a. Dynamic repays only $2 million of short-term debt in 2007. (Tables 20.1, 20.3–20.5)

b. Dynamic issues an additional $10 million of long-term debt in 2007 and invests $12 million in a new warehouse. (Tables 20.1, 20.3–20.5)

c. In 2007 Dynamic reduces the quantity of stuffing in each mattress. Customers don't notice, but operating costs fall by 10%. (Tables 20.1–20.5)

d. Starting in the third quarter of 2008, Dynamic employs new staff members who prove very effective in persuading customers to pay more promptly. As a result, 90% of sales are paid for immediately, and 10% are paid in the following quarter. (Tables 20.6 and 20.7)

e. Starting in the first quarter of 2008, Dynamic cuts wages by $4 million a quarter. (Table 20.7)

f. In the second quarter of 2008 a disused warehouse mysteriously catches fire. Dynamic receives a $10 million check from the insurance company. (Table 20.7)

g. Dynamic's treasurer decides he can scrape by on a $2 million operating cash balance. (Table 20.7)

6. True or false?

   a. Most commercial bank loans are made under commitment.

   b. A line of credit provides the lender with a put option.

   c. Bank term loans typically have a maturity of several years.

   d. If the interest rate on a one-year bank loan is stated as a discount of 10%, the actual yield on the loan is less than 10%.

   e. The interest rate on term loans is usually linked to LIBOR, the federal funds rate, or the bank's prime rate.

7. Complete the passage below by selecting the most appropriate terms from the following list: *floating charge, syndicated, commercial paper, warehouse receipt, arranger, collateral, commitment fee, line of credit, medium-term notes, collateralized loan obligation (CLO).*

   Companies with fluctuating capital needs often arrange a _____ with their bank. This is relatively expensive because companies need to pay a _____ on any unused amount.

   Secured short-term loans are sometimes covered by a _____ on all receivables and inventory. Generally, however, the borrower pledges specific assets as _____. For example, if goods are stored in a warehouse, an independent warehouse company may issue a _____ to the lender. The goods can then only be released with the lender's consent.

   Very large bank loans are often _____. In this case the lead bank acts as the _____ and will parcel out the loan among a group of banks.

   Banks also often sell loans. Sometimes they will put together a portfolio of loans and sell separate slices (or tranches). These are known as _____.

   Banks are not the only source of short-term debt. Many large companies issue their own unsecured debt directly to investors, often on a regular basis. If the maturity is less than nine months, this debt is generally known as _____. Companies also make regular issues of longer-term debt to investors. These are called _____.

8. In August 2004, six-month (182-day) Treasury bills were issued at a discount of 1.73%. What is the annual yield?

9. For each item below, choose the investment that best fits the accompanying description:

   a. Maturity often overnight (repurchase agreements/bankers' acceptances).

   b. Maturity never more than 270 days (tax-exempts/commercial paper).

   c. Often directly placed with investors (finance company commercial paper/ industrial commercial paper).

   d. Issued by the U.S. Treasury (tax-exempts/three-month bills).

e. Quoted on a discount basis (certificates of deposit/Treasury bills).

f. Sold by auction (tax-exempts/Treasury bills).

10. Consider three securities:

a. A floating-rate bond.

b. A preferred share paying a fixed dividend.

c. A floating-rate preferred.

A financial manager responsible for short-term investment of excess cash would probably choose the floating-rate preferred over *either* of the other two securities. Why? Explain briefly.

PRACTICE QUESTIONS

Visit us at
www.mhhe.com/bma1e.

11. Table 20.10 lists data from the budget of Ritewell Publishers. Half the company sales are for cash on the nail; the other half are paid for with a one-month delay. The company pays all its credit purchases with a one-month delay. Credit purchases in January were $30, and total sales in January were $180. Complete the cash budget in Table 20.11.

12. If a firm pays its bills with a 30-day delay, what fraction of its purchases will be paid in the current quarter? In the following quarter? What if the delay is 60 days?

TABLE 20.10

Selected budget data for Ritewell Publishers.

	February	March	April
Total sales	$200	$220	$180
Purchases of materials			
For cash	70	80	60
For credit	40	30	40
Other expenses	30	30	30
Taxes, interest, and dividends	10	10	10
Capital investment	100	0	0

TABLE 20.11

Cash budget for Ritewell Publishers.

	February	March	April
Sources of cash:			
Collections on cash sales			
Collections on accounts receivable	—	—	—
Total sources of cash			
Uses of cash:			
Payments of accounts payable			
Cash purchases of materials			
Other expenses			
Capital expenditures			
Taxes, interest, and dividends			
Total uses of cash	—	—	—
Net cash inflow			
Cash at start of period	100		
+ Net cash inflow			
= Cash at end of period			
+ Minimum operating cash balance	100	100	100
= Cumulative short-term financing required			

13. Which items in Table 20.8 would be affected by the following events?

   a. There is a rise in interest rates.

   b. Suppliers demand interest for late payment.

   c. Dynamic receives an unexpected bill in the third quarter from the Internal Revenue Service for underpayment of taxes in previous years.

14. Table 20.12 shows Dynamic Mattress's year-end 2005 balance sheet, and Table 20.13 shows its income statement for 2006. Work out statements of sources and uses of cash and sources and uses of funds for 2006.

Visit us at www.mhhe.com/bma1e.

15. Work out a short-term financing plan for Dynamic Mattress Company, assuming the limit on the line of credit is raised from $38 to $50 million. Otherwise keep to the assumptions used in developing Table 20.8.

16. Dynamic Mattress decides to lease its new mattress-stuffing machines rather than buy them. As a result, capital expenditure in the first quarter is reduced by $30 million, but the company must make lease payments of $1.5 million for each of the four quarters. Assume that the lease has no effect on tax payments until after the fourth quarter. Construct two tables like Tables 20.7 and 20.8 showing Dynamic's cumulative financing requirement and a new financing plan. Check your answer using the "live" spreadsheet on the book's Web site, **www.mhhe.com/bma1e.**

Visit us at www.mhhe.com/bma1e.

17. You need to borrow $10 million for 90 days. You have the following alternatives:

   a. Issue high-grade commercial paper, with a back-up line of credit costing .3% a year.

   b. Borrow from First Cookham Bank at an interest rate of .25% over LIBOR.

   c. Borrow from the Test Bank at prime.

   Given the rates currently prevailing in the market (see, for example, *The Wall Street Journal*), which alternative would you choose?

TABLE 20.12

Year-end balance sheet for Dynamic Mattress for 2005 (figures in $ millions).

Current assets:		Current liabilities:	
Cash	$ 4	Bank loans	$ 4
Marketable securities	2	Accounts payable	15
Inventory	20	Total current liabilities	19
Accounts receivable	22		
Total current assets	48	Long-term debt	5
		Net worth (equity and retained earnings)	60
Fixed assets:			
Gross investment	50		
Less depreciation	−14		
Net fixed assets	36	Total liabilities	
Total assets	84	and net worth	84

TABLE 20.13

Income statement for Dynamic Mattress for 2006 (figures in $ millions).

Note: Dividend = $1 million; retained earnings = $5 million.

Sales	$ 300
Operating costs	−285
	15
Depreciation	−2
	13
Interest	−1
Pretax income	12
Tax at 50%	−6
Net income	6

18. Suppose that you are a banker responsible for approving corporate loans. Nine firms are seeking secured loans. They offer the following assets as collateral:

a. Firm A, a heating oil distributor, offers a tanker load of fuel in transit from the Middle East.

b. Firm B, a wine wholesaler, offers 1,000 cases of Beaujolais Nouveau, located in a warehouse.

c. Firm C, a stationer, offers an account receivable for office supplies sold to the City of New York.

d. Firm D, a bookstore, offers its entire inventory of 15,000 used books.

e. Firm E, a wholesale grocer, offers a boxcar full of bananas.

f. Firm F, an appliance dealer, offers its inventory of electric typewriters.

g. Firm G, a jeweler, offers 100 ounces of gold.

h. Firm H, a government securities dealer, offers its portfolio of Treasury bills.

i. Firm I, a boat builder, offers a half-completed luxury yacht. The yacht will take four months more to complete.

Which of these assets are most likely to be good collateral? Which are likely to be bad collateral? Explain.

STANDARD &POOR'S

19. Use the Market Insight database (**www.mhhe.com/edumarketinsight**) to find recent balance sheets and income statements for two companies. Draw up a sources and uses of cash statement and a sources and uses of funds statement as in Tables 20.3 and 20.5.

STANDARD &POOR'S

20. Use the Market Insight database (**www.mhhe.com/edumarketinsight**) to compare the investment in current assets of different companies. Which of these companies make a heavy investment in inventories or receivables? Can you explain why?

21. A three-month Treasury bill and a six-month bill both sell at a discount of 10%. Which offers the higher annual yield?

22. In Section 20.6 we described a three-month bill that was issued on an annually compounded yield of 5.18%. Suppose that one month has passed and the investment still offers the same annually compounded return. What is the percentage discount? What was your return over the month?

23. Look again at Practice Problem 22. Suppose another month has passed, so the bill has only one month left to run. It is now selling at a discount of 5%. What is the yield calculated on a simple interest basis? What was your realized return over the two months?

24. Look up current interest rates offered by short-term investment alternatives. Suppose that your firm has $1 million excess cash to invest for the next two months. How would you invest this cash? How would your answer change if the excess cash were $5,000, $20,000, $100,000, or $100 million?

25. In August 2004 high-grade corporate bonds sold at a yield of 3.52%, while tax-exempts of comparable maturity offered 2.44% annually. If an investor receives the same *after-tax* return from corporates and tax-exempts, what is that investor's marginal rate of tax?

What other factors might affect an investor's choice between the two types of securities?

26. The IRS prohibits companies from borrowing money to buy tax-exempts and deducting the interest payments on the borrowing from taxable income. Should the IRS prohibit such activity? If it didn't, would you advise the company to borrow to buy tax-exempts?

27. Suppose you are a wealthy individual paying 35% tax on income. What is the expected after-tax yield on each of the following investments?

a. A municipal note yielding 7.0% pretax.

b. A Treasury bill yielding 10% pretax.

c. A floating-rate preferred stock yielding 7.5% pretax.

How would your answer change if the investor is a corporation paying tax at 35%? What other factors would you need to take into account when deciding where to invest the corporation's spare cash?

CHALLENGE QUESTIONS

28. Axle Chemical Corporation's treasurer has forecasted a $1 million cash deficit for the next quarter. However, there is only a 50% chance this deficit will actually occur. The treasurer estimates that there is a 20% probability the company will have no deficit at all and a 30% probability that it will actually need $2 million in short-term financing. The company can either take out a 90-day unsecured loan for $2 million at 1% per month or establish a line of credit, costing 1% per month on the amount borrowed plus a commitment fee of $20,000. If excess cash can be reinvested at 9%, which source of financing gives the lower expected cost?

29. Term loans usually require firms to pay a fluctuating interest rate. For example, the interest rate may be set at "1% above prime." The prime rate sometimes varies by several percentage points within a single year. Suppose that your firm has decided to borrow $40 million for five years. It has three alternatives. It can (**a**) borrow from a bank at the prime rate, currently 10%. The proposed loan agreement requires no principal repayments until the loan matures in five years. It can (**b**) issue 26-week commercial paper, currently yielding 9%. Since funds are required for five years, the commercial paper will have to be rolled over semiannually. That is, financing the $40 million requirement for five years will require 10 successive commercial paper sales. Or, finally, it can (**c**) borrow from an insurance company at a fixed rate of 11%. As in the bank loan, no principal has to be repaid until the end of the five-year period. What factors would you consider in analyzing these alternatives? Under what circumstances would you choose (**a**)? Under what circumstances would you choose (**b**) or (**c**)? (*Hint:* Don't forget Chapter 4.)

APPENDIX A

PRESENT VALUE TABLES

APPENDIX TABLE 1

Discount factors: Present value of $1 to be received after t years $= 1/(1 + r)^t$.

Number of Years	Interest Rate per Year														
	1%	2%	3%	4%	5%	6%	7%	8%	9%	10%	11%	12%	13%	14%	15%
1	.990	.980	.971	.962	.952	.943	.935	.926	.917	.909	.901	.893	.885	.877	.870
2	.980	.961	.943	.925	.907	.890	.873	.857	.842	.826	.812	.797	.783	.769	.756
3	.971	.942	.915	.889	.864	.840	.816	.794	.772	.751	.731	.712	.693	.675	.658
4	.961	.924	.888	.855	.823	.792	.763	.735	.708	.683	.659	.636	.613	.592	.572
5	.951	.906	.863	.822	.784	.747	.713	.681	.650	.621	.593	.567	.543	.519	.497
6	.942	.888	.837	.790	.746	.705	.666	.630	.596	.564	.535	.507	.480	.456	.432
7	.933	.871	.813	.760	.711	.665	.623	.583	.547	.513	.482	.452	.425	.400	.376
8	.923	.853	.789	.731	.677	.627	.582	.540	.502	.467	.434	.404	.376	.351	.327
9	.914	.837	.766	.703	.645	.592	.544	.500	.460	.424	.391	.361	.333	.308	.284
10	.905	.820	.744	.676	.614	.558	.508	.463	.422	.386	.352	.322	.295	.270	.247
11	.896	.804	.722	.650	.585	.527	.475	.429	.388	.350	.317	.287	.261	.237	.215
12	.887	.788	.701	.625	.557	.497	.444	.397	.356	.319	.286	.257	.231	.208	.187
13	.879	.773	.681	.601	.530	.469	.415	.368	.326	.290	.258	.229	.204	.182	.163
14	.870	.758	.661	.577	.505	.442	.388	.340	.299	.263	.232	.205	.181	.160	.141
15	.861	.743	.642	.555	.481	.417	.362	.315	.275	.239	.209	.183	.160	.140	.123
16	.853	.728	.623	.534	.458	.394	.339	.292	.252	.218	.188	.163	.141	.123	.107
17	.844	.714	.605	.513	.436	.371	.317	.270	.231	.198	.170	.146	.125	.108	.093
18	.836	.700	.587	.494	.416	.350	.296	.250	.212	.180	.153	.130	.111	.095	.081
19	.828	.686	.570	.475	.396	.331	.277	.232	.194	.164	.138	.116	.098	.083	.070
20	.820	.673	.554	.456	.377	.312	.258	.215	.178	.149	.124	.104	.087	.073	.061

Number of Years	Interest Rate per Year														
	16%	17%	18%	19%	20%	21%	22%	23%	24%	25%	26%	27%	28%	29%	30%
1	.862	.855	.847	.840	.833	.826	.820	.813	.806	.800	.794	.787	.781	.775	.769
2	.743	.731	.718	.706	.694	.683	.672	.661	.650	.640	.630	.620	.610	.601	.592
3	.641	.624	.609	.593	.579	.564	.551	.537	.524	.512	.500	.488	.477	.466	.455
4	.552	.534	.516	.499	.482	.467	.451	.437	.423	.410	.397	.384	.373	.361	.350
5	.476	.456	.437	.419	.402	.386	.370	.355	.341	.328	.315	.303	.291	.280	.269
6	.410	.390	.370	.352	.335	.319	.303	.289	.275	.262	.250	.238	.227	.217	.207
7	.354	.333	.314	.296	.279	.263	.249	.235	.222	.210	.198	.188	.178	.168	.159
8	.305	.285	.266	.249	.233	.218	.204	.191	.179	.168	.157	.148	.139	.130	.123
9	.263	.243	.225	.209	.194	.180	.167	.155	.144	.134	.125	.116	.108	.101	.094
10	.227	.208	.191	.176	.162	.149	.137	.126	.116	.107	.099	.092	.085	.078	.073
11	.195	.178	.162	.148	.135	.123	.112	.103	.094	.086	.079	.072	.066	.061	.056
12	.168	.152	.137	.124	.112	.102	.092	.083	.076	.069	.062	.057	.052	.047	.043
13	.145	.130	.116	.104	.093	.084	.075	.068	.061	.055	.050	.045	.040	.037	.033
14	.125	.111	.099	.088	.078	.069	.062	.055	.049	.044	.039	.035	.032	.028	.025
15	.108	.095	.084	.074	.065	.057	.051	.045	.040	.035	.031	.028	.025	.022	.020
16	.093	.081	.071	.062	.054	.047	.042	.036	.032	.028	.025	.022	.019	.017	.015
17	.080	.069	.060	.052	.045	.039	.034	.030	.026	.023	.020	.017	.015	.013	.012
18	.069	.059	.051	.044	.038	.032	.028	.024	.021	.018	.016	.014	.012	.010	.009
19	.060	.051	.043	.037	.031	.027	.023	.020	.017	.014	.012	.011	.009	.008	.007
20	.051	.043	.037	.031	.026	.022	.019	.016	.014	.012	.010	.008	.007	.006	.005

Note: For example, if the interest rate is 10% per year, the present value of $1 received at year 5 is $.621.

A

APPENDIX TABLE 2

Future value of $1 after t years $= (1 + r)^t$.

Number of Years	Interest Rate per Year														
	1%	2%	3%	4%	5%	6%	7%	8%	9%	10%	11%	12%	13%	14%	15%
1	1.010	1.020	1.030	1.040	1.050	1.060	1.070	1.080	1.090	1.100	1.110	1.120	1.130	1.140	1.150
2	1.020	1.040	1.061	1.082	1.102	1.124	1.145	1.166	1.188	1.210	1.232	1.254	1.277	1.300	1.323
3	1.030	1.061	1.093	1.125	1.158	1.191	1.225	1.260	1.295	1.331	1.368	1.405	1.443	1.482	1.521
4	1.041	1.082	1.126	1.170	1.216	1.262	1.311	1.360	1.412	1.464	1.518	1.574	1.630	1.689	1.749
5	1.051	1.104	1.159	1.217	1.276	1.338	1.403	1.469	1.539	1.611	1.685	1.762	1.842	1.925	2.011
6	1.062	1.126	1.194	1.265	1.340	1.419	1.501	1.587	1.677	1.772	1.870	1.974	2.082	2.195	2.313
7	1.072	1.149	1.230	1.316	1.407	1.504	1.606	1.714	1.828	1.949	2.076	2.211	2.353	2.502	2.660
8	1.083	1.172	1.267	1.369	1.477	1.594	1.718	1.851	1.993	2.144	2.305	2.476	2.658	2.853	3.059
9	1.094	1.195	1.305	1.423	1.551	1.689	1.838	1.999	2.172	2.358	2.558	2.773	3.004	3.252	3.518
10	1.105	1.219	1.344	1.480	1.629	1.791	1.967	2.159	2.367	2.594	2.839	3.106	3.395	3.707	4.046
11	1.116	1.243	1.384	1.539	1.710	1.898	2.105	2.332	2.580	2.853	3.152	3.479	3.836	4.226	4.652
12	1.127	1.268	1.426	1.601	1.796	2.012	2.252	2.518	2.813	3.138	3.498	3.896	4.335	4.818	5.350
13	1.138	1.294	1.469	1.665	1.886	2.133	2.410	2.720	3.066	3.452	3.883	4.363	4.898	5.492	6.153
14	1.149	1.319	1.513	1.732	1.980	2.261	2.579	2.937	3.342	3.797	4.310	4.887	5.535	6.261	7.076
15	1.161	1.346	1.558	1.801	2.079	2.397	2.759	3.172	3.642	4.177	4.785	5.474	6.254	7.138	8.137
16	1.173	1.373	1.605	1.873	2.183	2.540	2.952	3.426	3.970	4.595	5.311	6.130	7.067	8.137	9.358
17	1.184	1.400	1.653	1.948	2.292	2.693	3.159	3.700	4.328	5.054	5.895	6.866	7.986	9.276	10.76
18	1.196	1.428	1.702	2.026	2.407	2.854	3.380	3.996	4.717	5.560	6.544	7.690	9.024	10.58	12.38
19	1.208	1.457	1.754	2.107	2.527	3.026	3.617	4.316	5.142	6.116	7.263	8.613	10.20	12.06	14.23
20	1.220	1.486	1.806	2.191	2.653	3.207	3.870	4.661	5.604	6.727	8.062	9.646	11.52	13.74	16.37

Number of Years	Interest Rate per Year														
	16%	17%	18%	19%	20%	21%	22%	23%	24%	25%	26%	27%	28%	29%	30%
1	1.160	1.170	1.180	1.190	1.200	1.210	1.220	1.230	1.240	1.250	1.260	1.270	1.280	1.290	1.300
2	1.346	1.369	1.392	1.416	1.440	1.464	1.488	1.513	1.538	1.563	1.588	1.613	1.638	1.664	1.690
3	1.561	1.602	1.643	1.685	1.728	1.772	1.816	1.861	1.907	1.953	2.000	2.048	2.097	2.147	2.197
4	1.811	1.874	1.939	2.005	2.074	2.144	2.215	2.289	2.364	2.441	2.520	2.601	2.684	2.769	2.856
5	2.100	2.192	2.288	2.386	2.488	2.594	2.703	2.815	2.932	3.052	3.176	3.304	3.436	3.572	3.713
6	2.436	2.565	2.700	2.840	2.986	3.138	3.297	3.463	3.635	3.815	4.002	4.196	4.398	4.608	4.827
7	2.826	3.001	3.185	3.379	3.583	3.797	4.023	4.259	4.508	4.768	5.042	5.329	5.629	5.945	6.275
8	3.278	3.511	3.759	4.021	4.300	4.595	4.908	5.239	5.590	5.960	6.353	6.768	7.206	7.669	8.157
9	3.803	4.108	4.435	4.785	5.160	5.560	5.987	6.444	6.931	7.451	8.005	8.595	9.223	9.893	10.60
10	4.411	4.807	5.234	5.695	6.192	6.728	7.305	7.926	8.594	9.313	10.09	10.92	11.81	12.76	13.79
11	5.117	5.624	6.176	6.777	7.430	8.140	8.912	9.749	10.66	11.64	12.71	13.86	15.11	16.46	17.92
12	5.936	6.580	7.288	8.064	8.916	9.850	10.87	11.99	13.21	14.55	16.01	17.61	19.34	21.24	23.30
13	6.886	7.699	8.599	9.596	10.70	11.92	13.26	14.75	16.39	18.19	20.18	22.36	24.76	27.39	30.29
14	7.988	9.007	10.15	11.42	12.84	14.42	16.18	18.14	20.32	22.74	25.42	28.40	31.69	35.34	39.37
15	9.266	10.54	11.97	13.59	15.41	17.45	19.74	22.31	25.20	28.42	32.03	36.06	40.56	45.59	51.19
16	10.75	12.33	14.13	16.17	18.49	21.11	24.09	27.45	31.24	35.53	40.36	45.80	51.92	58.81	66.54
17	12.47	14.43	16.67	19.24	22.19	25.55	29.38	33.76	38.74	44.41	50.85	58.17	66.46	75.86	86.50
18	14.46	16.88	19.67	22.90	26.62	30.91	35.85	41.52	48.04	55.51	64.07	73.87	85.07	97.86	112.5
19	16.78	19.75	23.21	27.25	31.95	37.40	43.74	51.07	59.57	69.39	80.73	93.81	108.9	126.2	146.2
20	19.46	23.11	27.39	32.43	38.34	45.26	53.36	62.82	73.86	86.74	101.7	119.1	139.4	162.9	190.0

Note: For example, if the interest rate is 10% per year, the investment of $1 today will be worth $1.611 at year 5.

APPENDIX TABLE 3

Annuity table: Present value of $1 per year for each of t years $= 1/r - 1/[r(1 + r)^t]$.

Number of Years	Interest Rate per Year														
	1%	2%	3%	4%	5%	6%	7%	8%	9%	10%	11%	12%	13%	14%	15%
1	.990	.980	.971	.962	.952	.943	.935	.926	.917	.909	.901	.893	.885	.877	.870
2	1.970	1.942	1.913	1.886	1.859	1.833	1.808	1.783	1.759	1.736	1.713	1.690	1.668	1.647	1.626
3	2.941	2.884	2.829	2.775	2.723	2.673	2.624	2.577	2.531	2.487	2.444	2.402	2.361	2.322	2.283
4	3.902	3.808	3.717	3.630	3.546	3.465	3.387	3.312	3.240	3.170	3.102	3.037	2.974	2.914	2.855
5	4.853	4.713	4.580	4.452	4.329	4.212	4.100	3.993	3.890	3.791	3.696	3.605	3.517	3.433	3.352
6	5.795	5.601	5.417	5.242	5.076	4.917	4.767	4.623	4.486	4.355	4.231	4.111	3.998	3.889	3.784
7	6.728	6.472	6.230	6.002	5.786	5.582	5.389	5.206	5.033	4.868	4.712	4.564	4.423	4.288	4.160
8	7.652	7.325	7.020	6.733	6.463	6.210	5.971	5.747	5.535	5.335	5.146	4.968	4.799	4.639	4.487
9	8.566	8.162	7.786	7.435	7.108	6.802	6.515	6.247	5.995	5.759	5.537	5.328	5.132	4.946	4.772
10	9.471	8.983	8.530	8.111	7.722	7.360	7.024	6.710	6.418	6.145	5.889	5.650	5.426	5.216	5.019
11	10.37	9.787	9.253	8.760	8.306	7.887	7.499	7.139	6.805	6.495	6.207	5.938	5.687	5.453	5.234
12	11.26	10.58	9.954	9.385	8.863	8.384	7.943	7.536	7.161	6.814	6.492	6.194	5.918	5.660	5.421
13	12.13	11.35	10.63	9.986	9.394	8.853	8.358	7.904	7.487	7.103	6.750	6.424	6.122	5.842	5.583
14	13.00	12.11	11.30	10.56	9.899	9.295	8.745	8.244	7.786	7.367	6.982	6.628	6.302	6.002	5.724
15	13.87	12.85	11.94	11.12	10.38	9.712	9.108	8.559	8.061	7.606	7.191	6.811	6.462	6.142	5.847
16	14.72	13.58	12.56	11.65	10.84	10.11	9.447	8.851	8.313	7.824	7.379	6.974	6.604	6.265	5.954
17	15.56	14.29	13.17	12.17	11.27	10.48	9.763	9.122	8.544	8.022	7.549	7.120	6.729	6.373	6.047
18	16.40	14.99	13.75	12.66	11.69	10.83	10.06	9.372	8.756	8.201	7.702	7.250	6.840	6.467	6.128
19	17.23	15.68	14.32	13.13	12.09	11.16	10.34	9.604	8.950	8.365	7.839	7.366	6.938	6.550	6.198
20	18.05	16.35	14.88	13.59	12.46	11.47	10.59	9.818	9.129	8.514	7.963	7.469	7.025	6.623	6.259

Number of Years	Interest Rate per Year														
	16%	17%	18%	19%	20%	21%	22%	23%	24%	25%	26%	27%	28%	29%	30%
1	.862	.855	.847	.840	.833	.826	.820	.813	.806	.800	.794	.787	.781	.775	.769
2	1.605	1.585	1.566	1.547	1.528	1.509	1.492	1.474	1.457	1.440	1.424	1.407	1.392	1.376	1.361
3	2.246	2.210	2.174	2.140	2.106	2.074	2.042	2.011	1.981	1.952	1.923	1.896	1.868	1.842	1.816
4	2.798	2.743	2.690	2.639	2.589	2.540	2.494	2.448	2.404	2.362	2.320	2.280	2.241	2.203	2.166
5	3.274	3.199	3.127	3.058	2.991	2.926	2.864	2.803	2.745	2.689	2.635	2.583	2.532	2.483	2.436
6	3.685	3.589	3.498	3.410	3.326	3.245	3.167	3.092	3.020	2.951	2.885	2.821	2.759	2.700	2.643
7	4.039	3.922	3.812	3.706	3.605	3.508	3.416	3.327	3.242	3.161	3.083	3.009	2.937	2.868	2.802
8	4.344	4.207	4.078	3.954	3.837	3.726	3.619	3.518	3.421	3.329	3.241	3.156	3.076	2.999	2.925
9	4.607	4.451	4.303	4.163	4.031	3.905	3.786	3.673	3.566	3.463	3.366	3.273	3.184	3.100	3.019
10	4.833	4.659	4.494	4.339	4.192	4.054	3.923	3.799	3.682	3.571	3.465	3.364	3.269	3.178	3.092
11	5.029	4.836	4.656	4.486	4.327	4.177	4.035	3.902	3.776	3.656	3.543	3.437	3.335	3.239	3.147
12	5.197	4.988	4.793	4.611	4.439	4.278	4.127	3.985	3.851	3.725	3.606	3.493	3.387	3.286	3.190
13	5.342	5.118	4.910	4.715	4.533	4.362	4.203	4.053	3.912	3.780	3.656	3.538	3.427	3.322	3.223
14	5.468	5.229	5.008	4.802	4.611	4.432	4.265	4.108	3.962	3.824	3.695	3.573	3.459	3.351	3.249
15	5.575	5.324	5.092	4.876	4.675	4.489	4.315	4.153	4.001	3.859	3.726	3.601	3.483	3.373	3.268
16	5.668	5.405	5.162	4.938	4.730	4.536	4.357	4.189	4.033	3.887	3.751	3.623	3.503	3.390	3.283
17	5.749	5.475	5.222	4.990	4.775	4.576	4.391	4.219	4.059	3.910	3.771	3.640	3.518	3.403	3.295
18	5.818	5.534	5.273	5.033	4.812	4.608	4.419	4.243	4.080	3.928	3.786	3.654	3.529	3.413	3.304
19	5.877	5.584	5.316	5.070	4.843	4.635	4.442	4.263	4.097	3.942	3.799	3.664	3.539	3.421	3.311
20	5.929	5.628	5.353	5.101	4.870	4.657	4.460	4.279	4.110	3.954	3.808	3.673	3.546	3.427	3.316

Note: For example, if the interest rate is 10% per year, the investment of $1 received in each of the next 5 years is $3.791.

APPENDIX TABLE 4

Values of e^{rt}. Future value of $1 invested at a *continuously compounded* rate r for t years.

rt	.00	.01	.02	.03	.04	.05	.06	.07	.08	.09
.00	1.000	1.010	1.020	1.030	1.041	1.051	1.062	1.073	1.083	1.094
.10	1.105	1.116	1.127	1.139	1.150	1.162	1.174	1.185	1.197	1.209
.20	1.221	1.234	1.246	1.259	1.271	1.284	1.297	1.310	1.323	1.336
.30	1.350	1.363	1.377	1.391	1.405	1.419	1.433	1.448	1.462	1.477
.40	1.492	1.507	1.522	1.537	1.553	1.568	1.584	1.600	1.616	1.632
.50	1.649	1.665	1.682	1.699	1.716	1.733	1.751	1.768	1.786	1.804
.60	1.822	1.840	1.859	1.878	1.896	1.916	1.935	1.954	1.974	1.994
.70	2.014	2.034	2.054	2.075	2.096	2.117	2.138	2.160	2.181	2.203
.80	2.226	2.248	2.271	2.293	2.316	2.340	2.363	2.387	2.411	2.435
.90	2.460	2.484	2.509	2.535	2.560	2.586	2.612	2.638	2.664	2.691
1.00	2.718	2.746	2.773	2.801	2.829	2.858	2.886	2.915	2.945	2.974
1.10	3.004	3.034	3.065	3.096	3.127	3.158	3.190	3.222	3.254	3.287
1.20	3.320	3.353	3.387	3.421	3.456	3.490	3.525	3.561	3.597	3.633
1.30	3.669	3.706	3.743	3.781	3.819	3.857	3.896	3.935	3.975	4.015
1.40	4.055	4.096	4.137	4.179	4.221	4.263	4.306	4.349	4.393	4.437
1.50	4.482	4.527	4.572	4.618	4.665	4.711	4.759	4.807	4.855	4.904
1.60	4.953	5.003	5.053	5.104	5.155	5.207	5.259	5.312	5.366	5.419
1.70	5.474	5.529	5.585	5.641	5.697	5.755	5.812	5.871	5.930	5.989
1.80	6.050	6.110	6.172	6.234	6.297	6.360	6.424	6.488	6.553	6.619
1.90	6.686	6.753	6.821	6.890	6.959	7.029	7.099	7.171	7.243	7.316
2.00	7.389	7.463	7.538	7.614	7.691	7.768	7.846	7.925	8.004	8.085
2.10	8.166	8.248	8.331	8.415	8.499	8.585	8.671	8.758	8.846	8.935
2.20	9.025	9.116	9.207	9.300	9.393	9.488	9.583	9.679	9.777	9.875
2.30	9.974	10.07	10.18	10.28	10.38	10.49	10.59	10.70	10.80	10.91
2.40	11.02	11.13	11.25	11.36	11.47	11.59	11.70	11.82	11.94	12.06
2.50	12.18	12.30	12.43	12.55	12.68	12.81	12.94	13.07	13.20	13.33
2.60	13.46	13.60	13.74	13.87	14.01	14.15	14.30	14.44	14.59	14.73
2.70	14.88	15.03	15.18	15.33	15.49	15.64	15.80	15.96	16.12	16.28
2.80	16.44	16.61	16.78	16.95	17.12	17.29	17.46	17.64	17.81	17.99
2.90	18.17	18.36	18.54	18.73	18.92	19.11	19.30	19.49	19.69	19.89
3.00	20.09	20.29	20.49	20.70	20.91	21.12	21.33	21.54	21.76	21.98
3.10	22.20	22.42	22.65	22.87	23.10	23.34	23.57	23.81	24.05	24.29
3.20	24.53	24.78	25.03	25.28	25.53	25.79	26.05	26.31	26.58	26.84
3.30	27.11	27.39	27.66	27.94	28.22	28.50	28.79	29.08	29.37	29.67
3.40	29.96	30.27	30.57	30.88	31.19	31.50	31.82	32.14	32.46	32.79
3.50	33.12	33.45	33.78	34.12	34.47	34.81	35.16	35.52	35.87	36.23
3.60	36.60	36.97	37.34	37.71	38.09	38.47	38.86	39.25	39.65	40.04
3.70	40.45	40.85	41.26	41.68	42.10	42.52	42.95	43.38	43.82	44.26
3.80	44.70	45.15	45.60	46.06	46.53	46.99	47.47	47.94	48.42	48.91
3.90	49.40	49.90	50.40	50.91	51.42	51.94	52.46	52.98	53.52	54.05

Note: For example, if the continuously compounded interest rate is 10% per year, the investment of $1 today will be worth $1.105 at year 1 and $1.221 at year 2.

APPENDIX TABLE 5

Present value of $1 per year received in a continuous stream for each of t years (discounted at an *annually compounded* rate r) = $\{1 - 1/(1 + r)^t\}/\{\ln(1 + r)\}$.

Number of Years	Interest Rate per Year														
	1%	2%	3%	4%	5%	6%	7%	8%	9%	10%	11%	12%	13%	14%	15%
1	.995	.990	.985	.981	.976	.971	.967	.962	.958	.954	.950	.945	.941	.937	.933
2	1.980	1.961	1.942	1.924	1.906	1.888	1.871	1.854	1.837	1.821	1.805	1.790	1.774	1.759	1.745
3	2.956	2.913	2.871	2.830	2.791	2.752	2.715	2.679	2.644	2.609	2.576	2.543	2.512	2.481	2.450
4	3.922	3.846	3.773	3.702	3.634	3.568	3.504	3.443	3.383	3.326	3.270	3.216	3.164	3.113	3.064
5	4.878	4.760	4.648	4.540	4.437	4.337	4.242	4.150	4.062	3.977	3.896	3.817	3.741	3.668	3.598
6	5.825	5.657	5.498	5.346	5.202	5.063	4.931	4.805	4.685	4.570	4.459	4.353	4.252	4.155	4.062
7	6.762	6.536	6.323	6.121	5.930	5.748	5.576	5.412	5.256	5.108	4.967	4.832	4.704	4.582	4.465
8	7.690	7.398	7.124	6.867	6.623	6.394	6.178	5.974	5.780	5.597	5.424	5.260	5.104	4.956	4.816
9	8.609	8.243	7.902	7.583	7.284	7.004	6.741	6.494	6.261	6.042	5.836	5.642	5.458	5.285	5.121
10	9.519	9.072	8.657	8.272	7.913	7.579	7.267	6.975	6.702	6.447	6.208	5.983	5.772	5.573	5.386
11	10.42	9.884	9.391	8.935	8.512	8.121	7.758	7.421	7.107	6.815	6.542	6.287	6.049	5.826	5.617
12	11.31	10.68	10.10	9.572	9.083	8.633	8.218	7.834	7.478	7.149	6.843	6.559	6.294	6.048	5.818
13	12.19	11.46	10.79	10.18	9.627	9.116	8.647	8.216	7.819	7.453	7.115	6.802	6.512	6.242	5.992
14	13.07	12.23	11.46	10.77	10.14	9.571	9.048	8.570	8.131	7.729	7.359	7.018	6.704	6.413	6.144
15	13.93	12.98	12.12	11.34	10.64	10.00	9.423	8.897	8.418	7.980	7.579	7.212	6.874	6.563	6.276
16	14.79	13.71	12.75	11.88	11.11	10.41	9.774	9.201	8.681	8.209	7.778	7.385	7.024	6.694	6.390
17	15.64	14.43	13.36	12.41	11.55	10.79	10.10	9.482	8.923	8.416	7.957	7.539	7.158	6.809	6.490
18	16.48	15.14	13.96	12.91	11.98	11.15	10.41	9.742	9.144	8.605	8.118	7.676	7.275	6.910	6.577
19	17.31	15.83	14.54	13.39	12.39	11.49	10.69	9.983	9.347	8.777	8.263	7.799	7.380	6.999	6.652
20	18.14	16.51	15.10	13.86	12.77	11.81	10.96	10.21	9.533	8.932	8.394	7.909	7.472	7.077	6.718

Number of Years	Interest Rate per Year														
	16%	17%	18%	19%	20%	21%	22%	23%	24%	25%	26%	27%	28%	29%	30%
1	.929	.925	.922	.918	.914	.910	.907	.903	.900	.896	.893	.889	.886	.883	.880
2	1.730	1.716	1.703	1.689	1.676	1.663	1.650	1.638	1.625	1.613	1.601	1.590	1.578	1.567	1.556
3	2.421	2.392	2.365	2.337	2.311	2.285	2.259	2.235	2.211	2.187	2.164	2.141	2.119	2.098	2.077
4	3.016	2.970	2.925	2.882	2.840	2.799	2.759	2.720	2.682	2.646	2.610	2.576	2.542	2.509	2.477
5	3.530	3.464	3.401	3.340	3.281	3.223	3.168	3.115	3.063	3.013	2.964	2.917	2.872	2.828	2.785
6	3.972	3.886	3.804	3.724	3.648	3.574	3.504	3.436	3.370	3.307	3.246	3.187	3.130	3.075	3.022
7	4.354	4.247	4.145	4.048	3.954	3.865	3.779	3.696	3.617	3.542	3.469	3.399	3.331	3.266	3.204
8	4.682	4.555	4.434	4.319	4.209	4.104	4.004	3.909	3.817	3.730	3.646	3.566	3.489	3.415	3.344
9	4.966	4.819	4.680	4.547	4.422	4.302	4.189	4.081	3.978	3.880	3.786	3.697	3.612	3.530	3.452
10	5.210	5.044	4.887	4.739	4.599	4.466	4.340	4.221	4.108	4.000	3.898	3.801	3.708	3.619	3.535
11	5.421	5.237	5.063	4.900	4.747	4.602	4.465	4.335	4.213	4.096	3.986	3.882	3.783	3.689	3.599
12	5.603	5.401	5.213	5.036	4.870	4.713	4.566	4.428	4.297	4.173	4.057	3.946	3.841	3.742	3.648
13	5.759	5.542	5.339	5.150	4.972	4.806	4.650	4.503	4.365	4.235	4.112	3.997	3.887	3.784	3.686
14	5.894	5.662	5.446	5.245	5.058	4.882	4.718	4.564	4.420	4.284	4.157	4.036	3.923	3.816	3.715
15	6.010	5.765	5.537	5.326	5.129	4.945	4.774	4.614	4.464	4.324	4.192	4.068	3.951	3.841	3.737
16	6.111	5.853	5.614	5.393	5.188	4.998	4.820	4.655	4.500	4.355	4.220	4.092	3.973	3.860	3.754
17	6.197	5.928	5.679	5.450	5.238	5.041	4.858	4.687	4.529	4.381	4.242	4.112	3.990	3.875	3.767
18	6.272	5.992	5.735	5.498	5.279	5.076	4.889	4.714	4.552	4.401	4.259	4.127	4.003	3.887	3.778
19	6.336	6.047	5.781	5.538	5.313	5.106	4.914	4.736	4.571	4.417	4.273	4.139	4.014	3.896	3.785
20	6.391	6.094	5.821	5.571	5.342	5.130	4.935	4.754	4.586	4.430	4.284	4.149	4.022	3.903	3.791

Note: For example, if the interest rate is 10% per year, a continuous cash flow of $1 a year for each of 5 years is worth $3.977. A continuous flow of $1 in year 5 only is worth $3.977 − $3.326 = $.651.

APPENDIX TABLE 6

Cumulative probability [$N(d)$] that a normally distributed variable will be less than d standard deviations above the mean.

d	0	0.01	0.02	0.03	0.04	0.05	0.06	0.07	0.08	0.09
0	.5000	.5040	.5080	.5120	.5160	.5199	.5239	.5279	.5319	.5359
0.1	.5398	.5438	.5478	.5517	.5557	.5596	.5636	.5675	.5714	.5753
0.2	.5793	.5832	.5871	.5910	.5948	.5987	.6026	.6064	.6103	.6141
0.3	.6179	.6217	.6255	.6293	.6331	.6368	.6406	.6443	.6480	.6517
0.4	.6554	.6591	.6628	.6664	.6700	.6736	.6772	.6808	.6844	.6879
0.5	.6915	.6950	.6985	.7019	.7054	.7088	.7123	.7157	.7190	.7224
0.6	.7257	.7291	.7324	.7357	.7389	.7422	.7454	.7486	.7517	.7549
0.7	.7580	.7611	.7642	.7673	.7704	.7734	.7764	.7794	.7823	.7852
0.8	.7881	.7910	.7939	.7967	.7995	.8023	.8051	.8078	.8106	.8133
0.9	.8159	.8186	.8212	.8238	.8264	.8289	.8315	.8340	.8365	.8389
1	.8413	.8438	.8461	.8485	.8508	.8531	.8554	.8577	.8599	.8621
1.1	.8643	.8665	.8686	.8708	.8729	.8749	.8770	.8790	.8810	.8830
1.2	.8849	.8869	.8888	.8907	.8925	.8944	.8962	.8980	.8997	.9015
1.3	.9032	.9049	.9066	.9082	.9099	.9115	.9131	.9147	.9162	.9177
1.4	.9192	.9207	.9222	.9236	.9251	.9265	.9279	.9292	.9306	.9319
1.5	.9332	.9345	.9357	.9370	.9382	.9394	.9406	.9418	.9429	.9441
1.6	.9452	.9463	.9474	.9484	.9495	.9505	.9515	.9525	.9535	.9545
1.7	.9554	.9564	.9573	.9582	.9591	.9599	.9608	.9616	.9625	.9633
1.8	.9641	.9649	.9656	.9664	.9671	.9678	.9686	.9693	.9699	.9706
1.9	.9713	.9719	.9726	.9732	.9738	.9744	.9750	.9756	.9761	.9767
2	.9772	.9778	.9783	.9788	.9793	.9798	.9803	.9808	.9812	.9817
2.1	.9821	.9826	.9830	.9834	.9838	.9842	.9846	.9850	.9854	.9857
2.2	.9861	.9864	.9868	.9871	.9875	.9878	.9881	.9884	.9887	.9890
2.3	.9893	.9896	.9898	.9901	.9904	.9906	.9909	.9911	.9913	.9916
2.4	.9918	.9920	.9922	.9925	.9927	.9929	.9931	.9932	.9934	.9936
2.5	.9938	.9940	.9941	.9943	.9945	.9946	.9948	.9949	.9951	.9952

Note: For example, if d = .22, $N(d)$ = .5871 (i.e., there is a .5871 probability that a normally distributed variable will be less than .22 standard deviations above the mean).

ANSWERS TO QUIZZES

Chapter 1

1. (a) Real; (b) executive airplanes; (c) brand names; (d) financial; (e) bonds; (f) investment; (g) capital budgeting; (h) financing.

2. a. Financial assets, such as stocks or bank loans, are claims held by investors. Corporations sell financial assets to raise the cash to invest in real assets such as plant and equipment. Some real assets are intangible.
   b. Capital budgeting means investment in real assets. Financing means raising the cash for this investment.
   c. The shares of public corporations are traded on stock exchanges and can be purchased by a wide range of investors. The shares of closely held corporations are not traded and are not generally available to investors.
   d. Unlimited liability: investors are responsible for all the firm's debts. A sole proprietor has unlimited liability. Investors in corporations have limited liability. They can lose their investment, but no more.
   e. A corporation is a separate legal "person" with unlimited life. Its owners hold shares in the business. A partnership is a limited-life agreement to establish and run a business.

3. *c, d, e,* and *g* are real assets. Others are financial.

4. Double taxation and agency costs due to separation of ownership and control. Public organizations also face the higher costs of complying with legal requirements and communicating with dispersed shareholders.

5. *a, c, d.*

6. *c, d.*

7. Principal–agent issues, often amplified by asymmetric information.

Chapter 2

1. (a) Negative; (b) $PV = C_1/(1 + r)$; (c) $NPV = C_0 + (C_1/(1 + r))$; (d) r is the return foregone by investing in the project rather than the capital market; (e) the return offered by default-free U.S. Treasury securities.

2. $DF_1 = .867$; discount rate $= .154$, or 15.4%.

3. (a) .909; (b) .833; (c) .769.

4. (a) Return = profit/investment = $(132 - 100)/100 = .32$, or 32%; (b) Negative (if the rate of interest r equals 32%, NPV = 0); (c) PV $= 132/1.10 = 120$, or \$120,000; (d) NPV $= -100 + 120 = 20$, or \$20,000.

5. The return foregone by investing in a project rather than in securities. The opportunity cost of capital for a risk-free investment is the interest rate on government bonds. For risky investments firms need to estimate the return expected by investors from securities of similar risk.

6. Neither should invest in the office building. The ant should lend and receive $1.2 \times 185,000 = \$222,000$ at the end of the year (compared with a payoff of \$210,000 from the building). The grasshopper should consume his \$185,000 today rather than borrow $210,000/1.2 = \$175,000$ against the future value of the office building.

7. They will vote for *a* only. The other tasks can be carried out just as efficiently by stockholders.

8. To protect and enhance their reputations; because compensation is tied to earnings and stock price; supervision by the board of directors; the threat of takeover.

Chapter 3

1. \$1.00.

2. $125/139 = .899$.

3. $374/(1.09)^9 = \$172$.

4. $PV = 432/1.15 + 137/(1.15)^2 + 797/(1.15)^3 = 376 + 104 + 524 = 1,003$.

5. $100 \times (1.15)^8 = \$305.90$.

6. $NPV = -1,548 + 138/.09 = -\$14.67$.

7. $PV = 4/(.14 - .04) = \$40$.

8. (a) $PV = 1/.10 = \$10$; (b) $PV = (1/.10)/(1.10)^7 = 10/2 = \$5$ (approximately); (c) $PV = 10 - 5 = \$5$ (approximately); (d) $PV = C/(r - g) = 10,000/(.10 - .05) = \$200,000$.

9. a. $10,000/1.05^5 = \$7,840$.

b. You need to set aside $(12{,}000 \times 6\text{-year annuity factor}) = 12{,}000 \times 4.623 = \$55{,}476$.

c. At the end of 6 years you would have $1.08^6 \times (60{,}476 - 55{,}476) = \$7{,}934$.

10. (a) $1{,}000e^{.12 \times 5} = 1{,}000e^{.6} = \$1{,}822$; (b) $PV = 5e^{-.12 \times 8} = 5e^{-.96} = \$1.914$ million;

(c) $PV = C\left(\dfrac{1}{r} - \dfrac{1}{re^{rt}}\right) = 2{,}000\left(\dfrac{1}{.12} - \dfrac{1}{.12e^{.12 \times 15}}\right)$

$\quad\quad\quad = \$13{,}912$

11. (a) \$12.625 million; (b) \$12.705 million; (c) \$12.712 million.

Chapter 4

1. (a) Does not change; (b) Price falls; (c) Yield rises.

2. More than 8%.

3. Discount coupon payments of $12.5/2 = 6.25\%$ at $8.669/2 = 4.3345\%$ for $8 \times 2 = 16$ semiannual periods. Add the PV of the final payment in 2014. Price $= 121.78\%$.

4. Yields to maturity are about 4.3% for the 2% coupon, 4.2% for the 4% coupon, and 3.9% for the 8% coupon. The 8% bond had the shortest duration (7.65 years), the 2% bond the longest (9.07 years).

5. a. $PV = \dfrac{50}{1 + r_1} + \dfrac{1{,}050}{(1 + r_2)^2}$

b. $PV = \dfrac{50}{1 + y} + \dfrac{1{,}050}{(1 + y)^2}$

c. Less (it is between the 1-year and 2-year spot rates).

d. Yield to maturity; spot rate.

6. a. Fall (e.g., 1-year 10% bond is worth $110/1.1 = 100$ if $r = 10\%$ and is worth $110/1.15 = 95.65$ if $r = 15\%$).

b. Less (e.g., see 4(a)).

c. Less (e.g., with $r = 5\%$, 1-year 10% bond is worth $110/1.05 = 104.76$).

d. Higher (e.g., if $r = 10\%$, 1-year 10% bond is worth $110/1.1 = 100$, while 1-year 8% bond is worth $108/1.1 = 98.18$).

e. No, low-coupon bonds have longer durations (unless there is only one period to maturity) and are therefore more volatile (e.g., if r falls from 10% to 5%, the value of a 2-year 10% bond rises from 100 to 109.3 (a rise of 9.3%). The value of a 2-year 5% bond rises from 91.3 to 100 (a rise of 9.5%).

7. (a) The spot rates are 4.68% for 2007, 4.79% for 2008, 5.075% for 2009, and 5.38% for 2010; (b) upward-sloping; (c) lower (the yield is a complicated average of the different spot rates); (d) 5.65% from 2008–2009 and 6.31% from 2009–2010.

8. a. Price today is 108.425; price after 1 year is 106.930.

b. Return $= (106.930 + 8)/108.425 - 1 = .06$, or 6%.

c. If a bond's yield to maturity is unchanged, the return to the bondholder is equal to the yield.

9. a. False. Duration depends on the coupon as well as the maturity.

b. False. Given the yield to maturity, volatility is proportional to duration.

c. True. A lower coupon rate means longer duration and therefore higher volatility.

d. False. A higher interest rate reduces the relative present value of (distant) principal repayments.

10.

	Year	C_t	$PV(C_t)$	Proportion of Total Value	Proportion × Time
Security A	1	40	37.04	.359	.359
	2	40	34.29	.333	.666
	3	40	31.75	.308	.924
	V =		103.08	1.0	Duration = 1.949 years
Security B	1	20	18.52	.141	.141
	2	20	17.15	.131	.262
	3	120	95.26	.728	2.184
	V =		130.93	1.0	Duration = 2.587 years
Security C	1	10	9.26	.088	.088
	2	10	8.57	.082	.164
	3	110	87.32	.830	2.490
	V =		105.15	1.0	Duration = 2.742 years

Volatilities: A, 1.80; B, 2.40; C, 2.49.

11. a. $(1 + r_2)^2 = (1 + r_1)(1 + f_2)$
$1.03^2 = 1.01 \times (1 + f_2)$
$f_2 = .05$, or 5%.

b. The expected 1-year spot rate at time 1 equals the forward rate f_2.

c. Against (unless one believes that investors have generally expected interest rates to rise).

d. The forward rate equals the expected spot rate *plus* a risk premium.

e. Long-term bonds.

f. Short-term bonds.

Chapter 5

1. (a) True; (b) true.

2. Investors who buy stocks may get their return from capital gains as well as dividends. But the future stock price always depends on subsequent dividends. There is no inconsistency.

3. $P_0 = (5 + 110)/1.08 = \$106.48$

4. $r = 5/40 = .125$.

5. $P_0 = 10/(.08 - .05) = \$333.33$.

6. By year 5, earnings will grow to $18.23 per share. Forecasted price per share at year 4 is $18.23/.08 = \$227.91$.

$$P_0 = \frac{10}{1.08} + \frac{10.50}{(1.08)^2} + \frac{11.03}{(1.08)^3} + \frac{11.58}{(1.08)^4}$$
$$+ \frac{227.91}{(1.08)^4} = 203.05$$

7. $15/.08 + PVGO = 333.33$; therefore PVGO = $145.83.

8. Z's forecasted dividends and prices grow as follows:

	Year 1	Year 2	Year 3
Dividend	10	10.50	11.03
Price	350	367.50	385.88

Calculate the expected rates of return:

From year 0 to 1: $\dfrac{10 + (350 - 333.33)}{333.33} = .08$.

From year 1 to 2: $\dfrac{10.50 + (367.50 - 350)}{350} = .08$.

From year 2 to 3: $\dfrac{11.03 + (385.88 - 367.50)}{367.50} = .08$

Double expects 8% in *each* of the first 2 years. Triple expects 8% in *each* of the first 3 years.

9. (a) False; (b) true.

10. PVGO = 0, and EPS_1 equals the average future earnings the firm could generate under no-growth policy.

11. Free cash flow is the amount of cash thrown off by a business after all investments necessary for growth. In our simple examples, free cash flow equals operating cash flow minus capital expenditure. Free cash flow can be negative if investments are large.

12. The value at the end of a forecast period. Horizon value can be estimated using the constant-growth DCF formula or by using price–earnings or market–book ratios for similar companies.

13. If PVGO = 0 at the horizon date H, horizon value = earnings forecasted for $H + 1$ divided by r.

Chapter 6

1. (a) A = 3 years, B = 2 years, C = 3 years; (b) B; (c) A, B, and C; (d) B and C ($NPV_B = \$3,378$; $NPV_C = \$2,405$); (e) true; (f) It will accept no negative-NPV projects but will turn down some with positive NPVs. A project can have positive NPV if all future cash flows are considered but still do not meet the stated cutoff period.

2. Given the cash flows $C_0, C_1, \ldots, C_T$, IRR is defined by

$$NPV = C_0 + \frac{C_1}{1 + IRR} + \frac{C_2}{(1 + IRR)^2}$$
$$+ \cdots + \frac{C_T}{(1 + IRR)^T} = 0$$

It is calculated by trial and error, by financial calculators, or by spreadsheet programs.

3. (a) $15,750; $4,250; $0; (b) 100%.

4. No (you are effectively "borrowing" at a rate of interest higher than the opportunity cost of capital).

5. (a) Two; (b) −50% and +50%; (c) yes, NPV = +14.6.

6. The incremental flows from investing in Alpha rather than Beta are −200,000; +110,000; and 121,000. The IRR on the incremental cash flow is 10% (i.e., $-200 + 110/1.10 + 121/1.10^2 = 0$). The IRR on Beta exceeds the cost of capital and so does the IRR on the incremental investment in Alpha. Choose Alpha.

7. 1, 2, 4, and 6.

Chapter 7

1. *a, b, d, g, h.*

2. Real cash flow = 100,000/1.04 = $96,154; real discount rate = 1.08/1.04 − 1 = .03846

$$PV = \frac{96,154}{1.03846} = \$92,593$$

5.

	2007	2008	2009	2010	2011
Working capital	50,000	230,000	305,000	250,000	0
Cash flows	+50,000	+180,000	+75,000	−55,000	−250,000

6. Comparing present values can be misleading when projects have different economic lives and the projects are part of an ongoing business. For example, a machine that costs $100,000 per year to buy and lasts 5 years is not necessarily more expensive than a machine that costs $75,000 per year to buy but lasts only 3 years. Calculating the machines' equivalent annual costs allows an unbiased comparison.

7. PV cost = 1.5 + .2 × 14.09 = $4.319 million. Equivalent annual cost = 4.319/14.09 = .306, or $306,000.

8. **a.** NPV_A = $100,000; NPV_B = $180,000.
   b. Equivalent cash flow of A = 100,000/1.736 = $57,604; equivalent cash flow of B = 180,000/2.487 = $72,376.
   c. Machine B.

9. Replace at end of 5 years ($80,000 > $72,376).

Chapter 8

1. Expected payoff is $100 and expected return is zero. Variance is 20,000 (% squared) and standard deviation is 141%.

2. **a.** Standard deviation = 19.2%
   b. Average real return = 6.2%

3. Oblonsky did better, with an average return of 10.2% and standard deviation of 14.5%, vs. 9.1% and 19.2% for the market.

4. (a) False; (b) true; (c) false, (d) false, (e) true, (f) true; (g) true; (h) false.

5. *d.*

6.

$x^2_1\sigma^2_1$	$x_1x_2\sigma_{12}$	$x_1x_3\sigma_{13}$
$x_1x_2\sigma_{12}$	$x^2_2\sigma^2_2$	$x_2x_3\sigma_{23}$
$x_1x_3\sigma_{13}$	$x_2x_3\sigma_{23}$	$x^2_3\sigma^2_3$

3. (a) False; (b) false; (c) false; (d) false.

4. The longer the recovery period, the less the present value of depreciation tax shields. This is true regardless of the discount rate. If $r = .10$, then 35% of the 5-year schedule's PV is .271. The same calculation for the 7-year schedule yields .252.

7. (a) 26%; (b) zero; (c) .75; (d) less than 1.0 (the portfolio's risk is the same as the market, but some of this risk is unique risk).

8. 1.3 (Diversification does not affect market risk.)

9. A, 1.0; B, 2.0; C, 1.5; D, 0; E, −1.0.

Chapter 9

1. (a) 7%; (b) 27% with perfect positive correlation; 1% with perfect negative correlation; 19.1% with no correlation; (c) See Figure 1; (d) No, measure risk by beta, not by standard deviation.

2. **a.** Portfolio A (higher expected return, same risk); **b.** Cannot say (depends on investor's attitude toward risk); **c.** Portfolio F (lower risk, same expected return).

3. **a.** Figure 9.12*b*: Diversification reduces risk (e.g., a mixture of portfolios A and B would have less risk than the average of A and B).
   b. Those along line *AB* in Figure 9.12*a*.
   c. See Figure 2.

4. (a) See Figure 3; (b) A, D, G; (c) F; (d) 15% in C. (e) Put 25/32 of your money in F and lend 7/32 at 12%: Expected return = 7/32 × 12 + 25/32 × 18 = 16.7%; standard deviation = 7/32 × 0 + (25/32) × 32 = 25%. If you could borrow without limit, you would achieve as high an expected return as you'd like, with correspondingly high risk, of course.

5. **a.** 4 + (1.13 × 6) = 10.8%.
   b. Amazon: 4 + (2.2 × 6) = 17.2%.
   c. Heinz: 4 + (.36 × 6) = 6.2%.
   d. Lower. If interest rate is 4%, $r = 4 + (1.59 × 6)$ = 13.54%; if rate = 6%, $r = 6 + (1.59 × 4)$ = 12.36%.
   e. Higher. If interest rate is 4%, $r = 4 + (.65 × 6)$ = 7.9%; if rate = 6%, $r = 6 + (.65 × 4)$ = 8.6%.

6. (a) True; (b) false (it offers twice the market *risk premium*); (c) false.

7. (a) 7%; (b) 7 + 1(5) + 1(−1) + 1(2) = 13%; (c) 7 + 0(5) + 2(−1) + 0(2) = 5%; (d) 7 + 1(5) + (−1.5)(−1) + 1(2) = 15.5%.

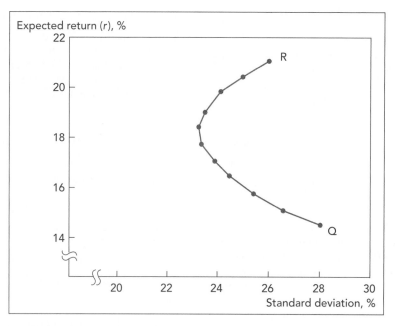

FIGURE 1

Chapter 9, Quiz Question 1(c).

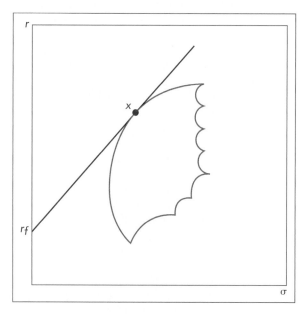

FIGURE 2

Chapter 9, Quiz Question 3(c).

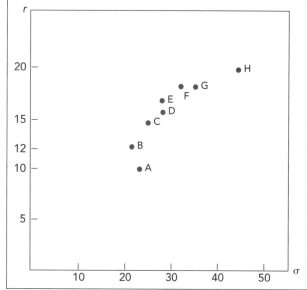

FIGURE 3

Chapter 9, Quiz Question 4(a).

Chapter 10

1. Overestimate.

2. 47% was explained by market movements, 53% by unique risk. Unique risk shows up as the scatter of points around the fitted line. The standard error is .30, so plus or minus two standard errors gives a range of 1.62 to 2.82.

3. $\beta_{assets} = 0 \times .40 + .5 \times .60 = .30, r = 10 + .30(18 - 10) = 12.4\%$.

4. Suppose that the cash flow in the event of success is $6 million. Then the *expected* flow is .5 × 6 = $3 million. If production of the potato in the event of success is normal risk, then this figure can be discounted back to the start of production at the company's ordinary cost of capital. For example, suppose the project lasts for 10 years. Then NPV = −15 + 3 × 5.65 = $1.95 million. Discounting the cash flow in the event of success at double the discount rate would not give the right answer (i.e., apparent NPV = −15 + 6 × 3.682 = $7.09 million). The required return for the period until the uncertainty about FDA approval is resolved depends on whether this risk is market risk.

5. (a) False; (b) false.

6. (a) A (higher fixed cost); (b) C (more cyclical revenues).

7. (a) True; (b) false; (c) true.

8. a. $PV = \dfrac{110}{1 + r_f + \beta(r_m - r_f)} + \dfrac{121}{[1 + r_f + \beta(r_m - r_f)]^2}$

   $= \dfrac{110}{1.10} + \dfrac{121}{1.10^2} = \$200$.

   b. $CEQ_1/1.05 = 110/1.10, CEQ_1 = \$105$; $CEQ_2/1.05^2 = 121/1.10^2, CEQ_2 = \$110.25$.

   c. $Ratio_1 = 105/110 = .95; Ratio_2 = 110.25/121 = .91$.

Chapter 11

1. (a) False; (b) true; (c) true; (d) false (they are capital expenditures even though not included in the capital budget); (e) true (examples include R&D, advertising, and marketing for new products, worker training); (f) false.

2. (a) Cash-flow forecasts overstated; (b) One project proposal may be ranked below another simply because cash flows are based on different forecasts; (c) Project proposals may not consider strategic alternatives.

3. a. Analysis of how project profitability and NPV change if different assumptions are made about sales, cost, and other key variables.

b. Project NPV is recalculated by changing several inputs to new, but consistent, values.

c. Determines the level of future sales at which project profitability or NPV equals zero.

d. An extension of sensitivity analysis that explores all possible outcomes and weights each by its probability.

e. A graphical technique for displaying possible future events and decisions taken in response to those events.

f. Option to modify a project at a future date.

g. The additional present value created by the option to bail out of a project, and recover part of the initial investment, if the project performs poorly.

h. The additional present value created by the option to invest more and expand output, if a project performs well.

4. (a) False; (b) true; (c) true; (d) true; (e) true.

5. a. Describe how project cash flow depends on the underlying variables.

   b. Specify probability distributions for forecast errors for these cash flows.

   c. Draw from the probability distributions to simulate the cash flows.

6. (a) True; (b) true; (c) false; (d) false.

7. Adding a fudge factor to the discount rate pushes project analysts to submit more optimistic forecasts.

Chapter 12

1. c.

2. Weak, semistrong, strong, strong, weak.

3. (a) False; (b) false; (c) true; (d) false; (e) false; (f) true.

4. (a) False; (b) false; (c) true; (d) false.

5. $6 - (-.2 + 1.45 \times 5) = -1.05\%$.

6. (a) True; (b) false; (c) true; (d) true.

7. Decrease. The stock price already reflects an expected 25% increase. The 20% increase conveys bad news relative to expectations.

8. a. An investor should not buy or sell shares based on apparent trends or cycles in returns.

   b. A CFO should not speculate on changes in interest rates or foreign exchange rates. There is no reason to think that the CFO has superior information.

   c. A financial manager evaluating the creditworthiness of a large customer could check the customer's stock price and the yield on its debt. A falling stock price or a high yield could indicate trouble ahead.

d. Don't assume that accounting choices that increase or decrease earnings will have any effect on stock price.

e. The company should not seek diversification just to reduce risk. Investors can diversify on their own.

f. Stock issues do not depress price if investors believe the issuer has no private information.

Chapter 13

1. **(a)**, A1, B5; A2, B4; A3, B3; A4, B1; A5, B2; **(b)** On March 7, the ex-dividend date; **(c)** $(.30 \times 4)/63.15 = .019$, or 1.9%; **(d)** $(.30 \times 4)/3.32 = .36$, or 36%; **(e)** The price would fall to $63.15/1.07 = \$59.02$.

2. **a.** False. The dividend depends on past dividends and current and forecasted earnings.
   b. True. Dividend changes convey information to investors.
   c. False. Dividends are "smoothed." Managers rarely increase regular dividends temporarily. They may pay a special dividend, however.
   d. False. Dividends are rarely cut when repurchases are being made.

3. **a.** Reinvest $1,000 \times \$.50 = \$500$ in the stock. If the ex-dividend price is $\$150 - \$2.50$, this should involve the purchase of 500/147.50, or about 3.4 shares.
   b. Sell shares worth $1,000 \times \$3 = \$3,000$. If the ex-dividend price is $\$200 - \$5$, this should involve the sale of 3,000/195, or about 15 shares.

4. Reduce repurchases by $10 million or issue new shares for $10 million.

5. **a.** Company value is unchanged at $5,000 \times 140 = \$700,000$. Share price stays at $140.
   b. The discount rate $r = (\text{DIV}_1/P_0) + g = (20/140) + .05 = .193$. The price at which shares are repurchased in year 1 is $140 \times (1 + r) = 140 \times 1.193 = \$167$. Therefore the firm repurchases $50,000/167 = 299$ shares. Total dividend payments in year 1 fall to $5,000 \times 10 = \$50,000$, which is equivalent to $50,000/(5000 - 299) = \$10.64$ a share. Similarly, in year 2 the firm repurchases 281 shares at $186.52 and the

dividend per share increases by 11.7% to $11.88. In each subsequent year, total dividends increase by 5%, the number of shares declines by 6% and, therefore, dividends per share increase by 11.7%. The constant growth model gives PV share $= 10.64/(.193 - .117) = \$140$.

6. **a.** $127.25.
   b. Nothing; the stock price will stay at $130. 846,154 shares will be repurchased.
   c. The with-dividend price stays at $130. Ex dividend it drops to $124.50; 883,534 shares will be issued.

7. *Current tax law (assuming gains tax cannot be deferred):* All investors should be indifferent except the corporation which prefers Hi.
   Zero tax on capital gains: As under the current tax law except that individuals now prefer Lo. (Note: corporations and security dealers treat capital gains as income).

Chapter 14

1. Note the market value of Copperhead is far in excess of its book value:

	Market Value
Common stock	$16,000,000
(8 million shares at $2)	
Short-term loans	$ 2,000,000

Ms. Kraft owns .625% of the firm, which proposes to increase common stock to $17 million and cut short-term debt. Ms. Kraft can offset this by (a) borrowing $.00625 \times 1,000,000 = \$6,250$, and (b) buying that much more Copperhead stock.

2. **(a)** $.5r_E + .5 \times 5\% = 12.5\%$; $r_E = 20\%$; **(b)** 12.5%; **(c)** E/P = 20%; P/E = 5; **(d)** $50; **(e)** $.5 \times \beta_E + .5 \times 0 = 1.0$; $\beta_E = 2.0$.

3. Expected return on assets is $r_A = .08 \times 30/80 + .16 \times 50/80 = .13$. The new return on equity will be $r_E = .13 + (20/60)(.13 - .08) = .147$.

4. **a.** See table below

Operating income ($)	500	1,000	1,500	2,000
Interest ($)	250	250	250	250
Equity earnings ($)	250	750	1,250	1,750
Earnings per share	.33	1.00	1.67	2.33
Return on shares (%)	3.3	10	16.7	23.3

b. $\beta_A = \left(\dfrac{D}{D+E} \times \beta_D\right) + \left(\dfrac{E}{D+E} \times \beta_E\right)$

$.8 = (.25 \times 0) + (.75 \times \beta_E)$

$\beta_E = 1.07$

5. **(a)** True; **(b)** True (as long as the return earned by the company is greater than the interest payment, earnings per share increase, but the P/E falls to reflect the higher risk); **(c)** False (the cost of equity increases with the ratio D/E); **(d)** False (the formula $r_E = r_A + (D/E)(r_A - r_D)$ does not require r_D to be constant); **(e)** False (debt amplifies variations in equity income); **(f)** False (value increases only if clientele is not satisfied).

6. **(a)** $r_A = .15$, $r_E = .175$; **(b)** $\beta_A = .6$ (unchanged), $\beta_D = .3$, $\beta_E = .9$.

7. See Figure 14.3.

8. Currently $r_A = r_E = .14$, or 14%. From proposition 2 the leverage causes r_E to increase to $r_E = r_A + (r_A - r_D)(D/E) = .14 + (.14 - .095) \times (45/55) = .1768$, or 17.68%.
   After-tax WACC $= .095 \times (1 - .40) \times .45 + .1768 \times .55 = .1229$, or 12.29%.

Chapter 15

1. The calculation assumes that the tax rate is fixed, that debt is fixed and perpetual, and that investors' personal tax rates on interest and equity income are the same.

2. **a.** PV tax shield $= T_c D = \$16$.
   b. $T_c \times 20 = \$8$.

3. Relative advantage of debt $= \dfrac{1 - T_p}{(1 - T_{pE})(1 - T_c)}$

   $= \dfrac{.65}{(1)(.65)} = 1.00$

   Relative advantage $= \dfrac{.65}{(.85)(.65)} = 1.18$

4. A firm with no taxable income saves no taxes by borrowing and paying interest. The interest payments would simply add to its tax-loss carry-forwards. Such a firm would have little tax incentive to borrow.

5. **a.** Direct costs of financial distress are the legal and administrative costs of bankruptcy. Indirect costs include possible delays in liquidation (Eastern Airlines) or poor investment or operating decisions while bankruptcy is being resolved. Also the *threat* of bankruptcy can lead to costs.
   b. If financial distress increases odds of default, managers' and shareholders' incentives

change. This can lead to poor investment or financing decisions.

   c. See the answer to 5(*b*). Examples are the "games" described in Section 15.3.

6. Not necessarily. Announcement of bankruptcy can send a message of poor profits and prospects. Part of the share price drop can be attributed to anticipated bankruptcy costs, however.

7. More profitable firms have more taxable income to shield and are less likely to incur the costs of distress. Therefore the trade-off theory predicts high (book) debt ratios. In practice the more profitable companies borrow least.

8. Debt ratios tend to be higher for larger firms with more tangible assets. Debt ratios tend to be lower for more profitable firms with higher market-to-book ratios.

9. When a company issues securities, outside investors worry that management may have unfavorable information. If so the securities can be overpriced. This worry is much less with debt than equity. Debt securities are safer than equity, and their price is less affected if unfavorable news comes out later.

   A company that can borrow (without incurring substantial costs of financial distress) usually does so. An issue of equity would be read as "bad news" by investors, and the new stock could be sold only at a discount to the previous market price.

10. **(a)** The cumulative requirement for external financing. **(b)** More profitable firms can rely more on internal cash flow and need less external financing.

11. Financial slack is most valuable to growth companies with good but uncertain investment opportunities. Slack means that financing can be raised quickly for positive-NPV investments. But too much financial slack can tempt mature companies to overinvest. Increased borrowing can force such firms to pay out cash to investors.

Chapter 16

1. Market values of debt and equity are $D = .9 \times 75 = \$67.5$ million and $E = 42 \times 2.5 = \$105$ million. $D/V = .39$.

   WACC $= .09(1 - .35).39 + .18(.61) = .1325$, or 13.25%.

2. Step 1: $r = .09(.39) + .18(.61) = .145$.

   Step 2: $r_D = .086$, $r_E = .145 + (.145 - .086)(15/85) = .155$.

   Step 3: WACC $= .086(1 - .35).15 + .155(.85) = .14$.

3. (a) False; (b) true; (c) true.

4. The method values the equity of a company by discounting cash flows to stockholders at the cost of equity. See Section 16.2 for more details. The method assumes that the debt-to-equity ratio will remain constant.

5. (a) True; (b) false, if interest tax shields are valued separately; (c) true.

6. APV = base-case NPV ± PV financing side effects
   a. APV = 0 − .15(500,000) = −75,000;
   b. APV = 0 + 76,000 = +76,000.

7. a. 12%, of course.
   b. r_E = .12 + (.12 − .075)(30/70) = .139, WACC = .075(1 − .35)(.30) + .139(.70) = .112, or 11.2%.

8. a. Base-case NPV = −1,000 + 1200/1.20 = 0.
   b. PV tax shield = (.35 × .1 × .3(1000))/1.1 = 9.55. APV = 0 + 9.55 = $9.55.

9. No. The more debt you use, the higher rate of return equity investors will require. (Lenders may demand more also.) Thus there is a hidden cost of the "cheap" debt: It makes equity more expensive.

10. Patagonia does not have 90% debt capacity. KCS is borrowing $45 million partly on the strength of its existing assets. Also the decision to raise bank finance for the purchase does not mean that KCS has changed its target debt ratio. An APV valuation of Patagonia would probably assume a 50% debt ratio.

Chapter 17

1. Call; exercise; put; European.

2. Figure 17.13a represents a call seller; Figure 17.13b represents a call buyer.

3. a. The exercise price of the put option (i.e., you'd sell stock for the exercise price);
   b. The value of the stock (i.e., you would throw away the put and keep the stock).

4. Value of call + PV(exercise price) = value of put + value of asset (e.g., share).
   See table below.
   Relationship holds only for European options with same exercise price.

5. Buy a call and lend the present value of the exercise price.

6. a. Keep gold stocks and buy 6-month puts with an exercise price equal to 83.3% of the current price.
   b. Sell gold stocks, invest £485,000 for 6 months at 6%. The remaining £115,000 can be used to buy calls on the gold stocks with the same exercise price.

7. (a) See Figure 4; (b) stock price − PV(EX) = 100 − 100/1.1 = $9.09.

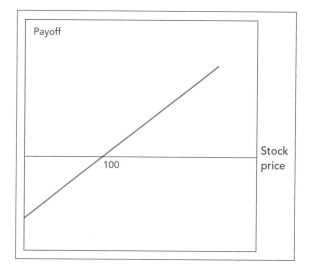

FIGURE 4

Chapter 17, Quiz Question 7.

8. Figure 17.13b doesn't show the cost of purchasing the call. The profit from call purchase would be negative for all stock prices less than exercise price plus cost of call. Figure 17.13a doesn't record the proceeds from selling the call.

9. (a) Zero; (b) Stock price less the present value of the exercise price.

10. The call price (a) increases; (b) decreases; (c) increases; (d) increases; (e) decreases; (f) decreases.

At Maturity:	Share Price Exceeds Exercise Price		Share Price below Exercise Price	
	Action	**Value**	**Action**	**Value**
Call + PV(EX)	Exercise call	Stock price	Don't exercise call	Exercise price
Put + share	Don't exercise put	Stock price	Exercise put	Exercise price

11. a. All investors, however risk-averse, should value more highly an option on a volatile stock. For both ExxonMobil and Genentech the option is valueless if final stock price is below the exercise price, but the option on Genentech has more upside potential.

b. Other things equal, stockholders lose and debtholders gain if the company shifts to safer assets. When the assets are risky, the option to default is more valuable. Debtholders bear much of the losses if asset value declines, but shareholders get the gains if asset value increases.

Chapter 18

1. a. Using risk-neutral method, $(p \times 20) + (1 - p)$ $(-16.7) = 1, p = .48$.

$$\text{Value of call} = \frac{(.48 \times 8) + (.52 \times 0)}{1.01} = 3.8.$$

b. $\text{Delta} = \dfrac{\text{spread of option prices}}{\text{spread of stock prices}}$

$$= \frac{8}{14.7} = .544.$$

c.

	Current Cash Flow	Possible Future Cash Flows	
Buy call	−3.8	0	+8.0
equals			
Buy .544 shares	−21.8	−18.2	+26.2
Borrow 18.0	+18.0	−18.2	−18.2
	−3.8	0	+8.0

d. Possible stock prices with call option prices in parentheses:

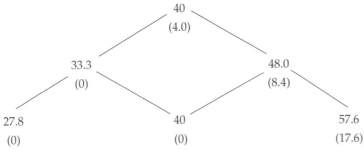

Option prices were calculated as follows:

Month 1: (i) $\dfrac{(.48 \times 0) + (.52 \times 0)}{1.01} = 0,$

(ii) $\dfrac{(.48 \times 17.6) + (.52 \times 0)}{1.01} = 8.4.$

Month 0: $= \dfrac{(.48 \times 8.4) + (.52 \times 0)}{1.01} = 4.0$

e. $\text{Delta} = \dfrac{\text{spread of option prices}}{\text{spread of stock prices}} = \dfrac{8.4}{14.7} = .57$

2. (a) No. The maximum delta is 1.0 when the ratio of stock price to exercise price is very high. **(b)** No. **(c)** Delta increases. **(d)** Delta increases.

3. Using the replicating portfolio method, delta $=$ $(31.67 - 0)/(106.67 - 60) = .6786$.

	Current Cash Flow	Possible Future Cash Flows	
Buy call	−14.56	0	+31.67
equals			
Buy .6786 shares	−54.29	+40.72	+72.39
Borrow 39.72	+39.72	−40.72	−40.72
	−14.56	0	+31.67

Using the risk-neutral method $(p \times 33.3) + (1 - p)(-25) = 2.5$, $p = .4715$.

$$\text{Value of call} = \frac{(.4715 \times 31.67) + (.5285 \times 0)}{1.025} = 14.56.$$

The put value is $14.56 + 75/1.025 - 80 = 7.73$.

4. Using the replicating portfolio method, delta = $(20 - 0)/(100 - 64) = .5556$.

	Current Cash Flow	Possible Future Cash Flows	
Buy call	−9.75	0	+20
equals			
Buy .5556 shares	−44.44	+35.56	+55.66
Borrow 34.69	+34.69	−35.56	−35.56
	−9.75	0	+20

Using the risk-neutral method $(p \times 25) + (1 - p)(-20) = 2.5$, $p = .5$

$$\text{Value of call} = \frac{(.5 \times 20) + (.5 \times 0)}{1.025} = 9.75$$

Lower risk means less upside for the call option. Thus option value falls.

5. **a.** Delta = $100/(200 - 50) = .667$.

b.

	Current Cash Flow	Possible Future Cash Flows	
Buy call	−36.36	0	+100
equals			
Buy .667 shares	−66.67	+33.33	+133.33
Borrow 30.30	+30.30	−33.33	−33.33
	−36.36	0	+100

c. $(p \times 100) + (1 - p)(-50) = 10$, $p = .4$.

d. Value of call = $\dfrac{(.4 \times 100) + (.6 \times 0)}{1.10} = 36.36$.

e. No. The true probability of a price rise is almost certainly higher than the risk-neutral probability, but it does not help to value the option.

6. **a.** Call value = $3.44.

b. Put value = call value + PV(exercise price) − stock price = $1.67.

7. True; as the stock price rises, the risk of the option falls.

8. **a.** You would exercise early if the stock price was sufficiently low. There may be little opportunity for further gains in the option value and it would be better to invest the exercise price to earn interest.

b. Don't exercise early. The interest savings from delaying payment of the exercise price is larger than the dividend foregone.

c. If the stock price and dividend are sufficiently high, it may pay to exercise early to capture the dividend.

Chapter 19

1. (a) $4357/(4357 + 2049) = .68$; (b) $(1010 + 264)/316 = 4.03$; (c) $2704/2018 = 1.34$; (d) $(446 + 1002)/2018 = .72$; (e) $(1010 - 251)/8643 = .088$; (f) $((1074 + 1257)/2)/(5550/365) = 76.7$ days; (g) $443/((2049 + 2603)/2) = .19$; (h) $408/443 = .92$.

2. The illogical ratios are $a, b, c, f,$ and i. The correct definitions are

$$\text{Debt-equity ratio} = \frac{\text{long-term debt} + \text{value of leases}}{\text{equity}}$$

$$\text{Return on equity} = \frac{\text{earnings available for common stockholders}}{\text{average equity}}$$

$$\text{Payout ratio} = \frac{\text{dividend per share}}{\text{earnings per share}}$$

$$\text{Current ratio} = \frac{\text{current assets}}{\text{current liabilities}}$$

$$\text{Average collection period} = \frac{\text{average receivables}}{\text{sales} \div 365}$$

3. (a) False; (b) true; (c) false; (d) false; (e) false—it will tend to increase the price–earnings multiple.

4. $365,000; 12.2.

5. (a) 12%; (b) 16%.

6. .25.

7. .73.; 3.65%

8. (a) 1.47; (b) Net working capital = 40. Total capitalization = 540. Debt to total capitalization = .52.

9. $10 million.

10. $82 million.

11. a. False (it is a process of deciding which risks to take).
    b. False (financial planning is concerned with possible surprises as well as expected outcomes).
    c. True (financial planning considers both the investment and financing decisions).
    d. False (a typical horizon for long-term planning is 5 years).
    e. True (perfect accuracy is unlikely to be obtainable, but the firm needs to produce the best possible consistent forecasts).
    f. False (excessive detail distracts attention from the crucial decisions).

12. (a) $2,900,000; (b) $225,000; (c) .25.

13. Archimedes will earn $550 and invest $320 to expand assets. Additional borrowing is $120, so retained earnings is $320 − 120 = $200. The residual dividend is $550 − 200 = $350.

14. (a) 8.6%; (b) 13.75%.

Chapter 20

1.

Cash	Working Capital
1. $2 million decline	$2 million decline
2. $2,500 increase	Unchanged
3. $5,000 decline	Unchanged
4. Unchanged	$1 million increase
5. Unchanged	Unchanged
6. $5 million increase	Unchanged

2. (a) Inventories go up (use). (b) Accounts receivable go up (use). (c) No change shown on the firm's books. (d) Increase in cash (source) and reduction in assets. A loss of $100,000 is deducted from retained earnings. (e) Cash declines (use) and equity declines. (f) Cash declines (use) (g) Cash unchanged, although net working capital increases (the debt issue is a source of *funds*).

3. Month 3: $18 + (.5 \times 90) + (.3 \times 120) + (.2 \times 100) = \$119,000.$
   Month 4: $14 + (.5 \times 70) + (.3 \times 90) + (.2 \times 120) = \$100,000.$

4. (a) 19.2, 16.8, 15, 13.2, 12, 12; (b) 19.2, 23.2, 20.6, 18.2, 16.4, 16.

5. a. Table 20.1: Bank loans = 3, Cash = 8, Current assets = 68, Current liabilities = 30, Total assets = Total liabilities and net worth = 118. Table 20.3 Repaid short-term bank loan = 2, Increase in cash balance = 4. Tables 20.4 and 20.5 unchanged.
   b. Table 20.1: Long-term debt = 22, Gross investment = 82, Net fixed assets = 62, Cash = 3, Total assets = Total liabilities and net worth = 125. Table 20.3: Issued long-term debt = 17, Total sources = 41, Invested in fixed assets = 26, Total uses = 42, Increases in cash balance = −1. Table 20.4: Fixed and Total assets change as in Table 20.1, as do Long-term debt and Total liabilities and net worth. Table 20.5: same changes as in Table 20.3, except Increase in net working capital = 6.
   c. Table 20.2: Operating costs = 289, Pretax income = 56, Net income = 28, Retained earnings = 27. Table 20.1: Net worth = 92, Total liabilities and net worth = Total assets = 131; Inventory = 22.5, Cash = 23.5. Table 20.4: Net worth = 92, Long-term liabilities and net worth = Total assets = 104, Net working capital = 54. Table 20.5: Net income = 28, increase in Net working capital = 24.
   d. Table 20.6: Third quarter, Total collections = 120.1, Ending receivables = 26.6. Fourth

quarter, Total collections = 129.5, Ending receivables = 28.1. Table 20.7: Third quarter: Sources minus uses and Cash at end of period increase by 11.6, Cumulative financing required decreases by 11.6. Fourth quarter: Sources minus uses increase by 1.5, Cumulative financing required decreases by 13.1 to −12.6.

e. Table 20.7: Labor, etc. = 26, Sources minus uses decrease by 4 in each quarter. Cumulative financing required decreases by 4 in first quarter, 8 in second, etc.

f. Table 20.7: Other sources of cash increase by 10 in the second quarter, increasing Sources minus uses and decreasing Cumulative financing required.

g. Table 20.7: Minimum operating cash balance = 2, Cumulative financing required decreases by 2 in all quarters.

6. (a) True; (b) false (borrower has a call); (c) true; (d) false (100/90 − 1 = .111, or 11.1%); (e) true.

7. Line of credit, commitment fee, floating charge, collateral, warehouse receipt, syndicated, arranger, CLOs or collateralized loan obligations, commercial paper, medium-term notes.

8. Price = 100 − (.5 × 1.73) = 99.135. Compound annual return = $(100/99.135)^2 - 1 = .0175$, or 1.75%. (More precisely, price = 100 − 1.73(182/360) = 99.125 and return = $(100/99.125)^{(365/182)} - 1 = .0178$, or 1.78%. See footnote 19.)

9. (a) Repurchase agreements; (b) commercial paper; (c) finance company commercial paper; (d) 3-month bills; (e) Treasury bills; (f) Treasury bills.

10. Only 30% of the floating-rate preferred dividend is taxed versus 100% of bond interest. The fixed-dividend preferred also has this advantage but its price fluctuates more than that of the floating-rate preferred.

GLOSSARY*

A number of Web sites contain comprehensive financial glossaries. See, for example, **www.finance-glossary.com** and **www.duke.edu/~charvey/Classes/wpg/glossary.htm.**

A

Abnormal return   Part of return that is not due to market-wide price movements.

Absolute priority   Rule in bankruptcy proceedings whereby senior creditors are required to be paid in full before junior creditors receive any payment.

Accelerated depreciation   Any *depreciation* method that produces larger deductions for depreciation in the early years of a project's life.

Accounts payable (payables, trade debt)   Money owed to suppliers.

Accounts receivable (receivables, trade credit)   Money owed by customers.

Accrued interest   Interest that has been earned but not yet paid.

ACH   *Automated Clearing House.*

Acid-test ratio   *Quick ratio.*

Adjusted present value (APV)   *Net present value* of an asset if financed solely by equity plus the *present value* of any financing side effects.

ADR   *American depository receipt.*

Adverse selection   A situation in which a pricing policy causes only the less desirable customers to do business, e.g., a rise in insurance prices that leads only the worst risks to buy insurance.

Affirmative covenant   Loan *covenant* specifying certain actions that the borrower must take.

Agency costs   Losses that arise when an agent (e.g., a manager) does not act solely in the interests of the principal (e.g., the shareholder).

Agency theory   Theory of the relationship between a principal, e.g., a shareholder, and an agent of the principal, e.g., the company's manager.

Aging schedule   Summary of age of *receivables* that are outstanding from each customer.

AIBD   Association of International Bond Dealers.

All-or-none underwriting   An arrangement whereby a security issue is canceled if the *underwriter* is unable to resell the entire issue.

Alpha   Measure of portfolio return adjusted for effect of market.

Alternative Minimum Tax (AMT)   A separately calculated minimum amount of tax that must be paid by corporations or individuals.

American depository receipt (ADR)   A certificate issued in the United States to represent shares of a foreign company.

American option   *Option* that can be exercised any time before the final exercise date (cf. *European option*).

Amex   American Stock Exchange.

Amortization   (1) Repayment of a loan by installments; (2) allowance for *depreciation*.

AMT   *Alternative minimum tax.*

Angel investor   Wealthy individual who provides capital for small start-up businesses.

Annual percentage rate (APR)   Annual interest rate calculated using *simple interest*.

Annuity   Investment that produces a level stream of cash flows for a limited number of periods.

Annuity due   *Annuity* whose payments occur at the start of each period.

Annuity factor   *Present value* of $1 paid for each of t periods.

Anticipation   Arrangement whereby customers who pay before the final date may be entitled to deduct a normal rate of interest.

Appraisal rights   A right of shareholders in a *merger* to demand the payment of a fair price for their shares, as determined independently.

Appropriation request   Formal request for funds for a capital investment project.

APR   *Annual percentage rate.*

APT   *Arbitrage pricing theory.*

APV   *Adjusted present value.*

Arbitrage   Purchase of one security and simultaneous sale of another to give a risk-free profit.

"Arbitrage" or "risk arbitrage"   Often used loosely to describe the taking of offsetting positions in related securities, e.g., at the time of a takeover bid.

Arbitrage pricing theory (APT)   Model in which expected returns increase linearly with an asset's sensitivity to a small number of pervasive factors.

Arranger   Lead *underwriter* to a syndicated loan.

Articles of incorporation   Legal document establishing a corporation and its structure and purpose.

Asian currency units   Dollar deposits held in Singapore or other Asian centers.

Asian option   *Option* based on the average price of the asset during the life of the option.

Ask price (offer price)   Price at which a dealer is willing to sell (cf. *bid price*).

Asset-backed securities   Securities issued by a special purpose company that holds a package of low-risk assets whose cash flows are sufficient to service the *bonds*.

Asset stripper   Acquirer who takes over firms in order to sell off a large part of their assets.

At-the-money option   Option whose exercise price equals the current asset price (cf. *in-the-money option, out-of-the-money option*).

Auction market   Securities exchange in which prices are determined by an auction process, e.g., *NYSE* (cf. *dealer market*).

Auction-rate preferred   A variant of *floating-rate preferred* stock where the dividend is reset every 49 days by auction.

Authorized share capital   Maximum number of shares that a company can issue, as specified in the firm's *articles of incorporation*.

Automated Clearing House (ACH)   Private electronic system run by banks for high-volume, low-value payments.

Automatic debit   *Direct payment*.

Availability float   Checks deposited by a company that have not yet been cleared.

Aval   Bank guarantee for debt purchased by *forfaiter*.

B

BA   *Banker's acceptance*.

Backwardation   Condition in which *spot price* of commodity exceeds price of *future* (cf. *contango*).

Balloon payment   Large final payment (e.g., when a loan is repaid in installments).

Bank discount   Interest deducted from the initial amount of a loan.

Banker's acceptance (BA)   Written demand that has been accepted by a bank to pay a given sum at a future date (cf. *trade acceptance*).

Barrier option   *Option* whose existence depends on asset price hitting some specified barrier (cf. *down-and-out option, down-and-in option*).

Basel Accord   International agreement on the amount of capital to be maintained by large banks to support their risky loans.

Basis point (bp)   0.01%.

Basis risk   Residual risk that results when the two sides of a hedge do not move exactly together.

Bearer security   Security for which primary evidence of ownership is possession of the certificate (cf. *registered security*).

Bear market   Widespread decline in security prices (cf. *bull market*).

Behavioral finance   Branch of finance that stresses aspects of investor irrationality.

Benchmark maturity   Maturity of a newly issued Treasury bond.

Benefit–cost ratio   One plus *profitability index*.

Bermuda option   *Option* that is exercisable on discrete dates before maturity.

Best-efforts underwriting   An arrangement whereby *underwriters* do not commit themselves to selling a security issue but promise only to use best efforts.

Beta   Measure of *market risk*.

Bid price   Price at which a dealer is willing to buy (cf. *ask price*).

Big Board   Colloquial term for the New York Stock Exchange.

Bill of exchange   General term for a document demanding payment.

Bill of lading   Document establishing ownership of goods in transit.

Binomial method   Method for valuing *options* that assumes there are only two possible changes in the asset price in any one period.

Blue-chip company   Large and creditworthy company.

Blue-sky laws   State laws covering the issue and trading of securities.

Boilerplate   Standard terms and conditions, e.g., in a debt contract.

Bond   Long-term debt.

Bond rating   Rating of the likelihood of bond's default.

Bookbuilding   The procedure whereby *underwriters* gather nonbinding indications of demand for a new issue.

Book entry   Registered ownership of stock without issue of stock certificate.

Book runner   The managing *underwriter* for a new issue. The book runner maintains the book of securities sold.

Bought deal   Security issue where one or two *underwriters* buy the entire issue.

BP   *Basis point*.

Bracket   A term signifying the extent of an *underwriter's* commitment in a new issue, e.g., major bracket, minor bracket.

Break-even analysis   Analysis of the level of sales at which a project would just break even.

Bridge loan   Short-term loan to provide temporary financing until more permanent financing is arranged.

Bull–bear bond   *Bond* whose *principal* repayment is linked to the price of another security. The bonds are issued in two *tranches*: In the first the repayment increases with the price of the other security; in the second the repayment decreases with the price of the other security.

Bulldog bond   *Foreign bond* issue made in London.

Bullet payment   Single final payment, e.g., of a loan (in contrast to payment in installments).

Bull market   Widespread rise in security prices (cf. *bear market*).

Bund   Long-term German government *bond*.

Buyback   *Repurchase agreement*.

C

Cable   The exchange rate between U.S. dollars and sterling.

Call option   Option to buy an asset at a specified exercise price on or before a specified exercise date (cf. *put option*).

Call premium   (1) Difference between the price at which a company can call its *bonds* and their *face value;* (2) price of a call *option.*

Call provision   Provision that allows an issuer to buy back the *bond* issue at a stated price.

Cap   An upper limit on the interest rate on a *floating-rate note.*

Capital asset pricing model   Model in which expected returns increase linearly with an asset's *beta.*

Capital budget   List of planned investment projects, usually prepared annually.

Capitalization   Long-term debt plus *preferred stock* plus *net worth.*

Capital lease   *Financial lease.*

Capital market   Financial market (particularly the market for long-term securities).

Capital rationing   Shortage of funds that forces a company to choose between worthwhile projects.

Capital structure   Mix of different securities issued by a firm.

CAPM   *Capital asset pricing model.*

Captive finance company   Subsidiary whose function is to provide finance for purchases from the parent company.

Caput option   *Call option* on a *put option.*

CAR   Cumulative *abnormal return.*

CARDs (Certificates for Amortizing Revolving Debt)   *Pass-through securities* backed by credit card *receivables.*

Carried interest   A proportion of the profits to which *private equity* partnerships, etc. are entitled.

Carry trade   Borrowing in country with low interest rate to relend in another country with a higher rate.

CARs (Certificates of Automobile Receivables)   *Pass-through securities* backed by automobile *receivables.*

Carve-out   Public offering of shares in a subsidiary.

Cascade   Rational herding in which each individual deduces that previous decisions by others may have been based on extra information.

Cash and carry   Purchase of a security and simultaneous sale of a *future,* with the balance being financed with a loan or *repo.*

Cash budget   Forecast of sources and uses of cash.

Cash cow   Mature company producing a large *free cash flow.*

Cash-deficiency arrangement   Arrangement whereby a project's shareholders agree to provide the operating company with sufficient *net working capital.*

CAT bond   *Catastrophe bond.*

Catastrophe bond (CAT bond)   *Bond* whose payoffs are linked to a measure of catastrophe losses such as insurance claims.

CBD   Cash before delivery.

CD   *Certificate of deposit.*

CDS (Credit default swap)   *Default swap.*

CEO   Chief executive officer.

Certainty equivalent   A certain cash flow that has the same present value as a specified risky cash flow.

Certificate of deposit (CD)   A certificate providing evidence of a bank time deposit.

CFTC   Commodity Futures Trading Commission.

CFO   Chief financial officer.

Chaebol   A Korean conglomerate.

Chapter 7   Bankruptcy procedure whereby a debtor's assets are sold and the proceeds are used to repay creditors.

Check conversion   When customer writes a check, information is automatically captured and his bank account immediately debited.

CHIPS   *Clearinghouse Interbank Payments System.*

Chapter 11   Bankruptcy procedure designed to reorganize and rehabilitate defaulting firm.

Chooser option   Holder decides whether it is a *call option* or *put option.*

Clean price (flat price)   *Bond* price excluding *accrued interest* (cf. *dirty price*).

Clearinghouse Interbank Payments System (CHIPS)   An international wire transfer system operated by a group of major banks for high-value dollar payments.

CLO   *Collateralized loan obligation.* Also CDO (collateralized debt obligation) and CMO (collateralized mortgage obligation).

Closed-end fund   Company whose assets consist of investments in a number of industrial and commercial companies.

Closed-end mortgage   Mortgage against which no additional debt may be issued (cf. *open-end mortgage*).

CMOs   *Collateralized mortgage obligations.*

COD   Cash on delivery.

Collar   An upper and lower limit on the interest rate on a *floating-rate note.*

Collateral   Assets that are given as security for a loan.

Collateralized loan obligation (CLO)   A security backed by a pool of loans, and issued in *tranches* with different levels of seniority.

Collateralized mortgage obligations (CMOs)   A variation on the mortgage *pass-through security* in which the cash flows from a pool of mortgages are repackaged into several *tranches* of *bonds* with different maturities.

Collateral trust bonds   *Bonds* secured by *common stocks* or other securities that are owned by the borrower.

Collection float   Customer-written checks that have not been received, deposited, and added to the company's available balance (cf. *payment float*).

Commercial draft (bill of exchange)   Demand for payment.

Commercial paper   Unsecured *notes* issued by companies and maturing within nine months.

Commitment fee   Fee charged by bank on an unused *line of credit.*

Common-size financial statements   Balance sheet where entries are expressed as proportion of total assets and income statement where entries are expressed as a proportion of revenues.

Common stock   Security representing ownership of a *corporation*.

Company cost of capital   The expected return on a portfolio of all the firm's securities.

Compensating balance   Non-interest-bearing demand deposits to compensate banks for bank loans or services.

Competitive bidding   Means by which public utility *holding companies* are required to choose their *underwriter* (cf. *negotiated underwriting*).

Completion bonding   Insurance that a construction contract will be successfully completed.

Composition   Voluntary agreement to reduce payments on a firm's debt.

Compound interest   Reinvestment of each interest payment on money invested to earn more interest (cf. *simple interest*).

Compound option   Option on an *option*.

Concentration banking   System whereby customers make payments to a regional collection center. The collection center pays the funds into a regional bank account and surplus money is transferred to the company's principal bank.

Conditional sale   Sale in which ownership does not pass to the buyer until payment is completed.

Conglomerate merger   *Merger* between two companies in unrelated businesses (cf. *horizontal merger, vertical merger*).

Consol   Name of a perpetual *bond* issued by the British government. Sometimes used as a general term for *perpetuity*.

Contango   Condition in which spot price of a commodity is below that of the *future* (cf. *backwardation*).

Contingent claim   Claim whose value depends on the value of another asset.

Contingent project   Project that cannot be undertaken unless another project is also undertaken.

Continuous compounding   Interest compounded continuously rather than at fixed intervals.

Controller   Officer responsible for budgeting, accounting, and auditing in a firm (cf. *treasurer*).

Convenience yield   The extra advantage that firms derive from holding the commodity rather than the *future*.

Conversion price   *Par value* of a *convertible bond* divided by the number of shares into which it may be exchanged.

Conversion ratio   Number of shares for which a *convertible bond* may be exchanged.

Convertible bond   *Bond* that may be converted into another security at the holder's option. Similarly convertible *preferred stock*.

Convexity   In a plot of a *bond*'s price against the interest rate, convexity measures the curvature of the line.

Corporate venturing   Practice by which a large manufacturer provides financial support to new companies.

Correlation coefficient   Measure of the closeness of the relationship between two variables.

Corporation   A business that is legally separate from its owners.

Cost company arrangement   Arrangement whereby the shareholders of a project receive output free of charge but agree to pay all operating and financing charges of the project.

Cost of capital   *Opportunity cost of capital*.

Counterparty   Party on the other side of a *derivative* contract.

Coupon   (1) Specifically, an attachment to the certificate of a *bearer security* that must be surrendered to collect interest payment; (2) more generally, interest payment on debt.

Covariance   Measure of the co-movement between two variables.

Covenant   Clause in a loan agreement.

Covered option   *Option* position with an offsetting position in the underlying asset.

Cramdown   Action by a bankruptcy court to enforce a plan of reorganization.

Credit derivative   Contract for *hedging* against loan default or changes in credit risk (e.g., *default swap*).

Credit scoring   A procedure for assigning scores to borrowers on the basis of the risk of default.

Cross-default clause   Clause in a loan agreement stating that the company is in default if it fails to meet its obligation on any other debt issue.

Cum dividend   *With dividend*.

Cum rights   *With rights*.

Cumulative preferred stock   Stock that takes priority over *common stock* in regard to dividend payments. Dividends may not be paid on the common stock until all past *dividends* on the *preferred stock* have been paid.

Cumulative voting   Voting system under which a stockholder may cast all of his or her votes for one candidate for the board of directors (cf. *majority voting*).

Current asset   Asset that will normally be turned into cash within a year.

Current liability   Liability that will normally be repaid within a year.

Current ratio   *Current assets* divided by *current liabilities*—a measure of liquidity.

Current yield   *Bond coupon* divided by price.

D

Data mining (data snooping)   Excessive search to find interesting (but probably coincidental) behavior in a body of data.

DCF   *Discounted cash flow*.

DDM   *Dividend discount model*.

Dealer market   Securities exchange in which dealers post offers to buy or sell, e.g., *Nasdaq* (cf. *auction market*).

Death spiral convertible   *Convertible bond* exchangeable for shares with a specified market value.

Debenture   Unsecured *bond*.

Debtor-in–possession financing (DIP financing)   Debt issued by a company in *Chapter 11* bankruptcy.

Decision tree   Method of representing alternative sequential decisions and the possible outcomes from these decisions.

Default swap   *Credit derivative* in which one party makes fixed payments while the payments by the other party depend on the occurrence of a loan default.

Defeasance   Practice whereby the borrower sets aside cash or *bonds* sufficient to service the borrower's debt. Both the borrower's debt and the offsetting cash or bonds are removed from the balance sheet.

Delta   *Hedge ratio.*

Depository transfer check (DTC)   Check made out directly by a local bank to a particular company.

Depreciation   (1) Reduction in the book or market value of an asset; (2) portion of an investment that can be deducted from taxable income.

Derivative   Asset whose value derives from that of some other asset (e.g., a *future* or an *option*).

Diff   *Differential swap.*

Differential swap (diff, quanto swap)   Swap between two *LIBOR* rates of interest, e.g., yen LIBOR for dollar LIBOR. Payments are in one currency.

Digital option   *Option* paying fixed sum if asset price is the right side of *exercise price*, otherwise zero.

Dilution   Diminution in the proportion of income to which each share is entitled.

DIP financing   *Debtor-in–possession financing.*

Direct deposit   The firm authorizes its bank to deposit money in the accounts of its employees or shareholders.

Direct lease   *Lease* in which the *lessor* purchases new equipment from the manufacturer and leases it to the *lessee* (cf. *sale and lease-back*).

Direct payment (automatic debit, direct debit)   The firm's customers authorize it to debit their bank account for the amount due, cf. *direct deposit.*

Direct quote   For foreign exchange, the number of U.S. dollars needed to buy one unit of a foreign currency (cf. *indirect quote*).

Dirty price   *Bond* price including *accrued interest*, i.e., the price paid by the bond buyer (cf. *clean price*).

Discount bond   Debt sold for less than its *principal* value. If a discount bond pays no interest, it is called a "pure" discount, or *zero-coupon,* bond.

Discounted cash flow (DCF)   Future cash flows multiplied by *discount factors* to obtain *present value.*

Discount factor   *Present value* of $1 received at a stated future date.

Discount rate   Rate used to calculate the *present value* of future cash flows.

Discounted payback rule   Requirement that discounted values of cash flows should be sufficient to pay back initial investment within a specified time.

Discriminatory price auction   Auction in which successful bidders pay the price that they bid (cf. *uniform price auction*).

Disintermediation   Withdrawal of funds from a financial institution in order to invest them directly (cf. *intermediation*).

Dividend   Payment by a company to its stockholders.

Dividend discount model   Model showing that the value of a share is equal to the discounted value of future *dividends.*

Dividend reinvestment plan (DRIP)   Plan that allows shareholders to reinvest dividends automatically.

Dividend yield   Annual *dividend* divided by share price.

Double-declining-balance depreciation   Method of *accelerated depreciation.*

Double-tax agreement   Agreement between two countries that taxes paid abroad can be offset against domestic taxes levied on foreign *dividends.*

Down-and-in option   *Barrier option* that comes into existence if asset price hits a barrier.

Down-and-out option   *Barrier option* that expires if asset price hits a barrier.

DRIP   *Dividend reinvestment plan.*

Drop lock   An arrangement whereby the interest rate on a *floating-rate note* or *preferred stock* becomes fixed if it falls to a specified level.

DTC   *Depository transfer check.*

Dual-class equity   Shares with different voting rights.

Dual-currency bond   *Bond* with interest paid in one currency and *principal* paid in another.

Dupont system   Formula expressing relationship between return on assets, sales-to-assets, profit margin, and measures of leverage.

Duration   The average number of years to an asset's *discounted cash flows.*

E

EBIT   Earnings before interest and taxes.

EBITDA   Earnings before interest, taxes, depreciation, and *amortization.*

EBPP   *Electronic bill presentment and payment.*

Economic exposure   Risk that arises from changes in real exchange rates (cf. *transaction exposure, translation exposure*).

Economic income   Cash flow plus change in *present value.*

Economic rents   Profits in excess of the competitive level.

Economic value added (EVA)   A measure of *residual income* implemented by the consulting firm Stern Stewart.

Efficient market   Market in which security prices reflect information instantaneously.

Efficient portfolio   Portfolio that offers the lowest risk (*standard deviation*) for its *expected return* and the highest expected return for its level of risk.

EFT   *Electronic funds transfer.*

Electronic bill presentment and payment (EBPP)   Allows companies to bill customers and receive payments via the Internet.

Electronic funds transfer (EFT)   Transfer of money electronically (e.g., by *Fedwire*).

Employee stock ownership plan (ESOP)   A company contributes to a trust fund that buys stock on behalf of employees.

Entrenching investment   An investment that makes particular use of the skills of existing management.

EPS   Earnings per share.

Equipment trust certificate   Form of *secured debt* generally used to finance railroad equipment. The trustee retains ownership of the equipment until the debt is repaid.

Equity   (1) *Common stock* and *preferred stock.* Often used to refer to common stock only. (2) *Net worth.*

Equity-linked bond   *Bond* whose payments are linked to a stock market index.

Equivalent annual cash flow (or cost)   *Annuity* with the same *net present value* as the company's proposed investment.

ESOP   *Employee stock ownership plan.*

ETF   *Exchange-traded fund.*

Euribor   *Euro interbank offered rate.*

Euro interbank offered rate (Euribor)   The interest rate at which major international banks in Europe lend euros to each other.

Eurobond   *Bond* that is marketed internationally.

Eurocurrency   Deposit held outside the currency's issuing country (e.g., euroyen, or *eurodollar deposit*)

Eurodollar deposit   Dollar deposit with a bank outside the United States.

European option   *Option* that can be exercised only on final exercise date (cf. *American option*).

EVA   *Economic value added.*

Event risk   The risk that an unanticipated event (e.g., a takeover) will lead to a debt default.

Evergreen credit   *Revolving credit* without maturity.

Exchange of assets   Acquisition of another company by purchase of its assets in exchange for cash or shares.

Exchange of stock   Acquisition of another company by purchase of its stock in exchange for cash or shares.

Exchange-traded fund (ETF)   A stock designed to track a stockmarket index.

Ex dividend   Purchase of shares in which the buyer is not entitled to the forthcoming *dividend* (cf. *with dividend, cum dividend*).

Exercise price (striking price)   Price at which a *call option* or *put option* may be exercised.

Expectations theory   Theory that *forward interest rate* (*forward exchange rate*) equals expected *spot rate.*

Expected return   Average of possible returns weighted by their probabilities.

Ex rights   Purchase of shares that do not entitle the owner to buy shares in the company's *rights issue* (cf. *with rights, cum rights, rights on*).

Extendable bond   *Bond* whose maturity can be extended at the option of the lender (or issuer).

External finance   Finance that is not generated by the firm: new borrowing or an issue of stock (cf. *internal finance*).

Extra dividend   *Dividend* that may or may not be repeated (cf. *regular dividend*).

F

Face value   *Par value.*

Factoring   Arrangement whereby a financial institution buys a company's *accounts receivable* and collects the debt.

Fair price provision   *Appraisal rights.*

Fallen angel   *Junk bond* that was formerly *investment grade.*

FASB   Financial Accounting Standards Board.

FCIA   Foreign Credit Insurance Association.

FDIC   Federal Deposit Insurance Corporation.

Federal funds   Non-interest-bearing deposits by banks at the Federal Reserve. Excess reserves are lent by banks to each other.

Fedwire   A wire transfer system for high-value payments operated by the Federal Reserve System (cf. *CHIPS*).

Field warehouse   Warehouse rented by a warehouse company on another firm's premises (cf. *public warehouse*).

Financial assets   Claims on *real assets.*

Financial engineering   Combining or dividing existing instruments to create new financial products.

Financial lease (capital lease, full-payout lease)   Long-term, noncancelable lease (cf. *operating lease*).

Financial leverage (gearing)   Use of debt to increase the *expected return* on *equity.* Financial leverage is measured by the ratio of debt to debt plus equity (cf. *operating leverage*).

Fiscal agency agreement   An alternative to a bond *trust deed.* Unlike the trustee, the fiscal agent acts as an agent of the borrower.

Flat price   *Clean price.*

Flipping   Buying shares in an *IPO* and selling immediately.

Float   See *availability float, collection float, payment float.*

Floating lien   General *lien* against a company's assets or against a particular class of assets.

Floating-price convertible   *Death spiral convertible.*

Floating-rate note (FRN)   *Note* whose interest payment varies with the short-term interest rate.

Floating-rate preferred *Preferred stock* paying dividends that vary with short-term interest rates.

Floor planning Arrangement used to finance inventory. A finance company buys the inventory, which is then held in trust by the user.

Foreign bond A *bond* issued on the domestic *capital market* of another country.

Forex Foreign exchange.

Forfaiter Purchaser of promises to pay (e.g., *bills of exchange* or *promissory notes*) issued by importers.

Forward cover Purchase or sale of forward foreign currency in order to offset a known future cash flow.

Forward exchange rate Exchange rate fixed today for exchanging currency at some future date (cf. *spot exchange rate*).

Forward interest rate Interest rate fixed today on a loan to be made at some future date (cf. *spot interest rate*).

Forward rate agreement (FRA) Agreement to borrow or lend at a specified future date at an interest rate that is fixed today.

FRA *Forward rate agreement.*

Free cash flow Cash not required for operations or for reinvestment.

Free-rider problem The temptation not to incur the costs of participating in a decision when one's influence on that decision is small.

FRN *Floating-rate note.*

Full-payout lease *Financial lease.*

Full-service lease (rental lease) *Lease* in which the *lessor* promises to maintain and insure the equipment (cf. *net lease*).

Fundamental analysis Security analysis that seeks to detect misvalued securities by an analysis of the firm's business prospects (cf. *technical analysis*).

Funded debt Debt maturing after more than one year (cf. *unfunded debt*).

Futures contract A contract to buy a commodity or security on a future date at a price that is fixed today. Unlike forward contracts, futures are traded on organized exchanges and are *marked to market* daily.

G

GAAP Generally accepted accounting principles.

Gamma A measure of how the *option delta* changes as the asset price changes.

Gearing *Financial leverage.*

General cash offer Issue of securities offered to all investors (cf. *rights issue*).

Gilt A British government *bond.*

Golden parachute A large termination payment due to a company's officers if they lose their jobs as a result of a *merger.*

Goodwill The difference between the amount paid for a firm in a *merger* and its book value.

Governance The oversight of a firm's management.

Gray market Purchases and sales of securities that occur before the issue price is set.

Greenmail Situation in which a large block of stock is held by an unfriendly company, forcing the target company to repurchase the stock at a substantial premium to prevent a takeover.

Greenshoe option *Option* that allows the *underwriter* for a new issue to buy and resell additional shares.

Growth stock *Common stock* of a company that has an opportunity to invest money to earn more than the *opportunity cost of capital* (cf. *income stock*).

H

Haircut An additional margin of *collateral* for a loan.

Hedge fund An investment fund charging a performance fee and open to a limited range of investors. Funds often follow complex strategies including *short sales*.

Hedge ratio (delta, option delta) The number of shares to buy for each *option* sold in order to create a safe position; more generally, the number of units of an asset that should be bought to hedge one unit of a liability.

Hedging Buying one security and selling another in order to reduce risk. A perfect hedge produces a riskless portfolio.

Hell-or-high-water clause Clause in a *lease* agreement that obligates the *lessee* to make payments regardless of what happens to the *lessor* or the equipment.

Highly leveraged transaction (HLT) Bank loan to a highly leveraged firm (formerly needed to be separately reported to the Federal Reserve Board).

High-yield bond *Junk bond.*

HLT *Highly leveraged transaction.*

Holding company Company whose sole function is to hold stock in the firm's subsidiaries.

Horizontal merger *Merger* between two companies that manufacture similar products (cf. *vertical merger, conglomerate merger*).

Horizontal spread The simultaneous purchase and sale of two *options* that differ only in their exercise date (cf. *vertical spread*).

Hurdle rate Minimum acceptable rate of return on a project.

I

IBF *International banking facility.*

IMM *International Monetary Market.*

Immunization The construction of an asset and a liability that have offsetting changes in value.

Imputation tax system   Arrangement by which investors who receive a *dividend* also receive a tax credit for corporate taxes that the firm has paid.

Income bond   *Bond* on which interest is payable only if earned.

Income stock   *Common stock* with high *dividend yield* and few profitable investment opportunities (cf. *growth stock*).

Indenture   Formal agreement, e.g., establishing the terms of a *bond* issue.

Indexed bond   *Bond* whose payments are linked to an index, e.g., a consumer price index (see *TIPS*).

Index fund   Investment fund designed to match the returns on a stock market index.

Indirect quote   For foreign exchange, the number of units of a foreign currency needed to buy one U.S. dollar (cf. *direct quote*).

Industrial revenue bond (IRB)   Bond issued by local government agencies on behalf of *corporations*.

Initial public offering (IPO)   A company's first public issue of *common stock*.

In-substance defeasance   *Defeasance* whereby debt is removed from the balance sheet but not canceled (cf. *novation*).

Intangible asset   Nonmaterial asset, such as technical expertise, a trademark, or a patent (cf. *tangible asset*).

Integer programming   Variant of *linear programming* whereby the solution values must be integers.

Interest cover   *Times interest earned.*

Interest rate parity   Theory that the differential between the *forward exchange rate* and the *spot exchange rate* is equal to the differential between the foreign and domestic interest rates.

Intermediation   Investment through a financial institution (cf. *disintermediation*).

Internal finance   Finance generated within a firm by *retained earnings* and *depreciation* (cf. *external finance*).

Internal growth rate   The maximum rate of firm growth without *external finance* (cf. *sustainable growth rate*).

Internal rate of return (IRR)   *Discount rate* at which investment has zero *net present value*.

International banking facility (IBF)   A branch that an American bank establishes in the United States to do eurocurrency business.

International Monetary Market (IMM)   The financial futures market within the Chicago Mercantile Exchange.

Interval measure   The number of days that a firm can finance operations without additional cash income.

In-the-money option   An *option* that would be worth exercising if it expired immediately (cf. *out-of-the-money option*).

Investment-grade bond   *Bond* rated at least Baa by Moody's or BBB by Standard and Poor's or Fitch.

IPO   *Initial public offering.*

IRB   *Industrial revenue bond.*

IRR   *Internal rate of return.*

IRS   Internal Revenue Service.

ISDA   International Swap and Derivatives Association.

ISMA   International Securities Market Association.

Issued share capital   Total amount of shares that are in issue (cf. *outstanding share capital*).

J

Junior debt   *Subordinated debt.*

Junk bond (high-yield bond)   Debt that is rated below an *investment-grade bond.*

Just-in-time   System of inventory management that requires minimum inventories of materials and very frequent deliveries by suppliers.

K

Keiretsu   A network of Japanese companies organized around a major bank.

L

LBO   *Leveraged buyout.*

Lease   Long-term rental agreement.

Legal capital   Value at which a company's shares are recorded in its books.

Legal defeasance   *Novation.*

Lessee   User of a leased asset (cf. *lessor*).

Lessor   Owner of a leased asset (cf. *lessee*).

Letter of credit   Letter from a bank stating that it has established a credit in the company's favor.

Letter stock   Privately placed *common stock,* so-called because the *SEC* requires a letter from the purchaser that the stock is not intended for resale.

Leverage   See *financial leverage, operating leverage.*

Leveraged buyout (LBO)   Acquisition in which (1) a large part of the purchase price is debt-financed and (2) the remaining *equity* is privately held by a small group of investors.

Leveraged lease   *Lease* in which the *lessor* finances part of the cost of the asset by an issue of debt secured by the asset and the lease payments.

Liabilities, total liabilities   Total value of financial claims on a firm's assets. Equals (1) total assets or (2) total assets minus *net worth.*

LIBOR   *London interbank offered rate.*

Lien   Lender's claims on specified assets.

Limited liability   Limitation of a shareholder's losses to the amount invested.

Limited partnership *Partnership* in which some partners have *limited liability* and general partners have unlimited liability.

Linear programming (LP) Technique for finding the maximum value of some objective function subject to stated linear constraints.

Line of credit Agreement by a bank that a company may borrow at any time up to an established limit.

Liquid asset Asset that is easily and cheaply turned into cash—notably cash itself and short-term securities.

Liquidating dividend *Dividend* that represents a return of capital.

Liquidator Person appointed by unsecured creditors in the United Kingdom to oversee the sale of an insolvent firm's assets and the repayment of debts.

Liquidity-preference theory Theory that investors demand a higher yield to compensate for the extra risk of long-term *bonds*.

Liquidity premium (1) Additional return for investing in a security that cannot easily be turned into cash; (2) difference between the *forward interest rate* and the expected *spot interest rate*.

Liquid yield option note (LYON) *Zero-coupon*, callable, puttable, *convertible bond*.

Lockbox system Form of *concentration banking*. Customers send payments to a post office box. A local bank collects and processes the checks and transfers surplus funds to the company's principal bank.

London interbank offered rate (LIBOR) The interest rate at which major international banks in London lend to each other. (LIBID is London interbank bid rate; LIMEAN is mean of bid and offered rate.)

Long hedge Purchase of a *hedging* instrument (e.g., a *future*) to hedge a short position in the underlying asset (cf. *short hedge*).

Longevity bonds *Bonds* that pay a higher rate of interest if a high proportion of the population survives to a particular age.

Lookback option *Option* whose payoff depends on the highest asset price recorded over the life of the option.

LP *Linear programming.*

LYON *Liquid yield option note.*

M

MACRS *Modified accelerated cost recovery system.*

Maintenance margin Minimum margin that must be maintained on a *futures* contract.

Majority voting Voting system under which each director is voted upon separately (cf. *cumulative voting*).

Management buyout (MBO) *Leveraged buyout* whereby the acquiring group is led by the firm's management.

Mandatory convertible *Bond* automatically convertible into equity, usually with a limit on the value of stock received.

Margin Cash or securities set aside by an investor as evidence that he or she can honor a commitment.

Marked to market An arrangement whereby the profits or losses on a *futures* contract are settled up each day.

Market capitalization rate *Expected return* on a security.

Market model Model suggesting a linear relationship between actual returns on a stock and on the market portfolio.

Market risk (systematic risk) Risk that cannot be diversified away.

Maturity factoring *Factoring* arrangement that provides collection and insurance of *accounts receivable*.

MBO *Management buyout.*

MDA *Multiple-discriminant analysis.*

Medium-term note (MTN) Debt with a typical maturity of 1 to 10 years offered regularly by a company using the same procedure as *commercial paper*.

Merger (1) Acquisition in which all assets and liabilities are absorbed by the buyer (cf. *exchange of assets, exchange of stock*); (2) more generally, any combination of two companies.

MIP (Monthly income preferred security) *Preferred stock* issued by a subsidiary located in a tax haven. The subsidiary relends the money to the parent.

Mismatch bond *Floating-rate note* whose interest rate is reset at more frequent intervals than the rollover period (e.g., a note whose payments are set quarterly on the basis of the one-year interest rate).

Modified accelerated cost recovery system (MACRS) Schedule of *depreciation* deductions allowed for tax purposes.

Modified IRR *Internal rate of return* calculated by first discounting later cash flows back to earlier periods so that there remains only one change in the sign of the cash flows.

Money center bank A major U.S. bank that undertakes a wide range of banking activities.

Money market Market for short-term safe investments.

Money market deposit account (MMDA) A bank account paying *money-market* interest rate.

Money-market fund *Mutual fund* that invests solely in short-term safe securities.

Monte Carlo simulation Method for calculating the probability distribution of possible outcomes, e.g., from a project.

Moral hazard The risk that the existence of a contract will change the behavior of one or both parties to the contract; e.g., an insured firm may take fewer fire precautions.

Mortality bonds *Bonds* that pay a higher rate of interest if there is a sharp rise in the death rate.

Mortgage bond *Bond* secured against plant and equipment.

MTN *Medium-term note.*

Multiple-discriminant analysis (MDA)   Statistical technique for distinguishing between two groups on the basis of their observed characteristics.

Mutual fund   Managed investment fund whose shares are sold to investors.

Mutually exclusive projects   Two projects that cannot both be undertaken.

N

Naked option   *Option* held on its own, i.e., not used for *hedging* a holding in the asset or other options.

Nasdaq   National Association of Security Dealers Automated Quote System. A U.S. stock exchange whose dealers tend to specialize in high-tech stocks.

Negative pledge clause   Clause under which the borrower agrees not to permit an exclusive *lien* on any of its assets.

Negotiated underwriting   Method of choosing an *underwriter*. Most firms may choose their *underwriter* by negotiation (cf. *competitive bidding*).

Net lease   *Lease* in which the *lessee* promises to maintain and insure the equipment (cf. *full-service lease*).

Net present value (NPV)   A project's net contribution to wealth—*present value* minus initial investment.

Net working capital   *Current assets* minus *current liabilities*.

Net worth   Book value of a company's *common stock*, surplus, and *retained earnings*.

Nominal interest rate   Interest rate expressed in money terms (cf. *real interest rate*).

Nonrefundable debt   Debt that may not be called in order to replace it with another issue at a lower interest cost.

Normal distribution   Symmetric bell-shaped distribution that can be completely defined by its mean and *standard deviation*.

Note   Unsecured debt with a maturity of up to 10 years.

Novation (legal defeasance)   *Defeasance* whereby the firm's debt is canceled (cf. *in-substance defeasance*).

NPV   *Net present value.*

NYSE   New York Stock Exchange.

O

Odd lot   A trade of less than 100 shares (cf. *round lot*).

Off-balance-sheet financing   Financing that is not shown as a liability in a company's balance sheet.

Offer price   *Ask price.*

OID debt   *Original issue discount debt.*

Old-line factoring   *Factoring* arrangement that provides collection, insurance, and finance for *accounts receivable*.

On the run   The most recently issued (and, therefore, typically the most liquid) government *bond* in a particular maturity range.

Open account   Arrangement whereby sales are made with no formal debt contract. The buyer signs a receipt, and the seller records the sale in the sales ledger.

Open-end mortgage   Mortgage against which additional debt may be issued (cf. *closed-end mortgage*).

Open interest   The number of currently outstanding *futures* contracts.

Operating lease   Short-term, cancelable *lease* (cf. *financial lease*).

Operating leverage   Fixed operating costs, so-called because they accentuate variations in profits (cf. *financial leverage*).

Opportunity cost of capital (hurdle rate, cost of capital)   *Expected return* that is foregone by investing in a project rather than in comparable financial securities.

Option   See *call option, put option.*

Option delta   *Hedge ratio.*

Original issue discount debt (OID debt)   Debt that is initially offered at a price below *face value*.

OTC   *Over-the-counter.*

Out-of-the-money option   An *option* that would not be worth exercising if it matured immediately (cf. *in-the-money option*).

Outstanding share capital   *Issued share capital* less the *par value* of shares that are held in the company's treasury.

Oversubscription privilege   In a *rights issue*, arrangement by which shareholders are given the right to apply for any shares that are not taken up.

Over-the-counter (OTC)   Informal market that does not involve a securities exchange. Specifically used to refer to the *Nasdaq dealer market* for *common stocks*.

P

Partnership   Joint ownership of business whereby general partners have unlimited liability.

Par value (face value)   Value of a security shown on the certificate.

Pass-through securities   *Notes* or *bonds* backed by a package of assets (e.g., mortgage pass-throughs, *CARs, CARDs*).

Path-dependent option   *Option* whose value depends on the sequence of prices of the underlying asset rather than just the final price of the asset.

Payables   *Accounts payable.*

Payback rule   Requirement that project should recover its initial investment within a specified time.

Pay-in-kind bond (PIK)   *Bond* that allows the issuer to choose to make interest payments in the form of additional bonds.

Payment float   Company-written checks that have not yet cleared (cf. *availability float*).

Payout ratio   *Dividend* as a proportion of earnings per share.

PBGC   Pension Benefit Guarantee Corporation.

P/E ratio   Share price divided by earnings per share.

PERC (Preferred equity redemption cumulative stock)   *Preferred stock* that converts automatically into equity at a stated date. A limit is placed on the value of the shares that the investor receives.

Perpetuity   Investment offering a level stream of cash flows in perpetuity (cf. *consol*).

PIK   *Pay-in-kind bond.*

PN   *Project note.*

Poison pill   An issue of securities that is convertible, in the event of a *merger,* into the shares of the acquiring firm or must be repurchased by the acquiring firm.

Poison put   A *covenant* allowing the *bond*holder to demand repayment in the event of a hostile *merger.*

Pooling of interest   Method of accounting for *mergers* (no longer available in the USA). The consolidated balance sheet of the merged firm is obtained by combining the balance sheets of the separate firms (cf. *purchase accounting*).

Position diagram   Diagram showing the possible payoffs from a *derivative* investment.

Postaudit   Evaluation of an investment project after it has been undertaken.

Praecipium   Arrangement fee for *syndicated loan.*

Preemptive right   Common stockholder's right to anything of value distributed by the company.

Preferred stock   Stock that takes priority over common stock in regard to *dividends.* Dividends may not be paid on *common stock* unless the dividend is paid on all preferred stock (cf. *cumulative preferred stock*). The dividend rate on preferred is usually fixed at time of issue.

Prepack   *Prepackaged bankruptcy.*

Prepackaged bankruptcy (prepack)   Bankruptcy proceedings intended to confirm a reorganization plan that has already been agreed to informally.

Present value   Discounted value of future cash flows.

Present value of growth opportunities (PVGO)   *Net present value* of investments the firm is expected to make in the future.

PRIDE   Similar to a *PERC* except that as the equity price rises beyond a specified point, the investor shares in the stock appreciation.

Primary issue   Issue of new securities by a firm (cf. *secondary issue*).

Prime rate   Benchmark lending rate set by U.S. banks.

Principal   Amount of debt that must be repaid.

Principal–agent problem   Problem faced by a principal (e.g., shareholder) in ensuring that an agent (e.g., manager) acts on his or her behalf.

Private equity   *Equity* that is not publicly traded and that is used to finance business start-ups, *leveraged buyouts,* etc.

Privileged subscription issue   *Rights issue.*

Production payment   Loan in the form of advance payment for future delivery of a product.

Profitability index   Ratio of a project's *NPV* to the initial investment.

Pro forma   Projected.

Project finance   Debt that is largely a claim against the cash flows from a particular project rather than against the firm as a whole.

Project note (PN)   *Note* issued by public housing or urban renewal agencies.

Promissory note   Promise to pay.

Prospect theory   A theory of asset pricing suggested by the observation of behavioral psychologists that investors have a particular aversion to losses even if very small.

Prospectus   Summary of the *registration* statement providing information on an issue of securities.

Protective put   *Put option* that is combined with holding in the underlying asset.

Proxy vote   Vote cast by one person on behalf of another.

Public warehouse (terminal warehouse)   Warehouse operated by an independent warehouse company on its own premises (cf. *field warehouse*).

Purchase accounting   Method of accounting for *mergers.* The assets of the acquired firm are shown at market value on the balance sheet of the acquirer (cf. *pooling of interest*).

Purchase fund   Resembles a *sinking fund* except that money is used only to purchase bonds if they are selling below their *par value.*

Put-call parity   The relationship between the prices of European *put* and *call options.*

Put option   *Option* to sell an asset at a specified *exercise price* on or before a specified exercise date (cf. *call option*).

PVGO   *Present value of growth opportunities.*

Pyramid   Created by forming a *holding company* whose only asset is a controlling interest in a second holding company, which in turn has a controlling interest in an operating company.

Q

q   Ratio of the market value of an asset to its replacement cost.

QIBs   *Qualified institutional buyers.*

Quadratic programming   Variant of *linear programming* whereby the equations are quadratic rather than linear.

Qualified Institutional buyers (QIBs)   Institutions that are allowed to trade unregistered stock among themselves.

Quanto swap   *Differential swap.*

Quick ratio (acid-test ratio)   Measure of liquidity: (*current assets* – inventory) divided by *current liabilities.*

R

Range forward   A *forward exchange rate* contract that places upper and lower bounds on the cost of foreign exchange.

Ratchet bonds   Floating-rate *bonds* whose coupon can only be reset downward.

Rate-sensitive bonds   *Bonds* whose coupon rate changes as issuer's credit-rating changes.

Real assets   *Tangible assets* and *intangible assets* used to carry on business (cf. *financial assets*).

Real estate investment trust (REIT)   Trust company formed to invest in real estate.

Real interest rate   Interest rate expressed in terms of real goods, i.e., *nominal interest rate* adjusted for inflation.

Real option   The flexibility to modify, postpone, expand, or abandon a project.

Receivables   *Accounts receivable.*

Receiver   A bankruptcy practitioner appointed by secured creditors in the United Kingdom to oversee the repayment of debts.

Record date   Date set by directors when making dividend payment. *Dividends* are sent to stockholders who are registered on the record date.

Recourse   Term describing a type of loan. If a loan is with recourse, the lender has a general claim against the parent company if the *collateral* is insufficient to repay the debt.

Red herring   Preliminary *prospectus.*

Refunding   Replacement of existing debt with a new issue of debt.

Registered security   Security whose ownership is recorded by the company's *registrar* (cf. *bearer security*).

Registrar   Financial institution appointed to record issue and ownership of company securities.

Registration   Process of obtaining *SEC* approval for a public issue of securities.

Regression analysis   In statistics, a technique for finding the line of best fit.

Regular dividend   *Dividend* that the company expects to maintain in the future.

Regulation A issue   Small security issues that are partially exempt from *SEC registration* requirements.

REIT   *Real estate investment trust.*

Rental lease   *Full-service lease.*

Repo   *Repurchase agreement.*

Repurchase agreement (RP, repo, buy-back)   Purchase of Treasury securities from a securities dealer with an agreement that the dealer will repurchase them at a specified price.

Residual income   After-tax profit less the *opportunity cost of capital* employed by the business (see also *Economic Value Added*).

Residual risk   *Unique risk.*

Retained earnings   Earnings not paid out as *dividends.*

Return on equity   Usually, equity earnings as a proportion of the book value of equity.

Return on investment (ROI)   Generally, book income as a proportion of net book value.

Reverse convertible   Bond that gives the issuer the right to convert it into common stock.

Reverse FRN (yield curve note)   *Floating-rate note* whose payments rise as the general level of interest rates falls and vice versa.

Revolving credit   Legally assured *line of credit* with a bank.

Rights issue (privileged subscription issue)   Issue of securities offered to current stockholders (cf. *general cash offer*).

Rights on   *With rights.*

Risk premium   Expected additional return for making a risky investment rather than a safe one.

ROI   *Return on investment.*

Roll-over CD   A package of successive *certificates of deposit.*

Round lot   A trade of 100 shares (cf. *odd lot*).

RP   *Repurchase agreement.*

R squared (R^2)   Square of the *correlation coefficient*—the proportion of the variability in one series that can be explained by the variability of one or more other series.

Rule 144a   *SEC* rule allowing *qualified institutional buyers* to buy and trade unregistered securities.

S

Sale and lease-back   Sale of an existing asset to a financial institution that then *leases* it back to the user (cf. *direct lease*).

Salvage value   Scrap value of plant and equipment.

Samurai bond   A yen *bond* issued in Tokyo by a non-Japanese borrower (cf. *bulldog bond, Yankee bond*).

SBIC   Small Business Investment Company.

Scenario analysis   Analysis of the profitability of a project under alternative economic scenarios.

Seasoned issue   Issue of a security for which there is an existing market (cf. *unseasoned issue*).

Season datings   Extended credit for customers who order goods out of the peak season.

SEC   Securities and Exchange Commission.

Secondary issue   (1) Procedure for selling blocks of *seasoned issues* of stock; (2) more generally, sale of already issued stock.

Secondary market   Market in which one can buy or sell *seasoned issues* of securities.

Secured debt   Debt that, in the event of default, has first claim on specified assets.

Securitization   Substitution of tradable securities for privately negotiated instruments.

Security market line   Line representing the relationship between *expected return* and *market risk.*

Self-liquidating loan   Loan to finance *current assets*. The sale of the current assets provides the cash to repay the loan.

Self-selection   Consequence of a contract that induces only one group (e.g., low-risk individuals) to participate.

Semistrong-form efficient market   Market in which security prices reflect all publicly available information (cf. *weak-form efficient market* and *strong-form efficient market*).

Senior debt   Debt that, in the event of bankruptcy, must be repaid before *subordinated debt* receives any payment.

Sensitivity analysis   Analysis of the effect on project profitability of possible changes in sales, costs, and so on.

Serial bonds   Package of *bonds* that mature in successive years.

Series bond   *Bond* that may be issued in several series under the same *indenture*.

Shark repellant   Amendment to company charter intended to protect against takeover.

Sharpe ratio   Ratio of portfolio's risk premium to its risk (*standard deviation*).

Shelf registration   A procedure that allows firms to file one *registration* statement covering several issues of the same security.

Shogun bond   Dollar *bond* issued in Japan by a nonresident.

Short hedge   Sale of a *hedging* instrument (e.g., a *future*) to *hedge* a long position in the underlying asset (cf. *long hedge*).

Short sale   Sale of a security the investor does not own.

Sight draft   Demand for immediate payment (cf. *time draft*).

Signal   Action that demonstrates an individual's unobservable characteristics (because it would be unduly costly for someone without those characteristics to take the action).

Simple interest   Interest calculated only on the initial investment (cf. *compound interest*).

Simulation   *Monte Carlo simulation.*

Sinker   *Sinking fund.*

Sinking fund (sinker)   Fund established by a company to retire debt before maturity.

Skewed distribution   Probability distribution in which an unequal number of observations lie below and above the mean.

SPE   *Special-purpose entity.*

Special dividend (extra dividend)   *Dividend* that is unlikely to be repeated.

Special-purpose entity   *Partnerships* established by companies to hold certain assets and obtain funding. May be used to obtain off-balance-sheet debt for the parent.

Specific risk   *Unique risk.*

Specialist   The individual who conducts the auction of a set of securities on the New York Stock Exchange.

Spinning   The *underwriter* of an *IPO* unethically allots a portion of offering to senior management of a client company.

Spin-off   Distribution of shares in a subsidiary to the company's shareholders so that they hold shares separately in the two firms.

Spot exchange rate   Exchange rate on currency for immediate delivery (cf. *forward exchange rate*).

Spot rate   Interest rate fixed today on a loan that is made today (cf. *forward interest rate*).

Spot price   Price of asset for immediate delivery (in contrast to forward or futures price).

Spread   Difference between the price at which an *underwriter* buys an issue from a firm and the price at which the underwriter sells it to the public.

Staggered board   Board whose directors are elected periodically, instead of at one time.

Standard deviation   Square root of the *variance*—a measure of variability.

Standard error   In statistics, a measure of the possible error in an estimate.

Standby agreement   In a *rights issue,* agreement that the *underwriter* will purchase any stock not purchased by investors.

Step-up bond   *Bond* whose *coupon* is stepped up over time (also step-down bond).

Stock dividend   *Dividend* in the form of stock rather than cash.

Stock split   "Free" issue of shares to existing shareholders.

Straddle   The combination of a *put option* and a *call option* with the same *exercise price.*

Straight-line depreciation   An equal dollar amount of *depreciation* in each period.

Strike price   *Exercise price* of an *option.*

Stripped bond   *Bond* that is subdivided into a series of *zero-coupon bonds.*

Strong-form efficient market   Market in which security prices reflect instantaneously all information available to investors (cf. *weak-form efficient market* and *semistrong-form efficient market*).

Structured debt   Debt that has been customized for the buyer, often by incorporating unusual *options.*

Subordinated debt (junior debt)   Debt over which *senior debt* takes priority. In the event of bankruptcy, subordinated debtholders receive payment only after senior debt is paid off in full.

Sum-of-the-years'-digits depreciation   Method of *accelerated depreciation.*

Sunk costs   Costs that have been incurred and cannot be reversed.

Supermajority   Provision in a company's charter requiring a majority of, say, 80% of shareholders to approve certain changes, such as a *merger.*

Sushi bond   A *eurobond* issued by a Japanese corporation.

Sustainable growth rate   Maximum rate of firm growth without increasing financial leverage (cf. *internal growth rate*).

Swap   An arrangement whereby two companies lend to each other on different terms, e.g., in different currencies, or one at a fixed rate and the other at a floating rate.

Swaption   *Option* on a *swap.*

Sweep program   Arrangement whereby bank invests a company's available cash at the end of each day.

Swingline facility   Bank borrowing facility to provide finance while the firm replaces U.S. *commercial paper* with eurocommercial paper.

Syndicated loan   A large loan provided by a group of banks.

Systematic risk   *Market risk.*

T

Take-or-pay   In *project finance,* arrangement where parent company agrees to pay for output of project even if it chooses not to take delivery.

Take-up fee   Fee paid to *underwriters* of a *rights issue* on any stock they are obliged to purchase.

Tangible asset   Physical asset, such as plant, machinery, and offices (cf. *intangible asset*).

Tax-anticipation bill   Short-term bill issued by the U.S. Treasury that can be surrendered at *face value* in payment of taxes.

T-bill   *Treasury bill.*

Technical analysis   Security analysis that seeks to detect and interpret patterns in past security prices (cf. *fundamental analysis*).

TED spread   Difference between *LIBOR* and U.S. *Treasury bill* rate.

Tender offer   General offer made directly to a firm's shareholders to buy their stock.

Tenor   Maturity of a loan.

Terminal warehouse   *Public warehouse.*

Term loan   Medium-term, privately placed loan, usually made by a bank.

Term structure of interest rates   Relationship between interest rates on loans of different maturities (cf. *yield curve*).

Throughput arrangement   Arrangement by which shareholders of a pipeline company agree to make sufficient use of pipeline to enable the pipeline company to service its debt.

Tick   Minimum amount the price of a security may change.

Time draft   Demand for payment at a stated future date (cf. *sight draft*).

Times interest earned (interest cover)   Earnings before interest and tax, divided by interest payments.

TIPS (Treasury Inflation Protected Securities)   U.S. Treasury *bonds* whose *coupon* and *principal* payments are linked to the Consumer Price Index.

Tolling contract   In *project finance,* arrangement whereby parent company promises to deliver materials to project for processing and then to repurchase them.

Tombstone   Advertisement listing the *underwriters* to a security issue.

Trade acceptance   Written demand that has been accepted by an industrial company to pay a given sum at a future date (cf. *banker's acceptance*).

Trade credit   *Accounts receivable.*

Trade debt   *Accounts payable.*

Tranche   Portion of a new issue sold at a point in time different from the remainder or that has different terms.

Transaction exposure   Risk to a firm with known future cash flows in a foreign currency that arises from possible changes in the exchange rate (cf. *economic exposure, translation exposure*).

Transfer agent   Individual or institution appointed by a company to look after the transfer of securities.

Translation exposure   Risk of adverse effects on a firm's financial statements that may arise from changes in exchange rates (cf. *economic exposure, transaction exposure*).

Treasurer   Principal financial manager (cf. *controller*).

Treasury bill (T-bill)   Short-term discount debt maturing in less than one year, issued regularly by the government.

Treasury stock   *Common stock* that has been repurchased by the company and held in the company's treasury.

Trust deed   Agreement between trustee and borrower setting out terms of *bond.*

Trust receipt   Receipt for goods that are to be held in trust for the lender.

Tunneling   Actions by a controlling shareholder to transfer wealth out of the firm (e.g., by supplying goods at an inflated price).

U

Underpricing   Issue of securities below their market value.

Underwriter   Firm that buys an issue of securities from a company and resells it to investors.

Unfunded debt   Debt maturing within one year (cf. *funded debt*).

Uniform price auction   Auction in which all successful bidders pay the same price (cf. *discriminatory price auction*).

Unique risk (residual risk, specific risk, unsystematic risk)   Risk that can be eliminated by diversification.

Unseasoned issue   Issue of a security for which there is no existing market (cf. *seasoned issue*).

Unsystematic risk   *Unique risk.*

V

Value additivity   Rule that the value of the whole must equal the sum of the values of the parts.

Value at risk (VAR)   The probability of portfolio losses exceeding some specified proportion.

Vanilla issue   Issue without unusual features.

Variable-rate demand bond (VRDB)   Floating-rate *bond* that can be sold back periodically to the issuer.

Variance   Mean squared deviation from the expected value; a measure of variability.

Variation margin   The daily gains or losses on a *futures* contract credited to the investor's margin account.

VAR   *Value at risk.*

Vega   A measure of how the *option* price changes as the asset's volatility changes.

Venture capital   Capital to finance a new firm.

Vertical merger   *Merger* between a supplier and its customer (cf. *horizontal merger, conglomerate merger*).

Vertical spread   Simultaneous purchase and sale of two options that differ only in their *exercise price* (cf. *horizontal spread*).

VRDB   *Variable rate demand bond.*

W

WACC   *Weighted-average cost of capital.*

Warehouse receipt   Evidence that a firm owns goods stored in a warehouse.

Warrant   Long-term *call option* issued by a company.

Weak-form efficient market   Market in which security prices instantaneously reflect the information in the history of security prices. In such a market security prices follow a random walk (cf. *semistrong-form efficient market* and *strong-form efficient market*).

Weighted-average cost of capital (WACC)   *Expected return* on a portfolio of all the firm's securities. Used as *hurdle rate* for capital investment.

White knight   A friendly potential acquirer sought out by a target company threatened by a less welcome suitor.

Wi.   When issued.

Winner's curse   Problem faced by uninformed bidders. For example, in an *initial public offering* uninformed participants are likely to receive larger allotments of issues that informed participants know are overpriced.

With dividend (cum dividend)   Purchase of shares in which the buyer is entitled to the forthcoming *dividend* (cf. *ex dividend*).

Withholding tax   Tax levied on *dividends* paid abroad.

With rights (cum rights, rights on)   Purchase of shares in which the buyer is entitled to the rights to buy shares in the company's *rights issue* (cf. *ex rights*).

Working capital   *Current assets* and *current liabilities*. The term is commonly used as synonymous with *net working capital*.

Workout   Informal arrangement between a borrower and creditors.

Writer   *Option* seller.

X

xd   *Ex dividend.*

xr   *Ex rights.*

Y

Yankee bond   A dollar *bond* issued in the United States by a non-U.S. borrower (cf. *bulldog bond, Samurai bond*).

Yield curve   *Term structure of interest rates.*

Yield curve note   *Reverse FRN.*

Yield to maturity   *Internal rate of return* on a bond.

Z

Zero-coupon bond   *Discount bond* making no *coupon* payments.

Z-score   Measure of the likelihood of bankruptcy.

GLOBAL INDEX

Note: Page numbers followed by *n* indicate material in source notes and footnotes.

INDEX

Note: Page numbers followed by *n* indicate material in source notes and footnotes.

SOME USEFUL FORMULAS

(The section number indicates the principal reference in the text.)

Perpetuity (3.2)

The value of a perpetuity of $1 per year is:

$$PV = \frac{1}{r}$$

Annuity (3.2)

The value of an annuity of $1 per period for t years (t-year annuity factor) is:

$$PV = \frac{1}{r} - \frac{1}{r(1+r)^t}$$

A Growing Perpetuity (the "Gordon" model) (3.3)

If the first period's cash flow is $1 at year 1 and if cash flows thereafter grow at a constant rate of g in perpetuity,

$$PV = \frac{1}{r-g}$$

A Growing Annuity (3.3)

If the first period's cash flow is $1 at year 1 and if the cash flow grows at a constant rate of g for t years,

$$PV = \frac{1}{r-g} - \frac{1}{r-g} \times \frac{(1+g)^t}{(1+r)^t}$$

Continuous Compounding (3.4)

If r is the continuously compounded rate of interest, the present value of $1 received in year t is:

$$PV = \frac{1}{e^{rt}}$$

Bond Duration and Volatility (4.2)

$$\text{Duration of T-period bond} = \frac{\sum_{t=1}^{T} t \times C_t/(1+y)^t}{\sum_{t=1}^{T} C_t/(1+y)^t}$$

Volatility (modified duration) = Duration/$(1+y)$

Equivalent Annual Cost (7.3)

If an asset has a life of t years, the equivalent annual cost is:

$$\frac{PV \text{ (costs)}}{t\text{-year annuity factor}}$$

Measures of Risk (8.2 to 8.4)

Variance of returns = σ^2
$\qquad\qquad$ = expected value of $(\tilde{r} - r)^2$

Standard deviation of returns = $\sqrt{\text{variance}} = \sigma$

Covariance between returns of stocks 1 and 2
= σ_{12} = expected value of $[(\tilde{r}_1 - r_1)(\tilde{r}_2 - r_2)]$

Correlation between returns of stocks 1 and 2:

$$\rho_{12} = \frac{\sigma_{12}}{\sigma_1\sigma_2}$$

Beta of stock $i = \beta_i = \dfrac{\sigma_{im}}{\sigma_m^2}$

The variance of returns on a portfolio with proportion x_i invested in stock i is:

$$\sum_{i=1}^{N} \sum_{j=1}^{N} x_i x_j \sigma_{ij}$$

Capital Asset Pricing Model (9.2)

The expected risk premium on a risky investment is:

$$r - r_f = \beta(r_m - r_f)$$

MM's Proposition II (14.2 and 16.3)

The required return on equity (r_E) increases in line with the debt–equity ratio calculated using market values (D/E):

$$r_E = r + (r - r_D)D/E$$

where r is the opportunity cost of capital.